At Your Service

Cooperative Information Systems
Michael Papazoglou, Joachim W. Schmidt, and John Mylopoulos, editors

Advances in Object-Oriented Data Modeling, Michael P. Papazoglou, Stefano Spaccapietra, and Zahir Tari, editors

Workflow Management: Models, Methods, and Systems, Wil van der Aalst and Kees Max van Hee

A Semantic Web Primer, Grigoris Antoniou and Frank van Harmelen

Meta-Modeling for Method Engineering, Manfred Jeusfeld, Matthias Jarke, and John Mylopoulos, editors

Aligning Modern Business Processes and Legacy Systems: A Component-Based Perspective, Willem-Jan van den Heuvel

A Semantic Web Primer, second edition, Grigoris Antoniou and Frank van Harmelen

Service-Oriented Computing, Dimitrios Georgakopoulos and Michael P. Papazoglou, editors

At Your Service: Service-Oriented Computing from an EU Perspective, Elisabetta Di Nitto, Anne-Marie Sassen, Paolo Traverso, and Arian Zwegers, editors

At Your Service

Service-Oriented Computing from an EU Perspective

edited by Elisabetta Di Nitto, Anne-Marie Sassen, Paolo Traverso, and Arian Zwegers

The MIT Press
Cambridge, Massachusetts
London, England

This book was set in Times New Roman and Syntax on 3B2 by Asco Typesetters, Hong Kong.

Library of Congress Cataloging-in-Publication Data

At your service : service-oriented computing from an EU perspective / edited by Elisabetta Di Nitto . . . [et al].
p. cm. — (Cooperative information systems)
Presents results of collaborative research projects of the European Community's Information Society Technologies Programme about service-oriented computing.
Includes bibliographical references and index.
ISBN 978-0-262-04253-6 (hardcover : alk. paper), 978-0-262-53730-8 (pb)
1. Web services—Research—Europe. 2. Internetworking (Telecommunication) 3. Application program interfaces (Computer software) 4. Business enterprises—Computer networks. I. Di Nitto, Elisabetta. II. Information Society Technologies Programme.
TK5105.88813.A85 2009
006.7′6—dc22 2008027498

Contents

Foreword

Today, it is almost impossible to remember what life was like with no computer, no mobile phone, and no Internet for exchanging e-mails and data. Organizations are doing business with each other by exchanging information via the Internet. People are filling in tax declarations online. Microcomputers are present in almost every electrically powered device we buy and use; most are controlled with dedicated forms of software, which often enable the device to be adapted, configured, or upgraded in some way. New application areas and the expansion of numbers and types of devices increase the demand for more and new services. Society is progressively using (and dependent on) software and services running on computers, connecting mobile phones, and other devices, and exchanging information on the Internet.

People like to shop and choose. Businesses and public administrations do this also. Today they obtain the most cost-effective or "optimal" solution to meet their needs, even if the match to needs is not perfect. Tomorrow, they may no longer have to compromise in this way.

Just imagine, from a consumer "demand" viewpoint, software that is provided as a service and computing power that is provided on request—and both of these provided via a communication network. Such an approach allows individuals and organizations to tap into, and to effectively harness, the immense wealth of information, knowledge, and analytical resources as and when they need them, paying only for what they use.

But what would this mean when seen from the supply side? What does it mean for you, as the designers and suppliers of software and services?

As changing demands from society influence what software you develop and how you develop it, you can expect your markets and the structure of your industry to evolve. Is it not true that patterns of competition and business are changing rapidly? It may not yet be so evident to people outside of the business, but the software industry itself is rapidly restructuring. For example, new business models are emerging as an alternative to the buying and selling of traditional packaged software, and as a real alternative to entire families of packaged software acquired from a single source.

For Europe and for its software industry, I believe that such a restructuring of the market and the industry represents a tremendous opportunity.

The European Community helps the industry to acquire more competitive positions by co-funding research in the area of service-oriented computing. Our Sixth Framework Programme for Research and Development (2002–2006) has invested more than 90 million euros in this area, which has led to joint projects of industry and academia in all European countries. In 2007, these efforts were reinforced with a further 120 million euros from our new Seventh Framework Programme.

This book presents the main results so far of European collaborative research in this field. It tells a story of the great potential, and of the continued strength, of European enterprises in many fields of software development. Just as ICT applications are drivers for economic growth, new jobs, and development in all industry sectors, software and services are key drivers for developments in ICT applications. Read on, and you will get a good glimpse of the technologies that help shaping our future.

Viviane Reding
Commissioner for Information Society and Media

Preface

This book is about service-oriented computing (SOC). Service-oriented computing decomposes the logic of an information system into services, which are smaller units of functionality. These services can be used as building blocks in the composition of larger systems. The philosophy of SOC is to build software applications by connecting different building blocks of software (i.e. services) in a loosely coupled way. The services are made available for use by publishing their interfaces. They can be provided in-house or by external parties. Service-oriented computing holds the potential to be an effective solution to letting software systems work together, even when they are developed by different organizations and are spread across the world.

Service-oriented computing is a key topic in the European Community's Information Society Technologies (IST) programme. The European Community co-funds research and technology development via its Sixth Framework Programme (FP6), which includes the IST programme. Since the start of FP6 in 2002, more than 3.5 billion euros have been allocated to collaborative research projects in the IST programme.

This book presents the results of some of those collaborative research projects on service-oriented computing. The book aims to highlight the value of the research performed with respect to the issues that are currently considered challenging in service-oriented computing. Furthermore, it seeks to assess the achievements of European research in the area, and to identify new and remaining research challenges in the field.

Audience

The book is targeted at researchers and practitioners in the field of service-oriented computing. Researchers will find some of the latest thinking in the domain and many examples of the state-of-the-art in service-oriented computing. Both researchers who are just beginning in the field and researchers with experience in the domain should find topics of interest. The references at the end of each chapter point to background topics and more research results.

Furthermore, practitioners will find the theory related to service orientation, which is behind many existing models, tools, and standards. Many chapters contain case studies that provide useful information about challenges, pitfalls, and successful approaches in the practical use of service-oriented computing.

The chapters were written in such a way that they are interesting and understandable for both groups. They assume some background knowledge of the domain, but no specialist knowledge is required. It is possible to read each chapter on its own.

Acknowledgments

Many people contributed in different ways to the realization of this book. First of all, we would like to thank the authors. They have put in considerable effort into writing their chapters. We very much appreciated their willingness and response to refine their contributions after yet another review round. We are very grateful to the reviewers, who provided their valuable feedback to draft versions of the chapters. We thank them for the time they dedicated to improving the quality of the book. Furthermore, we would like to thank John Mylopoulos and Mike Papazoglou, the series editors of the MIT Press Series on Information Systems, for giving us the opportunity to start this book in the first place. Finally, we would like to thank the MIT Press, and in particular Doug Sery, Alyssa Larose, and Mary Reilly, for their support in bringing the book to actual publication.

1 Introduction

Elisabetta Di Nitto, Anne-Marie Sassen, Paolo Traverso, and Arian Zwegers

1.1 Context

Service-oriented computing (SOC) represents one of the most challenging promises to support the development of adaptive distributed systems. Applications can open themselves to the use of services offered by third parties that can be accessed through standard, well-defined interfaces. The binding between applications and the corresponding services can be extremely loose in this context, thus making it possible to compose new services on the fly whenever a new need arises.

Around this idea a number of initiatives and standards have grown up, some of them focusing on how such roles need to interact with each other, and some others on how to engineer systems based on such a model and on how to provide foundational support to their development. In particular, so-called service-oriented applications and architectures (SOAs) have captured the interest of industry, which is trying to exploit them as the reference architecture to support B2B interaction. In this context, according to Forrester Research, the SOA service and market had grown by $U.S. 4.9 billion in 2005, and it is forecasted to have an interesting growth rate until 2010, with a compound annual growth rate of 88 percent between 2004 and 2009.[1]

In this scenario, with the actual adoption of SOA currently being at the level of focused experiments, a number of issues and challenges need to be addressed over both the long and the short term. Some of them are the following:

- The need to support the governance of complex SOA-based systems
- The need to properly address physical and conceptual interoperability among different integrated systems
- The need to properly guarantee the dependability of a system composed of parts owned by third parties
- The need to build approaches that support the (self-) adaptiveness of applications built upon the SOA model
- The opportunity to exploit distributed computational capabilities to achieve high-level objectives

- The possibility to adopt the SOA approach in contexts different from the classical B2B one and more oriented to the development of pervasive, multidevice systems.

In all these areas the research community is experimenting with different solutions and approaches, and we are witnessing the evolution of a melting pot of ideas and intuitions, coming from different fields, into more established and well-structured approaches. This is why we were asked to provide an overview on what is happening in the research projects funded by the European Community in this area, within the Information Society Technologies (IST) Sixth Framework Programme (FP6).[2]

The objectives of IST in FP6 are to ensure European leadership in domain-independent as well as domain-specific technologies at the heart of the knowledge economy. IST aims to increase innovation and competitiveness in European businesses and industries, and to contribute to greater benefits for all European citizens. Thus, the focus is on the future generation of technologies in which computers and networks will be integrated into the everyday environment, rendering accessible a multitude of services and applications through easy-to-use human interfaces. This vision of ambient intelligence places the user, the individual, at the center of future developments for an inclusive knowledge-based society for all.

Service-oriented computing is one of the research fields IST is focusing on, since it embodies relevant challenges for the vision of ambient intelligence, and appears to be one of the most promising topics for both research and industrial exploitation. For the projects that have been involved in the writing of this book, IST has contributed 94 million euros out of a total cost of these projects of about 153 million euros during 2002–2006. Such an investment, together with the establishment of the NESSI technology platform on services,[3] shows the willingness of Europe to act as a main player both at the institutional and at the industrial level.

This book shows how some of the most significant efforts funded by the European Community in the period when it was being written are addressing the open issues mentioned above. The presentation is structured to cover different aspects related to the development and operation of a service-based system. In the remainder of this chapter we briefly review the terminology that is used in the rest of the book, we provide an overview of the layers typical of a service-oriented application, and, finally, we outline the structure of the book.

1.2 Main Definitions and Terminology

As the various chapters of this book will show, services and SOAs can be used for purposes ranging from the most common applications on B2B integration to pervasive and autonomic systems. Of course, this means that the main concepts and definitions can vary from case to case. We have been trying to keep a uniform terminology by selecting the conceptual model for services (Colombo et al. 2005) developed within the SeCSE project (see chapter 10) as a common reference, and we have discovered that it should be extended

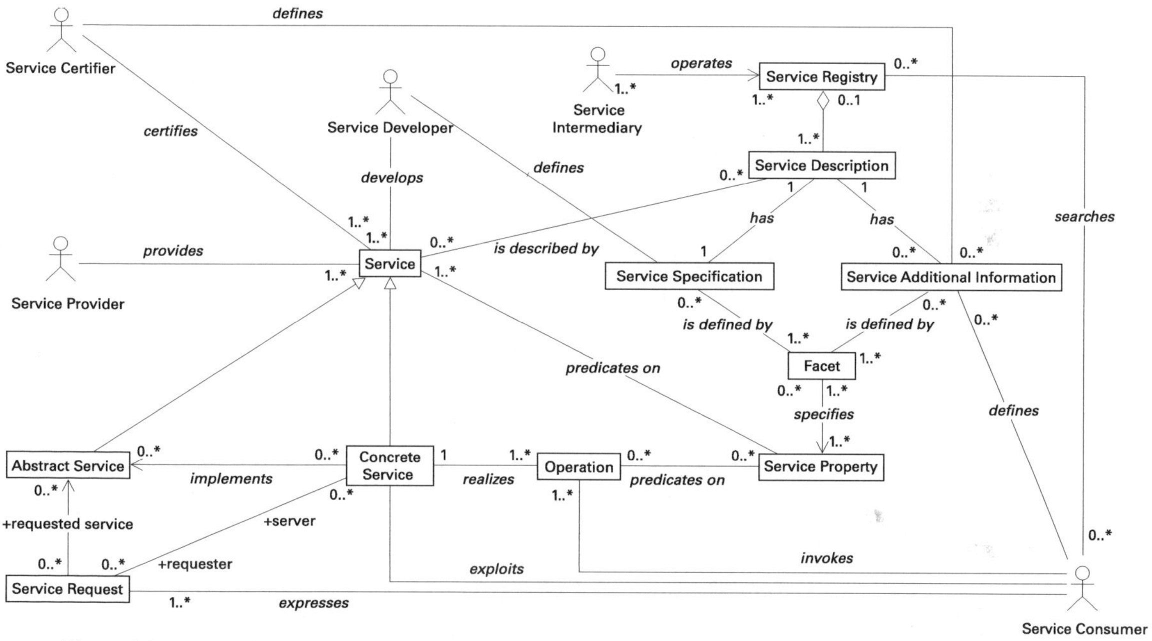

Figure 1.1
The core diagram of the SeCSE conceptual model

with new concepts in various directions to make it fully adequate to cover all concepts introduced in the various contributions. Its main core, however (see figure 1.1), remains unchanged, and represents the characteristic concepts of a service-oriented application. *Services*, in the context of this book, always represent the production of some result upon request. Such production is often performed by a software system that implements the service. However, it could also be performed by a human being or by cooperation between humans and computers.

In general, a service has a description associated with it. In the case of SeCSE such a description is organized in two parts, one that is defined when the service is designed and that contains all information needed to operate properly with the service (the service specification), and another that can be optionally used to incorporate additional information about the service. The service specification can include the signature of service operations, as well as behavioral constraints and properties, nonfunctional characteristics and so-called SLA templates that define the structure of the service-level agreements that the service can fulfill. The additional information contains information about the execution of services and is usually fed by the service users or by a third party, for instance, the party in charge of certifying the service. In SeCSE, service specifications and additional information are organized in facets, each of which provides a piece of the whole information about the service.

As will be discussed mainly in chapter 4, services can be implemented by using technologies ranging, for instance, from Web Services to P2P and Grid Services. Also, they can have specific characteristics, such as being dependable (see chapter 19) or collaborative (see chapter 5), and therefore can be exploited by multiple users at the same time through multiple interfaces and asynchronous and peer-to-peer interaction modes. Semantic services have an associated ontological description, provided in proper languages such as OWL-S or WSMO (see chapters 12, 13, and 14). Thanks to this description, the activities that require discovering and assembling compositions of services are greatly simplified. The explicit definition of semantics also allows the designer to focus more easily on a specific application domain, as happens in chapter 14, which focuses on services for the smart home application domain. Finally, services can be conversational (see chapters 8 and 9), as when they are used for business-to-business integration. In this context, interoperability issues have to be addressed as well (see chapter 18).

Software systems implementing the services can be autonomic or self-adaptive, in the sense that they are able to sense and adapt themselves, and their ability to offer services under different environmental conditions (see chapters 2, 6, and 9). Discovery of services also can happen by taking into account the environment and the context in which services operate (see chapters 3 and 4). Finally, services can be created not only by developers but also by end users (see chapter 11), by providing tools that allow for an easy end-user interaction.

1.3 Layers of a Service-Oriented Platform

Service-oriented computing is a research field that includes multiple aspects and facets. We have classified the chapters in this book according to two different and independent taxonomies. The first one is developed by the NESSI platform.[4] It aims to provide a unified view of European research in services architectures and software infrastructures. This view will be the basis for defining technologies, strategies, and deployment policies fostering new and open industrial solutions and societal applications that enhance the safety, security, and well-being of citizens.

The second taxonomy is "the SOC road map" (Papazoglou et al. 2006), which has been developed by researchers in the service-oriented community. It aims at identifying the specific research challenges arising mainly in the area of service integration. It is therefore more specific than the first one, and will be used to refine the classification of the projects dealing with service integration. The rest of this section describes the two taxonomies in more detail.

1.3.1 The NESSI Framework

Figure 1.2 shows the taxonomic framework of NESSI. It stretches from low-level infrastructure considerations (e.g., dealing with large-scale resource virtualization) to high-level

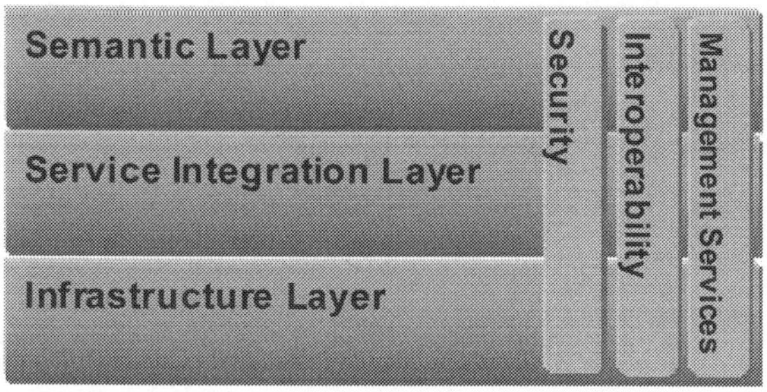

Figure 1.2
The NESSI framework

semantic considerations (e.g., supporting the definition and use of ontologies, reasoning with situations, and representing intentions). The framework also addresses concerns that span all these different levels of abstraction, covering cross-cutting issues such as security, system and service management, and interoperability. Below, we provide some details on the layers that are part of the road map. The reader should note that NESSI is using "service" in a broad sense, including network connectivity, computing hardware, application environments, and data and information, as well as application components.

Infrastructure The infrastructure domain aims at the virtualization of resources across servers, storage, distributed systems, and the network. Infrastructures have to be designed and implemented to be robust, fault-tolerant, and secure. From a user's perspective, infrastructures must be transparent (almost invisible) during the entire life cycle—allowing a plug-and-play approach to infrastructure use as well as to Grid provisioning and operation of services.

The internals of the infrastructure layer should be, in principle, completely transparent to the services being executed on top of it. The upper layer can, however, gain advantage from the Grid resource replication mechanisms and its autonomic capabilities for load balancing, clustering of similar/diverse components, and so on.

Service Integration In the NESSI vision, SOAs will become the primary architecture for business systems of the near future. SOAs provide means to create complex systems in a new modular way, simply by configuration and composition. This modularity will allow reusability of published services by other applications within a virtual organization paradigm. In this context, the general problem of configuring and composing a set of services, at both the functional and the business levels, is a difficult one: dependable systems can be built only from reliable configurations and compositions. Therefore, the service integration layer also aims at providing tools and methods for configuration and composition in the same way that existing CASE tools provide support for programming.

Moreover, the layer should also support dynamic reconfiguration by allowing software to be modified without stopping execution. The potential is great—dynamic reconfiguration allows systems to evolve and extend without loss of service, thus meeting the demands for high availability.

Semantics Semantics is a key element for the transformation of information into knowledge. One way to build knowledge will be through advanced search engines that allow fast search in a large body of unstructured data. Semantic Web technology based on ontologies will enable far more effective machine-to-machine communication.

On the business process level, business modeling provides the semantics that is required for business process management, process transformation, and intercompany cooperation. In a knowledge-based economy, learning and knowledge management finally will have to converge to a workplace utility.

Security and Trust Concern over security is one of the most significant barriers to acceptance of IT and digital services as a utility, becoming even more crucial in a highly dynamic environment. Security and trust in a utility-driven world can be achieved only by an end-to-end perspective that addresses all layers involved. An example is the consistent treatment of identity (of people, resources, and processes) balanced with mechanisms for providing levels of privacy and anonymity where required by the legal or regulatory environment or by user wishes. Related to this is the need for a practical yet rigorous approach to trust in large distributed systems, as well as models and mechanisms for secure and trusted interenterprise cooperation and cooperation in virtual organizations.

Management Services Central to the NESSI vision of a service-oriented utility are automated and autonomic management techniques for efficient and effective management of large, dynamic systems. These will include the following:

- Service life cycle management to support identification of components, their location, negotiation, and reservation, as well as their orchestration, configuration, and operational management. Life cycle management will also have to support the withdrawal and release of resources, accounting, and settlement.
- Trust, service-level agreements (SLAs), or contract management that deals with aspects such as the agreement over Quality of Service (QoS) provisioning mapped to SLAs, flexible QoS metrics, and the management of QoS violation. In addition, common principles for defining unambiguous SLAs that can be associated with a measurement and audit methodology will be necessary in a commercial environment.
- Managing of the complexity (including emergent properties) of global-scale, distributed ICT so that performance can be predicted and controlled.
- Mechanisms for controlled sharing of management information, end-to-end coordination, and performance prediction and management.

Interoperability and Open Standards Interoperability, including the use of open standards, when understood in its widest sense involves any kind of ICT at any level. It deals with aspects such as interfaces between different systems, abstraction between layers, connectivity, standardized protocols, interoperability to support dynamic composition of services, business process interfaces, standards for interenterprise cooperation, and integration with sensors and other devices. Industry-developed open standards will constitute the key mechanisms to overcome the current interoperability problems that generate frustration and distrust in new technology.

1.3.2 The SOC Road Map

The SOC road map (shown in figure 1.3) separates basic service capabilities provided by a services middleware infrastructure and conventional SOA from more advanced service functionalities that are needed for dynamically composing (integrating) services. It also

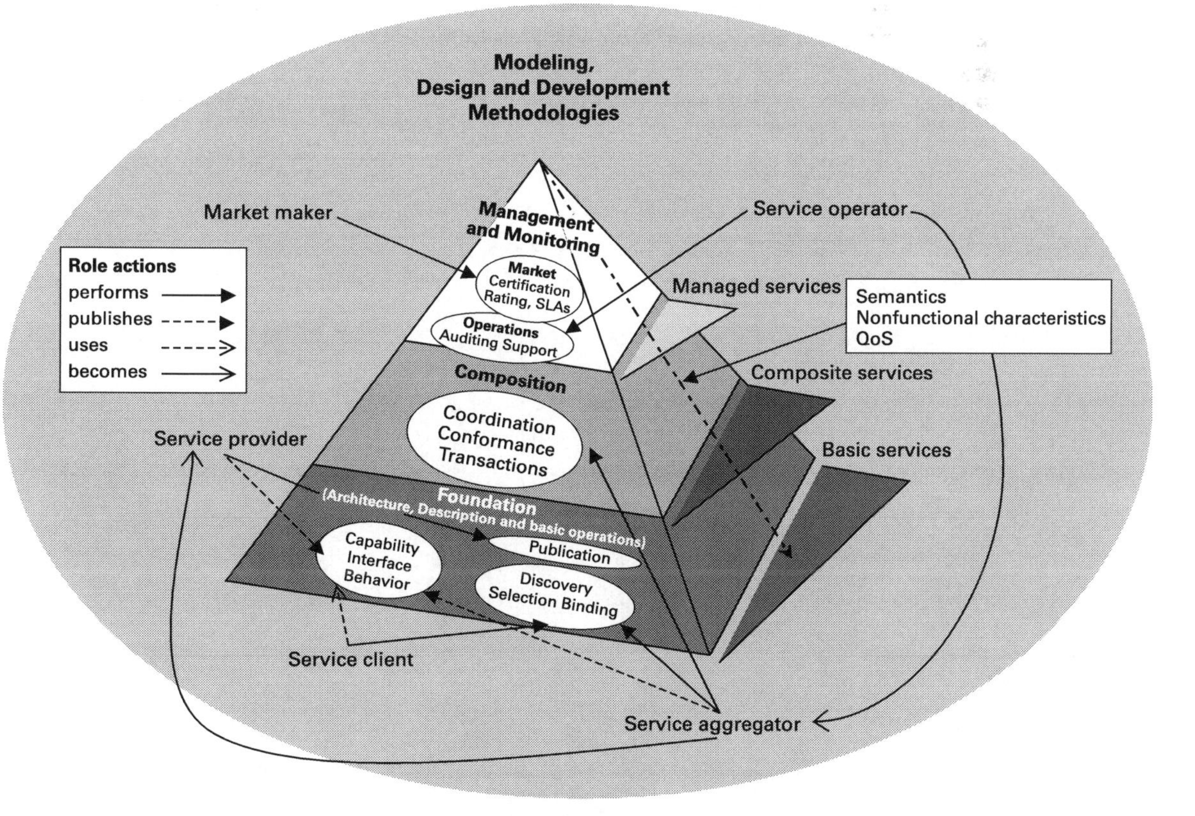

Figure 1.3
The SOC roadmap

distinguishes between a layer for composing services and a layer for the management of services and of their underlying infrastructure.

As shown in the figure, there are three planes. The bottom plane utilizes the basic service middleware and architectural constructs for describing, publishing, and discovering services, and the service composition and management planes are layered on top of it. The perpendicular axis indicates service characteristics that cut across all three planes. These include semantics, nonfunctional service properties, and quality of service (QoS). Quality of service encompasses important functional and nonfunctional service quality attributes, such as performance metrics (response time, for instance), security attributes, (transactional) integrity, reliability, scalability, and availability. Delivering QoS on the Internet is a critical and significant challenge because of its dynamic and unpredictable nature.

Figure 1.3 also highlights the importance of service modeling and service-oriented engineering (i.e., service-oriented analysis, design, and development techniques and methodologies that are crucial elements for the development of meaningful services and business process specifications). Service-oriented engineering activities help in developing meaningful services, service compositions, and techniques for managing services. Service engineering is thus applied to the three service planes shown in figure 1.3.

1.4 Structure of the Book

The chapters of this book have been organized according to the taxonomy shown in figure 1.4. The taxonomy was obtained by merging the two visions and road maps described in

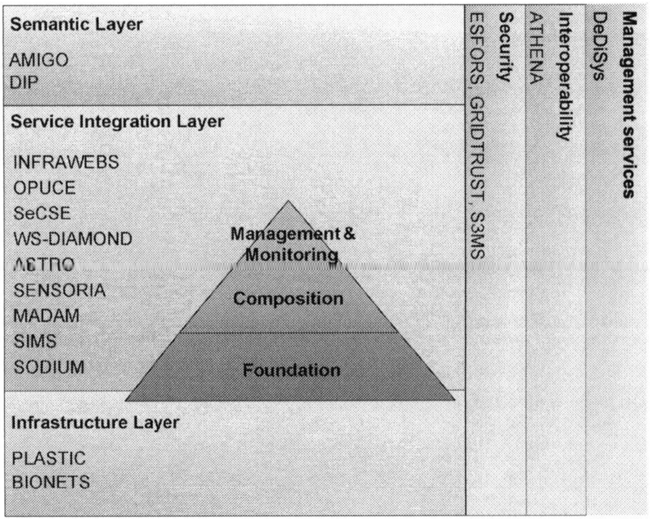

Figure 1.4
The structure of the book

the previous section. Indeed, the SOC road map can nicely detail one of the layers of the NESSI framework (i.e., the service integration layer).

The two projects that address the service infrastructure layer are BIONETS and PLASTIC (chapters 2 and 3). The emerging trends toward pervasive computing and communication environments will make it possible for user-oriented services to interface directly with the surrounding environment. This opens up enormous opportunities for context-related services, but also poses problems related to the management of these complex networks and services. Chapter 2 describes the biologically inspired approach of BIONETS on how to provide a fully integrated network and service environment that scales to large amounts of heterogeneous devices, and that is able to adapt and evolve in an autonomic way.

Pervasive computing will enable users to access information and computational resources anytime and anywhere. Such a setup is highly open and dynamic: pervasive computing systems should support ad hoc deployment and execution, integrating the available hardware and software resources at any given time and place. Service discovery will thus have an important role to play. Chapter 3 describes possible service discovery mechanisms in pervasive, heterogeneous environments.

Chapter 4 (on the SODIUM project) also deals with service discovery and heterogeneity, but at the service integration level of the NESSI framework. It provides innovative solutions for the description, discovery, and composition of heterogeneous services such as Web Services, Grid Services, or P2P services. In fact, SODIUM proposes an abstraction layer that hides the technical details of each service type from both developers and end users, without altering or modifying the distinct properties and characteristics of the underlying technologies.

Chapter 5, which describes the results of SIMS, introduces the concept of semantic interfaces for defining the collaborative behavior of services and the goals that can be achieved through collaborative behavior. Semantic interfaces are used to compose services and to ensure compatibility between the collaborating parts of the services at design time and runtime.

Chapter 6, which describes results of the MADAM project, proposes development approaches for self-adaptable, context-aware applications based on separation of concerns. Applications developed according to this approach dynamically optimize the end-user experience according to the context of the (mobile) user.

Chapter 7, which presents the results of the SENSORIA project, provides mathematically founded and sound methodologies and tools for dealing with the amount of flexibility and interoperability needed in next-generation service-oriented architectures. SENSORIA aims to support a more systematic and scientifically well-founded approach to engineering of software systems for service-oriented overlay computers.

Chapters 4, 5, 6, and 7 all concern the foundation layer of the SOC road map, since they provide basic principles and theory for describing and discovering services. Chapter 8, about the ASTRO project, covers a substantial part of the composition layer of the SOC road map, focusing essentially on the provision of innovative and powerful orchestration functionalities. ASTRO provides design-time support to composition, as well as runtime support by allowing the monitoring of composite services.

Chapter 9, on WS-DIAMOND, concerns the management layer of the SOC road map, since it describes a framework for self-healing Web Services.

The last category of project contributions to the service engineering issues identified by the SOC road map and the service integration layer of NESSI is represented by the SeCSE, OPUCE, and INFRAWEBS projects. All three projects provide useful principles and supporting tools to develop service-oriented systems. Chapter 10 (SeCSE) focuses on service description of both functional and nonfunctional properties of services, and how they can be composed into dependable service compositions. Chapter 11 (OPUCE) describes how end users can adapt and compose telecommunications services according to their needs while they are on the move. It tries to bring Web 2.0 principles to the telecommunications world. Chapter 12 (INFRAWEBS) describes a methodology and tools to develop semantic Web Services, either by starting from scratch or by converting nonsemantic Web Services into semantic Web Services.

Although placed in the semantics layer of the NESSI framework, chapter 13 is highly related to chapter 12, dealing also with the development of semantic Web Services. In particular, it describes some of the results of the DIP project and shows the real potential of semantics in a compelling real-world application in the e-government domain. Chapter 14, about the AMIGO project, shows how semantics may be used to realize the ambient intelligence vision of a networked home.

Chapters 15–19 deal with cross-cutting issues. Chapters 15, 16, and 17 deal with security. Chapter 15 describes the ESFORS project, which has identified security requirements for service-oriented systems and has done a survey on relevant research to address the requirements. Chapter 16 describes a fine-grained access control proposed by the GridTrust project that addresses the security challenges created by the next-generation grids where computing and storage power and services are shared among a (dynamic) pool of users. In chapter 17 the notion of security by contract ($S \times C$), developed by the S3MS project, is explained as a mechanism to create trust when nomadic users would like to download services that are useful for their context at a particular moment.

Chapter 18 presents the contribution of the ATHENA project within the cross-cutting issue of interoperability. In particular, ATHENA has developed an interoperability framework and a reference architecture that relate the areas in which interoperability issues can occur. They range from the business level down to the implementation level.

Chapter 19's focus is on dependability. If service-oriented computing is ever going to be used for mission-critical systems, the ability to prove the dependability of the system is crucial. The DeDiSys project proposes dependability techniques for both data-centric and resource-centric services.

Chapters 20 and 21 present an outlook to the future. How will all these valuable results be taken up by industry in order to create innovation and new jobs? In chapter 20, NESSI explains how this industry-driven initiative plans to take up these results and to fill the gaps.

Of course the issues that remain unsolved do not relate only to the industrial adoption of the results that have been developed so far. Basic research still needs to be further developed. In order to support this effort, in the first call of the new Framework Programme for Research (FP7) the European Commission has agreed to co-fund the S-Cube network of excellence in service-oriented computing. S-Cube's plans for further research are presented in chapter 21.

Acknowledgment

The work published in this chapter is partly funded by the European Commission under the Sixth Framework Programme. The work reflects only the authors' views. The Commission is not liable for any use that may be made of the information contained therein.

Notes

1. IDC, Enterprise Integration & SOA Conference, 2007. http://www.idc.com/italy/events/ei07/ei07.jsp.
2. http://cordis.europa.eu/ist/.
3. www.nessi-europe.eu.
4. http://www.nessi-europe.com/Nessi/Portals/0/Nessi-repository/Publications/Flyers/2006_02_NESSI_SRA_VOL_1.pdf.

References

M. Colombo, E. Di Nitto, M. Di Penta, D. Distante, and M. Zuccalà. 2005. Speaking a common language: A conceptual model for describing service-oriented systems. In *Service-Oriented Computing—ICSOC 2005: Third International Conference.... Proceedings*, ed. B. Benatallah, Fabio Casati, and Paolo Traverso. LNCS 3826, pp. 50–62. Berlin: Springer Verlag.

M. P. Papazoglou, P. Traverso, S. Dustdar, and F. Leymann. 2006. Service-oriented Computing Research Roadmap. http://infolab.uvt.nl/pub/papazogloump-2006–96.pdf.

2 BIONETS: Bio-Inspired Paradigms for Service Provisioning in Pervasive Computing Environments

Imrich Chlamtac, Daniele Miorandi, Stephan Steglich, Ilja Radusch, David Linner, Jyrki Huusko, and Janne Lahti

2.1 Introduction

The motivation for the BIONETS project (http://www.bionets.eu) comes from emerging trends toward pervasive computing and communication environments, characterized by an extremely large number of networked embedded devices (Weiser 1999). Such devices will possess sensing/identifying capabilities, making it possible for user-situated services to interface directly with the surrounding environment, entailing the possibility of introducing radically novel services able to enhance our five senses, our communication, and our tool manipulation capabilities.

These embedded devices will possess computing and (basic) communication capabilities having the potential to form a massively large networked system, orders of magnitude larger than the current Internet. Overall, the complexity of such environments will not be far from that of biological organisms, ecosystems, and socioeconomic communities. Conventional approaches to communications and service provisioning are ineffective in this context, since they fail to address several new features: a wide heterogeneity in node capabilities and service requirements, a huge number of nodes with consequent scalability issues, the possibly high node mobility, and the management complexity.

BIONETS aims at a novel approach able to address these challenges. Nature and society exhibit many instances of systems in which large populations are able to reach efficient equilibriums and to develop effective collaboration and survival strategies, able to work in the absence of central control, and able to exploit local interactions. We seek inspiration from these systems to provide a fully integrated network and service environment that scales to large numbers of heterogeneous devices, and that is able to adapt and evolve in an autonomic way.

BIONETS overcomes device heterogeneity and achieves scalability via an autonomic and localized peer-to-peer communication paradigm. Simple devices with sensing capabilities (T-nodes) are relieved from the burden of forwarding information (as is done in conventional wireless sensor networks solutions), acting as a distributed interface for services running in proximity. More powerful devices (U-nodes) are used to run services and to interface with the end users; in contrast to standard networking approaches, they do not form a connected topology, but live in an ecosystem in which highly dynamic islands of connected U-nodes form and disappear continuously.

Services in BIONETS are autonomic, and evolve to adapt to the surrounding environment, in the way living organisms evolve by natural selection. Network operations will be driven by the services, providing ad hoc support when and where needed to fulfill users' requests. Security issues will be considered as a fundamental part of the services themselves, representing a key ingredient for achieving a purposeful autonomic system. The network will become merely an appendix of the services, which in turn become a mirror image of the social networks of users they serve. This new people-centric paradigm breaks the barrier between service providers and users, and sets up the opportunity for "mushrooming" of spontaneous services, thereby paving the way to a service- and user-centric ICT revolution.

The BIONETS project, whose scope and impact are graphically depicted in figure 2.1, builds on two pillars, dealing with networks and services, respectively. Both are permeated by biologically inspired concepts and will, in the end, converge to provide a fully autonomic environment for networked services. The first pillar builds on a novel approach to information diffusion, communication, and filtering that aims at replacing the conventional end-to-end Internet approaches with localized service-driven communications. The

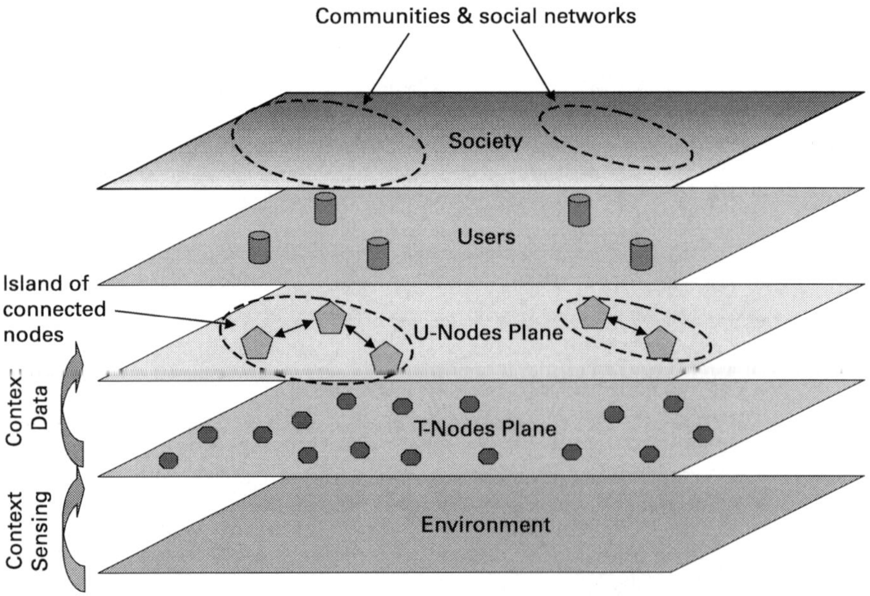

Figure 2.1
The large-scale BIONETS project picture

second one is a bio-inspired platform, centered on the concept of evolution, for the support of autonomic services. As shown in figure 2.1, in BIONETS, T-nodes gather data from the environment and are read by U-nodes that are in proximity. U-nodes form islands of connected devices, and may exchange information when they are in mutual communication range; decisions are taken by the service itself. Services are user-situated, and their interactions reflect the social networks/communities users belong to.

With respect to the taxonomy proposed by this book, the BIONETS project is a cross-cutting one, while remaining mostly focused on the infrastructure layer, owing to the tight coupling between networking and service issues.

In this chapter, we will introduce, present, and discuss the underlying concepts and some of the outcomes of the BIONETS project consortium efforts toward the definition of a bio-inspired, fully autonomic solution for pervasive computing/communications environments. In section 2.2 we review some of the most relevant related work. In section 2.3 we present the networking solutions introduced to ensure scalability and support heterogeneity in the networked BIONETS system. In section 2.4 we present the basic building blocks and architectural foundations of BIONETS services. Section 2.5 presents and discusses mechanisms and solutions for the provisioning of an autonomic support to the service life cycle. The chapter concludes with section 2.6, an analysis of the directions to be pursued within the project consortium.

2.2 Related Work

The foundations of pervasive computing can be traced back to the research undertaken at Xerox PARC at the end of the 1980s, which led to the milestone position paper by M. Weiser (1999). Though such a concept has expanded in many directions (including ubiquitous computing, ambient intelligence, and smart environments), the basis remains the vision of a fully distributed computing infrastructure in which smart objects are equipped with embedded electronics, enabling the seamless provisioning of services to the end user. Such vision included the possibility of interacting with the resulting "digital clouds" in a natural way, such as through haptic interfaces and other forms of noninvasive human–computer interaction means.

With the explosion of personal communication devices (PDAs, smart phones), the research focus has moved to mixed scenarios, where the underlying computing resources are coupled with the presence of more powerful personal devices which are used as interface to the final user. This is well exemplified by the Oxygen project run at the CSAIL lab of MIT (MIT Project Oxygen 2002). The BIONETS project builds on a similar two-tier architecture, where devices in the lower tier are used as distributed interface with the surrounding environment, and devices in the upper tiers provide the necessary computing power to provide context-aware services.

Opportunistic networking refers, broadly speaking, to a class of networked information systems where constituents (usually mobile devices) are connected only sporadically to each other, and opportunistically exploit contacts for forming ad hoc networks and exchanging information (HAGGLE Project 2006). In BIONETS, opportunistic networking is used to enlarge the set of services that can be offered in pervasive computing environments, by enabling the formation of temporary peer-to-peer wireless networks able to leverage the available resources.

The term "autonomic computing" was introduced by IBM to denote an innovative approach to innovation in the IT field (Kephart and Chess 2003). An autonomic computing system is characterized by possessing the self-CHOP features (self-configuration, self-healing, self-optimization, and self-protection). In other words, it is able to automate most of the management operations that, in current technologies, are carried out by human operators. The motivation for the autonomic computing initiative came from the observation that innovation in the IT field is hindered by the "complexity ceiling" characterizing IT systems. The final goal is to introduce techniques for letting computing systems become able to manage themselves without requiring any human intervention, and to seamlessly leverage the available resources in a goal-oriented way. Application of the autonomic concepts to communication systems was fostered by the EU initiative on "Situated and Autonomic Communication" (Sestini 2006), which targets the introduction of the next generation of autonomic communication systems.

In a broader sense, the autonomic properties (well represented by IBM's self-CHOP paradigm) are being applied to a variety of domains characterized by (1) systems whose complexity is reaching the limits of human ability to design and control them, and (2) the presence of computing logic, and therefore the possibility of automating tasks in the IT infrastructure. This field, which we will term autonomics, has its roots in cybernetics (Heylighen and Joslyn 2001), but builds on results from a variety of scientific domains, including complex systems science (Bar-Yam 1997; Pastor-Satorras et al. 2003), statistical physics, game theory, and systems biology.

Bio-inspired computing is a field of study that includes both the study of nature through the use of computing (e.g., bioinformatics) and the study of how nature can lead to new paradigms for computational machines (e.g., biocomputing; Timmis et al. 2006). The latter field includes approaches inspired by genetics, such as evolutionary computation (Foster 2001) as well as approaches inspired by developmental biology, such as artificial embryogeny (Stanley and Miikkulainen 2003). At a higher abstraction level, biology has been used as a source of inspiration for identifying design patterns for distributed computing systems (Babaoglu et al. 2006); the latter approach has represented the basis for two EU project, BISON (The BISON Project 2003) and DELIS (The DELIS Project 2005). In BIONETS, bio-inspired computing solutions are used as a means for achieving autonomicity at the service level.

Modeling distributed software systems with the notion of services gained momentum with the introduction of Web Services (Booth et al. 2004) and led to attempts to define an architectural style, referred to as service-oriented architecture (SOA; He 2003). SOA is still a living term, but all definition attempts have several characteristics in common. The central idea of SOA is to loose the coupling of service providers and service consumers, with loose coupling achieved in multiple steps. First, services are bound dynamically. Instead of defining fixed dependencies to remote components when implementing an application, only the required functionality is determined, and an appropriate implementation is utilized at runtime. Second, interface and exchanged data structures must be described in an open and implementation-independent manner. Third, the interactions between service consumer and service provider are atomic, uniform, and at best stateless.

The SOA concept of self-contained functional blocks that can be accessed by well-defined message choreographies promoted the idea for creating added value by composing services, and raised the need for considerations about the service life cycle (Wall 2006). Additionally, the promise of automatically generating added value led to several approaches for creating, adapting, and optimizing composite services (Oh et al. 2006; Küster et al. 2005; Gao et al. 2007), and describing the required service models by the use of ontologies (Roman et al. 2005; Battle et al. 2005; OWL Services Coalition 2004). The BIONETS service life cycle addresses automated and decentralized creation and adaptation of services, composite or atomic ones, with regard to a frequently changing computing environment characterized by unpredictable service availabilities.

2.3 The BIONETS Disappearing Network Architecture

2.3.1 Actors and Roles

The ability of the devices constituting pervasive computing/communication environments to connect to each other is expected to be one of the key properties for enabling the support of powerful user-centric services. The resulting large-scale computing and communication system will present features very different from those typical of existing models. First, the resulting system will comprise a huge number of nodes and will experience a potentially tremendous number of data flows, raising scalability issues for the underlying networking infrastructure. Further, these scenarios will be characterized by a large heterogeneity in terms of devices. These all-embracing networked environments will comprise devices ranging from simple passive RFID tags to standard sensor nodes up to smart phones, laptops, multimedia computers, and PDAs. All this heterogeneity represents a harmful feature for conventional IP-based networking paradigms, where the hourglass model imposes severe constraints on the needed resources of the networked entities. In BIONETS, such heterogeneity will be dealt with by splitting the devices into three categories (BIONETS 2006, 2007).

T-nodes are simple, inexpensive devices with sensing/identifying capabilities. They act as a form of distributed interface with the environment and are needed to provide context awareness to BIONETS services. T-nodes possess only a minimal set of requirements, so that even almost passive devices, such as TAGs or RFIDs, could satisfy them. T-nodes do not communicate among themselves but are able to interface only with U-nodes in proximity. Further, they present minimal requirements in terms of processing/storage/communications. In BIONETS, T-nodes can belong to different classes, where the classification is based upon the supported features. The classification is incremental, so that, for example, a T-node of class 2 presents all the features of a T-node of class 1 plus some additional ones. The features are defined in terms of offered primitives, including the ability to perform some (basic) information processing, encryption, storage, and so on (BIONETS 2006).

U-nodes are complex, powerful devices. No stringent limitation on requirements is encompassed for U-nodes. PDAs, laptops, smart phones, and multimedia computers represent examples of a U-node. U-nodes are carried around by users (hence they are inherently mobile) and run services. They interact with the environment through T-nodes, from which they gather information to run context-aware services. U-nodes may communicate among themselves to exchange information, whether environmental data or service-specific code (in order to enable service evolution).

Access points (APs) are complex, powerful devices that act as proxies with the IP world. APs do not run services, but enable BIONETS to leverage existing IP infrastructures.

The focus for the distinction between T-nodes and U-nodes is related to their different functional roles played with respect to the information gathered from the environment, necessary to enable the provisioning of context-aware services. Roughly speaking, T-nodes act as a distributed interface to the environment, whereas U-nodes carry all the "intelligence" in the system, including the possibility of running services. The overall system architecture and its relationship with the environment are depicted in figure 2.2.

Focusing on the information coming from the environment, we can see that two logical entities play a role in the network. The first one acts as source of information. According to standard terminology in data-centric wireless sensor networks (Krishnamachari 2005), we call these entities "data sources." Data sources can simply transmit raw (or processed in a basic way) information. The second entity, which we term "data consumers," is able to process/store/forward data. In the network, intelligence resides in data consumers; they can act as sinks of environmentally gathered data (which is then used to run context-aware services) and/or as routers, used to diffuse information within the system.

T-nodes can act only as data sources. On the other hand, U-nodes can act as both data sources and data consumers. (This accounts for the possibility of U-nodes integrating sensor units, such as cameras on smart phones.)

The resulting architecture is depicted in figure 2.3, where the logical entities and their features are sketched. Data sources perform sensing/identifying tasks, and are able to do

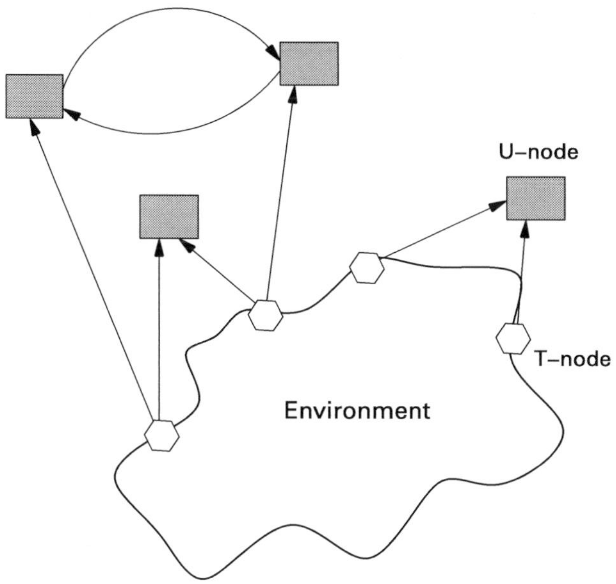

Figure 2.2
Logical structure of BIONETS network architecture and its relationship with the environment

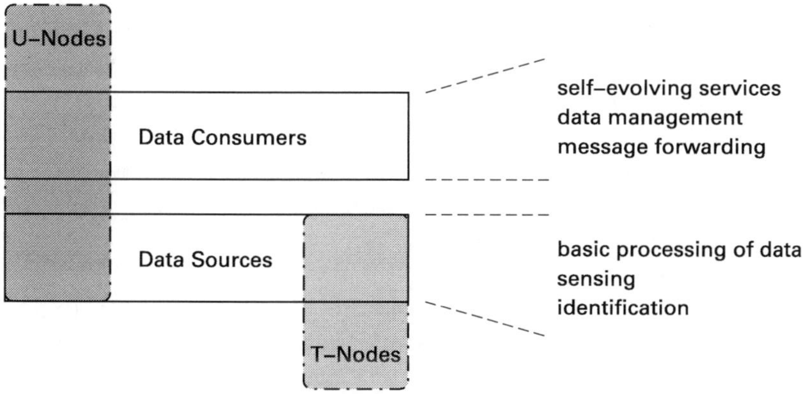

Figure 2.3
Logical roles in the BIONETS network architecture (Data Consumers and Data Sources), main features supported and mapping to device categories (T-Nodes and U-Nodes)

some basic processing of the collected data. Data management, message forwarding, and self-evolving services pertain to the data consumers' plane.

2.3.2 Communications in BIONETS Networks

The BIONETS communication model is based on a two-tier network architecture (Carreras et al. 2007) where nodes are divided according to the classification introduced in the previous section. This two-tier architecture aims at reflecting the need for supporting a wide range of very heterogeneous devices, where heterogeneity is expressed in terms of devices' functionalities and requirements.

The lower tier is composed of the T-nodes, as defined in the previous section. In contrast to conventional approaches in wireless sensor networks research (Akyildiz et al. 2002), T-nodes are not required to perform store-and-forward operations: this is a key design choice to lower the devices' complexity (and cost) and to increase their lifetime. On the other hand, U-nodes present computing/communication capabilities, are almost exempt from energy consumption and storage issues, and may be mobile in nature. U-nodes may communicate among themselves, but can also talk to T-nodes. They act both as sinks for sensor-gathered data and as sources/relays/sinks for communications among U-nodes.

Nodes in BIONETS communicate by exchanging messages, which are service data units (i.e., encapsulation of data items meaningful to a service). In general, messages will be much larger than standard IP packets. (This is because single IP packets usually do not expose meaningful data to the service layer.) Messages include metadata, in the form of ⟨attribute,value⟩ pairs (BIONETS 2007). This is consistent with the data-centric nature of BIONETS communications and allows services to expose messages' content. The approach is similar to what is proposed, in the wired domain, for content-based networking (Carzaniga and Wolf 2003). Destinations are specified using names, which again are described using ⟨attribute,value⟩ pairs. In this way BIONETS can seamlessly support unicast, multicast, and anycast message delivery (BIONETS 2007). Destinations are not necessarily bound to a given device, but can refer to a specific type of service, enabling transparent service-oriented communications.

The communication among U-nodes is based on opportunistic localized peer-to-peer interactions. (This is different from conventional communications in unstructured peer-to-peer networks, which do not account for intermittent connectivity and rely on the underlying IP infrastructure for performing the actual packet forwarding.) As opposed to the end-to-end semantics of standard Internet protocols, U-nodes communicate among themselves only when they are within mutual communication range, and when the service running on the user device requires the interaction to take place. In general, the BIONETS system will comprise a large number of disconnected islands, and no end-to-end connectivity will be present. Mobility of the devices is exploited to convey messages, and provides the means for systemwide dissemination of information. This localized nature of the interaction matches the localized nature of the information, which augments the services

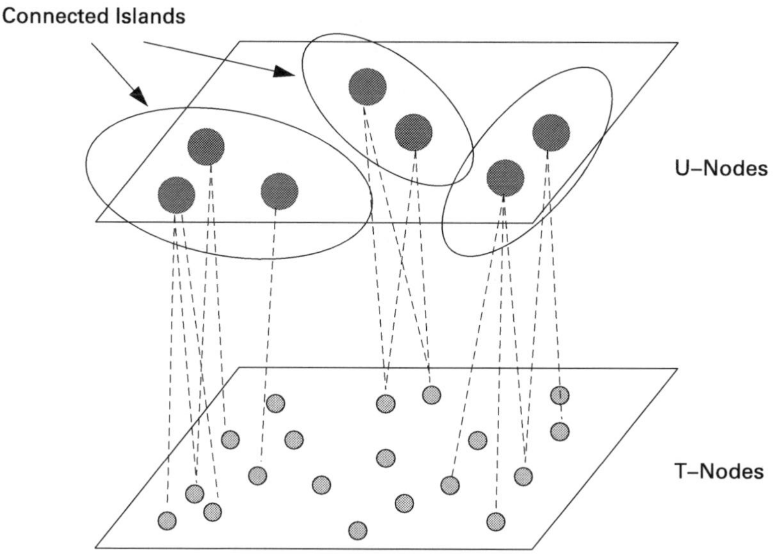

Figure 2.4
The two-tier BIONETS network architecture. Connected islands of U-Nodes interface with T-Nodes in proximity.

running on the users' devices. One of the main advantages of such a localized communication paradigm is that there is no need for (1) a global addressing mechanism or (2) a global routing mechanism, thus lowering the complexity of the network management tasks. The focus is indeed not on transmitting information to a particular node (address-based architecture) but, rather, to all the devices running the same service in proximity (localized service-oriented communication model). The described network architecture is depicted in figure 2.4.

It is worth recalling that the use of forwarding for relaying traffic in a highly partitioned network is consistent with some results in network information theory which show that (1) connected networks present poor scalability properties, owing to the massive interference generated, and that (2) throughput can be traded off for delay in the presence of nodes' mobility to achieve a scalable network model (Grossglauser and Tse 2002).

Clearly, the applicability of the BIONETS model is confined to a class of services requiring massive amounts of data retrieved locally and with relaxed delay constraints. (The picture changes if we also encompass the use of APs, which could provide, by means of an IP backbone, shortcuts to access remote data/services.)

Similar in spirit to the proposed network architecture are the works flourishing in the area of delay-tolerant or opportunistic networks (DTNs) (Fall 2003). With respect to the DTN approach, we are not interested in maintaining the end-to-end nature of communications (and, similarly, backward compatibility with IP); rather, we focus on localized interactions only. Remarkably, the BIONETS scenario also explicitly targets the presence of the environment as a key factor in providing personalized and localized context-aware services, which do not fit the basic DTN architecture. The common point with DTN approaches is the capability to operate in the presence of frequent disconnections, which are handled by means of a suitable relay protocol at the data transport level.

2.3.3 Scalability Issues

The basic way BIONETS deals with scalability issues is by giving up stringent connectivity requirements. In other words, BIONETS networks will almost always be highly partitioned. Nodes within mutual communication range will form what we term an island of nodes, the whole system looking like an archipelago. This leads to the necessity of rethinking the end-to-end communication paradigm typical of Internet-based applications. In BIONETS all operations should be performed on the basis of an intermittent connectivity, where the term "connectivity" does not mean, in general, the ability to join a backbone network and to establish a path toward a destination, but just to communicate with other devices (i.e., to be part of an island).

Since connectivity cannot be ensured, the way to diffuse information in the network remains to be addressed. Information dissemination in BIONETS will be based on relaying schemes in which a U-node "carries around" information that can be handed over to the other U-nodes it encounters on the move.

In BIONETS, mechanisms are needed to limit the diffusion of messages in the network, in order to prevent buffer overflows and enhance the scalability properties of the resulting system. On the one hand, information-filtering mechanisms (discussed below) will be applied to limit the diffusion of environmentally generated data. On the other hand, the significant but nonetheless limited amount of storage available on U-nodes places constraints on the number of copies of a message a node can inject in the system. The problem, roughly stated, lies in the fact that we are basically using flooding (even if controlled and acting over a disconnected network) to diffuse information. And flooding does not scale. Hence, we need techniques for controlling the diffusion of information. Many mechanisms studied in the context of routing protocols can be applied. The bottom line is that there is a fundamental trade-off between storage and packet delay. The more a message is retransmitted, the smaller (in a stochastic sense) the time necessary to reach a node. In a disconnected scenario, this implies the need for keeping the message longer in the memory, and hence the resulting storage–delay trade-off.

There are various mechanisms for controlling the diffusion of messages in BIONETS. One could employ timer-based mechanisms, where after the transmission of a message a node generates a time-out and waits to see if the message is being retransmitted by any other node. If a transmission of the same message is heard, the message is dropped and the memory released. In the other case, after the time-out has expired, the message is sent again. Another promising approach is that of K-copy relaying strategies (Carreras et al. 2007). Under the K-copy relaying strategy, each node receiving a message not destined for it can forward such message to K other nodes encountered on the way. The parameter K, which defines the number of copies of a message a node is allowed to make and disseminate, controls the delay–storage trade-off of the system. The larger the K, the faster the diffusion of a message in the network and the larger the amount of network resources (i.e., bandwidth, storage on devices, etc.) consumed. The case $K=0$ corresponds to the case in which only direct source–destination communication is possible. The case $K=N-1$, N being the number of nodes in the network, corresponds to the case of flooding. This family of protocols is of particular interest in that it naturally lends itself to a distributed stateless implementation. Also, assuming that the value of K can be stamped in the message header, there is the possibility of using different values of K for different applications, thus achieving application-dependent delay–storage trade-offs. Another possibility is to use probabilistic forwarding strategies, in which a message is propagated to a nearby node with a given probability (Lindgren et al. 2003). The ability to self-adapt the various parameters encompassed in such schemes can be introduced by employing distributed evolutionary mechanisms inspired by the genetic algorithms field (Alouf et al. 2007).

The relaying-based strategies outlined above target the scalability issues at the U-nodes level. In pervasive computing/communication environments, however, the number of tiny devices with sensing capabilities is expected to be some order of magnitude higher than that of user nodes. Thus, suitable techniques for limiting the diffusion of the data generated by T-nodes are a primary need to avoid network congestion and collapse. Information filtering (Carreras et al. 2007) plays a central role in ensuring the scalability properties of our architecture and applies to scenarios where sensors are used to gather information from the surrounding environment. Consider a U-node that issues a query at a given instant, from a given position, concerning the value of a given random field. A nearby sensor will answer with the data measured at its location at some previous time. The larger the distance between the sensor and the user, the longer the time it takes for the message to arrive at the U-node, and therefore the lower the usefulness (i.e., the information content) conveyed by the data because of its obsolescence. Roughly speaking, the message would contain information that is of little relevance owing to its low correlation with the actual query. From a sensor-centric perspective, we may then say that for such data, the information content decays over both time and space. On the other hand, from the user point of view, we define a "sphere of interest" that surrounds (again in time and space) the user's device and defines the local environment. Various mechanisms can be envisaged to implement such concepts, ranging from entropy-based coding (where the length of the coded data is adjusted depending on the mutual information conveyed) to wavelet-based coding (where the multiresolution property of the discrete wavelet transform is exploited to provide different levels of details).

2.4 BIONETS' Service Architecture

A disappearing network environment, where availability of resources, network conditions, and user requirements can change dynamically, and where the cooperation of nodes is not guaranteed and disconnected operations are common, generates huge challenges for the service architecture. In order to cope with issues such as service management, content and terminal adaptation, service discovery, deployment, deprecation, evolution, and security aspects in such a network environment, new approaches to build up a service architecture are needed. In BIONETS, we do not address a traditional client–server paradigm. In other words, all nodes are basically equal (i.e., peers) and exchanges are based on localized interactions. This kind of networking requirement generates additional challenges, and in many cases traditional service-oriented architecture solutions are not able to solve them. Even if we are talking about integrating the Web 2.0 community services and mechanisms with other arising trends, such as Semantic Web or Ubiquitous/Geospatial Web, to a new Web 3.0, it does not solve the problems rising from the connectivity and network access.

Based on the requirements arising from the different application scenarios, evolution, service autonomy, and underlying network architecture, a new BIONETS service framework was defined in order to cope with the aforementioned challenges in an efficient and cost-effective way.

In general, BIONETS aims at defining a joint network and service architecture (called as SerWork) by incorporating the disappearing network architecture and autonomous services in such a way that it is possible to utilize and benefit from the cross-scientific approaches in fulfilling the networking and service provisioning paradigms. This kind of approach distinguishes the BIONETS service architecture from conventional service-oriented architecture (SOA) frameworks (OASIS 2006; Erl 2005), whose foundation lies purely in software design paradigms, without taking into consideration the networking capabilities and restrictions caused by the underlying network architecture. For the same reasons it distinguishes itself from the Semantic Web and the other currently proposed Web 3.0 trends. The BIONETS SerWork architecture and its relationship with different study topics are depicted in figure 2.5.

2.4.1 BIONETS Services

Due to the constraints coming from the networking and several application scenarios (especially in terms of lack of guaranteed connectivity and locality of information), the BIONETS services need to be based on localized information. In addition, the applications usually require short response times and dynamic interaction with the end users. In BIONETS, we define the service as an entity which is capable of offering knowledge, content, or functionality to other services and users. Such a concept includes plain Web Services, user applications, application services, and protocol services. First, we need to determine in which aspects BIONETS services will differ from global mobile services, and what features

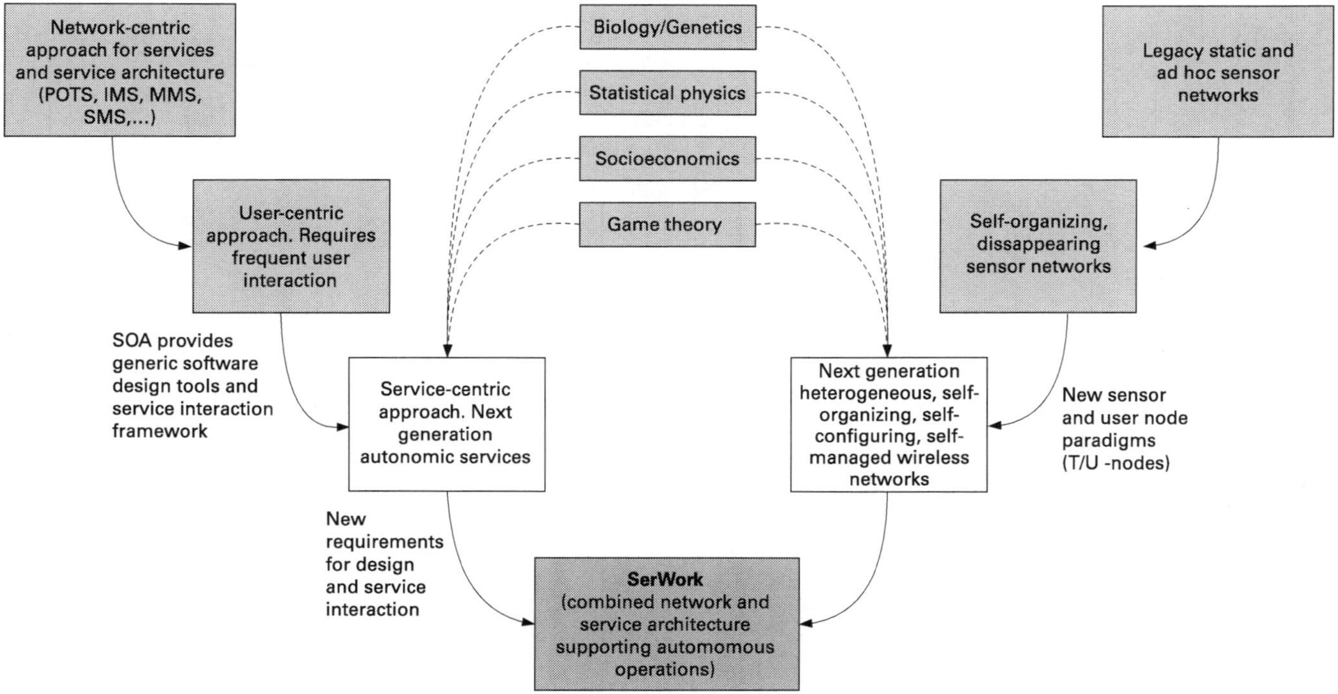

Figure 2.5
BIONETS network and services overview

can make BIONETS a widespread architecture: In BIONETS, services do not need to store and process the information in a centralized manner. Such tasks can be performed in the localized mobility area.

Since the users need up-to-date local information, it is necessary to collect and process information on the fly and on the spot, which will properly describe the actual status of that microenvironment.

The changes in the environment can happen very rapidly and affect a huge number of users in the corresponding mobility area. That is why a careful tracking of the actual conditions of the environment is required.

Information should be important for many users, making them interested in the further transmission of the information and spreading the service.

Service adaptation, self-improvement based on user feedback or on the popularity of the services, is a required feature of autonomic BIONETS services.

BIONETS services run on behalf of one or more users. They are spread across several physical or logical nodes of the network. To clarify descriptions, we henceforth distinguish between two basic service structures, service cells and service individuals, where the life cycle activities are operating. A service cell is an atomic service which cannot be broken up into more basic parts. A composition of service cells is called a service individual. Service individuals may also be composed of other service individuals in a recursive manner. However, completely decomposing service individuals results in a set of service cells which cannot subsequently be broken into parts.

Service individuals and service cells are supposed to have the same appearance, at least from an external point of view. So when we are using the term "service," either a service cell or a service individual is meant. This is possible because the external descriptions of service cells and service individuals are analog. The services can be categorized further to fixed and migrating services. Service cells, as well as composed service individuals, can be either fixed or migrating. From the architectural point of view, all service types are interfaced in the same way, but differ in their behavior and scope. Fixed services abstract functionalities of certain nodes (i.e., usually the features of physical devices abstracted by these nodes). For instance, a call setup service is supposed to be fixed, since this service can be executed only by a phone device, and its execution does not require nested services of other nodes. Migrating services are also based on the functionality of a single node (i.e., the features of the device abstracted by the node). In contrast to fixed services, the functionalities required for the execution of a migrating service are supposed to be provided by each U-node. Thus, only the nonfunctional characteristics of the nodes (e.g., execution speed, power consumption, etc.) may have an impact on the services. Migrating services may be moved between different nodes (i.e., the code of the service implementation is moved). Therefore, migrating services are represented in a platform-independent programming language that can be interpreted directly by the node hosting the services. The intention of migrating services is to have the opportunity to strategically decide which node will pro-

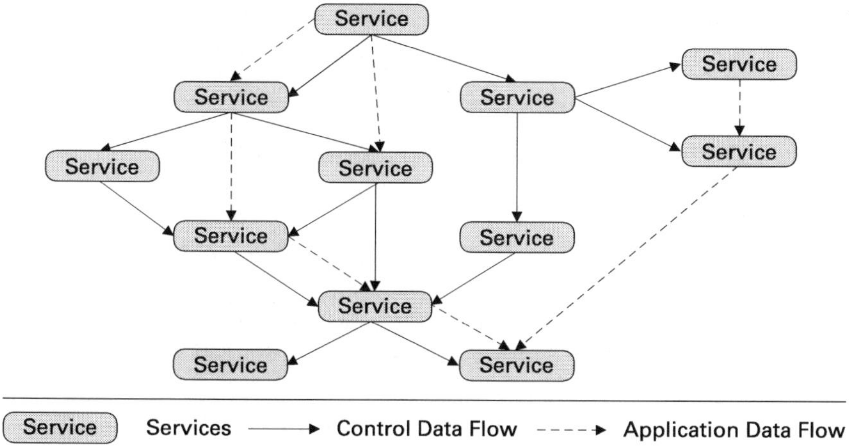

Figure 2.6
Exemplary visualization of service graphs

vide a certain service. Processing power, storage capacity, network connectivity, or even an exposed position in the network topology could be a criterion leading to this decision.

The composition that forms the service individual is a recursive process. Thus, each service individual is itself described by a set of services, either service cell or service individual, and at least two directed graphs representing the relations among these services, as illustrated in figure 2.6. The solid lines describe the flow of control data among the services and therefore, implicitly, the execution sequence. Hence, it determines an initiation cascade along with an appropriate parameterization of the services. The dotted lines describe the flow of application data among the services. With regard to our service model, we distinguish between these two types of flow because we do not expect each service in a composition to participate in the creation or processing of application data.

In the following subsection, we present one envisaged application scenario where BIONETS services can be applied. This is done to illustrate in which respect a bio-inspired evolution of the described system may be useful or, better, may be a good way for the entities to adapt in order to fulfill their final goals. Additionally, it might also be the case that only a bio-inspired evolution would permit such adaptation.

2.4.2 BIONETS Services: Wellness Use Case

Susan is an enthusiastic cyclist. She's planning to enter a cycle race with a couple of her friends. The evening before the race, she opens her laptop at home and starts her PersonalCoach Service. Her PersonalCoach Service is also able to adapt to a variety of other sport activities and is capable of evolving based on the user's needs and usage history. Susan communicates to the PersonalCoach Service that she is going to participate in the cycle race on the following day, and it automatically enrolls her in the race, using the available Internet connection (AP-node). The service automatically also downloads related information (map, weather forecast, etc.) about the race and predicts, based on previous experience, that Susan is going to need CyclingCoach-Service on the following day and that she is going to use her SmartWatch device (U-node) instead of her laptop at the race, so the Service migrates to the SmartWatch along with the CyclingCoach Service.

On the following day, Susan wears her SmartWatch and cycling clothes, and the SmartWatch automatically detects the sensors in Susan's clothes and automatically configures the body area network (BAN). At the racing location Susan mounts her bike and starts the race with her friends. They plan to cooperate and cycle the race as a group. When Susan is riding her bike, the body area network configures itself with the bike's sensors, creating a personal area network (PAN). The other cyclists in the group have their own PersonalCoach Services in their U-nodes, so the cyclists' PersonalCoach Services detect that there are other peer services in the vicinity and, based on previous information, find those reliable; hence they decide to engage in a cooperation and information exchange with those peer PersonalCoach Services. It might happen that one of the other users does not have CyclingCoach Service installed, so an instance of that service migrates from one of the cyclists' U-nodes to that user's U-node.

At the start of the race, hot spots offer wireless connections for the PersonalCoach Service. The Service is able, for example, to get the latest weather forecast or road condition information for the user. It can also benefit from distributed computing for calculating energy consumption, oxygen saturation, and possibly other services requiring lots of computing power. After a couple of kilometers the wireless network suddenly disappears, so the underlying network adapts itself to ad hoc communication. The PersonalCoach Service also adapts itself to the available communication mode and starts to use more localized data. For example, it starts to do the calculations in a SmartWatch and uses other U-nodes to convey data.

After the race, when Susan is back home, the PersonalCoach Service migrates again to Susan's laptop, analyzes all the data collected from the race, and presents the results to Susan It also suggests what to eat, how to stretch muscles, and how to train to get better results in the future.

2.4.3 BIONETS Scenario Analysis

In the story line presented above, we defined a personal coaching service in a BIONETS environment assisting users in their sport activities. The main idea of this scenario is the adaptation of the service to users' social networks and personal contexts, and to changing environmental conditions, such as existing network connections or lack of connections, thus enabling the user to access the service with any device and at any location.

Before the service can assist the user, the user needs to locate/find the service. In the BIONETS environment, where there is vast number of services available, the manual service discovery and installation procedures might not be feasible. Therefore, services in BIONETS need to be easily/automatically discovered.

It could even be possible that the service finds the user by using the user's contextual information and (semi)automatically deploying itself to the user's device. It could also be possible that the service autonomously emerges based on the data the user has, the features of the environment, and the past history of interactions with other networking and computing entities.

Based on these requirements, it can be seen that the BIONETS service should be autonomous with respect to service creation, announcement, discovery, and deployment. It is obvious that these requirements also raise security demands, in order to ensure that these sensitive operations are carried out in a secure way. Service creation will generate new security requirements for newly created services and change security policies; it also may create services which handle user information inadequately.

The service should also be able to extend its functionalities to other devices or deploy itself on a number of redundant nodes. This can be done to ensure a better availability of service building blocks, but at the same time it increases resources consumption. This self-deployment could take the form of service migration to other U-nodes, whereby the whole service logic is moved to another U-node; it could be a distributed approach where only fragments of the service logic are transferred to other devices; or it could take the form of service replication, where a service makes a copy of itself and sends it to (an)other node(s). Thus the secure distribution and execution of distributed code and/or code fragments are logical requirements for the service. Since the environment where the sport activity takes place and the type of available sensors may vary a lot, depending on which sport the user is practicing, the service needs to be highly adaptable. It has to be able to handle a massive amount of sensor information available in the environment, and to find the needed reliable information source.

Also, the type of the available sensor information may vary a lot. For example, there can be body area sensors (heart rate, blood pressure), personal area sensors (speed, location), or third-party sensors (weather, temperature). Data may also have a broad variety of security requirements. In particular, body area and personal area sensors provide information that is subject to a wide range of privacy concerns. If the sport activity takes place, for example, in a running lane, there might not always be a network connection available. So, although the service should use network connections whenever available, the service should perform reliably even in situations where no end-to-end network connections are available.

The service needs also to adapt itself to the changing needs of the user. For example, if the user needs a certain function that cannot be delivered by the service, the latter needs to cooperate with other services to fulfill the needs of the user. In some cases, it may be possible to leverage nearby users who are doing similar activities. In these cases, the service should be able to utilize the user's social networks and to engage in cooperation with nearby similar services. The services could, for example, share information or functionalities. At the same time, it has to be ensured that this cooperation does not penalize its users. An example might be a competition in which functionalities are shared between opposing teams.

In order to survive and evolve in these kinds of resource-constrained, dynamic, and heterogeneous environments without relying on a centralized control, the BIONETS service needs to be highly autonomous.

Even in this simple application scenario, we are combining several key functionalities of the evolution of Web 2.0 (i.e., Web 3.0), such as community services, location-based information, a web of intelligent agents, ontologies, metadata, trust, and security. The scenario also addresses the challenges of disappearing network and network access, which affect the service functionality and for which the SerWork architecture tries to find a proper solution.

2.4.4 Service Autonomicity

In the envisaged BIONETS environment, the number of small connected devices (U-nodes and T-nodes) will be much higher than that typical of current computing systems. Current technologies and service/network architectures will face severe limitations in operating in this kind of environment. The current service solutions need manual operations in all stages of their life cycle. They have to be created, deployed, and managed manually, and therefore need constant supervision from the human actors in the service chain.

In the BIONETS environment, the number of devices and the number of services running on those devices will exceed the number of human users by several orders of magnitude, making implementation of manual configuration and management unrealistic. The BIONETS environment is dynamic, heterogeneous, and resource-constrained. Therefore, in order to be able to survive and evolve in such an environment without relying on a centralized control, BIONETS services need to be able to automatically manage, optimize, monitor, repair, protect, and evolve. Therefore, in order to cope with this new situation, BIONETS services must be truly autonomic.

The essence of autonomic computing systems is self-management, the intent of which is to free the users from the burden of system operation and maintenance. In the BIONETS environment, service self-management implies some form of support for autonomous decision-making inside the services themselves. These autonomic services will maintain and adjust their operation in the face of changing components, workloads, demands, and external conditions.

The self-management procedures can be applied at many levels in an autonomic system. At first, automated functions can merely collect and aggregate the available information to support decisions by users. Alternatively, procedures can serve as advisers, suggesting possible courses of action for users to consider (Kephart and Chess 2003).

In some current systems, autonomic components can even make some lower-level decisions on behalf of the user. The purpose of the BIONETS system is to take the autonomic procedures even further. In BIONETS, the users will need only to make relatively less frequent, predominantly higher-level decisions, which the system will carry out automatically via more numerous, lower-level decisions and actions. Traditional service-oriented architectures such as Web and Grid services (Kreger 2001; Foster et al. 2002) can be used as foundations of future autonomic service environments, but they are far from representing a comprehensive solution to all the problems encountered. For example, when acting as a service provider, the autonomic service elements will not honor requests for service unquestioningly, as typical Web Service would do. Autonomic systems will provide a service only if it is consistent with their "higher" goal or individual benefit. Also, as consumers, autonomic elements will autonomously and proactively issue requests to other elements to carry out their objectives. Another difference from the traditional service-oriented concepts is that the autonomic elements will have complex life cycles, continually carrying on multiple threads of activity, and continuously sensing and responding to their environment (Farha and Leon-Garcia 2006).

2.4.5 Service Architecture Principles

Based on the previous requirements, we have defined the BIONETS service architecture principles. The requirements for the BIONETS services point out the necessity for a service to be able to change dynamically during its lifetime. In particular, a service must adapt its behavior to the changing environment and conditions. For this, services must have the capability to evolve. In other words, evolution is a means to achieve adaptation. In order to fulfill these requirements, we think that the way the service is defined and implemented, and the service framework that hosts services, must be sufficiently flexible. More concretely, we require that the service architecture be able to support the dynamic changes of the service and that the strategy used by the service to conduct these changes may be described as an evolutionary process.

The BIONETS principles distinguish between adaptation and evolution. Likewise, in biology, adaptation refers to the capacity of a given organism to sense, respond, and adapt to its environment, while evolution refers to emergence of new, better-adapted species in the long run. In terms of services, adaptation can be thought of as a mechanism, based on hardwired closed-loop algorithms, that observes the environment and acts accordingly. The adaptation is the modification of already existing functionalities in order to adapt to rapid environmental changes. Accordingly, the service evolution implies a long-term adaptation to changes in environment, especially the ability to acquire new functionality in the system (Yamamoto and Tschudin 2005; Miorandi et al. 2006).

In order to support the flexibility of the system, we have considered the layered approach for services, illustrated in figure 2.7. Based on the BIONETS T/U-node description, the three uppermost abstraction layers are unique to U-nodes. These layers handle

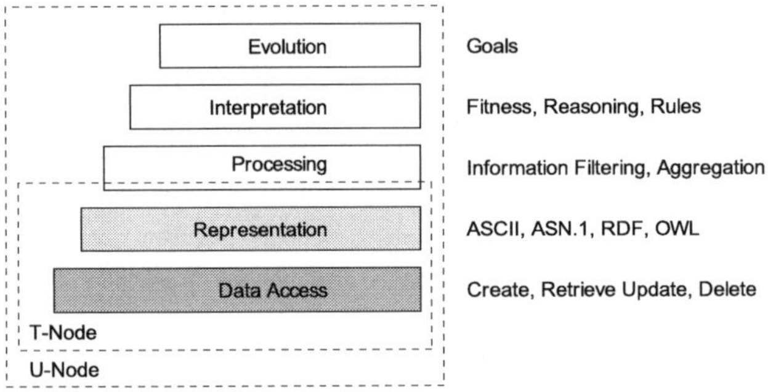

Figure 2.7
Layered view of BIONETS services

the processing of the information, the interpretation of the service fitness values, and the adaptation and the evolution of services according to their fitness to achieve their goals. For the T-nodes, only representation and data access are considered.

The general idea of the BIONETS service architecture is to break down a high-level user request to low-level service invocations. Each layer provides appropriate means to control the layer below. In other words, the evolution layer can modify the interpretation layer over time.

Figure 2.8a illustrates the different elements provided by the T- and U-nodes for the BIONETS service framework. The framework provides the generic interfaces for BIONETS networking concepts and also for the SOA, in order to provide support for traditional Web Services. Autonomicity, different evolution and adaptation strategies, life cycle, and service mobility are handled by the service mediator management functionalities. In the BIONETS framework one service mediator is bonded to certain service cells sharing the same management functionalities. The service cells, service individuals, and service mediators interact with other elements through the interaction framework and various shared data space interaction models. The purpose of the interaction framework is to provide flexibility in terms of having multiple concurrent and evolvable interaction model implementations. In order to implement the shared data space for the U-node, several interaction models can be considered (e.g., distributed hash tables, asynchronous publish/subscribe, etc.). The actual implementation of the shared data space needs verification, taking into consideration the different needs of different messaging and data delivery processes by using, for example, scalability as a metric when deciding the most suitable interaction model.

In order to cope more efficiently with the network communications and data and to control messaging through the whole BIONETS system, the control and data planes are segregated in BIONETS service architecture, as illustrated in figure 2.8b. In the communication framework, the data plane of the system provides the means for services to transfer the actual application/service data through the BIONETS network. The control plane provides the control and management messaging over the whole system. The control and data bearers (communication lines) are red arrows (representing the management and control bearers between different system blocks in the control plane) and blue arrows (representing the data bearers in the data plane).

Within the data plane, the service cells and service individuals can communicate either through the interaction framework or directly through the network. For example, in the case of service migration, the service needs to communicate directly through the network when migrating to another node. Within the control plane, the interactions between the upper layer services and the network are carried out through the interaction framework (see also figure 2.8a). In order to provide control and management for the whole service life cycle, a bidirectional control communication is required for the mediators, service cells, and interaction framework/framework footprint.

As mentioned earlier, the mediator is responsible for service life cycle management. Depending on the service cell and individual concentration and type in each U-node, the functionalities of mediators need to be changed accordingly. It can be done purely through the evolution and adaptation of service mediator functionalities or by replacing and adding new service mediator components from the existing network. In the latter case, the service mediator is also a part of the data plane, and in this case the communication is performed via data bearers, as in the case of service cells.

2.5 Service Life Cycle

The BIONETS service life cycle targets the autonomous adaptation of services, based on a formalized model of user goals, to continuously changing environmental conditions. For this purpose, we are investigating distributed means for creating and evolving services which require little or even no human intervention. As we stated, the idea of BIONETS services is ultimately to support three kinds of service emergence: (a) reactive emergence, (b) proactive emergence, and (c) spontaneous emergence. The first kind addresses the most typical case of service emergence. If conditions in the computing environment (resources of the runtime environment, connectivity, availability of computational entities, etc.) or the requirements of users change, the system is supposed to adapt accordingly, in order to remain valuable for the user. Proactive service emergence is intended to utilize information gathered from the environment and learned over time (e.g., descriptions, heuristics, etc.), in order to anticipate upcoming problems in the system or potential user actions. Anticipated events serve as a trigger for the creation of adapted service configurations. The third, and probably most experimental kind of, service emergence is the spontaneous one. Whereas reactive and proactive services emerge on the basis of proper knowledge about

(a)

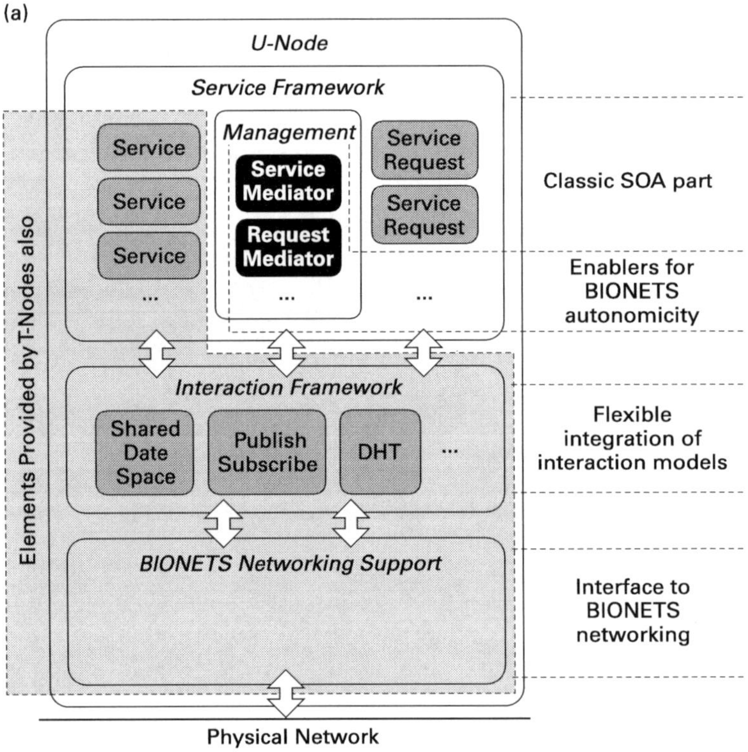

Figure 2.8
(a) Abstract view of BIONETS Service Framework. (b) BIONETS service architecture communication framework

events that either have occurred or are likely to occur, the idea of spontaneous service emergence is to create new functions by heuristically controlled randomization, which may be useful for the user. For all three cases, service emergence essentially requires means of automatic service verification, evaluation, and user rating.

2.5.1 Life Cycle Overview

The BIONETS service life cycle in its current version consists of four phases that comprise directly related activities. These phases are the initiation, the integration, the evolution, and the retirement of services (see figure 2.9). The initiation addresses the introduction of new services to BIONETS. The integration deals with deployment, discovery, and execution of services. The evolution phase addresses the evaluation of services, and their adaptation and transformation. The retirement phase covers all aspects of removing deprecated services from the BIONETS system. The phases and their constituent activities are introduced more in detail in the following sections.

(b)

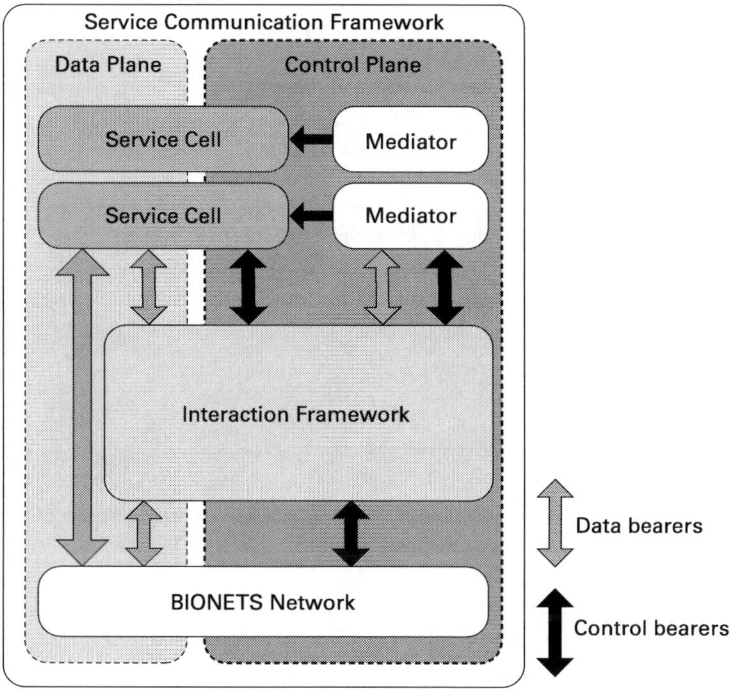

Figure 2.8
(continued)

Service Initiation The initiation phase originates new service individuals that satisfy a given functional model. This model can either represent goals requested directly by the user or reflect learned user preferences and heuristics. Therefore, the initiation phase comprises service request creation, service creation, and service verification. Our primary interest is the service creation on demand of the user. In this context, the service request represents the major orientation for the life cycle activities while containing a model of the functional and nonfunctional requirements. The service request creation addresses the creation of the model formally describing the user goals and also incorporates information about the context (i.e., current situation, user preferences, etc.). The service creation is intended for the creation of new services when no existing service can be found that matches the requirements defined by the service request. Basically this activity of the life cycle addresses service individuals, but we envision the extension of service creation to service cells as well. The service verification is a functional check of the created services, and determines whether a created service will meet the requirements of the service request. Thus, service verification is strongly interwoven with service creation, and proves the functional correctness of a service individual before it is integrated with the environment.

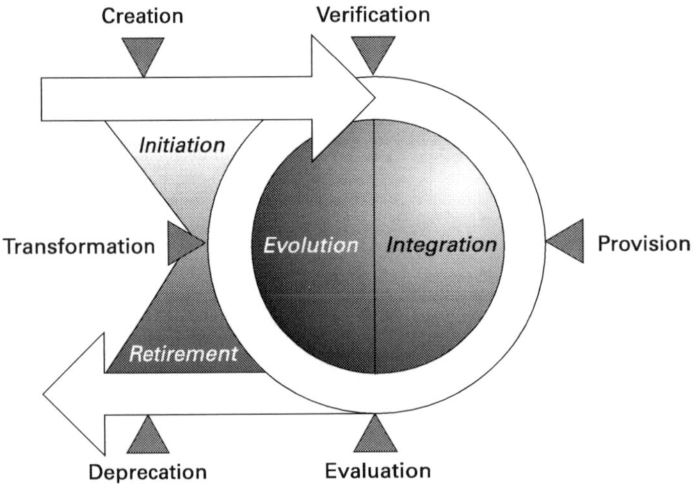

Figure 2.9
Abstract view on BIONETS Service life cycle

The service initiation can be realized in multiple ways that differ only in the grade of automation. Since we want to create a new service by combining existing services, the crucial factor for service initiation is the source of knowledge about the semantics of available services. In BIONETS we regard three possible sources for this knowledge: the user, the service developer, and the computing system. In the first case the user uses her/his own knowledge about services to compose them manually. She/he must define order, conditions, control, and data flow for the execution of the single constituting services. Hence, the user utilizes her/his own knowledge to add value to the service environment by creating new services. Although the approach of user-generated functionality is charming, the applicability decreases with the service complexity. Though simple problems can be addressed with simple service compositions, finding service compositions for the solution of complex problems may be very challenging for the user.

When regarding the service developer as the source of knowledge, we address knowledge that is delivered together with the service cell implementations. Thus, the service cell is sufficiently described with meta-information, which contains descriptions of interface semantics and functional semantics. This idea is, for instance, reflected in WSMO (Roman et al. 2005), SWSO (Battle et al. 2005), and OWL-S (OWL 2004), semantic description languages for the Web Service architecture. Semantic meta-information can be utilized by automatic composition processes to find a reasonable order for the execution of services and the data flow among them. Hence, in this approach the user is not required to define the composition of service himself/herself, he/she just needs to define the goals to be achieved (i.e., the problem but not the solution). Although automatic service composition based on semantic service descriptions is a theoretically promising and partially practically demonstrated concept, there is a trade-off between the required service development efforts and the actual applicability in large-scale open systems.

As third source of knowledge about service semantics, we identify the computing system itself. Instead of assuming services to be annotated with semantic descriptions, the service environment is supposed to "learn" how certain services can be composed. For that purpose, an initial description of user goals and successive user feedback can be utilized. A few predefined heuristics could additionally help to avoid critical malfunctions. Though positive examples of self-learning systems, such as heuristic error-feedback or Multilayer Perceptron-based systems are currently known only from other domains, some of their features would perfectly fit into the notion of self-evolving services.

Service Integration Once created, services need to be deployed to the service environment, so that they are available for execution when demanded. These activities (i.e., service deployment and service execution) are the main objectives of the integration phase.

Service deployment primarily deals with making services utilizable to the users of the BIONETS system in an efficient way. Service individuals and their constituting elements (i.e., service cells) need to be distributed across the nodes of the BIONETS environment, to make them physically available to users by their private equipment. This is required because services may "connect" multiple users, and therefore need to be present on the respective users' equipment. Additionally, there is all in all no guarantee for the lasting availability of remote access to services in the presence of disconnected networks. Hence, to make certain services continuously available, it may become necessary to migrate them from one node to another.

Service execution addresses the execution of previously created and positively verified service individuals in the current service environment. To avoid waste of resources with service creation, the service environment needs to be checked for already available services that can satisfy a service request. For this purpose we intend to follow two complementary approaches: the classical one, based on principles of service-oriented architecture as it is known today, and a novel, request-driven approach. The classic approach comprises a sequence of service publication, lookup by any arguments, binding, and execution. The request-driven approach is based on the publication of the service request in a one-to-many fashion, while the services (or their hosting nodes) themselves determine if they can answer the request in an appropriate way.

Another important matter of service execution we identified is the execution control. While controlling the execution of one service cell is a matter of the hosting node, controlling the execution of a service individual composed of several service cells and other service individuals is much more complex. Basically, we distinguish between centralized and decentralized control. Centralized control means that one node of the environment or one special service is selected to monitor and control the entire execution of a service individual. In contrast, decentralized control assumes that all nodes and services involved in a service individual execution are aware of ongoing actions and control the execution of their respective parts.

Service Evolution The service evolution phase comprises the service evaluation and the service transformation. The purpose of service evaluation is to estimate or test the performance of service individuals in the destination environment and select those that best match the requirement. However, the evaluation of service individuals in a certain computing environment mainly addresses the composition graph of service individuals or the code base of service cells. In contrast to the service verification in the initiation phase, the service evaluation ensures that services are not only functionally correct but also effective with regard to criteria such as required processing time, battery power, and storage consumption. Within the approach pursued, a system is regarded whose functionality does not have to be learned by the user, but gets to know the user self-reliantly. Therefore, the user should not define preferences explicitly on her (or his) own, but the system should learn user preferences with regard to the current context by means of user feedback. The performance of the service individuals already estimated to provide the requested functionality has to be evaluated according to these given criteria. However, the different natures of service cells and service individuals entail the need for different evaluation procedures, which are part of our ongoing work. In general, though, service evaluation needs to answer the following questions.

1. What is the fitness of all available service cells addressing the same type?
2. To what degree are service individuals fulfilling the high-level user goals determined by the service request, and also compared to equivalent service individuals?
3. How are general preferences of users (e.g., also of users not directly involved in service provision) considered by a service individual?

Earlier we identified four major objectives which are summarized as service evolution in the BIONETS service life cycle: (1) evolution of parameter sets for the configuration of services, (2) the evolution of service compositions (i.e., service individuals), (3) the evolution of native service implementations (i.e., evolution of service cells), and (4) the evolution of service interfaces. We started with addressing the first three objectives.

Service individuals are represented by graphs, as shown above. Therefore, we reduce the transformations at parameter granularity to modifications on the weights annotated on the edges of the functional graph. The second objective is in the service transformation and is mainly reflected by forming new variations of service individuals with differing compositions and configurations, while using all available service individuals and service cells. For this purpose we envision the utilization of graph manipulations that change the shape of the graph (i.e., by adding or deleting nodes and links). These graph manipulations are supposed to follow approved methods taken from genetic programming, such as mutation and crossover (Roman et al. 2005; Piszcz and Soule 2006), and evolutionary computing (Yamamoto and Tschudin 2005). The third of the above objectives is currently the most challenging one, since modifying running code in a nondisruptive way is currently an open research problem. To approach this challenge, we plan to use a gene expression model for code generation and regulation: code written in a chemical language may occur at varying concentrations in the system, and the system regulates these concentrations to achieve the desired behavior, guided by reward/punish fitness feedback signals coming from the clients (Yamamoto and Tschudin 2005).

2.5.2 Service Retirement

The service retirement phase generally addresses the removal of services from the BIONETS service environment, and is one possible consequence of service selection in the case of a negative service evaluation. Currently, service deprecation is the only life cycle activity in this phase. The main goal of service deprecation mechanisms in BIONETS is to save resources (mainly storage) by dropping service individuals and service cells which are no longer in use, either because they offer uninteresting features and functions or because they are outperformed by competing services. Service deprecation in BIONETS can be seen as an outcome of the natural selection process (i.e., the disappearing of services not able to achieve and maintain an adequate level of fitness). Also, aging is supposed to be taken into consideration for BIONETS. Indeed, BIONETS—like all evolutionary systems—tends to suffer from a problem which is known as the "rich get richer" paradigm (Clarke et al. 2002). These mechanisms tend inherently to favor old organisms (i.e., services) with respect to new ones. In this case, we envision implementing an opportune mechanism to slowly decrease the fitness of a service over time, in order to leave space for newcomers to grow and evolve.

2.6 Future Directions

In this chapter, we have briefly sketched some outcomes of the initial activities of the BIONETS project. BIONETS targets the introduction, by means of concepts and mechanisms inspired by biology and social sciences, of autonomic services for pervasive computing/communication environments.

Though the results presented in this chapter constitute a solid architectural foundation for the project to build on, much remains to be done. In particular, three main directions are currently envisaged by the project consortium to strengthen and refine the ongoing scientific activities:

1. Integration of security issues in the system architecture. This include issues related to integrity and accountability, as well as the integration of trust and reputation mechanisms into the various phases of the service life cycle.

2. Convergence of evolving services and disappearing networks support. In order to realize the vision of BIONETS SerWorks, a deep level of integration of the features provided by the disappearing network into the functioning of BIONETS services needs to be achieved. This is particularly relevant to service discovery and service execution operations.
3. Integration of advanced mechanisms, inspired by the functioning of real biological systems, in the service evolution phase. This aims at overcoming the limitation encompassed by classical evolutionary computing techniques (e.g., genetic algorithms) by exploiting results gathered by the project consortium on paradigms inspired by biology, and their possible mapping to the operations of BIONETS systems.

Acknowledgments

The work published in this chapter was partly funded by the European Community under the Sixth Framework Programme, contract FP6–027748, BIONETS (http://www.bionets.eu/). The work reflects only the authors' views. The Community is not liable for any use that may be made of the information contained therein. The authors acknowledge the contribution of all project partners to the material presented in this chapter.

References

Akyildiz, I. F., W. Su, Y. Sankarasubramaniam, and E. Cayirci. 2002. "Wireless sensor networks: A Survey." In Computer Networks (Elsevier) Journal, Vol. 38, No. 4, pp. 393–422.

Alouf, S., I. Carreras, D. Miorandi, and G. Neglia. 2007. Embedding evolution in epidemic-style forwarding. In *Proceedings of IEEE BioNetworks Workshop*, Pisa, Italy.

Babaoglu, O., G. Canright, A. Deutsch, G. Di Caro, F. Ducatelle, L. M. Gambardella, N. Ganguly, M. Jelasity, R. Montemanni, A. Montresor, and T. Urnes. 2006. Design patterns from biology for distributed computing." In *ACM Transactions on Autonomous and Adaptive Systems* 1(1): 26–66.

Bar-Yam, Y. 1997. *Dynamics of Complex Systems.* Boulder, Colo.: Addison-Wesley.

Battle, S., A. Bernstein, H. Boley, B. Grosof, M. Gruninger, R. Hull, M. Kifer, D. Martin, S. McIlraith, D. McGuinness, J. Su, and S. Tabet. 2005. Semantic Web Services Ontology (SWSO). http://www.daml.org/services/swsf/1.0/swso/.

BIONETS Project Consortium. 2006. WP1.1, Application Scenario Analysis, Network Architecture Requirements and High-level Specifications. BIONETS Project Deliverable D1.1.1, August. http://www.bionets.eu/docs/BIONETS_D1_1_1.pdf.

BIONETS Project Consortium. 2007. WP1.1, Requirements and Architectural Principles: Architecture, Scenarios, and Requirements Refinements. BIONETS Project Deliverable D1.1.2. htttp://www.bionets.eu/docs/BIONETS_D1_1_2.pdf.

The BISON Project. 2003. Biology-Inspired Techniques for Self-organization in Dynamic Networks. http://www.cs.unibo.it/bison/.

Booth, D., H. Haas, F. McCabe, E. Newcomer, M. Champion, C. Ferris, and D. Orchard. 2004. Web Services Architecture. http://www.w3.org/TR/ws-arch/.

Carreras, I., I. Chlamtac, F. De Pellegrini, and D. Miorandi. 2007. BIONETS: Bio-inspired networking for pervasive communication environments. *IEEE Transactions on Vehicular Technologies*, 56(1): 218–229.

Carzaniga, A., and A. L. Wolf. 2003. Forwarding in a content-based network. In *Proceedings of the ACM SIGCOMM, 2003.*

Clarke, I., O. Sandberg, B. Wiley, and T. Hong. 2002. Freenet: A distributed anonymous information storage and retrieval system. In *ICSI Workshop on Design Issues in Anonymity and Unobservability*, Berkeley, Calif., 2000.

The DELIS Project: Dynamically Evolving Large-scale Information Systems. 2005. http://delis.upb.de/.

Erl, T. 2005. *Service-Oriented Architecture: Concepts, Technology, and Design.* Upper Saddle River, N.J.: Prentice Hall PTR.

Fall, K. 2003. A delay-tolerant network Architecture for challenged internets. In *Proceedings of ACM SIGCOMM*, Karlsruhe, Germany.

Farha, R., and A. Leon-Garcia. 2006. Blueprint for an autonomic service architecture. In *International Conference on Autonomic and Autonomous Systems* (ICAS '06).

Foster, I., C. Kesselman, J. M. Nick, and S. Tuecke. 2002. The Physiology of the Grid: An Open Grid Services Architecture for Distributed Systems Integration. http://www.globus.org/alliance/publications/papers/ogsa.pdf.

Foster, J. A. 2001. Evolutionary computation. *Nature Reviews Genetics* (2): 428–436.

Gao, C., M. Cai, and H. Chen. 2007. QoS-aware service composition based on tree-coded genetic algorithm. In *31st International Computer Software and Applications Conference*, vol. 1, pp. 361–367.

Grossglauser, M., and D. Tse. 2002. Mobility increases the capacity of ad hoc wireless Networks. *IEEE/ACM Transactions on Networking* 10(4): 477–486.

Gupta, P., and P. R. Kumar. 2000. The capacity of wireless networks. *IEEE Transactions on Information Theory* 46(2): 388–404.

The HAGGLE Project. 2005. http://www.haggleproject.org/.

He, H. 2003. What Is Service-oriented Architecture. http://www.xml.com/pub/a/ws/2003/09/30/soa.html.

Heylighen, F., and C. Joslyn. 2001. Cybernetics and second-order cybernetics. In R. A. Meyers, ed., *Encyclopedia of Physical Science & Technology*, 3rd ed. New York: Academic Press.

Kephart, J. O., and D. M. Chess. 2003. The vision of autonomic computing. *IEEE Computer* 36(1): 41–50.

Kreger, H. 2001. Web Services Conceptual Architecture. Version1.0. http://www.cs.uoi.gr/~zarras/mdw-ws/WebServicesConceptualArchitectu2.pdf.

Krishnamachari, B. 2005. Modeling data gathering in wireless sensor networks. In Y. Li, M. Thai, and W. Wu, eds., *Wireless Sensor Networks and Applications*, sec. III, *Data Management*, pp. 572–591. Springer.

Küster, U., M. Stern, and B. König-Ries. 2005. A classification of issues and approaches in automatic service composition. In *Proceedings of the First International Workshop on Engineering Service Compositions* (WESC '05).

Lindgren, A., A. Doria, and O. Schelen. 2003. Probabilistic routing in intermittently connected networks. In *Proceedings of the SAPIR Workshop*, LNCS 3126, pp. 239–254. Springer.

Miorandi, D., L. Yamamoto, and P. Dini. 2006. Service evolution in bio-inspired communication systems. In *International Transactions on Systems Science and Applications* 2(1): 51–60.

MIT Project OXYGEN. 2002. Pervasive Human-Centered Computing. http://oxygen.csail.mit.edu/Overview.html.

OASIS Symposium: The Meaning of Interoperability. 2006. Reference Model for Service-Oriented Architecture 1.0. Committee specification 1. http://www.oasis-open.org/committees/download.php/19679/soa-rm-cs.pdf.

Oh, S., D. Lee, and S. R. Kumara. 2006. A comparative illustration of AI planning-based Web Services composition. *SIGecom Exchanges* 5(1): 1–10.

The OWL Services Coalition. 2004. OWL-S: Semantic Markup for Web Services. http://www.W3.org/Submission/OWL-S.

Pastor-Satorras, R., M. Rubi, and A. Diaz-Guiler. 2003. *Statistical Mechanics of Complex Networks.* Springer-Verlag.

Piszcz, A., and T. Soule. 2006. A survey of mutation techniques in genetic programming. In *Proceedings of the 8th Annual Conference on Genetics and Evolutionary Computation*, pp. 951–952.

Roman, D., U. Keller, H. Lausen, J. d. Bruijn, R. Lara, M. Stollberg, A. Polleres, C. Feier, C. Bussler, and D. Fensel. 2005. The Web Service modelling ontology. In Applied Ontology 1(1): 77–106.

Sestini, F. 2006. Situated and autonomic communication: An EC FET European initiative. *ACM Computer Communication Review* 36(2): 17–20.

Stanley, K. O., and R. Miikkulainen. 2003. A taxonomy for artificial embryogeny. *Artificial Life* 9(2): 93–130.

Timmis, J., M. Amos, W. Banzhaf, and A. Tyrrell. 2006. Going back to our roots: Second generation biocomputing. *International Journal of Unconventional Computing* 2: 729–735.

Tschudin, C., and Yamamoto, L. 2005. Self-evolving network software. *Praxis der Informationsverarbeitung und Kommunikation* (PIK) 28(4).

Wall, Q. 2006. Understanding the Service Lifecycle Within a SOA: Run Time. http://dev2dev.bea.com/pub/a/2006/11/soa-service-lifecycle-run.html.

Weiser, M. 1999. The computer for the 21st century. *ACM Mobile Computer Communications Review*, 3(3): 3–11.

Yamamoto, L., and C. Tschudin. 2005. Genetic evolution of protocol implementations and configurations. Paper presented at IFIP/IEEE International Workshop on Self-Managed Systems & Services (SelfMan '05), Nice, France.

3 Service Discovery in Pervasive Computing Environments

Sonia Ben Mokhtar, Nikolaos Georgantas, Valérie Issarny, Pierre-Guillaume Raverdy, and Marco Autili

3.1 Introduction

Pervasive computing envisions the unobtrusive diffusion of computing and networking resources in physical environments, enabling users to access information and computational resources anytime and anywhere. Mobile users take part in these pervasive environments by carrying tiny personal devices that integrate seamlessly into the existing infrastructure. Such a setup is highly open and dynamic: pervasive computing systems should thus support ad hoc deployment and execution, integrating the available hardware and software resources at any given time and place. Rendering such resources into autonomous, networked components facilitates their incorporation into a larger system.

The service-oriented architectures (SOA) computing paradigm is particularly appropriate for pervasive systems. In this architectural style, resources and applications on networked devices are abstracted as loosely coupled networked services. Service discovery is, then, an essential function within SOA since it enables the runtime association of clients with these networked services. Three basic roles are identified for service discovery in SOA: (1) *service provider* is the role assumed by a software entity offering a networked service; (2) *service requester* is the role of an entity seeking to consume a specific service; (3) *service repository* is the role of an entity maintaining information on available services and a way to access them. A *service description* formalism or language to describe the capabilities and other nonfunctional properties (such as quality of service, security, or transactional aspects), complemented with a *service discovery protocol* (SDP), allows service providers, requesters, and repositories to interact with each other.

Unfortunately, pervasive computing environments are highly heterogeneous, thus limiting actual interactions between users and services:

- First, pervasive services (assuming the role of service provider) and clients (assuming the role of service requester) are designed, developed, and deployed independently, using various middleware platforms. This results in the concurrent use of discovery and access protocols that do not directly interoperate with each other, owing to incompatible data representation and message formats.

- Second, the use of various wireless technologies (e.g., cellular networks, WiFi, or Bluetooth) and network management models (e.g., ad hoc or infrastructure-based) results in many independent networks being available to users at a given location. Since users can be connected to only a limited number of networks at the same time (often a single network), many services may not be visible/reachable.
- Finally, traditional service discovery protocols focus on capturing in their service advertisements and queries only the static characterization of services and clients. They do not take into account the user's current situation, such as location, activity, or type of terminal in use. In service-rich environments, such an approach performs highly inefficiently by providing users with long lists of services, only a few of which actually meet their expectations in terms of service quality, performance, cost, accessibility, and so forth. Guaranteeing more accuracy in the selection of available services is especially beneficial to mobile users, who are often equipped with resource-constrained devices.

This chapter discusses work undertaken within the IST AMIGO[1] and PLASTIC[2] projects to address the above issues. The AMIGO project targets an interoperable service-oriented middleware for the networked home, with the requirement of supporting legacy client and service applications. The PLASTIC project targets the development of adaptable services in a Beyond 3rd Generation (B3G) networking environment, thus providing context-aware service discovery in multinetwork environments.

Within the SeCSE[3] project, the service discovery research area is concerned with the delivery of innovative techniques and tools for service discovery to address the needs of service provision and integration. Figure 3.1 represents the service discovery diagram extracted from the current SeCSE conceptual model,[4] which reflects how the discovery phase can take place (1) at *requirements time* while gathering requirements for a service-based system to be developed (*early discovery*); (2) at *architecture time*, when the system is being designed and architected (*architecture time discovery*); and (3) at *runtime*, for service replacement while the system is running (*runtime discovery*). Based on when the discovery phase takes place, it is therefore possible to distinguish among *early discovery query*, *architecture time query*, and *runtime query*. In that respect, the IST AMIGO and PLASTIC projects address issues related to runtime discovery. Though both projects contribute to most of the layers of the NESSI technology platform road map[5] and the service-oriented computing (SOC) road map (Papazoglou and Georgakopoulos 2003), their service discovery solutions fall into the infrastructure layer of the NESSI Platform. Indeed, both solutions focus primarily on integrating legacy service discovery protocols and heterogeneous networks, thus providing a unified environment for client and service interactions.

Section 3.2 briefly outlines basic principles of service discovery protocols and details major features of four popular service discovery protocols. The subsequent sections concentrate on the interoperability solutions proposed by the AMIGO and PLASTIC projects, based on the underlying networking environment (section 3.3) and on the context-aware

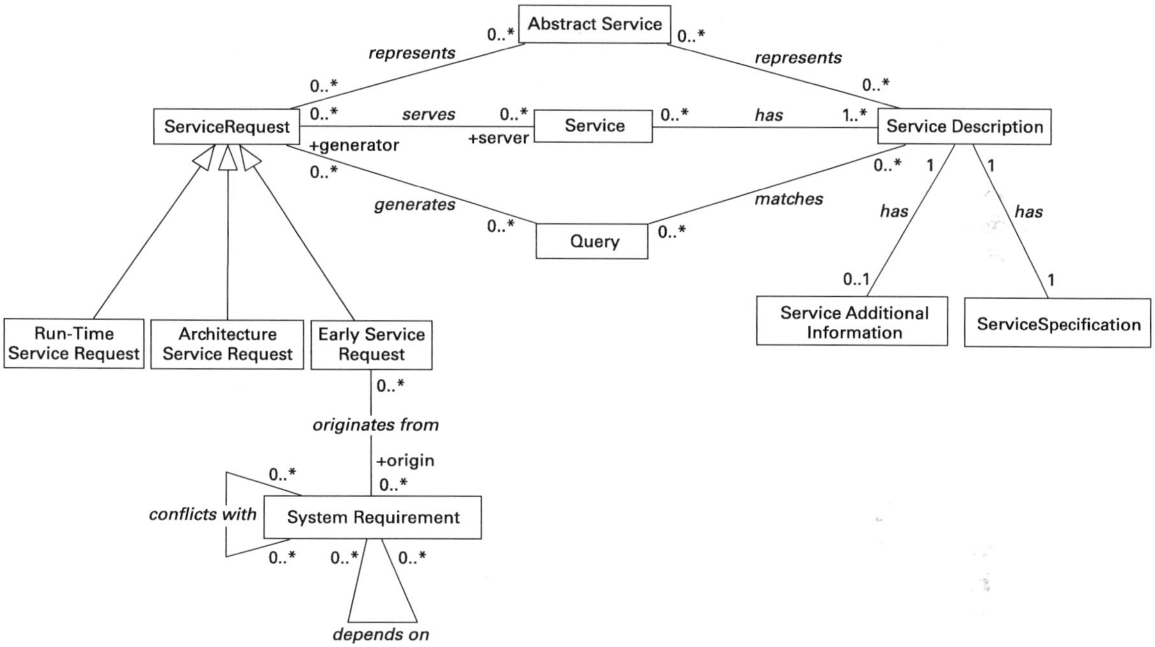

Figure 3.1
SecSE service discovery diagram

discovery of services in dynamic compositions of heterogeneous networks (section 3.4). We conclude with new directions for research on service discovery linked to the increasing capabilities and use of mobile devices (section 3.5).

3.2 An Overview of Service Discovery Protocols

Service discovery protocols enable components of a network to discover each other, express opportunities for collaboration, and compose themselves into larger collections that cooperate to meet application needs. SDPs can be classified (Maheswaran 2001; Zhu et al. 2005) as either

- Pull-based protocols, where clients send requests directly to service providers or to a third-party repository in order to get a list of services compatible with the request attributes or
- Push-based protocols, where service providers provide their service descriptions to all clients that locally maintain a list of networked services.

The pull-based protocols can further be divided into two subcategories: centralized pull-based protocols and distributed pull-based protocols.

In centralized pull-based discovery protocols (CORBA's Trading Object Service and Naming Service,[6] UDDI,[7] and Jini[8]), one or a few repositories are deployed in the network, and service information (i.e., service announcements and discovery requests) may be sent to one or all repositories. If clients and service providers interact with only one of the repositories, the repositories cooperate to distribute the service registrations or to route the clients' requests to the relevant repository. The location of the repository is usually assumed to be well known by the clients and service providers, though in some other protocols, clients and service providers broadcast a specific request on the network to locate the repository (e.g., Jini). Alternatively, a hash function may be used to transform a given service type or name into a numerical value which identifies one repository to use to register or request such service. This value can be computed independently from the discovery request (requester) or the service announcement (provider). It is then associated with the address of a device in a network that acts as a middleman (i.e., repository), storing the real location of the service and answering the clients' requests. Examples of systems implementing hash-based discovery protocols include Freenet (Clarke et al. 2000), Tapestry (Zhao et al. 2003), and Chord (Stoica et al. 2001). In large networks (e.g., Internet), the centralized approach raises scalability and reliability problems (i.e., number of entries). Relying on cooperative repositories to balance service information is a common technique to address these problems. In pervasive environments, the centralized approach further raises trust issues for the devices that host repositories, and require the management of network partitioning and device mobility. In both settings (Internet and pervasive environments), repositories require an explicit sign-off or a service announcement lifetime in order to remove stale entries.

In distributed pull-based discovery protocols, service providers store their descriptions locally, and therefore they are not distributed to the other nodes on the network. Clients send their requests using the broadcast/forward functionality provided by the network, and in fact flood the network to reach potential service providers. The flooding algorithm, however, tries to limit/prevent the duplication of queries. When receiving such a request, service providers compare it with the service descriptions stored locally to decide if they can satisfy the request. A typical representative of this approach is the simple service discovery protocol[9] (SSDP). The main drawbacks of the distributed pull-based approach are the network-flooding problem (Ni et al. 1999), the required support of multicast/broadcast communication by the underlying network, and the limited range (i.e., network hops) of the multicast/broadcast messages.

In the push-based approach, each device maintains a local repository of services found on the network. A service provider pushes its service descriptions to the network, typically by periodic unicast or multicast/broadcast messages. As a result, each device's local repository gradually collects all the announcements of the services in the environment. A client communicates directly with its local repository (i.e., on its device), which looks up its service entries for both local and distant services matching the request. IBM DEAPspace

(Hermann 2001) and SDS (Czerwinski et al. 1999) support push-based advertisements. SDS is in fact a hybrid protocol that supports both push- and pull-based service discovery methods. The main drawbacks of push-based protocols are related to the reachability of the services (similarly to the distributed pull-based discovery protocols) and to the setting of the broadcast interval. If it is set too short, the network is flooded with unnecessary advertisements, and if it is set too long, clients do not get an accurate listing of the available services.

SDPs for the Internet and intranets (e.g., CORBA and UDDI) use centralized pull-based protocols (often supporting association/collaboration between repositories) with complex service description formats and complete APIs for both service registration and requests. Leading SDPs for pervasive environments target small networks (e.g., home networks) and also use pull-based protocols (e.g., SSDP, SLP), often supporting both the distributed approach (for dealing with ad hoc/unmanaged networks) and the centralized approach (for bandwidth efficiency), but with limited service descriptions and matching capabilities. A main concern for the design of these SDPs was their reactiveness and the support of resource-constrained devices (typically consumer electronic devices such as TVs, camcorders, or digital video recorders). The increasing capabilities of mobile devices, however, now leave room for supporting more complex SDPs. Four of these protocols that target home and ad hoc networks (SSDP and WS-Discovery) and the Internet and intranets (CORBA and UDDI) are now presented.

3.2.1 SSDP

Simple service discovery protocol (SSDP) is the protocol defined within UPnP[10] for the dynamic discovery of services in home networks. In SSDP, clients looking for services multicast their discovery requests, and matching services respond via unicast directly to the client. Services may also periodically advertise themselves using multicast.

Services in SSDP are identified by a unique pairing of a *service-type* URI, which identifies the type of service (e.g., a printer, an alarm clock), and a *unique service name* (USN) URI, to differentiate various instances of the same type of service. Though the UPnP forum has defined a small set of services for home environments with standardized names and interfaces (e.g., media server, router), it is usually the responsibility of the client to know the exact type or name of the service it is looking for (exact syntactic matching). Service announcements and discovery results include both the service type and the USN, as well as location and expiration information. The location information (i.e., URL) identifies how one should access the service. Expiration information identifies how long a client should keep information about the service in its cache. SSDP services issue notification messages to announce their availability to the network, to update SSDP clients' cache entries, or to notify clients of changes in their location or of their intention to cease operating. The discovery request contains the type of service to discover, and only SSDP services that have a matching service type may respond.

Though SSDP provides only basic syntactic matching and limited information on the services, UPnP extends SSDP by defining how service providers can describe the hosting device and the interface (API and data types) of the hosted services in MXL. UPnP also defines how clients may retrieve these complete descriptions following a successful SSDP search. As mentioned earlier, the main drawback of multicast-based SDPs such as SSDP is that service discovery is limited by the reach of multicast packets (usually the local subnet).

3.2.2 WS-Discovery

WS-Discovery[11] provides an infrastructure for the dynamic discovery of Web services in ad hoc and managed networks. Derived from SLP (Guttman et al. 1999), WS-Discovery defines a multicast protocol between clients and target services (i.e., service providers) for queries and announcements. It defines a service repository, the d*iscovery proxy*, to reduce multicast traffic in networks with a large number of services.

Services in WS-Discovery can be discovered by their type (i.e., an identifier for a set of messages an endpoint sends and/or receives) and/or their scope (i.e., an extensibility point that may be used to organize target services into logical groups). Both clients and service providers may use compact signatures to secure protocol messages.

WS-Discovery is a lightweight protocol well suited for resource-limited devices, and leverages other Web Service specifications for secure, reliable, transacted message delivery. Owing to its hybrid solution, it can be deployed in ad hoc or managed networks of any size. WS-Discovery has its own shortcomings: it does not provide information about the status/liveness of the services, does not provide extended information on the service (context, semantics), and, like SLP or SSDP, is limited by the reach/scope of IP multicast. Discovery proxies may, however, be extended to support the tunneling of discovery requests between distant networks, as in mSLP (Zhao and Schulzrinne 2005).

3.2.3 CORBA

Service discovery in CORBA is supported by the Trading and Naming services, which act as centralized repositories. The Naming service provides a very basic lookup mechanism, and the Trading service allows objects that provide a service to register their characteristics, and then allows clients to locate those services by describing the functionality they require. The Trading service specification defines five functional interfaces (Lookup, Register, Admin, Link, Proxy). Most notably, the *Link* interface supports the linking (federation) of trading services for large-scale service discovery, and the *Proxy* interface can be used to encapsulate legacy systems. A given implementation of the Trading service may implement only a subset of these interfaces.

Service descriptions in CORBA are defined in IDL and contain the *service type*, which is composed of a *service name*, an *interface type*, and a set of *properties* used to differentiate between different service offerings. Service types can be hierarchical (i.e., a new service type can be declared a subtype of an existing type). Properties are typed values, and the types can be any arbitrarily complex IDL type. Clients specify their requirements in the form of a constraint, expressed in the Trading Service Constraint Language. The results of a query are returned as a list of matching offers that can be sorted according to the requirements of the client.

In most SDPs, service properties are static, meaning that the service provider sets their values at registration time. Some Trading service implementations, however, support dynamic properties, which are properties that are evaluated at the time of the lookup query (e.g., CPU load on the device hosting the service). When a server exports a service offer that contains a dynamic property, it also provides a reference to a dynamic property evaluation object, which is usually created by the service provider. When the Trading service evaluates a query involving a dynamic property, it invokes this evaluation object to get the runtime value of the property. The ability to evaluate property values dynamically results in the ability to make lookup queries based on the current state of a system, rather than on a snapshot state that can quickly become out of date. Another strength of the Trading service is that it can define policies for "Link following" (i.e., when, and to what extent, a link should be followed in the resolution of a query). A client can modify the link policy for an individual query, so that it can control and restrict the amount of searching that is performed.

3.2.4 UDDI

UDDI (Universal Description, Discovery, and Integration) is one of the core elements enabling Web Services, and is concerned with the publishing and discovery of Web Services in the Internet or intranets. The UDDI specification defines both the specific formats to use for service descriptions, and the repository with its APIs for publishing service information and for performing focused and unfocused discovery.

The initial UDDI description formats have been extended to allow the incorporation of WSDL,[12] which is the standard for Web Service description. In WSDL, Web Services are first described abstractly, as a collection of end points that process messages containing either document-oriented or procedure-oriented information. The operations and messages are then bound to a concrete network protocol and message format to complete the definition of an end point. UDDI provides a complete search API (complex single-step queries, extensible find qualifiers, sort orders, wild card, support for large result sets). UDDI supports multiregistries discovery and the modeling of business relationships (parent–child, peer-2-peer, and identity) so that a company can cooperatively manage multiple registries (i.e., model subsidiaries, internal departments, etc.), and defines partnerships with other businesses. UDDI also defines a subscription API to dynamically track changes in a (remote) repository and retrieve changes/updates synchronously or asynchronously.

Though UDDI's initial goal of becoming a public registry for Web Services on the Internet has failed, implementations of UDDI (or of Web Service discovery solutions derived from UDDI) are deployed in enterprise networks. The main shortcomings of UDDI when considering pervasive environments are that it assumes that services are always connected to the network, does not handle stale entries, and does not define how clients or service providers discover the UDDI registry. Furthermore, UDDI must also be deployed on powerful devices, and incurs a significant processing overhead and response time.

3.3 Multiprotocol Service Discovery

Existing SDPs do not directly interoperate with each other because they employ incompatible formats and protocols for service description, service advertisements, or discovery requests. Furthermore, they are often integrated in middleware platforms (e.g., SSDP and UPnP), thus complicating interoperability (i.e., incompatible data types or communication models). In fact, the diverse environment constraints and the de facto standard status of some of the existing protocols make it unlikely for a new and unique SD protocol to emerge. Several projects have thus investigated interoperability solutions (Grace et al. 2003), since requiring clients and service providers to support multiple SD protocols is not realistic.

SDP interoperability is typically achieved by using intermediate representations of service discovery paradigms (e.g., service description, discovery request) (Allard et al. 2003; Friday et al. 2004) instead of direct mappings (Koponen and Virtanen 2004), since the latter do not scale well with the number of supported protocols. Furthermore, two approaches are possible to interface with the various SDPs: transparent or explicit. In the transparent approach (Koponen and Virtanen 2004), the interoperability layer is located close to the network and directly translates messages to/from the various protocols. Clients and services are thus unaware of the translation process. In the explicit approach (Friday et al. 2004), the interoperability layer is located on top of the existing SDPs, and provides an API to the clients and sometimes to the service providers. Though the transparent approach eases the deployment and use of the interoperability solution by legacy clients and services, the explicit approach enables the extension of existing protocols with advanced features such as context management. We now detail and compare the INDISS and MUSDAC interoperability solutions proposed, respectively, by the IST AMIGO and IST PLASTIC projects that are, respectively, based on the transparent and explicit approaches.

3.3.1 The INDISS Interoperability Solution

The IST AMIGO project aims to improve the usability of home networks, and for that purpose investigates (1) interoperability issues arising from the use of heterogeneous networking technologies, devices, middleware platforms, and standards; (2) the automatic discovery of devices and services as well as their composability and upgradeability and self-administration; and (3) intelligent user interfaces. AMIGO assumes an all-IP networking environment, meaning that clients and services are using communication protocols built on top of IP, and that all devices within the pervasive environment (i.e., home network) are IP-reachable. Though different devices may belong to different subnets, unicast and multicast packets can reach all devices. Owing to the characteristics of the environment, SDPs in home environments are usually multicast-based and fully distributed.

In the context of the AMIGO project, INDISS (Interoperable Discovery System for Networked Services) (Bromberg and Issarny 2005) was designed to overcome SDPs' heterogeneity. In keeping with the goal of usability and the focus on dynamic home networks, INDISS is specifically designed as a transparent solution minimizing resource usage (i.e., memory, processing, and bandwidth), and introduces lightweight mechanisms that may be adapted easily to any platform. The transparent approach is also key to supporting legacy clients and services, which is crucial in AMIGO. INDISS is composed of a set of event-based components, and their composition is performed dynamically at runtime according to both the context and the device on which INDISS is deployed. INDISS operates close to the network, capturing and translating network messages without the need for client or service interactions. As a result, service discovery interoperability is provided to applications without altering them: applications are not aware of the existence of INDISS.

INDISS Architecture INDISS's main components are the *monitor*, the *parser*, and the *composer*:

- The *monitor component* detects the SDPs that are used, based on network activity on the assigned multicast groups and ports. This component also captures/collects network messages sent by clients and services onto these multicast groups, and forwards them to the appropriate parser components.
- The *parser* component, associated with a specific SDP, transforms the raw data flow (i.e., network messages) into series of events, extracting semantic SDP concepts from syntactic details in the SDP messages. The generated events are delivered to a locally deployed *event bus*.
- The *composer* component delivers a specific SDP message understood by the target clients and/or services, based on specific sets of events received from the *event bus*.

Parsers and composers are dedicated to specific SDP protocols. SDP interoperability comes from the composition of multiple parsers and composers dedicated to different SDPs, and from the implicit creation of an event bus shared between all composers and servers on a device. The communication between the *parser* and the *composer* does not depend on any syntactic detail of any protocol. They communicate at a semantic level through the use of events. A set of 20 events has been defined that can be combined to represent all common SD operations (i.e., service request, service registration, or service advertisements). This set comprises five categories: *SDP control events*, *SDP network events*, *SDP service events*, *SDP request events*, and *SDP response events*. Each SDP also

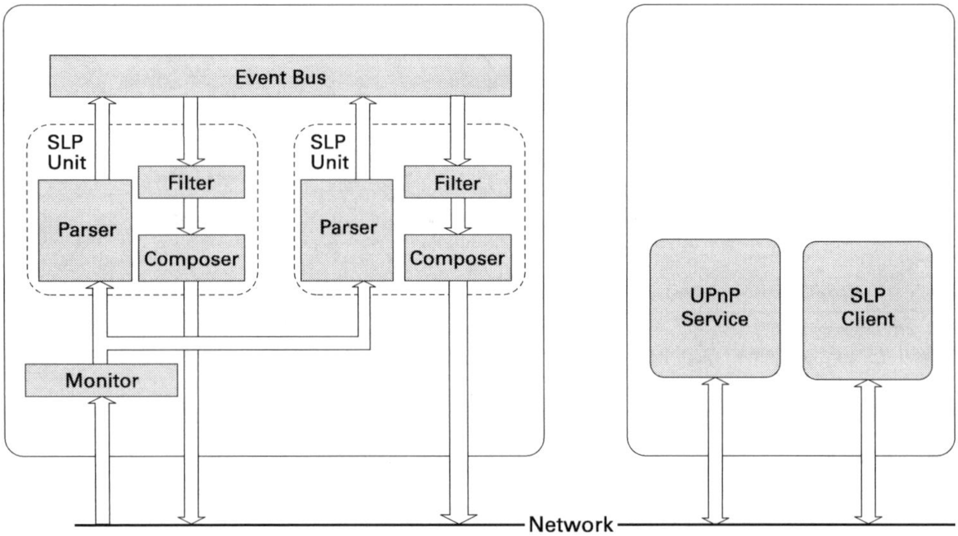

Figure 3.2
INDISS architecture

has a set of specific events that may or may not be used by other SDP units. Events that are not understood by a composer are simply discarded.

As depicted in figure 3.2, the monitor receives an incoming SLP request from the client, and forwards it to the parser of the SLP unit. The SLP parser then translates the message into a set of events. The UPnP composer receives the relevant (subset of) events according to its event filters, and composes the adequate UPnP messages. These messages are then sent to the UPnP multicast group and received by the service. As shown in table 3.1, an SLP search message is translated into a set of ten events. A UPnP composer will react on some of these events (i.e., SDP_NET_MULTICAST, SDP_SERVICE_REQUEST, SDP_SERVICE_TYPE), and in turn generate UPnP search messages.

In general, SDP functions such as service request, service registration, and service advertisements are complex distributed processes that require coordination between the actors of the specific service discovery function. It follows that the translation of SDP functions that is realized by INDISS is actually achieved in terms of translation of processes, and not simply of exchanged messages, thus requiring further coordination between the parser and the composer. This is realized by embedding the parser and the composer within a *unit* that runs coordination processes associated with the functions of the supported SDP. Specifically, the behavior of the unit is specified by using finite state machines.

INDISS Deployment INDISS may be deployed independently on one or more devices in the network. Each instance of INDISS dynamically instantiates parsers and composers

Table 3.1
Translation of SLP search request

Incoming SLP message	Events generated by the SLP Parser	UPnP Messages generated
SLP Search	SDP_C_START .... **SDP_NET_MULTICAST** SDP_NET_SOURCE_ **SDP_SERVICE_REQUEST** SDP_REQ_VERSION SDP_REQ_SCOPE SDP_REQ_PREDICATE SDP_REQ_ID **SDP_SERVICE_TYPE:** SDP_C_STOP	SSDP Search HTTP Get

for the SDPs it supports, and provides interoperability between these SDPs for all the devices in the network. Multiple instances of INDISS may provide interoperability between different sets of SDPs.

With INDISS, application components continue to use their native service discovery protocol; interoperability is achieved through a transparent integration of INDISS. Event streams are totally hidden from components outside INDISS, since they are assembled into specific SDP messages through composers. Consequently, interoperability is guaranteed to existing applications tied to a specific SDP without requiring any change to applications. Similarly, future applications do not need to be developed with a specific middleware API to benefit from SDP interoperability.

INDISS takes into account the resource-constrained nature of the devices found in home networks. Indeed, the memory footprint of the library is quite limited (40 KB for the core libraries and less than 100 KB, on average, for an SDP unit). The processing overhead (Bromberg and Issarny 2005) is also limited, compared with the native processing. Though INDISS can be deployed on a home gateway, and translate and forward all messages, it may take into account the consumer electronics nature of home networks, where some devices only provide services, and others only accesses them. Indeed, INDISS can be optimized for client-only or service-only devices by reducing the number of messages sent.

3.3.2 MUSDAC Platform

The IST PLASTIC project investigates the development and deployment of mobile, adaptive application services for B3G networks. As in AMIGO, PLASTIC considers an all-IP networking environment. However, PLASTIC assumes highly heterogeneous, loosely connected networks. Network heterogeneity arises from (1) the use of different networking technologies, (2) variations in the sets of IP-level configuration and communication functionality provided to devices by the network (e.g., IP multicast support, DHCP), and (3) networks belonging to different administrative domains (e.g., public/open vs. restricted/

secure) and management models (infrastructure-based vs. ad hoc). These networks may further target different classes of applications (e.g., sensor networks, home/automation networks, hot spots). The pervasive environment is thus modeled as a dynamic composition of heterogeneous and independent networks. A major assumption is that global IP routing is not guaranteed.

In this context, the *MUlti-protocols Service Discovery and ACcess* (MUSDAC) platform (Raverdy, Issarny, et al. 2006) was designed to facilitate service discovery and access in B3G environments. SDP interoperability is achieved using the explicit approach because MUSDAC provides an enhanced discovery API to MUSDAC-aware clients, while interacting on their behalf with existing SDPs to discover legacy services. To minimize complexity, MUSDAC registers this discovery API as a service (the *MUSDAC service*), using the various SDPs in use in the networks. Thus, MUSDAC-aware clients explicitly interact with MUSDAC, using their preferred discovery and access protocol. A MUSDAC-aware UPnP client will thus, as a first step, use SSDP to discover the UPnP MUSDAC service, and then access it, using SOAP, to discover services in the pervasive environment (i.e., advertised using other SDPs and/or in other networks).

Architecture The MUSDAC platform is composed of the following components (see figure 3.3):

- The *manager*, which controls discovery and access requests within the local network for both local and remote clients

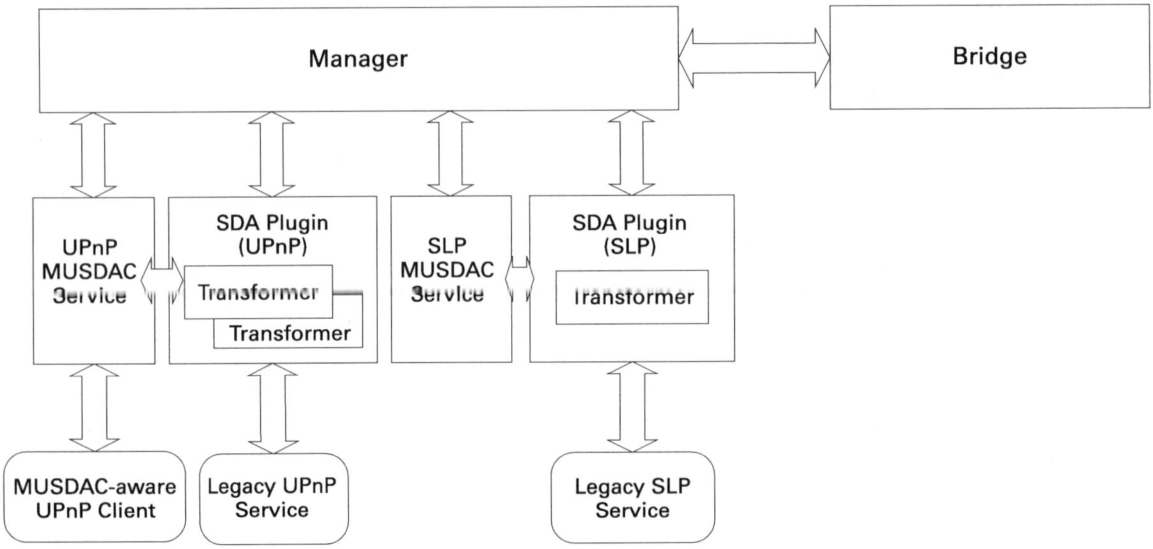

Figure 3.3
MUSDAC architecture

- *SDA plug-ins* that interact with specific SDPs to collect service information, register the *MUSDAC service* to be used by local clients, and perform service access on behalf of remote clients
- *Transformers* that extend service descriptions with context information
- *Bridges* that assist managers in expanding the service discovery and service access to other networks in the whole pervasive environment.

Services in the MUSDAC platform are described using the *MUSDAC Description* format, which is a generic and modular service description format able to hold both functional and nonfunctional characteristics of services. This description format is also used as a template for MUSDAC discovery requests. The MUSDAC description of a service is dynamically generated by the SDA plug-in on service announcements or when returning discovery results.

A client looking for a service in the environment first discovers the MUSDAC service using its preferred SDP, and sends its discovery request. Once received, the MUSDAC service forwards the discovery request to the manager, which sends it in parallel to the local SDA plug-ins (for discovering suitable services in the local network) and to the connected bridges (for propagation to nearby networks). A manager receiving a remote discovery request processes it as a local one (i.e., forwards it to its own SDA plug-ins and bridges) but returns the results to the originating bridge. Finally, the client's manager collects local and remote results, and returns them to the client via the MUSDAC service. As detailed in section 3.4, bridges disseminate discovery requests between networks based on context information.

Each SDA plug-in collects service information in a specific discovery domain (e.g., SLP, UPnP) on behalf of the manager. Depending on the SDP, the SDA plug-in either registers for service advertisements (i.e., push-based protocol) or directly performs service discovery (i.e., pull-based protocol). The SDA plug-in generates the initial MUSDAC service description based on the SDP-specific service description that it collects and on basic transformation rules. This initial description contains all the information available in the SDP-specific description and can be extended by transformers (see section 3.4). In the case of pushed protocols, the service description created by the SDA plug-in after a service announcement is sent to the manager, which records it in its local service description cache. For these push-based protocols, the manager directly evaluates incoming requests against the cache (i.e., without forwarding them to the SDA plug-in of these protocols), and returns the previously generated service descriptions.

Deployment The MUSDAC platform can be deployed on one or more devices in a network, and each device deploying MUSDAC may register to act as a manager, a bridge, or both. For each network, one manager is then dynamically elected. The manager is the central component of MUSDAC, as it processes, within its local network boundaries, discovery and access requests from local and remote clients. It is implemented as a centralized component, since the size of a network (e.g., subnet) is limited by nature (i.e., its number of devices and services is limited). The manager periodically sends presence beacons so that other MUSDAC devices in the network can detect its absence, as well as duplicates, and recover.

The elected manager then activates its SDA plug-ins and transformers, and discovers the bridges in its network. The manager dynamically activates some or all of these bridges based on several criteria (i.e., connectivity to other networks, expected lifetime, processing power, and cost), and then disseminates discovery requests between the networks on its different network interfaces. As devices hosting bridge components appear and disappear, the set of reachable networks (and thus services) in the multinetwork environment evolves.

Evaluations of the MUSDAC service discovery (Raverdy, Issarny, et al. 2006), as well as of the scalability of multinetwork service discovery (Raverdy, Armand, et al. 2006) have been performed. As can be expected, MUSDAC produces a significant overhead compared with simple, network-level protocols such as SSDP, WS-Discovery, or SLP. The main MUSDAC overhead is related to the cost of accessing the MUSDAC service (i.e., SOAP processing), whereas the overhead associated with the processing and dissemination of discovery requests through bridges is limited. However, exposing MUSDAC as a service to client is required to support enhanced service discovery. To truly benefit users, the MUSDAC platform must be deployed on a large number of devices, acting as bridges whenever possible. A high interconnectivity level allows for load balancing between bridges (that quickly become a bottleneck otherwise), and also increases the stability of the client/service communication.

3.3.3 Comparison

As shown in table 3.2, the IST AMIGO and PLASTIC projects first differ on the targeted networking environment, with the interconnection of different networks being managed either at the network level (INDISS) or at the application level (MUSDAC). This clearly has an effect on how SDP interoperability (i.e., the conversion of SDP paradigms such as service descriptions or discovery requests) is achieved in each project.

The two projects also differ on their deployment models. MUSDAC requires coordination between its components (e.g., between SD managers and between an SD manager and its connected bridges). This management overhead is, however, limited and independent of the number of clients and services. INDISS, on the other hand, does not provide nor require any coordination between multiple INDISS instances, and therefore does not generate any control overhead. However, since multiple instances of INDISS in a network operate independently, it may create unnecessary duplication of messages as requests and/or advertisements are translated and reemitted by each instance.

Since INDISS is targeted at home environment and consumer electronic (CE) devices, it focuses on responsiveness and low resource requirements. However, the service information carried over when translating between two SDPs corresponds to the intersection of

Table 3.2
INDISS and MUSDAC Comparison

	INDISS/AMIGO	MUSDAC/PLASTIC
Networking environment	Home networks • heterogeneous networks within same administrative domain	B3G networks • dynamic composition of independent networks
Interoperability requirements	Lightweight discovery Applicable to CE devices No infrastructure building	Enhanced discovery (context, security) Multinetworks discovery
Approach to SD interoperability	Translation of SDPs messages • transparent discovery • network messages interception • event-based parsing and composition	Integration of SDPs • explicit API • enhanced service description • client-side interoperability
Strengths	Transparent to clients and services Limited resources requirements Easy deployment	Context-aware discovery Multinetwork support Controlled dissemination
Weakness	Limited network reach Intersection of SD information	Requires client support High processing requirements

the two sets of service information. MUSDAC, on the other hand, is designed for B3G networks and focuses on extensibility. The MUSDAC service description format is designed to be extensible and corresponds to the union of the information contained in the service description formats of legacy SDPs, enriched with context information. INDISS and MUSDAC also differ on how the generation of the intermediate representation (INDISS events and MUSDAC descriptions/requests) to/from SDP specific messages can be reconfigured: in MUSDAC, a new SD plug-in (Java class) must be dynamically loaded and instantiated; in INDISS, the finite state machine (FSM) that performs the conversion of SPD messages can be dynamically reconfigured at runtime. The INDISS approach is therefore more efficient in the case of frequent fine-grain updates. More important, the INDISS approach benefits from the numerous tools available to optimize and validate FSMs.

Performance evaluation (Raverdy, Issarny, et al. 2006) highlighted the high cost of service discovery in MUSDAC compared with SDPs for pervasive environments (UPnP, SLP) and INDISS. This overhead is directly related to the service API of MUSDAC, which is required for any enhanced service discovery protocol.

As a conclusion, the INDISS approach is more appropriate within the same administrative domain, such as a home network, because it supports responsive applications, whereas service discovery solutions for B3G networks require multinetwork bridging or network overlays, as proposed in the MUSDAC approach.

Though not in the scope of this chapter, the interoperability of service access protocols must also be addressed. Indeed, clients and service providers using different SDPs are more than likely also to use incompatible protocols for communication. Translation of access messages may be achieved using techniques for service discovery similar to those in INMIDIO.[13]

3.4 Context-Aware Service Discovery for Pervasive Environments

A common limitation of the various SD protocols proposed over the years is that they were initially designed based on specific assumptions about the underlying network (e.g., Internet, home networks), the users' behavior, or the applications' needs. Though efficient for the targeted environment, these SD protocols prove to be inefficient or not applicable in different settings. A further limitation is that they support only selection based on the matching of service functional attributes, without taking into account the user's context information.

Relevant contextual information includes, for example, the situation of the user (e.g., location, activity, interests), the capabilities and status of the employed terminal (e.g., CPU status, screen resolution), or the computing environment (e.g., network connectivity, available bandwidth). Few projects have investigated how to practically integrate context-aware service selection support in existing service discovery protocols, such as Jini, Salutation, or UPnP. Lee and Helal (2003) extended Jini to support context awareness by means of dynamic context attributes in the service description. Though clients generate discovery requests in the original Jini format using only static attributes, the service descriptions may contain dynamic (context) attributes that are evaluated by the lookup service during the matching process. A key assumption behind this approach is that the context of the lookup service (e.g., location) used by the client approximates the context of the client/service.

Many projects have also proposed new context-aware service discovery protocols for infrastructure-based and ad hoc networks, and in particular for location-aware SDPs such as Splendor (Zhu et al. 2003). Lee (Lee et al. 2003) proposes an agent-based approach that aims to transparently and constantly provide users with the best networked service, based on their preferences and needs. Solar (Chen and Kotz 2002) is a middleware platform that enables context-aware applications to locate environmental services based on the current context. Q-CAD (Capra et al. 2005) is a QoS and context-aware resource discovery framework for pervasive environments. Each application dynamically specifies in its profile context parameters to be taken into account when discovering resources, and also specifies a utility function to be maximized when binding the most suitable resources.

3.4.1 Context Awareness in MUSDAC

As presented in section 3.3, MUSDAC enables service discovery in multinetwork environments, thus increasing the number of services accessible to users. Though multiple instances of the same service may be available, not all will provide the same quality of service. In such a service-rich environment, it becomes crucial to take context into account in order to return the best services to the client. In MUSDAC, context information is used not only for matching service requests with advertised services, but also for controlling the dissemination of service requests in the multinetwork environment. Indeed, context support in MUSDAC also aims at preserving available (and often limited) resources in the network and on (mobile) devices by avoiding unnecessary dissemination of service requests, and by providing users with services that best match their requirements.

In MUSDAC, service descriptions from legacy SDPs are translated into the MUSDAC description format, and are then extended with various types of context information (Raverdy, Riva, et al. 2006). In MUSDAC, *context information* of the networking environment, the interacting users, and the service instances are taken into account. The context of the networking environment aggregates information related to the specific network. It includes static context parameters (e.g., type of network, supported protocols, security level, etc.), dynamic context parameters (e.g., number of active users, number of available services, load, etc.), and admission control policies for incoming and outgoing messages. The context of the user includes information about the interacting user (e.g., location, credentials) and his control policies. Control policies express requirements on how the service instance should be selected and on how the discovery request should be propagated. Finally, the service context aggregates static and dynamic information about a service instance (e.g., cost, supported image format, waiting queue length, etc.) along with admission/security policies for regulating service access (e.g., reject uncertified requests).

Context information is modeled as the combination of *context parameters* and *context rules*. Context parameters correspond to the attributes characterizing the entity (e.g., bandwidth, expected lifetime, cost, security policy) and are stored in an open table of tuples (i.e., name and value pairs). Context rules express the preferences, choices, and filters for the control of the discovery process (propagation and matching). Context rules are expressed in the form of condition/action statements. Conditions are articulated as Boolean expressions, and the operators currently supported are *and*, *or*, *equal*, *not-equal*, *more than*, and *less than*. Actions currently supported are *propagate request*, *accept request*, and *select service*. Each rule is set as optional or mandatory, as the context parameter required to evaluate the rule may not be available. For example, a network may not be able to monitor the number of active users. Moreover, *and* and *or* operators permit flexible combining of elementary rules to build complex ones.

In order to illustrate our context model, examples of user, network, and service contexts are depicted in figure 3.4. The user context information associated with the discovery request sent by the user *Ratif* (step 1) specifies that the user's device has an audio output and a high-resolution screen, and that the user is looking for free and secure services in medium/high bandwidth networks. In *Network 2*, the service context associated with the video streaming service specifies that this service is free, secure, and currently idle, and requires devices with medium/high-resolution screen.

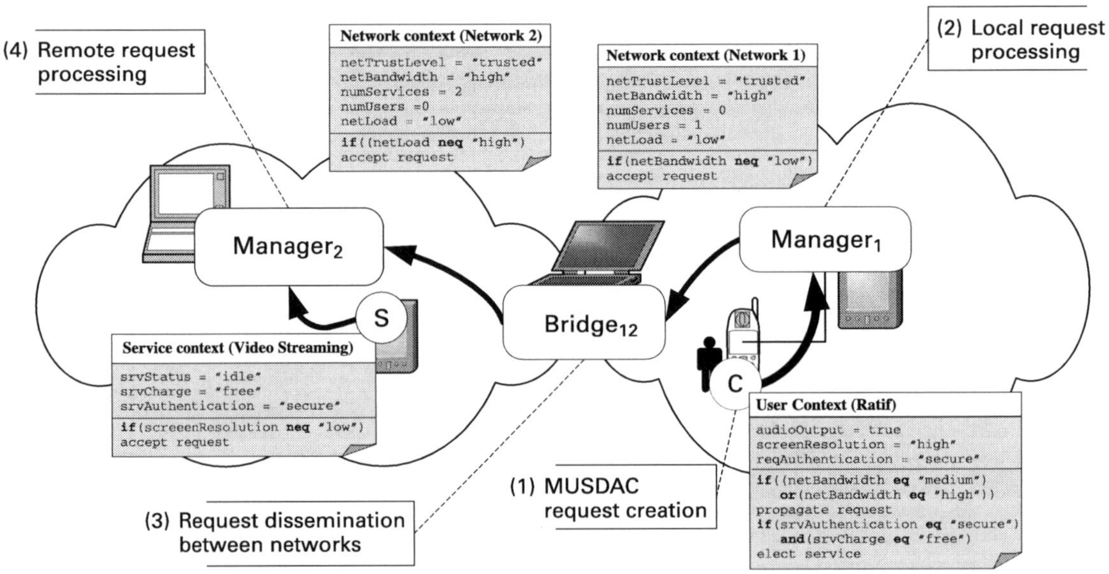

Figure 3.4
Context-awareness in MUSDAC

3.4.2 Context Information Provisioning and Utilization

Various components participate in the provisioning of context information used in MUSDAC: managers, users, SDA plug-ins, and transformers.

Managers initially gather static context information about the networking environment, and subsequently monitor the network activity to dynamically update context parameters such as number of active users, number of available services, current network load, and so forth. Moreover, the manager uses special control messages, called *context messages*, to periodically notify bridges within the domain about network context information. Nearby network domains can further exchange their network context information to gain knowledge about larger networking environments.

Users specify their context parameters and rules in the requests sent to the MUSDAC service. It is assumed that context monitors and device controllers are available on the user's terminal, and that the user is able to express his/her control policies in the form of semantically correct context rules.

Finally, SDA plug-ins and the associated transformers provide the service context information, which is carried by the service descriptions. As presented in section 3.3, SDA plug-ins generate the initial MUSDAC service description based on the SDP-specific service description. When context information is already available within the initial service description, the SDA plug-in automatically converts it, and adds it to the MUSDAC description. The initial description is then forwarded to the transformers associated with the

SDA plug-in. Transformers are external components, potentially provided by companies, consortiums, or interest groups, that extend initial MUSDAC descriptions with service-specific context information. A transformer may have a priori knowledge of certain services or may dynamically query specific context APIs of the service itself (or any third-party service) in order to collect service information (e.g., cost, availability status). Other transformers may add location or semantic information. Typically, transformers can be specified for interacting with a certain category of services (e.g., supplied by the same manufacturer) or for supporting a certain context interface (e.g., using a specific ontology). The benefit of using transformers is that they allow for the flexible integration of alternative methods for collecting service context information; as new context APIs are defined and implemented in services, new transformers can be deployed to support them. The enhanced service description is then forwarded to the manager that adds network-specific context information.

Managers and bridges are the components that directly process and utilize available context information. Managers are responsible for selecting instances of services that meet user requirements, and bridges are responsible for taking the decision on whether or not to propagate a discovery request to a certain network domain.

In the following, figure 3.4 is again used to explain how context information is utilized in the different phases of the service discovery process:

- Step 1: The user *Ratif* generates the discovery request, in which he specifies context parameters and rules.
- Step 2: Upon receiving this request, since no services are available in *Network 1*, *MUSDAC_Manager*$_1$ forwards it to *MUSDAC_Bridge*$_{12}$.
- Step 3: To decide whether the request has to be propagated, and the destination network (*Network 2*) can accept such request, *MUSDAC_Bridge*$_{12}$ processes applicable network context rules associated with *Network 1* and *Network 2*, and user context rules included in the discovery request (i.e., network load should not be high, and network bandwidth should be medium/high). Since all rules are positively matched, the request is forwarded to *MUSDAC_Manager*$_2$, which in turn forwards it to the local SDA plug-ins for processing.
- Step 4: Once *MUSDAC_Manager*$_2$ has received the result from the SLP SDA plug-in (i.e., the MUSDAC description for S2), it verifies the appropriate service and user context rules to ensure that the service matches the user requirements (i.e., secure and free of charge) and that the user's device is able to fully support the service (i.e., medium/high-resolution screen).

In Raverdy, Riva, et al. (2006), an evaluation of the context overhead in MUSDAC was conducted. Since managers and bridges can evaluate context rules directly, and use simple syntactic matching, the context-processing overhead during the request propagation and evaluation is limited (less than 30 ms for processing 30 context rules against 40 context parameters). This overhead occurs on each bridge forwarding the request and on each manager processing the request.

3.5 Conclusion

The pervasive computing vision is increasingly enabled by the large success of wireless networks and devices. In pervasive environments, heterogeneous software and hardware resources may be discovered and integrated transparently toward assisting the performance of users' daily tasks. An essential requirement for the realization of such a vision is the availability of mechanisms enabling the discovery of resources that best fit the client applications' needs among the heterogeneous resources that populate the pervasive environment. Based on the service-oriented architecture (SOA) paradigm, which allows the abstraction of the heterogeneous software and hardware resources as services described using structured service description languages, a number of service discovery protocols (SDPs) have emerged. However, these SDPs do not interoperate with each other, and provide limited support of service context and QoS properties, which is a key requirement for the realization of the user-centric vision aimed at by the pervasive paradigm. They also rely on the syntactic conformance of service interfaces or even service names; this requires a common agreement on syntax and ontology, which is hardly achievable in open pervasive environments.

In this chapter, we have presented the INDISS and MUSDAC service discovery solutions. INDISS targets service discovery in dynamic home networks and implements a transparent approach to SDP interoperability. It operates close to the network, capturing and translating network messages without the need for client or services interactions. On the other hand, the MUSDAC solution sits on top of existing SDPs and enables MUSDAC-aware clients to discover legacy services in the entire pervasive environment. Though both solutions primarily addressed the need for interoperability, IST AMIGO complemented INDISS with an interoperability solution for communication protocols (i.e., service access), whereas IST PLASTIC focused on providing context-aware service discovery in multinetwork environments.

The evolution of pervasive environments, characterized by increasing capabilities (memory, processing, connectivity) and popularity of mobile devices, and the need to support the dynamic composition of distributed services bring new requirements for a comprehensive service discovery solution:

- Proactive multiradio device management: Device connectivity and the dynamic composition of the various networks directly influence the set of reachable services, as well as the QoS that can be achieved. Existing SD solutions, however, do not control nor manage how devices connect to the available networks. A proactive approach must be devised to more effectively interconnect the various networks available at a location. While aiming at increasing the accessibility of services, such proactive management should also preserve the energy of the mobile device and meet the requirements of currently active applications.

- Mobility management: A challenging issue for service discovery and access in pervasive environments is to support the mobility of both clients and services as their location, and therefore their contextual information, evolve over time. Apart from the obvious objective of maintaining accurate service information, the service discovery component should also support various selection policies to deal with mobility, such as favoring interaction between nodes that will remain in network reach of each other for the duration of the session, or supporting the dynamic replacement of a service instance by another, more appropriate one on context changes.
- Semantic service discovery: In classic service discovery, the matching of service requests with service advertisements is based on assessing the conformance of related syntactic interfaces. However, an agreement on a single common syntactic standard is hardly achievable in the open pervasive environment. This problem becomes even more critical when service information contains extrafunctional information (i.e., context, QoS). Thus, higher-level abstractions, independent of the syntactic realizations in use, should be employed for denoting service information semantics.
- Security and privacy: Securing the exchange of service descriptions and discovery requests is crucial in pervasive environments, especially when such information is laced with service- or user-related contextual information. Secure service discovery primarily involves data integrity (e.g., service descriptions are not altered), authentication (e.g., only clients authorized in a network can perform a search), privacy (e.g., clients should not be able to track the requests of other clients), and confidentiality (e.g., some information within a service description may not be restricted).

Acknowledgment

This work was partially supported by the EC within the framework of the IST AMIGO project with FP6 contract 004182; the IST PLASTIC project with FP6 contract 26955; and the IST UBISEC[14] project with FP6 contract 506926.

Notes

1. http://www.hitech-projects.com/euprojects/amigo/.
2. http://www.ist-plastic.org/.
3. http://secse.eng.it/.
4. Refined Conceptual Model—A5.D9.1—http://secse.eng.it/.
5. http://www.nessi-europe.eu.
6. Object Management Group, "Trading Service Specification," OMG Technical Document number 00-06-27 (2000) http://www.omg.org/.
7. http://www.uddi.org/.

8. http://www.jini.org/.
9. Simple Service Discovery Protocol—Internet Draft—http://www.upnp.org/.
10. http://www.upnp.org/.
11. http://schemas.xmlsoap.org/ws/2005/04/discovery/.
12. http://www.w3.org/TR/wsdl.
13. http://www-rocq.inria.fr/arles/download/inmidio/index.html.
14. http://www.ubisec.org/.

References

Allard, J., V. Chinta, S. Gundala, and G. Richard III. 2003. Jini meets UPnP: An architecture for Jini/UPnP interoperability. In *Proceedings of the International Symposium on Applications and the Internet (SAINT)*, pp. 268–275. IEEE Computer Society.

Bromberg, Y.-D., and V. Issarny. 2005. INDISS: Interoperable Discovery System for Networked Services. In *Proceedings of ACM/IFIP/USENIX 6th International Middleware Conference (Middleware)*. LNCS 3790. Springer.

Capra, L., S. Zachariadis, and C. Mascol. 2005. Q-CAD: QoS and context aware discovery framework for mobile systems. In *Proceedings of the International Conference on Pervasive Services (ICPS)*, pp. 453–456.

Chen, G., and D. Kotz, 2002. Solar: An open platform for context-aware mobile applications. In *Proceedings of the 1st International Conference on Pervasive Computing (Pervasive 2002)*.

Clarke, I., O. Sandberg, B. Wiley, and T. W. Hong. 2000. Freenet: A distributed anonymous information storage and retrieval system. In *Proceedings of the ICSI Workshop on Design Issues in Anonymity and Unobservability*. Berkeley, CA, 2000.

Czerwinski, S. E., B. Y. Zhao, T. D. Hodes, A. D. Joseph, and R. H. Katz. 1999. An architecture for a secure service discovery service. In *Proceedings of the 5th Annual International Conference on Mobile Computing and Networking*, Seattle, WA.

Davies, N., K. Cheverst, K. Mitchell, and A. Friday. 1999. "Caches in the air": Disseminating tourist information in the Guide system. In *Proceedings of the Second IEEE Workshop on Mobile Computer Systems and Applications*, New Orleans, LA.

Friday, A., N. Davies, and E. Catterall. 2004. Supporting service discovery, querying and interaction in ubiquitous computing environments. *ACM Baltzer Wireless Networks (WINET)*, special issue on pervasive computing and communications, 10, no. 6: 631–641.

Grace, P., G. S. Blair, and S. Samuel. 2003. ReMMoC: A reflective middleware to support mobile client interoperability. In *Proceedings of the International Symposium on Distributed Objects and Applications*.

Guttman, E., C. Perkins, J. Veizades, and M. Day. 1999. Service location protocol, version 2. *IETF RFC* 2608 (June).

Hermann, R. 2001. DEAPspace: Transient ad hoc networking of pervasive devices. *Computer Networks* 35, no. 4: 411–428.

Koponen, T., and T. Virtanen. 2004. A service discovery: A service broker approach. In *Proceedings of the 37th Annual Hawaii International Conference on System Sciences (HICSS)*.

Lee, C., and S. Helal. 2003. Context attributes: An approach to enable context-awareness for service discovery. In *Proceedings of the 2003 Symposium on Applications and the Internet (SAINT)*. Orlando, FL.

Maheswaran, M. 2001. Data dissemination approaches for performance discovery in Grid computing systems. In *Proceedings of the 15th International Parallel and Distributed Processing Symposium*.

Ni, S.-Y., Y.-C. Tseng, Y.-S. Chen, and J.-P. Sheu. 1999. The broadcast storm problem in a mobile ad hoc network. In *Proceedings of the ACM/IEEE 5th International Conference on Mobile Computing and Networking (MobiCom)*, pp. 151–162. ACM.

Papazoglou, M. P., and D. Georgakopoulos. 2003. Service-oriented computing: Introduction. *Communications of the ACM* 46, no. 10: 24–28.

Raverdy, P.-G., S. Armand, and V. Issarny. 2006. Scalability study of the MUSDAC platform for service discovery in B3G networks. In *Proceedings of the Wireless World Research Forum Meeting (WWRF-17)*. Heidelberg, Germany.

Raverdy, P.-G., S. V. Issarny, R. Chibout, and A. de La Chapelle. 2006. A multi-protocol approach to service discovery and access in pervasive environments. In *Proceedings of the 3rd Annual International Conference on Mobile and Ubiquitous Systems: Networks and Services (MOBIQUITOUS)*. San Jose, CA.

Raverdy, P.-G., O. Riva, A. de La Chapelle, R. Chibout, and V. Issarny. 2006. Efficient context-aware service discovery in multi-protocol pervasive environments. In *Proceedings of the 7th International Conference on Mobile Data Management (MDM '06)*. Nara, Japan.

Stoica, I., R. Morris, D. Karger, F. Kaashoek, and H. Balakrishnan. 2001. Chord: A scalable peer-to-peer lookup service for Internet applications. In *Proceedings of the ACM SIGCOMM Conference*, pp. 149–160. San Diego, CA.

Zhao, B. Y., L. Huang, J. Stribling, S. C. Rhea, A. D. Joseph, and J. Kubiatowicz. 2003. Tapestry: A resilient global-scale overlay for service deployment. *IEEE Journal on Selected Areas in Communications* 22, no 1: 41–53.

Zhao, W., and H. Schulzrinne. 2005. Enhancing service location protocol for efficiency, scalability and advanced discovery. *Journal of Systems and Software* 75, no. 1–2: 193–204.

Zhu, F., M. Mutka, and L. Ni. Splendor: A secure, private, and location-aware service discovery protocol supporting mobile services. In *Proceedings of the 1st IEEE Annual Conference on Pervasive Computing and Communications (PerCom'03)*. Fort Worth, TX.

Zhu, F., M. Mutka, and L. Ni. 2005. Service discovery in pervasive computing environments. *IEEE Pervasive Computing* 4, no. 4: 81–90.

4 Unified Discovery and Composition of Heterogeneous Services: The SODIUM Approach

Aphrodite Tsalgatidou, George Athanasopoulos, Michael Pantazoglou, Arne J. Berre, Cesare Pautasso, Roy Grønmo, and Hjørdis Hoff

4.1 Introduction

Service-oriented computing (SOC) is an emerging software engineering trend that promises to reform the way applications are built. Services, the main building blocks in this new engineering trend, provide the means to utilize functionality that is offered by service providers via message exchanges over the Internet. The unique characteristics of a service have been a highly debated research issue (see, for example, Kozlenkov et al. 2006; Czajkowski et al. 2004; Vogels 2003, 59); nonetheless, all researchers agree that a service possesses properties such as self-description, Internet accessibility, and message-oriented communication. Normally, a service can be described, discovered, and invoked using XML-based protocols and standards which lie on top of other proven communication protocols, such as HTTP.

Web Services (Booth et al. 2004) is the best-known instantiation of the SOC paradigm. Other instantiations include Grid Services (Czajkowski et al. 2004), which emerged from the scientific application domain, and Peer-to-Peer (P2P) Services (Li 2001, 88), which originated from community-oriented systems and applications, such as instant messaging and file sharing.

All these services, regardless of their type, offer functionality which can be very useful in the development of service-oriented applications. For example, the applications in the crisis management domain require functionality, which may be provided by services from the health care domain, or services from the traffic management domain. However, such services are usually heterogeneous and are published in divers registries and networks. Thus, their distinct features, properties, supported protocols, and architectural models render them incompatible (Athanasopoulos, Tsalgatidou, and Pantazoglou 2006). Furthermore, it is notable that besides the interoperability issues between different service types, there are also interoperability concerns among services of the same type, for example, between P2P Services, as they mostly adhere to proprietary protocols and standards, or between Web Services, owing to different existing implementations. The latter has given rise to approaches such as the one undertaken by WS-I (Web Service Interoperability

Org.), which has established the basic interoperability profile (Ballinger et al. 2006) to deal with the discrepancies between Web Services.

The service heterogeneity and the lack of interoperability between services of the same type, as well as between services of different types, constitute a major obstacle to their widespread utilization in new service-oriented applications of diverse domains. Specifically, the activities of service discovery and service composition, which are two of the most important tasks in service-oriented engineering, become really cumbersome when one has to deal with services adhering to heterogeneous protocols and standards. We believe that this situation can be greatly improved by a unified approach toward the discovery and composition of heterogeneous types of services; such an approach can relieve the developer of a service-oriented application from the burden of dealing with the heterogeneity of the current service protocols, standards, and architectural models. This is the approach that is followed by the SODIUM (Service-Oriented Development In a Unified fraMework) project, which in this way supports the exploitation of the useful functionality offered by existing heterogeneous services and thus facilitates the development of service-oriented applications. Specifically, the goal of SODIUM is to create an open and extensible platform comprising appropriate tools and middleware that abstract developers from the underlying characteristics of the addressed service types. At the same time, SODIUM allows each type of service to retain its unique characteristics, without altering or enforcing any restrictions upon the underlying service provision platforms. Hence, developers are able to utilize the distinct traits of each service type. The types of services addressed by the current tools and languages of SODIUM are Web Services, P2P Services, and Grid Services. Nevertheless, the openness and extensibility of the SODIUM solution allow for the support of other service types, such as UPnP (Newmarch 2005) or sensor services (Gibbons et al. 2003, 22), by the provision of the appropriate extensions and plug-ins.

The contribution of SODIUM is mainly positioned in the service integration layer of the NESSI framework (NESSI), but it can also be positioned in the interoperability layer. Specifically, SODIUM lies in the bottom and middle layers of the SOC road map proposed in Papazoglou and Georgakopoulos (2003, 24), since it provides innovative solutions for the description, discovery, and composition of heterogeneous services. It also touches the upper layer of the SOC road map, as it provides some support related to the monitoring of compositions of heterogeneous services. Finally, it should be noted that the SODIUM solution for service discovery and composition exploits existing work on semantics and quality of service without, however, making a specific contribution in these areas.

In the following sections we present the approach employed by the SODIUM project and its outcomes as follows. We describe a motivating scenario that illustrates the need to integrate heterogeneous services (section 4.2). This scenario comes from the crisis management domain, and it was implemented by one of the pilot applications developed for the evaluation of the SODIUM platform (Hoff, Hansen, and Skogan 2006). We continue by illustrating the existing heterogeneity and discrepancies in the protocols and standards used for service description, discovery, invocation, and composition with respect to Web, P2P and Grid services which hinder the reuse of such services in other service-oriented applications (section 4.3). Then, we exemplify the SODIUM approach and present the main elements of the SODIUM platform (section 4.4). Finally, we compare our work with similar approaches (section 4.5) and present some concluding remarks (section 4.6).

4.2 Motivating Scenario

Our motivating scenario comes from the crisis management domain, where an important task is to determine how to get to a crisis location and dispatch the appropriate emergency units as fast as possible. For example, in case of an accident with severely injured people, it is critical to reach these persons with the appropriate equipment within minutes. In such cases, if the injury causes lack of oxygen to the brain for three to five minutes, brain cells start to die, and after approximately 15 minutes the damage is irreversible. Thus, it is vital that properly equipped ambulances and other rescue units be located within a 15-minute range at all times and places, to increase the possibility of reaching injured people before it is too late.

This requirement is hard to achieve owing to the vast set of parameters that need to be taken into account (e.g., accident/injury probability, population density and composition, accessibility, time of day/week/month/year, weather conditions, hospital locations, and many others). Furthermore, the integration of information stemming from various systems that calculate all these parameters (i.e., weather forecasting systems, traffic management systems, hospital information systems, etc.) is a complicated problem. Therefore, the use of a service-oriented approach in the development of applications satisfying the requirements mentioned above can be very beneficial. Some examples of services that provide useful functionality for the implementation of the above scenario are the following:

1. Web Services providing weather information, such as temperature and precipitation, or traffic conditions from roadside speed sensors and video surveillance cameras
2. Grid Services providing driving route calculations, weather forecasting information, and "response range" calculations based on current positions and conditions
3. P2P services providing information about the locations and status of emergency vehicles, and messaging facilities to the emergency vehicles with reposition message commands

Alas, such existing services and systems (e.g., services and systems from the health care management domain, weather forecasting systems, and so on) are highly heterogeneous, and thus difficult to be discovered and combined. Therefore, a service-oriented application supporting this scenario needs to be able to integrate heterogeneous services such as the ones mentioned above. Nevertheless, this is not an easy task, as was mentioned in the introduction, due to the incompatibility of the existing service types; some of the incompatibilities that need to be dealt with are presented in the following section.

The rest of the chapter presents the SODIUM approach, which provides a unified solution to the discovery and composition of heterogeneous services (i.e., Web, Grid, and P2P services) that has been used for implementing the motivating scenario described above.

4.3 Heterogeneous Services Computing

The requirements imposed by real-world applications, such as the ones presented in the previous section, induce the need for discovery and composition of various types of services. In the following paragraphs, we outline the results of a thorough analysis on the technologies of Web, P2P, and Grid services, conducted within the context of SODIUM, which revealed a number of heterogeneities, and discrepancies spanning across aspects such as service description, discovery, invocation, and composition. A detailed description of the state-of-the-art analysis is available in Tsalgatidou et al. (2005).

4.3.1 State of the Art in Service Description

The information conveyed by the description of a service generally falls into one or more of the following categories:

1. Syntactic information, which refers mainly to the structure of the service interface, and the provided operation signatures
2. Semantic information, which is provided to describe the capability of the service (i.e., its offered functionality)
3. Quality information, which describes the nonfunctional, qualitative characteristics of the service, such as its reliability, availability and performance.

The Web Services Description Language (WSDL) (Christensen et al. 2001) has been established as the de facto standard for syntactically describing a service. Still, the peculiarities of the various service types, such as Grid and P2P, have yielded numeral extensions to the standard. The Web Service Resource Framework (WSRF) (Banks 2006) defines a set of extension elements in WSDL in order to describe the properties of the resource being handled by a Grid Service. On the other hand, network topology concepts, such as peers or peer groups, need to be described in a P2P service description to allow its invocation. This requirement has yielded extensions, such as the ones described in Athanasopoulos, Tsalgatidou, and Pantazoglou (2006), to the WSDL standard.

Over the last years, a number of diverse protocols were proposed to address the lack of semantic information in WSDL descriptions. The Web Service Modeling Ontology

(WSMO) (Roman et al. 2005) and OWL-S (Martin et al. 2004) frameworks, along with the latest SAWSDL specification (Farrell and Lausen 2007), are the most prominent approaches in this direction. These protocols were further extended to meet the requirements of the Grid, as they were also utilized to provide semantic annotations to the descriptions of sharing resources (Babik et al. 2006).

Many heterogeneous protocols have also been proposed with respect to the quality of service (QoS). The Web Service Level Agreement (WSLA) (Keller and Ludwig 2003, 57), the WS-QoS (Tian et al. 2004), and the Web Service Offering Language (WSOL) (Tosic et al. 2003) are some of the proposed specifications that can be used to describe the QoS of a Web Service. As for Grid services, approaches such as the G-QoSM (Al-Ali et al. 2002) and the Globus Architecture for Reservation and Allocation (GARA) (Foster et al. 1999) cater for advanced quality specification and support management of services, resources, and the underlying network infrastructure. Finally, although not directly addressed in terms of language specifications, QoS has been taken into account in the P2P world, and many algorithmic approaches (Sahin et al. 2005; Vu, Hauswirth, and Aberer 2005) have been proposed to optimize the qualitative aspects of P2P networks.

4.3.2 State of the Art in Service Discovery

Besides the heterogeneity in their descriptions, Web, P2P, and Grid services have employed diverse publication and discovery mechanisms. Registries complying with the universal description, discovery, and integration specifications (UDDI; Clement et al. 2004) and the ebXML standard (EBXML 2002) are commonly used for publishing and discovering Web Services. On the other hand, Grid infrastructures, such as Globus (http://www.globus.org) or the latest gLite (http://glite.web.cern.ch/glite), have established their own mechanisms for publishing and discovering resources and services within virtual organizations. Such mechanisms utilize directories and services which rely on the Lightweight Directory Access Protocol (LDAP) (Koutsonikola and Vakali 2004, 66). Completely different discovery approaches are realized by P2P technologies, such as JXTA (Li 2001, 88) or Edutella (Nejdl et al. 2002), where services and resources are advertised and discovered in a distributed manner, all over the network.

4.3.3 State of the Art in Service Invocation

Web Services are traditionally communicated through the exchange of SOAP messages (Mitra 2003) over proven network protocols, such as HTTP and SMTP. The same invocation pattern is also applied to Grid Services, with the exception that the service client needs first to acquire the necessary credentials in order to gain access to a virtual organization. When it comes to P2P services, their invocation is tightly coupled with the specific P2P technology. Thus, services provided by peers in a Gnutella network (http://www.gnutella.com) are invoked in a different manner than services provided by peers in a JXTA network, and so on. Nevertheless, in most cases, the service client must either join the P2P network as a peer, or use an existing proxy peer to be able to invoke P2P services.

4.3.4 State of the Art in Service Composition

The Business Process Execution Language for Web Services (BPEL4WS) (Alves et al. 2007) has been established as a standard for composing Web Services into business processes. However, despite its wide adoption, BPEL4WS lacks the flexibility that would allow it to encompass other types of services as well, such as P2P and/or Grid services, also taking into account their specialized characteristics. Research efforts such as the Kepler engine (Altintas et al. 2004) have risen to support the execution of Grid Service scientific workflows in Grid environments. Other efforts, such as the one described in Gerke, Reichl, and Stiller (2005), have been proposed to enable the composition of P2P services in a P2P network. However, to the best of our knowledge, there is no approach, protocol, or standard to enable the composition of Web, P2P, and Grid services.

All the aforementioned protocols and standards suggest a heterogeneous situation that overwhelms developers and hinders the wide utilization of Web, P2P, and Grid services in a single service-oriented application. We believe that this challenge can be effectively addressed by establishing a unified approach in service-oriented computing as regards the various existing and emerging types of services. This is the exact contribution of the SODIUM project, the significant results of which we present in the following sections.

4.4 The SODIUM Approach to the Discovery and Composition of Heterogeneous Services

The primary goal of SODIUM is to facilitate the unified discovery and composition of heterogeneous services (with focus on Web, P2P, and Grid services), and thus to promote interoperability at the service discovery and composition levels. The SODIUM approach achieves this goal by providing an abstraction layer that hides the technical details of each service type from both developers and end users, without altering or modifying the distinct properties and characteristics of the underlying technologies. Specifically, the SODIUM solution comprises the following:

1. A generic service model (GeSMO) that supports the definition of the common as well as distinct characteristics of Web, P2P, and Grid services, thereby providing a solid conceptual basis to the SODIUM approach
2. A set of languages:
- The Visual Service Composition Language (VSCL), which supports the visual composition of heterogeneous services
- The Unified Service Query Language (USQL), which supports the unified discovery of heterogeneous services
- The Unified Service Composition Language (USCL), which provides a format for the executable representation of visual compositions made of heterogeneous services

3. A set of tools and supporting middleware:
• The composition visual editor, which implements the VSCL and supports the visual design of heterogeneous service compositions, as well as their translation to the USCL format
• The USQL service discovery engine, which implements the USQL and supports the unified discovery of different types of services from a wide spectrum of registries, repositories, and networks
• The USCL execution engine, which supports the execution and monitoring of heterogeneous service compositions that are expressed with the USCL format.

Figure 4.1 depicts the overall architecture of the SODIUM solution and also outlines the interactions between the constituent tools.

The SODIUM solution is divided in two main subsets, the composition suite and the runtime environment, which support the design and the runtime phases of the development process, respectively. Nevertheless, as figure 4.1 shows, the constituent tools are loosely coupled and communicate through document exchanges by means of well-defined

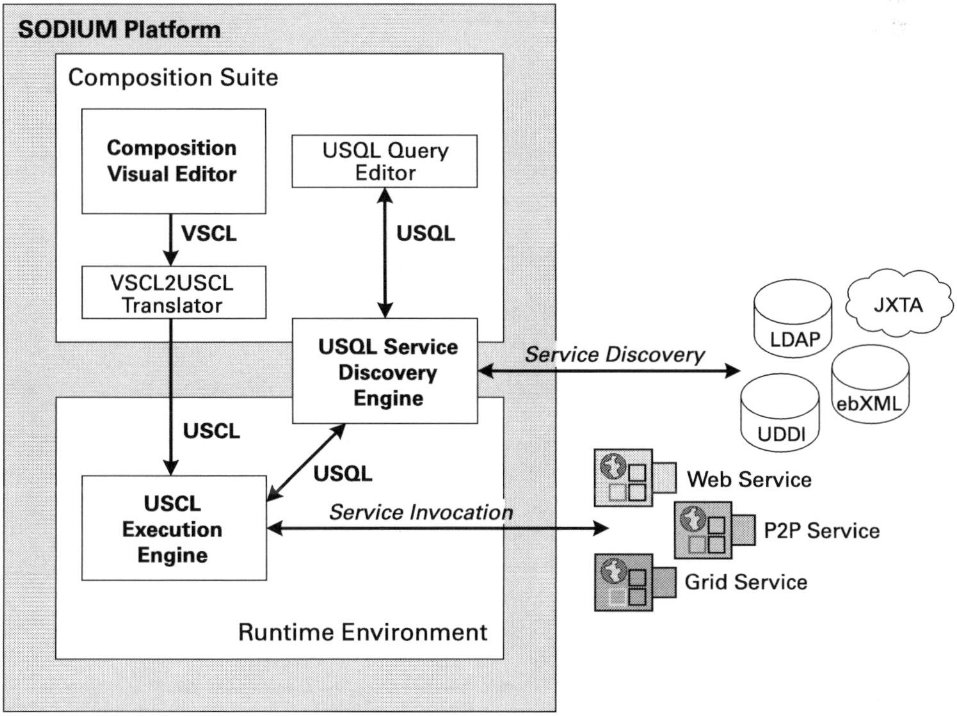

Figure 4.1
The SODIUM Platform

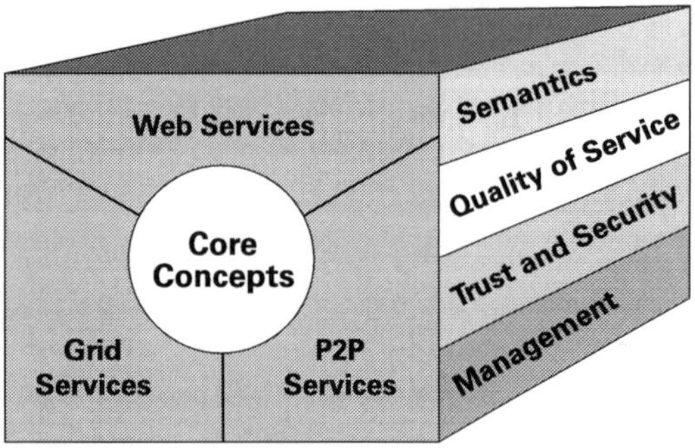

Figure 4.2
Architecture of the SODIUM Generic Service Model

interfaces. Therefore, they can be integrated with other tools in the future so as to create a customized service-oriented development environment.

Along with the SODIUM conceptual model, languages, and tools comes a model-driven methodology, which provides a way of composing existing yet heterogeneous services in order to execute a complex task.

In the following sections, we present and describe the SODIUM results.

4.4.1 The Generic Service Model

The generic service model (GeSMO) provides the conceptual basis upon which the SODIUM languages and tools were developed. Its specification was driven by the results of a thorough investigation of the state of the art in Web, P2P, and Grid service technologies outlined above. In general, the model is characterized by its generality, abstraction, simplicity, modularity, expressiveness, and extensibility.

GeSMO has adopted a layered architecture (see figure 4.2).

1. The *core layer*, which models all common concepts among the investigated service types (i.e., Web, P2P, and Grid services)
2. The extensions layer, which sits on top of the core layer and caters for the distinct features of each service type (i.e., Web, P2P, and Grid services)
3. A number of layers, orthogonal to the core and extensions layers, which model additional cross-cutting features, such as semantics, quality of service, trust and security, and management

Naturally, the fundamental concept of GeSMO is service. With the combination of concepts deriving from the layers described above, it is possible to describe a service from multiple points of view. Figure 4.3 outlines the different views that have been defined by GeSMO along with their interdependencies.

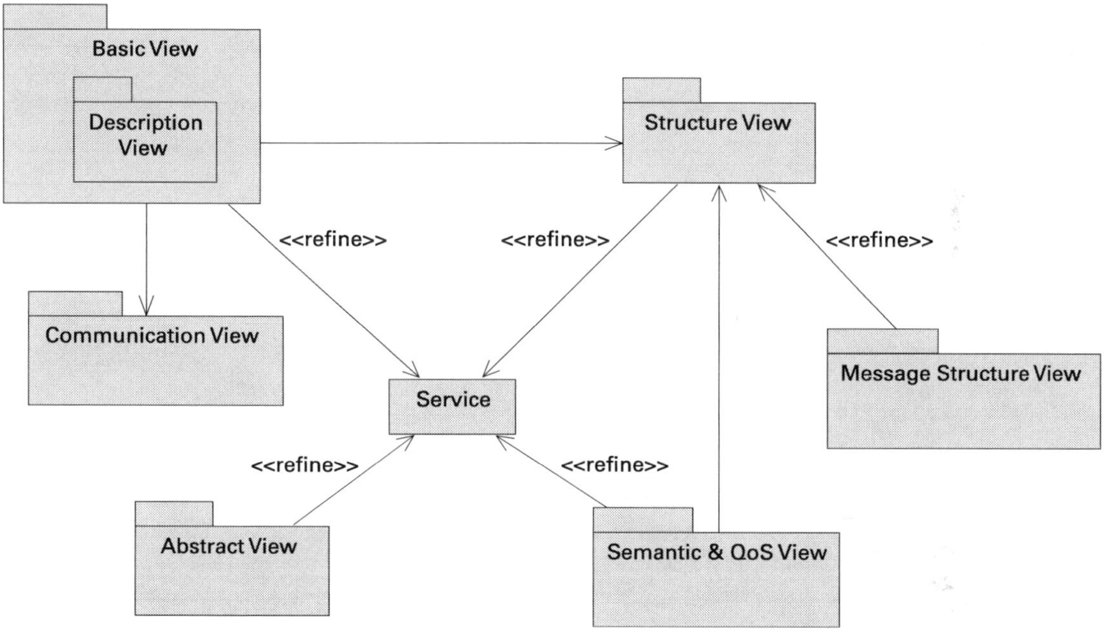

Figure 4.3
Views defined by the SODIUM Generic Service Model (GeSMO)

These service views are briefly described as follows.

1. Abstract view: It looks into the service notion from an abstract point of view and tries to identify its relationships with elements of the software engineering field.
2. Basic view: It pinpoints the minimal set of elements that need to be provided. The elements that are identified within this view may be further analyzed in other subviews.
3. Description view: This view focuses on the elements that are related to the description of a service.
4. Structure view: It identifies the structural elements that a service may comprise.
5. Semantics & QoS view: This view identifies the elements of the service model that may have semantic and QoS annotations.
6. Message Structure view: It provides a look into the structure and the elements of messages that are exchanged among a service and its clients.
7. Communication view: It identifies the elements related to the underlying network communication details (i.e., communication protocols that are used, network address, message wire format, etc.).

The basic, description, and structure views of GeSMO are shown in figures 4.4, 4.5, and 4.6.

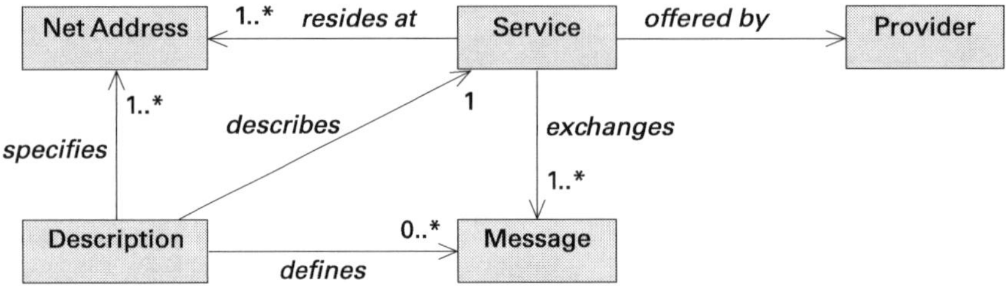

Figure 4.4
The Basic service view defined by GeSMO

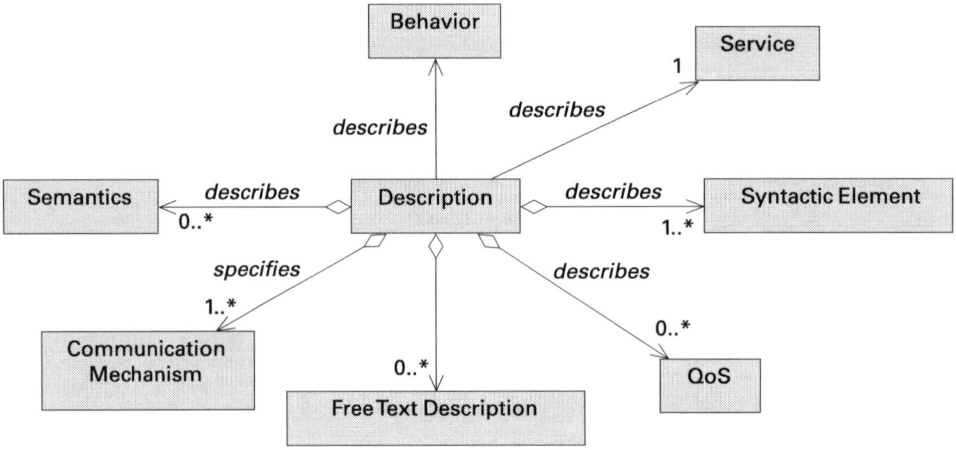

Figure 4.5
The Description service view defined by GeSMO

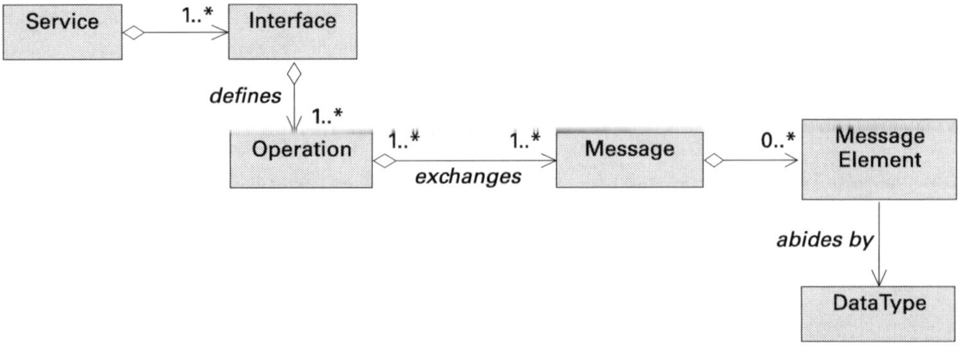

Figure 4.6
Structure view of a service as defined by GeSMO

The basic service model depicts a minimal set of concepts and their respective relationships that define the concept of service. This set of constructs, according to Vogels (2003, 59), suffices for the invocation of a service, but it needs to be further extended so as to facilitate the whole set of operations that are supported by the service model (i.e., publication, discovery, invocation, composition, etc.).

The service description model provides a detailed specification of the information that a description document may convey. A description document may provide descriptions or links to other documents for the whole or for parts of the information that is depicted in figure 4.5.

The structure model defines the set of structural elements that a service may be broken down into. A detailed description of all views defined in GeSMO is available in Tsalgatidou et al. (2005).

GeSMO shares many common concepts with the SeCSE Conceptual Model (Colombo et al. 2005). However, in GeSMO we focused primarily on the definition of different points of view, with the ultimate goal of describing services independently of their actual technology. In this respect, the conceptual service views provided by GeSMO may be considered as complementary to the SeCSE conceptual model.

Within the context of SODIUM, GeSMO served as a multipurpose tool. More specifically:

1. It was used as a conceptual basis for the specification of the three SODIUM languages (VSCL, USQL, and USCL), as well as for the development of the P2P Service Description Language (PSDL) (Athanasopoulos, Tsalgatidou, and Pantazoglou 2006), a WSDL-based format that was utilized in SODIUM for the description and invocation of JXTA P2P services.
2. It provided a common point of reference that facilitated communication and knowledge exchange among the project stakeholders.
3. Its abstraction and extensibility drove specific design decisions regarding the SODIUM tools, such as the plug-in–based architecture adopted by most of them.

In conclusion, the GeSMO specification currently caters for Web, P2P, and Grid services, nevertheless its extensibility allows for seamlessly accommodating other types of services.

4.4.2 Visual Service Composition

SODIUM supports the visual service composition through the Visual Service Composition Language (VSCL) and the Composition Suite.

The Visual Service Composition Language (VSCL) The VSCL is based on UML v2.0 (UML 2002), and supports the visual representation of service compositions which leverage Web, Grid, and P2P services. Specifically, the VSCL uses the concepts of the UML activity

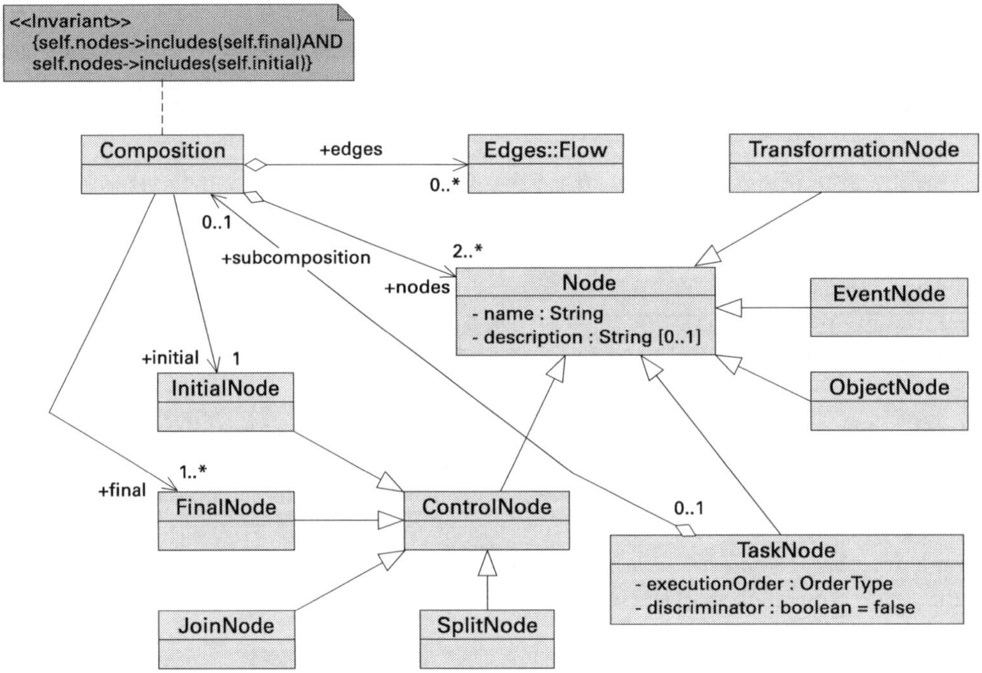

Figure 4.7
The VSCL conceptual meta-model

diagram as a basis for the provision of appropriate stereotypes that define all the necessary composition primitives. Nevertheless, the VSCL has a conceptual meta-model (see figure 4.7) that is independent of UML and other existing graphical modeling languages, however, it can be realized by a UML profile.

According to the VSCL meta-model, a service composition consists of nodes and flows/edges. The nodes are task nodes, control nodes, object nodes, event nodes, and transformation nodes; the different kinds of flow are used to specify flow of control and data between nodes. Hence, the main concepts of the VSCL are the tasks and the flow of data and control between tasks.

A task consists of both an abstract part and a concrete part. It may be coarse-grained, which means that it can be detailed in a sub-composition of tasks. The abstract part is service-independent and may be used as a starting point when querying for available and relevant heterogeneous services. The concrete part of a task has information about which service(s) to execute for this specific task. The strength of the task-based approach is that there is one composition graph, rather than two, incorporating both concrete and abstract parts. After services have been selected, the abstract part may still be used in order to check if new available and better-suited services have emerged. The possibility for defining

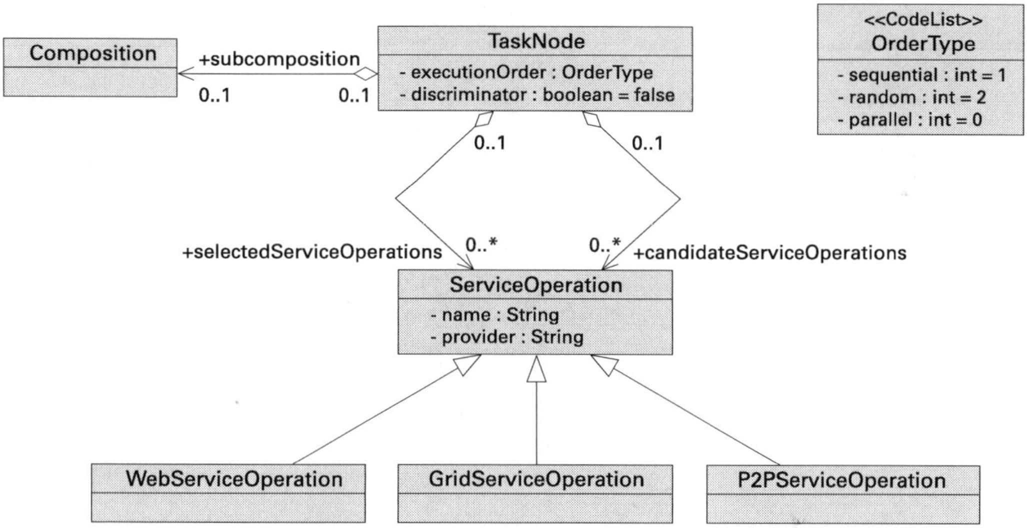

Figure 4.8
Relationship between tasks and services in the VSCL meta-model

transformations between the output(s) of a task and the input(s) of its successor task has also been included (Grønmo, Jaeger, and Hoff 2005). A task may itself be a composition, and thus it is decomposed into subtasks.

A heterogeneous composition in VSCL can consist of tasks executed by different kinds of services. The types defined in the context of SODIUM are P2P Services, Web Services, and Grid Services (see figure 4.8).

As shown in figure 4.8, one or more services may be selected to realize/execute a specific task. When more than one service operation is selected, the developer may state how the execution is to be done. There are three different possibilities. The service operations may be executed in parallel, sequential or in random order, the last two being associated with a response time limit. The service operations in the selectedServiceOperations list are considered "equal" with respect to the functionality they provide, but other aspects, such as QoS characteristics, may vary between them.

The detailed specification of the VSCL has been released as a public deliverable of SODIUM, and may be found in Hoff et al. (2005).

The SODIUM Composition Suite The SODIUM Composition Suite consists of the following main subcomponents:

1. The composition visual editor, for editing and analyzing service compositions with the use of the VSCL

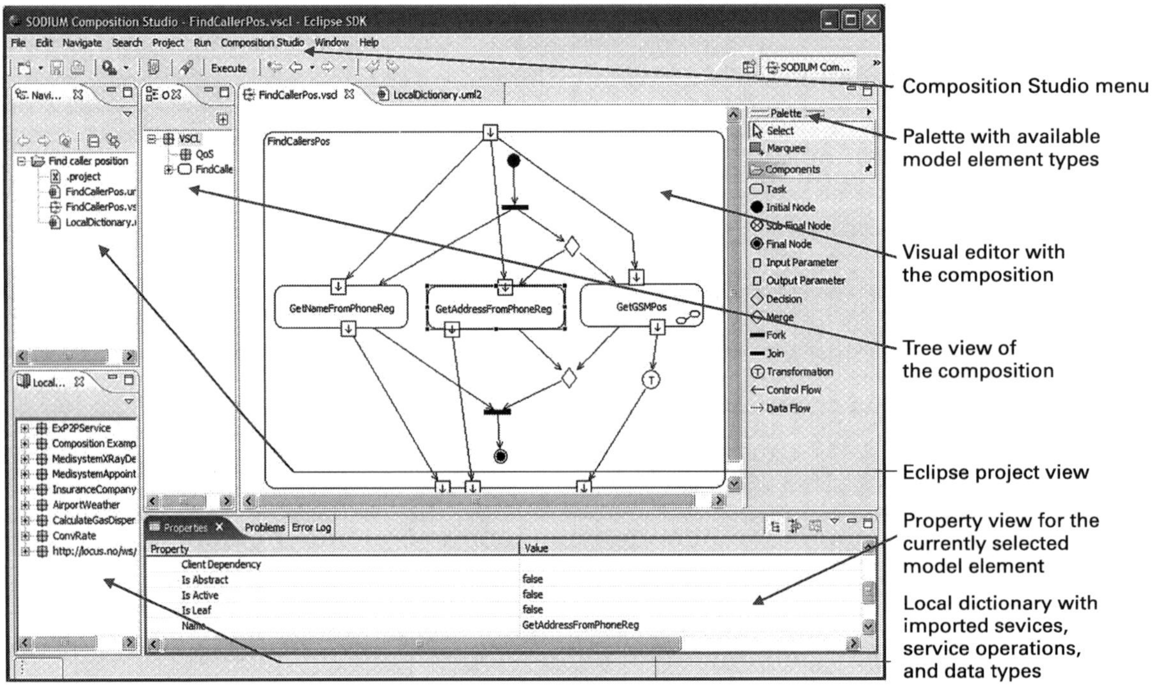

Figure 4.9
The SODIUM Composition Suite

2. The VSCL2USCL translator, which translates a service composition from a graphical notation (VSCL) to a lexical XML-based notation (USCL)
3. The USQL dialogue, for interacting with the USQL Engine in order to discover available Web, P2P, and Grid services.

The composition visual editor is the main component of the Composition Suite and has been developed as an Eclipse (http://www.eclipse.org) plug-in (see figure 4.9). It cooperates with the USQL Engine and the USCL Execution Engine in order to support the discovery of services and the deployment of executable service compositions. Moreover, it supports the following:

1. Specification of service compositions in multiple levels of abstraction
2. Static analysis of service compositions described in VSCL
3. Translation of VSCL graphs to USCL documents that can be executed by the Execution Engine.

The composition visual editor supports three approaches for defining heterogeneous service compositions:

1. Top-down approach for a task-oriented focus where tasks are identified, but no candidate service operations have yet been identified/selected
2. Bottom-up approach for a service-oriented focus when service operations to use are preknown
3. Dynamic approach for service operations to be discovered at execution time.

A typical use of the composition visual editor for the specification of service compositions based on the top-down approach is described as follows:

1. The first step in constructing VSCL graphs is to break down the composition into tasks, which interoperate in order to achieve the overall goal. This initial composition model of tasks is called an abstract model because no selected concrete services have yet been identified.
2. The abstract model is used as a basis for searching for appropriate candidate services which can realize each of the abstract tasks. When the appropriate services are discovered and selected, they are associated with the respective tasks and the result is a concrete model. Note that apart from selecting a specific service for the implementation of a task, developers are also allowed to assign USQL queries that will be executed at runtime, thus enabling the dynamic binding of services that are discovered, selected, and invoked at runtime.

More details regarding the SODIUM Composition Suite are available in Hoff et al. (2006).

4.4.3 Unified Service Discovery

Service discovery in SODIUM is supported by the Unified Service Query Language (USQL) and its associated engine, called USQL Engine, which are briefly described below.

The Unified Service Query Language (USQL) The USQL is an XML-based language providing the necessary structures for the formulation of service-type independent query documents and their responses. A rich yet extensible set of syntactic, semantic, and QoS search criteria enables service requesters to express their requirements in an accurate and intuitive manner. Moreover, with USQL, requesters can express their requirements toward a service and/or its operations, as well as the messages (i.e., input/output) exchanged by them. Hence, the USQL specification retains its consistency with GeSMO, specifically with respect to the structure view of a service (see figure 4.6).

Abiding by the principles of GeSMO, the USQL has established a certain level of abstraction so as to support mappings from/to a wide range of service description formats (e.g., WSDL, OWL-S, SAWSDL, etc.) and discovery protocols (e.g., UDDI, ebXML, JXTA, etc.). Thus, it can be used to discover services in a unified manner, regardless of how the latter have been described or where they have been published. The USQL specification defines two types of documents, the USQLrequest and USQLresponse. The former

```xml
<?xml version="1.0" encoding="UTF-8"?>
<USQL xmlns="urn:usql" version="1.1">
 <USQLRequest id="1167253624765">
  <SearchCriteria>
   <Service>
    <Provider><Value>Locus</Value></Provider>
    <Domain ontologyURI="urn:sodium:ont:crisis">
     <Value>CrisisManagement</Value>
    </Domain>
    <Operation>
     <Semantics ontologyURI="urn:sodium:ont:crisis">
      <Value>GetCallerPosition</Value>
     </Semantics>
     <Input>
      <Part>
       <Semantics ontologyURI="urn:sodium:ont:crisis">
        <Value>PhoneNumber</Value>
       </Semantics>
      </Part>
     </Input>
     <Output>
      <Part>
       <Semantics ontologyURI="urn:sodium:ont:crisis">
        <Value>CallerLocation</Value>
       </Semantics>
      </Part>
     </Output>
    </Operation>
   </Service>
  </SearchCriteria>
 </USQLRequest>
</USQL>
```

Figure 4.10
Example of a USQL request document

is used to express service type-independent queries, whereas the latter is used to convey the results of the query execution.

The snippet in figure 4.10 is an example USQL request document, in accordance with the motivating scenario presented earlier in the chapter.

The query is intended to search for services which retrieve the location of a caller based on its phone number. A closer look at the requirements included in the query reveals that there is nothing implying or bound to a specific service type; indeed, the USQL request is *service type-agnostic*. The requested service belongs to the domain of crisis management, as this is expressed by the Domain element. The desired functionality, as well as the input and output requirements, have been captured with the use of the Semantics elements specified into the Operation, and the requested Input and Output parts. The concepts used to popu-

```
<?xml version="1.0" encoding="UTF-8"?>
<USQL xmlns="urn:usql" version="1.1">
 <USQLResponsequeryId="1167253624765">
  <Services>
   <Entry rank="1.0">
    <WebService xmlns="urn:ws">
     <Name>CrisisMgmtService</Name>
     <Operation>GetCallerLocation</Operation>
     <Port>GetCallerPositionPort</Port>
     <WSDL>
      http://jemini.di.uoa.gr:8080/sodium/services/CrisisMgmtService.wsdl
     </WSDL>
    </WebService>
   </Entry>
   <Entry rank="0.833">
    <JXTAService xmlns="urn:jxta">
     <Name>PeerPositionService</Name>
     <Operation>GetPeerPosition</Operation>
     <Interface>PeerPositionServiceIF</Interface>
     <PSDL>
      http://www.s3lab.com/services/PeerPositionService.psdl
     </PSDL>
    </JXTAService>
   </Entry>
  </Services>
 </USQLResponse>
</USQL>
```

Figure 4.11
Example of a USQL response document

late the Semantics elements have been taken from a custom domain ontology that was developed for the purposes of SODIUM. However, the USQL is independent of the ontology being used to populate its semantic elements, and to this end, any ontology and/or semantic dictionary could be employed. To further constrain the query, and because of existing service level agreements and partnerships, the service requester has also specified the provider of the requested service.

An example USQL response document to the above USQL request is depicted in figure 4.11.

Apparently, the service discovery process yielded two matches, a standard Web Service and a JXTA P2P service, both delivering the desired functionality. The results have been prioritized according to their rank value, which quantifies their degree of match with respect to the search criteria of the USQL request. Note that although the USQL request was constructed in a service type-independent manner, the information conveyed by each of the corresponding entries in the USQL response is strongly associated with the type of the referred services and is adequate to enable their invocation.

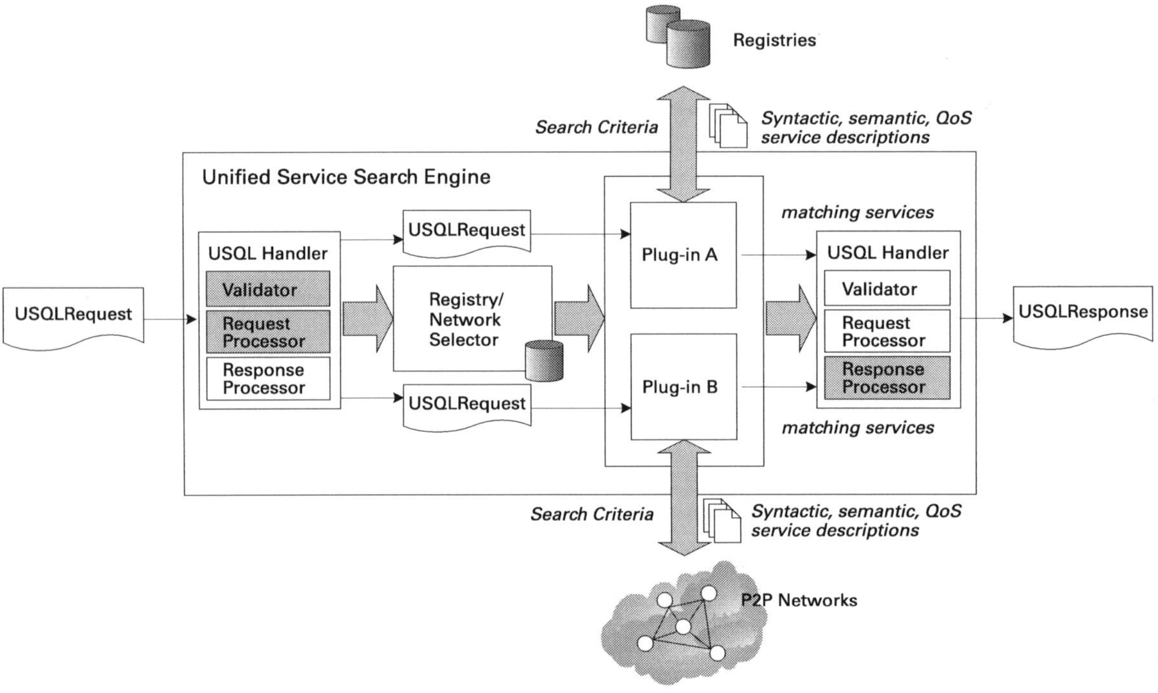

Figure 4.12
Architecture of the USQL Engine

The USQL Engine The USQL Engine is a powerful search tool enabling the discovery of heterogeneous services in various types of registries, repositories, and networks. As the name implies, the USQL Engine fully supports the USQL specification and acts as a black box from the user perspective: it accepts USQL request documents as input, and returns corresponding USQL response documents as output.

The architecture of the USQL Engine is depicted in figure 4.12.

The USQL Engine is characterized by a high degree of openness and extensibility, which is achieved by using plug-in mechanisms to accommodate the different types of services and registries. Specifically, the engine was extended in the context of SODIUM, and plug-ins were provided to support the discovery of services in UDDI and ebXML registries and JXTA networks. Moreover, appropriate extensions were developed to support the processing of WSDL, SAWSDL, OWL-S, and WS-QoS service descriptions.

Let us now briefly describe a typical service discovery process. Upon receiving a USQL request document, the USQL Engine engages the USQL handler to validate and forward it to appropriate registry plug-in components, which are coordinated by the registry selector and run in parallel. The service descriptions retrieved by the various registries are matched against the search criteria of the USQL request, and the ones that meet them are passed to the USQL handler. The latter consolidates the results from all registry plug-in components and prioritizes them, according to their degree of match, into a single USQL response document, which is returned to the service requester.

The USQL Engine provides both a graphical user interface (GUI) and a Web Service interface. The GUI, namely USQL Dialog, has been integrated with the SODIUM composition suite and is used by developers to formulate USQL queries, access the USQL Engine, and discover services at design time. At runtime, the USCL Execution Engine may invoke the USQL Engine Web Service and submit a predefined QoS-enhanced USQL query, in order to select and late-bind a service in a task from a set of alternative services having the same interface, yet characterized by different quality properties.

The architecture and functionality of the USQL Engine have been described in Pantazoglou, Tsalgatidou, and Athanasopoulos (2006b, 104). The definition of the matchmaking algorithm that has been implemented by the engine can be found in Pantazoglou, Tsalgatidou, and Athanasopoulos (2006a, 144).

4.4.4 Execution of Heterogeneous Service Compositions

In SODIUM, the execution of compositions consisting of Web, P2P, and Grid services is accomplished through the Unified Service Composition Language (USCL) and the related USCL Execution Engine.

The Unified Service Composition Language (USCL) The USCL is an XML-based language intended to be processed by machines, rather than humans. The main feature of the language consists of providing support for composing an open set of services, including Web, Grid, and P2P services. The description of the compositions is kept separate from the description of the software components, that are responsible for executing each composition task, in order to enhance the reusability of both. Compositions are modeled as processes whose structure defines the data and control flow dependencies between the service invocations, as well as the required exception handling behavior. Components are modeled as services, an abstraction that makes the mechanism used to access the corresponding implementation transparent.

Figure 4.13 depicts the structure of a USCL document.

The root element (USCL) of a USCL document can contain a set of process, service, and service type definitions. In practice, the service definitions and the required service type declarations are defined once and included from separate USCL documents. The external operation signature of a process is defined by a set of input and output parameters. Internally, a process contains the list of its component tasks and the data flow (parameters and edges). The service elements store the set of available service types that can be invoked. Similar to Processes, the operation signature of services is composed of a set of input and output parameters. Furthermore, a service can contain multiple access methods which define alternative ways to invoke the functionality provided by the service. Access

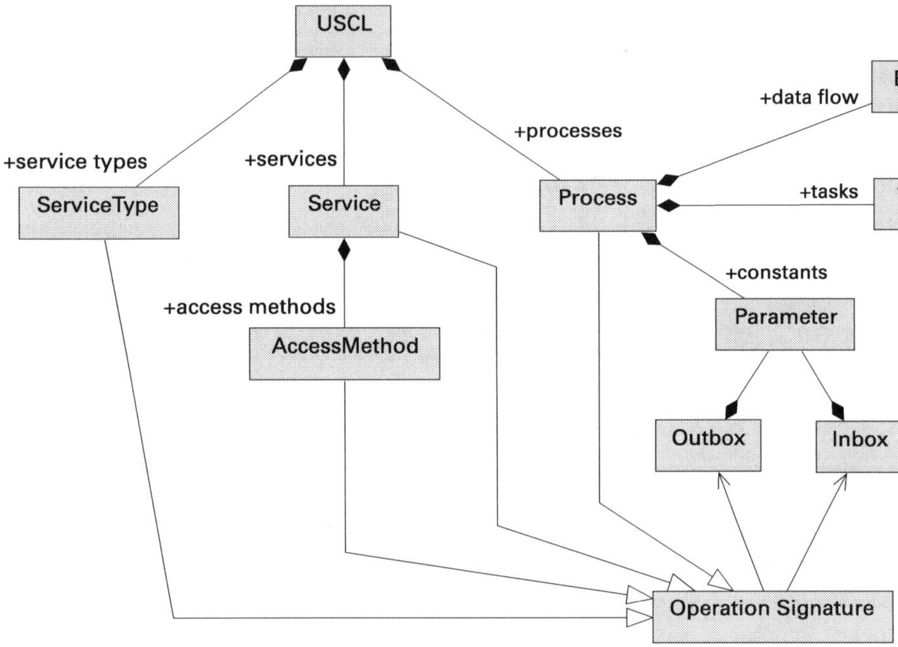

Figure 4.13
Overview of the structure of a USCL document

methods also have input and output parameters conforming to the template defined in the service type. By definition, the input and output parameters of an access method, and the ones belonging to the corresponding service type, are considered system parameters (Pautasso and Alonso 2004a).

Control flow is specified declaratively as a set of event-condition-action (ECA) rules, which are associated with each service invocation. The actions represent the actual invocation of the service, which is carried out only when the associated event fires and the condition evaluates to true. An event is defined as a predicate over the global state of the workflow (e.g., a rule should fire if a specific service has just successfully completed its invocation; another rule should fire if any one of a set of services has failed). A firing event will trigger the evaluation of the corresponding condition, which is a Boolean expression, over the values of data flow parameters. Nontrivial conditions are used to model alternative paths in the execution of the workflow. Moreover, they can also represent loop entry/exit conditions, since the rules associated with the service invocations can fire more than once during the lifetime of the workflow.

The data flow is also modeled declaratively as a graph of edges linking pairs of parameters. This fits quite well with the approach taken by VSCL, where such edges are visualized. Thus, it is intended to simplify the mapping between the two languages.

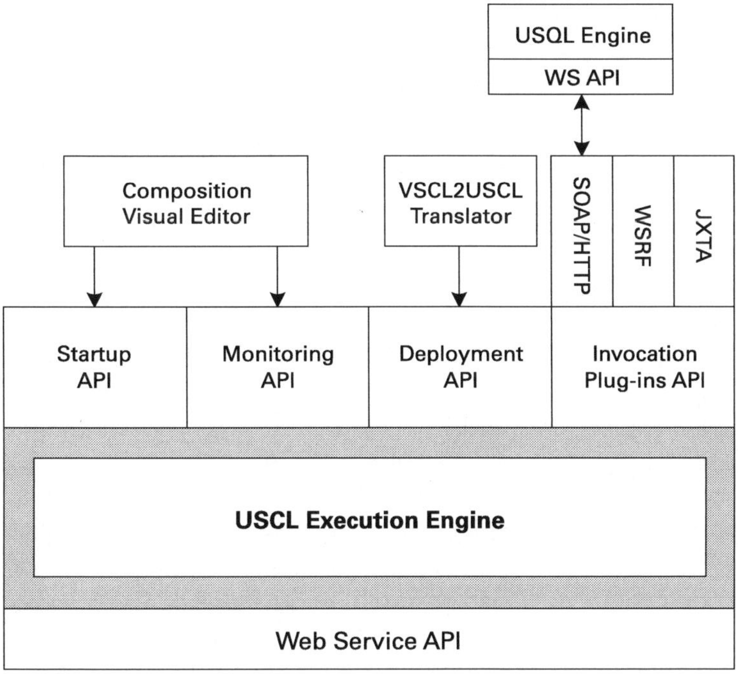

Figure 4.14
APIs provided by the USCL Execution Engine

In addition to control and data flow, USCL also features nesting, iteration, recursion, reflection, dynamic binding, and several other constructs specifically targeting the composition of heterogeneous kinds of services. The detailed specification of the USCL language is available in Pautasso, Heinis, and Alonso (2005).

The USCL Execution Engine The USCL Execution Engine provides a reliable and scalable platform for executing processes given in the USCL format, which are composed of heterogeneous services (Pautasso and Alonso 2004b). To do so, the architecture of the USCL Execution Engine employs plug-in components which enable it to support an open set of heterogeneous service invocation mechanisms.

The USCL Execution Engine provides a number of application programming interfaces (APIs) (see figure 4.14), which are used for communication with the rest of the SODIUM tools, as well as for the invocation of Web, P2P, and Grid services.

The functionality provided by the Deployment API is used to let the engine know that the processes and services declared in a USCL document are available, thus making the engine forget about the previously deployed items of the same USCL document. In this way, the USCL documents can be deployed to the USCL engine so the compositions stored in them can be prepared for execution. By means of this API, the VSCL2USCL translator component of the SODIUM Composition Suite is able to load USCL compositions to the USCL Execution Engine.

The Startup API is mainly used to initiate the execution of a new composition instance. In addition to starting an instance, this API allows clients to assign values to the input parameters of the newly created instance and to control how the state of the instance is managed by the engine (monitoring and logging). Once a process has been instantiated, it should be possible to identify it among others concurrently running inside the engine. Thus, after a process instance has been started, it is associated with a unique ID and then it is returned to the client that started its execution. No assumptions should be made about the format of such an ID, as this is left unspecified.

The Monitoring API allows accessing the execution logs of a given instance of a composition, identified by its ID. These logs provide information about the state of the execution of a composition and can be retrieved at any time during the execution of a composition. In general, the logs contain information about the data of a composition (current values of input/output parameters) as well as metadata (current execution state of a task, performance profiling information, error messages, and so on). Logs can be presented in a variety of formats (e.g., text, CSV, XML), depending on the intended usage.

The Invocation Plug-ins API addresses the requirement of dealing with heterogeneous services by providing a platform which can be extended to support the invocation of different kinds of services. This amounts to opening up the engine to use different mechanisms for invoking services of different kinds. The same API is also used by the engine for the execution of USQL queries at runtime, by submitting them to the USQL Engine through its Web Service interface.

The USCL Execution Engine supports both synchronous and asynchronous service invocation. For each service invocation to be performed, the engine instantiates a new object of the given service invocation plug-in class. Furthermore, the plug-in is executed in a dedicated thread. In this way, the USCL Execution Engine handles the multithreaded issues for the concurrent invocation of multiple services.

The USCL Engine provides for the persistence of the state information of the process instances. The design of this mechanism has been influenced by many requirements, such as performance, reliability, and portability across different data repositories. Access to the state information of the composition instances is provided in terms of a key-value pair which uniquely identifies a certain data (or metadata) value associated with a process (and task) instance. The state information data model is independent of the physical location of the data, so that it is possible to use caching to exploit locality and—for increased availability—replicate some of the values. Along these lines, in order to provide a level of scalability, state management can be optimized to keep only a subset of all of the composition instances in memory and, for instance, swap compositions whose execution has been completed to secondary storage, in a so-called process history space. In this way, the USCL Engine gives access to the state of past executions to enable composition profiling and optimization, caching of already computed results, and lineage tracking analysis.

Finally, in addition to the APIs previously described, the functionality of the USCL Execution Engine is also accessible through a WSRF Web services API (Heinis et al. 2005). This feature makes feasible the utilization of the USCL Execution Engine as a distinct component outside the SODIUM platform.

Thanks to its multithread support and efficient resource management, the USCL Execution Engine achieves considerable performance and scalability. A detailed description of these features, along with experiment measures, can be found in Pautasso, Heinis, and Alonso (2007, 65) and in Pautasso et al. (2006).

4.4.5 The SODIUM Service Composition Methodology

The SODIUM Service Composition Methodology provides a way of composing existing yet heterogeneous services, in an iterative, incremental four-phase evolving manner. (See figure 4.15.)

Let us proceed with a description of the four development phases defined by the SODIUM methodology. Along these lines, we exemplify the use of the various SODIUM tools in order to demonstrate how they should be used according to the principles of the methodology.

Phase 1: Modeling The first phase of the methodology consists of a number of activities. The first activity is to identify the task to be solved by a new service composition. The coarse-grained task is then refined into more detailed tasks. The relationships between tasks are modeled as flow of control and data, and may be characterized as a graph consisting of nodes (tasks) and directed edges (flows). To create complex control flow graphs, parallelism and choices may be introduced. Each of the tasks is given a unique name. In addition, expected input and output parameters may be specified. Expected service type(s) (Web Service, P2P Service, and Grid Service) can also be specified.

The next two activities may be done in parallel:

1. *Semantics* By associating the task name and its input/output parameters to a domain, the chance of discovering appropriate service(s) for the task increases. Therefore the user (1) identifies available ontologies in order to import a relevant subset of its concept definitions into the editor and then (2) uses these concepts to annotate the service category and input/output parameters of each of the tasks.
2. *QoS* For each of the tasks, the user may specify the QoS that must be offered by services executing the given task.

The final product of this phase is an abstract composition that serves as input to the next phase of the methodology.

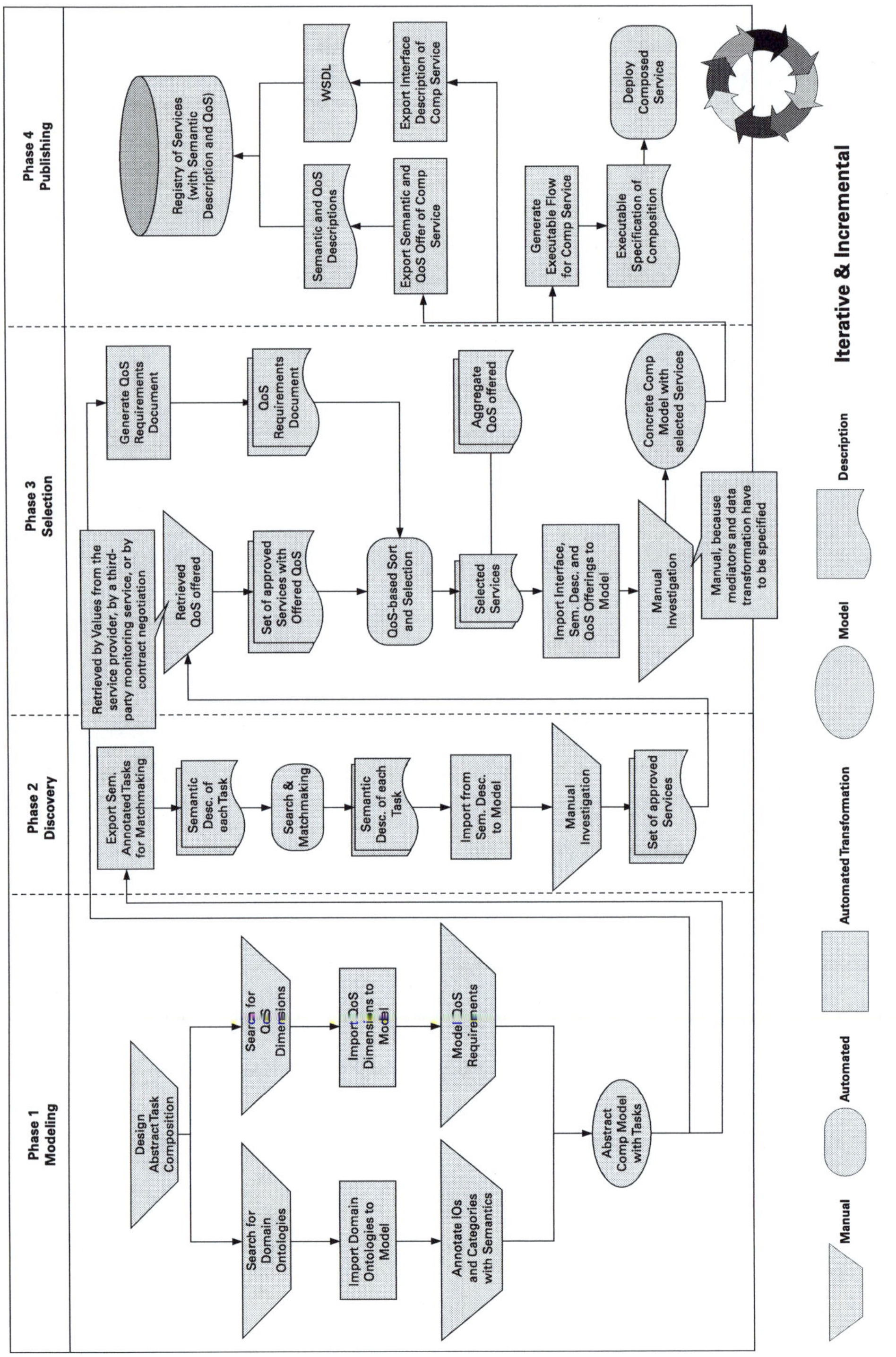

Figure 4.15
The SODIUM Heterogeneous Service Composition methodology

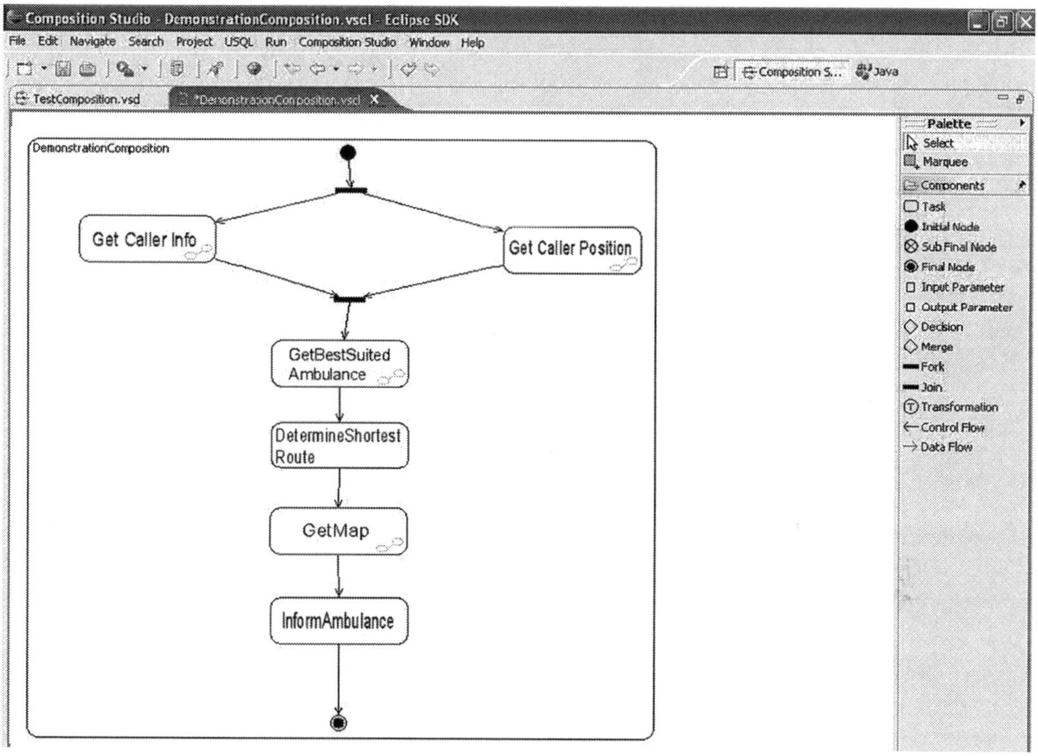

Figure 4.16
Abstract service composition created with the SODIUM Composition Suite

In SODIUM, the first phase of the methodology is supported by the Composition Suite. The screenshot in figure 4.16 illustrates an abstract composition that reflects the motivating scenario described in section 4.2.

Actually, the figure 4.16 depicts what happens when an emergency unit receives an emergency telephone call: it has to identify the location of an accident based on a caller's position, to find an ambulance which is closest to that location, and to dispatch it to that location. The outcome of the composition is a map with a route from the ambulance's current position to the accident location and a set of necessary command messages that are transmitted to the ambulance's personnel. Note that the Get Caller Info, Get Caller Position, Get Best Suited Ambulance, and Get Map tasks in the abstract graph are composite; thus they are decomposed into subtasks, as the little mark at the bottom right edge of each task denotes.

Phase 2: Discovery The second phase handles discovery of services that can satisfy the requirements of each task. The user may either go back and forth between phases 1 and 2 of the process, or create the whole abstract composition at once and then move on to phase 2 to populate the abstract composition with services, thereby transforming it into a concrete composition ready for execution. Since SODIUM aims at supporting dynamic service discovery at runtime, some tasks may be left without an associated service prior to runtime. Instead, these tasks are given a predefined service query, which will be executed at runtime.

Phase 2 is defined as a set of activities performed in sequence. The first activity is to make a semantic description (a query document) by using the query dialogue for each of the selected tasks. The query documents are passed directly to the query engine that supports the discovery process, based on matchmaking of semantic descriptions. It is assumed that a service registry is available with the following information provided for each service:

1. A service interface description
2. A semantic description that can be used for the matchmaking process
3. QoS offered that can be exploited for the selection in the next phase.

The final product of phase 2 is a list of candidate services per task.

The service discovery phase of the methodology is handled by the USQL Engine. More specifically, for each task that requires a service, the developer opens the USQL Dialogue (see figure 4.17) from the composition visual editor, creates a USQL query by setting a number of syntactic, semantic, and/or QoS search criteria, and executes the query by submitting it to the USQL Engine. The latter returns a list of matching services, which are appropriately displayed in the USQL Dialogue (see figure 4.17).

Phase 3: Selection In phase 3, the goal is to narrow down and rank the services based on the QoS requirements. The QoS requirements contain two parts (see Grønmo and Jaeger 2005 for further details). The first part contains the absolute QoS constraints that are used to exclude services. The second part contains the optimization criteria that are used to rank the services. Instead of applying a "greedy-based" approach (i.e., ensuring QoS optimization of each task in isolation), another approach could be used, as the one proposed in Grønmo and Jaeger (2005), which considers the composition as a whole or in subparts. However, the SODIUM platform supports only QoS optimization of single tasks in isolation.

The QoS-based prioritization and selection will return an assignment of a ranked list of candidate services for each task. Then, the composition designer chooses one or more concrete services for each task in the abstract composition model. In this way, the developer finalizes the concrete composition model, which is the outcome of phase 3. Often it can be wise to choose more than one service for a task. This is the case if during runtime a service becomes temporarily or permanently unavailable. Then, an alternative service, performing the same task, may compensate for the unavailable one.

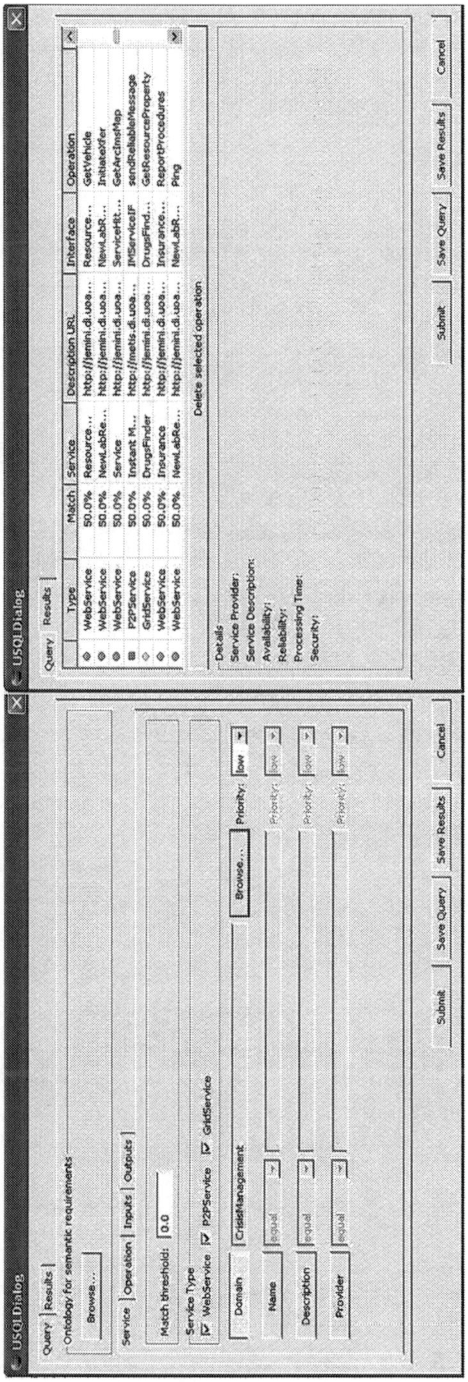

Figure 4.17
The USQL Dialog is used both for editing USQL queries and displaying search results

The outcome of phase 3 is a concrete service composition model with selected services. The SODIUM platform supports this phase via the use of the Composition Suite and the USQL dialogue. Having executed a USQL query, the developer needs to go through the list of matching services and manually select the one(s) that seem(s) to be most appropriate for the specific task.

Phase 4: Publishing In the fourth and final phase, the concrete composition model is used to generate different descriptions about the composed service:

1. A WSDL document describing the syntactic interface and its technical bindings
2. An executable flow document
3. Semantic Web Service documents (e.g., OWL-S, WSML etc.) and documents describing the offered QoS.

The WSDL file can be automatically generated as shown in Grønmo et al. (2004, 1), and the executable flow document can be generated as shown in Kath et al. (2004). The Semantic Web Service documents can be automatically generated by the transformation tool described in Grønmo, Jaeger, and Hoff (2005). All the generated information may be submitted to a Web Service registry where, third parties can discover and use the composed service. The transformation rules from the concrete composition model to QoS documents have not been specified within the context of SODIUM.

Publishing composite Web Service and registering service descriptions to a Web Service registry is not supported by the SODIUM platform, as it was considered outside the scope of the project. Thus, within the context of the SODIUM platform, only the generation of the executable USCL documents is supported, by means of the VSCL2USCL translator, which compiles and converts VSCL service compositions into USCL processes.

Figure 4.18 summarizes the involvement of the SODIUM tools in each phase prescribed by the methodology. In addition to the four phases of the methodology, a final step regarding the execution of the service composition has been included to show the involvement of the SODIUM execution engine.

A detailed view and description of the SODIUM Service Composition Methodology is given in Grønmo and Hoff (2007). Before concluding this section, we would like to note that although the intended users of the SODIUM Methodology are primarily the users of the SODIUM platform, the principles of this methodology can be applied to service composition in general, as a way of working.

4.5 Related Work

SODIUM provides for the development of service-oriented applications by supporting the unified discovery and composition of heterogeneous services. Its contribution lies in the areas of visual service composition (VSCL language and editor), execution of service com-

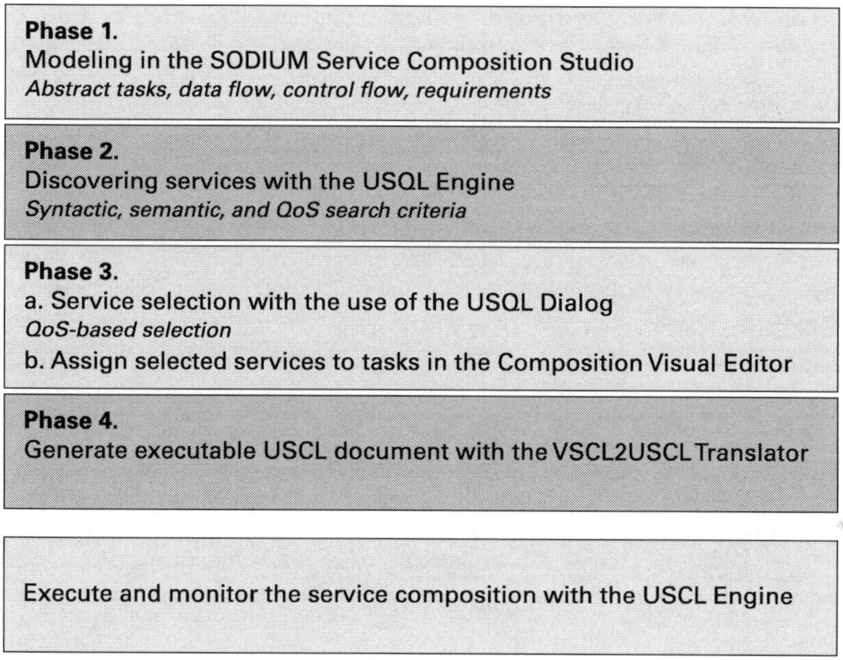

Figure 4.18
SODIUM methodology and SODIUM tools

positions (USCL language and execution engine), and service discovery (USQL language and engine). In the following we compare the SODIUM results with existing work in these areas.

The two SODIUM composition modeling languages (i.e., the VSCL and the USCL) accommodate the visual as well as the textual representation of service compositions. Similar to VSCL, the BPMN (BPMI 2004) notation supports the description of the control and data flow for a business process. BPMN is based on the UML activity diagram and facilitates the visual representation of business processes in a methodology-independent manner. The VSCL has been influenced by BPMN and, in addition, it provides constructs which facilitate the description of Web, Grid, and P2P services. Moreover, VSCL provides concepts which support the description of the non-functional aspects of a service, such as quality-of-service properties or associated semantics.

The USCL, on the other hand, is an XML-based service composition language which, like WS-BPEL (Alves et al. 2007), accommodates the description of the composition control and data flows. In contrast to WS-BPEL, USCL is independent of a specific service technology, and thus it may support the composition of services regardless of their type and underlying service provision platforms. Furthermore, the USCL, along with the

USCL Engine, accommodates the description of data transformations in a rich set of transformation techniques which include XSLT (Clark 1999), XQuery (Boag et al. 2007), and QVT (QVT-Merge Group 2004), so that the optimal one in terms of runtime performance and development effort can be applied.

The use of a service-oriented approach to software development introduces the need for service discovery, which is only partially addressed by other approaches to service composition development (Altintas et al. 2004). In the areas of Web, Grid, and P2P services, service discovery is performed with the use of custom and incompatible APIs and discovery mechanisms offered by registries and networks (Clement et al. 2004; Li 2001, 88). Over the last years, research in the area of service discovery was oriented toward improving and/or extending the existing discovery mechanisms (Paolucci et al. 2002; Li et al. 2004). Moreover, many approaches were proposed to enhance the overall discovery process and precision (Klein and Bernstein 2004, 30; Kozlenkov et al. 2006). Still, to the best of our knowledge, the SOC community lacks the means that would enable accessing and querying heterogeneous registries in a unified and standards-based manner. Moreover, exploitation of semantics and QoS within service descriptions proves to be a crucial part of service discovery. USQL and its enacting engine address these issues and constitute a stepping-stone to the unification of the various heterogeneous service areas.

4.6 Conclusions

Service-oriented computing is an emerging trend that promises to reform current software engineering approaches. Even though SOC aims at facilitating interoperability between the components required for building an application, it still has not come up to this expectation. The proliferation of various service-oriented technologies (e.g., Web, Grid and P2P services), which employ incompatible properties and characteristics, hinders the widespread utilization of those services. With the emerging need to compose such incompatible types of services, the support for their interoperation becomes an issue of high importance.

The SODIUM contribution in service interoperability and integration, presented in this chapter, provides an approach to unified discovery and composition of heterogeneous services. SODIUM provides a generic service model, a set of languages supporting the visual specification of service compositions, the unified querying for services, and the execution of heterogeneous service compositions, along with a set of tools that provide for the design, discovery, and execution of service compositions. Although the SODIUM platform was originally implemented to support the unified discovery and composition of Web, Grid, and P2P services, its extensibility and modularity features that are exhibited by the whole set of its components facilitate the accommodation of other types of services as well.

Other projects of the Information Society Technologies (IST) Priority of the 6th Framework Program (FP6) of the European Union which tackle issues similar to the ones tackled by SODIUM are SeCSE (http://secse.eng.it), ATHENA (http://www.athena-ip

.org/), PLASTIC (http://www-c.inria.fr/plastic/), and AMIGO (http://www.hitech-projects.com/euprojects/amigo/). The SeCSE project provides innovative technologies, methods, and tools for supporting service-oriented computing, but it does not explicitly tackle heterogeneity in service discovery and composition, which is the main focus of SODIUM. The ATHENA project addresses system and application interoperability and focuses mainly on bridging the gap between business and IT, whereas SODIUM concentrates on the interoperability between Web, P2P, and Grid services in the development of service-oriented applications. The PLASTIC and AMIGO projects tackle service interoperability in pervasive computing environments by taking advantage of context information to provide efficient service discovery in multi-network environments (the PLASTIC approach) and by establishing interoperability at a semantic level (the AMIGO approach), whereas SODIUM addresses service interoperability by offering a unified approach to the discovery and composition of existing heterogeneous services through the SODIUM languages and tools described in the previous sections.

The need to address heterogeneous types of services in a unified manner has also been identified by other organizations such as OMG, which released a request for proposal (UPMS RFP (UPMS 2006)) for the provision of a service meta-model that will leverage the description of services. Two SODIUM results, the VSCL language and the GeSMO model, have been submitted to OMG in order to address the needs of the UPMS RFP. Further to addressing the needs of standardization bodies, the SODIUM results have also been exploited through other venues. Thus, we would like to note that GeSMO has been used as input in the ATHENA project, whilst the USQL and the USQL engine have been extended and further utilized in the SeCSE project.

The SODIUM solution has been effectively applied to the construction of two pilot applications which integrate functionality from heterogeneous services in the crisis management and the health care domains. It is worth mentioning that the development of these two applications was greatly facilitated and improved by the SODIUM platform, despite the prototype phase of the provided tools. Furthermore, the independence of the SODIUM platform components facilitated the customization of the application development environment, since developers were given the liberty to tailor the deployment according to their needs.

All SODIUM tools are open source, provided under the LGPL license (http://www.gnu.org/licenses/lgpl.html) with the potential for integration in any commercial environment.

Acknowledgments

The work published in this chapter was partly funded by the European Community under the Sixth Framework Program, contract FP6–04559 SODIUM. The work reflects only the authors' views. The Community is not liable for any use that may be made of the information contained therein. The authors would like to thank the rest of the SODIUM project partners, namely: ATC, S.A., for the project management, Locus and MEDISYSTEM for contributing to the development of the pilots and the rest members of the NKUA, SINTEF, and ETHZ teams for their invaluable contribution to this work.

References

Al-Ali, R. J., Rana, O. F., Walker, D. W., Jha, S., and Sohail, S. 2002. G-QoSM: Grid Service discovery using QoS properties. *Computing and Informatics* 21: 363–382.

Altintas, I., Berkley, C., Jaeger, E., Jones, M., Ludäscher, B., and Mock, S. 2004. Kepler: An extensible system for design and execution of scientific workflows. In *16th International Conference on Scientific and Statistical Database Management*, pp. 423–424. Santorini, Greece.

Alves, A., Arkin, A., Askary, S., Bloch, B., Curbera, F., Goland, Y., Kartha, N., Liu, C., König, D., Mehta, V., Thatte, S., Rijn, D., Yendluri, P., and Yiu, A. eds. 2007. Web Services Business Process Execution Language Version 2.0. OASIS Standard, April 2007. http://docs.oasis-open.org/wsbpel/2.0/OS/wsbpel-v2.0–OS.html.

Athanasopoulos, G., Tsalgatidou, A., and Pantazoglou, M. 2006. Unified description and discovery of P2P services. 2006. In *First International Conference on Software and Data Technologies.* Setubal, Portugal. INSTICC Press.

Babik, M., Gatial, E., Habala, O., Hluchy, L., Laclavik, M., and Maliska, M. 2006. Semantic Grid services in K-Wf Grid. In *Second International Conference on Semantics, Knowledge, and Grid.* Guilin, China.

Ballinger, K., Ehnebuske, D., Ferris, C., Gudgin, M., Nottingham, M., and Yendluri, P., eds. 2006. Basic Profile Version 1.1, Web Services Interoperability Organization. http://www.ws-i.org/Profiles/BasicProfile-1.1-2006-04-10.html.

Banks, T. 2006. Web Services Resource Framework (WSRF)—Primer v1.2. OASIS, May. http://docs.oasis-open.org/wsrf/wsrf-primer-1.2–primer-cd-02.pdf.

Boag, S., Chamberlin, D., Fernández, M., Florescu, D., Robie, J., and Siméon, J., eds. 2007. XQuery 1.0: An XML Query Language. W3C, January. http://www.w3.org/TR/xquery/.

Booth, D., Haas, H., McCabe, F., Newcomer, E., Champion, M., Ferris, C., and Orchard, D., eds. 2004. Web Services Architecture. W3C Working Group Note, February. http://www.w3.org/TR/ws-arch/.

BPMI. 2004. Business Process Modeling Notation (BPMN) Version 1.0. OMG, May. http://www.omg.org/docs/bei/05-08-07.pdf.

Christensen, E., Curbera, F., Meredith, G., and Weerawarana, S., eds. 2001. Web Services Description Language (WSDL) 1.1. W3C note, March. http://www.w3.org/TR/wsdl.

Clark, J. 1999. XSL Transformation (XSLT) Version 1.0. W3C Recommendation, November. http://www.w3.org/TR/xslt.

Clement, L., Hately, A., von Riegen, C., and Rogers, T., eds. 2004. UDDI Version 3.0.2. OASIS, October. http://uddi.org/pubs/uddi_v3.htm.

Colombo, M., Di Nitto, E., Di Penta, M., Distante, D., and Zuccalà, M. 2005. Speaking a common language: A conceptual model for describing service-oriented systems. In *Service Oriented Computing, Computing ICSOC 2005: 3rd International Conference.* Amsterdam, Netherlands.

Czajkowski, K., Ferguson, D., Foster, I., Frey, J., Graham, S., Maguire, T., Snelling, D., and Tuecke, S. 2004. From Open Grid Services Infrastructure to WS-Resource Framework: Refactoring & Evolution, Version 1.0. The Globus Alliance. http://www.globus.org/wsrf/specs/ogsi_to_wsrf_1.0.pdf.

EBXML 2002, OASIS/ebXML Registry Services Specification v2.0. http://www.oasis-open.org/committees/regrep/documents/2.0/specs/ebrs.pdf.

Farrell, J., and Lausen, H., eds. 2007. Semantic Annotations for WSDL and XML Schema. W3C Recommendation, August. http://www.w3.org/TR/2007/REC-sawsdl-20070828.

Foster, I., Kesselman, C., Lee, C., Lindell, B., Nahrstedt, K., and Roy, A. 1999. A Distributed Resource management architecture that supports advance reservations and co-allocation. In *Proceedings of the International Workshop on Quality of Service.* London, England.

Gerke, J., Reichl, P., and Stiller, B. 2005. Strategies for service composition in P2P networks. In *Proceedings of the Second International Conference on E-Business and Telecommunication Networks*. Reading, U.K. INSTICC Press.

Gibbons, P., Karp, B., Ke, Y., Nath, S., and Seshan, S. 2003. IrisNet: An architecture for a world-wide sensor web. *IEEE Pervasive Computing* 2, no. 4: 22–33.

Grønmo, R., and Hoff, H. 2007. D19: SODIUM Service Composition Methodology. SODIUM, January. http://www.atc.gr/sodium.

Grønmo, R., and Jaeger, M. 2005. Model-driven methodology for building QoS optimised Web Service compositions. In *5th IFIP International Conference on Distributed Applications and Interoperable Systems* (DAIS 2005). Athens, Greece. LNCS 3543. Springer.

Grønmo, R., Jaeger, M., and Hoff, H. 2005. Transformations between UML and OWL-S. In *Foundations and Applications: Proceedings of the First European Conference on Model Driven Architecture* (ECMDA-FA), pp. 269–283. Nuremberg, Germany.

Grønmo, R., Skogan, D., Solheim, I., and Oldevik, J. 2004. Model-driven Web Service development. *International Journal of Web Services Research* 1, no. 4 (October–December): 1–13.

Heinis, T., Pautasso, C., Alonso, G., and Deak, O. 2005. Publishing persistent Grid computations as WS resources. In *Proceedings of the 1st IEEE International Conference on E-Science and Grid Computing* (e-Science 2005), pp. 328–335. Melbourne, Australia.

Hoff, H., Grønmo, R., Skogan, D., and Strand, A. 2005. D7: Specification of the Visual Service Composition Language (VSCL). SODIUM, June. http://www.atc.gr/sodium.

Hoff, H., Hansen, T., and Skogan, D. 2006. D5: Specification of Requirements for User Applications Part I: Requirements Specification for the Locus Pilot. SODIUM, February 2006. http://www.atc.gr/sodium.

Hoff, H., Skogan, D., Grønmo, R., Limyr, A., and Neple, T. 2006. D9: Detailed Specification of the SODIUM Composition Suite. SODIUM, February. http://www.atc.gr/sodium.

Kath, O., Blazarenas, A., Born, M., Eckert, K.-P., Funabashi, M., and Hirai, C. 2004. Towards executable models: Transforming EDOC behaviour models to CORBA and BPEL. In *8th International Enterprise Distributed Object Computing Conference* (EDOC 2004). Monterey, Calif.

Keller, A., and Ludwig, H. 2003. The WSLA framework: Specifying and monitoring service level agreements for Web Services. *Journal of Network and Systems Management* 11, no. 1 (March): 57–81.

Klein, M., and Bernstein, A. 2004. Toward high-precision service retrieval. *IEEE Internet Computing* 8, no. 1: (January–February): 30–36.

Koutsonikola, V., and Vakali, A. 2004. LDAP: Framework, practices, and trends. *IEEE Internet Computing* 8, no. 5 (September–October): 66–72.

Kozlenkov, A., Fasoulas, F., Sanchez, F., Spanoudakis, G., and Zisman, A. 2006. A framework for architecture-driven service discovery. In *2006 International Workshop on Service-Oriented Software Engineering*. Shanghai, China.

Li, G. 2001. JXTA: A network programming environment. *IEEE Internet Computing* 5, no. 3 (May–June): 88–95.

Li, Y., Zou, F., Wu, Z., and Ma, F. 2004. PWSD: A scalable Web Service discovery architecture based on peer-to-peer overlay network. In *6th Asia–Pacific Web Conference on Advanced Web Technologies and Applications*. Hangzhou, China. LNCS 3007.

Martin, D., Burstein, M., Hobbs, J., Lassila, O., McDermott, D., McIllraith, S., Narayanan, S., Paolucci, M., Parsia, B., Payne, T., Sirin, E., Srinivasan, N., and Sycara, K. 2004. OWL-S: Semantic Markup for Web Services. W3C, November. http://www.w3.org/Submission/OWL-S/.

Mitra, N., ed. 2003. SOAP Version 1.2 Part 0: Primer. W3C, June. http://www.w3.org/TR/soap12–part0/.

Nejdl, W., Wolf, B., Qu, C., Decker, S., Sintek, M., Naeve, A., Nilsson, M., Palmér, M., and Risch, T. 2002. EDUTELLA: A P2P networking infrastructure based on RDF. In *11th international Conference on World Wide Web* (WWW '02). Honolulu.

NESSI, Networked European Software & Services Initiative. http://www.nessi.com/Nessi/.

Newmarch, J. 2005. UPnP services and Jini clients. In *Proceedings of the 2005 Conference on Information Systems: Next Generations* (ICIS 2005). Las Vegas, Nev.

Pantazoglou, M., Tsalagatidou, A., and Athanasopoulos, G. 2006a. Quantified matchmaking of heterogeneous services. In *Proceedings of the 7th International Conference on Web Information Systems Engineering* (WISE 2006). Wuhan, China. LNCS 2455, pp. 144–155.

Pantazoglou, M., Tsalgatidou, A., and Athanasopoulos, G. 2006b. Discovering Web Services and JXTA peer-to-peer services in a unified manner. In *Proceedings of the 4th International Conference on Service-Oriented Computing* (ICSOC 2006). Chicago. LNCS 4294, pp. 104–115.

Paolucci, M., Kawamura, T., Payne, T., and Sycara, K., 2002. Importing the Semantic Web in UDDI. In *Proceedings of E-Services and the Semantic Web Workshop (WES 2002), CAiSE 2002 International Workshop.* Toronto.

Papazoglou, M., and Georgakopoulos, D. 2003. Service-oriented computing. *Communications of the ACM* 46, no. 10 (October): 24–28.

Pautasso, C., and Alonso, G. 2004a. From Web Service composition to megaprogramming. In *Proceedings of the 5th VLDB Workshop on Technologies for E-Services* (TES-04). Toronto.

Pautasso, C., and Alonso, G. 2004b. JOpera: A toolkit for efficient visual composition of Web Services. *International Journal of Electronic Commerce* 9, no. 2: 107–141.

Pautasso, C., Heinis, T., and Alonso, G. 2005. D6: Specification of the Unified Service Composition Language (USCL). SODIUM, June. http://www.atc.gr/sodium.

Pautasso, C., Heinis, T., and Alonso, G. 2007. Autonomic resource provisioning for software business processes. *Information and Software Technology* 49, no. 1: 65–80.

Pautasso, C., Heinis, T., Alonso, G., Pantazoglou, M., Athanasopoulos, G., and Tsalgatidou, A. 2006. D10: Detailed Specification of SODIUM Runtime Environment. SODIUM. http://www.atc.gr/sodium.

QVT-Merge Group. 2004. Revised Submission for MOF 2.0 Query/Views/Transformations RFP. QVT-Merge Group. http://www.omg.org/cgi-bin/apps/doc?ad/04-04-01.pdf.

Roman, D., Keller, U., Lausen, H., de Bruijn, J., Lara, R., Stollberg, M., Polleres, A., Feier, C., Bussler, C., and Fensel, P. 2005. Web Service modeling ontology. *Applied Ontology* 1, no. 1: 77–106.

Sahin, O. D., Gerede, C. E., Agrawal, D., El Abbadi, A., Ibarra, O., and Su, J. 2005. SPiDeR: P2P-based Web Service discovery. In *3rd International Conference on Service-Oriented Computing* (ICSOC 2005). Amsterdam.

Tian, M., Gramm, A., Ritter, H., and Schiller, J. 2004. Efficient selection and monitoring of QoS-aware Web Services with the WS-QoS framework. In *2004 IEEE/WIC/ACM International Conference on Web Intelligence*, pp. 152–158. Beijing.

Tosic, D. V., Pagurek, B., Patel, K., Esfandiari, B., and Ma, W. 2003. Management Applications of the Web Service Offerings Language (WSOL). In *15th Conference on Advanced Information Systems Engineering* (CAiSE'03). Velden, Austria. Published in Advanced Information Systems Engineering LNCS 2681 (2008), pp. 1029–1052.

Tsalgatidou, A., Athanasopoulos, G., Pantazoglou, M., Floros, V., Koutrouli, E., and Bouros, P. 2005. D4: Generic Service Model Specification. SODIUM, June. http://www.atc.gr/sodium.

UML. 2002. Unified Modeling Language: Superstructure, Version 2.0. OMG. http://www.omg.org/cgi-bin/doc?formal/05–07–04.

UPMS. 2006. UML Profile and Meta-model for Services (UPMS) Request for Proposal. OMG. http://www.omg.org/docs/soa/06–09–09.pdf.

Vogels, W. 2003. Web Services are not distributed objects. *IEEE Internet Computing* 7, no. 6 (November–December): 59–66.

Vu, L.-H., Hauswirth, M., and Aberer, K. 2005. Towards P2P-based semantic Web Service discovery with QoS support. Presented at Workshop on Business Processes and Services (BPS). Nancy, France. Published in *BPM Workshops*, LNCS 3812 (2006), pp. 18–31.

5 Compositional Service Engineering Using Semantic Interfaces

Jacqueline Floch, Richard T. Sanders, and Rolv Bræk

5.1 Introduction

This chapter introduces the model-driven service engineering approach developed as part of the IST FP6 SIMS project.[1] This approach focuses on precise modeling, analysis, and composition of collaborative services. Semantic interfaces are introduced to define the collaborative behavior of service components and the goals that can be achieved through collaborative behavior. They are used to compose services and to ensure compatibility between components at design time and runtime. A core idea of the SIMS project is to exploit the UML 2 collaboration concept to define semantic interfaces.

The main contribution of this chapter with respect to the SOC road map described in chapter 1 is in the "foundation" plane, since semantic interfaces provide a basis for describing, publishing, and discovering services.

5.2 SIMS Motivation: Better Tools for Service Engineers

The service engineers, the people who create service logic, can fulfill narrow time and cost constraints only if they have access to powerful development tools supporting efficient editing, consistency checking, validation, and automated code generation. Nonetheless, industrial service engineering is still largely implementation-oriented without any clear separation between service logic and implementation detail. Service logic is often developed by coding more or less directly in terms of platforms such as Java EE[2] or Web Services[3] (WS), resulting in platform dependency, low portability, and, for client–server platforms, a somewhat restricted range of service functionality. This is a paradox, since service orientation essentially means focusing on service functionality and hiding implementation detail, allowing different implementations of the same service functionality to be interchanged. This suggests that a higher level of abstraction would be more suitable, allowing the service engineer to focus on functionality and then use tools to derive alternative implementations automatically. In the model-driven architecture, one strongly argues the case for developing platform-independent models that are transformed into platform-specific models, and then to implementations, more or less automatically. This understanding is a driving force in SIMS.

5.2.1 Objective 1: Modular Composition with Proven Capabilities

One of the core challenges of service engineering is to find practical ways to model services and service features independently of each other, such that services may be composed into well-functioning systems that satisfy their requirements. Service composition in general involves static composition at design time as well as dynamic linking and binding at run-time. The new UML 2 collaboration concept (OMG 2004) provides a structured way to define partial functionalities in terms of collaborating roles, and therefore seems to offer a promising basis for service modeling. It allows service parts to be modeled as collaboration roles, and service behavior to be specified using interactions, activity diagrams, and state machines, as explained in Sanders et al. (2005), Castejón and Bræk (2006), Kraemer and Herrmann (2006), and Kraemer et al. (2006). Moreover, it provides means to compose and decompose services using collaboration uses and to bind roles to classifiers that define system components. In this way, UML 2 collaborations directly support service modeling and service composition at design time. They also enable services to be simulated and analyzed for errors so that correctness can be ensured at a very early stage. Implementations may subsequently be automatically generated for a range of different platforms.

5.2.2 Objective 2: A Wider Class of Services

Another challenge of service engineering is to define service architectures and service delivery platforms suitable for the application domain in question. The service-oriented architecture paradigm (SOA) is increasingly gaining acceptance, influencing the way people understand and define services. However, one should be aware of the fundamental limitation of SOA as it is currently understood. In SOA, services are provided by a service provider to a service consumer. This service provider is normally a "passive object," in the sense that it never takes any initiatives toward a service user. It merely awaits requests and responds to them. Collaborative services, on the other hand, are performed by objects that may take initiatives toward the service users. This is typical for telecom services, but also for many new services such as attentive services, context-aware services, notification services, and ambient intelligence. For example, we may consider a doorkeeper service where a doorkeeper agent integrated with a front door of a house acts as an intermediary between visitors and hosts, and also provides different forms of connectivity between visitors and hosts, no matter whether the latter are at home or not. The doorkeeper service involves at least three active objects: doorkeeper agent, visitor agent, and host agent that might all take initiatives such as leaving/retrieving a visitor card or a message, sending/retrieving a voice message, or setting up an instant messaging session or video connection. Such services in general entail a collaboration among several active objects, and therefore we call them collaborative services. Most contemporary uses of SOA fail to consider collaborative services. The SIMS project addresses this gap and defines a service architecture and delivery platform that support loosely coupled autonomous service components. This may be seen as a generalization of contemporary SOA, allowing for a wider class of services.

5.3 Overview of This Chapter

This chapter gives an introduction to the SIMS approach to service modeling and validation. Ontology and runtime issues, which also are addressed in the SIMS project, are not elaborated. The following contributions are presented:

- A UML-based approach for the precise definition of service component interfaces. The description of semantic interfaces overcomes the limitations of static interface descriptions that are typically used in contemporary service-oriented computing technologies such as Web Services.
- Techniques for defining interface goals and service goals in an implementation-independent way, allowing a precise characterization of collaborative services and service components.
- A UML-based approach for composing service components from service interfaces, and composing collaborative services from service components.
- Incremental validation techniques that ensure the well-formedness of semantic interfaces and the compliance of service components to interfaces.
- Validation techniques that ensure interoperability between collaborating service components at design time and at runtime.
- A set of mechanisms that support the discovery of service components based on their behavioral characteristics and service goals.

In the following, we first introduce the overall SIMS approach. We describe a collaborative service example, the "virtual meeting place" service that was defined to validate the approach. In the rest of this chapter, we exploit this service example to illustrate the proposed solutions. Further, we describe the main characteristics of collaborative services and identify the problems to be solved. Our experience is that collaborative services and the engineering solutions they require are not well understood outside the telecom domain. Therefore, we provide a survey of the main issues related to collaborative services. We introduce the SIMS modeling approach, the SIMS validation techniques, and the service discovery support. Finally, we discuss the SIMS techniques in the context of contemporary SOA and present some related work. At the time of writing, SIMS is still an ongoing project. We therefore conclude with a list of the expected project results rather than evaluation results.

As far as terminology is concerned, we use the term "services" to designate all kind of services, such as information services, business services, and telecom services as addressed by any service architecture (i.e., client–server architecture or peer-to-peer architecture). We will explicitly use a qualifier when designating a specific kind of service, such as "collaborative services" or "telecom services."

5.4 SIMS: Semantic Interfaces for Mobile Services

The SIMS project is a STREP project within the Sixth European IST Framework program. The SIMS consortium consists of a research institute, two universities, a mobile service operator, a telco service developer, a service platform provider, and a UML tool vendor. This mix of research institutions, universities, and industry encourages our research to follow a practical, industry-oriented approach. The project combines expertise in the areas of modeling and formal validation, tool development, middleware support, and industrial service development.

5.4.1 The SIMS Vision

The SIMS project concentrates on the problem of service creation and deployment for mobile collaborative services. The overall objective is to enable services to be developed rapidly in a modular fashion, and deployed in ways that enable automatic discovery of service opportunities at runtime, as well as dynamic service composition—but without sacrificing reliability. This calls for an approach to service engineering in which service components are independently developed and then validated with respect to their possible collaboration. In short, it requires a concept for service components with precise interface specifications that enable runtime discovery, composition, feature selection, and compatibility validation. It should enable interoperable service components to be developed by different service providers, and offered across terminal, network, and provider boundaries.

5.4.2 The Overall SIMS Approach

The overall SIMS approach is illustrated in figure 5.1. The approach enables compositional service specification and design. Services are specified as collaborations at an abstract level using UML 2 collaborations (OMG 2004); these are incrementally composed from subcollaborations representing partial service behaviors. At lower levels of composition, elementary collaborations are used to define the exact protocol behavior associated with a connection between two roles. Each of these roles is considered a semantic interface. In addition to defining a precise interface behavior, we also associate goals with the semantic interfaces (Sanders 2007; Sanders et al. 2005). Semantic interfaces are defined independently of particular components, and used to type components, making the approach modular and compositional. The precise modeling of interface behavior and goals enables safety and liveness properties to be checked effectively.

Following service specification, we design service components. A service component is a design time and/or runtime entity with the ability to participate in service collaborations

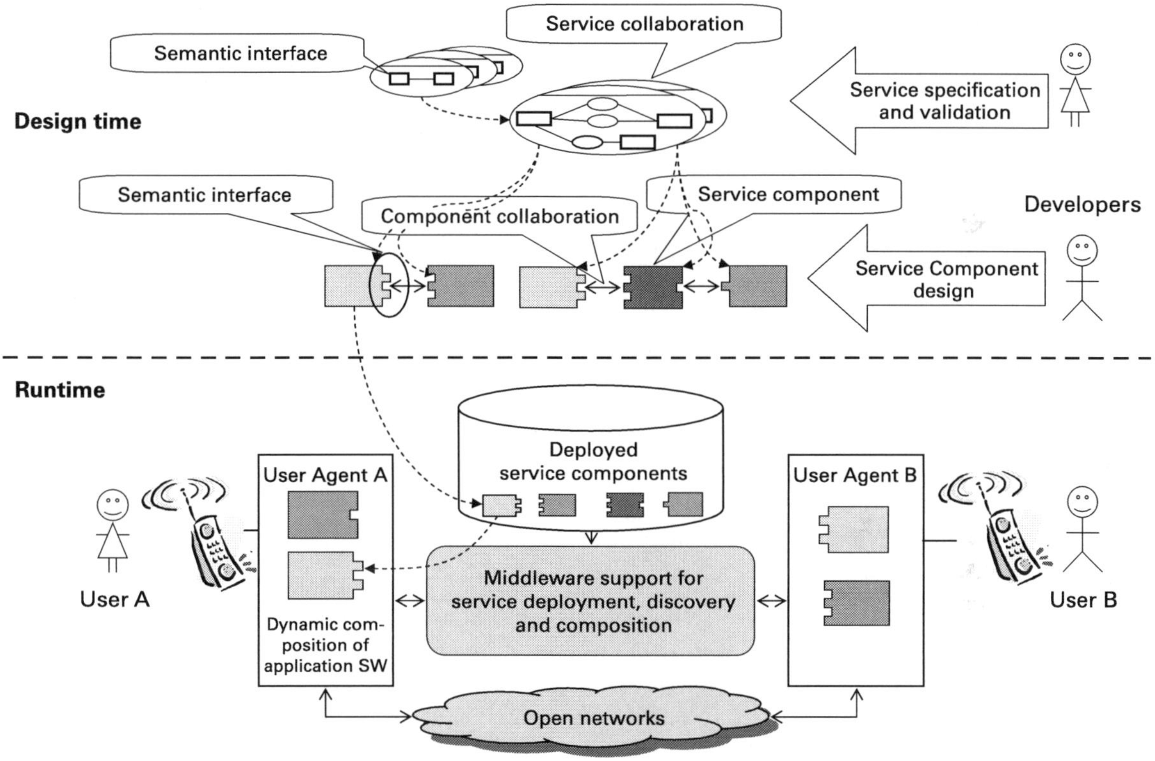

Figure 5.1
Exploiting semantic interfaces at design time and runtime

where they play service roles (i.e., as specified by UML collaboration roles). A service component may play one or more service roles and participate in one ore more services. It owns a thread of control and can initiate control activity. Service components communicate asynchronously with one another. The formal typing of components in terms of semantic interfaces enables service discovery and service composition at runtime with compatibility guarantees.

In addition to UML modeling concepts, the SIMS project exploits ontologies to provide a common and precise vocabulary and language for defining goals and properties of semantic interfaces. Artifacts defined using ontologies focus on the meaning and purpose of services and service components. They are less detailed than UML models, and therefore more easily understood by a developer or a service user. However, these aspects are not detailed here.

The SIMS project develops design tools and middleware that aim to support and validate the SIMS approach. The SIMS middleware supports service deployment and discovery. Tools and middleware are not elaborated in this chapter.

5.4.3 A SIMS Case Study: The Virtual Meeting Place

The virtual meeting place exemplifies the kind of collaborative services addressed in SIMS. It combines well-known Internet features, such as chat rooms and file sharing, with telecom services, such as voice conferencing and media streaming. The SIMS project has developed a set of service examples and service engineering scenarios to capture the requirements for the mobile service life cycle. The virtual meeting place is currently being developed and implemented in order to validate the SIMS approach.

Virtual meeting places are typically owned and configured by a person for some purpose, and individuals are invited to participate or may request to participate. Participation requires the use of some device in a session with the meeting place. What features are offered by the meeting place is determined by what initiatives the participants take at any particular time. The configuration should combine a set of service features that suits the purpose of each meeting place.

The service features include the following:

- Creating and configuring meeting places, which includes defining access rights to participants and what service features should be offered.
- Discovering meeting places. Users may browse for meeting places, typically based on interest in a topic or on context information, such as geographical position or status.
- Participating in meeting places. Users join meeting places using a device of their choice. This establishes a user session between the device and the meeting place.
- Initiating features of the meeting place. Users access the features enabled for the meeting place, which can typically include:
- Uploading or downloading digital content shared in the meeting place
- Chatting on message boards, or instant messaging to other joined users
- Voting on issues, for instance, on candidate participants
- Engaging in two-way calls or multi-way conference calls with joined users.

For such services to be appealing, the users should not need to worry about what software is required on their devices. Provided that their devices have the necessary capabilities, the underlying infrastructure should ensure that the appropriate service components are deployed for participation in the services available in a meeting place.

In the following we will consider a scenario where Richard creates the meeting place "MIT article," and invites Jackie, Rolv, and Anne Marie to participate. Anne Marie has a restricted access to the meeting place and cannot contribute with content. The meeting place is configured with conferencing capabilities. This is illustrated in figure 5.2. The example indicates that different devices and different user roles are supported.

5.5 Collaborative Services

Collaborative services entail collaborations between autonomous entities that may behave in a proactive manner. The nature and requirements of collaborative services are outlined

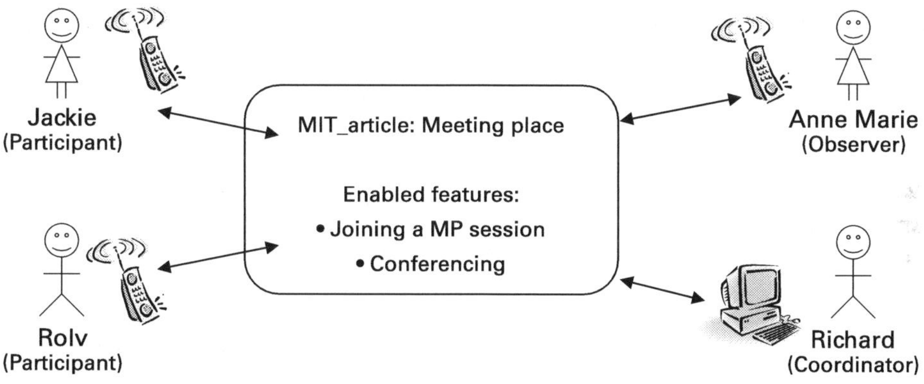

Figure 5.2
Example of a meeting place

in the following. We are familiar with collaborative services from the telecom domain and survey the main issues related to service engineering in that domain. The modeling techniques developed in that domain are a starting point to our approach.

5.5.1 Service Engineering in the Telecom Domain

The participants in a telecommunication service are distributed and behave independently. Therefore, distribution, concurrency, and peer-to-peer communication among users are inherent properties of the application domain, and not just implementation issues. The characteristics of the domain have influenced the engineering approach used in the domain (Bræk and Floch 2005). In the following we summarize this relationship.

The Concept of Service A telecom service is a functionality usually provided to a group of users. A telecom service results from the collaboration between a number of active objects in which several of these objects represent users. Even though each service user may access the service through one interface, there may be several users and interfaces involved. This is illustrated in figure 5.3. The meeting place service is a typical case in point. It entails collaboration between the parties taking part in the meeting place, and cannot be understood simply as an interface.

Domain Concepts The telecom domain may be characterized as follows:

- *Active objects with concurrent behavior* The telecom domain is characterized by real objects, such as users, that behave concurrently and need to interact and to be served concurrently. These are active objects executing their own behaviors and possibly taking initiatives independently of each other (without requiring invocation). Concurrency and communication among concurrent objects is at the heart of telecom applications.

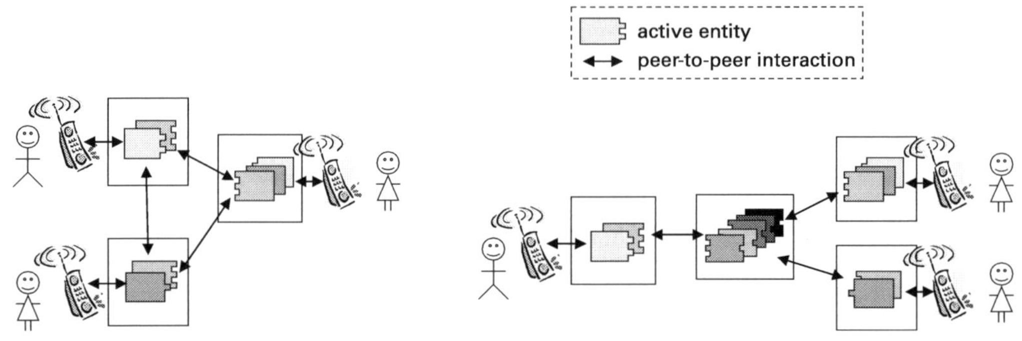

(a) direct collaboration between user agents

(a) collaboration through a server node

Figure 5.3
The concept of collaborative service

- *Stateful service sessions* A service session represents the relations and interactions between active objects involved in a service invocation. In many cases the behavior of a service session goes through distinct steps or phases, which means that the service can be classified as being stateful. For stateful services, it is not sufficient to view the service simply as a static set of inputs; one must also consider the causal ordering of inputs and their responses.
- *Asynchronous communication* It follows from the nature of active objects with concurrent behavior that they cannot communicate well by using control transfer. Communication by invocation is tied to a transfer of control from the calling entity to the called entity. The calling entity is blocked until control is returned from the called entity. Active objects are, in general, loosely coupled and autonomous. Asynchronous communication based on signal sending is therefore the preferred approach in the telecom domain.
- *Symmetrical or peer-to-peer interactions* One cannot in general assume that the active objects take on asymmetrical roles, but must allow objects to communicate on an equal basis, with few restrictions. Asymmetrical communication imposing asymmetric initiating roles and responding roles on interacting objects (e.g., client and server) is not appropriate. Asynchronous communication is the most general communication paradigm and may be used to realize any meaningful communication pattern. It is therefore well suited to implement symmetrical interactions. Communication between two active objects may generally flow in both directions and concurrently. Initiatives may be taken independently and simultaneously, leading to conflicts that must be resolved.

Another property of the domain is that different telecom service instances may contend for the same domain objects and resources. There is typically an n:m relationship between telecom services and objects involved in the services. For example, several users may want to call the same person.

Modeling Concepts Systems and service engineering is strongly biased by the concepts we use to model, communicate, and reason about a problem domain and its design solutions. Therefore, modeling concepts must be carefully chosen to reflect the domain they are intended for. Since the perspective and the concepts used in the models strongly influence the way we understand and deal with the topic domain, unsuitable modeling concepts may well lead to unsuitable system solutions. When the problem domain has active objects, asynchronous communication, and symmetrical interactions with multi-way initiatives, this should be reflected by corresponding modeling concepts. The domain requires support for the following:

- *Explicit states* Some form of state machine is useful to represent the active object behaviors. Objects may be involved in several interactions (i.e., interact with multiple objects), possibly in a concurrent manner.
- *Two-way interfaces and protocols* It follows from the symmetrical (peer-to-peer) nature that signals may flow both ways across an interface, and the ordering may be defined by a protocol. This means that interface definitions normally list the signals going both ways and possibly also specify the protocol.
- *General network structure* The overall system structure may form a network with few (if any) structural limitations.

Formal Modeling Abstract and formal modeling has gained a strong position in the telecom domain. Formal models of application functionality have been developed that can be understood and analyzed independently from implementations, and then automatically translated into efficient implementations. A conceptual abstraction that promotes human understanding and enables formal analysis of the correctness of complex behaviors has helped considerably to reduce the number of errors, and hence to increase the quality of systems. For example, SDL (ITU-T 2002) is widely used in the telecom industry, and a number of successful experiences have been reported (Færgemand and Reed 1991; Færgemand and Sarma 1993; Bræk and Sarma 1995; Cavalli and Sarma 1997; Dssouli et al. 1999; Reed and Reed 2001).

System Architecture Telecom systems are traditionally organized following an agent-oriented architecture. Agent-oriented architectures focus on the users and other entities in the environment that need to be represented and served. Components (agents) are defined to reflect or mirror these entities and represent their state. A system decomposition approach according to the active environment is sometimes called mirroring (Bræk and Haugen 1993).

The responsibility of an agent is to perform services on behalf of a user or another environment entity. In the telecom domain, a service user can usually access all services in a service provider domain through a single user agent that integrates the user state and preferences. Beyond users, agents may represent virtual entities such as meeting places, as well as physical entities such as users and terminals.

Mirroring differs from the functional decomposition which is often applied in contemporary SOA. A main advantage of mirroring is that it facilitates the specification of stateful and reactive behavior.

Computing Platforms Following from the characteristics outlined above, the computing platforms developed for the telecom domain are predominantly peer-to-peer oriented and based on asynchronous communication by messaging. Middleware platforms based on communication by remote invocation, such as CORBA, DCOM, and Java-RMI, are seldom used. Dealing with concurrency and two-way initiatives on such platforms requires multithreading and synchronization of invocations. However, multithreading is often not well understood by application programmers and thus a frequent source of error. (Thread programming can be tricky.[4])

Note that asynchronous communication is always required at the lower level of a distributed system. If communication by invocation in a distributed system is used, it needs to be layered on top of asynchronous communication. From a performance point of view, asynchronous communication will be the most efficient when it comes to networking.

5.5.2 Mixed Initiatives and Conflict Resolution

Mixed initiatives occur when interacting components simultaneously take the initiative to perform some actions that involve each other. Mixed initiatives must be properly handled in order to avoid safety problems such as deadlocks. A deadlock denotes a situation where two or more service components are unable to proceed because they wait endlessly for each other. A simple but illustrative example is the case of simultaneous call. A simultaneous call occurs when two users initiate a call to each other at the same time. It is necessary to resolve such conflicts by selecting one initiative, for instance, giving the incoming call request priority over the outgoing call request. Otherwise, each user will endlessly wait for a response from the other. Multiple cases of mixed initiatives are presented in SIMS Consortium (2007).

Mixed initiatives may result from the direct interaction between concurrent service components, or several parties may be involved. The problem of mixed initiatives is inevitable in collaborative services. When identified, it can be resolved simply.

Conflict Resolution Conflicts occur when two or more service components simultaneously take the initiative to divergent behaviors. For example, this would be the case when two users in a conference initiate two incompatible service features. The service components involved in a conflict should be able to detect conflict occurrence and to resolve the conflict through a common agreement. This problem is sometimes referred to as nonlocal choice (Gouda and Yu 1984). Conflict resolution is usually service-specific. Conflict resolution patterns can be defined as proposed in Floch (2003). Resolution may involve negotiation at runtime. More simply, a coordinator role may be assigned at design time.

Early Detection of Errors Formal modeling enables the validation of systems and the detection of errors. The aim of validation is to verify the system's logical consistency and completeness. Validation techniques are usually applied after the design phase. When the system has been designed, it is analyzed. If errors are found, the system has to be redesigned, reanalyzed, and so on, until no new errors can be detected. Differently, techniques that can be applied at design time are exploited in SIMS (Floch and Bræk 2003). They allow the developer to detect critical behavior patterns during service design, resulting in a shortened development process. For example, conflicts are critical behavior patterns. These techniques also include design rules that allow designers to avoid making certain dynamic errors and help them to develop well-formed behaviors.

5.6 SIMS Service Engineering Approach

The concepts used by SIMS and the UML concepts used to model SIMS concepts are defined in the metamodel presented in figure 5.4.

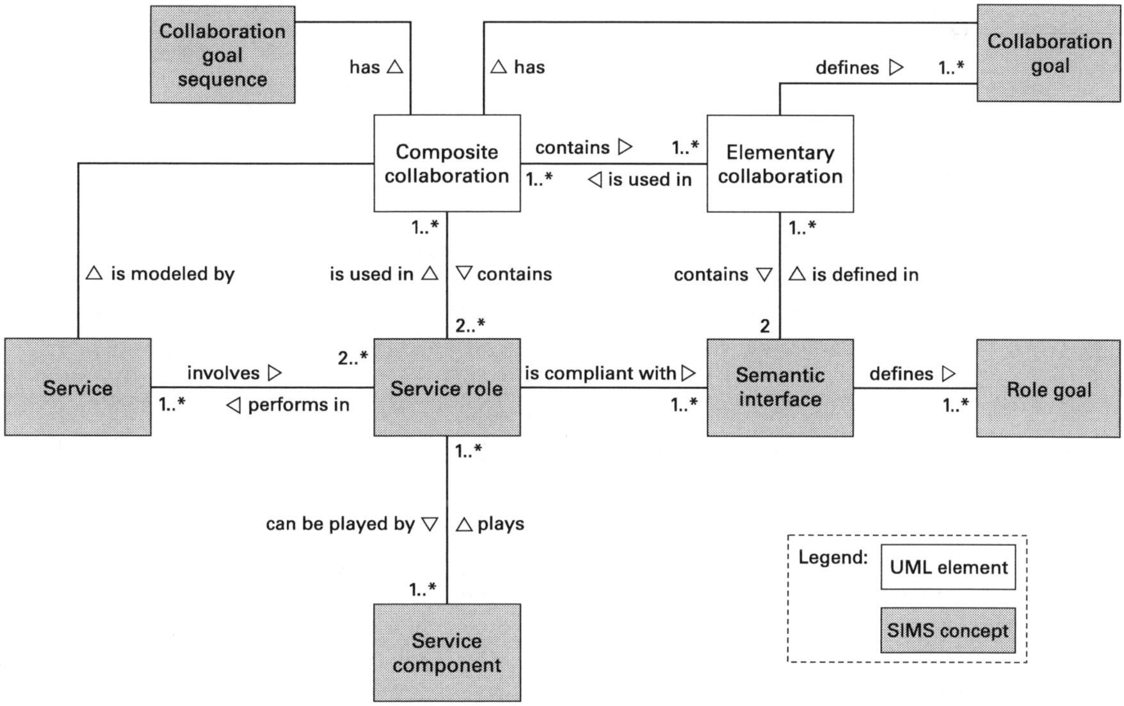

Figure 5.4
Meta model for SIMS basic concepts

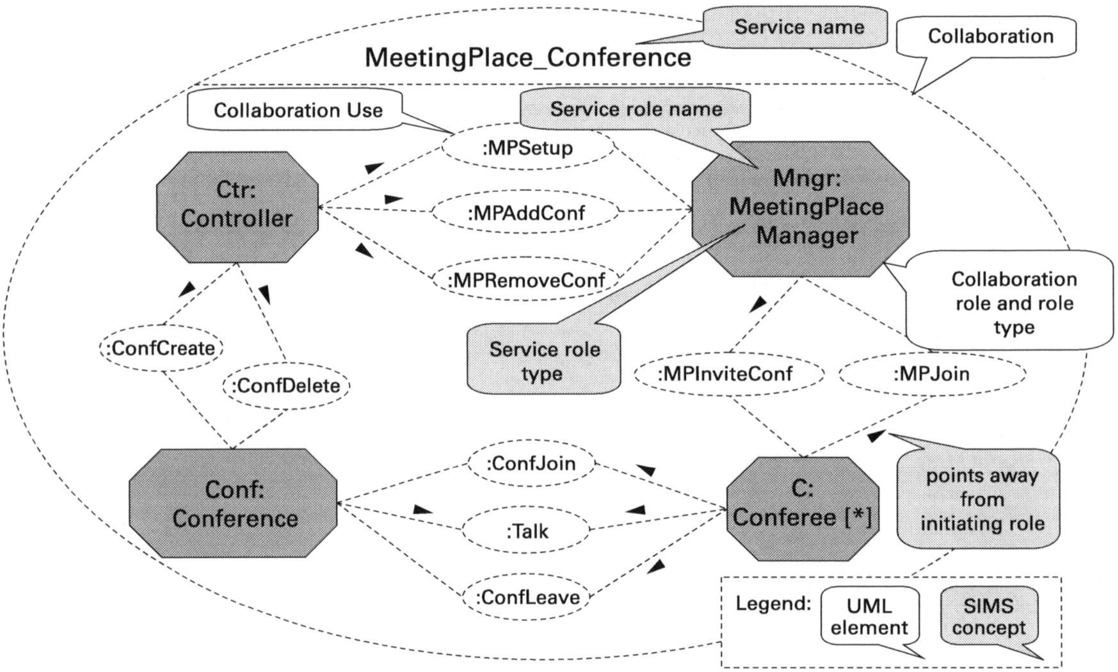

Figure 5.5
Service modeled by a composite collaboration

Service components are composition and deployment units that can play service roles. Services result from the collaboration between service roles. Service roles comply with a number of semantic interfaces, which are the lowest element of composition. Goals are defined for semantic interfaces and for collaborations, and are referenced in goal sequences.

Note: UML does not distinguish between composite collaborations (i.e., multirole collaborations) and elementary collaborations (i.e., binary collaborations).

5.6.1 Modeling Services

In SIMS, services are modeled using UML 2 Collaborations, as illustrated in figure 5.5. The figure models the MeetingPlace service with conferencing capabilities. It defines the service roles involved, and references the elementary collaborations it is composed from using UML2 Collaboration Uses. Here an octagonal stereotype is used for service roles, to distinguish the collaboration role from a semantic interface.

An elementary collaboration is the simplest possible form of UML Collaboration, defining exactly two roles (e.g., a client and a server). (See figure 5.6.) We call the role types defined by an elementary collaboration "semantic interfaces."

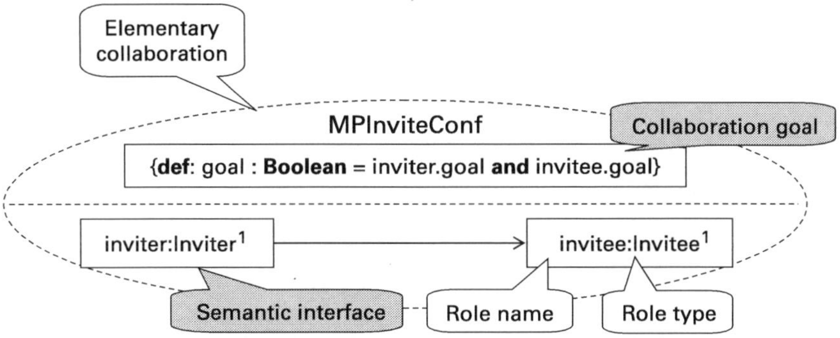

Figure 5.6
Elementary collaboration and a pair of semantic interfaces

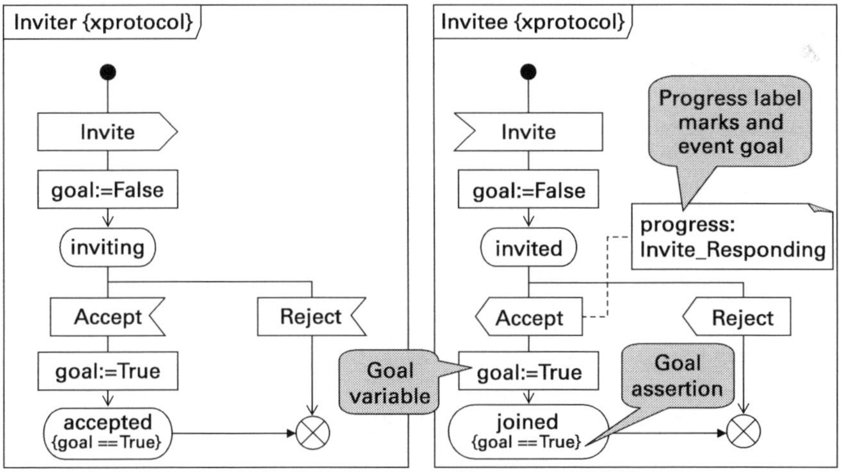

Figure 5.7
Interface behavior for semantic interfaces (with goals)

Semantic interfaces are either initiating or responding roles; initiating roles are ones that can take a first initiative (e.g., a client role in Web Services), whereas responding roles do not. An elementary collaboration can have two initiating roles (e.g., Talk, referenced in figure 5.5). This is indicated by connector end points in elementary collaborations, and by navigation arrows in composite collaborations, as shown in the figures above.

The behavior of a semantic interface is described by a state machine. Service goals are expressed by labeling events and states that it is desirable to reach. (See figure 5.7.) A service goal is a property that characterizes a desired or successful outcome of a service.

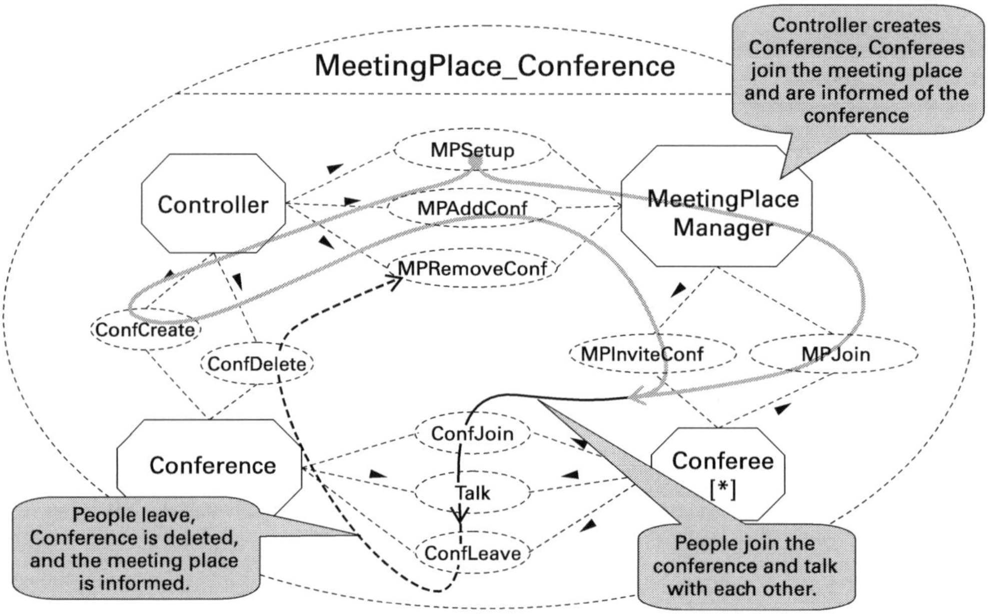

Figure 5.8
Informal representation of goal sequences

We can define a goal as a label related to a single event (e.g., the consumption or the sending of a signal); if that event occurs in the interaction between two semantic interfaces, the goal is achieved at that point. This kind of mark is called a progress label (Holzmann 1991). Goals can also be attributed to states, as goal assertions.

Semantic interfaces should be well formed. This means that they should be defined so that components providing these interfaces always collaborate safely and can collaborate in a useful way. Safety properties are checked through the validation of the detailed state machine behavior, and liveness properties are checked through the validation of goals. This is further explained in section 5.6.3.

Detailed goal relationships can be expressed in goal sequence diagrams. (See figure 5.8.) Goal sequences provide a high-level overview of the functionality of a service by stating in which order the goals of the elementary collaborations should be reached. In terms of UML, goal sequences can be expressed using state machine diagrams or interaction overview diagrams (not shown here).

5.6.2 Comparison of SIMS Approach with the SeCSE Model

The SIMS approach suggests a more general definition of the term "service," compared with that used by SeCSE (SeCSE—A5.D9 2006)—the one upon which this book is built (see chapter 1). In SIMS, services are viewed as collaboration between service components that deliver functionality to one or several end users—which can be humans or machines. With this definition, both collaborative services and two-party services of the client–server type can be supported. Collaborative services can involve several (i.e., more than two) collaborating components playing different service roles, as exemplified by the MeetingPlace service.

Referring to the SeCSE model, what is there denoted as "service" is more or less what SIMS calls the Service component. However, SeCSE does not distinguish between the functionality itself (i.e., the "service") and the component providing the functionality (the service component). In SIMS we separate the two, enabling service behavior to be packaged in a type, and expressing through role binding that components exhibit the properties needed to support the type.

Since SeCSE is limited to expressing services of the client–server type, and considering the interface to the server as constituting the service, the SeCSE model is restricted at this point. To allow both client and server sides to be expressed, and to support collaborative services as SIMS does, an SeCSE Service Description should describe "2..*" Service (or Service components according to SIMS parlance).

5.6.3 Validating Services

The purpose of service validation is to ensure that each component involved in a service will interact safely with the other components of the same service, and that those components can indeed achieve the goal of the service. SIMS takes interface behavior into consideration, exploiting model-checking techniques. Traditional model checking is performed on instances. SIMS extends the work of Floch (2003), and analyzes the types, not the instances. Much of the validation work can then be done once and for all at design time, thus ensuring correctness at an early stage of the development process.

SIMS addresses the following main validation steps:

- Semantic interfaces should be well-formed (i.e., they should not contain any design flaw that violates safety or liveness properties). State machines are reviewed for detection of design flaws, in particular ambiguous and conflicting behaviors that are symptoms of errors (Floch 2003).
- Each service role should comply with the semantic interfaces bound to it, which means the service role behavior should be according to the specification of its semantic interfaces. The validation makes use of projection as proposed in Floch and Bræk (2003).
- Each semantic interface should be compatible with the complementary semantic interface it interacts with.
- Each service role should be consistent with the role goal sequences related to the composite collaboration behavior the service role is involved in.

The validation guarantees the well-formedness of semantic interfaces, greatly simplifying consistency checking between semantic interfaces. The complexity of validation at runtime is also reduced.

The validation techniques are applied incrementally: we do not analyze the whole system, but validate partial behaviors separately, and then their composition. The validation of partial behaviors, such as checking the well-formedness of semantic interfaces and the compliance between service roles and semantic interfaces, is done at design time. The validation of their composition, such as compatibility between semantic interfaces and consistency of behaviors with goal sequences, is supported at design time, and may be supported at runtime. Dynamic systems that are modified and extended at runtime will then benefit from the approach.

Validation of behavior requires that the dynamic semantics is formally defined such that the system specification can be interpreted in an unambiguous way. UML deliberately does not define this, instead identifying a number of semantic variation points that can be bound by UML profiles. The SIMS approach to validation adopts the formal semantics of SDL-2000 (ITU-T 2002). Although work is in progress at the ITU-T to define an SDL profile for UML, no profile is available yet. We have therefore identified the "semantic variation points" of interest for our work and propose an SDL-like semantics for these variation points. The future SDL profile for UML will provide the formal basis needed to support our approach. Adopting the SDL semantics enables us to exploit the validation algorithms specified for projection, and to interface well-formedness checking and consistency checking developed in Floch (2003). The algorithms have been adapted to UML 2 and extended to support the validation of liveness properties using goals.

5.6.4 Discovering Services

Service discovery is a multifaceted term in SIMS. Service discovery is "a mechanism that enables a component to find complementary service capabilities in its environment." This definition embodies several types of service discovery:

- Discovery of compatible service components (i.e., other service components that can play compatibly in a service with a given component)
- Discovery of service opportunities before or at service session instantiation (i.e., enabling a service role to play in a service it was not originally designed for)
- Discovery of service opportunities within a service session (i.e., enabling a feature in a service depending on the outcome of the execution of previous features in the service session)
- Role learning (i.e., supporting service components to learn new service roles at runtime).

Each is detailed below.

Discovery of Compatible Service Components SIMS defines services as collaborations between service roles played by service components. One form of service discovery is for service components to find service component instances with which they can successfully achieve service goals. This means that the collaborating service component instances can interact through compatible semantic interfaces. We call this mechanism the discovery of compatible service components.

Compatibility can be calculated once and for all (provided the role-playing capabilities of service components are fixed), or possibly computed at runtime. Supplied with this knowledge, a service component can differentiate over or search for instances of compatible service component types in its environment, and be satisfied that they have the potential of reaching service goals when collaborating.

The discovery of compatible service components is an extension of the traditional form of service discovery, where the aim of the discovery mechanism is to find components (that provide services) for a client (e.g., as supported by CORBA's Trading Object Service [OMG 2000], JINI,[5] and UDDI.[6]) (An overview of some main service discovery protocols is provided in chapter 3 of this book.) SIMS differs from existing approaches in that the discovery is based on semantic interfaces rather than signatures of procedure calls.

How discovery of compatible components is initiated depends on the type of service and the situation in which a service is used. Discoverability assumes that devices register the semantic interfaces that their service components are able to provide. Service components should then explicitly request the discovery of compatible service components. Various types of discovery requests can be initiated:

- For some or all of its initiating semantic interfaces, the service component can request the SIMS middleware to retrieve component instances that offer compatible semantic interfaces.
- Similarly, for some or all of its responding semantic interfaces, the service component can request the SIMS middleware to retrieve component instances that offer compatible semantic interfaces.
- When requesting for discovery, a component may restrict the search to particular contexts. For example, a component may ask for discovery of compatible service components running on devices located within a specific area, or it may ask for the discovery of buddies able to participate in the service.

After discovery, the user is able to initiate services with compatible service components, or to identify from what other users a request may be initiated.

Discovery of Service Opportunities Before or at Service Instantiation This type of service discovery is closely related to the previous type, except that the service component is asked to participate in a service it is not originally designed for. For instance, assume we have designed a MeetingPlace service involving two service roles, "participant" and "coordinator," and that this service has been widely deployed. Assume also that a developer designs a new service, the IST Forum service, and reuses the service role "participant." This service is new and deployed on only a few devices. When the service IST Forum is instantiated, any user that can participate in MeetingPlace can also be invited to the IST Forum. In that way, users are given the opportunity to participate in a new service.

This kind of discovery can be seen as an extension of the discovery of compatible service components. When a new opportunity occurs, the end user can be informed. The information to be presented to the user may be either an informal description explicitly provided by the service designer or derived from the service ontology description.

Discovery of Service Opportunities within a Service Session This type of discovery is performed during service execution, and makes use of goal sequences. The opportunities for service components to initiate service features evolve as goals are achieved by those service components. For example, assume a meeting place with a conference where video is not activated. The controller reconfigures the conference to add video after a while. The video is not enabled for the participants unless it has been paid for. The goal "PayVideo" should be fulfilled by the controller in order to allow the conference to reach the goal "PlayVideo." Further, when this goal is reached, the participants are able to discover a new opportunity within the conference.

Given knowledge of goal sequences, the middleware is able to tell when a service feature is enabled between two service components. However, it then also needs to control and follow the state of each service role. This adds complexity to the middleware and increases middleware overhead. At the time of writing, SIMS has postponed implementing this type of discovery.

Role Learning Role learning consists of two activities: discovery of relevant service roles and installation on a device of a service component playing these service roles. We focus on the discovery activity. SIMS makes use of existing approaches for installation.

We consider the following cases of discovery in role learning:

- Discovery of new roles occurs during the discovery of compatible service components: a service component may discover compatible service components that have extended capabilities.
- Discovery of new roles occurs as part of service instantiation: either the requesting or the requested device may be informed of extended capabilities at the peer device.
- Discovery of new roles occurs within a service session. For example, in the case of the meeting place, the video feature may not be activated at meeting place instantiation, but be added later, during reconfiguration of the service by the controller. Participants that are not able to use this feature will then be informed of the availability of service roles that support this feature. SIMS does not support the replacement of a service role during a session. For using the new video feature, the participant should first terminate the current role, and then install and instantiate the new one.

- Discovery of new roles occurs as a regular background activity outside of any service execution. The middleware may check regularly (e.g., each morning) what new services, service components, or service roles have been released that are related to the service components and roles installed on a device, or related to the kinds of services that the user prefers to participate in. This kind of discovery is not a key functionality in SIMS. Rather, the project focuses on the other cases.

5.7 Applying the SIMS Approach in the Context of SOA

This section discusses the similarities and differences between the SIMS approach and SOA, and investigates the relevance of SIMS modeling and composition techniques in the context of SOA. Understanding SOA is not easy. There exists a multitude of definitions of what SOA is about (Mimoso 2004), and these definitions often fail to clearly distinguish between business, architecture, and engineering viewpoints. Therefore, we introduce our understanding of SOA before we identify the potential contributions of SIMS to SOA.

5.7.1 Service-Oriented Architectures

The initial overall goal of SOA was to enable flexible and agile business processes in a shifting market environment. To that end, SOA proposes a software architecture supporting interoperability between heterogeneous systems where the services or capabilities provided by the systems can be accessed without knowledge of the systems' implementation and management. There is no standard, universally accepted definition of service-oriented architectures. Erl (2005) proposes to characterize SOA by a set of fundamental design principles for service orientation, such as abstraction, reusability, composition, and loose coupling.

SOA can thus be considered as an evolution of component-based architectures. In component-based software engineering, applications are assembled from components that can be used without any knowledge of either their implementation or their underlying platform. SOA goes a step further by introducing an abstract business model that defines the concepts of functionality as a product or an enterprise resource, service provider, service consumer, and service contract. Though the owner of a component-based application is responsible for the instantiation of components, the service provider is responsible for the creation and the management of services. The most fundamental principle of service orientation is the standardized service contract (Erl 2007). In particular, services express their semantics and capabilities via a service contract.

Although SOA was initially proposed to organize business software, service orientation is applicable beyond that scope. For example, support has been developed for interface descriptions, QoS descriptions, semantics, discovery protocols, and binding frameworks. The SOA concepts are now also exploited in other types of producer/consumer systems, such as ubiquitous systems and even telecom.

SOA Enabling Technologies Thomas Erl, one of the most cited SOA experts, writes, "Contemporary SOA is intrinsically reliant on Web Services" (Erl 2005). Although Web Services is one of the leading SOA enabling technologies, several technologies may be used to build SOA services, such as .NET,[7] CORBA,[8] and Java EE.[9] They all support service interface description languages, service publication, service discovery, and communication needed to implement services. It is clear that standardization is necessary to achieve the vision of SOA. At the moment, the most intensive standardization effort is performed by W3C[10] and OASIS,[11] and relates to Web Services. We also observe that developers working with Web Services do not distinguish SOA from Web Services.

Because of the dominant use of Web Services in SOA, we will further discuss the techniques of SIMS with respect to the relevant standards for Web Services.

Service Composition Typically, a business scenario involves multiple partners providing services. This requires a more advanced model than the basic SOA consumer–provider model. Support for describing how services are coordinated is needed. SOA proposed two main composition approaches:

- Orchestration relies on a central business process that coordinates the execution of different operations on the services involved in the composition. Only the central coordinator of the orchestration is aware of the higher-level business process resulting from composition. WSBPEL (Web Services Business Process Execution Language) is the Web Services standard proposed for defining orchestrations (OASIS 2007).
- Choreography is concerned with collaborative business processes involving multiple autonomous services treated equally (Barros et al. 2005). Choreography involves different participants that can assume different roles and that have different relationships (Erl 2005). Each service involved in a choreography should know when to execute its operations and with whom to interact. WSCDL (Web Services Choreography Description Language) is the Web Services standard proposed for defining orchestrations (W3C 2005).

Note that service choreography and collaborative services in SIMS rely on the same main concepts: they both involve peer active roles and collaborative behaviors.

5.7.2 SIMS and SOA

Components and Interfaces The main difference between SOA and SIMS lies in the kind of component and interface used:

- The concept of service in SOA and the concept of semantic interface in SIMS are both means to hide and provide service logic. SOA is enterprise-oriented and seeks to support integration of services offered by different providers. At this level, service sessions and states are considered to be inconvenient details. In contrast, SIMS seeks to support the composition of collaborative behaviors that needs the representation of sessions and states.

- Composition in SIMS is applied to partial behaviors, either to service roles or to partial collaborative behaviors. This contrasts with composition in SOA, which is applied on full behaviors representing coherent and autonomous business activities or processes, and provided by service components.

Note that in addition to providing techniques for defining interfaces that hide the internal service logic, SIMS also provides an approach for developing the logic that realizes the service. The full service role and component behaviors can be specified using state machines, their compliance with interfaces can be validated, and code can be produced using transformation tools.

Model-Driven Engineering The applicability of model-driven engineering principles such as model-driven architecture (MDA) to SOA is clear: SOA would benefit from a platform-independent service model that conveys the business requirements for services to the developers and abstracts the functionality of the services to be implemented. The developers can then transform the service models to generate platform-dependent models.

SIMS proposes a platform-independent and abstract modeling approach that conforms to the MDA philosophy. As collaborative services addressed by SIMS are more general than consumer–provider services (or two-party services) in SOA, the SIMS modeling concepts are appropriate to model consumer–provider services. As the concept of SOA service corresponds to a service component with one semantic interface in SIMS, the modeling concepts used for semantic interfaces in SIMS can be applied to describe SOA services at an abstract level.

Current SOA composition approaches do not address model-driven service engineering, and they do not even support abstract modeling and validation of compositions (SeSCE-A3.D1 2006). Since service choreography can be understood as collaborations performed by distributed entities, composition modeling using UML 2 collaborations, as proposed in SIMS, is relevant for the modeling of service choreography.

Although SIMS does not address the transformation of SIMS service models to WS standard languages, initial experiments have been performed for transforming UML 2 collaborations to WSBPEL, using the customizable transformation tool Ramses.[12] This tool is also being used in the SIMS project for validation at design time.

Service Semantics The semantics of a service should describe the purpose of the service and other relevant information for sharing, discovering, and possibly composing a service. Goals as proposed in SIMS relate to the purpose of a service. Semantic interfaces also define the interaction behavior. This is required for guaranteeing safe interaction between components.

Although WSDL (Web Services Description Language) aims at providing a formal definition of the interface to a service, it is restricted to a static description of operations and associated messages. Service definitions expressed in WSDL are fundamental artifacts for service discovery. This is surprising, as static descriptions do not really tell much about a service. The document element in a WSDL definition allows the developer to include other information, such as the purpose of a service, the meanings of the messages, and the sequence in which operations should be invoked (W3C 2006). However, WSDL does not provide any formalism for defining a document element. The absence of semantic representation prevents services from being retrieved and composed dynamically. Goals and behavior semantics as described by the runtime representation of semantic interfaces in SIMS could be used to enrich WSDL descriptions.

Abstract WSBPEL can be used along with WSDL to describe the sequence of activities in a service, including waiting for the reception of messages or invocation of operations. WSBPEL supports complex sequence structures such as conditional behavior and repetition. Using WSBPEL, it is then possible to describe the behavior semantics of a process. However, BPEL focuses on the process activity rather than on collaborations with other services (see next point about service roles below). Like other WS standards, WSBPEL is an XML-based language and difficult to grasp. In our opinion, UML models as used in SIMS are easier to comprehend than XML descriptions.

Service Models and Roles Neither WSDL nor WSBPEL differentiates between different interfaces to a service: a service is defined to have a single interface. Thomas Erl (2006) proposes different service models where services can take different roles. For example, in the "controller service" model, services may take both a "service provider" role and a "service controller" role. The separation of interfaces related to the different service roles would facilitate the comprehension of these roles and would explicitly constrain what operations are allowed in different roles. Further, separation makes possible the validation of interactions between pairs of processes, which is the way SIMS validates a pair of semantic interfaces.

Service Choreography WSCDL addresses the collaborative composition of business processes and supports the description of interactions from a global perspective. It is still an immature standard. Barros et al. (2005) identify critical issues that make the standard barely applicable, among them the lack of formal foundation. Although WSCDL aims at providing a means to validate conformance of services with choreography descriptions and ensure interoperability between Web Services, the lack of any formal foundation prohibits validation. SIMS has a formal foundation in the SDL profile for UML.

WSCDL strongly depends on WSDL, and thus it is not possible to compose choreographies at runtime. The lack of support for describing service semantics prohibits the identification of functionally equivalent services at runtime. Exploiting the SIMS approach to formalize choreographies would enable dynamic composition and validation of choreographies.

5.8 Related Work

In this section we first consider the main concepts of the SIMS approach and explain their foundation in earlier work. Further, beyond individual concepts, we present some of the few comprehensive service engineering approaches.

The understanding that services involve collaboration between distributed components is not new; indeed, this was recognized in the early days of telecommunications. In terms of modeling the interaction of collaborations, various dialects of interaction diagrams existed prior to the first standardization of the ITU-T MSC language (ITU-T 2004) in 1994. A slightly different approach was taken in the use cases of OOSE (Jacobson et al. 1992), where interactions were described textually. However, interactions alone do not really cover structural aspects nor flexible binding of interfaces to roles in the way which is now made possible using UML 2 collaborations.

Collaborative designs such as protocols have traditionally been specified by state diagrams, using combinations of informal descriptions and formal models, such as using SDL (ITU-T 2002) or similar (Harel 1987; ISO 1989; Selic et al. 1994). But though state diagrams can be used with advantage to describe complete object behavior, the overall goals and the joint behavior tend to be blurred. Rößler et al. (2001) suggested collaboration-based design on a tighter integration between interaction and state diagram models, and created a specific language, CoSDL aligned with SDL, to define collaborations (Rößler et al. 2002). However, CoSDL fails to provide the high-level service specification offered by UML 2 collaborations and goal sequences.

The role concept was introduced in the late 1970s in the context of data modeling (Bachman and Daya 1977) and emerged again in the object-oriented literature. Using roles for functional modeling of collaborations was of primary concern in the OORAM methodology (Reenskaug 1992), and was one of the inputs influencing the UML work on collaborations in the OMG. Within teleservice engineering it has been a long-standing convention to describe telephone services using role names such as A and B or caller and callee. Bræk (1999) classified different uses of the role concept, and pointed out that UML 1 was too restrictive, since a classifier role could bind to only one classifier, and was not an independent concept that could be reused by different classes.

Goals have been used extensively in the requirements engineering domain (van Lamsweerde 2001; Yud 1997). However, to the best of our knowledge, no one has used goals before to represent the overall functionality of services, to compose them and express dependencies between them, or to validate service liveness properties.

Concerning service discovery, Klein and Bernstein (2004) propose a process-based approach based on service behavior description. Their aim is to provide techniques that support a higher level of precision than traditional techniques (i.e., matching the real user needs). They claim to obtain better results than in concept-based approaches that make use of ontologies. Although they focus on services as defined in client–server architectures, this result is of interest with respect to discovery of compatible components in SIMS. Discovery in SIMS combines the concept-based and behavior-based approaches. Collaboration goals can be expressed using ontologies, and thus are appropriate for concept-based discovery approaches. Discovery based on semantic interface descriptions is similar to process-based discovery.

Krüger et al. (2004) propose an approach to service engineering that has many commonalities with our own. As in SIMS, they consider services to be collaborations between roles played by components, and use a combination of use cases and an extended MSC language to describe them. Liveness is expressed by means of the operators provided by their MSC-like language, and service structure and role binding are described with so-called role and deployment domain models. In our work, UML collaborations are used to provide a unified way of describing service structure and role bindings, and to provide a framework for expressing liveness with goal sequences. Goal sequences provide interesting opportunities for validation and discovery. Further, maintaining the main concepts of that approach, Ermagan and Krüger (2007) define a UML profile for service-oriented systems.

Quartel et al. (2007) propose a conceptual framework for service modeling and refinement. They aim at defining a common semantic metamodel for different service modeling languages, thus allowing the checking of consistency between models. Their motivation is that service modeling languages are tailored to different service aspects, such as service behavior and information, or to different design tasks, such as modeling and analysis. The framework provides concepts to model and reason about services, and to support operations such as composition and discovery of services at design and runtime. In our opinion, this framework is interesting since it also provides a high level of abstraction allowing one to focus on service specification rather than on implementation details. Also, the framework takes into account different service definitions and proposes to model various service aspects, such as elementary interaction, choreography, structure, or behavior. A set of service modeling languages has been mapped to the conceptual framework, but collaborations like the ones we use in our approach have not been addressed.

Broy et al. (2007) propose a theoretical framework for service and component modeling and composition. Like us, they separate service modeling and component modeling. They adopt the view of services as crosscutting interaction aspects of software systems, and thus put emphasis on interaction modeling. They exploit mathematical models and argue that the complexity of software systems requires a purely theoretical framework. They recognize that this framework is not a viable approach for the practical engineer, but rather is a foundation of practical techniques for structuring and specifying services.

5.9 Closing Remarks

UML 2 collaborations have received little attention, and composite collaborations are not yet fully supported by current UML modeling tools. Even worse, the usefulness of collaborations has been questioned by one of the well-known UML book authors, Martin Fowler. Fowler (2004) writes about collaborations: "In practice, however, I've not found that they've been a compelling diagram type." The initial experimentation in SIMS shows that collaborations and roles are useful for the modeling and composition of partial behaviors.

The responses submitted to the OMG Request for Proposal (RFP), "UML Profile and Metamodel for Services (UPMS) RFP,"[13] indicate that UML 2 collaborations will gain importance in the future modeling of services. The SIMS metamodel (see figure 5.4) was itself part of the joint proposal submitted by a set of European IST research projects. The particularity of this joint proposal is that it reflects the need for UPMS to support various specific architectural styles and technologies, such as Web Services, service component architectures, P2P, Grid, and Agents. At the time of writing, the submitted responses to UPMS are under discussion.

The SIMS project is currently an ongoing activity. An initial validation of the proposed principles and associated design tools and middleware has been successfully performed on a simple extended instant messaging service. The principles and tools are currently being revised based on the feedback from this initial validation, but also to reach more ambitious goals as defined by the description of work. The main technical results we expect to achieve are the following:

- UML-based techniques for collaborative service modeling and composition
- Techniques for validating the safety and liveness properties of service components and their interoperability
- Ontology-based techniques for reasoning on service artifacts and a prototype ontology for representing the concepts of the telecom domain
- A development tool suite that includes support for modeling, validation, and ontology-based component retrieval and reasoning
- Transformation tools for the generation of component implementations from specifications
- Runtime mechanisms that exploit semantic interfaces for discovery of service components and service opportunities
- A middleware prototype that supports service discovery, composition, and validation as well as component instantiation and binding
- The specification and implementation of the MeetingPlace service with experimentation in a mobile telecom network, enabling us to assess the adequacy of the proposed technical solutions.

Multiple issues, including confidentiality and trust in discovered services, privacy, scalability, and business models, are not addressed by the SIMS project. A comprehensive solution for service composition at runtime should of course also address such issues.

Acknowledgments

The contribution of Cyril Carrez to the specification of the MeetingPlace service is gratefully acknowledged.

The work published in this chapter was partly funded by the European Community under the Sixth Framework Program, contract FP6–IST-027610 SIMS. The work reflects only the authors' views. The Community is not liable for any use that may be made of the information contained therein.

Notes

1. http://www.ist-sims.org/.
2. http://java.sun.com/javaee/.
3. http://www.w3.org/2002/ws/.
4. http://java.sun.com/docs/books/tutorial/essential/threads/.
5. http://www.jini.org/.
6. http://www.uddi.org/.
7. http://www.microsoft.com/net/.
8. http://www.corba.org/.
9. http://java.sun.com/javaee.
10. http://www.w3.org/.
11. http://www.oasis-open.org/home/index.php.
12. http://www.item.ntnu.no/lab/pats/wiki/index.php/Ramses_User_Page.
13. http://www.omg.org/cgi-bin/doc?soa/2006–9–9.

References

Bachman, C. W., and M. Daya. 1977. The role concept in data models. In *Proceedings of the 3rd International Conference on Very Large Data Bases*, pp. 464–476. Tokyo, Japan.

Barros, A., M. Dumas, and P. Oaks. 2005. A critical overview of the Web Services Choreography Description Language (WS-CDL). *BPTrends* (March): 1–17.

Bræk, R. 1999. Using roles with types and objects for service development. In *Proceedings of the 5th International Conference on Intelligence in Networks* (SMARTNET). Pathumthani, Thailand.

Bræk, R., and Ø. Haugen. 1993. *Engineering Real Time Systems*. Hemel Hempstaed, Great Britain: Prentice Hall.

Bræk, R., and A. Sarma, eds. 1995. *Proceedings of the 1995 SDL Forum*. Amsterdam, The Netherlands: North-Holland.

Bræk, R., and J. Floch. 2005. ICT convergence: Modeling issues. In *System Analysis and Modeling. 4th International SDL and MSC Workshop* (SAM). Ottawa. LNCS 3319, pp. 237–256.

Broy, M., I. H. Krüger, and M. Meisinger. 2007. A formal model of services. *ACM Transactions on Software Engineering and Methodology* 16(1).

Castejón, H. N., and R. Bræk. 2006. Formalizing collaboration goal sequences for service choreography. In *Formal Techniques for Networked and Distributed Systems* (FORTE). Paris: Springer. LNCS 4229, pp. 275–291.

Cavalli, A., and A. Sarma, eds. 1997. *Proceedings of the 8th International SDL Forum.* Amsterdam, The Netherlands: Elsevier.

Dssouli, R., G. v. Bochmann, and Y. Lahav, eds. 1999. *Proceedings of the 9th International SDL Forum*. Amsterdam, The Netherlands: Elsevier.

Ermagan, V., and I. H. Krüger. 2007. A UML2 profile for service modeling. In *10th International Conference on Model Driven Engineering Languages and Systems* (MODELS). Nashville, Tenn.: LNCS 4735, pp. 360–374.

Erl, T. 2007. *SOA: Principles of Service Design*. Upper Saddle River, N.J.: Prentice Hall.

Erl, T. 2005. *Service-Oriented Architecture (SOA): Concepts, Technology, and Design*. Upper Saddle River, N.J.: Prentice Hall.

Færgemand, O., and R. Reed, eds. 1991. *Proceedings of the 1991 SDL Forum*. Amsterdam, The Netherlands: North-Holland.

Færgemand, O., and A. Sarma, eds. 1993. *Using Objects: Proceedings of the 1993 SDL Forum*. Amsterdam, The Netherlands: North-Holland.

Floch, J. 2003. Towards plug-and-play services: Design and validation using roles. Ph.D. thesis, Norwegian University of Science and Technology.

Floch, J., and R. Bræk. 2003. Using projections for the detection of anomalous behaviours. In *Proceedings of SDL 2003: System Design, 11th International SDL Forum*. Stuttgart, Germany. LNCS 2708.

Fowler, M. 2004. *UML Distilled: A Brief Guide to the Standard Object Modeling Language*. Boston, MA: Addison-Wesley.

Gouda, M. G., and Y.-T. Yu. 1984. Synthesis of communicating finite state machines with guaranteed progress. *IEEE Transactions on Communications* 32(7): 779–788.

Harel, D. 1987. Statecharts: A visual formalism for complex systems. *Science of Computer Programming* 8: 231–274.

Holzmann, G. J. 1991. *Design and Validation of Computer Protocols*. London, UK: Prentice Hall International.

ISO. 1989. Estelle: A Formal Description Technique Based on an Extended State Transition Model. ISO 9074.

ITU-T. 2004. Recommendation Z.120: Message Sequence Charts (MSC).

ITU-T. 2002. Recommendation Z.100: Specification and Description Language (SDL).

Jacobson, I., M. Christerson, P. Jonsson, and G. Øvergaard. 1992. *Object-Oriented Software Engineering: A Case Driven Approach*. Reading, MA: Addison-Wesley.

Klein, M., and A. Bernstein. 2004. Toward high-precision service retrieval. *IEEE Internet Computing* 8(1): 30–36.

Kraemer, F. A., and P. Herrmann. 2006. Service specification by composition of collaborations—An example. In *Web Intelligence and International Agent Technology Workshops*. Hong Kong.

Kraemer, F. A., P. Herrmann, and R. Bræk. 2006. Aligning UML 2.0 state machines and temporal logic for the efficient execution of services. In *On the Move to Meaningful Internet Systems: Proceedings of the 8th International Symposium on Distributed Objects and Applications*. Montpellier, France. LNCS 4276.

Krüger, I. H., D. Gupta, R. Mathew, P. Moorthy, W. Phillips, S. Rittmann, and J. Ahluwalia. 2004. Towards a process and tool-chain for service-oriented automotive software engineering. In *First Workshop on Software Engineering for Automotive Systems* (SEAS). Edinburgh, UK.

Mimoso, M. S. 2004. A defining moment for SOA. *SearchWebServices.com*.

OASIS. 2007. Web Services Business Process Execution Language, Version 2.0, Committee Specification. January 1.

OMG. 2004. UML 2.0 Superstructure Specification, Revised Final Adopted Specification. ptc/04–10–02.

OMG. 2000. Trading Service Specification. td 00–06–27.

Quartel, D. A. C., M. W. A. Steen, S. V. Pokraev, and M. J. van Sinderen. 2007. COSMO: A conceptual framework for service modeling and refinement. *Information Systems Frontiers* 9: 225–244.

Reed, R., and J. Reed, eds. 2001. *Proceedings of the 10th SDL Forum*. Lutterworth, UK: Springer.

Reenskaug, T., E. P. Andersen, A. J. Berre, A. J. Hurlen, A. Landmark, O. A. Lehne, E. Nordhagen, E. Ness-Ulseth, G. Oftedal, A. L. Skar, and P. Stenslet. 1992. OORASS: Seamless support for the creation and maintenance of object-oriented systems. *Journal of Object-Oriented Programming* 5(6): 27–41.

Rößler, F., B. Geppert, and R. Gotzhein. 2002. CoSDL: An experimental language for collaboration specification. In *3rd International SDL and MSC Workshop* (SAM). Aberystwyth, UK.

Rößler, F., B. Geppert, and R. Gotzhein. 2001. Collaboration-based design of SDL systems. In *10th International SDL Forum.* Copenhagen.

Sanders, R. T. 2007. Collaborations, Semantic Interfaces and Service Goals: A Way Forward for Service Engineering. Ph.D. thesis, Norwegian University of Science and Technology.

Sanders, R. T., H. N. Castejón, F. A. Kraemer, and R. Bræk. 2005. Using UML 2.0 collaborations for compositional service specification. In *8th International Conference on Model Driven Engineering Languages and Systems* (MoDELS). Montego Bay, Jamaica.

SeCSE—A3.D1. 2006. SeCSE Consortium, Deliverable A3.D1: State of the Art on Architectural Styles and Validation.

SeCSE—A5.D9. 2006. SeCSE Consortium, Deliverable A5.D9: SeCSE Conceptual Model.

Selic, B., G. Gullekson, and P. T. Ward. 1994. *Real-Time Object-Oriented Modeling*. New York: John Wiley.

SIMS—D2.1. 2007. SIMS Consortium, Deliverable D2.1: Language and Method Guidelines. 1st version.

Van Lamsweerde, A. 2001. Goal-oriented requirements engineering: A guided tour. In *5th IEEE International Joint Conference on Requirements Engineering* (RE), pp. 249–263. Toronto.

W3C. 2006. Web Services Description Language (WSDL), Version 2.0, Part 2: Adjuncts. W3C Candidate Recommendation. March 27.

W3C. 2005. Web Services Choreography Description Language, Version 1.0. W3C Candidate Recommendation. November 9.

Yud, E. 1997. Towards modelling and reasoning support for early phase requirements engineering. In *3rd IEEE International Symposium on Requirements Engineering* (RE). Annapolis, Md.

6 Developing Self-Adaptive Mobile Applications and Services with Separation-of-Concerns

Nearchos Paspallis, Frank Eliassen, Svein Hallsteinsen, and George A. Papadopoulos

6.1 Introduction

Modern trends in mobile computing have inspired a new paradigm for the development of adaptive applications and services. Because of the variability which characterizes the context of such environments, it is important that the software used is developed so that its extrafunctional behavior is adapted at runtime with the aim of dynamically optimizing the end user's experience. This chapter proposes a novel approach for the development of adaptive, mobile applications and services using the separation-of-concerns paradigm (Parnas 1972), as it was studied and designed by the Mobility and Adaptation Enabling Middleware (MADAM) project (MADAM Consortium). The proposed approach specifies a set of steps for developing adaptive applications which can be automatically managed and dynamically adapted by an underlying middleware layer. Most notably, this approach treats the adaptive behavior of the corresponding application or service as a crosscutting concern in which the specification can be separated from the implementation of its functional logic.

In this approach, the applications are assumed to be composed of components and services which are systematically configured (and reconfigured) to offer the highest utility possible to the intended users. In this context, the utility refers to a broad term including both quality-of-service (QoS) metrics and nonquantifiable parameters which generally reflect the extent to which the provided service meets the user needs. The components and services are composed into alternative architectures by means of varying port and service bindings which, as a result, provide different levels of utility to the end users, depending on the context conditions.

In the literature, the separation-of-concerns approach is frequently described as one of three main technologies supporting compositional adaptation (the other two being computational reflection [Maes 1987] and component-based design [Szyperski 1997]). Additionally, the widespread use of middleware technology is typically considered as one of the major catalysts for enabling compositional adaptations (McKinley et al. 2004a). The proposed approach builds on top of these technologies and, furthermore, utilizes a middleware infrastructure which provides support services. These services include automatic detection and management of context changes, evaluation of the context conditions and user needs, and implementation of runtime service adaptation. The adaptation service relies on the dynamic publication and discovery of components and services, as well as the dynamic discovery of distributed services available in the context of the middleware-managed applications and services.

The developed applications are designed as per the component-oriented paradigm, where a component is understood to provide a service to its clients (i.e., other components and eventually the end users). In addition to this, the components are annotated with a set of metadata describing the relationship between their provided extrafunctional service properties and the required extrafunctional properties from collaborating services. Based on these metadata, and with the support of architectural reflection (Floch et al. 2006), the middleware is capable of dynamically selecting service implementations and applying adaptations as a response to context changes in a way which maximizes the benefit (i.e., utility) to the end users. Ubiquitous services are considered to be reusable and composable entities that can be exploited to improve the utility of a mobile application. In this way, the middleware seamlessly supports configurations based on both components and ubiquitous services.

Besides a middleware system, a development methodology is provided, comprising a set of models and tools which enable systematic and simplified development of adaptive applications and services. The latter is achieved by enabling the developers to concentrate on one aspect at a time, as per the separation-of-concerns paradigm. The relevant aspects in this case include the development of the functional parts of the system, and then the definition of its extrafunctional behavior. The actual aspect of defining the extrafunctional properties of a system is further refined into more granular concerns, such as the application of the where, when, and how of adaptations.

The SeCSE model (discussed in chapter 1) provides a loose and flexible definition of services. For the purposes of this chapter, the definition of services is adapted to better reflect the use of services from the perspective of the proposed approach. In particular, software components are considered as entities which offer and require services (also referred to as roles). Dynamic composition of components implies the binding of such services at either a local or a distributed (over-the-network) level. Support is also provided for leveraging common service technologies, such as Web Services, in parallel with the component-based applications. Concerning the taxonomy, presented in chapter 1, this work lies in the layer of service integration, and in particular it proposes development approaches for self-adapted, context-aware applications with emphasis on systems which aim for mobile and pervasive computing environments.

The rest of this chapter is organized as follows. Section 6.2 introduces the concepts of context awareness and adaptivity in the domain of mobile computing. Section 6.3 provides the first contribution of this work, which is the modeling of the context-awareness and adaptivity aspects as individual concerns. This provides the foundation for an elaborate development methodology and the required supporting tools which are thoroughly described in section 6.4. A case study scenario is then presented in section 6.5, with the purpose of better illustrating the use of the proposed methodology. Section 6.6 discusses related work and compares it with the proposed approach. Finally, section 6.7 concludes the chapter.

6.2 Context-Awareness and Adaptivity for Mobile Computing

Mobile computing is typically defined as "the use of distributed systems, comprising a mixed set of static and mobile clients" (Satyanarayanan 2001). As the popularity of mobile computing constantly increases, the study and adoption of relevant technologies, such as those studied in the ubiquitous (Weiser 1993), autonomic (Horn 2001), and proactive (Tennenhouse 2000) computing paradigms, is a necessity. Altogether, these paradigms suggest the need for a new generation of distributed and adaptive mobile systems, as a means for improving the quality of the services delivered to the end users.

Naturally, the development of software applications featuring such a sophisticated behavior is not easy. It has been suggested that although researchers have made tremendous progress in almost every aspect of mobile computing, major challenges still remain related to the increased complexity which characterizes the development of adaptive software (Horn 2001), and the necessary development methods and environments are still an area of ongoing research (McKinley et al. 2004a). It is also argued that the development complexity grows even further as the boundary between cyberspace and the real world becomes increasingly obscured. These arguments prompt the need for new development approaches and tools, with the goal of containing the development complexity and, consequently, its cost.

Any system which is designed to dynamically modify its implementation and behavior with the aim of optimizing the utility offered to the end users in environments of varying user needs and computing resources must possess two important properties: the ability to sense the environment and the ability to shape it. This is more apparent in applications following the pervasive computing paradigm, where computers are expected to be seamlessly embedded in the fabric of our everyday activities and automatically adapt their behavior (and as a result the environment) as a response to sensed context. In this respect, the following two subsections define and describe the scope of the proposed approach with respect to its context-awareness (environment-sensing) and adaptive behavior (environment-shaping) requirements.

6.2.1 Context Awareness

Context-awareness related mechanisms provide the primary means by which systems sense their environment. Context is commonly defined as "any information that can be used to characterize the situation of an entity; [where] an entity is a person, place, or object that is considered relevant to the interaction between a user and an application, including the user and the application themselves" (Dey 2000, 2001). This definition is followed by another definition that classifies context into three basic categories, based on the type of information it abstracts: user, computing, and environmental context types (Chen and Kotz 2000). The first group includes all types of information describing the physical and mental state of the users, such as whether they are driving, attending a lecture, sleeping, being anxious, or angry. The second group includes the information which can describe the computing infrastructure. This includes the memory and CPU usage of a computing node, the available networks and their characteristics, and the availability of software and hardware components. Finally, the environmental context describes the information which is related to the environment of the entity of interest (typically a user or a set of users), such as the location, the weather, the light and noise conditions, and even the time of the year (e.g., spring or autumn).

In pervasive computing applications, the context information is very important because it provides the primary means for enabling systems to intelligently adapt themselves (and consequently their offered services) to a changing environment. In the original description of ubiquitous computing (Weiser 1993), it was argued that the increasing ratio of computers to users leads to a situation where the users are simply overwhelmed by the demand for interaction. The Aura project (Sousa and Garlan 2002) reiterates this by stating how the increasing numbers of mobile and embedded computers render human attention as the scarcest resource of all, while at the same time resulting in a situation where many devices compete for a share of it. These ideas highlight the need for new channels of communication and interaction between users and computers. For example, the users could trigger appropriate actions in an implicit manner, simply by having the computers sense the context of interest to their domain without requiring explicit interaction with the users.

In this approach, the context information is primarily used with the aim of adapting the extrafunctional behavior of the applications. This is in agreement with the paradigm of developing context-unaware applications, and, as explained in the next section, it facilitates the development of self-adaptive software using the separation-of-concerns paradigm. Explicit use of context information in the functional logic of the applications (such as the use of location information for locating our position in a map tool) is also possible, although not the focus of this work.

6.2.2 Adaptive Behavior

Although context awareness enables sensing the environment, adaptations provide the main mechanisms to shape it. The adaptive behavior of the software refers to its ability to dynamically alter its behavior, using parameter and compositional adaptation. In the first case, a set of variables is defined so that they can be dynamically modified at runtime with the aim of changing the system behavior. A typical example of this is the Transmission Control Protocol (TCP). In TCP, some parameters can be dynamically adjusted to control the transmission window management as a response to the detected network congestion. By contrast, compositional adaptation enables the structural and algorithmic modification of a system, thus enabling, for example, the introduction of new behavior after deployment, or the correction of software without having to bring the system to a halt and then start it up again. For instance, a video teleconferencing tool could be designed to use alternative encoders and decoders, switching them at runtime without having to halt the system (and very likely terminate the active conferences).

Software adaptation is a well-studied field, and many experts have explored the aspects related to how, when, and where adaptations can be applied. For instance, McKinley et al. (2004a) discuss the most common answers to these questions and also provide an extensive taxonomy of related technologies for each of these questions, in which the where, when, and how are treated as orthogonal dimensions of the taxonomy.

In the approach proposed in this chapter, the adaptations are dynamic, triggered by context changes and enabled by architectural reflection, which allows the complete reconfiguration of service-oriented, component-based applications. Furthermore, the adaptations are enabled by allowing the restructuring of the application, and possibly the replacement of some of its components, or by rebinding to alternative service providers discovered in the environment of the application. Support for dynamic adaptation is an evident need, as mobile environments are naturally characterized by continuous context changes, which in turn require immediate corrective actions. In this way, the overall user experience can be optimized throughout time.

Finally, we examine adaptations at two levels: the application and the middleware. The applications are adapted as a means of changing their composition and/or rebinding to alternative service instances in the environment of the application, which is the primary goal of the system. The middleware itself can also be adaptive, in the sense that it can be reconfigured when necessary. For example, specific context sensors can be dynamically added to or removed from the middleware, depending on the runtime needs of the deployed applications for context information. Furthermore, protocols such as SOAP and RMI, and even proprietary protocols, can be dynamically used in order to bind to newly and dynamically discovered service instances.

In general, compositional adaptations are restricted to the middleware and the application layers, whereas parameter tuning also extends to the lower layers, such as the operating system, the communication protocols, and the hardware (McKinley et al. 2004a). Typical examples of hardware adaptations include the domains of ergonomics (e.g., adjusting the display brightness based on the ambient light conditions) and of power management (e.g., switching off unused or unnecessary network adapters to conserve the battery).

6.3 Crosscutting Concerns for Context-Aware, Adaptive Systems

This section studies different aspects of the services offered by mobile and distributed systems. Furthermore, it describes how mobile users perceive the interaction with a service as the combination of both its functional and its extrafunctional behavior (Paspallis and Papadopoulos 2006). This is followed by a discussion on how, when, and where the adaptations are applied. The results of this section are used to establish the foundation on which the proposed development approach is built.

We view an application as a system providing a service to an end user. Furthermore, applications may depend on the availability of other services which may have further service dependencies. Required services may be provided by bound components or by remote service instances. For example, consider a worker using a PDA to access information about her dynamically updated agenda. In this case the provided service could be implemented as a distributed system, where a local component on the PDA accesses a remote service on a corporate server to fetch task assignments. In addition to the functional properties of the service offered by the application, the user perceives the properties which characterize its extrafunctional behavior. For example, the user perceives the richness of the data (for instance, whether high- or low-resolution images are attached to her task assignments) and the service's responsiveness (for instance, how long it took for the PDA to get synchronized with the server, which is a function of the network latency and bandwidth).

Whether the effectiveness of a service is measured by the existence of some perceived results or the lack of such, as per the ubiquitous computing paradigm (Weiser 1993), a service can typically be analyzed into two parts. The first refers to the functional logic of the service, or simply delivering what the service was originally designed for. This behavior is also commonly referred to as the business logic of the application or service. In this example, the functional requirements include the functioning of the agenda application, which allows the user to dynamically access and update her task assignments.

As it has been already argued, though, real-world applications and services are also characterized by what is perceived by users as their extrafunctional behavior. This behavior is generally highly dynamic and is affected by numerous exogenous factors, such as the occupation or state of the users, the availability of resources such as memory and networks, and environmental properties such as location and light and noise status. In the worker example, the quality of the attached picture and the network latency or bandwidth are examples of how the user's perception is affected by the extrafunctional properties of the service.

As illustrated in figure 6.1, the user perceives the service as the combined result of both the service logic and its extrafunctional behavior. The main contribution of this chapter is the proposal of a software development methodology which enables the separation of the two concerns: developing the application logic and defining its adaptive behavior. With this approach, the application developers would be allowed to concentrate on the func-

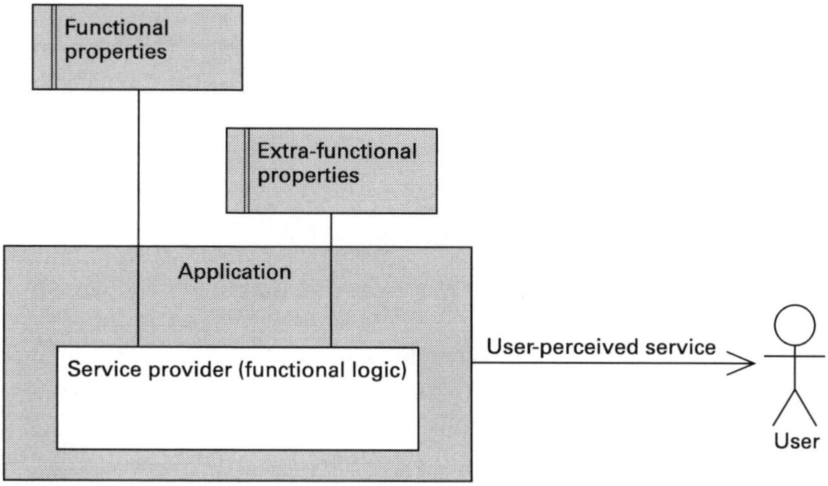

Figure 6.1
The user perceives the service as the combined result of both the application logic and its extra-functional behavior

tional requirements of their project only, rather than mixing the two concerns in the same development phase. The specification of the adaptive behavior would then be an additional aspect of the application or service, which could be developed independently and applied in a different layer (such as in the middleware) by the exploitation of reusable adaptation techniques. A detailed description of how this is achieved is in section 6.4.

6.3.1 Where, When, and How the Adaptations Are Enabled

In this chapter, "adaptations" refers to the runtime adjustment of the extrafunctional properties of an application or service by compositional or parameter adaptation, with the purpose of optimizing the utility delivered to the end users. Thus, it is important to study where, when, and how the different adaptations are applied.

Where Adaptations Are Enabled Compositional adaptations are typically applied at either of the middleware layers or at the application (or service) itself. In McKinley et al. (2004a), it is argued that adaptations can be applied in any of the four possible middleware layers, ranked based on the type of services they offer: domain-specific middleware services, common middleware services, distribution middleware, and host-infrastructure middleware. Nevertheless, adaptations (mostly in the form of parameter adaptations) can also be applied in additional layers of a typical computing node. For example, modern operating systems employ several adaptation techniques, mostly to accommodate power efficiency (for example, in the form of spinning a hard disk down, or adjusting the display brightness when a laptop is unplugged from the power outlet). Also, additional hardware devices can be adapted, usually as a result of an operating system module (for instance, some network cards can be switched off when not needed, whereas others adjust their transmission power based on their proximity to the base station).

When Adaptations Are Enabled Having detected where to apply the adaptations, the next step is to detect the events that trigger them. In the literature, adaptations are usually classified based on the phase of the system's lifetime: development time, compile (or link) time, load time, and runtime (McKinley et al. 2004a). Clearly, the first three imply static compositions, and runtime adaptations imply dynamic ones. The same classification is also used in Aspect-Oriented Software Development (AOSD) (Kiczales et al. 1997), where different aspects of a software system can be weaved during any of these phases. At development time, the adaptations are apparently hardwired into the code, and thus provide limited flexibility. At compile (or link) time, the main enabling technology involves customization of the components, which also provides limited flexibility. Finally, the load time adaptation is typically provided by editing configuration files before loading the software, which implies a slightly more flexible form of adaptivity. In the case of mobile and pervasive computing environments, however, the context changes rapidly, and consequently adaptations are primarily required to be applied at runtime. In the case of context-aware and self-adaptive applications, the decision of when the adaptations should take place is primarily a function on a set of predefined context data types. For example, an adaptation can be triggered by the level of remaining battery power, or by the availability of wireless networking, or, more commonly, by a combination of changes in several context types.

How Adaptations Are Enabled The last step in enabling adaptations concerns the decision on how the adaptations should be enabled. Although many techniques have been proposed, all of them are based on a fundamental approach: the creation of a level of indirection in the interaction between software entities (McKinley et al. 2004a). A large number of enabling technologies is described and evaluated in McKinley et al. (2004a), such as using specific software design patterns (Gamma et al. 1995), Aspects (Kiczales et al. 1997), reflection (both programmatic and architectural), and middleware-based adaptations. In the case of self-adaptive systems, the how question also applies to the approach used to take the decision on which adaptation must be selected. Actually, one of the promises of autonomic computing (Horn 2001) is that the composition of adaptive systems will be controlled by autonomous and completely automated software components. The current state of the art includes three types of adaptation approaches: action-based, goal-based, and utility-function-based (Walsh et al. 2004). Action policies dictate the adaptation action that the system should take whenever a context change occurs (condition for action). Action policies require policy makers to be familiar with the low-level details of the system such that the action policies cover the complete context and application state space, something that in practice is very challenging (especially as it requires handling of overlaps and conflicts). This is also incompatible with the long-term goal of elevating human administrators to a higher level of behavioral specification, as in our approach. Goal-based approaches define higher levels of behavioral specifications which set objectives (goals) for the state of the system, such as an upper bound for response time, while at the same time leaving the system to autonomously determine the actions required to achieve them. Conflicts arise when the system cannot satisfy all the goals simultaneously (e.g., which goals should be dropped?) or when multiple adaptation alternatives satisfy the goals (e.g., which one to select?). Finally, utility-function-based approaches assign values (utilities) to adaptation alternatives and provide even higher levels of abstraction by enabling on-the-fly determination of the optimal adaptation alternative (typically the one with the highest utility).

6.3.2 Developing Adaptive Applications with Separation-of-Concerns

This section proposes a development approach which consists of two steps, handling each of the two crosscutting concerns. In the first step, the developers break down the functionality of their applications or services into an abstract composition of roles. A role is the abstraction of a part of the application in terms of services provided and dependencies on services provided by other parts, or by the environment. In this phase, the developers need not worry about the potential adaptive behavior of their applications; rather, they simply concentrate on designing the basic components and services required for providing the main functionality (i.e., business logic). In the next phase the developers specify the adaptive behavior of their software. They do so by specifying the compositional and parameter-based reconfigurations which can be dynamically applied as a means of optimizing the utility as that is perceived by the end users. These adaptations are further refined into the more elementary steps of defining where, when, and how the adaptations take place.

The development of the basic functionality logic is the first and primary crosscutting concern to be handled when developing adaptive applications and services. In this respect, our methodology simply implies that the developers use the component-oriented paradigm for architecting and designing their applications and services, as is illustrated in figure 6.2 (part A). In this phase each component is specified by the role it has in the architecture, where a role refers to a service type (i.e., the type of service this role must provide in the composition).

Once the functional design phase is completed, the developers proceed to enable the adaptive behavior of their system by locating the variation points where adaptations are to be enabled. Potential variation points include the roles defined in the previous phase. These variation points are selected so that the users benefit from the resulting variability by being able to optimally exploit different functionality profiles, depending on the changing context. For example, if the service involves video streaming, then an apparent variation point corresponds to the selection of implementation for the compression code

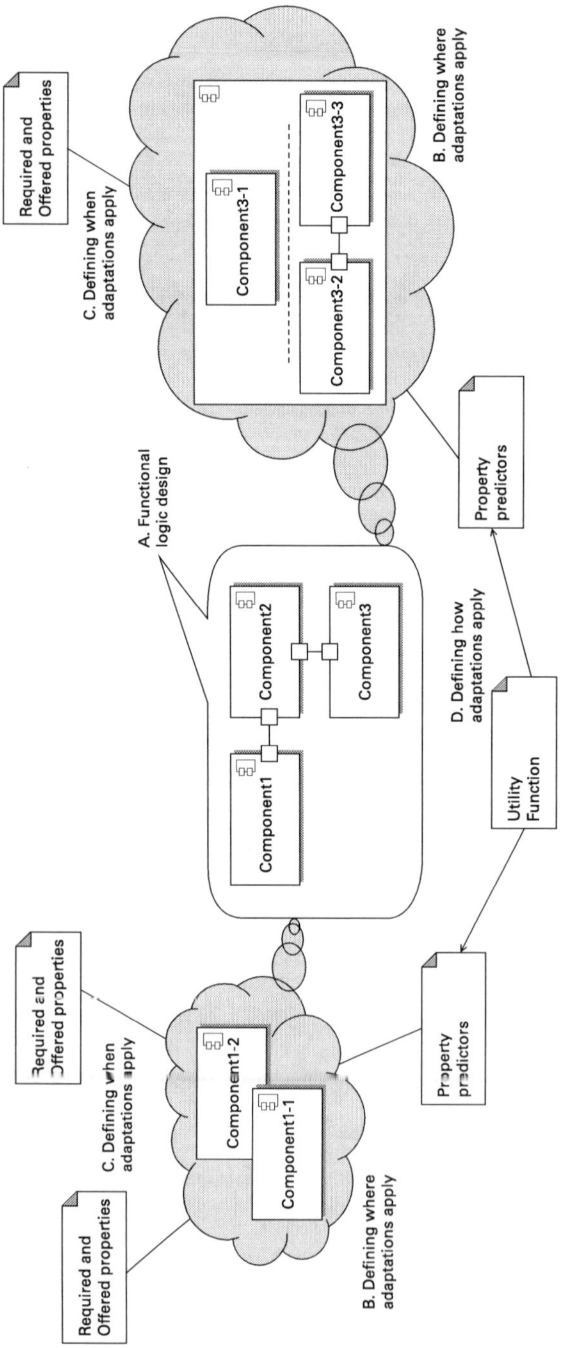

Figure 6.2
Developing with Separation-of-Concerns: specifying where, when and how adaptations take place

component to fill the corresponding role. This selection is naturally based on relevant context data, such as the networking conditions and the user status. Assuming that the users might be required to interact with the developed service in situations which require hands-free operation, the original design might then be extended with additional implementation alternatives to provide the GUI role in order to accommodate such a possibility. Consequently, the variation points might involve different implementation alternatives of existing roles only, or they might involve the introduction of additional composition alternatives which were not present in the original design.

This is illustrated in figure 6.2, where the transition from A to B indicates the specification of the variation points in the basic architecture (functional logic) of the basic application. For instance, in this example two implementation alternatives are specified for component 3: one atomic and one composite. At the same time, the role component 1-1 also has two implementation alternatives which are both atomic components.

In the MADAM approach, the variability is defined by means of three modeling artifacts: blueprint, composite, and service instance plans. The first one enables the use of atomic component realizations as building blocks for the applications. The composite plans are the main modeling artifact for enabling variation at the component level. Finally, the service instance plan enables the use of services for providing specific roles (i.e., subsets of the required functionality).

Following the determination of the application's variability, the developers proceed by specifying when the adaptations take place. This is accomplished by specifying the context and resource dependencies that affect the extrafunctional behavior of the application. Changes in these context and resource values are the triggers for adaptation. This knowledge of dependencies is encoded as metadata associated to individual components. The metadata can be used to characterize the offered extrafunctional properties of the service implemented by each component, as well as the corresponding extrafunctional properties of required collaborating services. They can, for example, be used to characterize some expected properties of the running environment (such as networking bandwidth of at least 10Kbps). Because sometimes the properties cannot be expressed by constant values, additional support for property predictors is also made available, which enables the expression of a property as a function of other properties and possibly context values. For instance, the responsiveness of a service offered by a component can be described as a function of the latency and the bandwidth of the network connection which is used to bind it to the remote service provider. This is illustrated in figure 6.2 as well, where the transition from B to C is achieved with the annotation of the different variation options with appropriate property metadata.

Finally, once the functional design and the specification of the variation points, context dependencies, and extrafunctional properties are completed, the developers need to describe how their applications and services must be adapted once an adaptation is triggered. As already discussed in section 6.3.1, autonomic systems typically employ action-based, goal-based, and utility-function-based approaches. In this approach, we opt for the last one, where the property predictors and the utility functions are designed so that they reason on the context situation by means of computing the utility of potential component compositions as numerical values. The task of planning the set of feasible compositions and computing the utility of each one is left to the composer, which in our approach is the adaptation manager described in document D2.3 of MADAM Consortium. Though the utility function provided by the developer determines the optimal configuration for a given context, the adaptation manager determines the detailed reconfiguration steps needed to bring the application into the selected configuration. Figure 6.2 (transition from C to D) illustrates the addition of the metadata required for the specification of the utility functions and the property predictors.

6.4 Development Methodology and Supporting Tools

This section describes a development methodology which is based on the approach outlined above and which addresses the different concerns in separate development steps. One of the main contributions of this proposal is a conceptual framework and modeling notation for adaptive applications meant to operate in mobile environments. The methodology applies this notation to gradually analyze and model the application in steps, tackling a different concern at each step. In the first step, the initial component architecture is developed based primarily on the functional requirements. Then, in the following steps, the three adaptation concerns (where, when, and how) are addressed. This section describes these steps by covering both the analysis and the modeling approaches.

6.4.1 Defining the Initial Architecture

Just as in traditional software engineering, the first step when designing a new adaptive system is the analysis of the problem domain, aiming to elaborate the understanding of the problem to be solved and to define the core functionality of the system and its interaction with its environment. This is followed by the derivation of the initial component architecture. The recommended notation for this step is UML composite structures, which allows defining the system and its environment as a set of entities along with the roles they should implement. In this case, the entities refer to anything that can affect the interaction of the user with the application, including the application and the user themselves (Dey 2000). The roles are simply used to denote the interaction between entities, and they can correspond to the binding between ports of interacting software components, or artificial ports representing the interaction between a user and an application (i.e., a user interface component).

For example, if the application requires vocal interaction with the user, then a component must be defined to transform text-based messages to speech. Additionally, a basic architecture for connecting these components must be provided so that the application is operational. This architecture specifies the structure of the application as a realization of a composite component, which itself can be recursively decomposed into further, possibly composite, components as well.

As the study of general techniques for the analysis and the design of the functional part of component-based applications is beyond the scope of this chapter, it is assumed that the developers exploit existing approaches for identifying their applications' functional and QoS requirements. This process is sufficient for the completion of the functional specification of the application, which is the first crosscutting concern of the proposed methodology.

6.4.2 Defining Where the Adaptations Take Place

The next step focuses on the adaptation concern: what requirements and constraints are likely to vary and where we have to insert variation points in the implementations in order to be able to adapt it. Typical factors that vary for mobile applications include the computing infrastructure, the environmental conditions, and the user. The anticipated variation is modeled by annotating the appropriate entities of the model developed in the previous step with varying properties, expressed as a property name and an associated set of possible values. In effect, this can be considered as an interaction-centered approach, as the two principal actors of the interaction are considered first (i.e., the user and the computing infrastructure) and the environmental context (i.e., surrounding the interaction) is considered next.

Having identified the adaptations, the next step includes the specification of a set of variation points to enable the adaptations of the application in order to suit the current requirements and constraints. In this step, the developers consider the implementation and realization of the components which are required to fulfill the roles defined in the initial architecture. Furthermore, they recursively abstract components by high-level roles, which in practice can be faced as generic (possibly composite) components or services exporting the same functionality (through the same role) and implementing the exact same logic. This abstraction enables the developers to provide different realizations for each role: either a component type, which can be realized by either a composite or an atomic component, or a service description type, which realizes an equivalent role. The atomic components provide a realization which cannot be decomposed any further, whereas the composite components can be further refined into additional component frameworks of more elementary components, in a recursive manner. Finally, the service description provides appropriate metadata describing alternative service instances that can be used to provide the corresponding role. The described variability model builds on original results from Geihs et al. (2006) and is depicted in figure 6.3.

In addition to local compositions, the composite component offers the possibility for defining distributed deployments for the application. This can be done by specifying where each component type of a composite composition is deployed (i.e., on the mobile device or

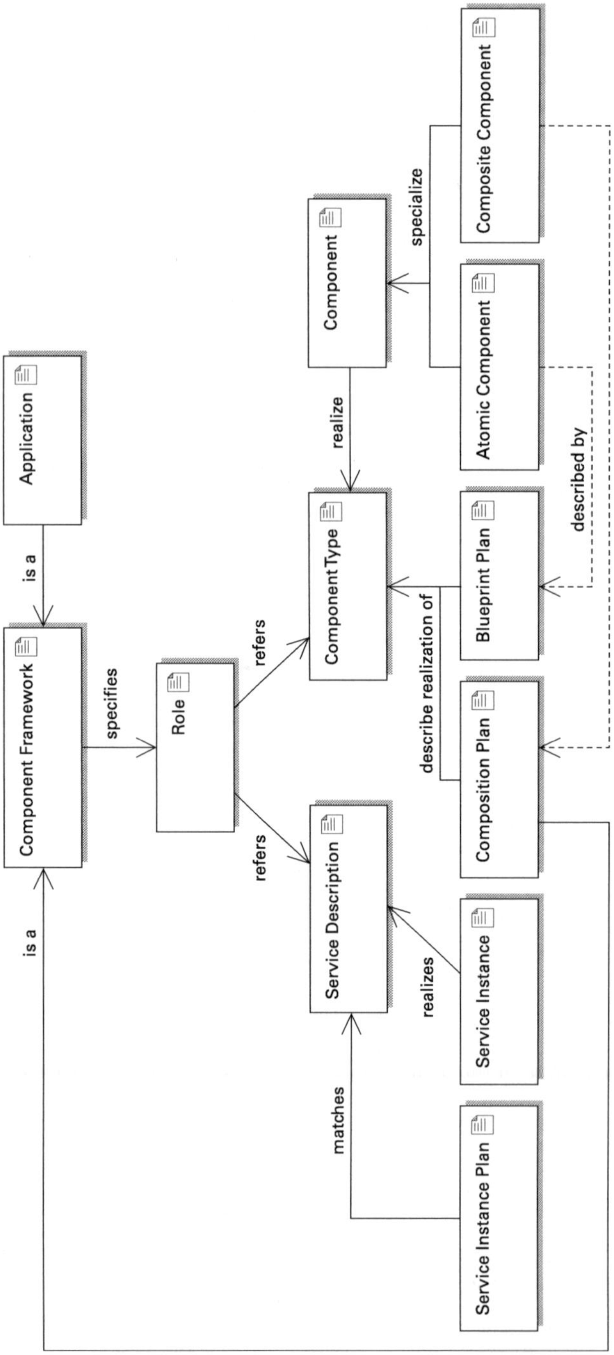

Figure 6.3
Variability model

on a server). As discussed in section 6.4.5, this approach supports a limited form of distribution in which some components are allowed to be deployed remotely, with the aim of optimizing the resource usage on the mobile device as well as the quality of service offered to the end user. In this respect, the developers should specify in this phase which components are subject to distribution, by modeling them with the corresponding composite composition. Further distribution is also achieved through the use of services (e.g., Web Services), but the difference in this case is that the actual implementation and management of the service is beyond the explicit control of the corresponding application.

Naturally, there are dependencies between variation points, in the sense that a choice at one variation point restricts the possible choices at others. To reflect such dependencies, the developers specify a set of variability constraints that determine which variants are feasible and which are not. For example, an application which provides the possibility for selecting alternative atomic realizations at two points can ensure that in no case is a composition chosen in which the two selected atomic components are contradicting (e.g., one instance requiring networking and the other compromising the user utility by avoiding network use to achieve lower power consumption). The details of this mechanism are outside the scope of this chapter; interested readers are referred to document D3.3 of MADAM Consortium.

From a practical point of view, this step results in the definition of the application's variability model, through the provision of a set of possible compositions. As is illustrated in figure 6.3, an application is defined as a component framework which specifies one or more roles. The roles are simple abstractions of a particular service, as it can be provided by a component type or a service, and provides a well-defined interface to enable this abstraction. On the component type side, multiple alternatives for atomic and composite components are enabled through their modeling as blueprint and composition plans, respectively. On the other hand, a role can also be provided by an instance of a service as it is modeled by a service instance plan. Given this variability model, the underlying middleware can dynamically generate the complete set of all possible variations. Furthermore, this model allows the consideration of components and component types which are dynamically added (or removed) at runtime, even after the initial application deployment.

Finally, the actual service instance plans can be provided either statically at development time or dynamically at runtime. In the first case, the developers specify a number of predefined service instance plans that correspond to actual, well-defined services (i.e., as they are specified by a URL). In the second case, the service instance plans provide just the specifications of the actual service instances, and an appropriate module in the underlying middleware actively searches for potential providers of the corresponding service. In both cases, the services are abstracted by a role which in practice can also be provided by a component type. This implies that alternative composition plans can be dynamically generated in parallel, so that some of them involve the use of services, and some others do not.

6.4.3 Defining When the Adaptations Take Place

By expressing the variability possibilities for an application, the developers implicitly define a number of possible variants, each one of which is better suited for a particular context. For example, one variant of a video codec component can be optimized for power efficiency but provide lower video quality, whereas another can be less power-efficient but provide better video quality. In this way, different variants offer varying levels of QoS (and thus utility) to the end users, and at the same time exhibit different patterns of resource consumption.

In order to support automatic adaptation, we need to model how the various choices at the variation points affect the properties of the system. This is done by defining property predictors associated with the components and the application. The property predictors are functions computing the varying properties of the component to which they are associated.

The analysis on the computing infrastructure includes reasoning on the context requirements (e.g., the selection of an appropriate variant might be affected by whether there is networking available, or whether there is sufficient free memory available). However, as the software components themselves are part of the computing context, the developers should also provide an analysis on the characterization of the components (e.g., the memory footprint of a component is 10kB or the minimum networking requirement for another component is bandwidth of 20Kbps). Additionally, the developers must reason about their applications' dependency on environmental and user properties, such as the ambient light and noise conditions, or the users' need for hands-free operation (e.g., while driving).

In conclusion, the result of this phase includes a set of context properties and related property predictor functions that allow the estimation of the properties of the application variants. This information abstracts offered and needed properties of the entities, whose values can be expressed either as constants or as functions on other properties.

6.4.4 Defining How the Adaptations Are Decided

The last step in the problem analysis includes the determination of how the application adaptations are decided (in other words, which variant should be selected for each possible combination of context conditions). In practice, this is the step where the developers are expected to specify the autonomous, self-adaptive behavior of their applications.

In this approach, a utility-function-based approach is used which is considered to be the most suitable for the proposed development approach and middleware design. In this approach, the developers are expected to specify a utility function that is used to rank the potential variants based on their fitness for a particular context. Ultimately, this utility function is used to select the most beneficial application variant. In practice, the utility functions are generally expressed as polynomials summing the weighted differences between the offered and needed properties of the examined variant. Eventually, a single utility function is associated to one application and is reused when evaluating the possible variants.

Currently, there are not many well-defined and structured methods for specifying such utility functions. Rather, this is an open problem in research areas such as autonomic systems and artificial intelligence. Concerning the approach proposed here, the developers are expected to collect as much information as possible about the desired behavior of the developed application and to use their personal experience and intuition in order to form good utility functions. Once this is complete, the resulting utility functions can be partly validated by testing them with the use of a simulation environment. Such a simulation can, for instance, benchmark the utility of all potential application variants, given a large set of context states.

6.4.5 Dealing with Distribution

An additional crosscutting concern which is automatically handled by the middleware is the support for distribution. Besides distribution at the context level (Paspallis et al. 2007), the proposed approach supports distributed application configurations. This is achieved through the formation of distributed adaptation domains (Alia et al. 2007a). Each adaptation domain corresponds to a collection of computing nodes along with their own resources and the communication networks they are connected to. It is assumed that within an adaptation domain, all computing nodes run an instance of the middleware, or at least a subset of it allowing the formation of distributed configurations. Each domain is associated with exactly one client node and zero or more server nodes. Additionally, the domains are formed dynamically through the use of a discovery protocol where the participating nodes periodically advertise their presence and form loosely coupled group memberships (Paspallis et al. 2007). Unlike clients, servers may be shared, which implies that they can participate in multiple adaptation domains.

The adaptation reasoning is centralized and is always performed under the control of the client node, whereas the adaptation reasoning can be performed at either the client node or the server node to save client node resources. The client node is typically a mobile device carried by the end user. In this case, the client side is granted complete control of the allocated resources on the server nodes (Alia et al. 2007b), and is fully responsible for making the adaptation decisions. Besides its local context information, the client node is provided with access to the available resources of other nodes, and thus it is rendered capable of making centralized decisions which include elements from the wider context of the distributed application. The resulting adaptation can involve the deployment of components on individual, remotely connected nodes, thus resulting in a distributed configuration.

Finally, the applications running inside a domain may depend on services provided outside the domain. These may include both Web Services and shared peripherals. Discovering, selecting, and binding to suitable service instances is also part of the responsibility of the adaptation management component. Naturally, this responsibility extends to replacing or removing the need for services that disappear or otherwise break the service-level agreement (SLA).

The general middleware functionality, as well as the behavior of the system in the case of distributed adaptations, is illustrated in section 6.5, where a case study example is described by providing information about both the development methodology and the deployment process.

6.4.6 Implementation and Testing

Just as in general software engineering, the completion of the problem analysis is followed by the implementation and the testing of the application. This facilitates the process for readying the application for deployment. Although the described approach is not dependent on any specific platform or programming language, it is assumed that an object-oriented language and an underlying virtual machine environment are used. The latter provides support for interfaces, computational reflection, and the creation of software components. In the MADAM project, the middleware and the applications were implemented using the Java language (Arnold et al. 2000) and were evaluated on mobile devices such as Windows Mobile-based iPAQ 6340 PDAs.

In practice, the proposed methodology is not dependent on any specific component technologies, as long as they support architectural reflection and dynamic reconfigurations. For example, in the MADAM prototype implementation, a simple and custom component framework was defined. In this case, the developers were simply expected to define the functional aspects of their applications by developing the required components and the basic architecture. Both the basic component functionality and the application's extrafunctional features are expressed programmatically by reusing and extending custom-made APIs. For instance, a utility function is expressed by implementing a specific interface and by programmatically defining how the utility is computed as a function of other parameters, including the context.

Besides this programmatic approach, a Model Driven Development (MDD)-based methodology was proposed by MADAM Consortium. This approach includes a set of required models which are based on and extend the Unified Modeling Language (UML) 2.0 standard. The provided modeling artifacts enable the software developers to visually design their applications and express their extrafunctional properties. For this purpose, a number of UML extensions (also denoted as UML profiles) are provided, including the Context, the Resource and Deployment, the Property, the Utility, and the Variability profiles. These profiles are used to incrementally model the different aspects of the functional and extrafunctional parts of an application. As per the MDD approach, a complete set of tools is provided, which not only enables the design of the Platform Independent Model (PIM) of the application, but also allows for the automatic generation of Platform Specific Model (PSM) implementations.

As a proof of concept, a tool chain was implemented for generating application code targeting the Java Virtual Machine (JVM) (Lindholm and Yellin 1999). Although these tools produce code which is complete with respect to their adaptation functionality, in some cases the developers are still expected to fill in some gaps and provide code snippets which cannot be automatically generated. For instance, utility functions and property predictors are generally defined manually. A detailed description of the corresponding MDD-based methodology is presented in document D3.3 of the MADAM Consortium.

Concerning the testing phase, there is currently limited automated support. Most notably, all context parameters can be simulated at runtime, and thus allow a developer to more easily evaluate the behavior of the application. However, a missing part of the testing framework is a suite which could automatically build the set of possible variants while off-line, and dynamically evaluate the utility of each of them for different context values. Such a tool would be of great assistance to developers during the specification of the utility functions and the property evaluators, as it would provide instantaneous feedback concerning the adaptive behavior of the designed application. Although not available yet, there are plans for providing such functionality as part of the MADAM project's successor, MUSIC (MUSIC Consortium).

6.5 A Case Study Example

To illustrate the proposed methodology, this section explains the development of an example application following the steps described above. The case study also illustrates how self-adaptation is important to mobile users for retaining both the usefulness and the QoS of the provided service. The purpose of the example application is to assist a satellite antenna installer with aligning the antenna to the appropriate satellite. This task requires the use of hands and eyes to manipulate the antenna equipment, and therefore the installer in some periods prefers an audio-based interface, whereas a traditional interface using the keyboard and display is preferred in other periods.

The application includes signal analysis, which is quite heavy for a handheld device in terms of both memory and processing requirements, and consequently there is a concern about battery lifetime. Also there is a need to coexist with other applications, for example, a chatting program to be able to communicate with the company's headquarters. Therefore the application should provide the possibility to offload some of the computation to a server available over the network. However, the network connection available varies as the user moves about. Some places feature WLAN coverage, and some others feature weak GSM signals only. Furthermore, the precision required for the signal analysis varies during the alignment operation. The initial steps require lower precision, as opposed to the final fine-tuning steps. To further illustrate the adaptation aspect of this example application, let us consider a typical usage scenario.

First the worker is still in the office, using the PDA to prepare for the day, with several onsite visits scheduled. In this situation, the application has the full attention of the user, and consequently the visual interaction mode is preferred, as it is more responsive and more resource efficient (it requires less memory, less CPU use, and no networking, which results in lower power consumption). Then the worker moves onsite and starts working on the alignment of an antenna, and the application switches to the audio interaction mode to allow the worker to use her hands and eyes to manipulate the antenna. Later in the day, the worker moves to a site where the network is sufficiently fast and cheap but the memory and CPU resources are running low (e.g., because the PDA starts other applications as well). At that point, the application switches to the audio mode, where the speech-to-text component is either hosted by a remote server or the equivalent role is provided by a service provider.

As is illustrated by this scenario, the self-adaptation mechanism has to monitor the context (i.e., the status of the hosting device, the user, and the surrounding environment) and dynamically respond to context changes by selecting and applying the most suitable application variant at any time. To keep things simple, the further elaboration of this scenario considers two variation points only: the selection of a UI modality (i.e., visual or audio) and the choice between high- and low-precision calculations. For the audio UI case we also consider alternative implementations with different quality and resource needs.

6.5.1 Designing the Example's Initial Architecture

In this phase, the developers detect the primary requirements for the development of the application and break it down into a composition of abstract components or roles. The resulting component architecture for the example includes five abstract components, as is illustrated in figure 6.4.

These abstract components are the UI, the Main Logic, the Analyzer, the Satellite Adapter and the Math Processor. The UI component implements the user interface. The Main Logic component provides the basic business logic of the application, which primarily gathers information from the Analyzer and communicates it to the UI in a human-understandable way. The Analyzer is responsible for reading the received satellite signal

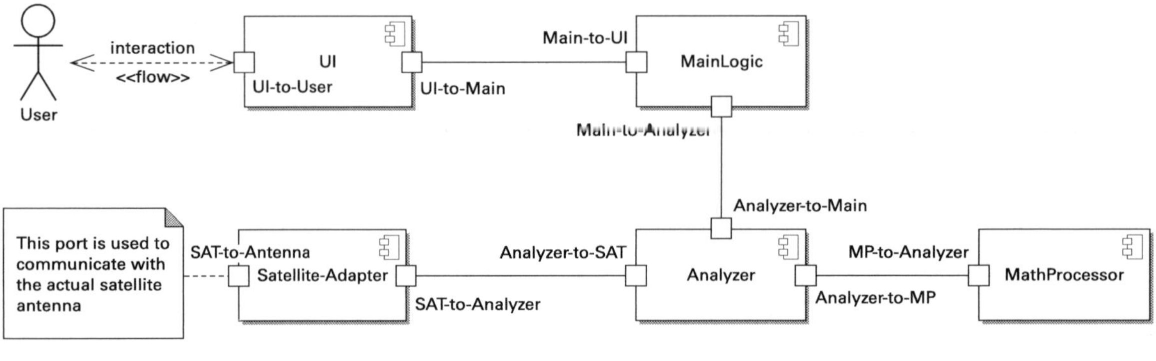

Figure 6.4
Specifying the functional architecture of the case study example

and extracting the information which is required by the user in order to fulfill her assignment. The Analyzer interacts with the Satellite Adapter, which transforms satellite data to an appropriate, computer-usable form, and with the Math Processor, which provides mathematical methods needed for signal analysis. The architecture diagram also specifies how the components are connected in terms of ports and connectors.

Figure 6.5 specifies the relation to the user and the environment. The user is depicted as the corresponding actor using the application, and the Satellite Adapter is shown to interact with the satellite equipment.

6.5.2 Design of Where the Adaptations Take Place

From the description of the requirements for the example application and the scenario, we conclude that the properties relevant to adaptation for this application are audio or visual interaction, the precision of the signal analysis, the need for memory, the need for network capacity, and the power consumption.

Apparently, the selection of where to enable adaptations is driven by the need for adaptation on individual components, as well as on the compositions of the components. For instance, in this case a developer would consult the scenario analysis, which hints at two variation points: the first one involves the selection of an appropriate UI mode, and the second one involves the selection of a realization of the Math Processor type. It is worth noting that although the scenario analysis is the primary input available to the developers, additional input might also be considered, such as whether alternative realizations of relevant component types are available, and whether their properties make them better suited for varying context situations. Additional factors affecting this creative process include considerations on the distribution of components, and whether the distribution of selected component types is desired in certain contexts (or even inevitable in some others).

Though numerous adaptations could be possible in this scenario, for the sake of simplicity it is assumed that the Main Logic, the Analyzer, and the Satellite Adapter are provided by concrete atomic realizations (not shown). The UI, on the other hand, is assumed to be adaptable, and thus abstracted by a composite realization. The Math Processor is also assumed to be adaptable, by providing alternative atomic realizations to fill in the corresponding component type.

The basic variation in the UI consists of the choice between a visual-based and an audio-based interface for the user. In the first case, the user interacts by pressing buttons in the application's display window and by reading the displayed messages. In the case of audio-based interaction, the user makes selections in the application using voice-activation technology, and the application notifies him or her with messages played on the device's speakers. The visual interaction component can be easily implemented by an atomic realization, whereas in the case of audio-based interaction, the implementation is further decomposed into three additional components: the audio controller, the player, and the text-to-speech (TTS), as shown in figure 6.5. Again, for the sake of simplicity, we consider

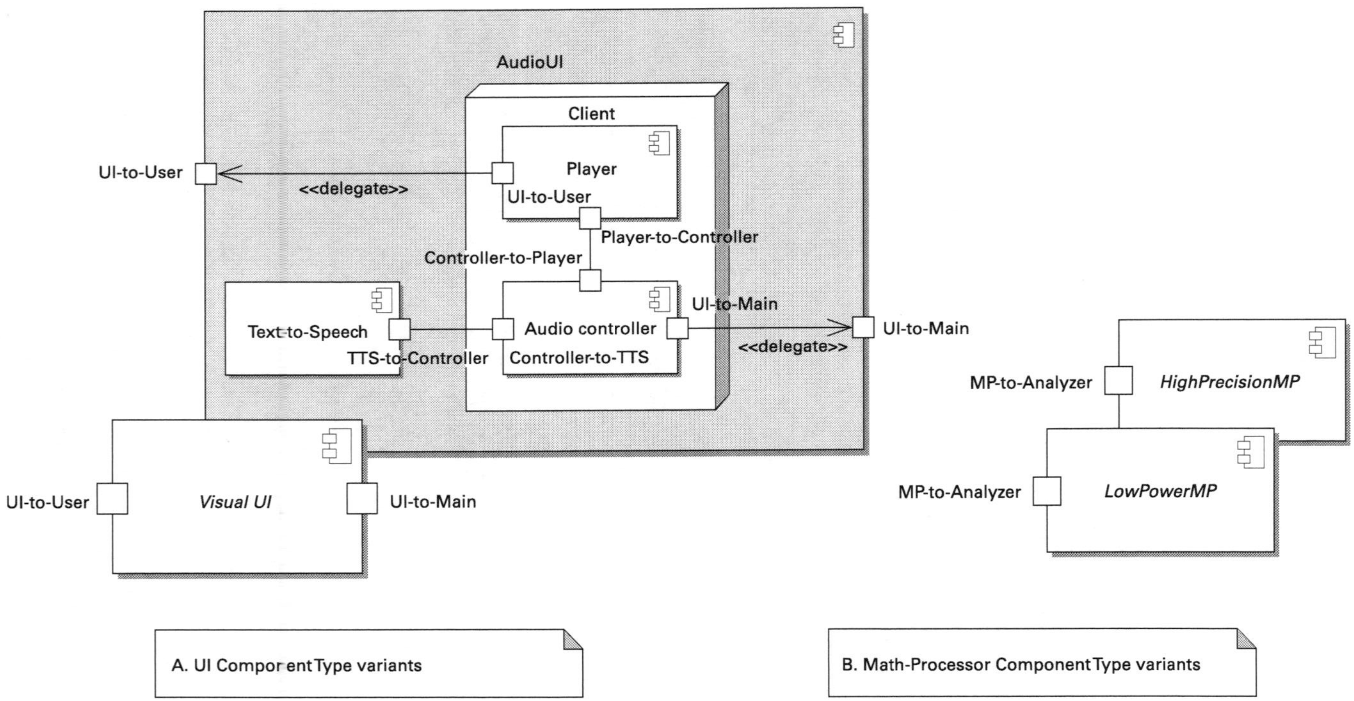

Figure 6.5
Specifying the variability model of the case study example

only the speech output part of the audio UI. The player plays a given audio stream on the device's speakers. The TTS implements speech-synthesis functionality, and the audio controller interacts with the rest of the application and coordinates the TTS and the player.

The player and the audio controller are constrained roles that can be bound only by a component instance deployed on the client device. The TTS role, on the other hand, is an open role that can be filled either by a component instance deployed in the client device or by a remote service providing the same functionality. In our case, we assume that the TTS component takes text as input and returns that text as synthesized speech encoded in the output byte stream. Evidently, the speech synthesis is a very demanding process, requiring significant resources in terms of CPU and memory. For this reason, using a remote service to provide this functionality will in many situations be more suitable.

Figure 6.5 (part B) depicts the two possibilities for realizing the Math Processor component type. In this case, the variability is simply denoted by the availability of the two atomic realizations of the matching component type. Since the selection of the UI component type is orthogonal to the selection of the Math Processor type, the two Math Processor realizations double the number of possible variants to six. Furthermore, assuming that the TTS functionality can also be available as a service, then additional variations are also possible: two for each TTS service provider available. For example, assuming that there is one well-known service type offering the TTS service, then a well-defined TTS proxy can replace the TTS component in the audio UI composition, thus adding an additional composition for the UI component, and two additional compositions to the overall application (corresponding to the two combinations possible with each of the two Math Processor components). Note that in figure 6.5 the visual UI and the two Math Processor components are underlined to indicate their status as atomic realizations rather than composite plans. In the case of the audio UI composition plan, the player, audio controller, and TTS are all abstracted as roles, to indicate that different realizations of each one of them might be plugged in their role.

6.5.3 Design of When Adaptations Take Place

Having specified the variation points, the developers next need to specify when the adaptations are triggered. More specifically, the types of events that can potentially cause the selection of a different variant must be detected. This type of analysis is partly dependent on the previous step, since the developers need to evaluate which types of context changes can potentially trigger the adaptation at any variation point.

With regard to the UI variation point, a developer can detect numerous factors affecting the ultimate selection of interaction with the user. Such factors include the resources of the mobile device (for example, its memory and CPU), the network availability (along with properties such as bandwidth, latency, etc.), and of course the user's needs, such as the need for hands-free operation. Also, the availability of suitable TTS service providers is a significant factor affecting the adaptation decisions. Concerning the second variation

Table 6.1
Resources required by the application and by component realizations

	Memory	CPU	Net bandwidth	Net latency
Minimum resources required by compositions				
Application	UI.mem + MP.mem + 100	UI.cpu + MP.cpu + 30	UI.net bandwidth	UI.net latency
Audio UI	PL.mem + AC.mem + TTS.mem	PL.cpu + AC.cpu + TTS.cpu	TTS.net bandwidth	TTS.net latency
Minimum resources required by atomic component realizations				
Visual UI	40	20	0	0
TTS component	80	40	0	0
TTS service	5	5	20	40
Player	30	30		
Audio controller	10	10		
High-precision MP	70	50		
Low-precision MP	50	30		

point, the selection of the Math Processor realization can be influenced by factors such as the available resources (memory and CPU), the user need for short response times, and the user need for precision.

Besides the contextual factors that affect the QoS offered to the end user, an additional concern is the actual requirements of the component realizations with regard to resources. Evidently, before the developers can even start thinking about optimizations through adaptation, the possible variants must be compared against the available resources in order to reason whether they can be realized at all. For example, variations which include component realizations that require networking when that is not available should not be considered at all.

The result of this phase is a matrix with the offered and the needed properties of the involved component types and their corresponding component realizations. Table 6.1 illustrates an example of resource requirements of the individual component types and their realizations. Furthermore, this table depicts the offered utility of the relevant component types (as constants or property predictors), as well as the offered utility of the whole application, as a utility function. For simplicity, it is assumed that all values in this table are in the range of 1 to 100.

As illustrated in this table, both component types specify needed and offered properties as functions on the chosen component realizations. This is compatible with the general approach of both dynamically generating the possible variants (using the variability model) and computing their required and offered properties. Furthermore, the component realizations also specify some of their context dependencies as functions (possibly including conditional expressions) on other context entities, although most of their values are

Table 6.2
Offered properties of compositions and component realizations and utility of the application

	Hands-free	Response	Precision
Properties offered by the component realizations			
Visual UI	0	70	
TTS component	100	50	
TTS service	100	if(ctxt.bandwidth>50) then 70 else 20+ctxt.bandwidth	
High-precision MP		75	80
Low-precision MP		90	60
Properties (utility) offered by abstract component types			
Application	UI.hands-free	$c_1 \cdot$ UI.response + $c_2 \cdot$ MP.response	MP.precision
AudioUI	100	TTS service.response	
Utility function			
Application	utility = $c_H \cdot$ (hands-free=ctxt.hands-free) + $c_R \cdot$ (if (response>ctxt.response) then 1 else (ctxt.response-response)/100) + $c_P \cdot$ (if (precision>ctxt.precision) then 1 else (ctxt.precision-precision)/100)		

specified as constants. In the case of functionally specified properties, the context prefix is used to denote a value read from the context system.

6.5.4 Design of How Adaptations Are Decided

The last step in the specification of the application's adaptive behavior concerns the definition of an appropriate decision mechanism. Although it would be possible to consider any of the three classes of solutions that were discussed in section "Where, When, and How the Adaptations Are Made," in this approach we focus on the use of utility functions, which match the concepts of properties and property predictors perfectly, and thus provide an ideal candidate for the proposed methodology.

In this methodology, the users specify only a single utility function which can be interchangeably applied to any possible variant. In table 6.2, the utility function is defined as the weighted sum of a fitness metric for the three main properties needed: the hands-free, the response time, and the precision. This is expressed in the Utility function cell by comparing the required properties (e.g., hands-free) with the provided properties as specified in the context (e.g., ctxt.hands-free). The results of these comparisons are then accumulated and weighted to derive the final utility value which is used to compare the different variants.

For instance, when the hands-free property is evaluated to match (i.e., it is both offered and required), then the first section of the utility function evaluates to 1 and is multiplied by its corresponding weight (i.e., C_H). Furthermore, as also shown in table 6.2, the required properties are computed as constants (e.g., the response property offered by the visual UI is 70), or they are dynamically computed through property predictors (e.g., the response of the audio UI remote variant is computed as a function of the available bandwidth, and the application's hands-free property is computed as a delegate of the UI type's hands-free property).

The computed values are finally summed up based on their assigned weights. The three weights c_H, c_R, and c_P encode the importance of each of the three properties to the final variant selection. Typically, these weights are directly related to the user preferences. For example, someone might rank support for hands-free higher than that for precision, whereas someone else might value precision as the most desired property.

Though the weights should generally be defined so that adaptations would match the preferences of the most typical users, it should be possible to let the users adjust these values if they need to. In the prototype implementation of MADAM, this was possible through a GUI that enabled users to edit their preferences in the same way they edited the values of the simulated context types. Though more sophisticated techniques could be applied to allow for automated adjustment of these parameters, at this point simplicity was chosen over complexity. In the future, we will endeavor to investigate the application of known algorithms, such as from machine learning (Alpaydin 2004), with the purpose of enabling automated adjustment of the adaptation weights as a self-learning system.

6.6 Related Work

There is a substantial amount of literature on adaptive mobile systems. The Reconfigurable Ubiquitous Networked Embedded Systems (RUNES) middleware (Costa et al. 2005) targets embedded environments and aims at enabling advanced scenarios in which devices leverage off each other and exhibit autonomous and coordinated behavior. Similar to the MADAM middleware, RUNES specifies components which interact with each other exclusively via interfaces (i.e., offered services) and receptacles (i.e., dependencies). Additionally, the RUNES middleware specifies a reconfiguration metamodel based on logical mobility, as described in Zachariadis and Mascolo (2003).

The Odyssey project (Noble 2000; Noble and Satyanarayanan 1999) consists of a set of extensions to the NetBSD operating system which aim at supporting adaptation for a broad set of applications. These applications run on mobile devices but access data on servers. Odyssey supports fast detection and response to resource availability (i.e., agility), but the applications are still expected to independently decide how to adapt to the notified changes.

The Aura project (Sousa and Garlan 2002) primarily targets pervasive applications, and for this reason it introduces auras (which correspond to user tasks) as first-class entities. To this direction, the same project categorizes the techniques which support user mobility into use of mobile devices, remote access, standard applications (ported and installed at multiple locations), and use of standard virtual platforms to enable mobile code to follow the user as needed.

A communication-oriented approach is proposed by LIME (Picco et al. 1999), in which the mobile hosts are assumed to communicate exclusively via transiently shared tuple spaces. The model used offers both spatial and temporal decoupling and allows adaptations through reactive programming (i.e., by supporting the ability to react to events). Although this middleware architecture supports seamless support for distribution, it does not go far with regard to providing support for generic context-aware adaptations.

The Quality of Service Aware Component Architecture (QuA) project investigates how component architectures can preserve the safe-deployment property for QoS-sensitive applications (Amundsen et al. 2004). Similar to the MADAM approach, the QuA project envisages platform-managed QoS, where the platform is able to reason about how end-to-end QoS depends on the quality of component services.

In another work (Lundesgaard et al. 2006), a service model is proposed which classifies services in three levels: service, subservice, and atomic service. This classification is similar to what is used in service-oriented computing (SOC), where applications can be seen in terms of service levels of abstraction (Huhns and Singh 2005). This model is also similar to the one we described, although in our case the basic abstraction is provided by roles which can be provided by both components and services, whereas in this case the abstraction is provided on the basis of services only. In the latter, atomic services are used at the lowest level for forming subservices at the intermediate level, which are eventually used to compose high-level services.

Additional projects also aim to address the complete life cycle of QoS-aware applications. Similar to the MADAM approach, $2K^{Q+}$ (Duangdao et al. 2001) provides a QoS software engineering environment for specifying alternative component compositions and their QoS properties, which are then appropriately compiled for deployment on a specialized middleware. A platform-dependent compiler is provided, which produces executable code for reconfiguring the application at runtime by probing the QoS and resource availability.

The Quality Objects (QuO) framework (Loyall et al. 1998) relies on a suite of description languages for specifying QoS requirements. These specifications are compiled into executable code which is used for monitoring QoS and for controlling the interaction between distributed objects running on top of a CORBA-based middleware. This approach has the limitation that the specifications are platform-specific, as opposed to the composition and service plans we have described.

With concern to the SOC approach, many similarities are found in relation to our approach. For instance, SOC utilizes services as fundamental elements for developing applications and systems (Papazoglou and Georgakopoulos 2003). However, the area of adding context awareness to services is a new and promising one (Maamar et al. 2006). The proposed approach adds context awareness to some extent, although the entire decision making is centralized on the client side. However, more general approaches are currently under investigation.

Unlike the existing literature, the proposed approach offers a well-defined methodology for developing context-aware, adaptive applications. The underlying middleware supports automatic and autonomous reasoning on the possible adaptations for the selection of the most beneficial one. To the best of our knowledge, no related work proposes such a structured methodology for developing context-aware, adaptive applications. Additionally, a novel approach is proposed for the support of dynamically considering and exploiting services in the composition of component-based applications. Although in its infancy, this approach appears very promising and is one of the major points of focus of the MUSIC project (MUSIC Consortium).

6.7 Conclusions

This chapter described a novel methodology which utilizes an underlying middleware layer to ease the task of developing adaptive mobile applications. This methodology was partly studied and developed in the context of the MADAM project.

The proposed development methodology enables the design and implementation of adaptive applications for the mobile user, using the Separation-of-Concerns paradigm. In this approach, the developers are enabled to design the functional aspects of their applications independently of the specification of their extrafunctional behavior. An underlying middleware system is assumed to provide runtime support for the automatic self-adaptation of the deployed applications. It is argued that the proposed methodology, in combination with the provided middleware support, can significantly ease the effort required for the development of adaptive, mobile applications.

Additionally, it is important to state that although the MADAM results are novel and impact several software practitioners, more work is under way as part of a follow-up project: the Self-Adapting Applications for Mobile Users in Ubiquitous Computing Environments (MUSIC Consortium). Besides improving the existing results, MUSIC aims at providing additional support for ubiquitous computing environments, and also at providing better integration with SOA-based systems.

Acknowledgments

The work published in this chapter was partly funded by the European Community under the Sixth Framework Program, contracts FP6–4169 (IST-MADAM) and FP6–35166 (IST-MUSIC). Some of the ideas expressed in this chapter are the result of extensive collaboration among the partners of these projects. The authors would like to thank these partners and acknowledge the impact of their ideas on this work. The work reflects only the authors' views. The Community is not liable for any use that may be made of the information contained therein.

References

Alia, M., V. S. W. Eide, N. Paspallis, F. Eliassen, S. O. Hallsteinsen, and G. A. Papadopoulos. 2007a. A utility-based adaptivity model for mobile applications. In *Proceedings of the IEEE International Symposium on Ubisafe Computing* (UbiSafe), pp. 104–118. Niagara Falls, Canada.

Alia, M., S. Hallsteinsen, N. Paspallis, and F. Eliassen. 2007b. Managing distributed adaptation of mobile applications. In *Proceedings of the 7th IFIP International Conference on Distributed Applications and Interoperable Systems* (DAIS), pp. 556–563. Paphos, Cyprus.

Alpaydin, E. 2004. *Introduction to Machine Learning.* Cambridge, Mass.: MIT Press.

Amundsen, S., K. Lund, F. Eliassen, and R. Staehli. 2004. QuA: Platform-managed QoS for component architectures. Paper presented at the Norwegian Informatics Conference (NIK).

Arnold, K., J. Gosling, and D. Holmes. 2000. *The Java^{TM} Programming Language*, 3rd ed. Upper Saddle River, N.J.: Prentice Hall.

Chen, G., and D. Kotz. 2000. A Survey of Context-Aware Mobile Computing Research. Technical Report TR2000–381. Department of Computer Science, Dartmouth College.

Costa, P., G. Coulson, C. Mascolo, G. P. Picco, and S. Zachariadis. 2005. The RUNES middleware: A reconfigurable component-based approach to networked embedded systems. In *Proceedings of the 16th International Symposium on Personal, Indoor and Mobile Radio Communications* (PIMRC), pp. 806–810. Berlin.

Dey, A. K. 2000. Providing Architectural Support for Building Context-Aware Applications. Ph.D. thesis, College of Computing, Georgia Institute of Technology.

Dey, A. K. 2001. Understanding and using context. *Personal and Ubiquitous Computing* 5, no. 1: 4–7.

Duangdao, W., K. Nehrstadt, X. Gu, and D. Xu. 2001. "2K^{Q+}: An integrated approach of QoS compilation and reconfigurable, component-based run-time middleware for the unified QoS management framework. In *Middlesex 2001: Proceedings of the IFIP/ACM International Conference on Distributed Systems Platforms*, pp. 373–394. Heidelberg, Germany.

Floch, J., S. Hallsteinsen, F. Eliassen, E. Stav, K. Lund, and E. Gjørven. 2006. Using architecture models for runtime adaptability. *IEEE Software* 23, no. 2: 62–70.

Gamma, E., R. Helm, R. Johnson, and J. Vlissides. 1995. *Design Patterns: Elements of Reusable Object-Oriented Software.* Boston: Addison-Wesley.

Geihs, K., M. U. Khan, R. Reichle, A. Solberg, S. Hallsteinsen, and S. Merral. 2006. Modeling of component-based adaptive distributed applications. In *Dependable and Adaptive Distributed Systems (DADS Track): Proceedings of the 21st ACM Symposium on Applied Computing* (SAC), pp. 718–722. Dijon, France.

Horn, P. 2001. Autonomic Computing: IBM's Perspective on the State of Information Technology. http://www.research.ibm.com/autonomic/manifesto/autonomic_computing.pdf. (Accessed November 30, 2007.)

Huhns, M. N., and M. P. Singh. 2005. Service-oriented computing: Key concepts and principles. *IEEE Internet Computing* 9, no. 1: 75–81.

Kiczales, G., J. Lamping, A. Mendhekar, C. Maeda, C. Lopes, J.-M. Loingtier, and J. Irwin. 1997. Aspect-oriented programming. In *Proceedings of the European Conference on Object-Oriented Programming*, LNCS 1241, pp. 220–242.

Lindholm, T., and F. Yellin. 1999. *The Java^{TM} Virtual Machine Specification*, 2nd ed. Upper Saddle River, N.J.: Prentice Hall.

Lundesgaard, S. A., K. Lund, and F. Eliassen. 2006. Utilizing alternative application configurations in context- and QoS-aware mobile middleware. In *Proceedings of the 6th IFIP International Conference on Distributed Applications and Interoperable Systems* (DAIS). LNCS 4025, pp. 228–241. Bologna, Italy. Springer Verlag.

Loyall, J. P., D. E. Bakken, R. E. Schantz, J. A. Zinky, D. A. Karr, R. Vanegas, and K. R. Anderson. 1998. QoS aspect languages and their runtime integration. In *Proceedings of the 4th Workshop on Languages, Compilers, and Run-time Systems for Scalable Computers* (LCR), pp. 303–310. Pittsburgh, Penn.

Maamar, Z., D. Benslimane, and N. Narendra. 2006. What can context do for Web Services? *Communications of the ACM* 49, no. 12: 98–103.

MADAM Consortium. Mobility and Adaptation Enabling Middleware (MADAM). http://www.ist-madam.org.

Maes, P. 1987. Concepts and experiments in computational reflection. *ACM SIGPLAN Notices* 22, no. 12: 147–155.

McKinley, P. K., S. Masoud Sadjadi, E. P. Kasten, and B. H. C. Cheng. 2004a. Composing adaptive software. *IEEE Computer* 37, no. 7: 56–64.

McKinley, P. K., S. Masoud Sadjadi, E. P. Kasten, and B. H. C. Cheng. 2004b. A Taxonomy of Compositional Adaptation. Technical Report MSU-CSE-04–17. Department of Computer Science and Engineering, Michigan State University.

MUSIC Consortium. Self-Adapting Applications for Mobile Users in Ubiquitous Computing Environments (MUSIC). http://www.ist-music.eu.

Noble, B. 2000. System support for mobile, adaptive applications. *IEEE Personal Communications* 7, no. 1: 44–49.

Noble, B., and M. Satyanarayanan. 1999. Experiences with adaptive mobile applications in Odyssey. *Mobile Networks and Applications* 4, no. 4: 245–254.

Papazoglou, M. P., and D. Georgakopoulos. 2003. Service oriented computing: Introduction. *Communications of the ACM* 46, no. 10: 24–28.

Parnas, D. L. 1972. On the criteria to be used in decomposing systems into modules. *Communications of the ACM* 15, no. 12: 1053–1058.

Paspallis, N., A. Chimaris, and G. A. Papadopoulos. 2007. Experiences from developing a distributed context management system for enabling adaptivity. In *Proceedings of the 7th IFIP International Conference on Distributed Applications and Interoperable Systems* (DAIS), pp. 225–238. Paphos, Cyprus.

Paspallis, N., and G. A. Papadopoulos. 2006. An approach for developing adaptive, mobile applications with separation of concerns. In *Proceedings of the 30th Annual International Computer Software and Applications Conference* (COMPSAC), pp. 299–306. Chicago.

Picco, G. P., A. L. Murphy, and G.-C. Roman. 1999. LIME: Linda meets mobility. In *Proceedings of the 21st International Conference on Software Engineering* (ICSE), pp. 368–377. Los Angeles.

Satyanarayanan, M. 2001. Pervasive computing: Vision and challenges. *IEEE Personal Communications* 8, no. 4: 10–17.

Sousa, J. P., and D. Garlan. 2002. Aura: An architectural framework for user mobility in ubiquitous computing environments. In *Proceedings of the 3rd Working IEEE/IFIP Conference on Software Architecture*, pp. 29–43. Montreal.

Szyperski, C. 1997. *Component Software: Beyond Object-Oriented Programming*, 2nd ed. Essex, England: Addison-Wesley.

Tennenhouse, D. L. 2000. Proactive computing. *Communications of the ACM* 43, no. 5: 43–50.

Walsh, W. E., G. Tesauro, J. O. Kephart, and R. Das. 2004. Utility functions in autonomic systems. In *Proceedings of the International Conference on Autonomic Computing* (ICAC), pp. 70–77. New York.

Weiser, M. 1993. Hot topics: Ubiquitous computing. *IEEE Computer* 26, no. 10: 71–72.

Zachariadis, S., and C. Mascolo. 2003. Adaptable mobile applications through SATIN: Exploiting logical mobility in mobile computing middleware. Paper presented at the 1st UK-UbiNet Workshop. London.

7 Sensoria: Engineering for Service-Oriented Overlay Computers

Martin Wirsing, Laura Bocchi, Allan Clark, José Luiz Fiadeiro, Stephen Gilmore, Matthias Hölzl, Nora Koch, Philip Mayer, Rosario Pugliese, and Andreas Schroeder

7.1 Introduction

The last decades have shown tremendous advances in the field of information technology (IT). In fact, with online access to vast amounts of information, states offering their services for citizens on the World Wide Web, and software in control of critical areas such as flight control systems, information systems now lie at the very foundations of our society. But it is the business sector where IT has had the most impact. Driven by the need to stay competitive in an environment of rapid change in global markets and business models, as well as local regulations and requirements, organizations now strongly depend on a functional and efficient IT infrastructure which is flexible enough to deal with unexpected changes while still offering stability for business processes and connections to customers, partners, and suppliers.

With the emerging trend of automating complex and distributed business processes as a whole, many organizations face the problem of integrating their existing, already vastly complicated, systems to reach yet another layer of sophistication in the interconnection of business value, business processes, and information technology. Many IT systems are difficult to adapt and work with; progress in the world of businesses is often impeded by the difficulty of changing the existing IT infrastructure. Service-oriented computing (SOC) is a new approach to software development and integration that addresses these challenges. SOC provides the opportunity for organizations to manage their heterogeneous infrastructures in a coherent way, thus gaining new levels of interoperability and collaboration within and across the boundaries of an organization. In addition, SOC promises new flexibility in linking people, processes, information, and computing platforms.

The IST-FET Integrated Project Sensoria[1] is a European Community-funded project that develops methodologies and tools for dealing with service-oriented computing. It addresses major problems found in current approaches to SOC and provides mathematically founded and sound methodologies and tools for dealing with the amount of flexibility and interoperability needed in these next-generation infrastructures. Sensoria aims to support a more systematic and scientifically well-founded approach to engineering of software systems for service-oriented overlay computers. At the core of our research is a concept of service that generalizes current approaches such as Web Services and Grid Computing. Sensoria provides the scientific foundations for a development process where developers can concentrate on modeling the high-level behavior of the system and use transformations for deployment and analysis. To this end we investigate programming primitives supported by a mathematical semantics; analysis and verification techniques for qualitative and quantitative properties such as security, performance, quality of service, and behavioral correctness; and model-based transformation and development techniques.

In the NESSI road map most of the research of Sensoria is located in the service integration layer, although the research touches both the semantic layer and the infrastructure layer, as well as the crosscutting areas of management services, interoperability, and security. Sensoria addresses grand challenges from the areas of service foundations (dynamic reconfigurable architectures, end-to-end security), service composition (composability analysis operators for replaceability, compatibility, and conformance; QoS-aware service composition; business-driven automated composition); service management (self-configuring services); and service engineering (design principles for engineering service applications, associating a service design methodology with standard software development, and business process modeling techniques). In the addressed grand challenges, the Sensoria research consortium focuses on solid mathematical foundations—the project as a whole therefore is located in the "foundational plane" of the SOC Road Map (see chapter 1).

In the remaining sections, we present the Sensoria development approach and illustrate its building blocks. Section 7.2 contains an overview of the Sensoria project and introduces the case study that will be used throughout the chapter.

Today, both UML and SCA are commonly used to specify service-oriented systems, either individually or in combination. Therefore we show two alternative approaches to modeling: the Sensoria UML extension for services and the SCA-inspired SRML, in sections 7.3 and 7.4, respectively.

When orchestrating service-oriented systems it is often necessary to find trade-offs between conflicting system properties. In section 7.5 we show how soft constraints can be used to model context-dependent restrictions and preferences in order to perform dynamic service selection.

To illustrate our approach to qualitative and quantitative analysis, we show two of the calculi which are used in the Sensoria development environment, but normally hidden from the developers. The COWS calculus presented in section 7.6 can be used for performing security modeling and enforcement on service orchestrations; in particular, we add annotations for ensuring confidentiality properties. The PEPA process algebra is used to validate the performance of orchestrations regarding previously defined service-level agreements in section 7.7.

An expanded version of this paper is available as LMU-IFI-PST technical report 0702 (Wirsing et al. 2007a).

7.2 Sensoria

Sensoria is one of the three integrated projects of the Global Computing Initiative of FET-IST, the Future and Emerging Technologies section of the European Commission. The Sensoria Consortium consists of 13 universities, two research institutes, and four companies (two SMEs) from seven countries.[2]

7.2.1 Sensoria Approach

The core aim of the Sensoria project is the production of new knowledge for systematic and scientifically well-founded methods of service-oriented software development. Sensoria provides a comprehensive approach to the visual design, formal analysis, and automated deployment of service-oriented applications. The Sensoria techniques enable service engineers to model their applications on a very high level of abstraction, using service-oriented extensions of the standard UML or standard business process models, and to transform those models to be able to use formal analysis techniques as well as generate executable code.

The Sensoria techniques and tools are built on mathematical theories and methods. These formal results are complemented by realistic case studies for important application areas including telecommunications, automotive, e-learning, and e-business. The case studies are defined by the industrial partners to provide continuous practical challenges for the new techniques of services engineering and for demonstrating the research results. This approach is shown in figure 7.1.

An important consideration of the Sensoria project is "scalable analysis for scalable systems." Our vision is that developers of service-oriented systems can develop at a high level of abstraction with support from tools that analyze the system models, provide feedback about the reliability of the system and possible problems, establish the validity of functional and nonfunctional requirements, and manage the deployment to different platforms. We base our tools on formal languages with well-defined properties which make it possible to establish their correctness. Two aspects are particularly important to make the process practical for commercial software development: (1) analysis results are translated back into the familiar modeling notations so that developers do not need to understand the calculi used to perform the analysis, and (2) the analyses not only are usable for "toy examples," but also scale to realistic problems. The process may be customized to various application domains and different iterative and agile process models, such as the Rational Unified Process (RUP), Model-Driven Development (MDD), or Extreme Programming (XP). Figure 7.2 displays one step in this development process.

The developer usually works with higher-level input models, but also with program code, and uses the Sensoria development environment (downloadable from Sensoria project) to perform qualitative or quantitative analysis and to generate output (e.g., new models or code that can be deployed on various platforms). Our tools within the qualitative and

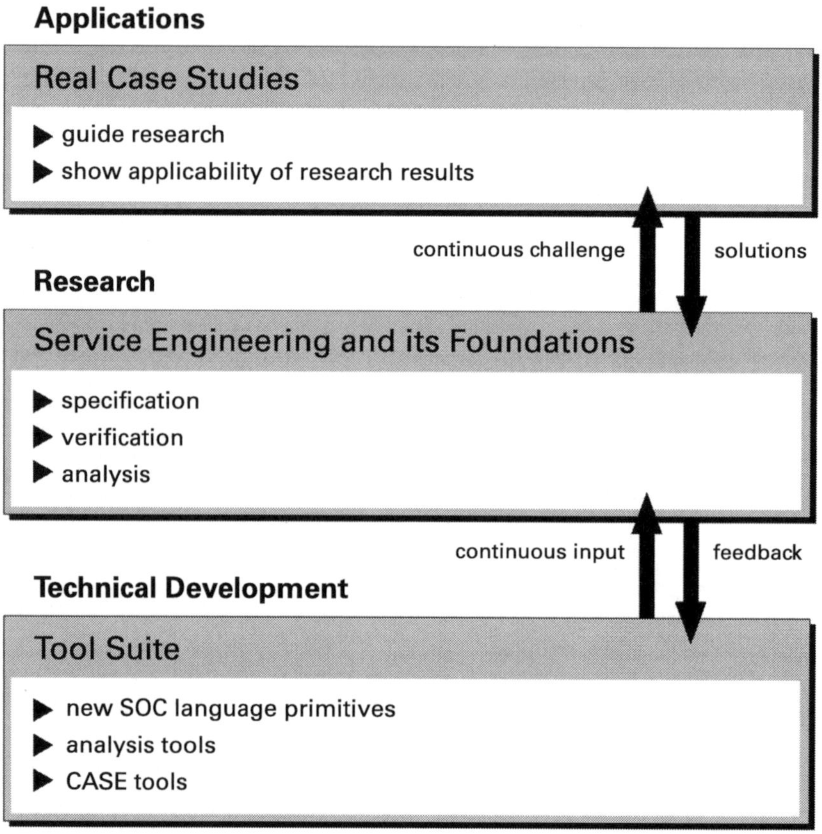

Figure 7.1
Sensoria innovation cycle

quantitative analyses can, for example, perform checks of functional correctness of services, early performance analysis, prediction of quantitative bottlenecks in collaborating services, and verification of service-level agreements.

7.2.2 Research Themes

The research themes of Sensoria range across the whole life cycle of software development, from requirements to deployment, including reengineering of legacy systems.

Modeling Service-Oriented Software The definition of adequate linguistic primitives for modeling and programming service-oriented systems enables model-driven development for implementing services on different global computers, and for transforming legacy systems into services using systematic reengineering techniques. Modeling frontends allows

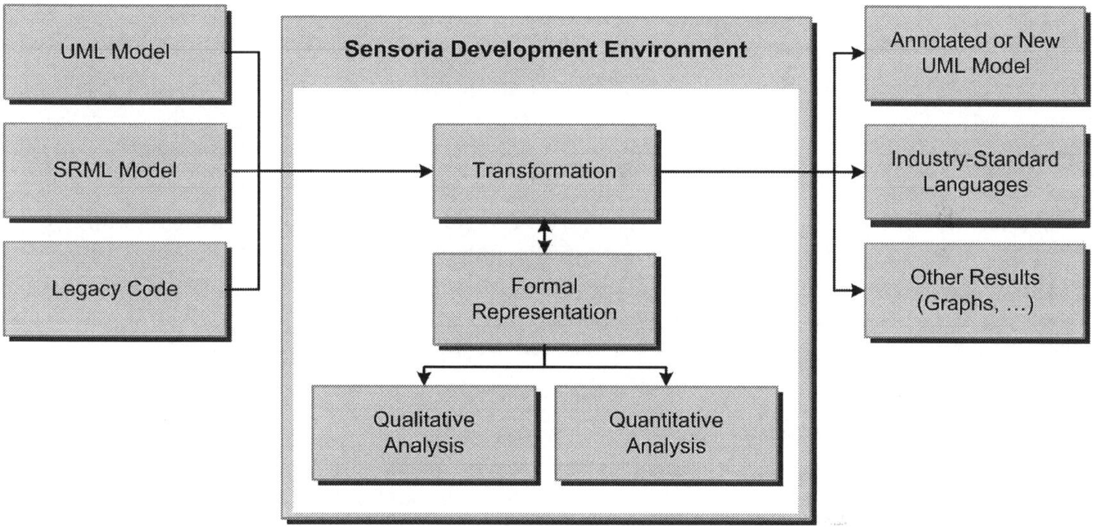

Figure 7.2
Sensoria development process

designers to use high-level visual formalisms such as the industry standard UML. Automated model transformations allow generation of formal representations from engineering models for further development steps.

Formal Analysis of Service-Oriented Software Based on Mathematically Founded Techniques Mathematical models, hidden from the developer, enable qualitative and quantitative analysis supporting the service development process and providing the means for reasoning about functional and nonfunctional properties of services and service aggregates. Sensoria results include powerful mathematical analysis techniques, particularly in program analysis techniques, type systems, logics, and process calculi for investigating the behavior and the quality of service of properties of global services.

Deployment and Runtime Issues of Service-Oriented Software The development of sound engineering techniques for global services includes deployment mechanisms with aspects such as runtime self-management, service-oriented middlewares, and model-driven deployment, as well as reengineering legacy systems into services, thus enabling developers to travel the last mile to the implementation of service-oriented architectures.

7.2.3 Automotive Case Study

Today, computers embedded in cars can access communication networks such as the Internet, and thereby provide a variety of new functionalities for cars and drivers. In the future, instead of having to code these functionalities, services will be able to be discovered at run-time and orchestrated so as to deliver the best available functionality at agreed levels of quality. A set of possible scenarios of the automotive domain are examined to illustrate the scope of the Sensoria project. In the following we focus on one of them, the car repair scenario.

In this scenario, the diagnostic system reports a severe failure in the car engine that implies the car is no longer drivable. The in-vehicle repair support system is able to orchestrate a number of services (garage, backup car rental, towing truck) that are discovered and bound at that time according to levels of service specified at design time (e.g., balancing cost and delay). The owner of the car deposits a security payment before the discovery of the services is triggered.

7.3 UML Extension for Service-Oriented Architectures

Within the Sensoria approach, a service engineer can model services using a specialization of the UML covering static, dynamic, and quality-of-service aspects of services.

For the static aspects of service-oriented software systems, the UML specialization ranges from rather simple, stereotyped language extensions for introducing services to more complicated structures such as dependency relations between services and their contextual relationships to resources and legacy systems. Modeling dynamics of service-oriented software, in particular orchestration and choreography of services, is supported by primitives for interaction and activity modeling that take into account possible failures and quality-of-service aspects. (These nonfunctional extensions are not covered in this chapter. Interested readers are referred to Wirsing et al. 2006.)

7.3.1 Modeling Structures of SOA

The structure of a service-oriented architecture can be visualized by UML deployment and composite structure diagrams. A deployment diagram is used to represent the—usually nested—nodes of the architecture (i.e., hardware devices and software execution environments). Figure 7.3 shows a UML deployment diagram of the car and its environment as first approximation to an architecture model. The nodes are connected through communication paths that show the three types of communication that characterize the automotive domain: intravehicle communication (nonnamed connections), intervehicle communication, and communication among vehicle and environment, such as the communication with the car manufacturer or a remote discovery server. The components that are involved in the execution of service orderings are a service discovery which may be local or external to the car, a reasoner for service selection, and a service orchestrator.

In addition to UML deployment diagrams, which give a static view of the architecture, we use UML structure diagrams to represent the evolving connections within the service-oriented architecture of the vehicle and its environment. Three types of connections are

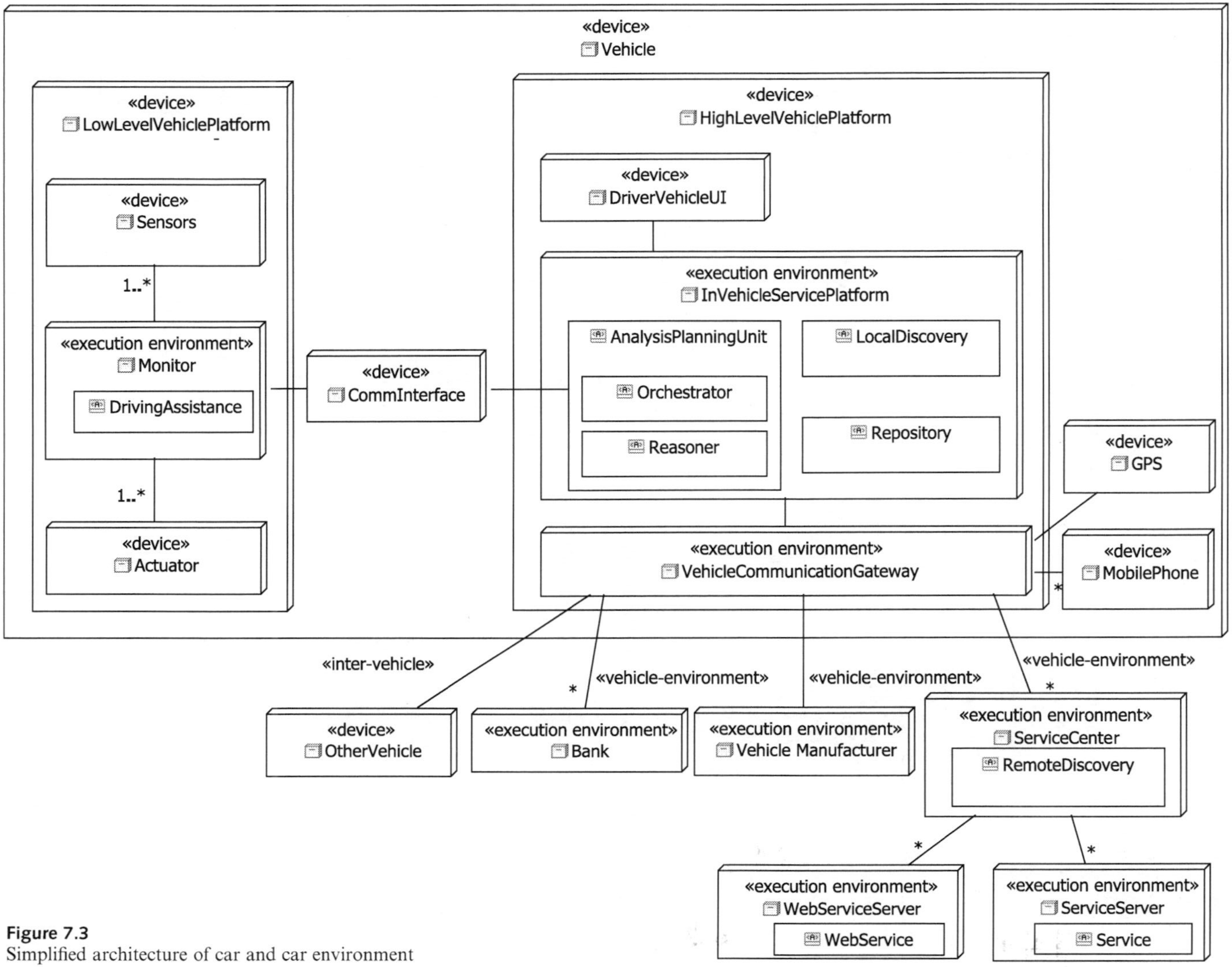

Figure 7.3
Simplified architecture of car and car environment

identified: discovery connection, permanent connection (as in modeling of non-service-oriented architectures), and temporary connections. In order to be invoked, services need to be discovered before the binding to the car's onboard system takes place. Thus the discovery connection is based on the information provided by a discovery service. We distinguish a temporary connection which is, for example, one from the car's onboard system to a known service, such as the car manufacturer's discovery service, from a permanent connection. Permanent connections wire components as in traditional software. For a graphical representation and more details about these connections, the reader is referred to Wirsing et al. (2006).

7.3.2 Modeling Behavior of SOA

The behavior of a service-oriented system is mainly described by the service orchestration which defines the system's workflow. Modeling orchestration of services includes specifying interactions among services, modeling transactional business processes using concepts developed for long-running transactions, and specifying nonfunctional properties of services.

In the modeled business process of the on-road car repair scenario, the orchestration is triggered by an engine failure or a sensor signal such as low oil level. The process starts with a request from the orchestrator to the bank to charge the driver's credit card with the security deposit payment, which is modeled by an asynchronous UML action `requestCardCharge` for charging the credit card. The number of the card is provided as output parameter of the UML stereotyped call action. In parallel to the interaction with the bank, the orchestrator requests the current position of the car from the car's internal GPS service. The current location is modeled as input to the `requestLocation` action and subsequently used by the `findLocalServices` and `findRemoteServices` interactions, which retrieve a list of services. For the selection of services the orchestrator synchronizes with the reasoner to obtain the most appropriate services. Service ordering is modeled by the UML actions `orderGarage`, `orderTowTruck`, and `orderRentalCar`, following a sequential and parallel process, respectively.

Figure 7.4 shows a UML activity diagram of the orchestration of services in the on-road car repair scenario. We use stereotyped UML actions indicating the type of interactions (`send, receive, sendAndReceive`), and model input and output parameters of the interactions with UML pins stereotyped with outgoing and incoming arrows (abbreviations for send and receive, respectively). These pins are not linked to any edge, but specify variables containing data to be sent or target variables to accept the data received; constraints prohibit illegal combinations such as send actions with input pins. Interactions match operations of required and provided interfaces of the services. Services are defined as ports of UML components.

The key technique to handle long-running transactions is to install compensations (e.g., based on the Saga concepts; Bruni et al. 2005). Modeling of compensations is not directly supported in UML. We provide a UML extension within Sensoria for the modeling of these compensations. The extension consists of two modeling primitives—`Scope` and `CompensationEdge`—and corresponding stereotypes for UML activity diagrams. A `Scope` is a structured activity node that groups activity nodes and activity edges. The grouping mechanism provided is convenient for the definition of a compensation or fault handler for a set of activities; at the same time, fault and compensation handlers can also be attached directly to actions. Compensation handlers are defined by linking an activity or scope with a `compensationEdge` stereotyped activity edge to the compensation handler. The handler in turn may again consist of a single action (e.g., see `cancelGarage` in figure 7.4). On completion of an activity node with an associated compensation handler, the handler is installed and is then executed through an explicit `compensate` action in the continued execution of the orchestration.

The UML stereotypes defined for orchestration are part of the Sensoria UML Profile. The use of such a UML extension has direct advantages for the design of model transformations, especially for deployment transformations.

7.4 The Sensoria Reference Modeling Language

SRML is a language for modeling composite services understood as services whose business logic involves a number of interactions among more elementary service components as well the invocation of services provided by external parties. SRML offers modeling primitives inspired by the Service Component Architecture (SCA) (Beisiegel et al. 2005) but addressing a higher level of abstraction in which one models the business logic of the domain. SRML models both the structure of composite services and their behavioral aspects. As in SCA, interactions are supported on the basis of service interfaces defined in a way that is "independent of the hardware platform, the operating system, the hosting middleware and the programming language used to implement the service" (Fiadero et al. 2006).

An SRML module declares one or more components, a number of "requires-interfaces" which specify services that need to be provided by external parties, and (at most) one "provides-interface" that describes the properties of the service offered by the module. Components have a tight coupling (performed at design time) and offer a distributed orchestration of the parties involved in the service. The coupling between components and external parties is looser and is established at runtime through the discovery, selection, and binding mechanisms that are supported by the underlying service middleware.

A number of wires establish interaction protocols among the components and between the components and the external parties that instantiate the interfaces. A wire establishes a binding between the interactions that both parties declare to support and defines the interaction protocol that coordinates those interactions. Figure 7.5 illustrates the SRML module for the on-road car repair scenario.

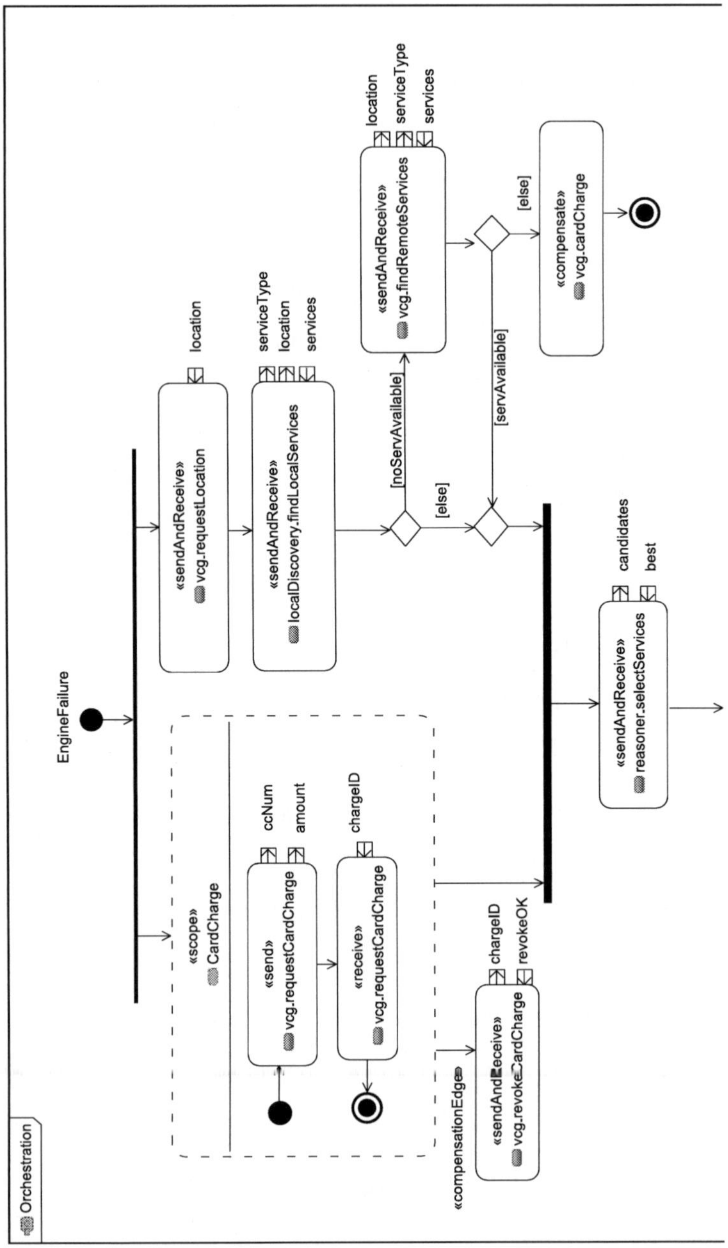

Figure 7.4
Orchestration in the on road car repair scenario

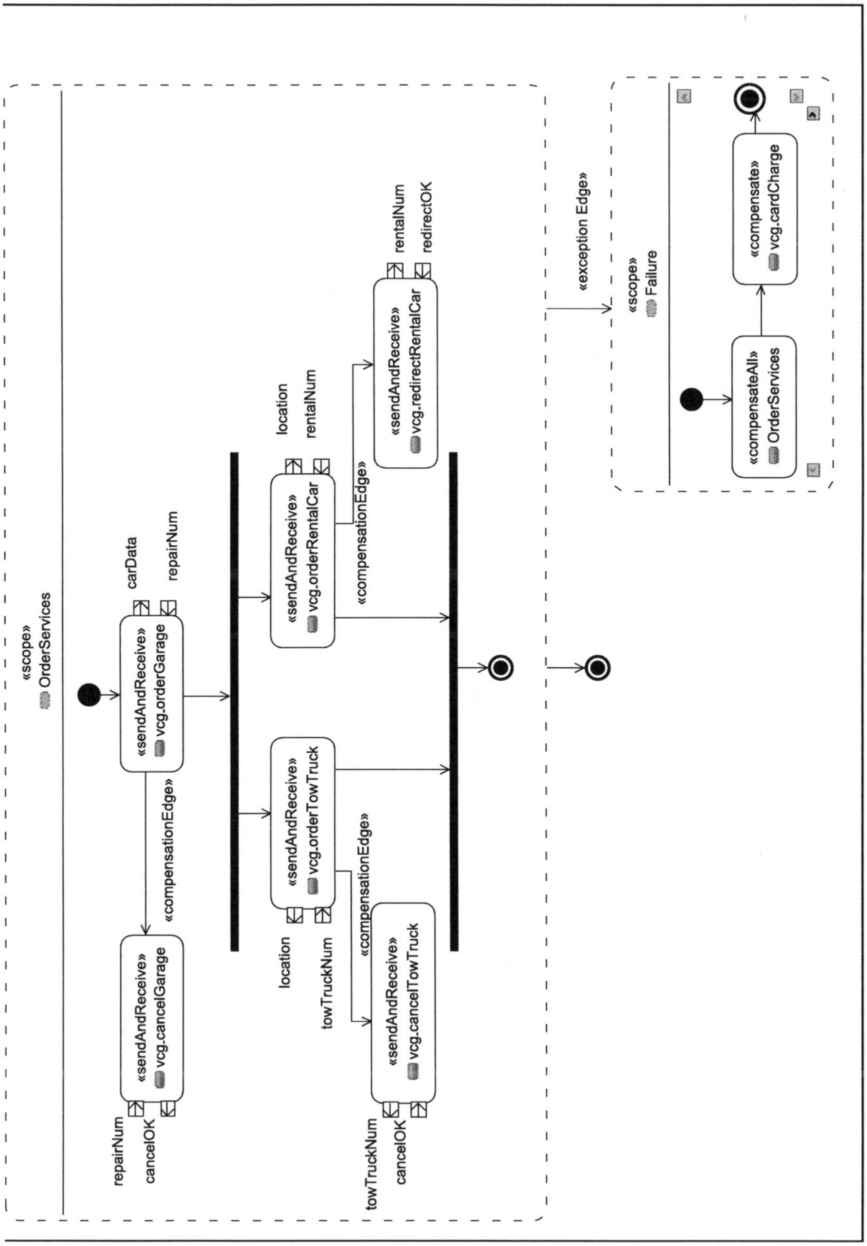

Figure 7.4
(continued)

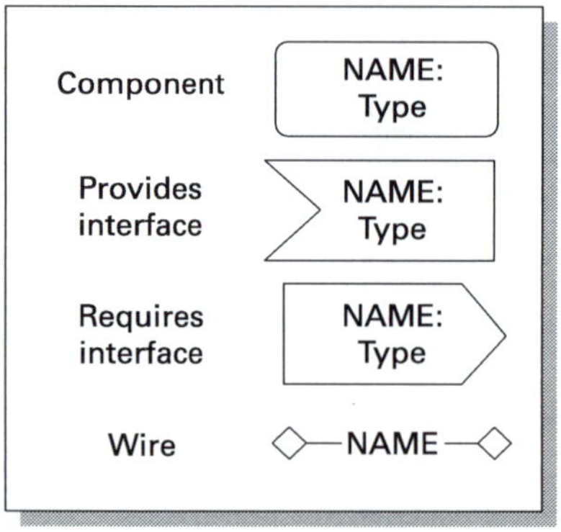

(a)

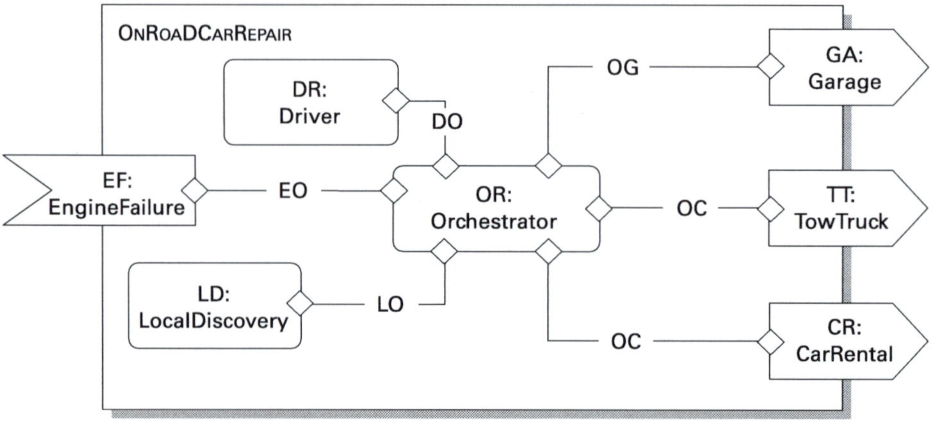

(b)

Figure 7.5
(a) Entities in a SRML module, (b) SRML module for the on road car repair scenario

We are developing an editor for SRML based on Eclipse Modeling Framework (EMF). The editor relies on an SRML metamodel consisting of an EMF tree; graph transformation techniques can be used to automate the encoding between (parts of) SRML and other languages for which an EMF metamodel exists. Thus, for example, we are providing an encoding from BPEL processes into SRML modules (Bocchi et al. 2007). More specifically, we extract high-level declarative descriptions of BPEL processes that can be used for building more complex modules, possibly including components defined in other (implementation or modeling) languages for which an encoding into SRML exists. We are using the same approach to develop mappings between SRML and other modeling

```
INTERACTIONS

    rcv engineFailure

    s&r askUsrDetails

        ⊠ cust:customerID

          ccID:bankAccountID

          dest:location

          workRelated:boolean

          ⊿t:time

    s&r currentLocation

        ⊠ l:location

    snd confirmation

    s&r requestCharge

        🔔 cust:customerID

           ccID:bankAccountID

           amount:moneyVal

        ⊠ certif:paymentCertificate

    s&r orderGarage

        🔔 ...

    s&r rentACar

        🔔 ...

    s&r orderTowTruck

        🔔 ...
```

Figure 7.6
Specification of the interactions for the business role *Orchestrator*

languages/calculi developed in Sensoria. For instance, we are encoding SRML into COWS in order to provide SRML with an operational semantics for the process of service discovery.

7.4.1 Specifying SRML Entities

The specification of each SRML entity (components, external interfaces, and wires) addresses properties of the interactions supported by that entity.

Figure 7.6 presents the interactions specified in the business role fulfilled by the orchestrator. SRML supports conversational interaction types—send-and-receive (s&r) and receive-and-send (r&s)—involving initiation (`interaction`🔔 denotes the event of `initiating interaction`), reply (`interaction`⊠ denotes the reply event of `interaction`), and other events for handling specific aspects of conversations, such as committing, canceling, and revoking a deal (see Fiadero et al. 2006 for an exhaustive list of types of interactions and interaction events). Interactions can have 🔔-parameters for transmitting data when the interaction is initiated and ⊠-parameters for carrying a reply.

The different types of entities involved in a module are specified in SRML using three different but related languages. All the languages provide a specification of the supported interactions. The languages for defining business roles, business protocols, and interaction protocols differ in the way they define the behavioral interface.

A component is a computational unit represented in a module by what we call a business role. A business role declares the interactions in which the component can become involved, as well as the execution pattern that orchestrates those interactions (i.e., the orchestration). The orchestration is specified through a set of variables that provide an abstract view of the state of the component and by a set of transition rules.

The transition rules can be derived from UML sequence or activity diagrams and refined with additional information. Each transition has a *trigger*, typically the occurrence of an interaction event, a *guard* identifying the states in which it can take place, the *effects* that change the local state (s′ denotes the value of the local variable s after the transition), and the *sends* which specify the interaction events that are sent. The following is a transition of the business role *Orchestrator*.

```
transition startProcess
  triggeredBy engineFailure🔔?
  guardedBy s=Begin
  effects s'=FailureDetected
  sends currentLocation🔔!
    ∧ askUsrDetails🔔!
```

The external interfaces are defined in a module through what we call business protocols. Business protocols specify the interactions similarly to business roles. Their behavior abstracts from details of the local state of the co-party and specifies the protocol that the co-party adheres to as a set of properties concerning the causality of the interactions. The following is the behavior for the business protocol *EngineFailure*.

```
initiallyEnabled engineFailure🔔?
engineFailure🔔? enables confirmation🔔!
```

The behavior is described by two statements. The first one ensures that the interaction *engineFailure*🔔? is enabled from the beginning of the session and that it remains enabled until it occurs. In the second one, confirmation🔔! will be accepted only after the occurrence of *engineFailure*🔔?.

7.4.2 Service-Level Agreement

SRML offers primitives for modeling "dynamic" aspects concerned with configuration, session management, and service-level agreement (SLA). In particular, SRML supports the definition of attributes and constraints for SLA, using the algebraic techniques developed in Bistarelli et al. (1997) and Bistarelli (2004) for constraint satisfaction and optimization. Section 7.5 presents this calculus in more detail, together with an example, and shows how the constraints can be modeled in SRML.

7.5 Soft Constraints for Selecting the Best Service

The reasoning component of a service-oriented system (see figure 7.3) has to achieve a compromise between different goals of the system. Soft constraints are a promising way to specify and implement such reasoning mechanisms.

Soft constraints are an extension of classical constraints to deal with nonfunctional requirements, overconstrained problems, and preferences. Instead of determining just a subset of admissible domain elements, a soft constraint assigns a grade to each element of the application domain. Bistarelli, Montanari, and Rossi (Bistarelli et al. 1997) and Bistarelli (2004) have developed a very elegant theory of soft constraints where many different kinds of soft constraints can be represented and combined in a uniform way over so-called constraint semirings (*c-semirings*).

In Sensoria we are developing a language which extends the c-semiring approach with possibilities to specify preferences between constraints and to vary the constraints according to a context. This simplifies the description of behaviors of systems in a dynamically changing environment and with complex trade-offs between conflicting properties.

A context is a boolean expression which can guard a constraint. For example, the distance to the destination might determine whether the quick availability of a rental car is important or not. In this case, "distance $<$ 20km" is a context that can restrict the applicability of a constraint. Variables appearing in contexts are called *context variables*; variables appearing only in constraints but not in contexts are called *controlled variables*. In the car repair scenario, the context variables will specify, among other things, the *distance* to the destination or whether the journey is *work-related*. The controlled variables represent properties of offers (e.g., the cost or quality of an offer). A soft constraint is a mapping from (domains of) controlled variables into a c-semiring.

In the car repair scenario we use soft constraints to specify the preferences of the users. The constraints map the controlled variables into a c-semiring where values are natural numbers; 0 means not acceptable, 1 means barely acceptable, and higher numbers represent higher values of acceptance. For example, the user may prefer a garage that can repair the car as quickly as possible, with a duration of more than two days not being acceptable:

$\mathit{fastRepair}$: $[\mathit{garage\text{-}duration} \mid n \mapsto \lfloor 48/n \rfloor]$

We also may want the repair to be done cheaply, but only if the trip is not work-related. Repairs costing more than 1000 euros are still acceptable, but only barely:

$\mathit{cheapRepair}$: **in context** $\neg \mathit{work\text{-}related?}$
assert $[\mathit{garage\text{-}cost} \mid n \mapsto \lceil 1000/n \rceil]$ **end**

Users might not consider all constraints to be equally important. For example, a user who prefers fast but expensive repairs can specify this as a preference between constraints: fastRepair $>$ cheapRepair. In this case an offer that results in a faster repair will always be preferred; the price will be used only to break ties between equally fast repairs.

From a set of constraints and preferences the reasoner can compute either the best solutions or a set of all solutions that are better than a certain threshold. Two techniques that are used for solving soft constraint systems are branch search and bound search (Wirsing et al. 2007c) and dynamic programming (Bistarelli 2004).

The constraints presented in this section can be modeled in SRML using the following syntax, where S is a c-semiring, D is a finite set (domain of possible elements taken by the variables), and V is a totally ordered set (of variables).

7.5.1 Constraint System

S is `<[0..1000],max,min,0,1000>`
D is $\{n \in \mathbb{N} : 1 \leq n \leq 1000\}$
V is `{DR.askUsrDetails⊠.workRelated, GA.cost, GA.duration,...}`

The variable *DR.askUsrDetails⊠.workRelated* is a Boolean context variable that is true if the trip is work-related. The variables *GA.cost* and *GA.duration* represent the cost and availability of the garage service, respectively. We show the SRML specification of the *fastRepair* and *cheapRepair* constraints. Notice that we represent the context as a variable of the constraint.

7.5.2 Constraints

```
fastRepair is  <{GA.duration},def1>
           s.t. def1(n)=floor(48/n)
cheapRepair is <{GA.cost},def2> s.t. def2(n)=
           if DR.askUsrDetails⊠.workRelated
                then 1000 else ceiling(1000/n)
```

7.6 A Process Calculus for Service-Oriented Systems

COWS (Calculus for Orchestration of Web Services [Lapadula et al. 2007b]) is a recently designed process calculus for specifying, combining, and analyzing service-oriented applications while modeling their dynamic behavior. We present (an excerpt of) COWS's main features and syntax while modeling some simplified components of the on-road car repair scenario. The type system of COWS (Lapadula et al. 2007a) enables us to verify confidentiality properties (e.g., that critical data such as credit card information is shared only with authorized partners). The complete specification, including compensation activities, can be found in Wirsing et al. (2007b).

7.6.1 Service Orchestration with COWS

To start with, we present the COWS term representing the "orchestration" of all services within the scenario of section 7.3:

$[p_{car}]$ $(Orchestrator \mid LocalDiscovery \mid Reasoner \mid SensorsMonitor)$
$\mid$ Bank $\mid$ OnRoadRepairServices

The services above are composed by using the *parallel composition* operator $\_ \mid \_$ that allows the different components to be concurrently executed and to interact with each other. The *delimitation* operator $[\_]\ \_$ is used here to declare that p_{car} is a (partner) name known to all services of the in-vehicle platform (i.e., *Orchestrator*, *LocalDiscovery*, *Reasoner*, and *SensorsMonitor*), and only to them.

Orchestrator, the most important component of the in-vehicle platform, is

$$[\mathrm{x}_1, \ldots, \mathrm{x}_\mathrm{n}]\ (p_{car} \cdot o_{engfail}?\langle x_1, \ldots, x_n\rangle.s_{engfail} + p_{car} \cdot o_{lowoil}?\langle x_1, \ldots, x_n\rangle.s_{lowoil})$$

This term uses the *choice* operator $\_+\_$ to pick one of those alternative "recovery" behaviors whose execution can start immediately. For simplicity, only "engine failure" and "low oil" situations are taken into account.

The *receive-guarded prefix* operator $p_{car} \cdot o_i?\langle x_1, \ldots, x_n\rangle.\_$ expresses that each recovery behavior starts with a *receive* activity of the form $p_{car} \cdot o_i?\langle x_1, \ldots, x_n\rangle$ corresponding to reception of a request emitted, when a failure arises, by *SensorsMonitor* (a term representing the behavior of the "low level vehicle platform" of figure 7.3). *Receives*, together with *invokes*, written as $p \cdot o!\langle e_1, \ldots, e_n\rangle$, are the basic communication activities provided by COWS.

Besides input parameters and sent values, they indicate an *end point* (i.e., a pair composed of a partner name p and an operation name o), through which communication should occur. $p \cdot o$ can be interpreted as a specific implementation of operation o provided by the service identified by the logic name p. An interservice communication takes place when the arguments of a receive and of a concurrent invoke along the same end point do match, and causes replacement of the variables arguments of the receive with the corresponding values arguments of the invoke (within the scope of variables declarations). For example, variables $x_1, \ldots, x_n$, declared local to *Orchestrator* by means of the delimitation operator, are initialized by the receive leading the recovery activity with data provided by *SensorsMonitor*.

The recovery behavior $\mathrm{s}_{\mathrm{engfail}}$, executed when an engine failure occurs, is

$$[p_e, o_e, x_{loc}, x_{list}]\ ((requestCardCharge \mid requestLocation.findServices)$$
$$\mid p_e \cdot o_e?\langle\rangle.p_e \cdot o_e?\langle\rangle.selectServices.orderGarage.\ (orderTowTruck \mid orderRentalCar))$$

$p_e \cdot o_e$ is a scoped end point along which successful termination signals (i.e., communications that carry no data) are exchanged to orchestrate execution of the different components. Variables x_{loc} and x_{list} are used to store the value of the current car's GSP position and the list of closer on-road services discovered. To present the specification of $s_{engfail}$ in terms of the UML actions of figure 7.4, we have used an auxiliary "sequence" notation (e.g., in *requestLocation.findServices*). This notation indicates that execution of *requestLocation* terminates before execution of *findServices* starts. Indeed, *requestLocation .findServices* actually stands for the COWS term

$$p_{car} \cdot o_{reqLoc}!\langle\rangle \mid p_{car} \cdot o_{respLoc}?\langle x_{loc}\rangle.$$
$$(p_{car} \cdot o_{findServ}!\langle x_{loc}\rangle$$
$$\mid p_{car} \cdot o_{found}?\langle x_{list}\rangle.p_e \cdot o_e!\langle\rangle + p_{car} \cdot o_{notFound}?\langle\rangle)$$

where *requestLocation* and *findServices* are

$$requestLocation \triangleq p_{car} \cdot o_{reqLoc}!\langle\rangle \mid p_{car} \cdot o_{respLoc}?\langle x_{loc}\rangle$$
$$findServices \triangleq p_{car} \cdot o_{findServ}!\langle x_{loc}\rangle \mid p_{car} \cdot o_{found}?\langle x_{list}\rangle.p_e \cdot o_e!\langle\rangle + p_{car}o_{notFound}?\langle\rangle$$

Bank, the last service we show, can serve multiple requests simultaneously. This behavior is modeled by exploiting the *replication* operator * _ to spawn in parallel as many copies of its argument term as necessary. The definition of *Bank* is

$$* \; [x_{cust}, x_{cc}, x_{amount}, o_{checkOK}, o_{checkFail}]$$
$$p_{bank} \cdot o_{charge}? \; \langle x_{cust}, \; x_{cc}, \; x_{amount}\rangle.$$
$$(\langle \text{perform some checks and reply on } o_{nocheckOK} \text{ or } o_{checkFail}\rangle$$
$$\mid p_{bank} \cdot o_{checkOK}?\langle\rangle \cdot x_{cust} \cdot o_{chargeOK}!\langle\rangle$$
$$+ \; p_{bank} \cdot o_{checkFail}? \; \langle\rangle \cdot x_{cust} \cdot o_{chargeFail}!\langle\rangle)$$

Once prompted by a request, in contrast to *Orchestrator*, *Bank* creates one specific instance to serve that request and is immediately ready to concurrently serve other requests. Notably, each instance exploits communication on "internal" operations $o_{checkOK}$ and $o_{checkFail}$ to model a conditional choice.

7.6.2 Using Types for Verifying Service Properties

One advantage of using COWS as modeling language is that it already provides some tools for analyzing the models and verifying the properties they enjoy. For example, the type system introduced in Lapadula et al. (2007a) for checking data security properties on COWS terms is a practical and scalable way to provide evidence that a large number of applications enjoy some given properties: from the *type soundness* of the language as a whole, it follows that all well-typed applications do comply with the properties stated by their types. The types permit expression of policies constraining data exchanges in terms of *regions* (i.e., sets of partner names attachable to each single datum). Service programmers can thus settle the partners usable to exchange any given datum (and then the services that can share it), thus avoiding the datum's being accessed (by unwanted services) through unauthorized partners. The language operational semantics uses these annotations to guarantee that computation proceeds according to them.

To provide a flavor of the properties that can be expressed and enforced by using the type system, we illustrate some properties relevant for the scenario modeled above. First, a driver in trouble must be assured that information about his credit card and GSP position cannot become available to unauthorized users. To this aim, the credit card identifier *ccId*, communicated by activity *requestCardCharge* to the service *Bank*, can be annotated with the policy $\{p_{bank}\}$, which allows *Bank* to receive the datum but prevents it from transmitting the datum to other services. Similarly, the car's GSP position stored in x_{loc}, used by services *orderGarage*, *orderTowTruck*, and *orderRentalCar*, can be annotated with the regions $\{x_{garage}\}$, $\{x_{towTruck}\}$, and $\{x_{rentalCar}\}$, respectively, to specify different policies for the same datum, according to the invoked services. Notably, these policies are not statically fixed, but depend on the partner variables x_{garage}, $x_{towTruck}$, and $x_{rentalCar}$, and thus will be determined by the values that these variables assume as computation proceeds. As a final example property, we mention that by using appropriate regions only, including the customer partner name, one can guarantee that critical data of on-road services, such as cost and quality of the service supplied, are not disclosed to competitor services.

7.7 Quantitative Analysis of Service-Level Agreements

In the car repair scenario the quantitative issue of concern relates to how long it will take from the point of engine failure until both a tow truck and a garage have been ordered, and the tow truck is on its way to help the stranded driver. If the duration of each of the service activities which need to take place along the way (*requestLocation*, *findServices*, *orderGarage*, ...) was known exactly, then this calculation would simply involve adding up these times to give the total duration. However, as is usual in service-oriented systems, none of these durations will be known exactly in this case, and the calculation needs to be based on the expected average duration of each of the atomic service events. In this setting, where only the average duration is known, and not the variance or higher moments, the correct distribution to model with is the exponential distribution. Thus, this aspect of the problem naturally lends itself to Markovian representation and analysis, and that is the approach we will take here.

For the quantitative analysis of such systems we use Performance Evaluation Process Algebra (PEPA) (Hillston 1996), which extends classical process algebras by associating a duration with each activity. Thus, where classical process algebras such as CCS and CSP deal with instantaneous actions which abstract away from time, PEPA has continuous-time activities whose durations are quantified by exponentially distributed random variables. Thus PEPA is a *stochastic* process algebra which describes the evolution of a process in continuous time. The operational semantics of the language gives rise to a continuous-time, finite-state stochastic process called a continuous-time Markov chain (CTMC), which can be used to find the steady-state probability distribution over a model. From this it is straightforward to compute conventional performance measures such as utilization or throughput. Here we are instead performing transient analysis of the CTMC, where one considers the probability distribution at a chosen instant of time. It is possible to use these results to perform more complex quantitative analysis, such as computing response-time measures and first passage-time quantiles, as used in service-level agreements. It is also possible to perform scalability analysis by using an altogether different

Table 7.1
Activities and minimum and maximum values of the rates from the model

Activity	Rate	Value min	Value max	Meaning
EngineFailure	r_1	1.0	1.0	Arbitrary value—measurement only begins at the end of this event
RequestLocation, FindServices	r_2	0.9	1.1	Location information can be transmitted in one minute, with little variance, service discovery is similar
CurrentLocation	r_3	0.25	1.25	The driver processes location information and decides to act on this, with high variance
SelectServices	r_4	1.9	2.1	The reasoner takes around thirty seconds to make a decision, with little variance
SelectServices	r_5	0.25	1.25	The on-road repair service takes slightly less than one minute to process orders, with high variance

All times are expressed in minutes. Thus a rate of 1.0 means that something happens once a minute (on average). A rate of 2.0 means that the associated activity happens twice a minute on average, or that its mean or expected duration is thirty seconds, which is an equivalent statement.

representation based on ordinary differential equations. For example, we have investigated with PEPA how models of Web Service execution scale with increasing client population sizes (see Wirsing et al. 2006).

The PEPA process algebra is a compact formal language with a small number of combinators. Components perform activities. Activities have a type and rate specified using *prefix* (.) so that (α, r) denotes performing activity α at rate r and $(\alpha, \top)$ is a partner for this where the other partner in the cooperation determines the rate. Alternative behaviors can be composed in a choice (+). Parallel composition of components uses CSP-style synchronization over a set of activity types ($\bowtie$). Private behavior can be hidden (/).

To perform quantitative analysis, we assign exponentially distributed rates to the activities of our model. Table 7.1 explains the meaning of these. In our modeling we were unwilling to assume that we even knew precisely the average duration of the atomic service events, and required only that these values lie in a range between some minimum and some maximum average value. The less certainty we have about the actual value of the rate, the wider this range must be.

We analyzed the model first using the PEPA Workbench (Gilmore and Hillston 1994), which confirmed that the model had no deadlocks and no transient states, and that all local states of all components were reachable and that all activities were live. We used the ipc/Hydra tool chain (Bradley and Knottenbelt 2004) to assess the service against the following compound service-level agreement (SLA-1) on the orchestration overall.

At least 30 percent of engine failures lead to the tow truck being ordered within 15 minutes and at least 60 percent of engine failures lead to the tow truck being ordered within 30 minutes.

At first sight it might seem that SLA-1 is so generous with the time bounds and confidence bounds that it will easily be satisfied, and that a more demanding SLA-2 could be posed instead: "30 percent of failures dealt with in 10 minutes, 90 percent in 30." However, there is a possibility that each atomic service event in the orchestration will take longer than average and that each of these is operating at its minimum rate, leading to a much longer overall time than might be expected.

We assess SLA-1 using the passage-time quantile computation capabilities provided by ipc/Hydra. We vary rates r2 to r5 across five possible values, leading to $5 \times 5 \times 5 \times 5 = 625$ experiments to be performed. The graphs of computed probability against experiment number for time bounds of 15 minutes and 30 minutes for all 625 experiments are shown in figure 7.7. Using both of these graphs, we determine that SLA-1 is satisfied across the values of the rates of the model, but that the time bounds and confidence bounds are tight, and the more demanding SLA-2 would not be satisfied by some of the combinations of rate values used in the model.

7.8 Concluding Remarks

Service-oriented computing and service-oriented architectures are having a huge impact on IT-based business organizations across the world. However, there are still many open issues regarding the development, analysis, and deployment of such software, some of which touch the very foundations of service-oriented computing.

As a remedy, the EU project Sensoria is developing a novel comprehensive approach to the visual design, formal analysis, and automated deployment of service-oriented software systems where foundational theories, techniques, and methods are fully integrated in a pragmatic software engineering approach.

Compared to other research projects in the field of service-oriented computing, Sensoria focuses heavily on scalable quantitative and qualitative analysis techniques based on formal foundations which can be embedded into a practical software development process. SODIUM,[3] in contrast, focuses on service-modeling semantic support for service discovery, but leaves aside dynamic reconfiguration, model transformation, service deployment, service extraction, and analysis techniques. PLASTIC,[4] on the other hand, is more focused toward development, deployment, and management of service-oriented adaptive applications. Resource management is a major aspect in the PLASTIC approach. The SeCSE project[5] is geared toward development and runtime support for service-oriented computing, again considering formal analysis techniques of services as a secondary field of activity. Sensoria's main research focus and asset in the service-oriented community is therefore the combination of a pragmatic approach with formal theories for service-oriented computing, supporting both development and analysis of service-oriented systems.

We have illustrated service modeling in high-level languages such as SRML or the Sensoria extension of UML, service selection with soft constraints, and analysis of qualitative

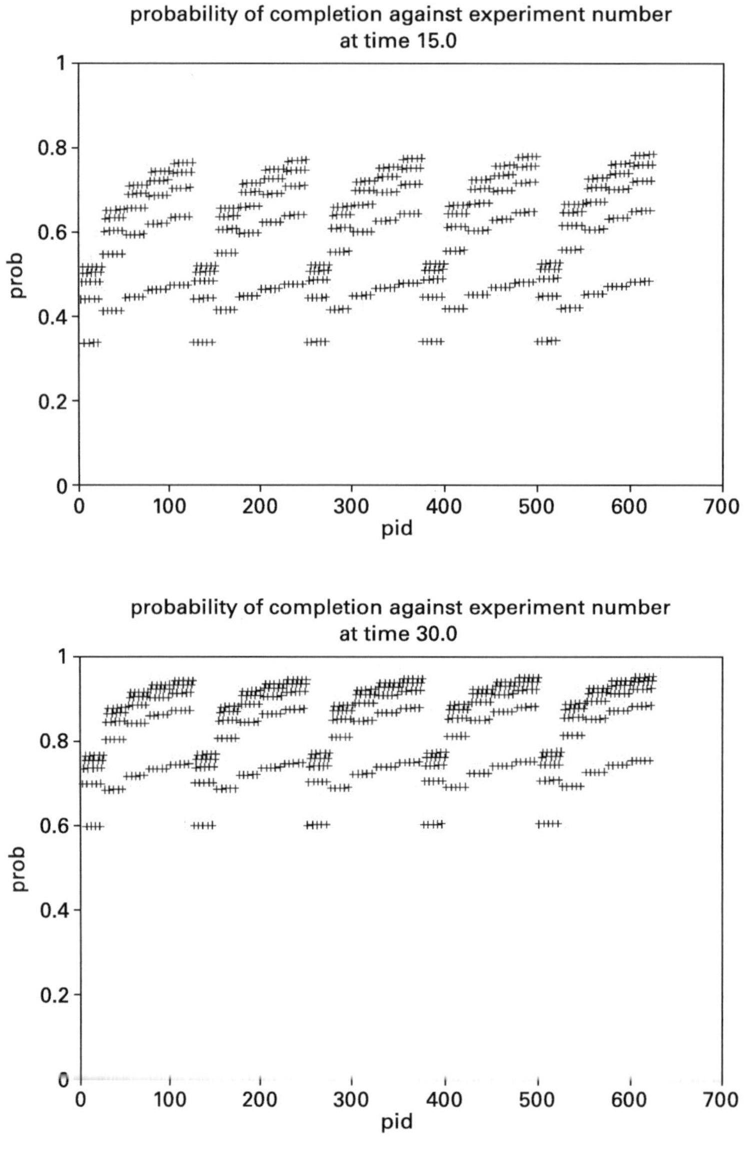

Figure 7.7
Graph of probability of completing the passage from engine failure to completion of order of tow truck within fifteen and thirty minutes plotted against experiment number over all 625 experiments

and quantitative service properties with process calculi such as COWS and PEPA. Further research of the Sensoria project addresses topics including resource consumption of services, security, reconfiguration, deployment, and reengineering of legacy systems into services. To facilitate practical application of these results, we are distributing the Sensoria development environment under an open-source license.

To learn more, please visit our website http://www.sensoria-ist.eu/.

Acknowledgment

The work published in this chapter is partly funded by the European Community under the Sixth Framework Program, contract FP6–IST-2005–016004 SENSORIA. The work reflects only the authors' views. The Community is not liable for any use that may be made of the information contained therein.

Notes

1. http://www.sensoria-ist.eu/.
2. LMU München (coordinator), Germany; TU Denmark at Lyngby, Denmark; FAST GmbH München, S and N AG, Paderborn (both Germany); Budapest University of Technology and Economics, Hungary; Università di Bologna, Università di Firenze, Universitá di Pisa, Universitá di Trento, ISTI Pisa, Telecom Italia Lab Torino, School of Management Politecnico di Milano (all Italy); Warsaw University, Poland; ATX Software SA, Universidade de Lisboa (both Portugal); Imperial College London, University College London, University of Edinburgh, University of Leicester (all United Kingdom).
3. http://www.atc.gr/sodium/.
4. http://www.ist-plastic.org/.
5. http://secse.eng.it/.

References

Beisiegel, Michael, Henning Blohm, Dave Booz, Jean-Jacques Dubray, Adrian Colyer, Mike Edwards, Don Ferguson, Bill Flood, Mike Greenberg, Dan Kearns, Jim Marino, Jeff Mischkinsky, Martin Nally, Greg Pavlik, Mike Rowley, Ken Tam, and Carl Trieloff. 2005. Building Systems Using a Service Oriented Architecture. White paper, SCA Consortium. htttp://www.oracle.com/technology/tech/webservices/standards/sca/pdf/SCA%'_White_Paper1_09.pdf.

Bistarelli, Stefano. 2004. *Semirings for Soft Constraint Solving and Programming*. LNCS 2962. Berlin: Springer.

Bistarelli, Stefano, Ugo Montanari, and Francesca Rossi. 1997. Semiring-based constraint satisfaction and optimization. *Journal of the ACM* 44(2): 201–236.

Bocchi, Laura, Yi Hong, Antónia Lopes, and José Luiz Fiadeiro. 2007. From BPEL to SRML: A formal transformational approach. In *Proceedings of the 4th International Workshop on Web Services and Formal Methods* (WS-FM '07). Berlin: Springer.

Bradley, Jeremy T., and William J. Knottenbelt. 2004. The ipc/HYDRA tool chain for the analysis of PEPA models. In *Proceedings of the 1st International Conference on the Quantitative Evaluation of Systems* (QEST 2004), pp. 334–335.

Bruni, Roberto, Gianluigi Ferrari, Hernán Melgratti, Ugo Montanari, Daniele Strollo, and Emilio Tuosto. 2005. From theory to practice in transactional composition of web services. In M. Bravetti, L. Kloul, and G. Zavattaro, eds., *Formal Techniques for Computer Systems and Business Processes: Proceedings of WS-FM 2005, 2nd International Workshop on Web Services and Formal Methods*. LNCS 3670, pp. 272–286. Berlin: Springer Verlag.

Fiadeiro, José Luiz, Antónia Lopes, and Laura Bocchi. 2006. A formal approach to service component architecture. In *Web Services and Formal Methods*. LNCS 4184, pp. 193–213. Beerlin: Springer.

Gilmore, Stephen, and Jane Hillston. 1994. The PEPA Workbench: A tool to support a process algebra-based approach to performance modelling. In *Proceedings of the 7th International Conference on Modelling Techniques and Tools for Computer Performance Evaluation*. LNCS 794, pp. 353–368. Berlin: Springer Verlag.

Hillston, Jane. 1996. *A Compositional Approach to Performance Modelling*. Cambridge: Cambridge University Press.

Lapadula, Alessandro, Rosario Pugliese, and Francesco Tiezzi. 2007a. Regulating data exchange in service oriented applications. In *Proceedings of the IPM International Symposium on Fundamentals of Software Engineering* (FSEN '07). LNCS 4767, pp. 223–239. Berlin: Springer.

Lapadula, Alessandro, Rosario Pugliese, and Francesco Tiezzi. 2007b. A calculus for orchestration of Web Services. In *Proceedings of the 16th European Symposium on Programming* (ESOP '07). LNCS 4421, pp. 33–47. Berlin: Springer.

Sensoria Project. Web site for the Sensoria Development Environment. http://svn.pst.ifi.lmu.de/trac/sct.

Wirsing, Martin, Allan Clark, Stephen Gilmore, Matthias Hölzl, Alexander Knapp, Nora Koch, and Andreas Schroeder. 2006. Semantic-based development of service-oriented systems. In E. Najn et al., eds., *Proceedings of the 26th IFIP WG 6.1 International Conference on Formal Methods for Networked and Distributed Systems* (FORTE '06). LNCS 4229, pp. 24–45. Berlin: Springer.

Wirsing, Martin, Laura Bocchi, Allan Clark, José Luiz Fiadeiro, Stephen Gilmore, Matthias Hölzl, Nora Koch, Philip Mayer, Rosario Pugliese, and Andreas Schroeder. 2007a. Sensoria: Engineering for Service-Oriented Overlay Computers. Technical Report 0702, Ludwig-Maximilians-Universität München, Institut für Informatik, PST.

Wirsing, Martin, Rocco De Nicola, Stephen Gilmore, Matthias Hölzl, Roberto Lucchi, Mirco Tribastone, and Gianluigi Zavattaro. 2007b. Sensoria process calculi for service-oriented computing. In Ugo Montanari, Don Sannella, and Roberto Bruni, eds., *Second Symposium on Trustworthy Global Computing* (TGC 2006). LNCS 4661. Berlin: Springer.

Wirsing, Martin, Grit Denker, Carolyn Talcott, Andy Poggio, and Linda Briesemeister. 2007c. A rewriting logic framework for soft constraints. *Electron. Notes in Theoretical Computer Science* 176(4): 181–197.

8 ASTRO: Supporting the Composition of Distributed Business Processes in the E-Government Domain

Marco Pistore, Pietro Braghieri, Piergiorgio Bertoli, Antonio Biscaglia, Annapaola Marconi, Stefano Pintarelli, and Michele Trainotti

8.1 Introduction

Several service-oriented applications require the development and execution of distributed business processes that cross organizational boundaries. This is the case, for example, with applications in the e-government domain, where services realize complex and long-running procedures, in most cases spread across different offices and departments. Similarly, in e-commerce applications, services consist of distributed business processes that communicate with various online entities, such as online shops and e-banking applications. In all these process-oriented, service-based applications, the idea is that new services, implementing processes that are spread among different offices, departments, companies, and organizations, are obtained by composing already available component services, often developed by third parties.

The ASTRO (http://www.astroproject.org/) project aims at supporting the automated composition of process-oriented, service-based systems, both at design time and at runtime, and at developing techniques and tools that enact the effective, reliable, low-cost, and time-efficient composition and monitoring of distributed business processes.

Design-time support to the composition of process-oriented services is achieved by the automated synthesis of executable composite Web Services, expressed in WS-BPEL (Andrews et al. 2003). WS-BPEL is an XML-based language that provides an operational description of the stateful behavior of Web Services on top of interfaces defined via WSDL specifications (Christensen et al. 2001). WS-BPEL comes in two variants; the first, called *abstract* WS-BPEL, allows third parties to expose their services as abstract stateful protocols which may hide details on the actual implementation of their internal logics—a crucial feature in a distributed setting where internal procedures must be carefully kept private. In contrast, *executable* WS-BPEL programs specify every detail and are used to implement a process defining a service which can be run on engines such as the ActiveBPEL[1] engine or the Oracle BPEL[2] Process Manager.

Starting from a set of component services published as abstract WS-BPEL programs, and given a set of requirements that model the desired properties of the composite service we aim at, we automatically generate an executable WS-BPEL (i.e., a fully instantiated WS-BPEL program that, by interacting with the component services, implements the desired composite Web Service).

To keep composition requirements as simple as possible, our approach clearly separates different aspects of such requirements, splitting them into control, data, and flow requirements. *Control requirements* define constraints, based on semantic annotations of the components services that control the interaction flow among different processes (e.g., termination conditions and transactional issues). For instance, actors taking part in an e-government tax payment procedure may foresee different behaviors associated with failures of different procedure steps; this originates a variety of termination conditions, only some of them being deemed acceptable. *Data requirements* specify how data should be exchanged among component services, stating how incoming and outgoing messages should be forwarded and manipulated among services. For instance, in a tax payment scenario, complex data structures that carry information about the citizen, his work, and other properties must be communicated and used by different actors. Finally, *flow requirements* serve to deal with the fact that real-world business processes usually do not handle a single item at a time, but process sets of items at once. For instance, e-government procedures for tax payment usually process all the requests that must be considered in a given period of time. That is, though the business process for a single item can be rather simple, the real implementation must handle sets of items each of which can follow a different flow.

Runtime support for the composition of process-oriented services is necessary in the case of distributed business processes to monitor the behavior of the system and its distributed components. In particular, the presence of aggregate flows of information makes monitoring a crucial activity to gather statistics over such flows, and to identify situations which, even though admissible in single instances, are unexpectedly frequent (e.g., an online bank refuses money transfers most of the time). A further motivation is the fact that, owing to the lack of control on the way third-party services are implemented and modified, even compositions that are designed and implemented correctly can violate requirements at runtime, and such violations need to be reported promptly.

ASTRO provides runtime support to the composition of process-oriented services by allowing the monitoring of composite services, and realizing a clear separation between the business logic of a Web Service and its monitoring. The ASTRO architecture supports both monitors that deal with the execution of a single instance of process and monitors that report aggregated information about sets of instances of a process type. Properties and situations to be monitored are specified in language that allows for expressing boolean, statistical, and time-related properties, and for automatic conversion into monitoring agents.

ASTRO's contributions to support service composition at design time and runtime fit essentially into the service integration layer of the NESSI taxonomic framework. More specifically, in terms of the research plans of the SOC road map, the ASTRO tool set covers a substantial part of the composition layer, focusing essentially on the provision of innovative and powerful orchestration functionalities. To a lesser extent, ASTRO also contributes to the management and monitoring layers by allowing the establishment and runtime checking of SLA rules through automated monitoring functionalities.

In this work, we describe in detail the ASTRO approach, and the results of applying the techniques developed in ASTRO to a real application in the e-government sector, involving the payment of municipal taxes on solid waste. Section 8.2 introduces the case study, describing the tax payment procedure and the protocols realized by the involved actors. Section 8.3 describes the ASTRO approach to service composition, and its application to the case study. Section 8.4 describes the ASTRO approach to service composition and its application to the case study. Section 8.5 draws conclusions and describes lines of work for further extensions to the ASTRO approach.

8.2 The Case: Citizen Tax Payment System

The payment of municipal taxes in Italy consists of a number of complex processes that involve different and independent public administration offices, as well as citizens, companies, and banks. In this chapter we will consider the process of paying a specific municipal tax, the TARSU (TAssa sui Rifiuti Solidi Urbani, i.e., municipal solid waste tax). The TARSU is used by the municipality to pay for the collection and the disposal of solid waste, and is calculated on the basis of the size of the house occupied and of the number of persons living in the house.

In order to ease the understanding of the process, we first provide an overview of the TARSU payment process, which describes the way the process is conducted in order to carry out a single procedure for tax payment; then we focus on the actual implementation of the actors taking part in the procedure.

8.2.1 The TARSU Procedure

Figure 8.1 shows the TARSU payment process, which involves three actors: the Ufficio Tributi (i.e., the Tax Office), the Ufficio Ragioneria (i.e., the Accounting Office), and the Banca Tesoriere (i.e., the Treasury). The process is initiated by the Ufficio Tributi, which calculates the tax amount and sends a tax account registration request to the Ufficio Ragioneria and a payment request to the Banca Tesoriere, suspending for a response. At this stage, the Banca Tesoriere handles the payment request by forwarding it to the citizen's bank, and notifies Ufficio Tributi of the result. Then, if the tax payment request has been successful, the Ufficio Tributi notifies the Ufficio Ragioneria, which, in turn, generates an account receipt and sends it back to both Banca Tesoriere and Ufficio Tributi.

The implementation of the TARSU procedure described in figure 8.1 requires cooperation between the heterogeneous and distributed procedures of the three actors (Ufficio Tributi,

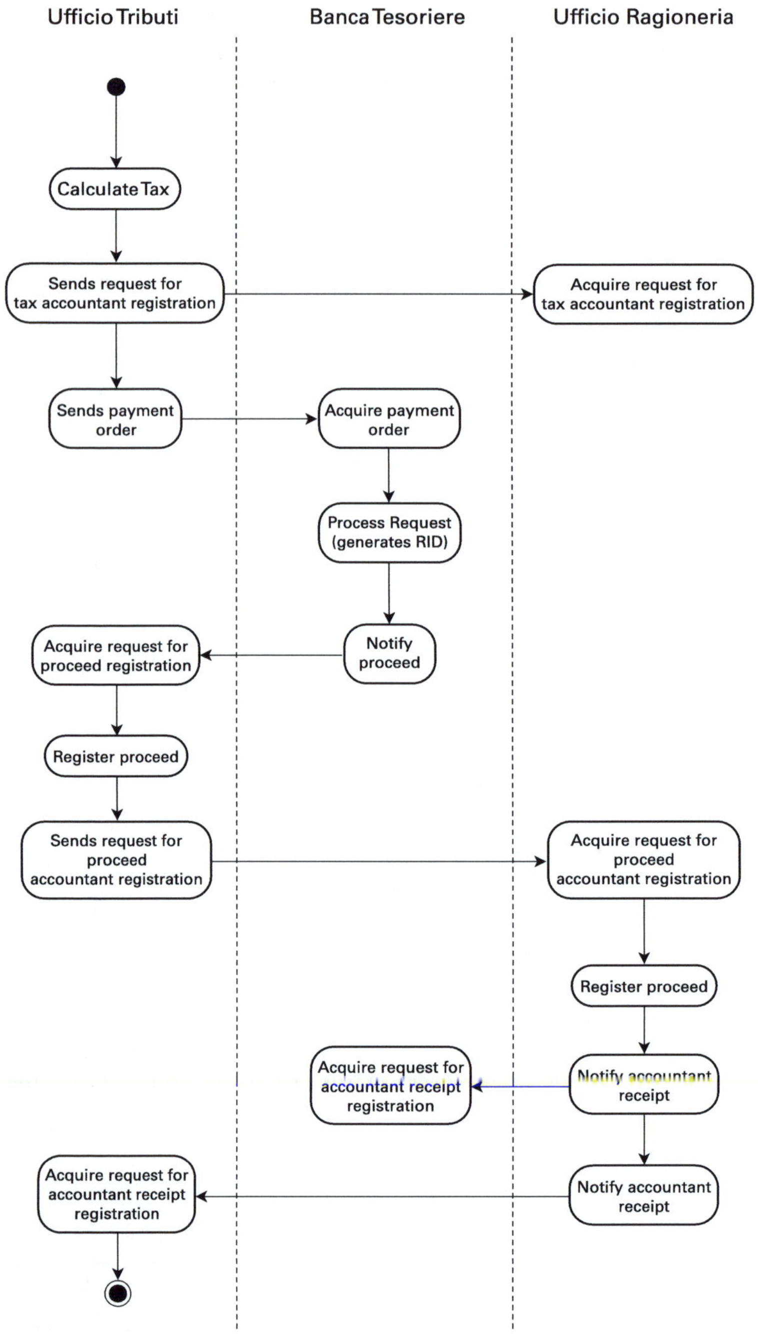

Figure 8.1
TARSU process activity diagram

Banca Tesoriere, Ufficio Ragioneria). This requires the presence of a further "orchestrating" actor that links the actors in a proper way, by passing around and manipulating the information they produce. Though the process in figure 8.1 is rather simple and very generic, its implementation is far from trivial. Indeed, the process as shown does not consider a variety of issues that arise in its actual implementation. In particular:

- Several *non-nominal* behaviors diverge from the nominal case depicted in figure 8.1. For instance, the citizen may not be able to pay his tax; the payment may take an unacceptably long time to complete; or errors may arise in the transfer of personal data implied by the procedure. Often, in real-world workflow, specifications are informally described using natural language instead of being embodied in the protocol definition. This is also the case for our TARSU scenario; however, in order to present the TARSU as a Web Service that can be further reused by other services, non-nominal cases must be incorporated into the actors' protocol instead of being embodied in the protocol definition.
- The business logic schematically described in figure 8.1 involves transferring and manipulating *complex data structures*. For instance, the data needed to handle payment requests consist of structured records, including bank account information that are necessary to proceed to payment emission.

  Different services, developed by different partners, may represent equivalent information in different ways or make use of different abstractions. For instance, one service may require the full address of a customer, and another may need only the town he resides in. Identifying the proper way to match different representations of information is a difficult and error-prone task. To tackle this problem it is necessary to devise easy-to-use tools for specifying data-matching templates.
- Though figure 8.1 represents a TARSU process being enacted for a single tax payment, the actual implementation of the process follows a rather different line. Indeed, e-government procedures almost never handle each citizen request separately; for practical reasons, requests are usually handled in batches, based on the enforcement of deadlines. For instance, in Italy, waste taxes must be paid once a year; for this reason, the Ufficio Tributi service accumulates requests and sends them out every six months. In contrast, private actors (e.g., an online bank) usually process single requests. That is, data produced by different actors need to be suitably dispatched or aggregated, depending on the design of flows of data.

The actual enactment of the procedure by means of an orchestrating actor will need to consider the way these aspects are modeled by the specific implementations of the Ufficio Tributi, Ufficio Ragioneria, and Banca Tesoriere.

8.2.2 The Actors

We now describe in a more detailed way the implementation of the actors involved in the TARSU, referring specifically to the one provided by the province of Trento (which we slightly abridge for ease of understanding). In such a context, each of the three involved public administration partners (Ufficio Tributi, Ufficio Ragioneria, and Banca Tesoriere) has been developed independently, based on different technologies and software systems. For example, Ufficio Tributi uses the Civilia platform developed by DeltaDator, and relies on J2EE technology. Banca Tesoriere uses an AS/400 legacy system. This situation is rather typical at the current stage of development of distributed applications; these technological gaps must be solved to achieve the complete interoperability of the functionalities realized by the partners in order to realize the TARSU process. This is achieved by wrapping each of the existing functionalities within a WS-BPEL interface that exposes the protocol (accompanied by a WSDL interface that defines its static counterpart in terms of inputs/outputs). As a result, we obtain the protocols discussed below.

Ufficio Tributi The main role of the Ufficio Tributi is to manage calculation and collection of municipal taxes such as TARSU and ICI (Imposta Comunale sugli Immobili, i.e., local taxation on buildings). Tax amounts depend on data such as the number of family members and the size of the house. It is Ufficio Tributi's responsibility to obtain and maintain all the data needed to calculate municipal tax amounts, and to verify that the information declared by the citizens is correct.

Figure 8.2 shows the WS-BPEL for the Ufficio Tributi service, as represented by Active-BPEL Designer,[3] one of the several WS-BPEL Designer tools that have been proposed to ease the work of business experts/analysts when defining WS-BPEL business processes. Such a graphical notation maps an XML format of the language and hides several details of each WS-BPEL activity. A more synthetic view of the control flow of the service is depicted as a state-transition system (STS), in figure 8.3.

The "?" and "!" notations are used to represent, respectively, reception and transmission of messages. Remaining activities consist of internal manipulations of data. Annotations attached to the final states of the protocol ("$\surd$" and "$\times$") are used for distinguishing different termination cases, and will be explained in section 8.3. Finally, the figure also shows, on the left side, the input/output data exchanged by the service, which in the actual service are presented by means of a WSDL specification.

The process starts when the system needs to compute the TARSU tax amount, as indicated by the first activity in figure 8.2. First, the citizen must be registered into a payment system and be sent a prepared payment request. Then, once the tax amount is computed using the available data, the Ufficio Tributi service prepares a payment request and waits for notification of whether or not payment has been successfully completed. If payment is not completed, the process aborts (left branch of the *Pick* activity). Otherwise (right branch of the *Pick* activity), the data needed to execute the payment are sent. If the payment is completed, it is returned, together with the confirmation and an accountant's receipt that is used to update the citizen's tax payment position.

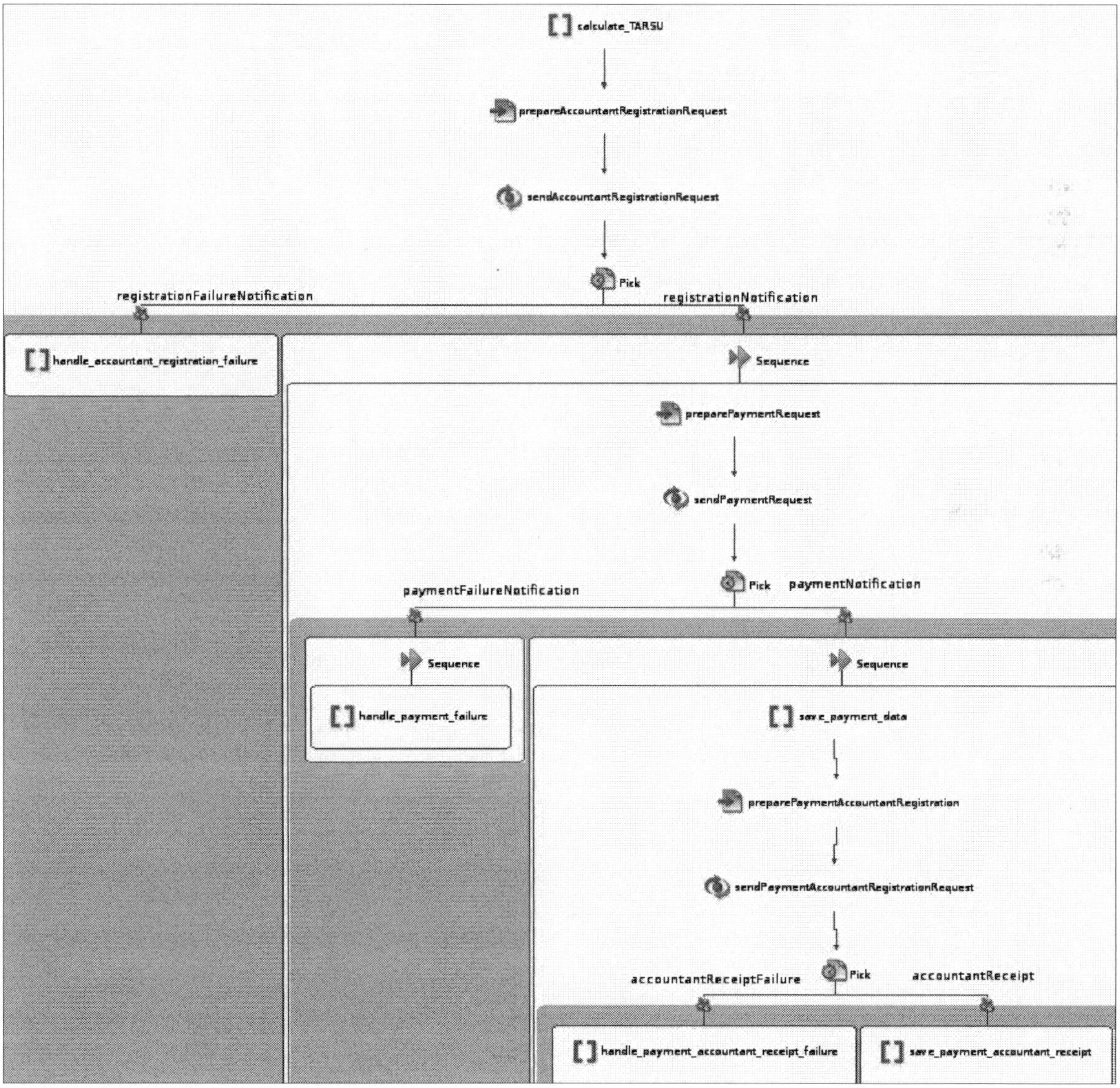

Figure 8.2
Abstract WS-BPEL for Ufficio Tributi service

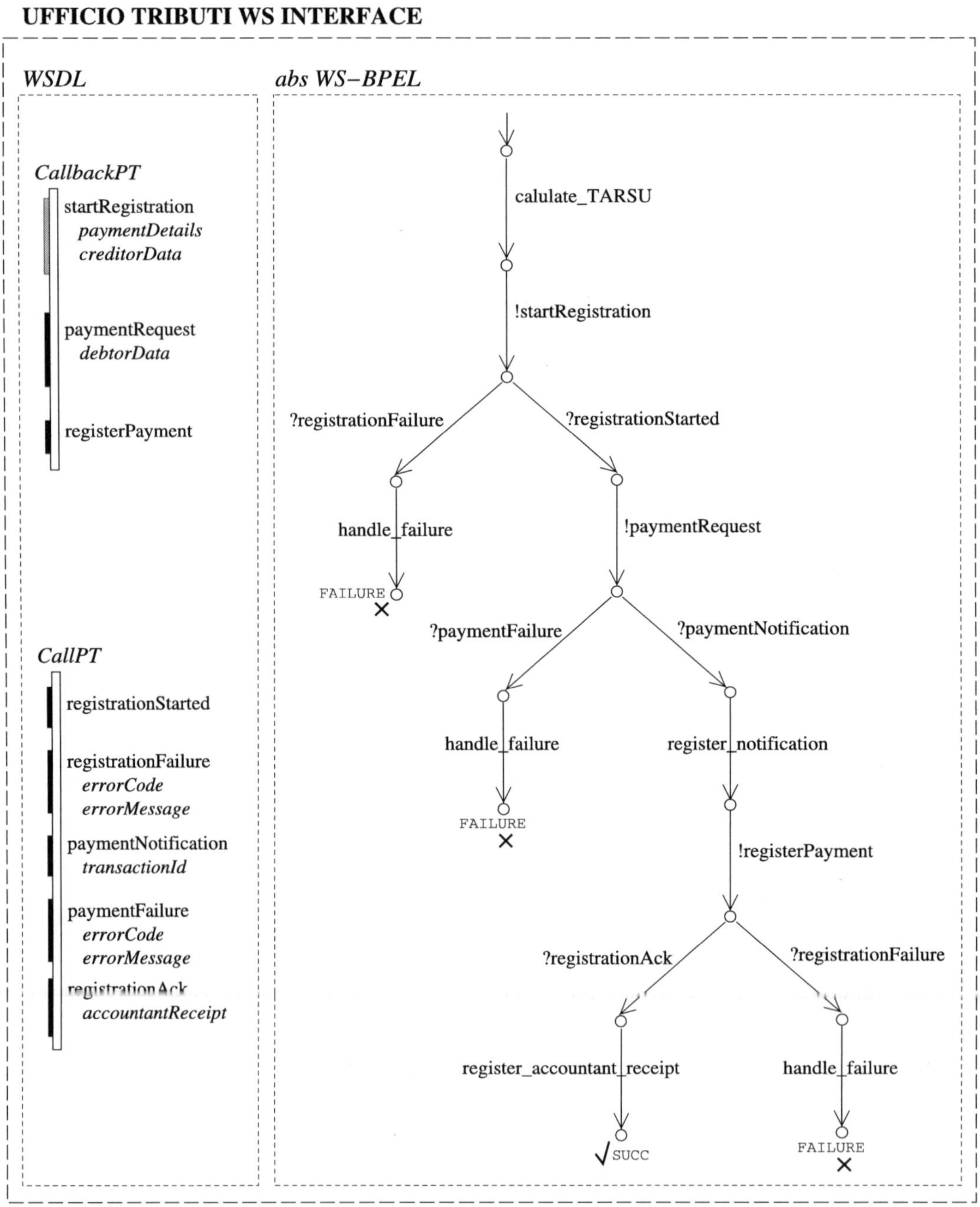

Figure 8.3
Control flow (as STS) for the Ufficio Tributi service

Banca Tesoriere The Banca Tesoriere service has the main role to hold and manage the municipal funds by implementing functionalities related to the payment of public office accounts, in a way similar to those of a bank. Indeed, in several cases, this service is farmed out to a private bank by the municipality. The abstract WS-BPEL of the Banca Tesoriere is depicted in figure 8.4, and its corresponding view as an STS appears in figure 8.5. The process starts when a payment request is received. The data received include the identity of the tax payer and the amount due to the municipality. The Banca Tesoriere handles the payment request and then notifies the requester whether or not the payment has been made. If the payment is completed, Banca Tesoriere waits for the accountant's receipt.

Ufficio Ragioneria The Ufficio Ragioneria deals with municipal accounting. Its main roles are managing public budgets and handling public finances. The Ufficio Ragioneria interface protocol is shown in figure 8.6; we do not report its abstract WS-BPEL view for reasons of space. The process first receives a request for registering a possible tax payer; however, the registration procedure may fail for structural reasons, and in which case, an explanation is sent to the requester. Otherwise, the service waits for a request to register the payment of the citizen or to abort the procedure altogether. Also, whether the registration of the payment succeeds or fails, an appropriate message is sent to the requester.

8.3 Supporting the Process: Composition

In order to enforce the TARSU procedure, the actors involved must be coordinated appropriately. The construction of the logic that realizes such a coordination is the goal of the composition task. In particular, ASTRO envisages an automated composition approach, based on the ideas expressed in Pistore, Traverso, et al. (2005), Pistore, Marconi, et al. (2005), and Marconi, Pistore, and Traverso (2006); in this approach, an orchestrator process is constructed that establishes a dialogue with the component services such that the established protocol obeys some formal constraints that represent the expected behavior of the overall process. The orchestrator itself is constructed as a WS-BPEL process, enabling the uniform treatment of composite and component services by means of standard tools (e.g., the ActiveBPEL platform). Thus, starting from the abstract WS-BPEL of the available components, and based on formal composition requirements, the outcome of the composition is the executable WS-BPEL composite service implementation, together with its external interface (abstract WS-BPEL and WSDL).

The composite service must be satisfactory under all the aspects discussed in the introduction. It must deal with nominal as well as non-nominal behaviors of the components services; it must match and combine the complex data structures they exchange; it must deal with flows of information that aggregate and dispatch results from single requests.

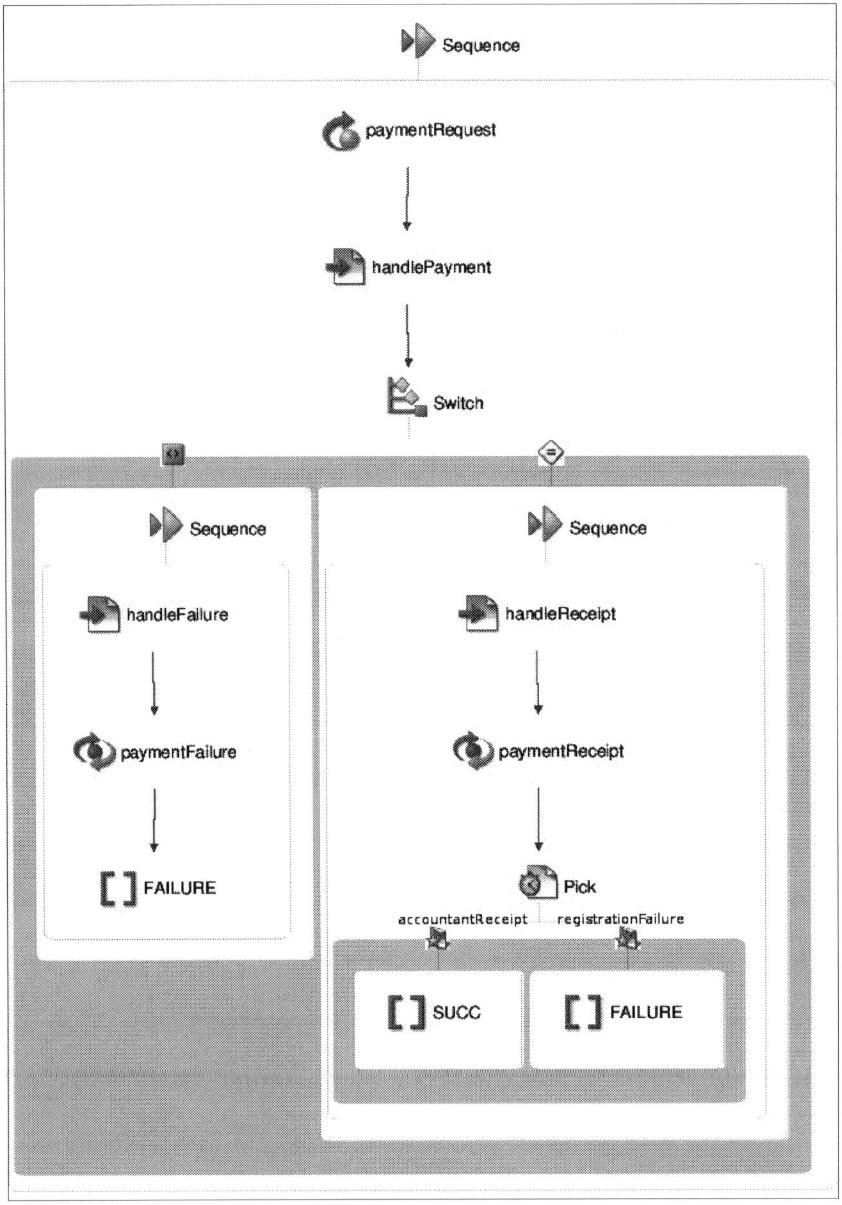

Figure 8.4
Abstract WS-BPEL for Banca Tesoriere service

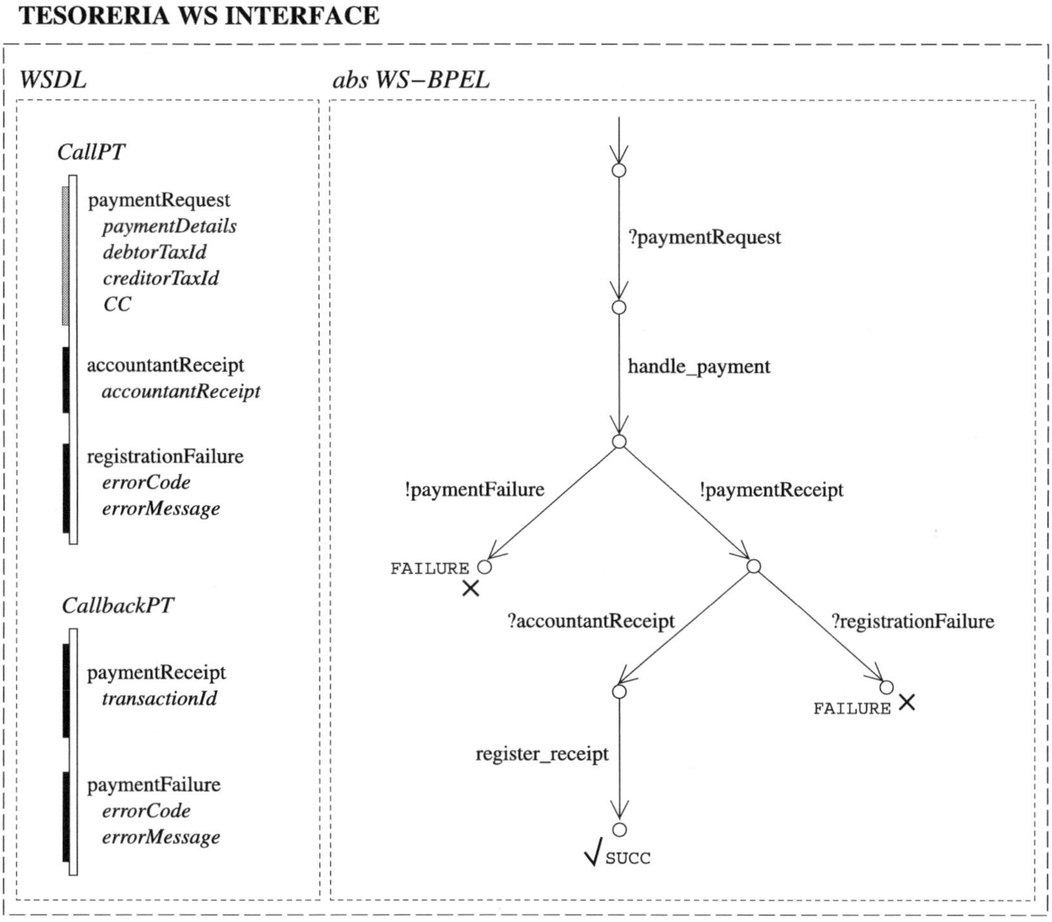

Figure 8.5
Control flow (as STS) for the Banca Tesoriere service

Each of these orthogonal aspects is associated with specific requirements; for this reason, our methodology foresees a structured description of requirements in terms of separate components: *data requirements*, *control requirements*, and *flow requirements*, which answer the issues mentioned above in a direct way.

8.3.1 Control Requirements

Control requirements are used to handle the presence of different (nominal and nonnominal) behaviors of component services by allowing the description of "allowed combinations of behaviors" at different levels of preferences.

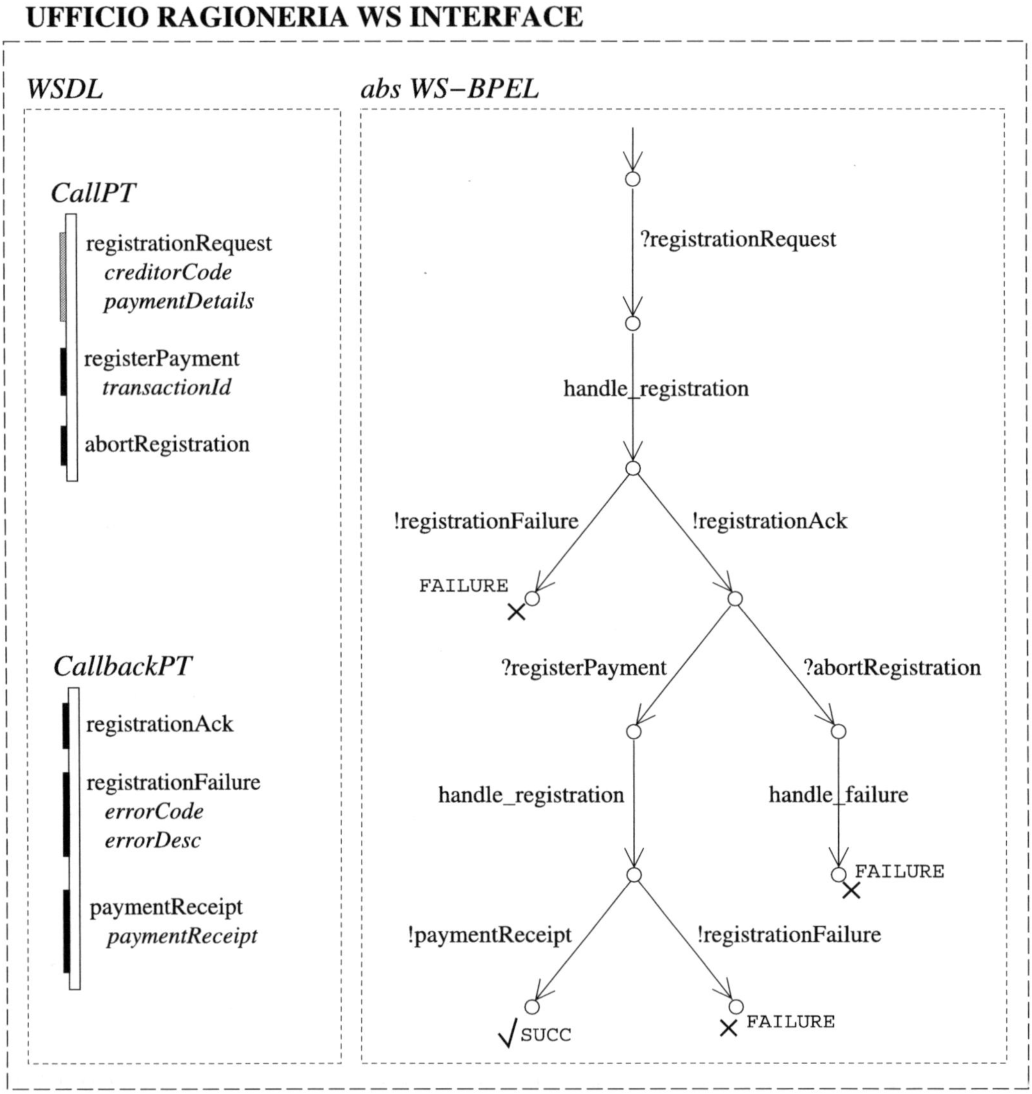

Figure 8.6
Control flow (as STS) for the Ufficio Ragioneria service

Table 8.1
Logical requirements for the TARSU domain

	Ufficio Tributi	Banca Tesoriere	Ufficio Ragioneria
Primary	$\surd$	$\surd$	$\surd$
Secondary	$\times$	$\times$	$\times$

In order to achieve this, the developer must first define termination conditions by annotating the abstract WS-BPEL of the component services with simple semantic information. In particular, in the specification of each service abstract WS-BPEL protocol, we must mark some states as successful (symbol $\surd$) and others as failing (symbol $\times$). Consider, for instance, the Ufficio Tributi service in figure 8.3. When it receives a message carrying the accountant's receipt information, the tax payment has been registered and the protocol terminates successfully. The protocol terminates in failure if the payment is not made.

Then, based on the termination conditions of the component services, the allowed combinations are layered into a primary and a secondary control requirement. The former identifies the "desirable" final situations, and the latter identifies the "acceptable" ones. Such control requirements can be specified in a very simple way by the developer through tables (in our case, the layering is expressed in table 8.1).

The primary requirement is to reach a situation where all the services are in a successful state, modeling the fact that the TARSU payment procedure completed successfully. The secondary requirement is that it is also acceptable to reach a situation where Ufficio Tributi, Banca Tesoriere, and Ufficio Ragioneria are unsuccessful. In our approach, such a table is automatically translated into an intermediate internal formal language that represents requirements in terms of automata that impose constraints on the behavior of the composite service.

As a result, the execution of a composite service obeying such a requirement may reach a state in which it is not possible to satisfy the primary requirement (e.g., the citizen does not pay on time); but even when such a state is reached, the secondary requirement must be guaranteed.

As also shown by our experience in different settings (Marconi, Pistore, and Traverso (2007); Pistore, Traverso, and Bertoli (2005); Marconi, Pistore and Traverso (2006); Pistore et al. (2005)), our table-based language for control requirements is an appropriate compromise that provides the ability to express requirements about the possible behaviors exposed by real-life services, while keeping the interface reasonably intuitive and simple.

8.3.2 Requirements

Control requirements abstract completely from the relationship between the data exchanged between the component services and the composite service. This crucial aspect is taken in charge by data requirements. In particular, data requirements concern the specification of how incoming messages must be used by the composite service (from simple forwarding to complex data manipulation) to obtain outgoing messages.

In the ASTRO approach, data requirements are specified using the formal modeling language proposed in Marconi, Pistore, and Traverso (2006), which adopts an intuitive and easy-to-define graphical notation to specify complex requirements concerning data manipulation and exchange. All these requirements are collected in a diagram called a data net. A data net is a graph whose elements are nodes, arcs, and gates. Nodes are used as either entry or exit points to/from the net, and represent sources of messages (input nodes) or the consumption of messages (output nodes). For instance, in figure 8.7, the input node (full circle) labeled *paymentDetails* indicates that some payment details are provided by the (interface of the) Ufficio Tributi; the output node (empty circle) with the same label indicates that such data are read by the Banca Tesoriere. Different types of gates are available; each type of gate features one or more entry points and one or more exit points, and it represents a specific constraint on the way the messages flowing in via the entry points are propagated to the exit points. For instance, a specific kind of gate is used to "multiplex" its only input to all of its outputs; this is the case of the leftmost gate in figure 8.7, which serves to duplicate payment details data coming from the Ufficio Tributi to both the Banca Tesoriere and the Ufficio Ragioneria. A different kind of gate, with one input and one output, is used to compute a function. (See, e.g., the *get_creditorTaxId* gate in figure 8.7.)

This is useful to define data mediation operations, when the output data of one service and the input data of another service do not match. Other kinds of gates are used to combine several input messages into a single output message, to keep echoing a single input message in output, and so on. Arcs are used as links between nodes and gates; they represent the flow of messages from the input nodes to the output nodes, possible via some gates.

A complete and formal description of the language is reported in Marconi, Pistore, and Traverso (2006); intuitively, the semantics of a data net is based on representing each component of the net as a state transition system (STS) that progresses on the basis of input messages, and in doing so, may produce output messages. Naturally, each kind of gate is associated with a specific STS schema. Then, the service that is to be composed according to a data requirement must conform to the behaviors accepted by the set of synchronized STSs associated with the data net.

In our example the data requirements are represented by the data net in figure 8.7. For instance, considering the excerpt in figure 8.8, the *paymentDetails* information received in the *startRegistration* message from the Ufficio Tributi must be forwarded both to the Banca Tesoriere service (through the *paymentRequest* message) and to the Ufficio Ragioneria (through the *registrationRequest* message). Also, the *creditorTaxId* information to be sent in the Banca Tesoriere *paymentRequest* message must be extracted from the *creditorData*

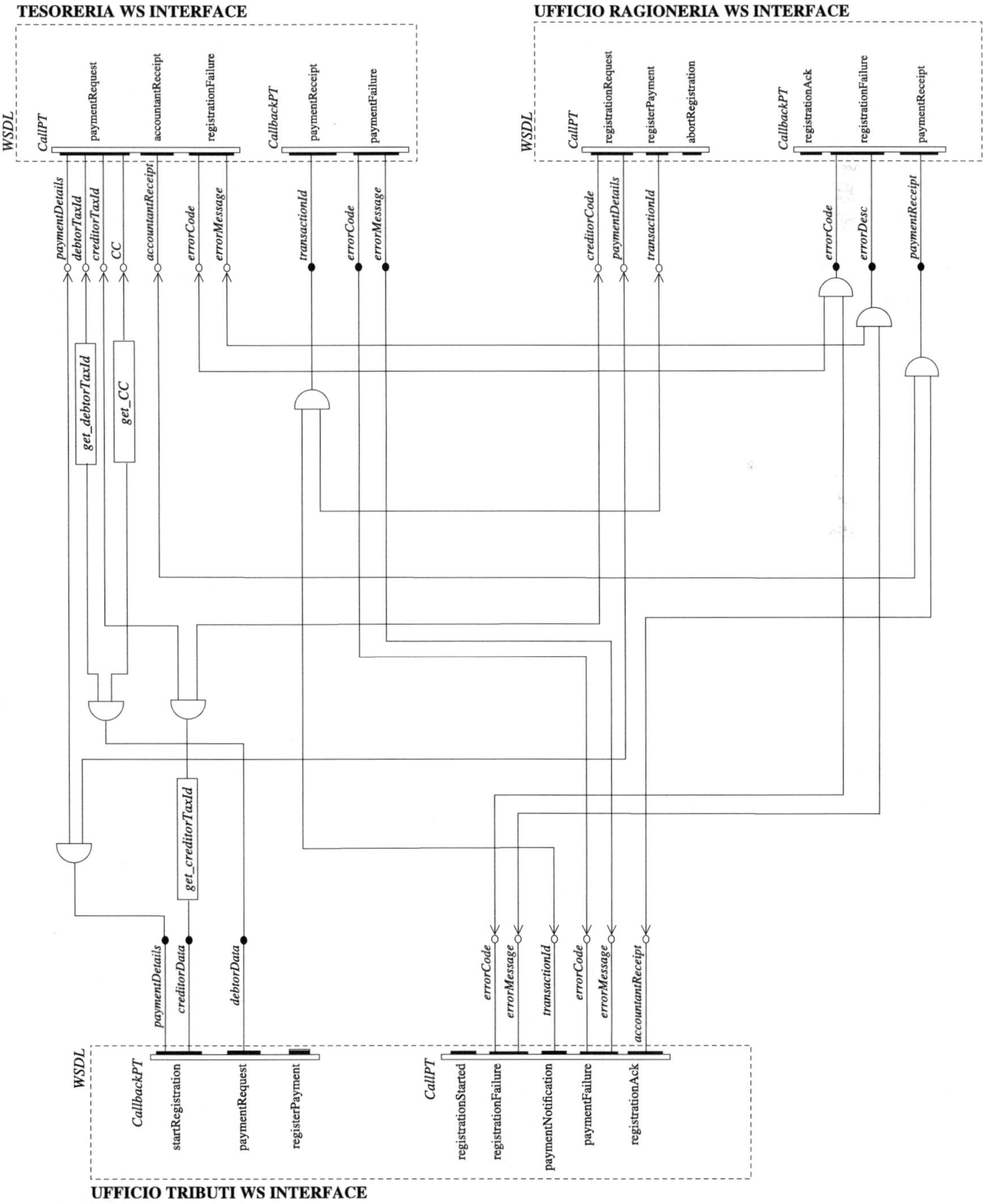

Figure 8.7
Data requirements

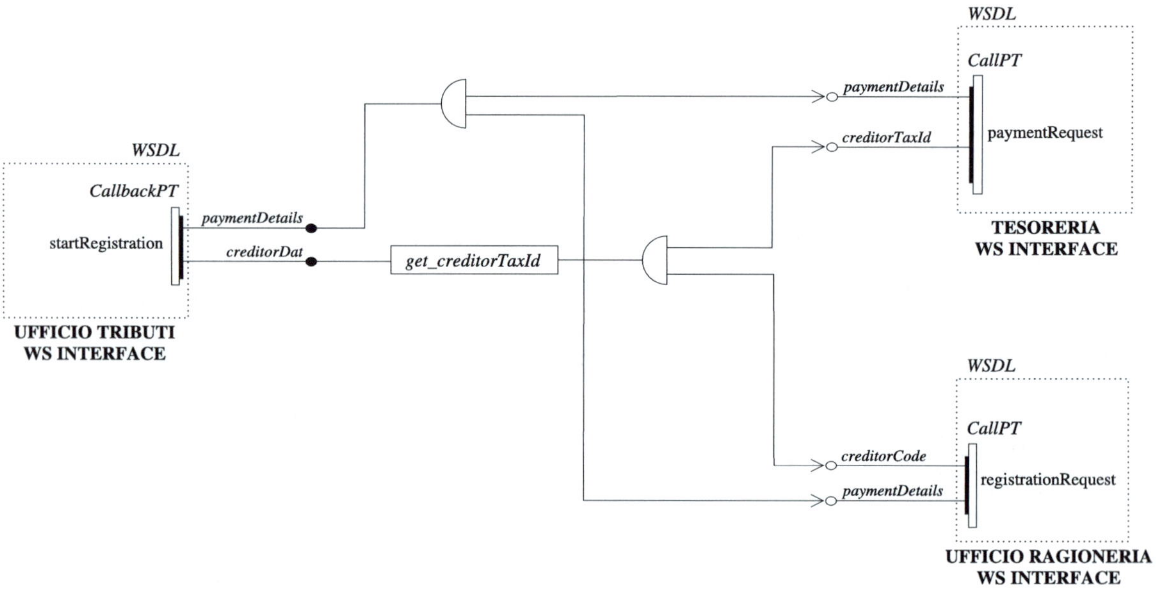

Figure 8.8
An excerpt of the data requirements

part of the *paymentRequest* message received by the Ufficio Tributi; the internal function (*get_creditorTaxId*) has been defined for this purpose, and will be used by the composite service to properly manipulate data. More specifically, such an internal function is specified as an expression using XPath, the standard language used in WS-BPEL assignments. XPath is an expression language for addressing portions of an XML document, or for computing values (strings, numbers, or boolean values) based on the content of an XML document. For instance, the XPath specification of *get_creditorTaxId*, defining how to obtain the *creditorTaxId* navigating the XML tree structure of part *creditorData*, is the following:

get_creditorTaxId =
/nsUT:paymentRequestMsg/nsUT:creditorData/nsUT:taxCode

Similarly to the above, all outgoing message parts are obtained by properly aggregating, manipulating, or simply forwarding incoming message parts.

8.3.3 Flow Requirements

Neither control requirements nor data requirements take into account the issue of aggregating the behavior of single instances of services execution according to flow annotations. For instance, in the TARSU scenario, the composite service needs to take into account that the Ufficio Tributi service works on a batch basis, once a year, whereas the Ufficio Ragioneria acts on a "per request" basis; to synchronize these services, the composite service must suitably dispatch the batches coming from the Ufficio Tributi to the Ufficio Ragioneria. At the same time, the service must collect the single instances from the Ufficio Ragioneria so as to build batches for the Ufficio Tributi.

These kinds of constraints are captured by the "flow" component of requirements, which consists of annotating the input/output ports of the composite service with flow annotations, analogously with what is done for the inputs/outputs of component services. This is performed by enriching the data net language, and in particular input/output nodes, with annotations that specify the way instances are aggregated into data flows. Once more, our aim is to propose a language simple enough to express the vast majority of real-life scenarios, yet simple enough to be fully and easily understood by the developer.

We are currently identifying standard patterns in flow requirements, and using them to define a standard language of annotations that can be attached to WS-BPEL, and that allow the specification of aggregation conditions on the basis of temporal constraints, of constraints on the number of instances, and on constraints on data values.

For instance, it is possible to say that a certain action takes place every twelve months, collecting all the instances in that period; or that batches of 100 requests are grouped together; or that requests are grouped together until the sum of their values exceeds a given amount. Figure 8.9 presents the annotated diagram for the TARSU scenario: the Ufficio Tributi office must compute taxes for all citizens, and acts by collecting requests and propagating them once a year. The following annotation is anchored to the top-level scope of the (WS-BPEL of) the Ufficio Tributi service, and indicates that actions in that scope must be instantiated for all citizens and must be collected into sequences of values.

```
⟨flow⟩
⟨anchor name=''seq_1''\⟩
⟨range property=''all'' value=''citizen''⟩
⟨grounding type=''sequence''⟩
⟨\flow⟩
```

Similar annotations are used for the Ufficio Ragioneria and Banca Tesoriere services, which take a different design choice and act on a "per day" basis.

8.3.4 Data Composition and Control Composition

Our automated techniques, introduced in Marconi, Pistore, and Traverso (2006), fully support data and control flows, and have their foundations on the formal framework introduced in Pistore, Traverso, and Bertoli (2005); see also Pistore et al. (2005); and Pistore, Marconi, et al. (2005). In such a formal framework, automated composition of services is recast as a planning problem: component services define the planning domain,

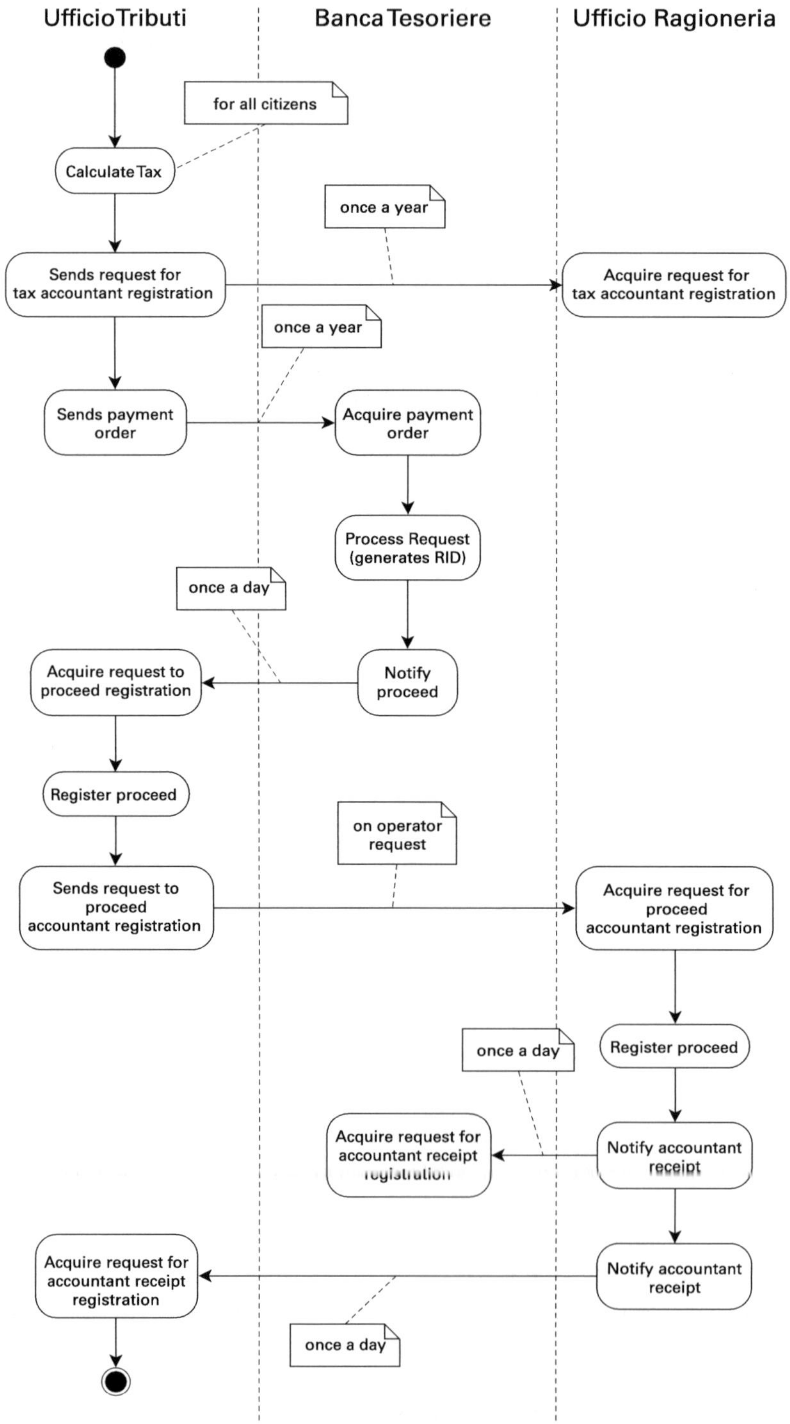

Figure 8.9
TARSU process activity diagram

composition requirements are formalized as a planning goal, and planning algorithms are used to generate the composite service.

In particular, it has to be noted that the framework of Pistore, Traverso, and Bertoli (2005), which we rely upon, differs substantially from other planning frameworks, since different agents in the framework, which represent the component services, may communicate by means of asynchronous, message-based interactions—rather than by acting in a synchronous way. This allows a faithful representation of the features of the way that distributed services interact.

More specifically, the composition domain is modeled as a state transition system (STS from now on) which models the set of component services, and describes a dynamic system that can be in one of its possible states and can evolve to new states as a result of performing some actions. Actions are distinguished in input actions, which represent the reception of messages; output actions, which represent messages sent to external services; and internal actions, which represent internal evolutions that are not visible to external services (i.e., data computation that the system performs without interacting with external services). A transition relation describes how the state can evolve on the basis of inputs, outputs, or internal actions.

The domain is obtained by means of an automated translation step, starting from the abstract WS-BPEL specification of component services. (Details on the translation can be found at http://astroproject.org.) Such a domain is, in general, *nondeterministic*: since some components may act based on their internal logics, their actions may not be predicted a priori.

Once the domain Σ is built, the automated synthesis problem consists of identifying another state transition system Σ_c that, once connected to Σ, satisfies the composition requirements ρ.

As shown in Pistore, Traverso, and Bertoli (2005), this problem can be recast in terms of a planning problem: Σ_c is the plan to look for, which, controlling the domain, satisfies the goal ρ. In particular, the "Planning as Model Checking" approach is particularly apt for this purpose, owing to its ability to deal effectively with large nondeterministic domains, and with requirements whose semantics are represented in terms of STSs and can therefore model layered preferences together with data constraints. Such an approach stands on the shoulders of powerful BDD-based techniques developed for Symbolic Model Checking to efficiently explore domain Σ during the construction of Σ_c.

Once the state transition system Σ_c has been generated, it is translated into WS-BPEL to obtain the new process which implements the required composition. The translation is conceptually simple; intuitively, input actions in Σ_c model the receiving of a message from a component service, output actions in Σ_c model the sending of a message to a component service, and internal actions model manipulation of data by means of expressions and assignments.

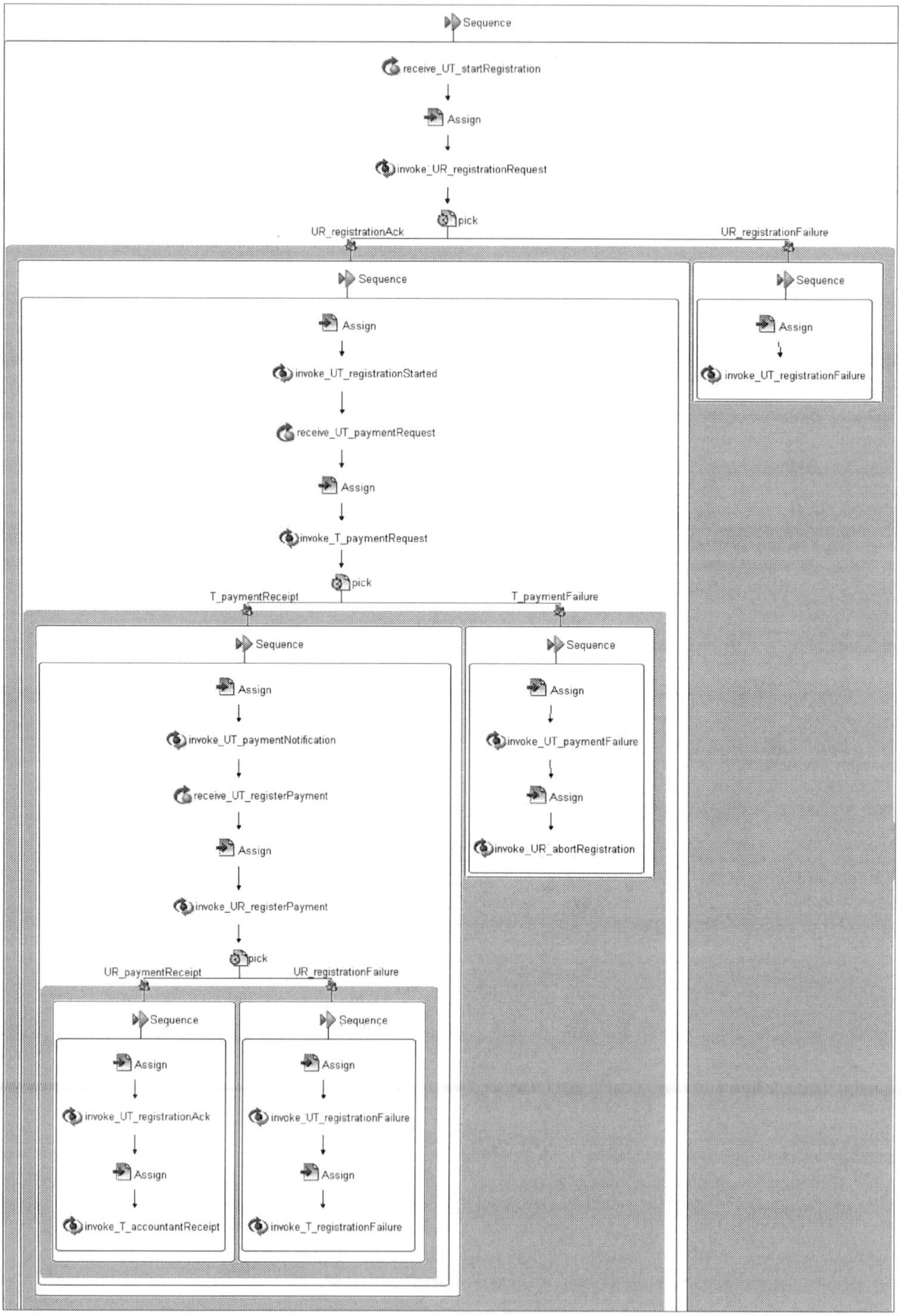

Figure 8.10
The composite service

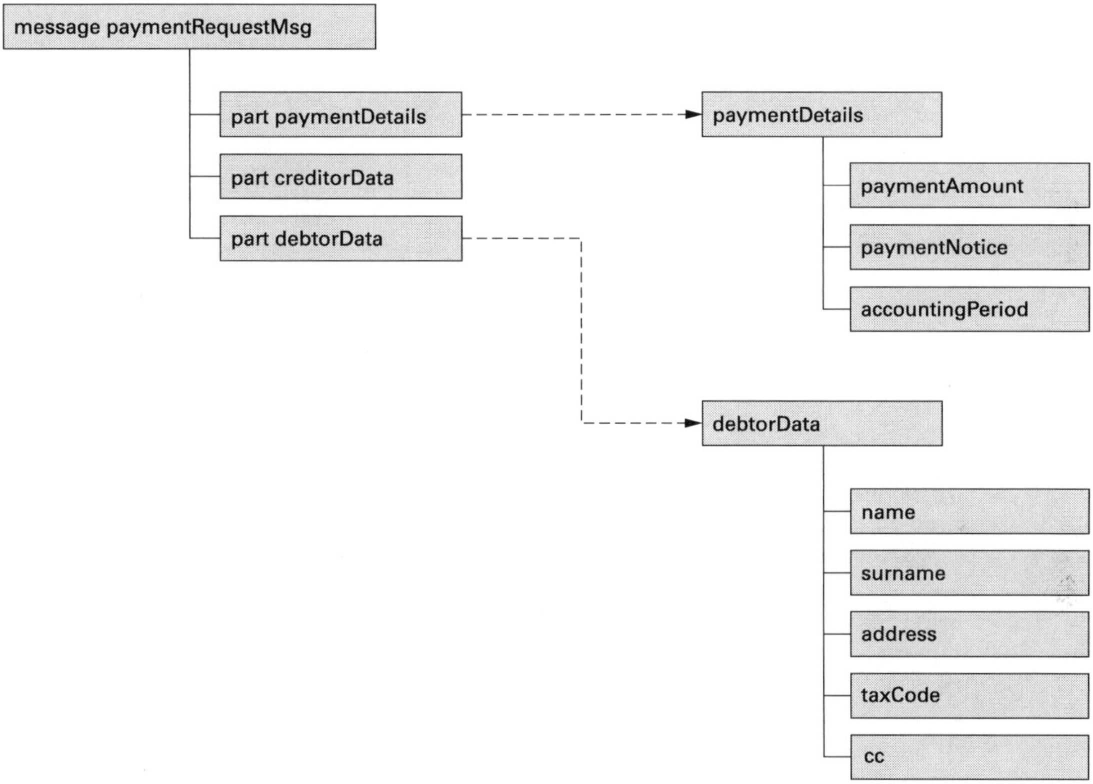

Figure 8.11
The WSDL data structure for payment requests

In our scenario, the application of techniques has led to automatic generation, in a matter of seconds, of the composite service represented in figure 8.10, which orchestrates the TARSU actors obeying the data and control requirements discussed in this section. Two observations are in order. First, notice that, as expected, this orchestrator responds to the different possible contingencies by taking different action paths. Second, the graphical notation of the produced WS-BPEL hides the fact that assignments are actually quite complex, since they involve complex data structures. For instance, figure 8.11 reports the data structure for the payment request.

8.3.5 Flow-Supporting Composition

Once data and control requirements are handled and a centralized orchestrator is obtained that handles single instances of tax payments, flow requirements need to be suitably injected so that the orchestrator collects and dispatches data according to such constraints.

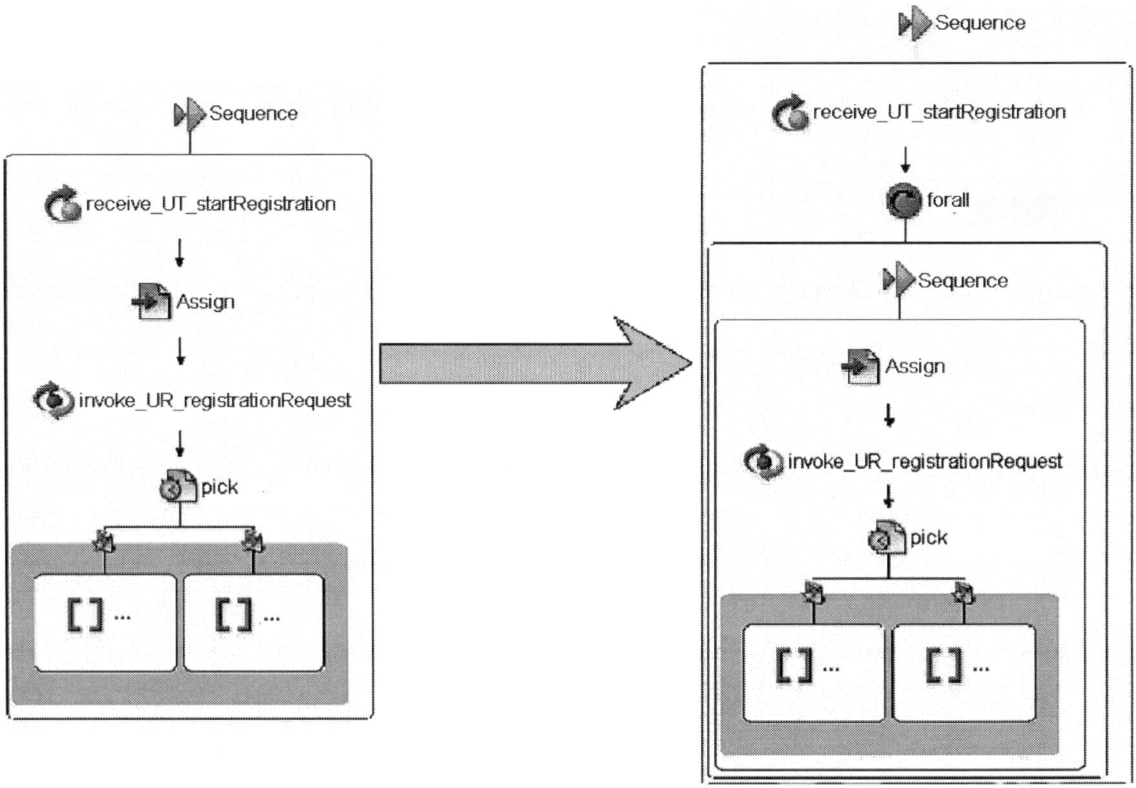

Figure 8.12
The WS-BPEL revised for handling flows

This can be done by modifying the code produced by the automated control- and data-composition step, in order to take flow requirements into account. This means that each flow requirement is injected into a specific portion of code, adding loops that perform the collection and distribution of data.

For instance, in figure 8.12, we show how the constraint of handling payments for all citizens, which was described in section 8.3.3, implies that a "for" loop wraps around that step of the process. So far, this step of the composition is still semiautomatic and relies on the application of transformation templates over the WS-BPEL code; in particular, we rely on the XSL Transformation language (XSLT[4]) to put in place transformations that simply embed code into loops, such as the one needed in this case. However, we can easily foresee the need for more complex transformations, which cannot be directly supported via XSLT—for instance, concerning the need for aggregations based on data contents; this constitutes a clear development direction for the research carried out in ASTRO.

8.4 Supporting the Process: Monitoring

Once a service has been developed by a third party, manually, or by an automated composition step, it is deployed and executed over a platform that supports the linkage with the other available services on the Web. In this runtime phase, which is supported by tools such as ActiveBPEL, the ability to monitor the execution of services is crucial to promptly detecting problems and to checking whether the execution profile conforms to the expectations.

In particular, the presence of aggregated flows of information makes it very valuable not only to monitor single instances of processes, but also to collect runtime statistical information about aggregated flows. For instance, the fact that a significant percentage of citizens refuse to pay a tax has to be reported as soon as possible to the business analyst, so that prompt actions can be taken. Some problems can be detected only at runtime: some situations can be admissible in general at design time, but must be promptly revealed when they happen (e.g., the fact that a bank payment procedure fails repeatedly). Finally, it has to be considered that in distributed, service-oriented applications, where services are independently developed by third parties prior to being combined within novel functionalities, even properties and requirements that are verified at design time can be violated at runtime—for instance, since services may be modified autonomously and without notification. All these aspects strongly motivate the need for monitoring the execution of Web Services (compositions) and of distributed business processes.

In ASTRO, the approach to monitoring is characterized by three main features. First, monitors are independent software modules that run in parallel to WS-BPEL processes, observe their behavior by intercepting the input/output messages that are received/sent by the processes, and signal some misbehavior or, more generally, some situation or event of interest. That is, our approach does not require the monitored services to be decorated or modified to any extent in order to guarantee direct usage of third-party services.

Second, we are interested in supporting monitoring by providing two different kinds of tools: instance monitors, which observe the execution of a single instance of a WS-BPEL process, and class monitors, which report aggregated information on all the instances of a given WS-BPEL process. Though the former are the usual monitors that need to be used, for instance, to identify and correct failures of single instances of processes, the latter assume a crucial importance to enact the computation of statistics and to monitor processes that must obey information flow constraints, and that therefore aggregate multiple executions of other processes.

Third, we envisage the automated generation and deployment of monitors on the basis of a clearly defined monitoring language which is based on events and combines past-time linear logics and numerical functionalities. In the following, we detail our monitoring approach, sketching the underlying architecture and describing our monitoring language and support tools.

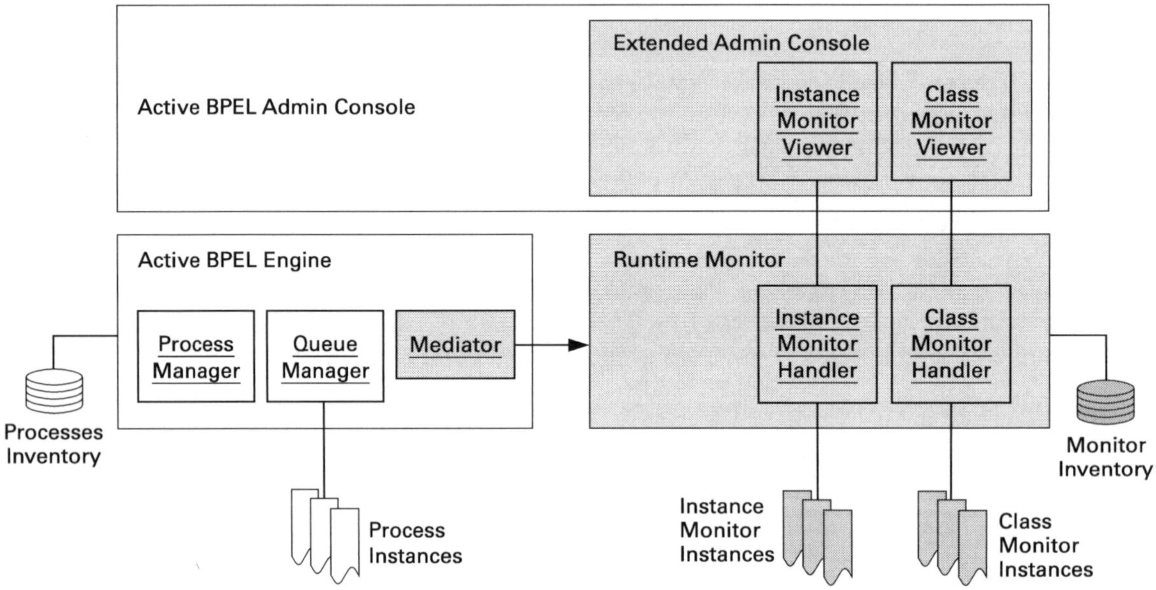

Figure 8.13
The ActiveBPEL engine extended with the run-time monitor environment

8.4.1 Monitoring Architecture, Specification, and Generation

Our monitoring architecture is based on extending ActiveBPEL, one of the most diffused engines for designing and executing WS-BPEL processes. As shown in figure 8.13, the environment is extended with five new components (shaded in figure). A mediator allows the environment to intercept input/output messages and to capture other relevant events, such as the creation and termination of process instances. These are passed to a runtime monitor (RTM), which is responsible for supporting the life cycle and the evolution of the monitor instances, and handles the sets of instance monitors and class monitors. Finally, an extended admin console extends the ActiveBPEL admin console with a cockpit that presents, along with other information on the WS-BPEL processes, the information on the status of the corresponding monitors.

To specify monitoring properties, both at the level of instance monitors and at that of class monitors, we devised a language named RTML (Runtime Monitor specification Language). RTML stands on the notion of monitorable event, defining what can be immediately tracked by a monitoring process which observes the behavior of services. In particular, in RTML basic events are message exchanges (for instance, *msg*(Banca Tesoriere.*input* = *paymentRequest*) denotes the receipt of a payment request message by the Banca Tesoriere), and creation and termination of service instances (denoted by the start and end keywords).

Based on this, for what concerns instance monitor properties, RTML offers the ability to obtain both logical and quantitative monitor information. The logical portion of RTML consists of a past-time linear temporal logic over boolean formulas on events; that is, RTML allows for specifying properties on the whole history of a given instance monitor, using "temporal" operators such as *since*, *once*, and *yesterday*. Such kinds of RTML expressions are particularly useful to track down unexpected behaviors of a service, which in most cases can be represented by simple linear logic formulas. The numeric portion of RTML allows counting events in time and computing the discrete time span between events; this is very useful for obtaining quantitative measures that can be used to check, for instance, the QoS of the service instance being monitored. Indeed, the numeric and logical portions of RTML are closely integrated, so that it is possible to count the occurrences of complex behaviors (represented by temporal formulas) or, vice versa, to trigger a boolean monitoring condition based on comparisons among numerical quantities (for instance, a certain event taking place more often than expected). Such an ability to integrate events and quantitative measures is crucial to allow monitoring both behavioral conformance and QoS requirements of processes.

This is pushed even further for class monitor properties. Here, RTML adds the ability to aggregate monitoring results over sets of process instances, so as to obtain numerical aggregate values. For instance, using an appropriate "class count" operator, it is possible to compute the total number of times a certain property holds or to detect, for instance, how many non-nominal behaviors take place. Similarly, by using an appropriate "class average" operator, it is possible to compute the percentage of times where services of a certain kind respond in a certain way. (A full report on the language can be found in Barbon et al. 2006.)

The ASTRO approach to support monitoring is based on converting RTML properties into STSs that evolve on the basis of trapped events, and where certain states are associated with the satisfaction of requirements. Then, these STSs are embedded within Java classes that are deployed in order to "sniff" the events from the WS-BPEL engine.

The possibility to specify properties of classes of processes in an easy way, and to automatically generate the monitors, is particularly relevant in scenarios such as TARSU. For instance:

- It is possible to monitor how often the whole procedure fails, so as to check that a reasonable success ratio is maintained at runtime. Recalling that failure states are annotated by ×, this is expressed by the formula *avg*(*end* & (Ufficio Tributi.× | Ufficio Ragioneria.× | Banca Tesoriere.×)), which, intuitively, computes the average number of times (*avg*) where the process ends (*end*) and some of the components fail.
- More specifically, it is possible to monitor the frequency of the cases where the Ufficio Ragioneria is first notified of a citizen who needs to be recorded, but then the payment for that citizen fails. Since in this case some effort is wasted, it is important to monitor that

such cases, though deemed possible, take place only seldom. This is represented by the formula avg (*once msg*(Ufficio Ragioneria.*input* = *abortRegistration*)), which intuitively computes the average number of times that, somewhere in time (*once*), an input is received that corresponds to such abortion case.

- It is possible to monitor the average elapsed time of the process with the formula *avg*(*running*), where running expands into a logical statement that collects the elapsed time between the start of a process and its termination.
- It is possible to monitor the average time spent by one of the actors in the process (e.g., by the Ufficio Ragioneria), to check whether one of them constitutes a bottleneck at execution time. The formula *avg* (*time* (*msg* (Banca Tesoriere.*input* = *paymentRequest*)) + *time* (*msg* (Banca Tesoriere.*input* = *accountantReceipt*))) does this, by taking the reception of messages that trigger the activation of the service as reference points to measure time.

8.5 Related and Future Work

In this chapter we have presented the ASTRO approach to support the automated composition of distributed processes expressed in WS-BPEL, both during the design phase and at runtime. In particular, we considered a case study taken from a real e-government application, and we have shown results of our approach, both in terms of generating an orchestrator capable of dealing with a complex tax payment procedure, and of expressing and deploying monitors that signal relevant events and data at runtime. Concerning both composition and monitoring, we identified a relevant aspect of distributed processes, namely, the presence of aggregated flows of information, which requires specific and nontrivial handling, and which is not currently supported by any other proposed approaches for service composition and monitoring. (See, e.g., (Wu et al. 2003; McDermott et al. 1998; Shesagiri et al. 2003; Hull et al. 2003; Berardi et al. 2003). We identified some key patterns in that respect, and we are in the course of designing a full-fledged language to support flow annotations. Already at this stage, we are able, by means of XML template transformations, to deal with relevant information requirements during service composition. Moreover, our ability to support monitoring of classes of services already proves sufficient in allowing runtime detection of relevant properties that capture features of information flows.

The powerful composition and monitoring functionalities embedded within the ASTRO platform involve the interaction of a relevant set of actors and concepts among those defined within the SeCSe conceptual framework. Indeed, concerning service composition, the ASTRO platform manipulates stateful services of both concrete and abstract form, enacting the automated synthesis of composite (concrete) services which satisfy given service properties by orchestrating sets of existing (abstract) services. Thus, the platform is directly operated by service developers, and the resulting composite services are subject to interactions with service consumers, which perform specific requests, and with service certifiers. Similarly, concerning service monitoring, the ASTRO platform considers abstract descriptions of stateful services together with service properties, to automatically obtain concrete service monitors that can be directly deployed and executed. Such concepts and actors are also central for several of the projects described in this book, and especially for some of those that fall into the NESSI infrastructure and service integration layer, whose conceptual views can be closely related to the one behind ASTRO—more specifically, PLASTIC, WS-DIAMOND, and SODIUM.

The SYNTHESIS tool used within the PLASTIC project offers a form of automated composition, enabling the assembly of third-party components, also based on nonfunctional QoS requirements. However, the context of SYNTHESIS is rather different from that of ASTRO—component assembly vs. Web Service composition. This implies remarkable differences in the technologies and representational tools adopted in the respective platforms. In particular, SYNTHESIS works on behavioral descriptions based on message sequence charts (MSCs) and on coordination requirements expressed as Büchi automata, synthesizing sets of (C++) wrappers that adapt each component behavior to obey the coordination requirements by means of MSC-specific algorithms. Though QoS is a key issue in service composition as well, so far the ASTRO platform deals with QoS requirements only at the qualitative level and to a limited extent, by layering composition requirements according to preference values. Quantitative QoS can, however, be monitored at runtime, thanks to the statistical constructs present in RTML. The integration of RTML-like constructs as composition requirements, and QoS-based extension to service representation, are in the research agenda of ASTRO.

In the WSDIAMOND project, the long-term goal is to make use of monitoring information to automatically adapt (“heal”) the running system so as to restore its correct functioning. Different from ASTRO’s approach, WSDIAMOND relies on techniques borrowed from model-based diagnosis, based on establishing a distributed diagnoser that relies on the local specification of expected behaviors for each component.

In the SODIUM project, an integrated approach is presented that tackles both service composition and service discovery by providing an array of graphical languages to specify and interoperate services independently from their actual implementation. Though SODIUM extends ASTRO’s approach by also integrating discovery in its process, it must be noted that it does not feature any of the powerful automated composition or monitoring capabilities at the core of the ASTRO tool set.

Future prospects for ASTRO include a deeper investigation of flow requirements, based on a wider analysis of scenarios in e-government, as well as in other areas such as e-commerce and telecommunication, in order to achieve a complete definition of a flow requirement language. Furthermore, we intend to investigate the issue of distributing the orchestration and monitoring of distributed processes, taking into account deployment requirements that may force us to depart from the idea of having orchestration performed in a centralized way.

Acknowledgments

The work published in this chapter is partly funded by the European Community under the Sixth Framework Programme, contracts FP6–016004 SENSORIA and FP6–507482 KnowledgeWeb, and by the FIRB-MIUR project RBNE0195K5, "Knowledge Level Automated Software Engineering." The work reflects only the authors' views. The Community is not liable for any use that may be made of the information contained therein.

Notes

1. ActiveBPEL. The Open Source BPEL Engine—http://www.activebpel.org.
2. Oracle BPEL Process Manager—http://www.oracle.com/products/ias/bpel/.
3. Active Endpoints. ActiveBPEL Designer—http://www.active-endpoints.com/.
4. XSL Transformations (XSLT 1.0)—http://www.w3.org/TR/xslt.

References

Andrews, T., Curbera, F., Dholakia, H., Goland, Y., Klein, J., Leymann, F., Liu, K., Roller, D., Smith, D., Thatte, S., Trickovic, I., and Weerawarana, S. 2003. Business Process Execution Language for Web Services (version 1.1).

Barbon, F., Traverso, P., Pistore, M., and Trainotti, M. 2006. Run-time monitoring of instances and classes of Web Service compositions. In *Proceedings of the IEEE Conference on Web Services*, pp. 63–70.

Berardi, D., Calvanese, D., De Giacomo, G., Lenzerini, M., and Mecella, M. 2003. Automatic composition of e-services that export their behaviour. In *Proceedings of the First International Conference on Service-Oriented Computing*. LNCS 2910.

Berglund, A., Boag, S., Chamberlin, D., Fernandez, M. F., Kay, M., Robie, J., and Siméon, J. 2007. XML Path Language (XPath 2.0). http://www.w3.org/TR/xpath20/.

Christensen, E., Curbera, F., Meredith, G., and Weerawarana, S. 2001. Web Service Definition Language (WSDL 1.1). http://www.w3.org/TR/wsdl.

Hull, R., Benedikt, M., Christophides, V., and Su, J. 2003. E-services: A look behind the curtain. In *Proceedings of PODS '03.*

Marconi, A., Pistore, M., and Traverso, P. 2006. Specifying data-flow requirements for the automated composition of Web Services. In *Proceedings of the 4th IEEE International Conference on Software Engineering and Formal Methods*, pp. 147–156.

Marconi, A., Pistore, M., Poccianti, P., and Traverso, P. 2007. Automated Web Service composition at work: The Amazon/MPS case study. In *Proceedings of the IEEE International Conference on Web Services*, pp. 767–774.

McDermott, D., Ghallab, M., Howe, A., Knoblock, C., Ram, A., Veloso, M., Weld, D., and Wilkins, D. 1998. The Planning Domain Definition Language Manual. Technical Report 1165, Yale Computer Science University. CVC Report 98–003.

Pistore, M., Marconi, A., Bertoli, P., and Traverso, P. 2005. Automated composition of Web Services by planning at the knowledge level. In *Proceedings of the International Joint Conference on Artificial Intelligence.*

Pistore, M., Traverso, P., and Bertoli, P. 2005. Automated composition of Web Services by planning in asynchronous domains. In *Proceedings of the International Conference on Automated Planning and Scheduling.*

Pistore, M., Traverso, P., Bertoli, P., and Marconi, A. 2005. Automated synthesis of composite BPEL4WS Web Services. In *Proceedings of the 3rd IEEE International Conference on Web Services.*

Sheshagiri, M., desJardins, M., and Finin, T. 2003. A planner for composing services described in DAML-S. In *Proceedings of the AAMAS '03.*

Wu, D., Parsia, B., Sirin, E., Hendler, J., and Nau, D. 2003. Automating DAML-S Web Services composition using SHOP2. In *Proceedings of ISWC '03.*

9 WS-DIAMOND: Web Services—DIAgnosability, MONitoring, and Diagnosis

Luca Console, Danilo Ardagna, Liliana Ardissono, Stefano Bocconi, Cinzia Cappiello, Marie-Odile Cordier, Philippe Dague, Khalil Drira, Johann Eder, Gerhard Friedrich, Mariagrazia Fugini, Roberto Furnari, Anna Goy, Karim Guennoun, Andreas Hess, Volodymyr Ivanchenko, Xavier Le Guillou, Marek Lehmann, Jürgen Mangler, Yingmin Li, Tarek Melliti, Stefano Modafferi, Enrico Mussi, Yannick Pencolé, Giovanna Petrone, Barbara Pernici, Claudia Picardi, Xavier Pucel, Sophie Robin, Laurence Rozé, Marino Segnan, Amirreza Tahamtan, Annette Ten Tejie, Daniele Theseider Dupré, Louise Travé-Massuyès, Frank Van Harmelen, Thierry Vidal, and Audine Subias

9.1 Introduction

The goal of this chapter is to present the guidelines and achievements of the WS-DIAMOND STREP Project, funded by the EU Commission under the FET-Open Framework, grant IST-516933. It started in September 2005 and ended in June 2008.

The project aims at making a step in the direction of self-healing Web Services. In the framework of the book, WS-DIAMOND deals with service architectures, mechanisms to achieve integration and interoperation among services, and engineering approaches for developing dependable services (Console et al. 2007a). In particular, it addresses two very different issues concerning self-healing capabilities:

1. To develop a framework for self-healing Web Services. A self-healing Web Service is able to monitor itself, to diagnose the causes of a failure, and to recover from the failure, where a failure can be either functional, such as the inability to provide a given service, or nonfunctional, such as a loss of service quality. Self-healing can be performed at the level of the single service and, at a more global level, with support to identify critical misbehavior of groups of services and to provide Web Services with reaction mechanism to global-level failures. The focus of WS-DIAMOND is on composite and conversationally complex Web Services, where "composite" means that the Web Service relies on the integration of various other services, and "conversationally complex" means that during service provision a Web Service needs to carry out a complex interaction with the consumer application in which several conversational turns are exchanged between them.
2. To devise guidelines and support tools for designing services in such a way that they can be easily diagnosed and recovered during their execution. Moreover, software tools to support this design process will be developed.

According to the principle of service integration in the NESSI road map (see chapter 1), WS-DIAMOND aims at developing a service integration platform that provides tools and methods for configuration and composition of self-healing units able to self-diagnose and self-repair. Moreover, WS-DIAMOND develops a platform for dynamic reconfiguration where software can be modified without stopping execution, thus meeting the demands for high availability. In fact, as computing facilities are increasing at a very rapid pace, presenting new forms of interaction, such as portable and mobile devices, home and business intelligent appliances, new technology shows a tremendous potential for the development of complex services to support human activities (e.g., work, health care, communities of workers, leisure, etc., possibly in a mobile context), in particular creating networks of cooperating services (Web Services).

According to the Services Research road map (see chapter 1), WS-DIAMOND addresses mainly the service composition and management planes and w.r.t. service characteristics that cut across the two planes; it also tackles nonfunctional service properties and quality of service (QoS).

The availability of reliable self-diagnostic and repairable services will be critical to enable activities to be carried on in dynamically reconfigurable runtime architectures, as required in the Service Foundation Grand Challenges, as well as for infrastructure support for process integration and for QoS-aware service composition. In the same way as today, we cannot work without access to corporate or external knowledge sources, on a broader prospective. Business-to-business and business-to-customer activities will be enriched with advanced capabilities and functionalities, thus enhancing business integration. Complex services will be made available through networks of cooperating services (Web Services). These networks are open, and may dynamically accommodate the addition and removal of new services and the disappearance of other ones. The availability and reliability of services (especially complex ones) will be of paramount importance. Indeed, the reliability and availability of software, together with the possibility of creating self-healing software, is recognized as one of the major challenges for IST research in the next years, according to ISTAG 2004.[1]

WS-DIAMOND studies and develops methodologies and solutions for the creation of self-healing Web Services able to detect anomalous situations, which may manifest as the inability to provide a service or to fulfill QoS requirements, and to recover from these situations (e.g., by rearranging or reconfiguring the network of services). WS-DIAMOND will also provide methodologies for the designer of services, supporting service design and service execution mechanisms that guarantee diagnosability and reparability of runtime failures (e.g., thanks to the availability of sets of observables or of sets of redundancies in the services or alternatives in the execution strategies). These goals are achieved by combining results from different research areas, as will be outlined in section 9.2.

WS-DIAMOND research concerns a number of "grand challenges," as described within the Service Research road map, at all levels: in the service foundations WS-DIAMOND studies dynamic connectivity capabilities, based on service discovery; at the service composition level, QoS-aware service composition is considered; in the service management level, self-healing services are developed as a main goal of the project; finally, at the service design and development level, design principles for self-healability are defined.

This chapter describes the results achieved in the first phase of the WS-DIAMOND project and is organized as follows. After framing the project in the literature context, section 9.3 introduces an application scenario. Section 9.4 presents the conceptual framework and architecture we developed for the platform supporting self-healing service execution, considering the requirements addressed in the first year of the project (namely, the design and development of a platform supporting self-healing execution of Web Services). Sections 9.5, 9.6, and 9.7 detail the three main components of such a framework: the self-healing layer supporting service execution (section 9.5), the diagnostic algorithm (section 9.6), and the approach to repair planning and execution, with a sample scenario (section 9.7). Section 9.8 concludes the chapter, discussing current and envisioned directions of research in the project.

9.2 Related Work

An area which considers self-healing systems is autonomic computing, proposed in the literature (Kephart and Chess 2003) to create systems capable of self-management, in particular, systems with self-configuration, self-optimization, self-healing, and self-protection properties. In the service area Papazoglou and Georgakopoulos (2003) advocate the need for extending the service-oriented approach in regard to service management. Several approaches have been proposed in the composed services and workflows systems areas to provide adaptive mechanisms, in particular for such process-based systems. In Mosaic (Benatallah et al. 2006) a framework is proposed for modeling, analyzing, and managing service models, focusing on systems design. Meteor-S (Cardoso and Sheth 2003) and other semantic-based approaches (e.g., WSMO) explicitly define the process goal as the basis both for service discovery and for composition. In WSMO, a goal-based framework is proposed to select, integrate, and execute semantic Web Services. No separation between design and runtime phases is proposed, nor is specific support to design adaptivity addressed. However, whereas goal-based approaches open up the possibility of deriving service compositions at runtime, their applicability in open service-based applications is limited by the amount of knowledge available in the service. In Meteor-S, semantically annotated services are selected, focusing on the flexible composition of the process and also on QoS properties, but runtime adaptivity to react to changes and failures is not considered. More recently, autonomic Web processes have been discussed in Verma and Sheth (2005), where a general framework for supporting self-* properties in composed Web Services is advocated. In the workflow area, the work of Hamadi and Benatallah (2004) presents SARN (Self-Adaptive Recovery Net), a Petri Net-based model for specifying exceptional behavior in workflow systems at design time. Following a failure, the standard behavior of the workflow is suspended and a recovery transition is enabled and fired. Hamadi and Benatallah (2004) also specify a set of recovery policies that can be applied in SARN both on single tasks and on workflow regions. The work in Eder et al. (1996) presents WAMO, which widely supports recovery actions in composed services. WAMO enables a workflow designer to easily model complex business processes in a simple and straightforward manner. The control structure is enriched by transactional features.

Other proposals tackle single aspects of adaptation. In business process optimization approaches, the process specification is provided and the best set of services is selected at runtime by solving an optimization problem (Zeng et al. 2004). In a similar way, in Grid systems, applications are modeled as high-level scientific workflows where resources are selected at runtime in order to minimize, for example, workflow execution time or cost. Even if runtime reoptimization is performed and provides a basic adaptation mechanism, user context changes and self-healing are not addressed.

In the SeCSe project (SeCSE Team 2007), self-healing is addressed in terms of QoS optimization and reconfiguration. Dynamic binding is supported through dynamic service selection and through adapters, based on optimization and reoptimization of QoS (Di Penta et al. 2006). Reconfiguration, as described in SCENE (Colombo et al. 2006), is based on the definition of rules for activating repair actions such as alternative services, rebinding, and process termination.

Self-healing processes in the Dynamo approach (Baresi and Guinea 2007) combine monitoring and reactions associated with pre- and post-conditions for activities.

The approach proposed in WS-DIAMOND is based on the infrastructure provided by PAWS (Processes with Adaptive Web Services) (Ardagna et al. 2007), a framework and tool kit for designing adaptable services, defining QoS agreements, and optimizing service selection, substitution, and adaptation at runtime. In WS-DIAMOND, such an approach has been coupled with the ability to automatically derive a repair plan based on repair actions provided by the PAWS self-healing interface. The strategy for deriving repair plans has its basis on the WAMO (Eder and Liebhart 1996) approach, where workflow transactions are supported by repair plans which have the goal of minimizing the impact of repair on the executed activities. To support such an approach, the definition of compensation operations, in addition to retry and substitution of service operations, as well as execution sequences for such actions, have been defined in WS-DIAMOND.

QoS has been the topic of several researches efforts crossing distinct communities, in particular the Web and Web Service community (Keller and Heiko 2003; Ran 2003) and the networking and internetworking communities. The highly fluctuating radio channel conditions, jointly with the heavy resource request deriving from multimedia applications, force thinking in terms of adaptive QoS or soft QoS, the opposite of the traditional hard QoS or static QoS idea.

In Marchetti et al. (2003) the representation of quality aspects in Web Services is discussed in the context of multichannel information systems. Their proposal includes the concept of service provider communities as a basis for a homogeneous definition of quality, and a classification of quality parameters, based on negotiable/nonnegotiable parameters and on provider/user perspectives. Zeng et al. (2004) provides a thorough analysis of quality evaluation in the context of adaptive composed Web Services, focusing on price, duration, reputation, success rate, and availability as quality parameters.

An important need which is emerging for highly distributed processes is execution monitoring. Mechanisms for automatically augmenting processes with monitoring functionalities have been proposed in Spanoudakis et al. (2005), considering that traditional monitoring tools cannot be applied to a heterogeneous environment such as the Internet.

Last but not least, a methodological approach is needed to design all aspects of such systems, focusing on exception handling and compensation mechanisms (Alonso and Pautasso 2003).

In the MAIS project, adaptive Web-based process execution has been developed based on flexible services, considering service similarity and QoS, and runtime service substitution mechanisms (Pernici 2006). Extended Petri nets have been used as a modeling technique and a basis for building analysis tools in process modeling (van der Aalst et al. 2003). However, little attention is paid to conforming to patterns of interactions between organizations and to providing inherent flexibility and fault tolerance in process execution.

Basic recovery is being proposed in the literature with retry and substitution operations. In Web-based process evolution, recovery has been proposed in Erradi et al. (2006), based on adaptive service composition and service substitution. Research work in Grid services is based on retry and substitution operations, but a more comprehensive approach to service repair is advocated in Candea et al. (2006), considering also the context of execution.

However, the above-mentioned approaches focus only on a direct repair of failed services, based on monitoring of failures; the link between failures and the causes of failures (faults) is not considered as a basis for repair strategies.

Current standards for Web Service markup describe operational behavior and syntactic interfaces of services, but they do not describe the semantics of the operations performed by the Web Services. Such a description is required to enable diagnosable and self-healing Web Services.

Research in Meteor-S has proposed a template-based process representation to enhance flexibility of processes through a dynamic selection of component services, based on service semantic similarity and QoS properties (Patil et al. 2004). The Semantic Web community is working toward markup languages for this Web Service semantics. The most prominent initiatives in this area are OWL-S (Martin et al. 2005), developed by a joint US/EU consortium, and the EU-based WSMO initiative (Web Service Modeling Ontology), developed by the EU-funded DIP consortium (Fensel and Bussler 2002).

These efforts, joined with proposals about discovery and dynamic composition (Spanoudakis et al. 2005; Colombo et al. 2006), aim at supporting retrieval and automatic composition of services (for example, the EU-funded consortium on Semantically Enabled Web

Services (SWWS; swws.semanticweb.org). However, aspects of diagnosability have been largely ignored until now by these Semantic Web initiatives. In order to enable diagnosable and self-healing Web Services, we will build upon and extend the currently proposed markup languages. In particular, the current semantic service markup languages focus on functional properties of the service (the input/output behavior), but are limited with respect to nonfunctional aspects. To enable diagnosability, the existing markup languages have to be extended to deal with such nonfunctional aspects as QoS descriptions, monitoring information, and repair options in case of failure.

In the research on automated monitoring and diagnosis, through the 1990s the model-based approach emerged as extremely interesting and led to several studies, methodologies, solutions, and applications (Hamscher et al. 1992; AI Magazine 2003). The approach focused mainly on the diagnosis of artifacts (moving from electronic circuits to more complex systems, such as subsystems in automotive or aerospace domains).

A current trend of research in diagnosis is the analysis of complex systems, taking into account the dynamic and distributed nature of the systems to be diagnosed. Indeed, focus has moved progressively from static to dynamic and then time-evolving systems, where parameters or structure itself (reconfigurable systems) can vary over time, and from global to hierarchical and then distributed systems, where components can communicate with each other.

Moreover, the focus has moved from "traditional" application areas to new ones such as economic systems, software, communication networks, and distributed systems. Particularly significant with respect to this project is the application to software diagnosis in which the same basic technologies have been successfully applied to debug programs (Mateis et al. 2000; Wotowa et al. 2002) and component-based software (Grosclaude 2004; Peischl et al. 2006). The same approach defined for debugging and diagnosing software has also been applied to Web Services (Mayer and Stumptner 2006). The focus of that work is different from our approach in that it aims at debugging (and diagnosing) problems in the composition of services (orchestration), rather than diagnosing and repairing problems arising during service execution.

9.3 An Application Scenario

The application scenario used in the project is an e-commerce application, concerned with a FoodShop company that sells food products on the Web.

The company has an online shop (that does not have a physical counterpart) and several warehouses ($WH_1, \ldots, WH_n$) located in different areas that are responsible for stocking nonperishable goods and physically delivering items to customers, depending on the area each customer lives in.

Customers interact with the FoodShop Company in order to place their orders, pay the bills, and receive their goods.

In the case of perishable items that cannot be stocked, or of out-of-stock items, the FoodShop Company must interact with one or more suppliers ($SUP_1, \ldots, SUP_m$).

In the following we describe the business process from the customer order to the parcel delivery, which is executed through the cooperation of several services. In particular, in each business process instance we have one instance of the Shop service, one instance of a Warehouse service, and one or more instances of Supplier services.

It is important to point out that the business process includes activities that are carried out by humans, such as the preparation of the order package or the physical delivery to the customer. However, we will assume that these activities have an electronic counterpart (a so-called wrapper) in the Web Services whose goal is to track the process execution. For example, when a Supplier physically sends supplies to a Warehouse, we assume that the person responsible for assembling the supply clicks on a "sent" button on her PC that saves the shipping note. On the other side, the person receiving the physical supply clicks on a "received" button on her PC, entering the data shown on the shipping note.

9.3.1 The FoodShop Business Process

Figure 9.1 depicts a high-level view of the business process, using a simplified UML-like representation. When a customer places an order, the Shop service selects the Warehouse that is closest to the customer's address, and that will thus take part in process execution.

Ordered items are split into two categories: perishable (they cannot be stocked, so the warehouse will have to order them directly) and nonperishable (the warehouse should have them in stock). Perishable items are handled directly by the Shop, exploiting the services of a Supplier, whereas nonperishable items are handled by the Warehouse; all of them are eventually collected by the Warehouse in order to prepare the parcel for the customer.

The Shop checks whether the ordered items are available, either in the Warehouse or from the Supplier. If they are, they are temporarily reserved in order to avoid conflicts between orders.

Once the Shop receives all the information on item availability, it can decide whether to give up on the order (to simplify, this happens whenever there is at least one unavailable item) or to proceed. In the former case, all item reservations are canceled and the business process ends.

If the order proceeds, the Shop computes the total cost (items plus shipping) with the aid of the Warehouse, which provides the shipping costs, depending on its distance from the customer location and the size of the order. Then it sends the bill to the customer, who can decide whether to pay or not. If the customer does not pay, all item reservations are canceled and, again, the business process terminates.

If the customer pays, then all item reservations are confirmed and all the Suppliers (in the cases of perishable and out-of-stock items) are asked to send their goods to the Warehouse. The Warehouse will then assemble a package and send it to the customer.

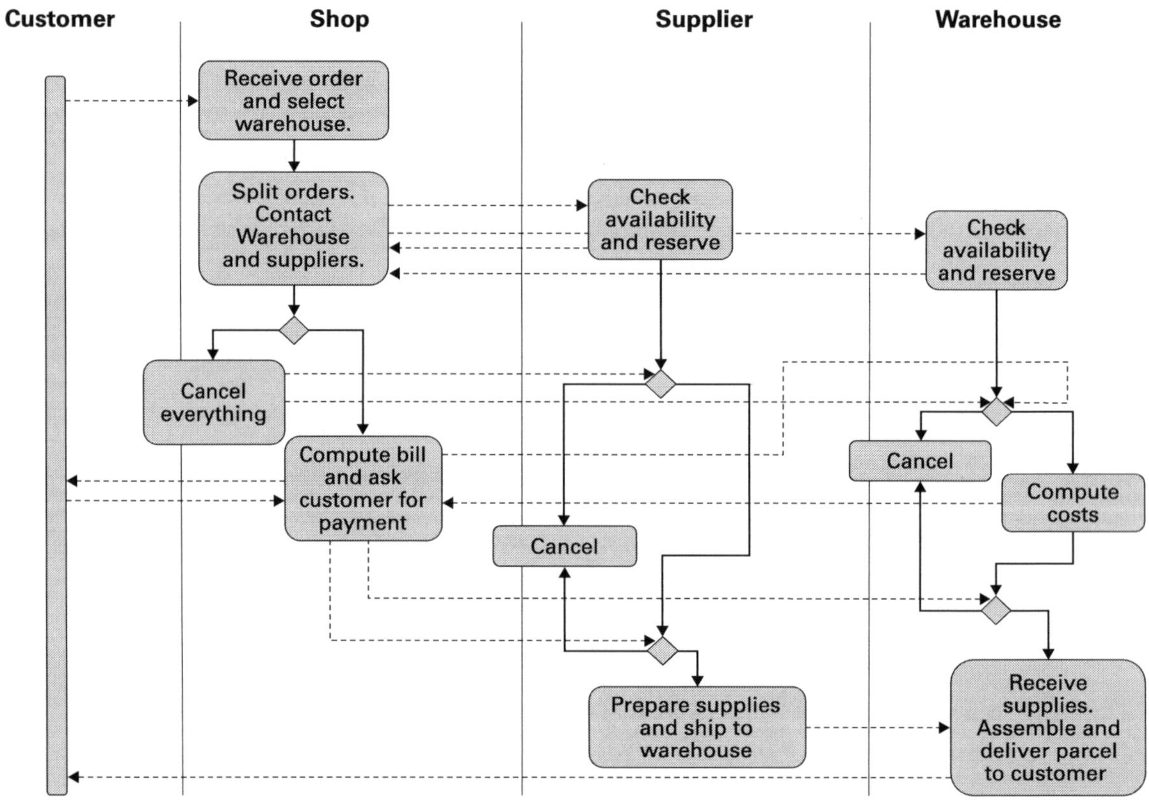

Figure 9.1
An abstract view of the FoodShop business process

9.4 WS-DIAMOND Architecture

In the first phase of the project, we concentrated on the design and development of a platform supporting the self-healing execution of Web Services. This means that we concentrated on the runtime problems, and design issues were faced in the second phase. A second very general consideration is that we are focusing on diagnosing problems that occur at runtime and we are not considering the issue of debugging a service (we assume that code has been debugged).

This led us to the definition of the following:

1. The types of faults that can occur and that we want to diagnose:

a. Functional faults, and specifically semantic data errors (such as wrong data exchanges, wrong data in databases, wrong inputs from the users, and so on).

b. QoS faults.

In this chapter, we will focus on the first ones.

2. The types of observations/tests that can be available to the diagnostic process:
a. Alarms raised by services during their execution.
b. Data possibly exchanged by services.
c. Data internal to a service (we will return later to privacy issues).
3. The types of repair/recovery actions that can be performed, such as compensating for or redoing activities.

We also decided to concentrate on orchestrated services, although some of the proposed solutions are also valid for choreographed services.

The main achievements in the first phase of the project are the following:

- We proposed a Semantic Web Service definition language which includes features needed to support the diagnostic process (e.g., observable parameters). Moreover, we started to analyze how these semantic annotations can be learned from service execution logs.
- We extended Web Service execution environments to include features which are useful to support the diagnostic/fault recovery process.
- In particular, an architecture supporting self-healing service execution has been defined, as described in section 5.
- We characterized diagnosis and repair for Web Services. In particular, we defined a catalog of faults (Fugini and Mussi 2006) and possible observations, and proposed an architecture for the surveillance platform (diagnostic service; see above). The core of the platform is a diagnostic problem solver, and thus we proposed algorithms for performing the diagnostic process, focusing attention on functional faults. In particular, the diagnostic architecture is decentralized; a diagnoser is associated with each individual service. A supervisor is associated to the orchestrator service or to the process owner. We defined a communication protocol between local diagnosers and the supervisor, assuming that no knowledge about the internal mechanisms of a Web Service is disclosed by its local diagnoser. The correctness of the algorithms has been proved formally.
- We defined repair as a planning problem, where the goal is to build the plan of the recovery actions to be performed to achieve recovery from errors. The actions are those supported by the execution environment and involve backtracking the execution of some services, compensating for some of the actions that were performed, redoing activities, or replacing faulty activities (or services) with other activities (services).

9.4.1 DIAMONDS: Diagnostic Services

A diamond (in charge of the enhanced service execution and monitoring, diagnosis, and recovery planning and execution) is associated with each service and with the orchestrator (figure 9.2).

Web Service's DIAMONDS The DIAMOND associated with a basic service is depicted in figure 9.3.

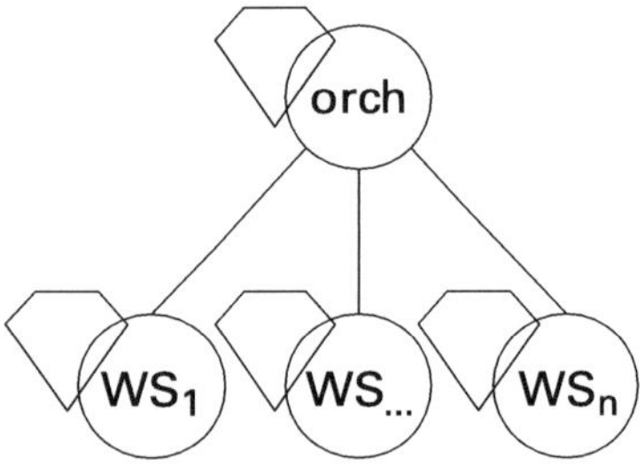

Figure 9.2
Services and DIAMONDS

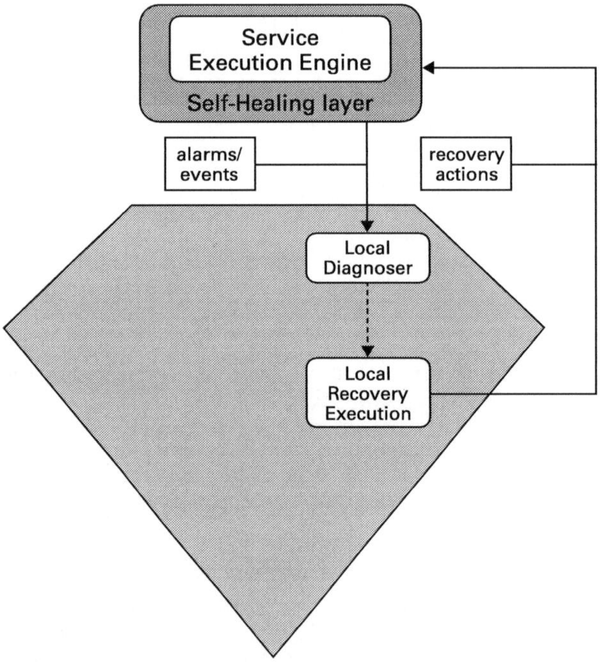

Figure 9.3
Web Service's DIAMOND

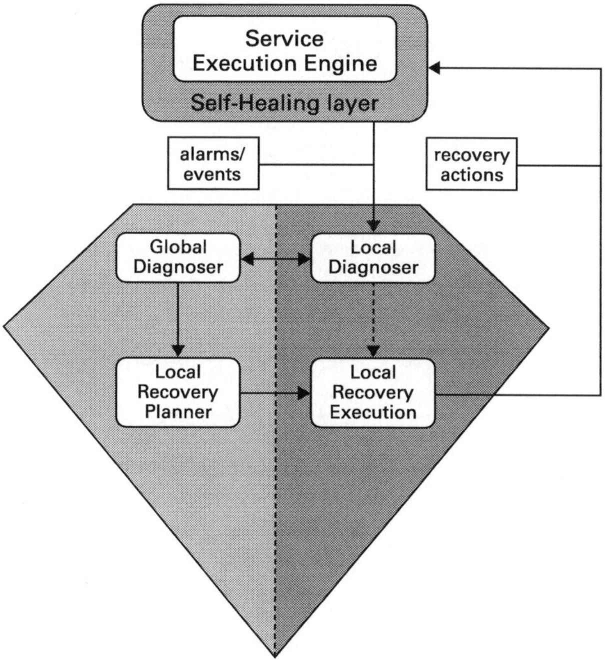

Figure 9.4
Orchestrator's DIAMOND

The self-healing layer is the set of extensions to the service execution engine designed in the project, which enables monitoring, diagnosis, and repair.

The diagnosis and repair include the following events:

1. Alarms and events generated by the service go to the diamond (to local diagnoser).
2. Local diagnoser privately owns the model of the service and is in charge of explaining alarms (events) by either
a. Explaining them with internal faults.
b. Blaming other services (from which inputs have been received) as the cause of the problem.
3. The local recovery execution module receives recovery actions to be performed from the global recovery planner (see below). Repair actions can also be selected by the local diagnoser.
4. Recovery actions are passed to the self-healing layer.

Orchestrator's DIAMONDS The diamond associated with the orchestrator is made up of two parts (see figure 9.4).

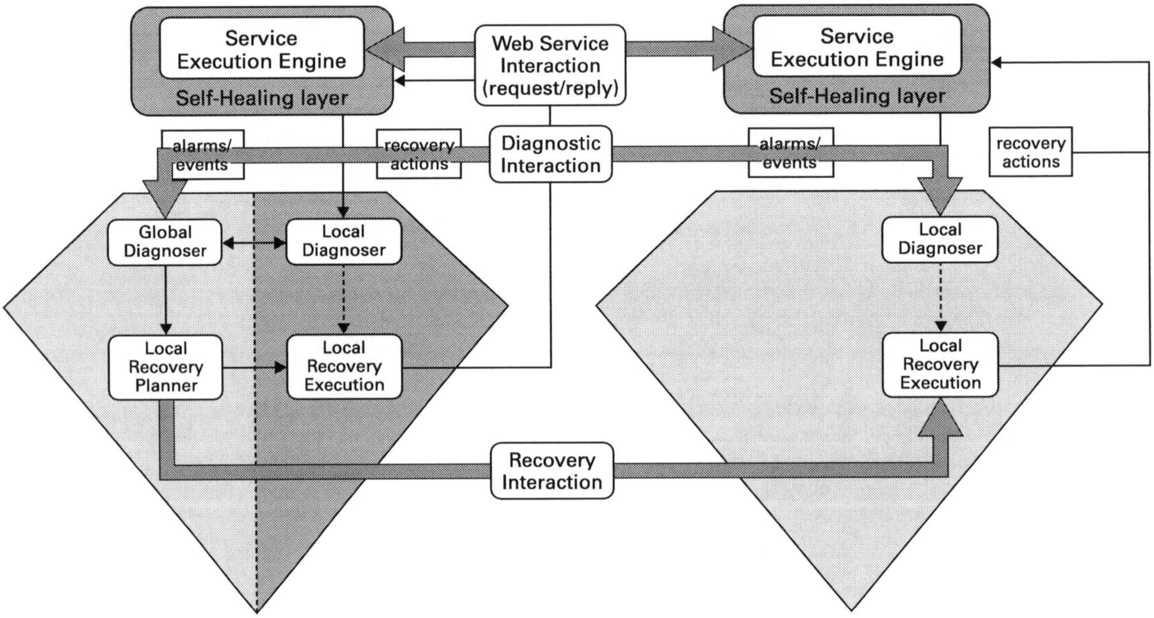

Figure 9.5
Overall Architecture

- Global diagnoser and global recovery planner modules (left part).
- Local diagnoser and local recovery execution modules (right part).

The latter is relevant because an orchestrated service may in turn be a subservice of a higher-level orchestrated service. The global diagnoser interacts with local diagnosers to compute a global diagnosis; it does not have access to local models. The diagnosis is computed in a decentralized way.

The recovery planner operates sequentially after a global diagnosis has been computed. It generates a plan for recovery and passes it to local recovery execution modules.

9.4.2 Overall Architecture

Figure 9.5 depicts the overall architecture with interaction between a service (and its diamond) and the orchestrator (and its diamond). In particular, it shows the following:

- The two-way interaction between the local diagnoser(s) and the global diagnoser, to compute a global diagnosis in a centralized way.
- The sequential interaction between the global diagnoser and the recovery planner.
- The one-way interaction from the recovery planner to the local recovery execution module(s).

9.5 Self-Healing Layer

In this layer of WS-DIAMOND, anomalous situations may become evident at application runtime as the inability to provide a service or to fulfill a contracted QoS. To recover from these situations, various actions can be undertaken, depending on where the fault has occurred (in the network, in a server, in the application flow, etc.) and on the type of fault (blocking, interapplication, intraapplication, owing to missing data or faulty actions performed by human actors, and so on).

The methodologies provided by WS-DIAMOND for the design of self-healing services supporting service design and service execution mechanisms are embedded in this layer. These guarantee the diagnosis and repair of runtime failures through a set of observables, of exception handlers, or of sets of redundancies in the services or alternatives in the application execution strategies.

This layer handles the correct execution of complex services. The process is described using process description languages, in particular WS-BPEL (Business Process Execution Language). Process representation in the self-healing environment allows monitoring of Web Service choreography/orchestration and of its conversational behavior, as well as of data and temporal dependencies among process activities. The activity performed in this layer is the execution of mechanisms for the evaluation of actual and potential violations of process functions and quality, and for the concretization of self-healing composed services, through exploitation of diagnosis and actuation of repair actions.

The service execution engine uses, executes, and coordinates recovery actions. Recovery acts both on single Web Services and on processes composed of several Web Services. A list of repair actions is available for the service execution engine; such list can be extended when global repair strategies involve several processes. Repair actions are based on the selection of alternative services, on compensation actions, on ad-hoc exceptions handling actions, and on renegotiation of quality parameters.

The service engine is in charge of selecting the most suitable service able to provide a requested service. Services and processes have a management interface, as explained below. Compared with the existing Web Service-enabled application servers, a WS-DIAMOND server provides an environment in which to run adaptive Web Services on the basis of a QoS-driven approach. QoS is managed as a contract between the Web Service provider and the Web Service requester. The requester may specify quality requirements at Web Service invocation time, or these requirements may be implicitly specified as annotations of the services. If the WS-DIAMOND platform realizes that the QoS of a Web Service is decreasing to an unacceptable level, then sample strategies that can be adopted are channel switching, to provide the Web Service on a channel with better QoS characteristics, or Web Service substitution, selecting an alternative Web Service for the user. Alternatively, concurrent Web Services can be started to obtain the "first responding" best result. The substitution of alternative Web Services of course depends on an appropriate choice of a service with similar functionality. Such similarity computation is based on a semantic-based analysis of the involved Web Service and is supported by a Web Service ontology. Since substituted and substituting Web Services may have different signatures, a wrapper is used to conciliate such differences. The wrapper is created on-the-fly according to information contained in the mapping document, a configuration file that lists the set of transformations to apply on exchanged messages in order to conciliate their different schemas. The mapping document is predefined by designers at design time, with the support of the WS-DIAMOND design tools.

Monitoring is provided to capture process-related, potentially faulty behaviors and to trigger recovery actions. The focus is on aspects which are not treated in the diagnostic modules, such as proactively monitoring time constraints that can anticipate possible future time violations; monitoring errors owing to architectural problems or to QoS violations; and monitoring conversations and analyzing their behavior with respect to their expected behavior.

Different measuring and monitoring functionalities may be associated with the execution environment. Some are directly related to the execution of a service, and provide metering services to observe the service behavior, either externally or through its management interface. Other monitoring functionalities are provided, with alarms generated by monitoring process execution and exchanged messages.

Monitoring is performed at different levels, from the infrastructure, where suitable mechanisms and probes are provided, to the Web Service and the process levels, where other mechanisms are provided, such as time-outs.

Monitoring also deals with time management of Web Services, to cope with situations when, for example, several messages are to be exchanged and delivered within the communication patterns in a timely manner, in order to meet internal and external deadlines. In fact, composite self-healing Web Services often include several service providers and/or consumers, and span different companies to support the business processes. Time management is included in the core concept of Web Service functionality at the provider's side. Besides these considerations, it is necessary that the flow of work and information be controlled in a timely manner by temporal restrictions, such as bounded execution durations and absolute deadlines often associated with the activities and subprocesses. However, arbitrary time restrictions and unexpected delays can lead to time violations, increasing both the execution time and the cost of the process because they require some kind of exception handling.

Time management for Web Services is performed using predictive time management, proactive time management, and reactive time management. At design time, the process designer enriches the process with temporal information and time-related properties (execution, duration, earliest allowed start, latest allowed end, implicit and explicit temporal constraints between tasks, and so on) (Eder et al. 2006).

Repair actions are located at various levels of the self-healing architecture and may be involved in a whole plan (Modafferi and Conforti 2006). Repair can act at the instance level (e.g., redo an operation) and at the class level, modifying the service class characteristics (e.g., change the QoS profile or modify the process structure for the service and not only for a specific instance).

Repair actions are performed on Web Services through a management interface which is part of the self-healing layer. Through the management interface, particular instances of Web Services, involved in a particular instance of a process, can be repaired from a failed state. Repair actions are the following:

- Infrastructural actions: These allow reconfiguring the set of interacting Web Services through reallocation of services and resources at the infrastructural level.
- Service-level actions: These allow retrying service invocation, redoing operations with different parameters, and compensating for previous operations performed on the service; a substitution operation can also be performed at the service level.
- Flow-level actions: These act at the process level, changing the execution flow (skip, re-execute from) or modifying the process variables, or acting on parts of the process with process-level compensation, such as in fault handlers in BPEL (Modafferi and Conforti 2006).

An example of execution of repair actions in the self-healing layer is shown in figure 9.6.

If the Warehouse service invoked in the Foodshop has a permanent fault, and this fault is identified (e.g., during the calculation of costs), the process administrator is notified through the management interface (Modafferi et al. 2006).

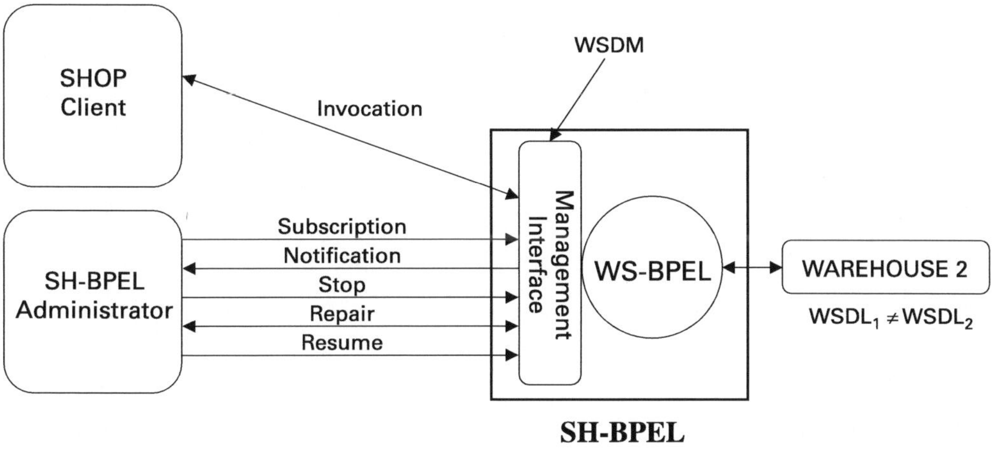

Figure 9.6
Self-healing process execution

The process manager chooses the substitution of the Warehouse as a repair action. Substitution is performed at runtime and services with compatible, even if not identical, interfaces may be invoked, through an adaptation mechanism provided in the self-healing interface.

This also implies that previous actions involving the Warehouse have to be redone (check availability of goods and calculation of costs). Then normal execution can be resumed.

9.6 Diagnostic Algorithm

The adopted diagnosis approach is model-based diagnosis (MBD). MBD (Hamscher et al. 1992) was originally proposed and used within the artificial intelligence community for reasoning on possibly faulty physical systems, especially in technical domains, from electronic circuits to cars and spacecraft (Console and Dressler 1999), but it has also been applied in other domains.

Most MBD approaches rely on a component-oriented model of the system to be diagnosed:

- The system to be diagnosed is modeled as a set of components (e.g., for physical systems, hydraulic pipes or electric resistors) and interconnections between components.
- The behavior of each component is modeled as a relation on component variables. Such a model is provided for the correct and/or faulty behavior of the component; in technical domains, in particular, the behavior under alternative known fault modes can be provided.
- Variables typically range on discrete, finite domains, which in the case of physical systems may also correspond to qualitative abstractions of continuous domains.
- Component variables include interface variables, used to define component interconnections in the system by equating interface variables of different components (e.g., an output variable of a component with an input variable of another component). Therefore, a model for the overall system, as a relation on all component variables, is at least implicitly given.
- The model of component behavior can be a static, temporal model that relates values that different variables take at the same time, but it can also relate values at different times; a way to do this is constraining changes of state variables, thus providing a dynamic model.

The resulting overall model of the system is therefore able to predict, or at least constrain, the effect of the correct and incorrect behavior of a component, as well as of variables that are not directly related to the component.

Diagnostic reasoning should identify diagnoses as assignments of behavior modes to components that explain a given set of observations (values for observable variables). A diagnostic engine should, in general, explore the space of candidate diagnoses and discriminate among alternative candidates, possibly suggesting additional pieces of information to be acquired for this purpose. Discrimination should be performed only toward a given diagnostic goal (e.g., selecting an appropriate repair action).

There are several formalizations of MBD (Hamscher et al. 1992). Consistency-based diagnosis (Reiter 1987) is used in our approach: a diagnosis is an assignment of behavior modes to components that is consistent with observations. For static models this means that the candidate predicts, for observable variables, a set of possible values which includes the observed one.

In WS-DIAMOND, diagnosis is decentralized. This means the following:

- We associate with each basic service a local diagnoser owning a description of how the service is supposed to work (a model). The role of local diagnosers is to provide the global diagnoser with the information needed for identifying the causes of a global failure.
- We provide a global diagnoser which is able to invoke local diagnosers and relate the information they provide, in order to reach a diagnosis for the overall complex service. If the supply chain has several levels, several global diagnosers may form a hierarchy where a higher-level global diagnoser sees the lower-level ones as local diagnosers.

This approach enables recursive partition of Web Services into aggregations of subservices, hiding the details of the aggregation from higher-level services. This is in accordance with the privacy principle which allows designing services at the enterprise level (based on intra-company services) and then using such services in extranets (with other enterprises) and public internets. The global diagnoser service only needs to know the interfaces of local services and share a protocol with local diagnosers. This will mean, in particular, that the model of a service is private to its local diagnoser and need not be made visible to other local diagnosers or to the global one.

Each local diagnoser interacts with its own Web Service and with the global diagnoser. The global diagnoser interacts only with local diagnosers. More precisely, the interaction follows this pattern:

- During service execution, each local diagnoser should monitor the activities carried out by its Web Service, logging the messages it exchanges with the other peers. The diagnoser exploits an internal "observer" component that collects the messages and locally saves them for later inspection. When a Web Service composes a set of subsuppliers, the local diagnoser role must be filled by the global diagnoser of the subnetwork of cooperating services. On the other hand, an atomic Web Service can have a basic local diagnoser that does not need to exploit other lower-level diagnosers in order to do its job. Local diagnosers need to exploit a model of the Web Service in their care, describing the activities carried out by the Web Service, the messages it exchanges, the information about dependencies between parameters, and alarm messages.
- When a local diagnoser receives an alarm message (denoting a problem in the execution of a service), it starts reasoning about the problem in order to identify its possible causes,

which may be internal to the Web Service or external (erroneous inputs from other services). The diagnoser can do this by exploiting the logged messages.

- The local diagnoser informs the global diagnoser about the alarm it received and the hypotheses it made on the causes of the error. The global diagnoser starts invoking other local diagnosers and relating the different answers, in order to reach one or more global candidate diagnoses that are consistent with reasoning performed by local diagnosers.

According to the illustrated approach, each local diagnoser needs a model of the service it is in charge of. We assume that each Web Service is modeled as a set of interrelated activities which show how the outputs of the service depend on its inputs. The simplest model consists of a single activity; the model of a complex one specifies a partially ordered set of activities which includes internal operations carried out by the service and invocations of other suppliers (if any).

The model of a Web Service enables diagnostic reasoning to correlate input and output parameters and to know whether an activity carries out some computation that may fail, producing an erroneous output as a consequence.

Symptom information is provided by the presence of alarms, which trigger the diagnostic process; by the absence of other alarms; or by additional test conditions on logged messages introduced for discrimination.

The goal of diagnosis is to find activities that can be responsible for the alarm, performing discrimination for the purpose of selecting the appropriate recovery action.

When an alarm is raised in a Web Service W_i, the local diagnoser A_i receives it and must give an explanation. Each explanation may ascribe the malfunction to failed internal activities and/or abnormal inputs. It may also be endowed with predictions of additional output values, which can be exploited by the global diagnoser in order to validate or reject the hypothesis. When the global diagnoser receives a local explanation from a local diagnoser A_i, it can proceed as follows:

- If a Web Service W_j has been blamed for incorrect outputs, then the global diagnoser can ask its local diagnoser A_j to explain them. A_j can reject the blame, or explain it with an internal failure, or blame it on another service that may have sent the wrong input.
- If a fault hypothesis by A_i has provided additional predictions on output values sent to a Web Service W_k, then the global diagnoser can ask A_k to validate the hypothesis by checking whether the predicted symptoms have occurred, or by making further predictions.

Hypotheses are maintained and processed by diagnosers as partial assignments to interface variables and behavior modes of the involved local models. Unassigned variables represent parts of the overall model that have not yet been explored, and possibly do not need to be explored, thus limiting invocations to local diagnosers.

The global diagnoser sends hypotheses to local diagnosers for explanation and/or validation. Local diagnosers explain blames and validate symptoms by providing extensions to partial assignments that assign values to relevant unassigned variables. In particular, the global diagnoser exploits a strategy for invoking as few local diagnosers as possible, excluding those which would not contribute to the computation of an overall diagnosis (explanation).

Details on the strategies adopted by the global diagnoser about the communication protocol between global and local diagnosers, and about local diagnosers, can be found in Console et al. 2007b), where properties of the correctness of the adopted algorithms are also proved.

9.7 Planning and Execution of Repair

The WS-DIAMOND part devoted to repair actions aimed at recovering the failed services at runtime is now presented. We have seen how the diagnosis specifies the execution of distributed conversations among local and global diagnosis services (Console et al. 2007b). We assume that the Shop is the process and that each service has its own local database, where faulty data can exist.

In general, within an organization, a process P based on Web Services invokes both operations of internal services, located within the organization boundaries, and operations of external services, located outside the organization boundaries. Both kinds of services are invoked by sending messages and receiving response messages synchronously or asynchronously. In this chapter, we consider that process services are "WS-Diamond enabled" (i.e., they are endowed with self-healing capabilities).

We define $P_j = \langle IS\_OP_j, ES\_OP_j \rangle$, where IS_OP_j is the set of the operations of the internal services and ES_OP_j is the set of operations of the external services. For each invoked service operation S_OP, its input, output, and fault messages are defined, that is, $S\_OP_i = \langle IM_i, OM_i, FM_i \rangle$. Each of these messages is composed of data parts (i.e., $M_k = \{D\}$). External services can in turn be complex processes and invoke other services. Failures (i.e., the observed symptoms of faults) can occur during the execution of the process, and manifest as fault messages for which a fault handler has not been defined. Failures occur during the execution of actions in the process, where actions are either the execution of internal service operations or invocation of external service operations.

Repair is based on repair plans (generated online or prepared offline for a given process) which are executed if a failure occurs in the process and a fault has been diagnosed. Faults are diagnosed in a distributed way, indicating which service originated the fault and faulty messages, in particular the erroneous message(s) deriving from the faulty execution in the faulty service. Hence, a fault is identified by a service-message pair $F = \langle S,M \rangle$, where S is the faulty service and M is the erroneous message originating subsequent failures. In particular, from the diagnosis we get the faulty operation and (if diagnosis allows that), in addition, the faulty output of the operation (e.g., the message which is faulty). For each failure-fault pair, a plan contains the repair actions needed to resume the correct execution of a process. The plan is sequential, and can contain alternative paths which define alternative repair action sequences, whose execution depends on conditions on the variables evaluated during repair plan execution. The plan is generated on the basis of the analysis of which of the actions following the erroneous messages have been affected during their execution.

Repair actions are the following:

- Retry an operation
- Redo an operation: re-execute with different message data
- Compensate for the effects of an operation: invoking an operation which is defined as a compensation for a given operation in a given state
- Substitute a service.

Faults can be either permanent or temporary. If a fault is permanent, invoking the same operation of the service again will result in a failure again. If a fault is temporary, reinvocation of the operation originating the erroneous message in the F = ⟨S,M⟩ pair may result in a correct message. *Retry* addresses temporary faults of services, and *redo* addresses temporary faults on data (e.g., a wrong item code), whereas *compensate* can be a complex sequence of actions aimed at rolling back to a safe process state. Finally, *substitute* addresses permanent faults (e.g., a service does not answer within a given deadline). In a repair plan, other actions allow changing data values and evaluating conditions, in addition to normal service operation execution.

9.7.1 Sample Failures and Faults

In figure 9.7, the Web Services of the FoodShop interact to fulfill an order from a customer. For the sake of simplicity, we consider that the order is a list of requested items and does not exist explicitly. We assume that a failure (that is, the symptom of an error) occurs in the ForwardOrder step of the Shop service workflow. The diagnosis step detects which of the three possible faults (F1, F2, F3 in figure 9.7) has originated the failure, and then a repair action or plan is executed.

In the example, we consider the following:

1. Item_description = "lasagna"
2. Shipping_note = item_code+item_description
3. Warehouse crosschecks the item description, the shipping note, and the package before sending the package upon receipt of the request to perform ForwardOrder.

We assume that faults occur one at a time, and that *retry* and *substitute* actions are always successful.

During the diagnosis, the possible faults F are as follows:

Possible faults F = ⟨S,M⟩
F1 = ⟨SHOP, Item_code⟩

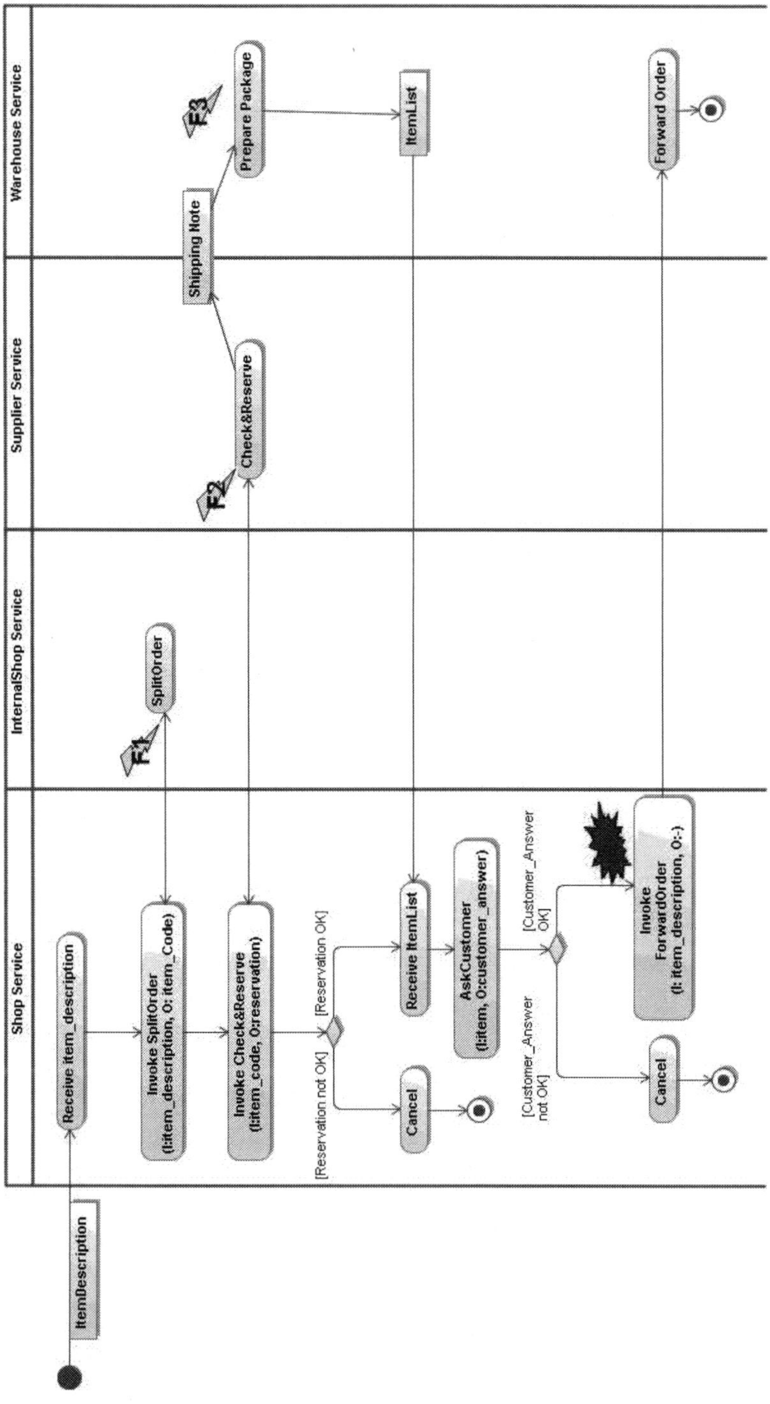

Figure 9.7
UML-like representation of the application scenario: interacting Web Services, symptoms and fault

F2 = ⟨SUPPLIER, reservation⟩
F3 = ⟨WAREHOUSE, ItemList⟩—the WAREHOUSE fills a package with wrong goods.

In F3 the customer has to confirm the correctness of the package contents by checking the list of items.

Let us examine the case of a fault in the SUPPLIER service (F2). This service has a wrong correspondence between the name of the item and its code. It thus sends a wrong shipping note to the warehouse (and possibly a wrong response to the shop), and the warehouse (provided the goods exist) prepares the package. When the warehouse receives the item description from the shop with the ForwardOrder operation, it verifies that the ordered goods (item_description in figure 9.7), the shipping note, and the package are not consistent, and then it raises failure `Fail`. However, exactly the same failure can occur if the SHOP sent the wrong code to the supplier and if the warehouse prepared the wrong package.

To decide which action(s) need to be performed during repair, diagnosis can be beneficial to select the right strategy. In fact, even with the same failure, in the three cases above, three different repair plans should be executed. For instance, if the error were in SHOP, the shop can send the correct data to the supplier and compensate for affected actions (see, for instance, plan P1 below), whereas if SUPPLIER has a permanent fault in providing a given item, the most convenient action to get the right package would be to substitute the supplier, if the supplier cannot be repaired.

9.8 Execution and Repair Actions in Plans

Table 9.1 summarizes some possible situations of faults in the various Web Services of the example. In addition, a fault type characterization is given. To test the approach, a fault injection tool has been developed that acts on data faults and on service delays (Fugini et al. 2007).

Three different plans can be generated, depending on the fault and on the infected Web Services. In table 9.2, the possible repair plans are reported. The repair strategies that can be adopted are reported in table 9.3. The plan generation is built on top of the DLV (Eiter et al. 2004) reasoning framework. DLV offers disjunctive Datalog and the handling of incomplete knowledge by negation as failure. Consequently, by exploiting DLV, we are able to model rich background theories. Such background theories are necessary in order to asses the quality of objects (faulty or correct) produced by a fault workflow instance and by subsequent repair actions. Depending on the result of repair actions, the quality of objects is changed (e.g., faulty objects may be turned into correct ones). However, in order to handle conditional branches of the plan, we had to extend the basic time model of the DLV planning system into a forward-branching time model in order to reflect different continuations of the current state of the world.

Table 9.1
Faults characterization

Correct execution	F1 (SHOP)	F2 (SUPPLIER)	F3 (WAREHOUSE)
Receive (lasagna)	Receive (lasagna)	Receive (lasagna)	Receive (lasagna)
SplitOrder (lasagna, O4)	SplitOrder (lasagna, O5)	SplitOrder (lasagna, O4)	SplitOrder (lasagna, O4)
Check&Reserve (O4)	Check&Reserve (O5)	Check&Reserve (O4)	Check&Reserve (O4)
Prepare-package (O4, lasagna)	Prepare-package (O5, spaghetti)	Prepare-package (O4, spaghetti)	Prepare-package (O4, lasagna)
Package: lasagna	Package: spaghetti	Package: spaghetti	Package: spaghetti
ForwardOrder: lasagna *OK*	ForwardOrder: lasagna *Failure Fail*	ForwardOrder: lasagna *Failure Fail*	ForwardOrder: lasagna *Failure Fail*
Fault type	Permanent (error in SHOP DB)	Permanent (error in SUPPLIER DB)	Temporary (error WAREHOUSE in filling package; when detected by diagnosis, is corrected by WAREHOUSE)

Table 9.2
Three possible repair plans

P1	P2	P3
Repair after SplitOrder	Repair after SplitOrder	Retry ForwardOrder(lasagna)
Change value: item-code=O4	Compensate(Check&Reserve)	
Compensate(Check&Reserve)	**Substitute** SUPPLIER	
Redo Check&Reserve(O4)	Invoke Check&Reserve(O4)	
IF reservation=OK	IF reservation=OK	
Retry ForwardOrder(lasagna, *OK*)	Retry ForwardOrder (lasagna, *OK*)	
Resume after ForwardOrder	Resume after ForwardOrder	
OTHERWISE	OTHERWISE	
Compensate(AskCustomer)	Compensate(AskCustomer)	
Compensate(ForwardOrder)	Compensate(ForwardOrder)	
Invoke Cancel	Invoke Cancel	

Table 9.3
Repair strategies

Failure	Fault	Plan
Fail	F1: SHOP, item code	P1
Fail	F2: SUPPLIER, reservation	P2
Fail	F3: WAREHOUSE, ItemList	P3

The execution of repair plans is based on the PAWS adaptive process execution framework (Ardagna et al. 2007). PAWS provides a set of design support tools to select candidate services for execution and substitution from an enhanced UDDI registry (URBE); to configure service mediators to enable dynamic binding and runtime substitution when service interfaces are different; to design compensate operations and a process management interface (SH-BPEL) to control process execution (start repair and resume process execution), the repair operations (retry, substitute, compensate, change values of variables), and their effects on the process execution state.

9.9 Discussion and Future Work

In this chapter, we have presented the approach of the WS-DIAMOND project to self-healing Web Services. The approach consists of a set of methodologies, design-time tools, and runtime tools to design and develop a platform for observing symptoms in complex composed applications, for diagnosis of the occurred faults, and for selection and execution of repair plans.

The chapter has presented the main results achieved in the first phase of WS-DIAMOND, where we concentrated on some specific problems, making assumptions in order to constrain the problem.

Such assumptions are being progressively relaxed or removed in the final part of the project; this approach is allowing us to manage the complexity of the problem and of the task.

A first major assumption is that we are considering orchestrated services. We are currently extending the approach to deal with choreographed services. This actually does not impact the overall diagnostic architecture (which is not influenced by this distinction, except that the global diagnoser must be associated with the owner of the complex process rather than with the orchestrator).

On the other hand, repair and the self-healing layer are being modified. In the current approach, we are also assuming that all services are WS-DIAMOND enabled, that is, that they have an associated diagnostic service. Such an assumption is being removed, and we are considering the case where some services are black boxes.

Another major assumption in the first phase is that we are concentrating on functional errors, whereas in the second phase we also consider problems related to the QoS. We will also extend the range of functional faults we are considering. This means, in particular, that the self-healing layer is being modified to include modules for monitoring QoS parameters.

Still regarding faults, we are currently concentrating on "instance-level diagnosis," that is, diagnosis and recovery (repair) of problems arising during a single execution of a service. We are currently moving to analyze issues related to multiple execution of the same service, which is especially important for QoS faults.

As regards repair, we worked with a limited set of repair primitives, and we are currently extending this set to include further alternatives to be considered during repair planning. However, in the project we do not expect to remove the general assumption that diagnosis and repair are performed sequentially. The issue of interleaving repair/recovery with diagnosis, which is a very important one in diagnostic problem solving, will be a topic for future investigations outside the project.

In addition, we assumed that the model of service activities which is needed by its local diagnoser is handmade. However, the dependencies that are needed can be derived from the service description, and we are currently investigating how the model can be produced in a partially automated way. The approach to diagnosis presented in the chapter is the one that in our view is best suited for the problem of explaining the causes of errors. We are currently investigating an alternative approach which is more integrated with monitoring service execution and that could be useful to detect situations that may lead to error during monitoring.

Finally, other issues that are considered in WS-DIAMOND regard security and trust in the selection of substitute services. A first approach is presented in Fugini and Pernici (2007).

Acknowledgment

The work published in this chapter is partly funded by the European Community under the Sixth Framework Programme, contract FP6–IST-516933 WS-DIAMOND. The work reflects only the authors' views. The Community is not liable for any use that may be made of the information contained therein.

Note

1. http://cordis.europa.eu/ist/istag-reports.htm.

References

AI Magazine. 2003. Special issue on model-based diagnosis (Winter 2003).

Alonso, G., and C. Pautasso. 2003. Visual composition of Web Services. In *Proceedings of the 2003 IEEE Symposia on Human Centric Computing Languages and Environments*, pp. 92–99.

Ardagna, D., M. Comuzzi, E. Mussi, B. Pernici, and P. Plebani. 2007. PAWS: A framework for processes with adaptive Web Services. *IEEE Software* (November/December), pp. 39–46.

Baresi, L., and S. Guinea. 2007. Dynamo and self-healing BPEL compositions. In *Proceedings of ICSE Companion 2007*, pp. 69–70.

Benatallah, B., F. Casati, F. Toumani, J. Ponge, and H. R. M. Nezhad. 2006. Service Mosaic: A model-driven framework for Web Services life-cycle management. *IEEE Internet Computing* 10(4): 55–63.

Candea, G., E. Kiciman, S. Kawamoto, and A. Fox. 2006. Autonomous recovery in componentized Internet applications. *Cluster Computing Journal* 9(1): 175–190.

Cardoso, J., and P. Sheth. 2003. Semantic e-workflow composition. *Journal of Intelligent Information Systems* 21(3): 191–225.

Console, L., L. Ardissono, S. Bocconi, C. Cappiello, L. Console, M. O. Cordier, J. Eder, G. Friedrich, M. G. Fugini, R. Furnari, A. Goy, K. Guennoun, V. Ivanchenko, X. Le Guillou, S. Modafferi, E. Mussi, Y. Pencole, G. Petrone, B. Pernici, C. Picardi, X. Pucel, F. Ramoni, M. Segnan, A. Subias, D. Theseider Dupré, L. Travé Massuyès, and T. Vidal. 2007a. WS-DIAMOND: An approach to Web Services—DIAgnosability, MONitoring and Diagnosis. In *Proceedings of the E-Challenges Conference*, pp. 105–112.

Console, L., and O. Dressler. 1999. Model-based diagnosis in the real world: Lessons learned and challenges remaining. In *Proceedings of the 16th International Joint Conference on Artificial Intelligence*, pp. 1393–1400.

Console, L., C. Picardi, and D. Theseider Dupré. 2007b. A framework for decentralized qualitative model-based diagnosis. In *Proceedings of the 20th International Joint Conference on Artificial Intelligence*, pp. 286–291.

Colombo, M., E. Di Nitto, and M. Mauri. 2006. SCENE: A service composition execution environment supporting dynamic changes disciplined through rules. In *Proceedings of the 4th International Conference on Service Oriented Computing*, pp. 191–202.

Di Penta, M., R. Esposito, M. L. Villani, R. Codato, M. Colombo, and E. Di Nitto. 2006. WS Binder: A framework to enable dynamic binding of composite Web Services. In *Proceedings of the International Workshop on Service Oriented Software Engineering, Workshop at ICSE 2006*, pp. 1036–1037.

Eder, J., M. Lehmann, and A. Tahamtan. 2006. Choreographies as federations of choreographies and orchestrations. In *Advances in Conceptual Modeling—Theory and Practice.* Berlin: Springer. LNCS 4231, pp. 183–192.

Eder, J., and W. Liebhart. 1996. Workflow recovery. In *Proceedings of the Conference on Cooperative Information Systems IFCIS (CoopIS)*, pp. 124–134.

Eiter, T., W. Faber, N. Leone, G. Pfeifer, and A. Polleres. 2004. A logic programming approach to knowledge-state planning: Semantics and complexity. *ACM Transactions on Computational Logic* 5(2): 206–263.

Erradi, A., P. Maheshwari, and V. Tosic. 2006. Policy-driven middleware for self-adaptation of Web Services compositions. In *Middleware 2006*. Berlin: Springer. LNCS 4290, pp. 62–80.

ESSI WSMO Working Group. Web Service Modeling Ontology. http://www.wsmo.org.

Fensel, D., and C. Bussler. 2002. The Web Service modeling framework WSMF. *Electronic Commerce Research and Applications* 1(2): 113–137.

Fugini, M. G., and E. Mussi. 2006. Recovery of faulty Web applications through service discovery. In *Proceedings of the 1st SMR-VLDB Workshop, Matchmaking and Approximate Semantic-based Retrieval: Issues and Perspectives*, pp. 67–80.

Fugini, M. G., and B. Pernici. 2007. A security framework for self-healing services. In *Proceedings of the 5th UMICS Workshop at CAiSE 2007.*

Fugini, M. G., B. Pernici, and F. Ramoni. 2007. Quality analysis of composed services through fault injection. In *CBP 2007 International Workshop on Collaborative Business Processes, Workshop at 15th International Conference, BPM 2007.* LNCS 4714.

Grosclaude, I. 2004. Model-based monitoring of component-based software systems. In *Proceedings of the 15th International Workshop on Principles of Diagnosis* (DX '04), pp. 155–160.

Hamadi, R., and B. Benatallah. 2004. Recovery nets: Towards self-adaptive workflow systems. In *Web Information Systems Engineering (WISE).* Berlin: Springer. LNCS 3306, pp. 439–453.

Hamscher, W., J. de Kleer, and L. Console. 1992. *Readings in Model-Based Diagnosis.* San Francisco: Morgan Kaufmann.

Keller, A., and L. Heiko. 2003. The WSLA Framework: Specifying and monitoring service level agreements for Web Services. *Journal of Network and Systems Management* 11(1): 57–81.

Kephart, J. O., and D. M. Chess. 2003. The vision of autonomic computing. *IEEE Computer* 36(1): 41–50.

Marchetti, C., B. Pernici, and P. Plebani. 2003. A quality model for e-service based multi-channel adaptive information systems. In *4th International Conference on Web Information Systems Engineering, Workshops*, pp. 165–172.

Martin, D., M. Paolucci, S. McIlraith, M. Burstein, D. McDermott, D. McGuinness, B. Parsia, T. Payne, M. Sabou, M. Solanki, N. Srinivasan, and K. Sycara. 2005. Bringing semantics to Web Services: The OWL-S approach. In *Semantic Web Services and Web Process Composition.* Berlin: Springer. LNCS 3387, pp. 26–42.

Mateis, C., M. Stumptner, and F. Wotawa. 2000. Modeling Java programs for diagnosis. In *Proceedings of the 14th European Conference on Artificial Intelligence*, pp. 171–175.

Mayer, W., and M. Stumptner. 2006. Debugging failures in Web Services coordination. In *Proceedings of the 17th International Workshop on Principles of Diagnosis* (DX '06), pp. 171–178.

Modafferi, S., and E. Conforti. 2006. Methods for enabling recovery actions in Ws-BPEL. In *On the Move to Meaningful Internet Systems: Proceedings of the International Conferences CoopIS, DOA, GADA, and ODBASE.* Berlin: Springer. LNCS 4275, pp. 219–236.

Modafferi, S., E. Mussi, and B. Pernici. 2006. SH-BPEL: A self-healing plug-in for Ws-BPEL engines. In *Proceedings of the 1st Workshop on Middleware for Service Oriented Computing.* New York: ACM Press. ACM Conference Proceedings 184, pp. 48–53.

Papazoglou, M. P., and D. Georgakopoulos. 2003. Service-oriented computing. *Communications of the ACM* 46(10): 24–28.

Patil, A., S. A. Oundhakar, A. P. Sheth, and K. Verma. 2004. Meteor-S Web Service annotation framework. In *Proceedings of the 13th International Conference on the World Wide Web*, pp. 553–562. New York: ACM Press.

Peischl, B., J. Weber, and F. Wotawa. 2006. Runtime fault detection and localization in component-oriented software systems. In *Proceedings of the 17th International Workshop on Principles of Diagnosis* (DX '06), pp. 195–203.

Pernici, B., ed. 2006. *Mobile Information Systems—Infrastructure and design for adaptivity and flexibility*, Berlin: Springer.

Ran, S. 2003. A model for Web Services discovery with QoS. *SIGecom Exchanges* 4(1): 1–10.

Reiter, R. 1987. A theory of diagnosis from first principles. *Artificial Intelligence* 32(1): 57–95.

SeCSE Team. 2007. Designing and deploying service-centric systems: The SeCSE way. In *Service Oriented Computing: A Look at the Inside* (SOC@Inside '07).

Spanoudakis, G., and K. Mahbub. 2006. Nonintrusive monitoring of service based systems. *International Journal of Cooperative Information Systems* 15(3): 325–358.

Spanoudakis, G., A. Zisman, and A. Kozlenkov. 2005. A service discovery framework for service centric systems. In *Proceedings of the IEEE International Conference on Services Computing*, vol. 1, pp. 251–259.

van der Aalst, W. M. P., ter Hofstede, A. H. M., and Weske, M. 2003. Business process management: A survey. In *Business Process Management: International Conference* (BPM 2003). Berlin: Springer. LNCS 2678, pp. 1–12.

Verma, K., and Sheth, A. P. 2005. Autonomic Web processes. In *Proceedings of the 3rd International Conference on Service Oriented Computing*, pp. 1–11.

Wotowa, F., Stumptner, M., and Mayer, W. 2002. Model-based debugging or how to diagnose programs automatically. In *Proceedings of IEA/AIE 2002.* LNAI, pp. 746–757.

Zeng, L., Benatallah, B., Ngu, A. H. H., Dumas, M., Kalagnamam, J., and Chang, H. 2004. QoS-aware middleware for Web Services composition. *IEEE Transactions on Software Engineering* 30(5): 311–327.

10 SeCSE—Service-centric System Engineering: An Overview

Massimiliano Di Penta, Leire Bastida, Alberto Sillitti, Luciano Baresi, Neil Maiden, Matteo Melideo, Marcel Tilly, George Spanoudakis, Jesus Gorroñogoitia Cruz, John Hutchinson, and Gianluca Ripa

10.1 Introduction

The service-oriented paradigm is fostering a new breed of software system development. Complex applications are seen as compositions of remote services often owned by different organizations. This approach is one of the pillars behind the NESSI vision of "the user, the individual, at the centre of future developments for an inclusive knowledge-based society for all,"[1] but requires methods and tools for its full and seamless adoption.

The SeCSE project contributes to the definition of a sound service-oriented development discipline by means of some innovative solutions. Starting from existing standards, research achievements, and stakeholders' expectations, the project aims at the following:

1. Extending existing approaches to service specification to include additional special-purpose information, offering quality of service (QoS) and dependability statements, and supporting the use of such specifications for discovery and dynamic binding.
2. Developing linguistic mechanisms and methodological approaches for the development of self-adaptive service compositions where non-service-based parts can be integrated seamlessly to create a hybrid system. It also offers solutions for the validation, testing, and runtime monitoring of services and service-centric systems (SCSs).
3. Verifying the SeCSE methods, tools, and techniques against real-world problems and scenarios provided by the industrial partners.

This chapter provides a general overview of the main results of the project based on the following motivating case study from the automotive and telco domains:

> A carmaker wants to equip its top-level models with an onboard device to allow drivers to interact with the remote services offered by its portal. Among the features, there is a service that allows drivers to plan a trip according to their appointments. The service uses a navigation system to get the geographical position of the car, and automatically checks the driver's agenda to see if she/he is on time for scheduled appointments. If the driver is late, the service automatically phones her/his secretary to change the schedule as needed. Otherwise, all the appointments are confirmed. As soon as the driver arrives at the destination, the service provides the list of parking lots close to the destination with some free spots.

This chapter's structure belongs to the service engineering area, given the support that the SeCSE results aim at offering to the service development life cycle. Clearly there is still a long way to go before a comprehensive and precise engineering approach for service-based applications is defined. As we will discuss in the rest of this chapter, SeCSE provides some bricks in this area.

The rest of the chapter is organized as follows. Section 10.2 sketches the SeCSE development process. Section 10.3 introduces the different activities of the methodology, and section 10.4 describes the SeCSE integrated platform. Section 10.5 surveys related approaches, and section 10.6 ends the chapter.

10.2 SeCSE Development Process

This section, starting from the scenario described in the previous section, introduces the main elements of the SeCSE approach for conceiving service-centric applications. The concepts, artifacts, and activities are fully defined in the SeCSE conceptual model (Colombo et al. 2005), and the different steps of the process itself are presented in the SeCSE methodology.

The proposed scenario foresees the development of a composed service, hereafter called DriveWorkAndPark, that fulfills the scenario described in the previous section. We start with eliciting the requirements and, based on these, discovering services that might partially address these requirements. As a result of this phase the system integrator is provided with the following:

- A number of functional and nonfunctional requirements: for example, the fact that the call to the secretary to change the appointment has to pass through a telecom network that depends on the preferences of the end user (the driver), and the fact that the cost of the DriveWorkAndPark service must be low (in any case not higher than 1.5 euros per user session).
- A first set of potential services able to support parts of the DriveWorkAndPark. In this specific case, these are services offering parking places, supporting the execution of phone calls among third parties, and allowing users to access their agendas remotely. This set of services is useful to check the feasibility of developing DriveWorkAndPark. The system integrator in fact realizes that most of the steps to be executed as part of DriveWorkAndPark can be implemented by exploiting these services, and therefore, as soon as she/he moves to the design phase, she/he can start understanding how to integrate them.

As soon as the requirements are set, we can start the design phase to define the workflow in charge of orchestrating the interactions with the external services identified in the previous step (see figure 10.1).

The system integrator can also exploit architecture-based service discovery to design composed services and discover that only a subset of the parking services previously discovered share the same WSDL interface. The integrator also discovers that no service for

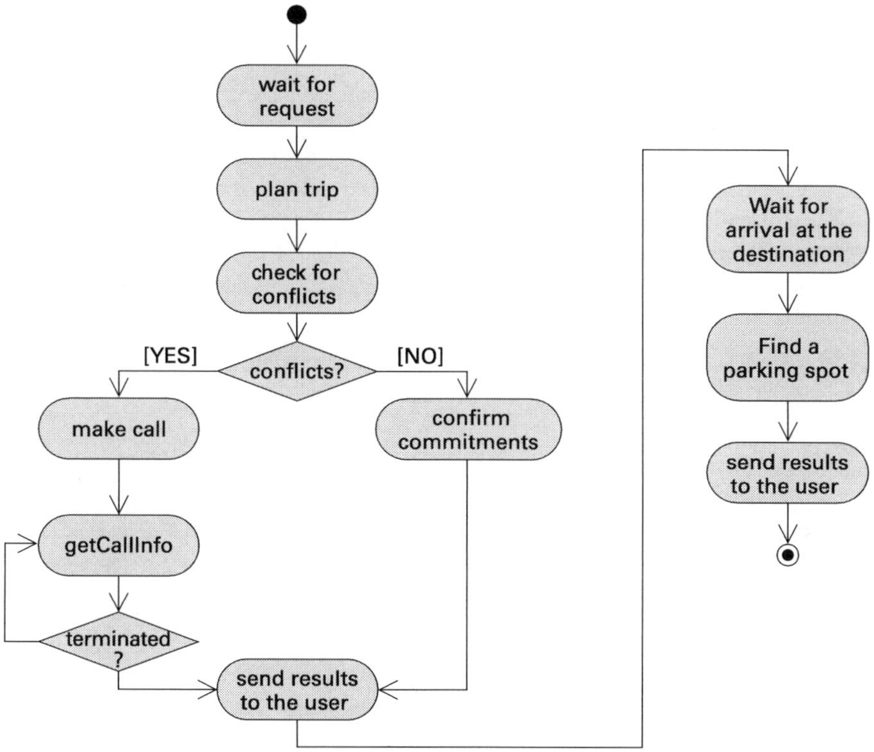

Figure 10.1
DriveWorkAndPark workflow

third-party calls is able to fulfill the interface foreseen by the workflow, where this service is supposed to send an event to the workflow as soon as the phone call between the service consumer and his/her secretary ends. Based on these findings, the system integrator decides to develop some adapters for the interactions with selected services, and to modify the structure of the composition to comply with the interface of the actual third-party call service. In this phase, the system integrator can also negotiate some service-level agreement (SLA) with the owners of some of the component services in order to ensure that the requirement that has been set on the cost of the service is actually fulfilled.

During design, the system integrator also identifies constraints on modeled workflow. In the example, the service DriveWorkAndPark works correctly only if the agenda used by the service consumer is accessible via a Web Service. When this does not apply, the service is not able to check the conflicts and limits itself to providing information about the duration of the trip and about the parking spots available at the destination. After finalizing the core part of the workflow, which is written in BPEL, the system integrator focuses on the definition of monitoring and binding constraints (in conjunction with runtime service discovery), which allows the process to be configured with respect to usage context. As for the service DriveWorkAndPark, this means determining, for instance, the criteria for selecting the telecommunication service for third-party calls, and being able to react to faulty/unforeseen situations. When this happens, the faulty service is added to a "blacklist" and is not selected anymore (or until a given time-out expires).

As result of the design phase, the composed service (augmented BPEL process) is ready for testing, deployment, publication, and execution. In the testing phase the system integrator will check whether the service fulfills the functional and nonfunctional requirements.

After deployment, a specification for the DriveWorkAndPark service is defined and is published in the SeCSE registry located at the carmaker's site. At this point the carmaker can start integrating this service with the onboard device that is installed on its cars.

In the next section we describe in detail the main activities of the SeCSE process.

10.3 Main Activities

10.3.1 Service Specification

Service specification refers here to the service's capabilities as defined by the service developer/provider. The provider describes and makes available such services, and the integrator/user can discover and use them on the base of such a service specification. Different types of specifications are required to support specific SCS engineering processes. The ability of a potential service consumer to exploit these processes, therefore, is dependent upon appropriate service specifications that are available.

There are a number of different specification mechanisms for advertising services, such as UDDI, WSDL, and OWL-S. Some focus on describing different properties, but there is much overlap, with many concentrating on describing bindings and signatures. Motivated by the growing need for service consumers to use semantics to distinguish between competing services, the SeCSE approach is to provide support for the specification of a range of service properties. Rather than inventing a new language, we have developed a framework of partial specifications.

A SeCSE service specification is defined as a set of facets (Walkerdine et al., 2007). Each facet describes one or more functional and nonfunctional service properties. Facets are essentially a way of packaging service specifications, providing meta-information that supports the management and discovery of what information is available about a service. Within SeCSE we have developed a number of facets that capture information relating to a service's general description, signature, commercial information (e.g., service-level agreement), QoS values, test cases, and behavioral information. Figure 10.2 shows a section of the QoS facet specification that was developed for the DriveWorkAndPark service.

This service specification states an availability > 96 percent for the service as a whole, and a mean time to complete for the parkRequest operation of <1000 ms. The specification also links to a QoS ontology which all of the QoS attributes, metrics, and units reference, and which in turn can be referenced by the service consumer.

```
<FacetSpecificationData>
  <QoSSpec>
    <QoSOntologyReferences>
      <Reference>http://www.comp.lancs.ac.uk/owl_qos/qosont2.owl</Reference>
    </QoSOntologyReferences>
    <QoSCharacteristic>
       <Name>Availability</Name>
       <Metrics>
       <Metric>
         <Name>AvailabilityAsPercentageUptime</Name>
         <MinValue>96</MinValue>
         <Unit>percent</Unit>
         </Metric>
       <Metric>
         <AssociatedOperation>parkRequest</AssociatedOperation>
         <Name>MeanTimeToComplete</Name>
         <MaxValue>1000</MaxValue>
         <Unit>milliseconds</Unit>
         </Metric>
       </Metrics>
    </QoSCharacteristic>
  </QoSSpec>
</FacetSpecificationData>
```

Figure 10.2
Sample of the DriveWorkAndParck QoS Facet Specification

Typically, a service provider selects a subset of the available SeCSE facet types to describe its services. Where an appropriate mix of facets is used, powerful support for service discovery is provided, which enables selection between competing services. The facet approach is therefore tolerant of the range of ways in which a potential service consumer can search for services and parameterize their registry queries.

10.3.2 Service Discovery

An important issue in developing SCSs is the static and dynamic discovery of services that can fulfill the functional and nonfunctional requirements of the system, and can be combined to compose the system. In SeCSE, we have developed new processes, methods, and tools to extend current software development practices and support SCS development.

We divide the process for service discovery in SCSs into three main activities: (a) requirement-based service discovery, (b) architecture-based service discovery, and (c) run-time service discovery.

Requirement-Based Service Discovery This is a requirement-driven discovery activity concerned with both the specification of the requirements of the system under development

> **A driver is driving his car. The driver needs to find a space in a car park close to his destination. The driver activates Fiat's car park booking service. The car park booking service finds the car park nearest to that destination. The service will check if there is a space in that car park, and if so it books the space.**

Figure 10.3
A simple use case précis for an in-car route planner application, which is used to formulate queries with which to discover services

> **FR:** The vehicle shall locate available car parks relative to the vehicle's geographical coordinates.
> **PR:** The vehicle shall provide a list of available car parks within 1 minute of the driver's request for the list.

Figure 10.4
Requirements on the application

and the identification of the services that can satisfy those requirements (Zachos et al. 2007). The process is iterative, and the initially available candidate services are identified based on high-level descriptions of the system requirements.

During this activity, service consumers develop simple use case précis that describe the required behavior of the service-centric application. Figure 10.3 shows a use case précis that describes the use of an in-car application which allows the user to find and book a parking lot space close to her/his destination. Figure 10.4 expresses some simple requirements that are associated with the précis for that application. The first, a functional requirement, specifies what the service shall do, and the second, the nonfunctional requirement, specifies desirable qualities of the service.

The identified services clarify and describe the requirements in more detail or specify other system requirements generating a new set of requirements. This new set of requirements is the base for discovering other services that can fulfill the functionality and quality of the system. The results of this process are (1) specification of SCS requirements, (2) an outline of the architecture models of the SCS, and (3) a list of candidate services that can satisfy the requirements.

We use query expansion and word disambiguation techniques to match stakeholder requirements with metadata annotations of service descriptions, using the WordNet online lexicon. It is achieved in a four-stage iterative process that consists of requirements expression, discovery of services using the queries extracted from the expressed requirements, service explanation and selection, then discovery of new requirements and reexpression of current ones in light of the selected services.

The requirement-based service discovery has four key components. In the first, a service query generated from the natural language requirements is divided into sentences, then tokenized and part-of-speech tagged and modified to include each term's morphological root (e.g., "driving" to "drive," and "drivers" to "driver"). Second, the algorithm applies procedures to disambiguate each term by defining its correct sense and tagging it with that sense (e.g., defining a driver to be a vehicle rather than a type of golf club). Third, the algorithm expands each term with other terms that have similar meaning according to the tagged sense, to increase the likelihood of a match with a service description (e.g., the term "driver" is synonymous with the term "motorist," which is also included in the query). In the fourth component the algorithm matches all expanded and sense-tagged query terms to a similar set of terms that describe each candidate service such as the DriveWorkAndPark service, expressed using the service description facet, in the SeCSE service registry.

Architecture-Based Service Discovery This activity deals with the identification of services that not only can provide the functionality and quality properties identified during requirement-based service discovery, but also fit within specific architectural and detailed design models of the system under development. Architecture-based discovery follows requirement-based service discovery and can identify subsets of services identified during it which can also fulfill specific architectural and behavioral constraints or identify new candidate services based on such constraints.

This discovery activity is driven by evolving models of the architecture and detailed design of the SCS by taking into account constraints that have been specified as part of these models. Such constraints may include, for example, the data types of the services identified in an architecture model, any behavioral models that may have been identified for these services, and other QoS properties that may have been specified for services and/or the operations that they provide. The activity can also result in amendments of architectural models if such amendments become necessary owing to decisions to select specific services identified by the discovery process.

The architecture-driven discovery process (Kozlenkov et al. 2007) is based on a query engine that supports the matching of service interfaces, behavioral models of services, and quality of service constraints. The matching algorithms which are deployed in this process are based on the computation of distances between different types of service facets, including the signature, operational semantics, description, and quality of service facets. Key features of these algorithms are that they treat service matching as an optimal assignment problem, can perform inexact matching (e.g., when matching), and distinguish between hard and soft constraints by generating results that are guaranteed to satisfy the former but satisfy the latter only if this will result in the optimization of an overall objective function, taking into account different search criteria.

In reference to the example workflow that we introduced in section 10.2, suppose that the design model of a system that implements part of the DriveWorkAndPark workflow is expressed in UML according to the sequence diagram shown in figure 10.5.[2] This diagram specifies eight operations that a haptical device of the car should use in order to realize part of the DriveWorkAndPark workflow. These operations are the following:

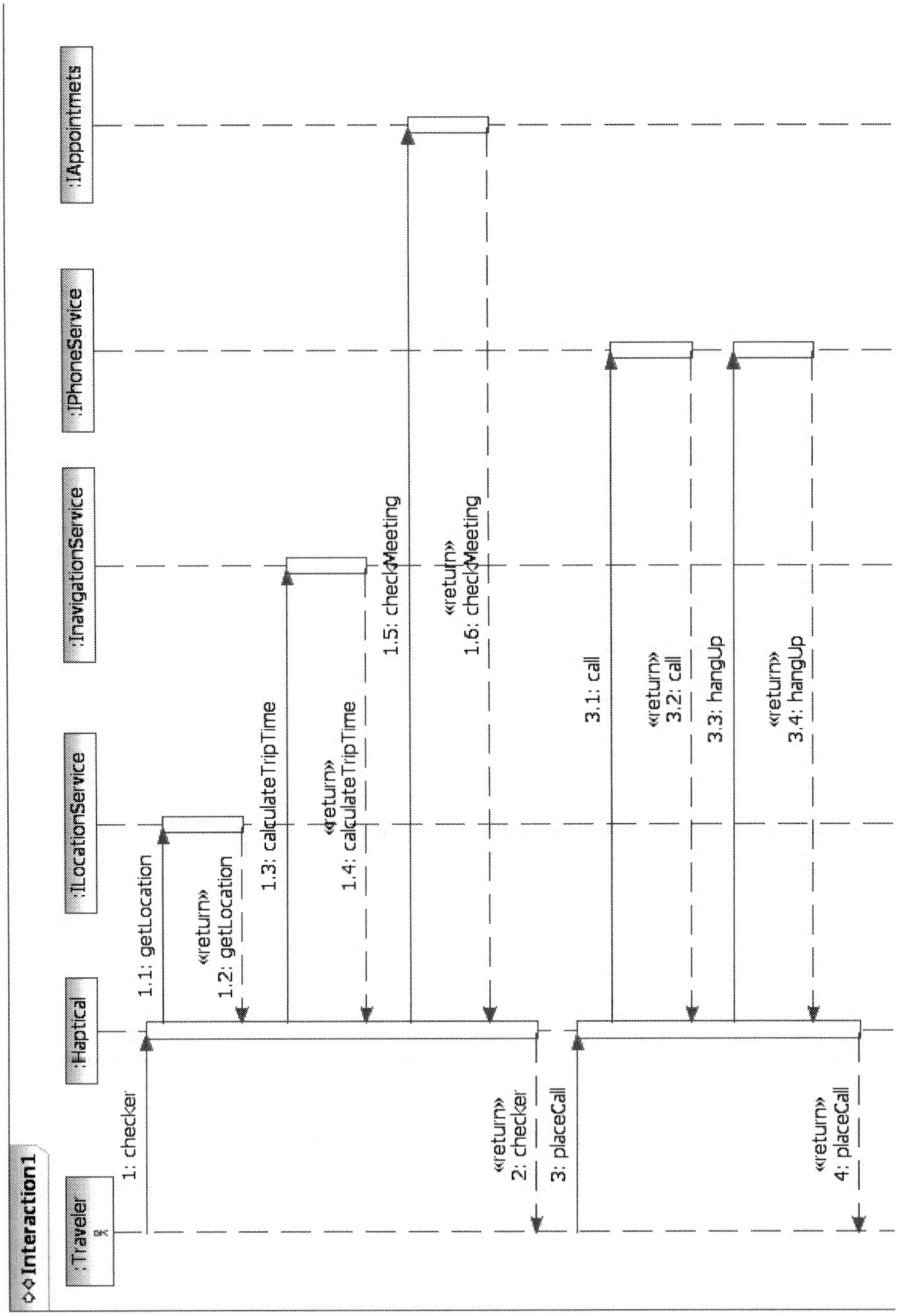

Figure 10.5
UML design model for DriveWorkAndPark workflow

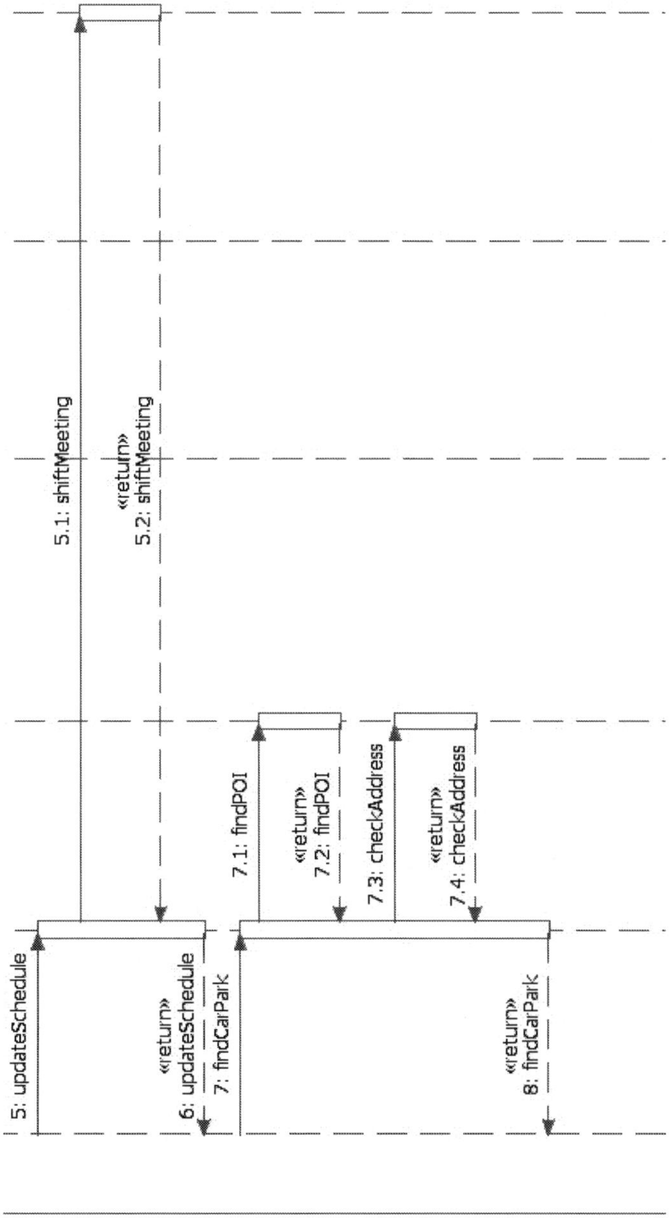

Figure 10.5
(continued)

- getLocation—This operation returns the location of the driver in terms of its geographical coordinates, given a destination address.
- calculateTripTime—This operation returns the arrival date/time of the driver, given the profile of the car.
- checkMeeting—This operation verifies if there is a conflict between the time of a meeting and the arrival time of the driver, given information about the meeting and the arrival times.
- call and hangup—These operations perform a phone call, given a phone number.
- shiftMeeting—This operation reschedules a meeting, given new start and end dates and times for it.
- findPOI—This operation identifies the position of a point of interest (POI) close to a specified location, given the name and type of this point.
- checkAddress—This operation checks the correctness of a given address.

Given the above diagram, a service discovery query could be specified by identifying the messages in the diagram for which service operations should be discovered (also known as "query messages" in Kozlenkov et al. (2007). Assuming a query that identifies as query messages, the messages GetLocation and findPOI in figure 10.6, the architecture-driven service discovery process of SeCSE would return the following candidate service operations:

1. Candidate service operations for GetLocation:

• GeocodingService.getLocationsList( )	0.11374[3]
• WNavigation.getPosition( )	0.14051
• YNavigation.getPosition( )	0.15241
• ReverseGeocodingService.getLocations List( )	0.15941

2. Candidate service operations for FindPOI:

• FindNearbyPOIService.getPoiList( )	0.19936
• ReverseGeocodingService.getLocations List( )	0.20578
• RouteCalculationService.getRoute( )	0.21203
• FindNearbyPOIService.getCompactPOI List( )	0.21276

To understand the matching process of the architecture-driven discovery process of SeCSE, consider the candidate operations getPOIList( ) and getCompactPOIList( ) for the query message FindPOI. The distances between these candidate operations and FindPOI were 0.19936 and 0.21276, respectively. These distances were computed by matching, among other elements in the specifications of these operations, the data types of their input and return parameters with the data types of the input and return parameters of FindPOI.

Figure 10.6 shows how the return data type POI of FindPOI was mapped onto the return data types of the operations getPOIList( ) and getCompactPOIList( ), namely, tns1:FindLocations and tns1:FindPOI.

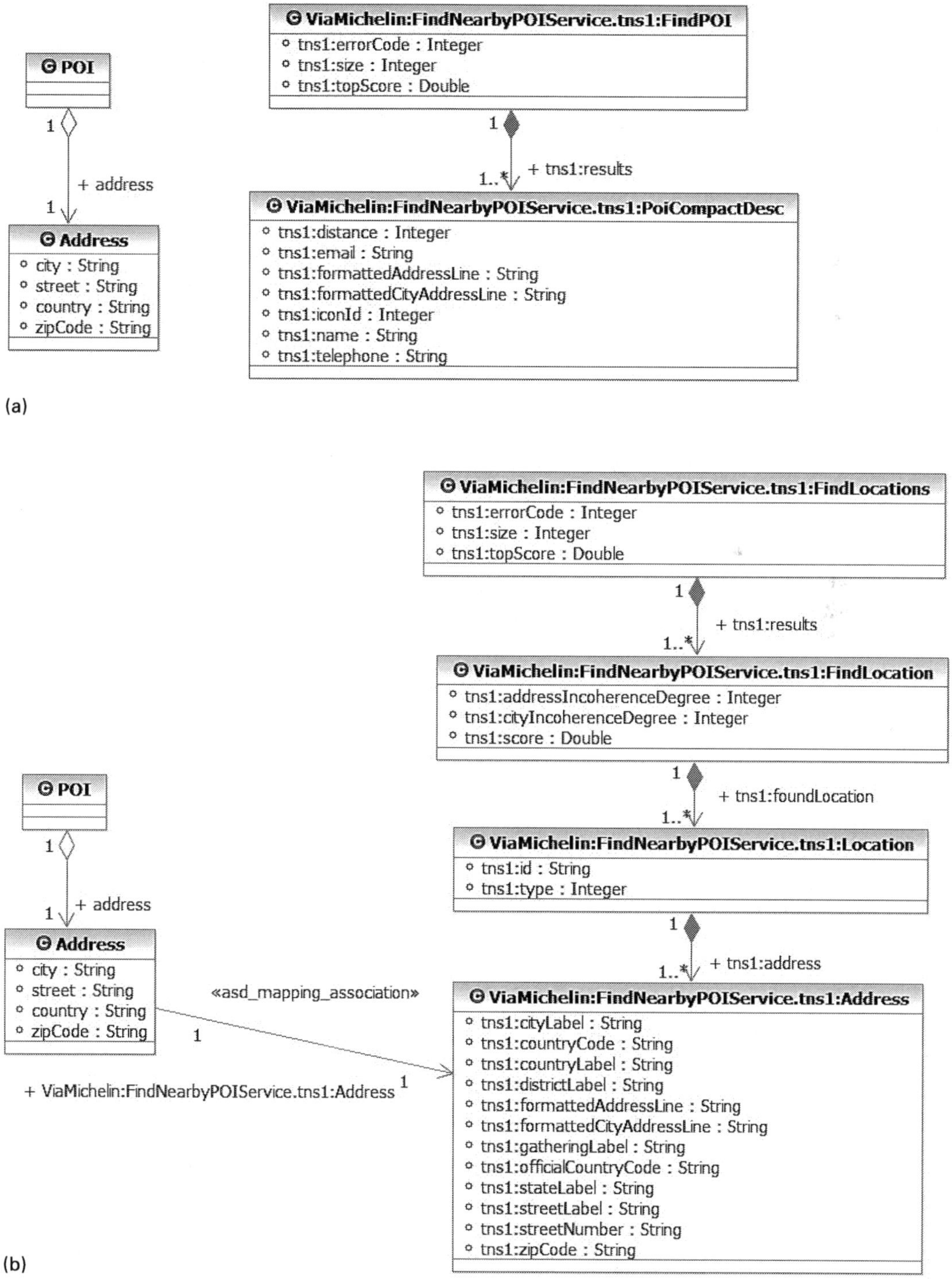

Figure 10.6
Matching of service operation data types. (a) Mapping of output data type of FindPOI onto output data type of getPOI. (b) Mapping of output data type of Find POI onto output data type of getCompactPOIList

As shown in part (a) of figure 10.6, the class Address that is part of the return data type POI of FindPOI is mapped onto the class FindNearbyPOIService.tns1:Address that is part of the data type of the return parameter of getPOIListReturn. This mapping was created because the two classes have attributes with similar names and identical types, including the following:

- Address.city:String, and FindNearbyPOIService.tns1:Address.tns1:cityLabel:String
- Address.street:String, and FindNearbyPOIService.tns1:Address.tns1:streetLabel:String
- Address.country:String, and FindNearbyPOIService.tns1:Address.tns1:countryCode: String
- Address.zipCode:String, and FindNearbyPOIService.tns1:Address.tns1:zipCode:String

In the case of the return data type of getCompactPOIListReturn, however, none of its attributes was similar to the attributes of the return data type of FindPOI. Thus, as shown in part (b) of figure 10.6, there was no matching between it and the return data type of FindPOI. These structural differences were one of the factors that gave rise to the difference between the distance of FindPOI and getPOIList( ) and the distance between FindPOI and getCompactPOIList( ). Other factors underpinning the calculation of the above distance measures included structural differences between the input parameters of the relevant operations, as well as differences in their names and behavioral models of the services that offered them. A more detailed account of the matching process and the computation of distances during the architecture-driven discovery process is given in Kozlenkov et al. (2007).

Runtime Service Discovery This activity (Spanoudakis et al. 2007) involves identifying alternative services to replace services already participating in an SCS that may become unavailable or fail to meet specific functional and quality requirements or context-related conditions during system execution. Runtime service discovery is a challenging activity since it requires efficient discovery of alternative services that precisely match the functional and quality requirements of the SCS and enable replacement of these services during runtime execution in an efficient and nonintrusive way.

Suppose, for instance, that at runtime there was a need for discovering alternative service operations for the operation findPOI in the implementation of the system presented in figure 10.5, as this operation might be found to be unavailable following a call made to it. In this case, none of the candidate operations getPOIList( ) and getCompactPOIList( ) that were identified for findPOI by the architecture-driven service discovery process would be an acceptable result. The reason for this is that there is no guarantee that the return types of these operations would be compatible with the use of the results of findPOI in the implemented workflow. To guarantee this, the return data types of candidate operations for findPOI would need to be subtypes of the return type of this operation. On the other hand, an operation with a return type that is a subtype of POI in figure 10.6 would be acceptable in this respect (other criteria would also need to be satisfied in this case, as described in Spanoudakis et al. (2007).

After surveying discovery tools supplied by the project, we are now ready to concentrate on the actual composition of services.

10.3.3 Composition Design

Service-centric system engineering covers the development of complex SCSs by providing mechanisms for selecting and composing different component services. The dynamic nature of SCSs precludes the a priori identification of the services defining the system and demands for discovery and selection of services at runtime. Thus, designers and developers require the proper tools to determine, for example: (1) when binding happens during system execution; (2) what criteria selected services should fulfill; (3) under which conditions services should be replaced with other services; and (4) what aspects of service provision can be negotiated with service providers.

To define the high-level design of an SCS, we suggest the adoption of a product lines engineering approach called variability. Using this approach, some of the abstract tasks required of the system being developed can be defined as variables at design time. They can then be implemented using different services (expressed as alternatives). This involves (Nieto et al. 2007):

- Variation point management: the variable parts of the workflow and possible alternatives are defined.
- Variation point realization: the services to be used in the implementation of the alternatives are selected.

Consistent with the approach based on variability, the language used to develop an SCS should support the designer not only in the definition of the way service invocations are sequenced in a workflow, but also in the definition of self-configuration policies that will discipline the selection of services and negotiation actions at runtime.

To address these requirements, a composition language has been proposed (Colombo et al. 2006) to describe service compositions in terms of two distinct parts: (1) a process part, described using WS-BPEL, to define the main business logic of the composition, and (2) a declarative part, described using binding constraints and event-condition-action (ECA) rules (Colombo et al. 2006). Constraints and rules are used to associate a BPEL workflow with the declaration of the policy to be used during (re)configuration. In particular, constraints define the aspects that always need to be met by an SCS; rules define the self-organization actions to be executed when some situations occur.

Figure 10.7 shows a sample of a rule that triggers the reconfiguration of the composition in response to an event generated by a monitoring component. In fact, if some failure occurs in a service, all bindings to component services should be reconsidered.

```
<!– processInfo enad eventList are global variables -->
<rule name="service violation event">
    <scope>
        <all/>
    <scope>
    <event>
        <name>violationEvent</name>
        <type>rulelanguge.datamodel.events.ServiceViolationEvent</type>
    </event>
    <consequence description="the service endpoint is stored into the endpoint black list">
        processInfo.updateBlackList(violationEvent.getServiceDetails());
        CacheUpdatingActionRequest actionRequest = new CacheUpdatingActionRequest();
        actionReqeust.setServiceEndpoint(violationEvent.getServiceDetails().getEndpoint());
        actionRequest.setMode("delete");
        eventList.addExternalEvent(new Event(actionRequest));
    </consequence>
</rule>
```

Figure 10.7
Example of reaction rule

10.3.4 Negotiation of Contractual Agreements

Automated SLA negotiation can be used during the discovery and selection of services both at design time and at runtime. Various negotiation protocols can be used to support the matching between service requests and service offers on QoS attributes, such as 1:1 bargaining or multiparty cooperative and competitive negotiations. At design time, the negotiation can be auction-type, to determine the best candidate(s) for the binding among the services that are returned by the discovery tool. At runtime the use of negotiation is likely only in exceptional cases because it is a time-consuming activity. Negotiation can be used as an alternative to global rebinding as a recovery action in the event of risks of a global QoS constraints violation (i.e., an SLA violation). In such a case, the estimation of the QoS of the workflow slice still to be executed can be adjusted through negotiation and, if successful, the existing bindings can be kept. The SeCSE negotiation platform offers the possibility to adopt various negotiation protocols and also to define new ones. Moreover, it offers an efficient search-based approach to help the parties converge toward an agreement (see Di Nitto et al. 2007 for more details).

For example, the system integrator may want to negotiate the QoS of one of the services she/he is going to integrate into the composition, for example, the Microsoft MapPoint Service. In the negotiation the integrator specifies preferences, such as her/his ranges of admissible values for cost (e.g., between 1 and 4 euros) and response time (e.g., between 2 and 6 ms). Such ranges are used to perform a negotiation with the provider, using, for example, an automatic, search-based negotiation strategy described in Di Nitto et al. (2007). As a result, the provider is able to guarantee to the integrator a response time of 4 ms for a cost of 2.5 euros.

10.3.5 Service Verification/Validation

Verification and validation are crosscutting processes that highlight the dual-perspective nature of testing in SCSs.

Among different verification and validation activities, testing is a valuable means to ensure high reliability for business-critical, service-oriented architectures, and a lot can be learned from testing techniques conceived for traditional systems, for component-based systems, and for distributed or Web-based systems. However, when dealing with service-oriented architectures, it is necessary to take the following factors into account:

- Service integrators and service consumers, in general, are not aware of how a service can evolve. Service providers can change a service implementation without, however, updating the service interface (e.g., because only the service's internal logic has changed. As a result, the functional and/or nonfunctional behavior of applications or other services integrating this service can be affected.
- Providing a given piece of functionality with a QoS level that does not violate the service-level agreement (SLA) is also important. However, the provider may stipulate an SLA with a consumer without being aware that there may be some conditions for the service for which such an SLA cannot be guaranteed.

To tackle the first issue, we propose that services be accompanied with a testing facet containing test cases and nonfunctional assertions. When someone acquires the service, this facet constitutes part of the contract (Di Penta et al. 2007a) between the service consumer/integrator and the provider. SeCSE provides a tool kit composed of the following:

1. A tool for the automatic generation of testing facets starting from system test cases, for example, written using the JUnit framework.
2. A tool, to be used at a composition stage, by the service integrator to retest the service and verify whether the service still provides the same level of functionality and of QoS as when it was acquired.

It can happen, for example, that when the service integrator acquires the Exchange Server Calendar service, such a service returns appointments in a proprietary format. At a given point, the provider decides to modify such a service, so that it returns appointments in a vCal format. When the integrator is going to use such a service in the DriveWorkAndPark composition, she/he retests it with the regression testing tool, using the testing facet downloaded when the service was acquired. The regression testing tool might indicate that the service has changed its behavior. SeCSE also provides a tool that generates contexts—consisting of inputs, bindings between abstract and concrete services (in the case of compositions)—which cause SLA violations (Di Penta et al. 2007b). The tool is based on the use of evolutionary testing strategies, in particular genetic algorithms. In service-oriented development, this kind of testing has to be performed by a service provider

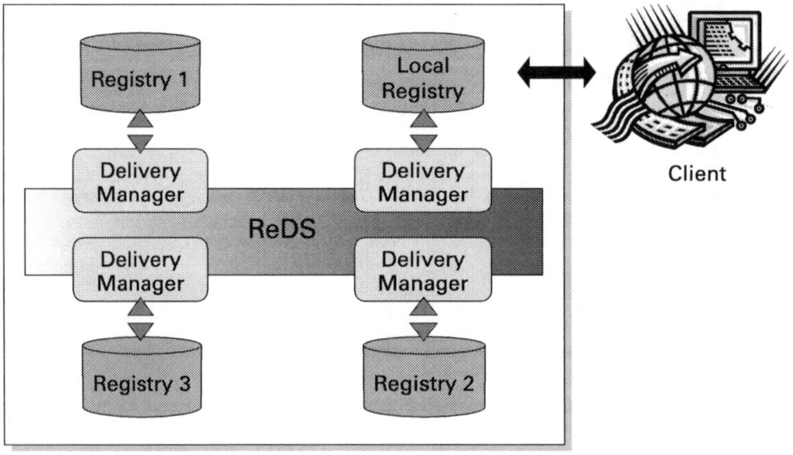

Figure 10.8
SeCSE Distributed Registry

before publishing a simple or composite service and starting negotiations with service consumers about SLAs.

For example, let us suppose the system integrator assumes that, for any binding and input, the DriveWorkAndPark composition ensures a response time of 15 s. She/he could therefore generate an SLA template for the composition with such a value. However, the SLA testing is able to indicate that, for particular itinerary options, the MapPoint service takes longer than expected. As a consequence, the overall response time will be 18 s. This may suggest that the integrator declare, for the composition, a response time upper bound of 20 s.

10.3.6 Service Delivery

Service delivery focuses on the mechanism by which services are made available to potential consumers. This is done by the SeCSE Distributed Registry (DIRE), (figure 10.8), our proposal to support loose interactions among registries. DIRE aims at fostering communication among different proprietary registries by means of two elements: a distributed communication bus and a delivery manager associated with each registry. The bus is introduced to connect the delivery managers, and is based on REDS (Cugola and Picco 2006), a distributed publish-and-subscribe middleware. The delivery manager acts as facade: it is the intermediary between the registry and the bus, and manages the information flow in the two directions.

The distributed registry allows the integration of heterogeneous registries and supports the creation of special-purpose filters to retrieve services efficiently.

Distributed registries are organized in a federation to allow them to "share" services. Each member of a federation can redistribute the information it gets about a service to every registry of the federation. A registry can promote both proprietary services and services received from others. Federations are special-purpose subscriptions. Usually, we adopt content-based subscriptions, but federations exploit topic-based subscriptions. Each federation is associated with a topic, which becomes the name of the federation. When a registry joins a federation, it must subscribe to the associated topic. This ensures that every time there is a message for that topic, the participants in the federation receive it, and thus we have a multicast communication group.

Services are published by providing the delivery manager with the data that should be shared. A company can choose to share data created on its registry or information retrieved from others. In both cases, only the owner of the published data can update them. Since the infrastructure is a decoupled distributed system, a registry can join and declare its interests at any time. The infrastructure guarantees that a registry can always retrieve the information it is interested in. For this purpose, the propagation of information is subject to lease contracts, a typical concept of many distributed systems (e.g., Jini[4]). When the lease expires, the information is no longer considered to be valid and must be retransmitted to extend its validity. The delivery manager can perform this operation automatically, guaranteeing that when the information is re-sent, all interested registries retrieve it.

Because of commercial agreements between the parties, a service consumer may want to use exactly one specific service. In this case, the selection can be precise: the delivery manager uses the unique identifiers of interested elements to create a filter and subscribe to them through the dispatcher.

When the client does not know the services it wants, the infrastructure allows the client to retrieve all the services whose descriptions comply with specified properties. If the property is encoded in a standard facet, the client can use the unique identifier of the facet and select all the services that have a relationship with the selected property.

10.3.7 Dynamic Binding

When an SCS is deployed, binding and recovery are triggered at runtime by the execution of the rules defined as part of the service composition according to the approach discussed in section 10.3.3. As for binding, two complementary approaches are possible: global and local (re)binding (Di Penta et al. 2006). They address two different types of problems. Global binding refers to the selection of all the services needed by the composition in order to satisfy some global QoS constraints and an objective function in terms of some QoS attributes. For example, a system integrator might want to limit the maximum cost for the DriveWorkAndPark composition to 10 euros while minimizing the response time and maximizing the availability of the services. Such an objective can cause the choice of the

Exchange Server Calendar service, of the Microsoft MapPoint service, and of the Telecom SendSms and ThirdPartyCall services among the available concrete services. Bindings are determined based on a single service-declared QoS, and also on the likelihood that different paths in the workflow will be executed, because different paths will involve different services and produce different global QoS values.

A monitoring mechanism (see section 10.3.8) detects risks of possible violations of the QoS constraints during execution. These violations can be due to some unforeseen behavior (e.g., a service takes more time than expected, a service is not available, or an unlikely path is executed). In case of such events, the monitoring mechanism triggers a recovery action, as specified in the rule set. One possible recovery action is to rebind the workflow slice still not executed, in order to try to improve the final QoS by using the actual QoS values of the executed part (Canfora et al. 2005).

Alternatively, it is possible to pursue a local (re)binding strategy, which permits the selection of a service binding while the composition is running, just before the service is invoked. This selection is based on local QoS constraints only, or else on information about context. In our DriveWorkAndPark example, the selection of a car parking lot is based on the position of the car at the moment the service is requested.

10.3.8 Service Monitoring

In SeCSE, the monitoring of functional and QoS properties is the responsibility of data collectors, which are in charge of capturing and extracting the data needed to perform monitoring; data analyzers, which are responsible for analyzing collected data and checking whether they satisfy set constraints; and a monitoring manager, which is in charge of initiating and controlling the whole monitoring process.

The SeCSE monitoring subsystem supports the specification of the monitoring policies and rules in a single common language, called SECMOL (SErvice Centric MOnitoring Language), which has been developed and integrated with the major standard for specifying and monitoring service-level agreements: WS-Agreement.

This way, the monitoring manager receives specifications of the monitoring policy and the rules to be monitored in the SECMOL. Following the receipt of these specifications, the manager assesses whether the agreement can be monitored, and identifies the data collectors and analyzers that will undertake responsibility for collecting the primitive information needed for monitoring and checking the rules, respectively. After selecting the appropriate data collectors and analyzers, the monitor manager does the following things:

- Extracts the specification of the data to be collected at runtime from the input service-level agreement and passes it to the data collectors, and
- Extracts the specification of the rules to be monitored from the input service-level agreement and passes it to the data analyzers.

The monitoring manager also has the responsibility to connect the selected data collector(s) and analyzer(s) so as to enable them to exchange data directly at runtime, receive the results of the monitoring process, and report these results to the interested parties.

In SECMOL, a monitoring rule specifies logical conditions over one or more data streams which are generated either directly, by extracting data from messages that are captured at runtime (data extraction), or indirectly, by computations that are performed upon data which are extracted from runtime messages. For example, a rule specifying a guarantee term regarding the maximum response time of a service operation may be defined as a condition over a stream of data that constitute the response times of all the calls of the relevant operation.

Furthermore, the language requires the specification of the machine that will perform the relevant processing for each rule, computation, and data extraction. This is specified by a runtime element. Also, each data extraction and computation is associated with a schedule specifying the interval at which data should be extracted or the computation should be performed.

Since SECMOL rules are encoded in XML, complete examples would be too verbose. This is why we think that it is better if we introduce a simple example only informally. The following excerpt checks whether the average response time of service gplanTrip is "always" less than 15 seconds:

```
let lastTen = retrieve('pID', null, null,
'planTrip', 'postcondition', 10)
(avg rt in lastTen; rt) < 15
```

We approximate the "always" with the last 10 invocations and use a *retrieve* statement to get them. The parameters say that we want to get the values from a process identified by pID, and we use the XPath expression planTrip to identify the postcondition we are interested in. Then "let" assigns lastTen with returned data and "avg" computes the average value of all the last 10 invocations. The monitoring expression states that the average value must always be less than 15 (seconds).

10.4 SeCSE Integrated Platform

All SeCSE tools are integrated in a software suite named SeCSE Development Environment (SDE). It is Web-based and incorporates the following tools:

1. Early Service Discovery Suite (ESD), which supports requirement elicitation and early service discovery.
2. Testing tools (Service Regression Testing Tool, RTT) and Service Quality of Service Tool, QST) that aim at building confidence in the service's functional and nonfunctional features.

3. Composition design tools (Composition Designer, CD; and Architecture Time Discovery, ASD) that support the design of adaptable composition of services conforming to the BPEL standard and the identification of services compatible with the architectural constraints of the composition.
4. Runtime environment that supports the execution of the new enriched BPEL services by offering negotiation and binding mechanisms as well as runtime service discovery.
5. Service Specification Tool (SST) that supports the description of dependable services by means of facets expanding the semantic descriptions. A core set of facets is provided by default, but it is possible to extend and customize these facets according to the specific customer needs.
6. Monitor platform that checks service-centric systems for compliance with functional and nonfunctional requirements to offer a basis for providing service failure recovery mechanisms that allow business continuity. The monitoring mechanisms work both at the process level (loose monitoring) and at the single operation level (tight monitoring).
7. Service delivery platform that supports the exposition of services in different repositories (SeCSE registry, UDDI, ebXML, etc.) by means of a delivery manager offering push/pull policies, community of interest creation, and a flexible and extensible infrastructure to federate registries.

The SDE architecture (figure 10.9) allows a seamless and loosely coupled integration of the SeCSE tools by means of Web Service technologies and has been conceived having these main layers in mind:

- A view layer, the SDE-Web, that is a Web-based application usable by means of any browser and is responsible for interacting with the users, capturing their inputs (as actions) and presenting the results of those actions. In particular, this layer offers all those functionalities necessary for the development of SCS at design time.
- A control layer, the SDE-IF, built upon an ESB which delivers the user's request (sent by SDE-Web) to the appropriate SeCSE tool, and also manages the message exchanges among the SeCSE tools themselves and supports the runtime of the SCS. It offers special features to extend and to simplify the use of this ESB when integrating hybrid systems (i.e., services and legacy systems) to transform them to an SOA, including message exchange patterns and message transformations, using technologies such as XSLT.

This SDE has been released together with another supporting component, the SeCSE Registry, which manages and stores the service descriptions according to the SeCSE approach. In the next section, the SeCSE Registry will be further described.

10.4.1 SeCSE Registry

One of the main components of an SOA is the registry, or service directory, that stores all the information about known services. An accurate description of the services and the ability to extract such information from a repository is a key element for implementing easily

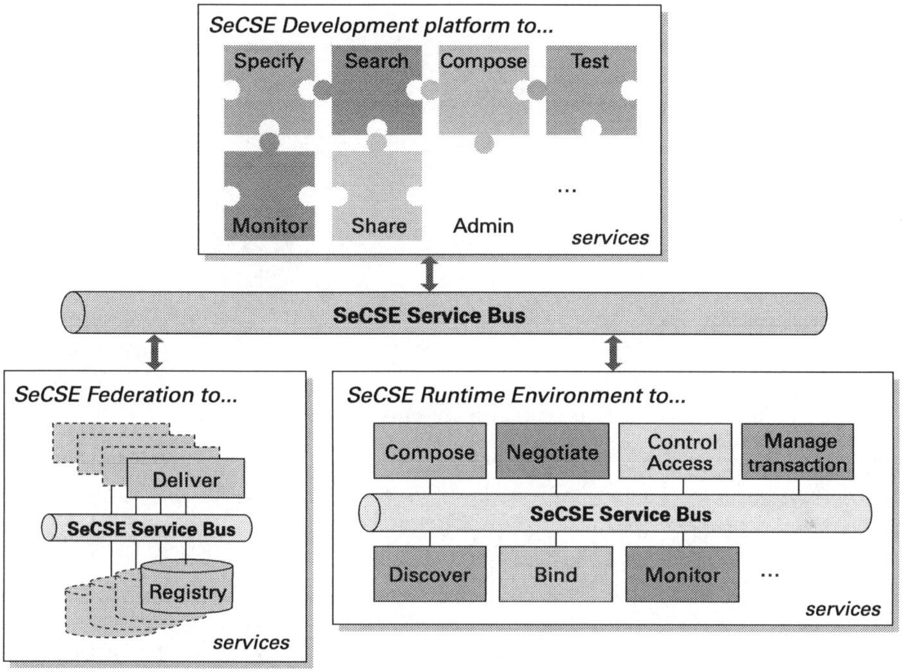

Figure 10.9
SeCSE Development Environment architecture

configurable systems, and one which is able to adapt automatically to any changes that may occur in the system context. The registry has the goal of supporting both the advanced classification and the search technologies. It provides several features that are not included in the commonly used UDDI registries or in the recently proposed ones, such as ebXML. In particular, in this registry the services are described through a complex set of facets (Prieto-Diaz and Freeman 1987) that are detailed XML descriptions of the different aspects of a service defined by an XML schema that defines the structure and an XML file that describes the facet itself.

Complex searches can be performed easily through the investigation of the XML description of the facets and the associated XML schema, using the XPath and XQuery technologies. This is important because it allows SeCSE's discovery tools to identify and evaluate services according to the needs of the potential service consumer.

10.4.2 Deployed DriveWorkAndPark Example

The DriveWorkAndPark example has been developed as part of our case studies and is deployed on the platform shown in figure 10.10. The composition is running on the runtime platform installed at secse.cefriel.it. On the same machine other components of the

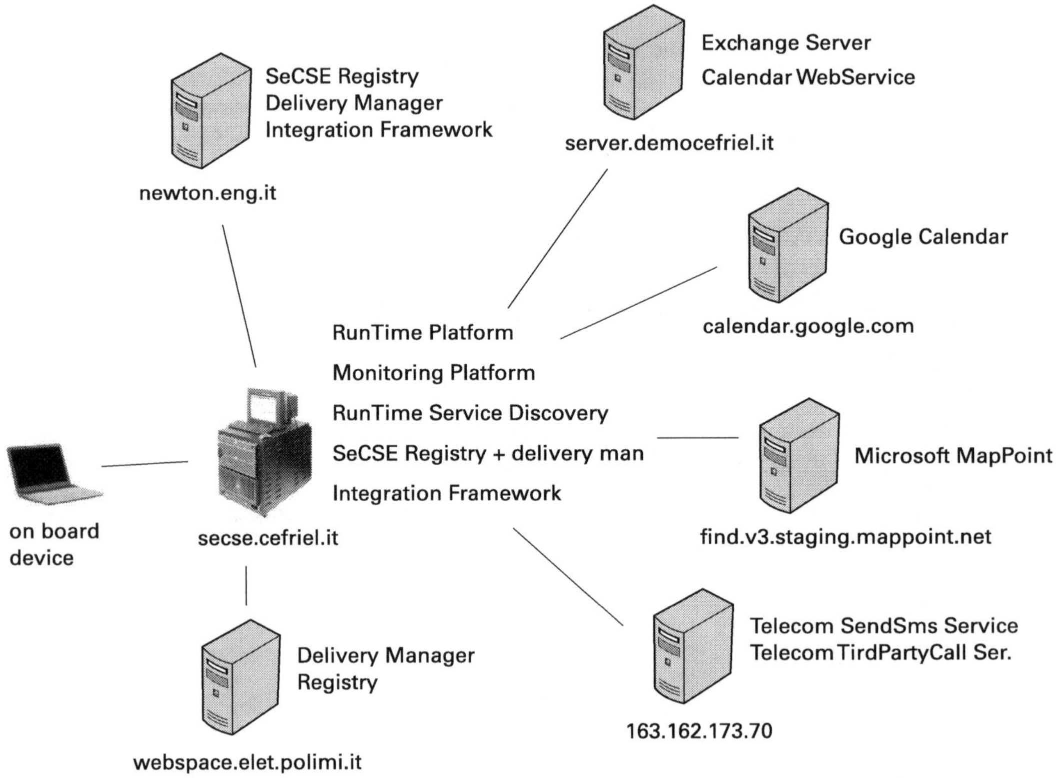

Figure 10.10
Deployment of DriveWorkAndPark

SeCSE SDE run and interact with those installed on different domains (Engineering and Politecnico di Milano). The composition executes services either hosted in the same domain (such as the Exchange calendar service) or in different domains (such as Google, Microsoft, and Telecom Italia).

10.5 Related Work

This section presents a brief description of the state of the art related to all aspects of service-centric applications and provides a comparison between SeCSE outcomes and the results achieved in other initiatives.

10.5.1 Specification

Current approaches to service specification, such as WSDL[5] and UDDI,[6] suffer from weakness in specifying semantics, but in most cases this weakness can be resolved by extending them in some way. WSDL 2.0, for instance, will go some way to addressing the lack of semantics in earlier versions of the language. Even technologies such as OWL-S,[7] which purport to address the issue of semantic service specification, are lacking in the semantics which they allow to be expressed and have not gained widespread uptake. Specifying service quality, despite attracting research interest in recent years, is an area in which there is no standard solution. Emerging techniques, such as WS-POLICY, still require a more complete quality model. On top of this, the issue of expressing semantics in quality specification is an open one.

Our faceted approach is a way to address this issue. The various facets we have developed enable the definition of syntactical, operational, and quality characteristics of a service. Moreover, given the possibility of introducing new facets within our framework, it is possible to continuously extend the pieces of information that constitute the description of a service.

10.5.2 Discovery

Syntactic-based matching techniques are now widely recognized as ineffective for service discovery. Therefore, semantics has been proposed as key to increasing automation in applying Web Services (Ankolenkar et al. 2002). Although some approaches (Sycara et al. 2002; Paolucci et al. 2002; Wang and Stroulia 2003; Klein and Ries 2004) overcome the weaknesses of syntactical matching methods, each also has its own weaknesses. Approaches such as Paolucci et al. (2002) rely on the message flow only, which can lead to different problems. For example, services with identical message flows may offer completely different functionality. Services with identical functionality may use different message flows to achieve this functionality. Thus, if matching is based on the comparison of message flows, services offering functionality different from the one intended by the consumer may be invoked. All of the reported approaches also depend on well-defined semantics through use of standards for service specification and models of internal service behavior—semantics that cannot be assumed for heterogeneous services available in diverse locations. Rather, more flexible approaches that assume less about how services are specified are needed. Query expansion is an established technique in information retrieval. Balke and Wagner (2003) present techniques toward advanced personalization of Web Service selection. Query expansion in information retrieval is often associated with word sense disambiguation to determine the correct sense of terms in order to enable correct expansion. Most word sense disambiguation algorithms exploit WordNet,[8] an online lexical reference system whose design is inspired by current psycholinguistic theories of human lexical memory. WordNet offers costfree use and well-documented open code, making it an ideal tool for disambiguation of meaning, semantic tagging, and information retrieval. Though the approaches that we have reviewed so far concern mainly the efficacy of discovery but make the hypothesis work with services built using a homogeneous technology, the peculiarity of SODIUM (an FP6 IST European STREP project[9]) is to focus on supporting discovery in a heterogeneous setting where services and service registries are built by using different technologies.

In SeCSE we adopt a very flexible approach to service discovery by providing tools with different capabilities that address specific needs at different times in the service life cycle. In particular, in the early phases we adopt the flexible approach based on query expansions and disambiguation. In the design phases we take into account architectural constraints concerning the way the service to be found is supposed to interact with the composition. In the runtime phase we look for services that are fully compatible with the structure of the BPEL process implementing the composition.

10.5.3 Composition of Services and Dynamic Binding

The typical approach to building service compositions is based on the ideas of exploiting BPEL as the language to express the way component services have to be combined and of relying on external, nonparametric tools to support everything has to do with the reconfiguration of the composition itself. An example of this approach is the MAIS framework (De Antonellis et al. 2006), which offers a specific component to support dynamic binding according to a hard-coded policy.

METEOR-S (Verma et al. 2005) overcomes this restriction because it exploits semantic Web languages to describe both domain constraints and services. The composition is divided into scopes, and matchmaking algorithms are used to associate each scope with a concrete set of services. The binding to concrete services is enabled at design time, deployment time, and just before execution. Though this approach requires that a semantic description be attached to each potential service, our approach works with both complete and lightweight service descriptions, and also supports runtime bindings that do not seem to be addressed in METEOR-S.

Mandel and McIlraith (2003) exploit DAML-S technologies to support semantic discovery of services and their runtime integration into the composition, but the approach does not account for dependences among service invocations, such as the ones that occur in our DriveWorkAndPark example, between the invocation activities related to the usage of an agenda service. Similarly, Orriens et al. (2003) present an initial rule-based approach to govern the semiautomatic development of compositions. Our approach builds on this to fully automate the evolution of compositions at runtime.

The combination of rules and workflow languages in service-oriented computing has already been proposed as a way to define conditional business logic that is not directly captured in the workflow (Rosenberg and Dustdar 2005). In contrast, our rules are not designed to encapsulate fragments of business logic, but work at a lower level of abstraction to support the definition of policies for dynamic binding and negotiation.

10.5.4 Negotiation

Research on automated negotiation is mainly related to architectural solutions for negotiation or algorithms and models for protocols and negotiator strategies. In Chhetri et al.

(2006) a multiagent framework with a two-layered architecture is presented, in which local QoS negotiations for finding a binding to the same invoke activity are coordinated to satisfy global QoS constraints of a composition. Local constraints have to be inferred from the global ones and from the workflow topology. The model presented in Comuzzi and Pernici (2005) consists of a negotiation broker carrying out one-to-one negotiations on behalf of both service consumers and providers. The decision model of the negotiators is expressed by a hard-coded parametric function which needs to be instantiated by the parties before negotiation starts. In contrast, a marketplace-based architecture is presented in Rolli et al. (2004), in which the marketplace mediates all the communication among negotiation parties, but it does not take part in the negotiations. In Ncho and Aimeur (2004), the multiagent system paradigm is combined with the Web Service technology to enable distributed online bargaining applications. However, only two negotiation processes are supported, bilateral and trilateral. The latter uses a third entity to authenticate the trading agents and to validate the deals.

In contrast to the other approaches, the main characteristics of the SeCSE negotiation platform are to be able to support various kinds of negotiation processes, explicitly expressed as state machines, and to plug in agents with different negotiation strategies.

10.5.5 Validation and Verification

Many testing approaches used for traditional software systems, such as unit or regression testing, can be adapted or reused for service-oriented systems. However, there are some peculiarities that need to be tackled with customized approaches. Although research on testing of services and service-oriented systems is still at an early stage, a number of approaches dealing with various testing levels and activities have been developed. Tsai et al. (2002) and Bertolino and Polini (2005) proposed a framework to extend the UDDI registry to support Web Service testing. As discussed in the introduction, the lack of observability is a relevant issue when testing services. Recently, Martin et al. (2006) proposed a framework to automatically perform Web Service robustness testing. With respect to this state of the art, the contribution of verification and validation approaches developed in SeCSE is twofold:

- Providing a support for regression testing, that is, letting a service integrator test whether during its evolution a service still preserves its functional behavior and its QoS properties. The SeCSE approach is able to transform legacy system unit test suites into service test suites and to automatically generate QoS assertions, to support regression testing execution at a minimum cost in terms of service invocations and resource usage.
- Automatically generating test cases with the purpose of testing service-level agreements. Although other approaches, such as Martin et al. (2006), perform service stress-testing, the SeCSE approach is novel in that it automatically generates test cases to cause violations to constraints related to any possible QoS attribute, and also considers dynamic binding as one of the factors affecting the overall QoS of a composite service.

10.5.6 Service Delivery

As for the cooperation and coordination among registries, the different approaches can roughly be classified in two main groups: approaches based on selective replication and approaches based on semantic annotations.

UDDI and ebXML belong to the first family. UDDI extends the replication and distribution mechanisms offered by the previous versions to support complex and hierarchical topologies of registries, identify services by means of a unique key over different registries, and guarantee the integrity and authenticity of published data by means of digital signatures. ebXML is a family of standards based on XML to provide an infrastructure to ease the online exchange of commercial information. In contrast to UDDI, ebXML allows for the creation of federations among registries (all the elements are replicated on the different registries) to foster the cooperation among them. The idea is to group registries that share the same commercial interests or are located in the same domain.

Even if these approaches foster the cooperation among registries, they imply that all registries comply with a single standard, and the cooperation needs a setup phase to manually define the information contributed by each registry. Moreover, given the way relations are managed by UDDI, the more registries we consider, the more complex the management of relations becomes, and the cost of publishing or discovering a service increases.

METEOR-S (Verma et al. 2005) and PYRAMID-S (Pilioura et al. 2004) are the two main representatives of the second family. They support the creation of scalable peer-to-peer infrastructures for the publication and discovery of services. METEOR-S supports only UDDI registers, whereas PYRAMID-S supports both UDDI and ebXML registries. Both the approaches adopt ontology-based meta-information to allow a set of registries to be federated: each registry is "specialized" according to one or more categories it is associated with. This means that the publication of a new service requires the meta-information needed to categorize the service within the ontology. This information can be specified manually, or it can be inferred semiautomatically by analyzing an annotated version of the WSDL interface of the service. If the same node of the ontology is associated with more than one registry, the publication of the services that "belong" to that node must be replicated on all the registries.

The distinguishing feature of SeCSE compared with the other approaches is the support offered to user-defined replication of services on the different registries. This element allows users to decide the kinds of services they want to interact with and to move their information close to where the services might be used. The second characterizing approach is federation, where different registries can easily cooperate to share the information about mutually known services. Both the benefits derive from the adoption of a publish-and-subscribe infrastructure as underlying communication means and from the flexibility offered by the filters used by the communication bus to deliver service data.

10.5.7 Monitoring

As for service monitoring, there are several works that define specification languages for SLAs and propose appropriate monitoring architectures. Sahai et al. (2002) describes an automated and distributed SLA monitoring engine. Keller and Ludwig (2002) presents the Web service-level agreement (WSLA) framework. It defines and monitors SLAs for Web Services, focusing on QoS properties such as performance and costs. Skene et al. (2007) describes a model and an analysis technique for reasoning on the monitorability of systems. SLAs are expressed using the SLAng language. All these approaches focus on formally defining high-level contracts among parties (typically, between a service consumer and a service provider); hence, they do not allow properties with a fine-grained granularity, such as those needed for activities in a workflow.

Barbon et al. (2006) presents an approach for monitoring BPEL service compositions. Monitors can be attached to a single instance or to the whole class of process instances; they can check temporal, Boolean, time-related, and statistical properties, expressed in RTML (Runtime Monitoring Specification Language). Business and monitoring logics are kept separated by executing the monitor engine and the BPEL execution engine in parallel; code implementing monitors are automatically generated from high-level specifications. With respect to our approach, they do not allow for dynamic (re-)configuration of the monitoring system in terms of rules and metalevel parameters; moreover, they don't deal with external variables, thus limiting the expressiveness of the language.

Another interesting approach that we see as orthogonal to SeCSE is the one proposed by WS-DIAMOND (FP6 IST European FET Project[10]). It introduces an interesting taxonomy of possible classes of problems arising during the execution of a composition, together with a classification of the possible repair strategies. Though the classes of problems could be used in SeCSE to create proper policies for monitoring, the repair strategies could be triggered by the rules defined within the SeCSE composition.

10.6 Conclusions

This chapter presents an overview of the SeCSE project by introducing the methods, tools, and techniques developed within the project. Such methods and tools support the development and the runtime of service-centric systems in different aspects, such as the following:

- Specifying the service characteristics by means of an extensible mechanism, where different facets specify various aspects of the service, such as the interface, the behavior, the QoS, and commercial aspects
- Discovering a service needed to build a service-oriented system during the requirement elicitation and specification phase, during the design phase, and at runtime
- Composing services and hybrid components to build service-oriented systems
- Negotiating the service-level agreement

- Testing the service's functional and nonfunctional behavior
- Supporting the publication of services through federations of distributed registries
- Supporting the dynamic binding between service-centric systems and available services based on functional and nonfunctional preferences and constraints
- Monitoring the operation of service-centric systems, enacting recovery actions whenever necessary.

The main characteristic of SeCSE is that it aims at offering a comprehensive and integrated solution for SCSs, and focuses on the development of flexible and dependable SCSs that can adapt dynamically to the environment and interact with other systems that are not service-based.

The chapter presents some interesting achievements, but other key issues remain as subject of our future work:

- A first problem concerns the transparency level of service descriptions. Clearly, the more transparent it is (i.e., the more it describes the internals of a service), the more the encapsulation principle is broken, but, on the other hand, service consumers can clearly decide on it and its characteristics with more information.
- An important aspect is the definition and the enforcement of proper security policies for services. Though current technologies provide some support for this, when services are composed in a complex whole, the problem of understanding if the policies of the composition are compatible with the policies of the composed services is still unclear.
- In many examples, the self-adaptation of SCSs depends on the context in which systems are deployed. In SeCSE, we have no explicit and comprehensive definition of contexts, but this is left implicit in some events and values that determine the execution of some self-adaptation procedures.
- So far, we have considered only orchestrated SCSs, that is, systems where a central workflow acts as the only coordinator of the composition. When integrating preexisting B2B services as well as pervasive services, the interaction among them is performed on a peer-to-peer basis and usually does not require the existence of a workflow coordinating the various actions.

Acknowledgments

The work published in this chapter is partly funded by the European Community under the Sixth Framework Programme, contract FP6–511680 SeCSE. The work reflects only the authors' views. The Community is not liable for any use that may be made of the information contained therein. The authors would like to thank the whole SeCSE consortium and in particular all the people who provided feedback and contributions for this chapter.

Notes

1. http://www.nessi.europe.eu.
2. This design model can be specified either directly in UML using v1.0 of the architecture driven service discovery tool of SECSE or extracted from a specification of the workflow in the BPEL-based workflow specification language of the composition designer tool of the project.
3. Distance between candidate service operation and the query operation.
4. http://www.jini.org/.
5. http://www.w3.org/TR/wsdl.
6. http://www.oasis-open.org/specs/index.php#uddiv3.0.2.
7. http://www.w3.org/Submission/OWL-S/.
8. Http://www.cogsci.princeton.edu.
9. http://www.atc.gr/sodium.
10. http://wsdiamond.di.unito.it.

References

Ankolenkar, A., M. Burstein, J. Hobbs, O. Lassila, D. Martin, D. McDermott, S. McIlraith, S. Narayanan, M. Paolucci, T. Payne, and K. Sycara. 2002. Daml-S: Web service description for the semantic web. In *The First International Semantic Web Conference* (ISWC). LNCS 2342.

Balke, W.-T., and M. Wagner. 2003. Towards personalized selection of Web Services. In *Proceedings of the International World Wide Web Conference.*

Barbon, F., P. Traverso, M. Pistore, and M. Trainotti. 2006. Run-time monitoring of instances and classes of Web Service compositions. In *Proceedings of the International Conference on Web Services*, pp. 63–71.

Baresi, L., and S. Guinea. 2005. Dynamo: Dynamic monitoring of WS-BPEL processes. In *Proceedings of the 3rd International Conference of Service-oriented Computing.* LNCS 3826, pp. 269–282.

Bertolino, A., and A. Polini. 2005. The audition framework for testing Web Services interoperability. In *31st EUROMICRO Conference on Software Engineering and Advanced Applications*, pp. 134–142.

Chhetri, M., Lin, J., Goh, S., Zhang, J., Kowalczyk, R., and Yan, J. 2006. A coordinated architecture for the agent-based service level agreement negotiation of web service composition. In *Proceedings of the Australian Software Engineering Conference* (ASWEC'06), pp. 90–99. Washington, DC: IEEE Computer Society.

Canfora, G., M. Di Penta, R. Esposito, and M. L. Villani. 2005. QoS-aware replanning of composite Web Services. In *Proceedings of the IEEE International Conference on Web Services*, pp. 121–129.

Colombo, M., E. Di Nitto, M. Di Penta, D. Distante, and Maurilio Zuccalà. 2005. Speaking a common language: A conceptual model for describing service-oriented systems. In *Proceedings of the 3rd International Conference on Service-oriented Computing.*

Colombo, M., E. Di Nitto, and M. Mauri. 2006. SCENE: A service composition execution environment supporting dynamic changes disciplined through rules. In *Proceedings of the International Conference on Service-oriented Computing.* LNCS, pp. 191–202.

Comuzzi, M., and B. Pernici. 2005. An architecture for flexible Web Service QoS negotiation. In *Proceedings of the Ninth IEEE International EDOC Enterprise Computing Conference*, pp. 70–82. Washington, DC: IEEE Computer Society.

Cugola, G., and G. P. Picco. 2006. REDS: A Reconfigurable Dispatching System. http://zeus.elet.polimi.it/reds.

De Antonellis, V., M. Melchiori, L. De Santis, M. Mecella, E. Mussi, B. Pernici, and P. Plebani. 2006. A layered architecture for flexible e-service invocation. *Software Practice and Experience* 36, no. 2: 191–223.

Di Nitto, E., M. Di Penta, A. Gambi, G. Ripa, and M. L. Villani. 2007. Negotiation of service level agreements: An architecture and a search-based approach. In *Proceedings of the Fifth International Conference on Service-Oriented Computing*, pp. 295–306. Berlin: Springer.

Di Penta, M., M. Bruno, G. Esposito, V. Mazza, and G. Canfora. 2007. Web Services regression testing. In *Test and Analysis of Web Services*, L. Baresi and E. Di Nitto, eds. Springer.

Di Penta, M., G. Canfora, G. Esposito, V. Mazza, and M. Bruno. 2007. Search-based testing of service level agreements. In *Proceedings of the 9th Annual Conference on Genetic and Evolutionary Computation*, pp. 1090–1097. London: ACM.

Di Penta, M., R. Esposito, M. L. Villani, R. Codato, M. Colombo, and E. Di Nitto. 2006. WS-Binder: A framework to enable dynamic binding of composite Web Services. In *Proceedings. International Workshop on Service Oriented Software Engineering*, pp. 74–80. Shanghai. ACM Digital Library.

Keller, A., and H. Ludwig. 2002. Defining and monitoring service level agreements for dynamic e-business. In *Proceedings of the 16th USENIX System Administration Conference* (Lisa '02), pp. 189–204.

Klein, M., and B. K. Ries. 2004. Coupled signature and specification matching for automatic service binding. In *Proceedings of the European Conference on Web Services* (ECOW), pp. 183–197.

Kozlenkov, A., G. Spanoudakis, A. Zisman, V. Fasoulas, and F. Sanchez Cid. 2007. Architecture-driven service discovery for service centric systems. *International Journal of Web Services Research* 4, no. 2: 81–112.

Mandell, D. J., and S. A. McIlraith. 2003. Adapting BPEL4WS for the semantic Web: The bottom–up approach to web service interoperation. In *Proceedings of the 2nd International Semantic Web Conference.*

Martin, E., S. Basu, and T. Xie. 2006. Automated robustness testing of Web Services. In *Proceedings of the 4th International Workshop on SOA and Web Services Best Practices.*

Ncho, A., and E. Aimeur. 2004. Building a multi-agent system for automatic negotiation in web service applications. In *Proceedings of the Third International Joint Conference on Autonomous Agents and Multiagent Systems*, vol. 3, pp. 1466–1467. New York: IEEE Computer Society.

Nieto, F. J., L. Bastida, M. Escalante, and A. Gortazar. 2007. Development of dynamic composed services based on the context. In *Proceedings of the 2nd International Conference on Interoperability of Enterprise Software and Applications.*

Orriens, B., J. Yang, and M. P. Papazoglou. 2003. A framework for business rule driven service composition. In *Proceedings of the 3rd VLDB Workshop on Technologies for e-Services.*

Paolucci, M., T. Kawamura, T. R. Payne, and K. Sycara. 2002. Semantic matching of Web Services capabilities. In *Proceedings of the First International Semantic Web Conference.* LNCS 2348, pp. 333–347.

Pilioura, T., G.-D. Kapos, and A. Tsalgatidou. 2004. PYRAMID-S: A scalable infrastructure for semantic Web Services publication and discovery. In *Proceedings of the 14th International Workshop on Research Issues on Data Engineering.*

Prieto-Diaz, R., and P. Freeman. 1987. Classifying software for reusability. *IEEE Software* 4, no. 1: 6–16.

Rolli, D., S. Luckner, C. Momm, and C. Weinhardt. 2004. A framework for composing electronic marketplaces—From market structure to service implementation. In *Proceedings of the 3rd Workshop on e-Business.*

Rosenberg, F., and S. Dustdar. 2005. Towards a distributed service-oriented business rules system. In *Proceedings of the 3rd European Conference on Web Services* (ECOWS 2005), pp. 14–24.

Sahai, A., V. Machiraju, M. Sayal, L. J. Jin, and F. Casati. 2002. Automated SLA monitoring for web services. In *DSOM '02 Proceedings.* LNCS 2506, pp. 28–41. Berlin: Springer.

Skene, J., Skene, A., Crampton, J., and Emmerich, W. 2007. The monitorability of service-level agreements for application service provision. In *Proceedings of the 6th International Workshop on Software and Performance*, pp. 3–14. New York: ACM Press.

Spanoudakis, G., K. Mahbub, and A. Zisman. 2007. A platform for context aware runtime Web Service discovery. In *Proceedings of the IEEE 2007 International Conference on Web Services*, pp. 233–240.

Sycara, K., S. Widoff, M. Klusch, and J. Lu. 2002. LARKS: Dynamic matchmaking among heterogeneous software agents in cyberspace. In *Autonomous Agents and Multi-Agent Systems*, pp. 173–203. Kluwer Academic Publisher.

Tsai, W. T., R. Paul, Y. Wang, C. Fan, and D. Wang. 2002. Extending WSDL to facilitate Web Services testing. In *7th IEEE International Symposium on High-Assurance Systems Engineering*, pp. 171–172.

Verma, K., K. Gomadam, A. P. Sheth, J. A. Miller, and Z. Wu. 2005. The METEOR-S approach for configuring and executing dynamic Web processes. *Technical Report TR-6-24-05*, Large Scale Distributed Information Systems lab, University of Georgia.

Walkerdine, J., J. Hutchinson, P. Sawyer, G. Dobson, and V. Onditi. 2007. A faceted approach to service specification. In *Proceedings of the Second International Conference on Internet and Web Applications and Services.* May 13–19, 2007, Le Morne, Mauritius, IEEE Computer Society Press.

Wang, Y., and E. Stroulia. 2003. Semantic structure matching for assessing Web-Service similarity. In *First International Conference on Service Oriented Computing*.

Zachos, K., N. A. M. Maiden, X. Zhu, and S. Jones. 2007. Discovering Web Services to specify more complete system requirements. In *Proceedings of CAiSE '07, 19th Conference on Advanced Information System Engineering*, pp. 142–157.

11 User-centric Service Creation and Execution

Antonio Sánchez, Carlos Baladrón, Javier Aguiar, Belén Carro, Laurent-Walter Goix, Jürgen Sienel, Isabel Ordás, Rubén Trapero, and Alejandro Bascuñana

11.1 Introduction

Telecommunication markets are flooded with new applications. Operators and their suppliers usually implement solutions with a great potential market, but these services require long deployment times and redundant work to adapt the logic to the different access networks, and do not always satisfy the specific user needs.

In recent times the requirements of the users have evolved rapidly. Small companies are interested in developing specific applications and services to satisfy these requirements, but the network resources and required data (user profile, user behavior, user location, etc.) are under the control of the operators. At the same time, users are given a passive role, as there is no way for them to personalize their services according to their needs.

In parallel, today's services are becoming more complex, requiring the collaboration of an increasing number of telecommunication network resources of various technologies, which are managed by various types of operators or private individuals, or are part of complex industrial installations.

The answer given by operators is a paradigm known as Open Service Marketplace (Glitho et al. 2003, 446), a market model that mirrors the outsourcing trend of European economics during recent times and brings it into the communications world. According to this model, operators open their infrastructures and information systems to third parties, to let them perform the role of service providers without directly owning the networks. This approach results in benefits for both sides; third parties can access markets that would otherwise be closed to them, and the operators increase their service portfolios with highly focused services while also getting additional income from the rent of their infrastructures.

On the other hand, the Web 2.0 paradigm is quickly transforming the Web from the asymmetric broadcast means it was at its beginning (when end users pulled contents from providers) to a symmetric exchanging network, where pairs share contents among themselves as prosumers. The Web is no longer just a database of contextualized data, but a computation platform that offers remote access to applications, so Web 2.0 is in fact a web of services. The result of this paradigm shift is that end users are now in the center of the Web, and thus they are even given the role of service developers. Specific creation environments based on graphical user interfaces have been designed to let nonexperts create simple Web applications, known as mashups.

Currently the Open Service Marketplace paradigm is mostly applied to the communications world, whereas Web 2.0 and user centricity are part of the information technologies side. A merger of the two philosophies would result in a converged Web of information technologies and communication services where users could design their own highly personalized integrated services, relieving operators from the pressure of service development and deputing it to the customers' bases.

OPUCE (Open Platform for User-centric Service Creation and Execution) is an integrated project aimed at developing a complete platform for the dynamic user-centric creation, deployment, and execution of services including information technologies and communication features. Thus, it is the meeting point for the Open Service Marketplace and user-centricity paradigms.

The goal of the OPUCE platform is to put the end users in the center of the whole life cycle of a service, to let them become at the same time the creator, the manager, and the consumer of services. The OPUCE platform hence provides the necessary automation at each step of the whole process to allow nonexpert individuals to step into this user-centric paradigm. The project has delivered the first functional prototype of the platform in October 2007.

OPUCE brings tangible benefits to end users in the form of a greatly widened service pool and better fitting to requirements. Service providers gain easy service creation and an extended scope of services that can be offered and of the markets that can be targeted. Furthermore, the business of SMEs is leveraged by allowing quick creation and deployment of a new range of services by ad hoc cooperation with other business players.

In the taxonomy of this book, this chapter is placed in the section on service engineering. It in fact provides an overview of how users themselves can engineer the services they need in the context of a particular moment in an easy way.

11.2 What Is OPUCE?

In order to have a better understanding of OPUCE, it is useful to consider a use case to see what the platform is capable of. For instance, an executive is waiting for an e-mail of critical importance and needs to read it as soon as it arrives. As he is a busy person, he cannot spend all day at the office refreshing his in-box, so he would like the e-mail to be forwarded according to his context. For this he would subscribe to a forwarding service to filter his e-mail account and send an SMS when the appropriate message arrives, unless he is driving, in which case the service should make a text-to-speech call for him to listen to the e-mail's content. This example, along with the rest of the document, will be referred to as message reachability, and will be used to illustrate some concepts related to the OPUCE platform.

Currently, it is nearly impossible to find such a highly personalized service as a direct offer from any telco operator. In a current typical situation the executive of the example would contact his telco operator to request the message reachability service, triggering at best a market analysis to evaluate potential benefits, then entering the process to design the service logic and deploy it, meaning that it will take a long time for the service to become available.

Some technologies (that will be detailed in the next section) have recently appeared that allow operators to open their networks so that external entities can personalize or even implement their own services. However, even if the executive of the message reachability example had access to such tools, he would typically need a deep knowledge of the operator's infrastructure to write the service logic and deploy it over the network (if allowed). Traditionally, the skills requested to handle such tasks are very specialized, and the process of getting the service up and running is still long. Therefore, such a solution is adequate only for specific entities such as specialized third parties; it is obviously not viable for the vast majority of end users.

The OPUCE platform offers intuitive and automated tools for end users without specific knowledge to design, implement, deploy, and execute their own personalized communication services. Using the OPUCE platform, the executive of the example would first search the pool of services implemented by other users. If he does not find anything fitting his needs, he would access one of the OPUCE service editors to specify the service logic as a composition of basic building blocks. When the service is finished, the executive would simply click the *deploy* button on the OPUCE portal, and the OPUCE service life cycle manager would automatically take the necessary actions to translate the graphical composition into an executable script and deploy the required software components into the distributed OPUCE service execution environment (SEE). Finally, the executive, or anyone else allowed to do so, could click the *run* button and the script would be executed in the SEE. All the operations related to the control of the overall service life cycle are performed inside the intuitive Web-based OPUCE portal.

This approach is beneficial for both the users and the operator. The former are capable of designing their own highly personalized services, and the latter is able to use the OPUCE tools to reduce the time and effort to market new services. Also, the service catalog is greatly widened and the usage of networks increases.

11.3 State of the Art

11.3.1 Service Creation in Communications

Today's business climate demands a high rate of change in market conditions, driving the need for the IT infrastructure of an organization to respond quickly in support of new business models and requirements (Papazoglou et al. 2006).

While the market for broadband services continues to grow, to remain competitive, operators must address two challenges (EmergeCore Networks): the need for additional revenue paths as the price for bandwidth decreases, and the need to bolster customer retention in a crowded market.

Therefore, telco operators need a way to rapidly create services adapted to the users in order to be able to compete in a fierce market environment. Services not only should be created fast, but also adapted to the user needs and as personalized as possible. Traditional monolithic approaches perform very poorly in this environment, as the development process is longer if feedback is expected from users and the service is adapted accordingly. Thus, a new development paradigm is required in order to face the challenges the present market poses.

The first answer of the operators has been the Network Services middleware (Glitho et al. 2003, 446): an additional layer that wraps the network capabilities of the infrastructure, offering high-level abstractions to deal with communication functionalities. Additionally, the service logic is completely decoupled from the underlying infrastructure. These two features yield easier service development and deployment, respectively. In the form of APIs such as JAIN or Parlay (Moerdijk and Klostermann 2003, 58), the network services layer has greatly improved development and deployment times of value-added services from the operators' side.

11.3.2 Service-Oriented Computing

The SOC paradigm, implemented via service-oriented architectures (SOA) (Huhns and Singh 2005, 75; Papazoglou 2003; Curbera et al. 2002, 86), sees the world as a collection of basic entities called services. Each of these services represents a specific functionality, such as presence, location, or call control. The main feature of services is that they are able to interoperate, so they can be linked together in order to offer higher-level software solutions to end users. Several different applications can then be built out of a combination of services with little effort, simply by changing the workflow and parameters of the service but still using the same basic services. These are known as composed services.

The concept of an application being a collection of services also has the advantage of loose coupling (Stal 2006, 54; Kaye 2003): services are independent from each other and from the composed services which employ them, so these blocks could be constantly changing and being updated internally without affecting the rest of the elements in the architecture.

The way to achieve such cooperation is a new paradigm in programming languages called orchestration. Orchestration languages (Peltz 2003, 46), such as BPEL (Pasley 2005, 60), aim at defining how a set of smaller atomic entities interact, specifying the sequence in which those entities should be invoked (Kloppmann et al. 2004).

The next step in the chain of research is expected to fully couple the SOA approach with the emerging semantic trends. In a distant future this integration will allow automatic discovery, creation, and execution of services with semantic input from the human user (McIlraith et al. 2001, 46). In the meanwhile, other approaches aim at partial coupling of semantic technologies, mainly to allow more efficient semantic-based discovery (Sycara et al. 2003, 27) and interaction control (Paolucci and Sycara 2003, 34).

Though its origin is in the information technologies, SOC is entering the telco world (Pollet et al. 2006, 529). The principle of loose coupling has also proved to be useful for the rapid creation and deployment of communication services, since it allows composition of value-added services by simply plugging together some basic services. Large and small companies are already moving their systems to SOAs (EmergeCore Networks; Erl 2005), but this philosophy also allows the construction of larger interenterprise systems, such as the World Wide Web.

11.3.3 Web 2.0, User Centricity, and Mashups

The Web 2.0 paradigm describes the World Wide Web of today as a symmetric computation platform in which users exchange information and services (O'Reilly).

Therefore, although at its origin the Web was an asymmetric means for content broadcasting from providers to users, Web 2.0 is completely centered on end users, who act not only as consumers but also as providers of content and services.

According to user centricity, several enhancements have been proposed in the literature in order to complete the SOA approach, involving end users in the chain of service development. Most of them (Tsai et al. 2006; Chang et al. 2006, 248) include feedback channels in the chain, in order to let users publish the features of the services they require so developers can implement them, but what is really needed is to let end users create their own services.

Recently the concept of mashup has brought the loose coupling philosophy to the service creation in the Web 2.0. Mashups are simple Web applications made by the interconnection of remote services available on the Web. A very good example is Google Maps (Google Maps), a cartographic service that has been plugged to all kinds of databases to create innovative and personalized location mashups.

But even though they are simple, mashups require specific knowledge in order to be created, so they cannot be considered truly user-centric. Additional higher-level environments are needed in order to allow nonexpert individuals to create their own Web services.

Mashup creation environments are the next step in service creation inside the Web. They are graphical tools designed to translate a graphical workflow representing the service being designed into an executable script. Two of the most important companies in the Internet world, Microsoft and Yahoo!, have already released their own mashup creation environments, Microsoft Popfly (Microsoft Popfly) and Yahoo! Pipes (Yahoo! Pipes). In these environments basic services are represented by boxes that can be dragged and dropped, and then inputs and outputs can be linked with arrows in order to design a workflow without requiring any further knowledge.

Though services created with these environments are simple and limited, they are in fact the first tools that allow end users to truly develop their own Web applications.

11.4 OPUCE: Innovations and Motivation

The tools provided by the OPUCE platform allow individuals with no specific knowledge to create, deploy, share, publish, advertise, manage, execute, and personalize services, and third parties to enter the service creation market using the operator's communications infrastructure. Therefore, the OPUCE platform is a complete service marketplace that evolves around the user applying Web 2.0 principles to the telco world.

OPUCE presents several advantages over Web mashup editors. First, it offers not only IT-based capabilities but also convergent communication services. Its SOA-based execution environment is designed to handle innovative NGN communication capabilities. Though both mashups and OPUCE are based on SOA principles, the former are implemented with lightweight technologies that heavily restrict the services they can offer. OPUCE, on the contrary, is based on state-of-the-art Web Services technology that is much more flexible and reliable. Mashups are suitable for casual and leisure purposes, but OPUCE services are designed to satisfy the requirements of professional applications.

On the other hand, research in the telco world has given birth to a variety of high-level, user-oriented creation and execution environments for communication services based on the Network Services middleware (such as Glitho et al. 2003, 446). However, although these environments also rely on loose coupling and building of high-level applications as composition of basic services, they are not truly SOA. Instead, they are heavily tied to a specific technology, and thus interoperation of heterogeneous entities is not possible. The Web Services middleware of OPUCE, on the contrary, allows a seamless integration of every service as long as it is wrapped as an OPUCE Web Service. This eases cooperation with external third-party service providers.

Moreover, whereas other high-level user-centric environments offer only a creation-execution pair, OPUCE is a complete platform that provides an integrated experience to the user, putting him in control of the whole life cycle of a service. It offers support features such as automatic deployment, user-driven sharing and advertising, or implicit personalization.

Additionally, OPUCE has been designed with context-aware capabilities for service adaptation since its very beginning, so it offers personalization at every stage of the service life cycle. For instance, user interfaces are automatically adapted to the capabilities of the device employed, services can be designed with context-aware workflows (e.g.: "if the user is at work, do one thing, and if not, do something else"), and notifications about services are adapted to user presence.

In conclusion, OPUCE merges the advantages of every approach for user-centric service creation. Communications are lagging behind in the Web 2.0 paradigm because telco operators lack a marketable solution to merge their infrastructures with the Web, and because OPUCE covers the whole life cycle of services and is implemented with reliable technology, it offers a viable market solution for professional and casual user-centric converged services.

11.5 User-centric Service Management in OPUCE

11.5.1 User-centric Service Life Cycle

The core of the OPUCE platform is a triplet formed by a service creation environment (SCE), a service execution environment (SEE), and a service life cycle manager (SLM). End users compose new services using the intuitive graphical SCE and execute them in the SEE, and the SLM controls the life cycle of a service inside the platform: it translates the graphical composition into an executable script, stores the services in a repository, deploys the necessary software components into the distributed SEE, issues orders for advertising of services, and removes services when they are no longer used. A set of support modules provides additional functionalities: a portal acts as a Web-based front end for controlling services within the platform, a service advertiser (SA) sends notifications about services, a user information manager (UIM) stores and retrieves all user-related information, and, based on that information, an adaptation module automatically personalizes all the stages of the service life cycle for each user. Every module is designed to offer enough automation to let nonexpert end users control each step of the service life cycle.

A fundamental concept of OPUCE services is that they are built out of a collection of base services. Base services are functional units deployed by the platform owner (typically the service provider) or authorized third parties, which can be connected according to suitable composition rules in order to create more complex OPUCE services. Base services wrap a single or limited set of either telco or IT capabilities. When encapsulating telco resources or network capabilities, they are able, for example, to send SMSs or instant messages, place a phone call, set up an audio conference, or monitor a friend's presence.

In the context of this chapter, user-centric service life cycle management is intended as the process of enabling end users (not technically skilled) to create their own services and manage their life cycles autonomously within the service provider platform. Such a process allows the users to share their own services with a community, thus creating a powerful and self-increasing ecosystem.

Figure 11.1 illustrates the approach considered for user-centric services. Three major roles are identified:

- The service provider, focused on learning information about end users (both creators and final users), including context information, service usage statistics, and preferences. The service provider is typically also hosting and operating the platform to run services created by end users. In the message reachability example, the service provider should retrieve the context information of the executive in order to detect his presence and activity status (whether he is driving or not).

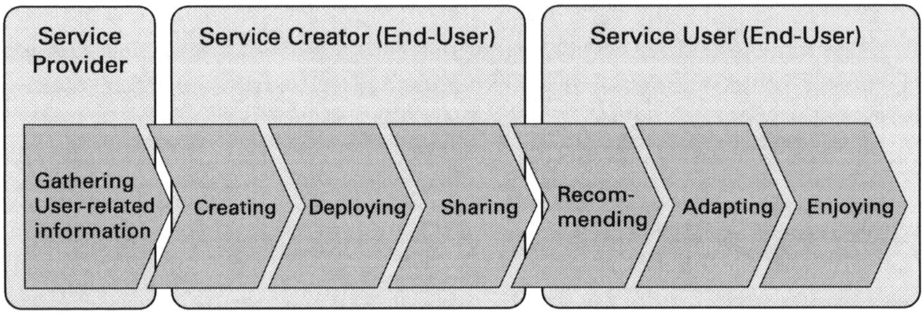

Figure 11.1
Overview of the OPUCE approach to User Centric Services

- The service creator, an end user creating her/his own services, also in charge of managing their life cycles, such as deploying, sharing, and notifying her/his social network or interest groups about them.
- The final service user, an end user of the platform interested in services of some kind that receives updates about newly available services and can execute them after some context-aware adaptation step.

Each step along the overall life cycle directly involves the end user as an entity either releasing some personal information (such as context, preferences, etc.) to the service provider, or as being a fundamental actor of the community, designing, managing, and sharing services autonomously. All platform users ultimately benefit from a wide range of services designed by other users that are automatically adapted to their own context.

The concept of user sphere is used to support this separation of roles between creators and final users. It describes the information related to each individual's reality, such as her/his relationships, interests, well-known places, phone numbers, and e-mail addresses. Referencing the user sphere throughout this life cycle is essential to address relative information, whose actual value may vary across users. The $me notation is used to access the final user's user sphere (e.g., $me.phone_number, employed by the creator at creation time, references the final user's phone number at execution time). In the message reachability example, the executive creating the service could specify the value $me.phone_number as the target of the SMS and the text-to-speech call instead of his fixed phone number. At execution time, the service would retrieve the phone_number of the user executing it, so it is useful not only for its creator but also for whoever may use it.

11.5.2 Architecture of the OPUCE Platform

The OPUCE platform architecture is shown in figure 11.2. Each of its six top-level blocks is in charge of a set of separated functionalities, and the links between them represent the different interfaces used during the whole life cycle of a service. The OPUCE project (2007) defines the following set of functionalities for each of the top-level blocks:

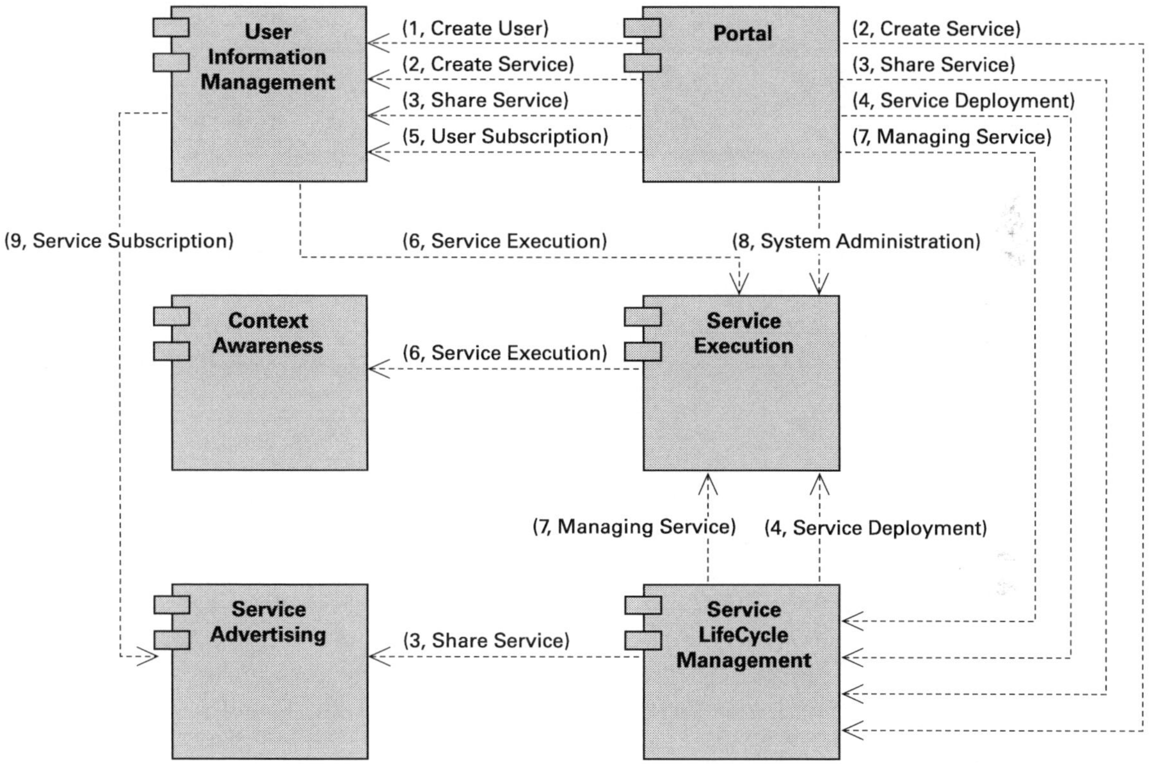

Figure 11.2
OPUCE platform high level architecture

The portal module provides the front end interfaces for the different actors to access the platform for service creation, service management, and platform administration. It also includes an intuitive graphical service creation environment.

User information management (UIM) is a distributed module in the OPUCE architecture to manage, elaborate, and keep in a secured way critical and sensitive information about users, such as credentials, location, context, service subscriptions, and personalization preferences.

The service advertising (SA) module allows notification of services based on an intelligent matching of user profiles with the characteristics of services to be advertised. In addition, the notification process follows a context-aware paradigm in which the user is able to configure notification preferences.

Context awareness (CA) is an intelligent element adapting services to a rapidly changing end user environment. It retrieves this information from the UIM and performs the necessary changes in the workflow and the data handled in order to adapt the service to the context of each user.

The task of the service life cycle management (SLM) block is to implement centralized control over the entire life cycle of all services, from creation until removal from the platform. It stores the descriptions of newly created services, validates them, deploys them over adequate resources, issues orders for advertising over potentially interested users, monitors services, deactivates them for upgrading tasks, redeploys newly needed components, and withdraws them when expiration time arrives or upon request from the service creator.

The service execution environment (SEE) module provides an event-driven orchestrator for high-level service logic and several low-level environments for the execution of base services on top of IT or telco resources.

11.6 OPUCE Platform

11.6.1 Service Description

The service representation in OPUCE is achieved by a set of XML documents linked together and addressing different aspects of the service life cycle. Each of these files is called facet. The main advantages of the faceted approach are the modularity and the flexibility. This approach allows separate access to each facet by the different platform elements, and use of different third-party XML languages to describe any required facet inside the service description.

The faceted approach followed in OPUCE has been taken mainly from the work done inside the SeCSE (Service Centric System Engineering; SeCSE project 2005) European project. It is depicted in figure 11.3.

Service specification is depicted in detail in figure 11.4. Due to the different objectives of the OPUCE and SeCSE projects, the set of facets used in the service specification was redesigned following functional requirements of the project.

OPUCE considers three sets of facets. The facets for each of these sets are listed below:

1. Functional facets
• Service logic, to define the workflow of the composed service.
• Service interface, which describes the external interfaces which might be offered by the service.
• Context Awareness, which describes ambience information that may be used to change the behavior of a service at runtime.
2. Nonfunctional facets
• Graphical representation, which includes the serialization of the graphical representation of the service in the service creation environment.
• Security and Privacy, which describes the privacy policy to be agreed by the user and to be fulfilled by the service providers. This allows OPUCE to protect and control the access to user's personal information.

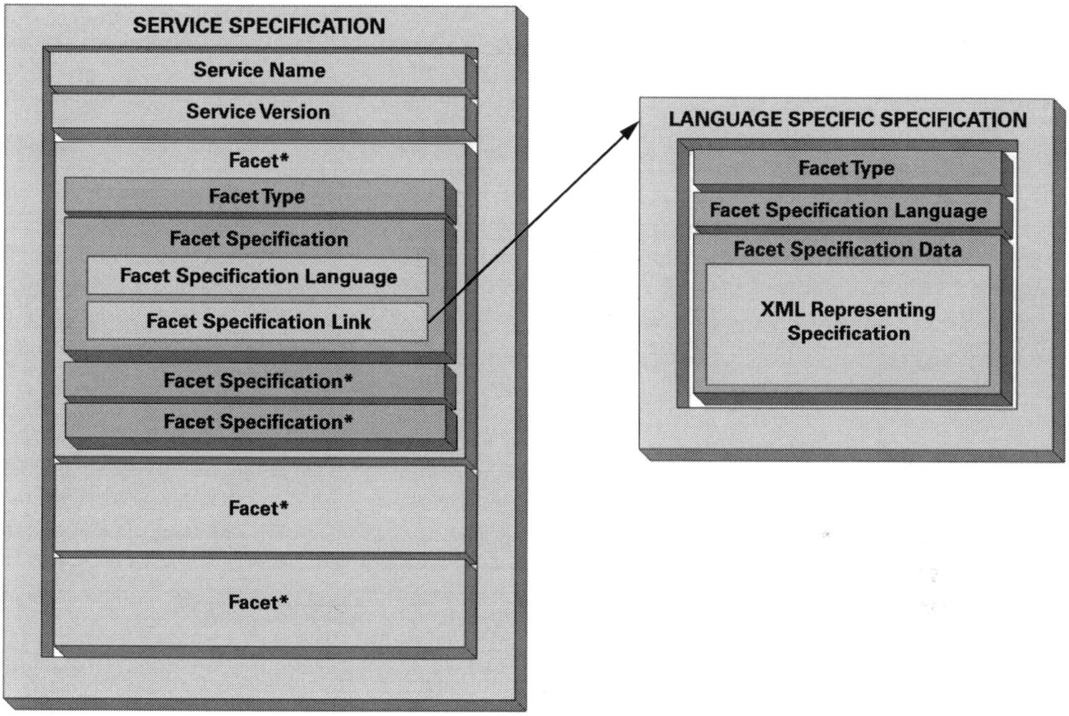

Figure 11.3
Faceted approach used to describe services

- Group Management, which provide the services with social capabilities (sharing, recommendation, etc. between groups of people etc).
- Service Behavior Constraints, which provide an internal security mechanism to ensure that a composition has been correctly created.
- Semantic Description, which provides advanced searching and categorization capabilities.
- Scheduling, used to define the timing information decided by the user (as service creator) for both activating and deactivating the service.

3. Management facets

- Accounting, which is used to define the accounting policy to do for a certain service and for those base services involved in the composition.
- Service-level agreement, to define conditions when creating and using the service. It is also used to define the business model to be applied for that service.
- Service deployment, to define deployment information prior to the activation of the service.
- Service Provisioning, which is used to define all those activities to be done in the platform, in the base services and in the user side prior to activate the service. Some of them are the configuration of databases, creation of users accounts, resources reservation etc.

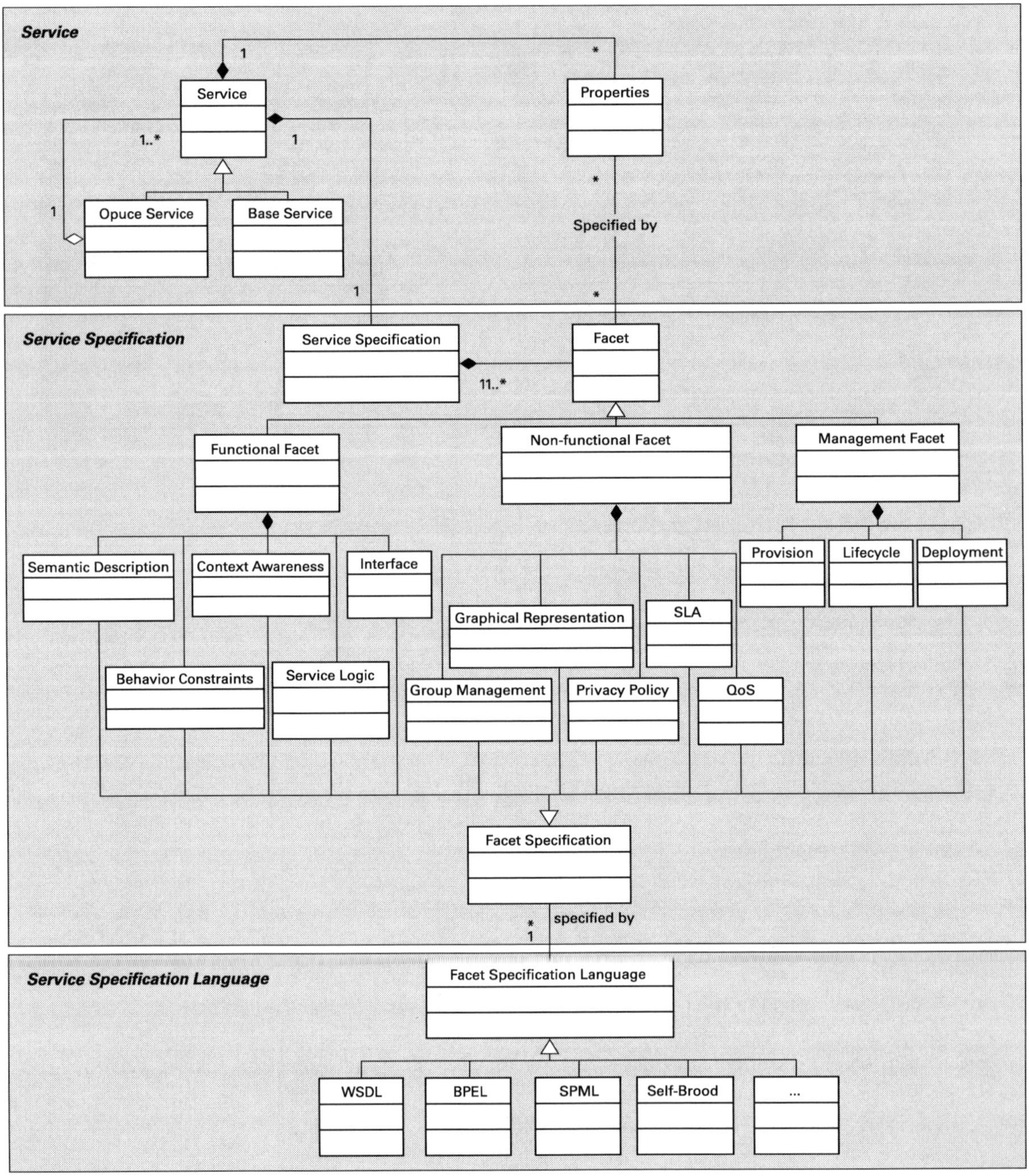

Figure 11.4
Service specification in OPUCE

Table 11.1
Facets' usage in service descriptions

Facet Type	Facet	Base Service	OPUCE service
Functional facets	Service logic	n/a	Mandatory
	Service interface	Mandatory	n/a
	Context awareness	Optional	n/a
Non-functional facets	Security and privacy	Optional	Optional
	Group management	n/a	Optional
	Scheduling	n/a	Optional
	Graphical representation	n/a	Optional
	Service behavior constraints	Optional	n/a
	Semantic description	Mandatory	Mandatory
Management facets	Accounting	Optional	Optional
	Service-level agreement	Optional	Optional
	Service deployment	Optional	Optional
	Service provisioning	Optional	Optional

All services are represented with the same service specification, but there will be a different subset of mandatory facets depending on the nature of the service (whether it is a base service or an OPUCE service). Table 11.1 summarizes the facets defined inside OPUCE service specifications and details, whether they are mandatory or optional for base or composed OPUCE services.

11.6.2 Accessing: Portal

The OPUCE portal offers a front end to drive the user through the creation, deployment, and sharing phases from the service creator point of view, and usage and rating from the service user perspective.

Figure 11.5 illustrates the functions provided by the OPUCE portal.

The most innovative user-centric features present in the portal are the following:

- *Service edition* User-friendly tools to edit a composed service. This environment enables the creation of service logics, allowing the linking and configuring of base services together in a chain that helps to reference the user's sphere dynamically or statically.
- *Service profile management* Supports collecting metadata (e.g., description, name, tags, semantic descriptions, etc.) that will be stored in the OPUCE service descriptor described above.
- *Service test and simulation* Service test functions are designed to help service creators verify the correctness of service compositions by simulating their execution, since service creators are also responsible for them and the OPUCE platform will guarantee the safe execution of services.
- *Service life cycle management* Service creators use these features to manage deployment and execution of their services.

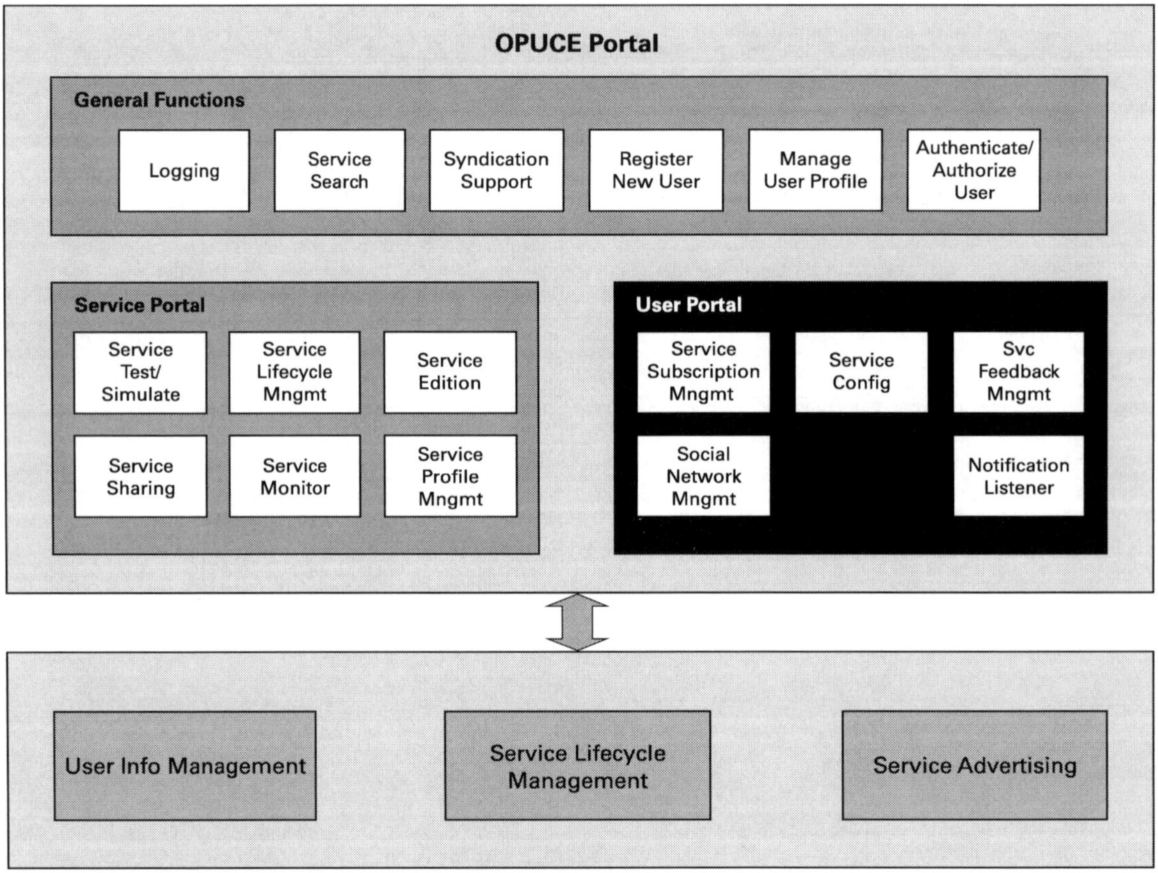

Figure 11.5
OPUCE Portal functions

- *Sharing* service creators can set the sharing policy for a specific service and define a list of target users with whom they wish to share their services. The "sharing" information can be linked to the user's social network so she/he can share services with a restricted number of acquaintances.
- *Service feedback management* Allows users to provide feedback on received and/or used services by means of voting or recommendation functions.

11.6.3 Creation: Service Creation Environment (SCE)

A dynamic service creation environment is one of the pillars on which a user-oriented service ecosystem can be built. The SCE covers the central steps of the service life cycle.

OPUCE provides two different SCEs: a basic one to run on mobile devices such as PDAs and a Web-based advanced one accessible through the portal. Indeed, users can enjoy their new role of service creators, using every device and access whether at home or on the move. Service creators can further perform "cross-editing" (i.e., switching between the two editors when conditions are applicable, since they share the same graphical service description and back-end service repository. Figure 11.6 shows a screenshot of the Advanced Editor interface, with the palette of base services on the left and the canvas for service design on the right.

The two editors share a common service composition model (Cipolla et al. 2007) defined in OPUCE that seamlessly integrates IT and telco resources. The main feature of this model is the event-driven approach which defines the execution of complex, high-level services in a way that nonexpert end users feel is natural: users are exposed to a friendly way of dealing with resources (e.g., "place a call," "line is busy," "read RSS feed," etc.). To support such an approach, the OPUCE service composition model requires that the interaction with the resources happen in terms of events and actions, and the fundamental composition rules for building complex services are event-triggered patterns. The basic pattern is "When event E occurs, then execute action A"; other patterns are modeled after this, but include flow control constructs, borrowed from the world of programming languages (condition testing, etc.). The main advantage of this paradigm is that the description of the service logic is simple and straightforward, since it is close to natural language.

The resources available to create OPUCE services are building blocks called base services. From this set of base services high-level services can be composed by combining these elements through event-triggered patterns (explained later) and their corresponding data flows. A base service used inside a service composition is called a base service instance (BSI).

Each base service is identified by a unique name inside the platform, and is specified by three sets of information:

- *Properties* Variables that represent the internal status of the BSI.
- *Actions* Operations that a BSI can perform when requested. The behavior of an action can depend on the value of the properties associated with the instance. After the invocation of an action, the BSI can fire one or more events.
- *Events* Events are the means a BSI can use to proactively communicate that something has happened (a change of state, the arrival of a message, etc.). The events fired by a BSI can trigger the invocation of an action on a (possibly different) BSI.

An OPUCE service composition is defined by a set of base service instances, a set of connections between the events and the actions of the base service instances, and by an initial event. In order to compose services, the user first defines an initial event to trigger the instantiation of the service composition. Then, the user creates connections between BSIs according to the event-triggered patterns.

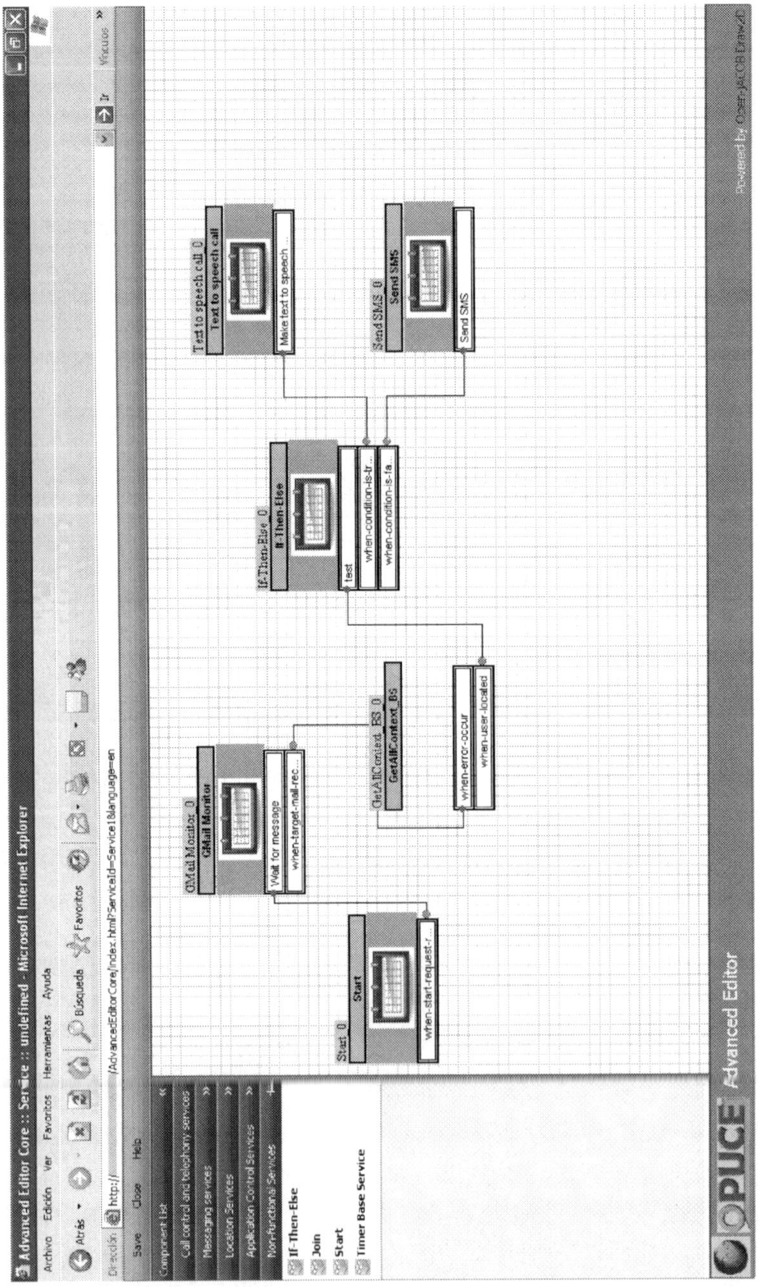

Figure 11.6
OPUCE Advance Editor

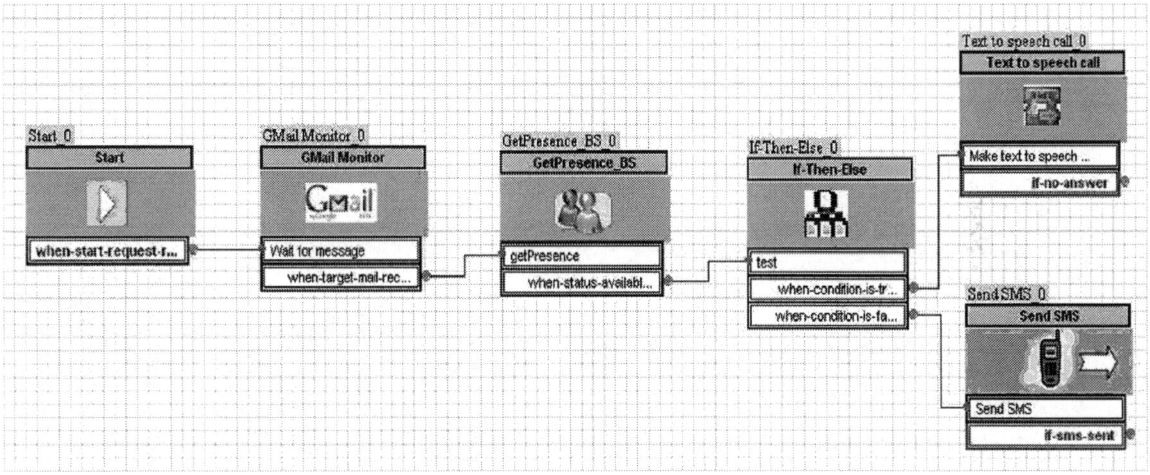

Figure 11.7
Message reachability service composition

The output of the SCE (both mobile and advanced editors) is a graphical service description (GSD) that will be translated to an executable BPEL script upon deployment on the SEE.

Figure 11.7 depicts the graphical composition designed by the executive in the message reachability example. The first block, Start, is mandatory for all services, and is in charge of activating the service when the user clicks the *run* button on the portal. Then the GMail Monitor fires an event when an e-mail reaches the in-box according to the properties selected. The GetPresence base service retrieves the presence activity of the user from the UIM, and the If-Then-Else block fires a True event if presence activity is *driving* and a False one otherwise. Finally, the Text-To-Speech Call or Send SMS block is invoked, depending on the event fired by the If-Then-Else block.

11.6.4 Deployment: Service Life Cycle Manager (SLM)

User-created services impose new requirements on the telecom platforms, because they must be able to cope with a huge set of dynamically generated services, each one orchestrating a subset of telecom-oriented base services. Thus, effective life cycle management has to take place:

- To allow users to decide when and how long their services must be available (i.e., the life cycle schedule).
- To be able to automatically perform the provisioning of base services and platform elements, and to register and to publish new services in order for them to be available to end users.

- To avoid interference of services that act on the same set of control flow (e.g., SIP messages) or detect such feature interaction in advance, to define rules to cope with it.
- To provide scalable execution architectures in a heterogeneous environment allowing the orchestration of enablers residing on different platforms. This scalability should also avoid execution hot spots in case specific services become successful.

Automatic deployment is nothing new in the telco world; however, the traditional deployment, automatic or not, has always been instigated and determined by operators. OPUCE goes a step further: the SLM (Yelmo et al. 2007) allows service creators to take control of some aspects of the deployment.

Thus, there is no need for any human intervention from the operator either when triggering the service deployment process or during the deployment itself; the service description contains all data necessary to deploy the service.

Leaving out physical installation activity, the rest of the deployment process is as follows:

- *Service provisioning* Traditionally, provisioning requires a manual participation to create accounts for users, reserve resources, and so on. In OPUCE all these processes are carried out automatically, using the service description to specify the provisioning details for each service.

Three provisioning tasks have been identified, each one impacting different elements of the platform.

- *Component provisioning*, which considers the provisioning tasks to be done in those base services that the service creator has combined, such as reservation of resources or configuration of permissions.
- *Platform provisioning*, which considers the provisioning tasks to be carried out in the OPUCE platform components, such as updating the service repository or, in the future, the billing systems.
- *User provisioning*, which considers the provisioning tasks to be performed on the user side at subscription time, such as installing a dedicated application in the user's mobile device or accepting a certain SLA before using the service.

Each type of provisioning is a set of different tasks or activities. Thus, separate facets for each of them are nested within the main provisioning facet. Figure 11.8 depicts the service description structure for this facet and the relationship of each type of provisioning with the corresponding architecture module.

- *Service registration* In this activity the platform registers all the information needed to access the service once it is activated, such as end points if it is a Web Services-based access, a phone number to send an SMS to start the service, or a simple URL if the access uses a simple Web-based interface.

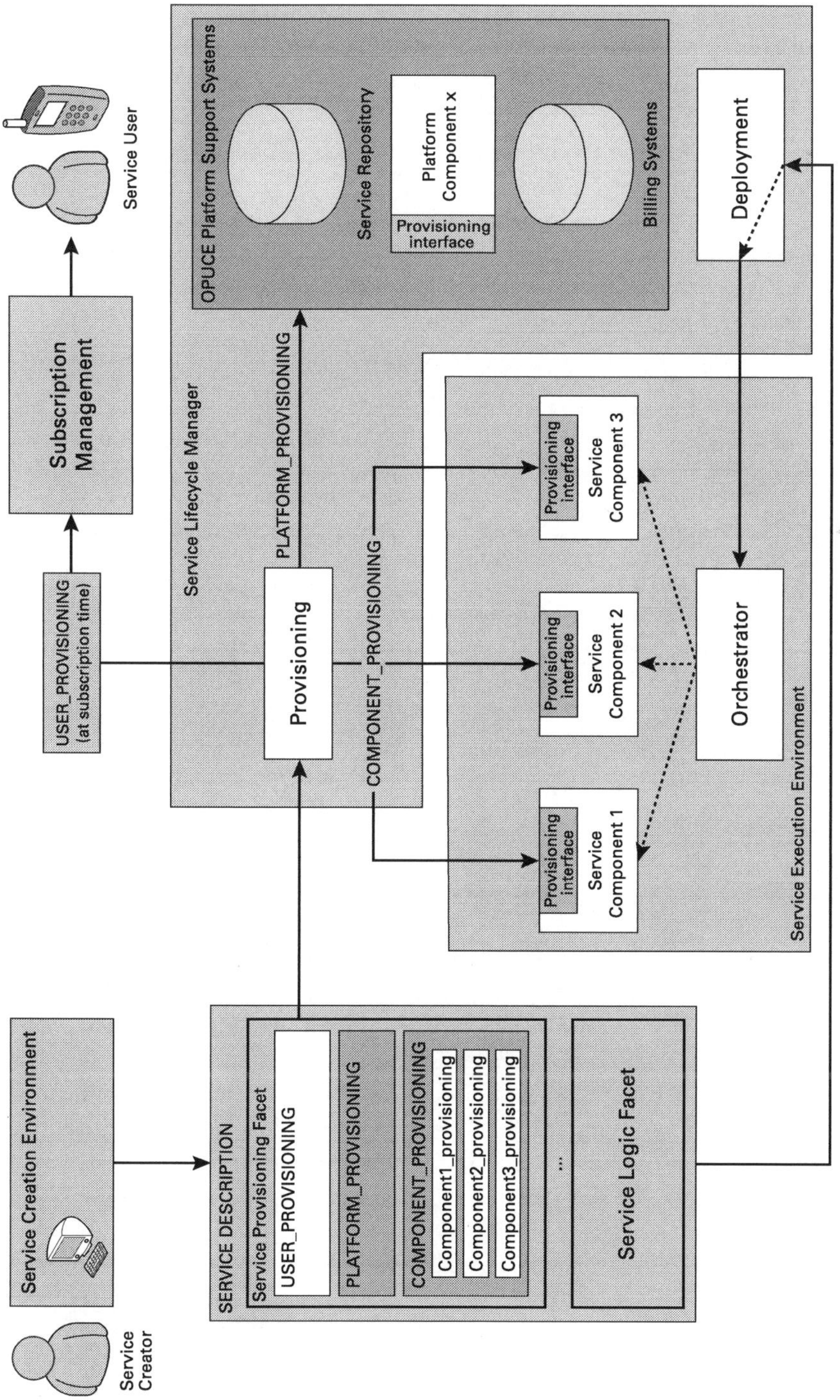

Figure 11.8
Service Deployment and Provisioning

- *Service publication* In this activity the service is officially published, including all associated attributes (e.g., service type, descriptions, terms and conditions of use), thus making service discovery easier. These data are taken from the service description, such as the service name and the semantic facet.
- *Service test* The aim of this activity is to ensure that a new service is ready to be subscribed to and consumed by end users.
- *Service activation* This is the last step of the service deployment process. Once the service has been activated, it becomes publicly available and ready for subscription. This activity is triggered by using the information included within the service life cycle schedule facet of the service description.

Once the service creator finishes the composition of the service in the editor, she/he can click the *deploy* button in the service management section of the portal. This action invokes the SLM, which first translates the graphical composition into an executable script to be stored in a facet of the service description (service logic). Then, during provisioning, the software components corresponding to the base services used in the composition are deployed in the proper execution environments. For this concrete example, IT base services (Start, GmailMonitor, GetPresence, and If-Then-Else) are deployed into a J2EE execution environment, and communication base services (Text-To-Speech call and Send SMS) into a Mobicents-based JAIN-SLEE environment. The service logic script is deployed into the OPUCE service execution engine (described later on).

After provisioning, the SLM registers the service, setting up the required end points to invoke, and publishes it, issuing the command to the service advertiser to start the notification process. Finally, the service is activated, allowing OPUCE users, including the creator of the service, to subscribe and use it.

11.6.5 Discovering, Publishing, and Sharing: Service Advertiser (SA)

For service discovery, the portal offers interfaces to access the browsing capabilities of the service repository. In addition, a "push mode" discovery mechanism is provided.

The service advertiser subsystem (OPUCE project 2007; Baladrón et al. 2007) enables notification of services to users via multiple channels. It also allows sharing of services between various levels of system participants—from operators to end users.

Whenever a service is created, it becomes necessary to advertise it to users of the platform in order to let them know about the newly created item. The SA offers automatic and intelligent correlation of user interests and service descriptions to determine the individuals potentially interested in the particular kind of service, resulting in a fine-targeted system.

When sharing, a user is able to specifically notify other users (typically her/his friends) about interesting services.

The result of both processes is a notification (i.e., a message which is sent to a set of target users). Context-awareness techniques are employed for low-intrusive sending. Each user is able to select a set of preferences specifying how to receive these messages. For example, a user can elect to receive notifications via instant messaging if her/his presence status is online, via SMS if the presence status is offline and location is at home, and via e-mail otherwise.

In any case, anti-spam tools inside the service advertiser module avoid message flooding. The user is able to select the entities she/he trusts or distrusts in order to avoid or block, respectively, notifications from those entities.

In order to facilitate the advertising process, the composer specifies in the portal, at creation time, a set of defining keywords for the service. For the message reachability, some keywords could be "SMS," "Phone Call" and "e-mail." At deployment time, the SA automatically notifies all users who have subscribed to those keywords according to their individual preferences. Additionally, every OPUCE user aware of the service can access the notification capabilities of the SA through the portal, selecting further target users from their contact list to notify them about it, thus enabling viral marketing inside the community.

11.6.6 Adaptation and Personalization

In order to reach high levels of service personalization in OPUCE, adaptation is performed at each step of the whole service life cycle and particularly during deployment, notification, and invocation. It involves mainly the following modules: service composition, service execution, notification to end users, and remote service management. Such adaptation relies heavily upon user information provided by the user information management module, which encompasses user profile, preferences, and context.

Adaptation during service composition and execution is performed both explicitly and implicitly:

- The service creation environment allows the user to define context-aware execution flows by means of context-dependent control sentences. For instance, in the message reachability service, the workflow depends on the presence status of the user because of the chaining of GetPresence and If blocks.
- The service creator can also rely on context-aware base services. These base services have hard-coded access to the context information, and their internal execution behavior depends on it.
- Content adaptation is performed through the context-awareness block, which offers transcoding and multipresentation features to the service execution environment.

Context information used for adaptation is provided by two submodules within the user information management module: the context enabler (CER) and context and usage feeds (CUF). The CUF is an application running on the end user device that captures all context data related to the user (and is provided for desktop and mobile devices), including location, presence, nearby resources, and device status and capabilities. The CER is a distributed framework that handles data coming from the CUF and stores it using a common format, applying reasoning techniques capable of inferring higher-level information (e.g., current user activity) and improving its quality and usability within the platform. This information is either pushed to or polled (regularly pulled) by the specific base service, which can use user context at execution time to enrich service information, select service flow branch, trigger events based on a change, or optimize internal base service logic.

Remote service management (RSM) is another aspect of the service life cycle enabling adaptation, in that it enables the dynamic configuration of services of end-user devices. The RSM is a submodule of the SLM and offers the following functionalities:

- The RSM deployment feature provides the means to successfully deploy components on the end-user device and allows the platform to activate and deactivate them, using an interface module. This effectively extends the OPUCE execution environment, allowing the inclusion of client-side execution.
- The RSM monitor provides end-user device-related service information, including management and runtime parameters of service components.
- Finally, the RSM hot updating takes care of the updating of service components that are running on the end-user device.

11.6.7 Enjoying: Service Execution Engine (SEE)

OPUCE aims at unifying heterogeneous execution environments in a scalable and reliable manner. In this context a generic platform model is required. This was achieved by introducing an orchestration layer to decouple the implementation of the base services from the description of the high-level service logic.

This abstraction layer allows incorporating base services in different execution environments such as JSLEE, J2EE, or .NET, and also enables service execution on the client side, using widgets or other Web 2.0 client technologies.

Figure 11.9 depicts the implemented service execution environment and the deployment system that will instantiate the components and the services on the platform. The service execution environment (Cipolla et al. 2007) consists of a set of execution containers which can host the components, protocol resource adaptors, and support functions.

Base services wrap basic functionalities. Each base service exposes a unified interface that enables the invocation of actions, and the storing and retrieval of parameters and state information, and is exposed through a platform-specific Web Service interface. On JAIN SLEE containers, two different mediator interfaces are provided: a generic Web Service resource adaptor and an OPUCE-specific broker resource adaptor. Other resource adaptors can be plugged in, for example, to handle asynchronous events coming from underlying network resources, such as call termination or incoming SMS.

Telco-oriented applications need to handle an event-driven execution model for invoking new service instances or continuing an existing service logic flow. In order to integrate this model in the OPUCE SEE, the event gateway module was introduced in the platform.

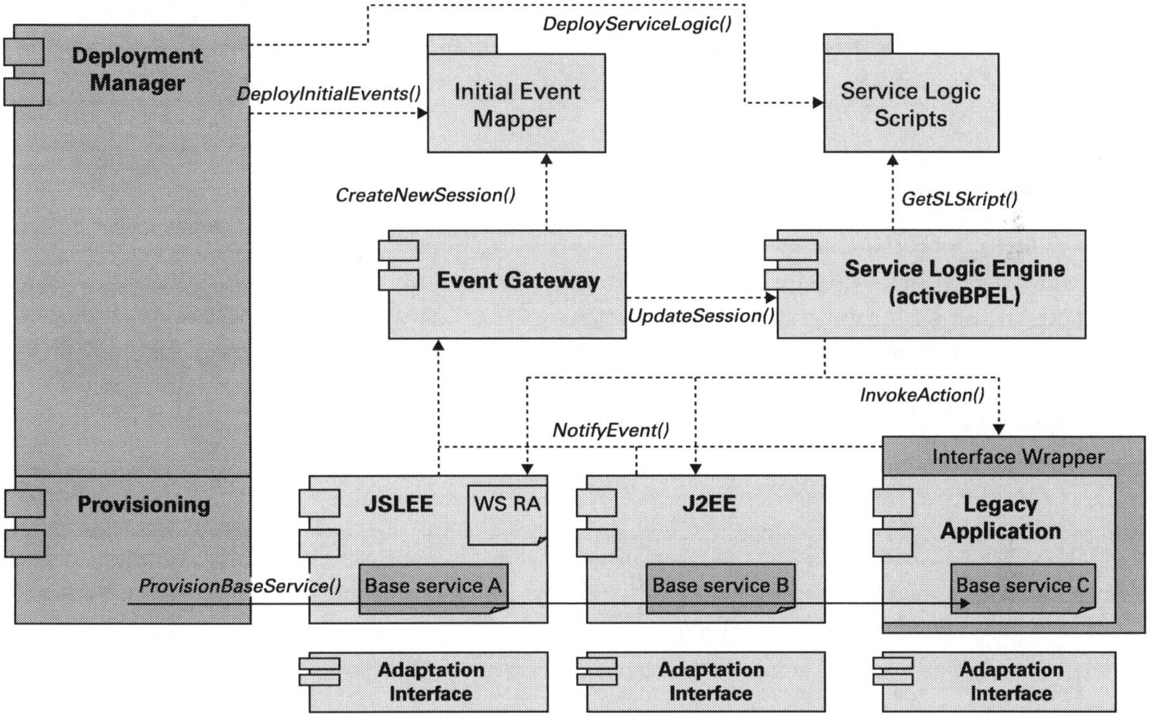

Figure 11.9
OPUCE SEE

This component is the end point for all event notifications generated by the base services and forwards these notifications to the service logic engine, thereby contributing to decoupling base services from the high-level service logic engine. Upon an event notification, the event gateway has two main tasks:

- If the event is the initial event for some service, create a new service instance on the service logic engine that will handle the forwarded events.
- Forward the received event to the end point associated with the appropriate service instance.

The service composition model described is based on an event-driven paradigm in which every base service instance (BSI) gets actions invoked, fires events, and keeps track of some properties (which represent the internal state of the component). The service logic of an OPUCE service describes how different BSIs interact with each other, using event-triggered patterns to make a higher-level service. This service logic is specified by a set of connections between events and actions, together with the initial and final events. The execution of the functionalities of a base service is the responsibility of the base service implementation; the execution of the service logic, as defined above, is up to the service logic engine (SLE), which belongs to the orchestration layer. The SLE will enable the execution of the service logic by performing the following functionalities:

- Invoke actions on base services
- Wait for event notifications from the event gateway
- Manage the life cycle of OPUCE services.

The SLE exposes one end point per OPUCE service, on which it receives all the event notifications forwarded by the event gateway. Once a notification has been correlated with the OPUCE service instance it belongs to, the SLE will process the event according to the appropriate event-triggered pattern and will invoke one or more actions on the base service execution containers. Before invoking actions, some flow control may be performed if the pattern associated with the event involves a nonfunctional block.

11.7 Conclusions and Future Work

The OPUCE platform is the next step in the evolution of the SOA paradigm, putting the user at the center of the service life cycle. Inside OPUCE, the end user is not only a consumer but also a creator. The tools offered by the platform allow users to control every step of the service life cycle: creation, deployment, advertising, sharing, execution, and withdrawal.

Currently, the SOA approach is being adopted by small and large enterprises, but the end user is demanding more and more prominence in the ICT world, as demonstrated by the Web 2.0 paradigm (O'Reilly) and the raising of user-centered tools for "service/application creation."

The OPUCE platform falls into the center of this paradigm shift toward user centricity and offers an intuitive and highly automated platform to put users in the lead of their telco experience (Sánchez et al. 2007). This also has the benefit of enabling new business models and relieving some pressure from the operators by allowing services created by end users. Operators are able to share some of the revenues with the more active service creators of the community, and in turn greatly widen the target audience since user-made services can now fulfill the requirements of niche markets impossible to reach by traditional approaches.

The first prototype of the OPUCE platform was successfully integrated in October 2007. It includes operative implementations of five of the six top-level blocks of the OPUCE architecture: portal (including SCEs), SLM, SEE, SA, and UIM. The context-awareness block has not yet been implemented as a stand-alone module at the time of writing, but some adaptation capabilities have been added to other modules or at the base service level, as described in section 11.6.6. All functionalities described in this chapter are currently fully implemented, unless explicitly stated otherwise.

This first prototype is capable of hosting the entire life cycle defined for an OPUCE service: a user can access the platform through the portal, compose a service in the SCE, deploy it on the platform through the SLM, notify other users about it with the SA, and execute it in the SEE. The UIM stores relevant user-related information, allowing composition of context-aware services, personalization at the platform level, and configuration of services and basic AAA functionalities.

The OPUCE project will continue until February 2009. The first prototype of the platform still lacks some features to allow its usage in a real market environment, such as a complete security/AAA framework, a billing system, SLA support, or interfaces for third parties to put their base services into the platform. At the time of writing, these features are planned to be implemented in the final prototype of the OPUCE platform, along with the results of research in other innovative areas, such as semantics, learning/reasoning, and adaptation, which will also be conducted in parallel during the remaining phase of the project.

As the OPUCE platform is already completely functional, a validation stage will enable usability experts and selected test groups of potential end users to evaluate it and provide feedback during the upcoming months.

Therefore, the OPUCE platform, as the ultimate combined application of the SOA paradigm and the user-centricity trend, represents the telco response to the Web 2.0 revolution in the Internet and opens an entire world of possibilities to users, communities, and operators.

Acknowledgments

The work presented in this chapter is executed as part of the OPUCE project and partly funded by the European Union under contract IST-034101. OPUCE is an integrated project of the 6th Framework Programme, IST Priority.

The work reflects only the authors' views. The Community is not liable for any use that may be made of the information contained therein.

References

Baladrón, Carlos, Javier Aguiar, Belén Carro, Jürgen Sienel, Rubén Trapero, Juan Carlos Yelmo, José María del Álamo, Jian Yu, and Paolo Falcarin. 2007. Service discovery suite for user-centric service creation. In *Proceedings of Service Oriented Computing: A Look at the Inside* (SOC@Inside '07).

Chang, Mark, Jackson He, W. T. Tsai, Bingnan Xiao, and Yinong Chen. 2006. UCSOA: User-centric service-oriented architecture. In *Proceedings of the IEEE International Conference on e-Business Engineering* (ICEBE '06), pp. 248–255.

Cipolla, Davide, Fabrizio Cosso, Matteo Demartini, Marc Drewniok, Francesco Moggia, Paola Renditore, and Jürgen Sienel. 2007. Web Service based asynchronous service execution environment. In *Proceedings of TSOA-07, First International Workshop on Telecom Service Oriented Architectures.*

Curbera, Francisco, Matthew Duftler, Rania Khalaf, Willian Nagy, Nirmal Mukhi, and Sanjiva Weerawarana. 2002. Unraveling the Web Services web: An introduction to SOAP, WSDL, and UDDI. *IEEE Internet Computing* 6, no. 2 (March/April): 86–93.

EmergeCore Networks. Trends in Service Provider Solutions. http://www.emergecore.com/products/downloads/WhitePaper_trends-in-service.pdf.

Erl, Thomas. 2005. *Service-Oriented Architecture: Concepts, Technology, and Design*. Upper Saddle River, N.J.: Prentice Hall.

Glitho, Roch H., Ferhat Khendek, and Alessandro De Marco. 2003. Creating value added services in Internet telephony: An overview and a case study on a high-level service creation environment. *IEEE Transactions on Systems, Man and Cybernetics*, Part C: *Applications and Reviews* 36, no. 4: 446–457.

Google Maps. http://maps.google.com/.

Huhns, Michael N., and Munindar P. Singh. 2005. Service-oriented computing: Key concepts and principles. *IEEE Internet Computing* 9, no. 1 (January/February): 75–81.

Kaye, Doug. 2003. *Loosely Coupled: The Missing Pieces of Web Services.* RDS Press.

Kloppmann, Matthias, Dieter König, Frank Leymann, Gerhard Pfau, and Dieter Roller. 2004. Business process choreography in WebSphere: Combining the power of BPEL and J2EE. *IBM Systems Journal* 43, no. 2.

McIlraith, Sheila A., Tran C. Son, and Honglei Zeng. 2001. Semantic Web Services. *Intelligent Systems* 6, no. 2: 46–53.

Microsoft Popfly. http://www.popfly.ms/.

Moerdijk, Ard-Jan, and Lucas Klostermann. 2003. Opening the networks with Parlay/OSA APIs: Standards and aspects behind the APIs. *IEEE Network* 17, no. 3 (May/June): 58–64. OPUCE project. 2007. Deliverable D2.3_1: Description of OPUCE Platform Elements.

O'Reilly, Tim. What Is Web 2.0. O'Reilly Network. http://www.oreillynet.com/pub/a/oreilly/tim/news/2005/09/30/what-is-web-20.html.

Paolucci, Massimo, and Katia P. Sycara. 2003. Autonomous semantic Web Services. *IEEE Internet Computing* 7, no. 5 (September/October): 34–41.

Papazoglou, Michael P., Paolo Traverso, Schahram Dustdar, Frank Leymann, and Bernd J. Krämer. 2006. Service oriented computing research roadmap. In *Dagstuhl Seminar. Proceedings.* Seminar at the International Conference and Research Center for Computer Science of Schloss Dagstuhl.

Papazoglou, Mike P. 2003. Service-oriented computing: Concepts, characteristics and directions. In *Proceedings of the Fourth International Conference on Web Information Systems Engineering* (WISE 2003), p. 3. Pasley, James. 2005. How BPEL and SOA are changing Web Services development. *IEEE Internet Computing* 9, no. 3 (May/June): 60–67.

Peltz, Chris. 2003. Web services orchestration and choreography. *Computer* 36, no. 10 (October): 46–52.

Pollet, Thierry, Gerard Maas, Johan Marien, and Albert Wambecq. 2006. Telecom services delivery in a SOA. In *20th International Conference on Advanced Information Networking and Applications* (AINA 2006), vol. 2, pp. 529–533.

Sánchez, Antonio, Belén Carro, and Stefan Wesner. 2008. Telco services for end customers. European perspectiva. *IEEE Communications* 46, no. 2 (February): 14–18.

SeCSE project. 2005. Doc. A1.D1a: State of the Art—Service Engineering.

SeCSE: Service Centric System Engineering. http://secse.eng.it/.

Stal, Michael. 2006. Using architectural patterns and blueprints for service-oriented architecture. *IEEE Software* 23, no. 2 (March/April): 54–61.

Sycara, Katia P., Massimo Paolucci, Anupriya Ankolekar, and Naveen Srinivasan. 2003. Automated discovery, interaction and composition of semantic Web Services. *Journal of Web Semantics* 1, no. 1 (September): 27–46.

Tsai, W. T., Bingnan Xiao, Raymond A. Paul, and Yinong Chen. 2006. Consumer-centric service-oriented architecture: A new approach. In *Proceedings of the Fourth IEEE Workshop on Software Technologies for Future Embedded and Ubiquitous Systems (SEUS 2006) and the Second International Workshop on Collaborative Computing, Integration, and Assurance (WCCIA 2006)*, p. 6. Yahoo! Pipes. http://pipes.yahoo.com/.

Yelmo, Juan C., Rubén Trapero, José M. del Álamo, Juergen Sienel, Marc Drewniok, Isabel Ordás and Kathleen McCallum. 2007. User-driven service lifecycle management—Adopting Internet paradigms in telecom services. In *Service-Oriented Computing* (ICSOC 2007). LNCS 4749, pp. 342–352.

12 INFRAWEBS—A Framework for Semantic Service Engineering

Gennady Agre, Tomás Pariente Lobo, Zlatina Marinova, Joahim Nern, Andras Micsik, Andrei Boyanov, Tatiana Atanasova, James Scicluna, José-Manuel López-Cobo, and Elpida Tzafestas

12.1 Introduction

The IST research project INFRAWEBS,[1] completed in the beginning of 2007, focused on developing a semantic service engineering framework enabling creation, maintenance, and execution of WSMO-based Semantic Web Services, and supporting Semantic Web Service applications within their life cycle. Being strongly conformant to the current specification of various elements of the Web Service Modeling Ontology (WSMO)[2]—ontologies, goals, semantic services, and mediators—the INFRAWEBS framework manages the complex process of creation of semantic descriptions by identifying different types of actors (users) of Semantic Web Service technologies; clarifying different phases of the semantic service engineering process; and providing a specialized software tool set oriented to the identified user types and intended for usage in all phases of the Semantic Web Service engineering process.

The viability of the INFRAWEBS approach has been tested by two pilot applications with a high level of complexity. The first application is the STREAM Flows! system (SFS), in which customers can create and reuse travel packages (López et al. 2005). The second application is based on an e-government scenario. It illustrates interactions carried out by Semantic Web Services in the scope of public administration and interactions between administrations, citizens, and enterprises, with emphasis on the enterprise-to-administration integration (Riceputi 2006).

As a service-oriented framework, the contribution of the INFRAWEBS project is mainly positioned in the service integration layer of the NESSI framework.[3] However, it can also be positioned in its semantic layer since the project results improve the state of the art on semantic tools. The set of tools developed during the project makes the otherwise arduous process of constructing a WSMO-based Semantic Web Service application, requiring expert knowledge of the WSMO model, and the Web Service Modeling Language (WSML), a task achievable by ordinary Web Service developers. Facilitating the task of WSMO object construction is an achievement of the project that has a potential impact on the adoption of Semantic Web Services on a larger scale.

The set of software modules and tools developed during the INFRAWEBS project provides some innovative solutions for semantic service description, publishing, discovery, and dynamic composition, with the main focus on solving problems occurring in the process of creating real service-based applications. Through tight integration of traditional design principles for engineering service applications with WSMO methodology for Semantic Web Service description and use, the INFRAWEBS framework can be considered as the first framework for semantic service engineering that covers the whole Semantic Web Service life cycle and allows creation of complex semantically enabled applications. That is why, from the point of view of the service-oriented computing road map (Papazoglou and Georgakopoulos 2003), the INFRAWEBS contribution lies in the service engineering plane because it supports the engineering of service-based applications in a semantic-oriented manner.

12.2 INFRAWEBS Framework

Conceptually, the INFRAWEBS framework is a service-oriented architecture (SOA) comprising coupled and linked INFRAWEBS Semantic Web units. Each unit provides tools and components for analyzing, designing, and maintaining WSMO-based Semantic Web Services (SWS) and SWS applications within the whole life cycle. The INFRAWEBS framework is developed to support all stages of the Semantic Web Service life cycle presented in figure 12.1 (see Agre and Marinova 2007 for more details).

A very important aspect, concerning the development and operation of any SOA-based application, is to identify the actors and their roles in the scope of the application (Colombo et al. 2005). The following actors have been identified as potential users of the INFRAWEBS framework:

1. *Semantic Web Service provider* Any provider of already existing Web Services who would like to convert them to Semantic Web Services and to publish them.
2. *Semantic Web Service broker (aggregator)* A provider who would like to create and publish a service with some desired functionality via composition of several existing Semantic Web Services.

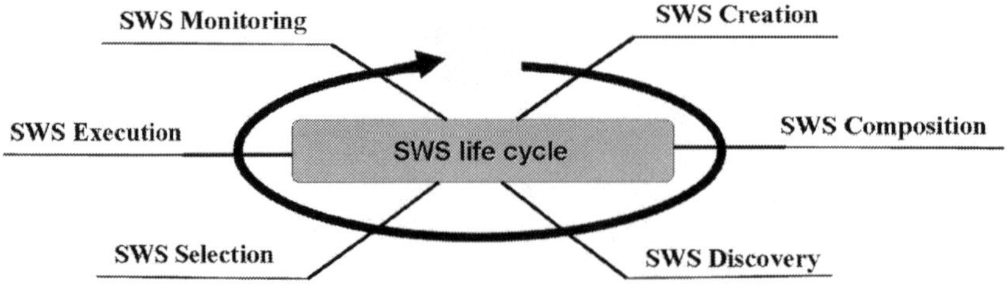

Figure 12.1
INFRAWEBS SWS life cycle

3. *Semantic Web Service application provider* An organization that would like to design its own application based on Semantic Web Service technology.
4. *Web Service application consumer* An "ordinary" end user of a Web Service application who transparently uses the INFRAWEBS framework (while using the application) for finding and executing a Web Service or a composition of Web Services able to satisfy his/her request (goal).

The proposed categorization of INFRAWEBS framework users allows identification of the set of different tasks that the framework is able to accomplish in order to satisfy the objectives of these users, to define the set of necessary components, and to specify the framework architecture.

12.2.1 INFRAWEBS Conceptual Architecture

The INFRAWEBS conceptual architecture consists of two main elements: a design-time part (Semantic Web unit) and a runtime part (runtime environment) (figure 12.2).

All Semantic Web unit components are organized in two directions: (1) problem solving based on semantic information (or logic-based problem solving) versus problem solving

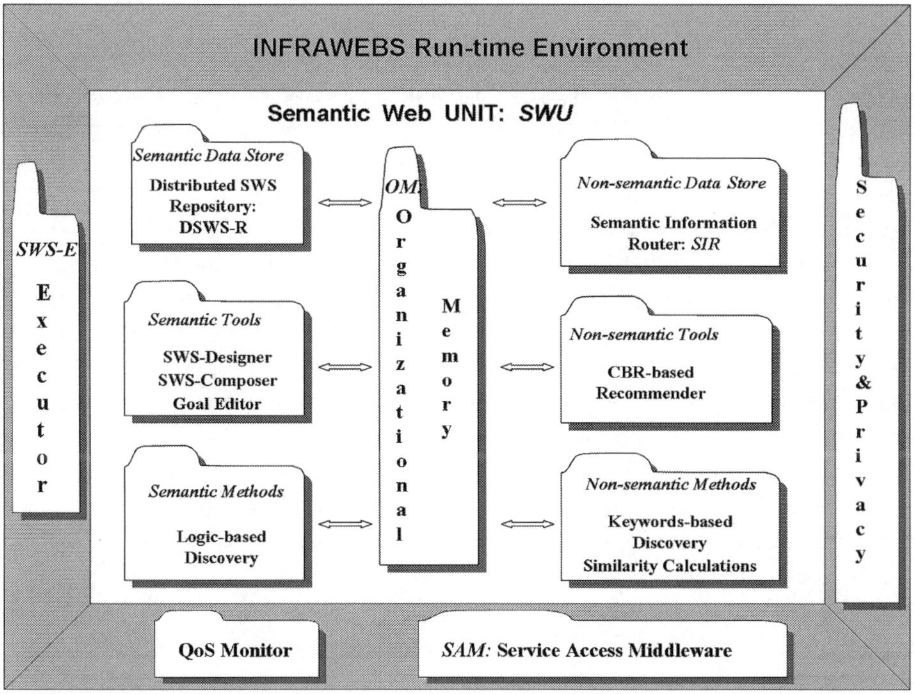

Figure 12.2
INFRAWEBS Conceptual Architecture

based on nonsemantic information (similarity-based problem solving), and (2) different types of information needed for both kinds of problem solving. From these points of view the Semantic Web unit proposes information structures for storing and retrieving semantic and nonsemantic data: distributed Semantic Web Service repository (DSWS-R) enables efficient storage and retrieval of all elements of the Semantic Web (WSMO objects): goals, ontologies, Semantic Web Services and mediators. Each DSWS-R consists of two components: the local repository, a place where all WSMO objects created in this Semantic Web unit are stored; and the local registry, a place where publicly available (i.e., published) advertisements of WSMO objects are stored. Advertisements contain the minimal necessary information needed to locate the advertised document: an identifier of the described WSMO object, the end point of the owner registry, and the policy for propagating this advertisement. Advertisements are published in the local registry by their owner and are then propagated to partner registries, depending on their policy. The process of publication of advertisements is described in more detail in section 12.3.4 (see also Marinova et al. 2007).

The semantic information router (SIR) contains annotated metadata about Web Services (WSDL files), used for grounding of Semantic Web Services created in a Semantic Web unit and for their subsequent execution. The semantic information router provides a graphical user interface for Web Services annotation and categorization (Saarela 2006).

Similarity-based organizational memory (OM) contains a special representation (so-called knowledge objects) of both semantic and nonsemantic objects stored in other INFRAWEBS information structures (DSWS-R and SIR). Organizational memory is a Web Service implementation of the INFRAWEBS case-based memory, allowing effective retrieval of objects based on their content (Andonova et al. 2006).

There are also tools for creation and maintenance of both semantic and nonsemantic data. The Semantic Web Service designer (SWS-Designer) enables design of WSMO-based Semantic Web Services on the basis of existing nonsemantic Web Service descriptions stored in the semantic information router and WSML ontologies, as well as by reusing existing WSMO semantic service descriptions stored in the DSWS-R (Agre and Dilov 2007).

The Semantic Web Service composer (SWS-Composer) is a tool for design-time creation of new Semantic Web Services through composition of other existing WSMO-based Semantic Web Services stored in the repository (DSWS-R) (Atanasova et al. 2006).

The goal editor provides means for creation of WSMO-based goal templates used for the design of Semantic Web Service-based applications and also is used at runtime for creation of specific application user goals (Agre and Marinova 2007).

The case-based reasoning recommender is a similarity-based tool facilitating operation of all INFRAWEBS "semantic-based" components by utilizing "past experience." Knowledge objects stored in the organizational memory are used as case descriptions analyzed for determining the most similar solutions to the current problem (Nern et al. 2007). The tool is implemented as a component integrated with the organizational memory.

The problem-solving methods used for creating and maintaining Semantic Web Services are logic-based discovery (Kovács et al. 2007), some application-specific decision-support methods are used for service composition, compensation, and monitoring (Agre and Marinova 2007) as well as some structural linguistic and statistical methods for calculating similarity (Agre 2006).

The INFRAWEBS runtime environment is responsible for communication with different INFRAWEBS users and other Semantic Web units, ensuring security and privacy of these operations. The runtime environment consists of the service access middleware (SAM; Kovács et al. 2007), the Semantic Web Service executor (SWS-E; Scicluna et al. 2007), the quality of service (QoS) monitor (Scicluna et al. 2006), and security and privacy components (Tzafestas 2006).

The INFRAWEBS conceptual architecture presents a novel approach to facilitating the process of creating and maintaining Semantic Web Services and SWS applications. It is based on tight integration of similarity-based and logic-based reasoning. Similarity-based reasoning is used for fast finding of approximate solutions, which are further concretized by the logic-based reasoning.

The following sections show how the architecture described supports different kinds of INFRAWEBS framework users (see Agre et al. 2007 for more details).

12.2.2 Support for Web Service Providers

In INFRAWEBS a Semantic Web Service can be created in two ways: by converting an existing nonsemantic Web Service into a semantic one (this process is called Semantic Web Service design) or by composition of several existing Semantic Web Services (Semantic Web Service composition). This section describes the process of creating Semantic Web Services from existing, nonsemantic ones. This process is realized by creating semantic service descriptions on the basis of existing WSDL descriptions, as well as by reusing already created semantic descriptions of similar services.

Semantic Web Service Design Life Cycle The life cycle of the Semantic Web Service design process is defined by both the static structure of the semantic description of a WSMO-based semantic service and certain assumptions on what kind of additional semantic information is needed, where it is stored, and how it can be found. From this point of view, we assume that nonsemantic Web Services are implemented and formally described (as WSDL definitions) outside the INFRAWEBS framework and are stored in some UDDI-like repositories.

In order to facilitate finding such Web Services, the service provider can annotate them with natural language-based metadata (for example, according to the Dublin Core[4] schema). It is necessary to emphasize that the addition of such metadata does not convert a Web Service into a WSMO-based Semantic Web Service. It simply enables the process of finding the annotated service by users or business partners. In the INFRAWEBS framework this service annotation activity is considered as the first, preliminary step of the Semantic Web Service design process, and it is seen as a process of registration of Web Services into the INFRAWEBS framework.

The INFRAWEBS framework supports this activity through a dedicated component, the semantic information router, which is a metadata-based content management and aggregation platform for storing and annotating Web Services (Saarela 2006).

The next step of the Semantic Web Service design process is the creation of its logical description according to the WSMO framework. However, in order to facilitate this very complicated activity, we have split it into several substeps:

1. Finding a desired nonsemantic Web Service (WSDL).
2. Finding a set of appropriate ontologies to be used for semantic reformulation of the main Web Service functionality in ontological terms.
3. Creating the semantic description of the Web Service behavior—service grounding, determining the correspondence between data structures in the semantic and nonsemantic descriptions of a WSMO service, and the service choreography describing how it is possible to communicate with the semantic service in order to properly execute the nonsemantic Web Service grounded to it.
4. Creating the semantic description of service functionality, advertising what the service can do. Such semantic service capability description is used for discovery.
5. Publishing semantic descriptions. In the INFRAWEBS framework such descriptions are stored in the local (belonging to the concrete local Semantic Web unit) distributed repositories (DSWS-R). The DSWS-R component is then responsible for propagating the advertisement of published objects within the framework.

All these substeps (except the last one) can be done in the INFRAWEBS by means of a special tool, the INFRAWEBS Designer (SWS-Designer), which is described in more detail in section 12.3. The publishing activity is performed by the SWS-Designer and DSWS-R components, as described in section 12.3.4.

12.2.3 Support for Web Service Aggregators

INFRAWEBS enables Web Service aggregators to compose, in design time, already existing semantic descriptions of Web Services in order to provide new value-added services. Composed services are also defined as WSMO-based Semantic Web Services, and can then be discovered and used in the same way as atomic services. Semantic Web Service application providers can also be considered as Web Service brokers if they provide composed services as part of their application functionality.

The INFRAWEBS design-time composer tool (SWS-Composer) enables the combination of different Semantic Web Services to obtain a new, complex Semantic Web Service. It uses adapted workflow methodology for creating WSMO-based service compositions, as well as for the determination and visualization of data and control flow within the composed service (Atanasova et al. 2006).

Services to be included in a composition can be selected either directly, by browsing available services, or found through INFRAWEBS's similarity search. In the latter case, a plain-text request is defined and the organizational memory—a dedicated component playing the role of a case-based memory in the INFRAWEBS framework—is queried to provide the most similar services. The result of composition is represented as semantic description of the service and can be stored in the distributed repository.

At present, WSMO orchestration is still in the stage of language design and specification. For this reason, the design-time compositions are described as a choreography combining the choreography descriptions of participating services. In the future, when orchestration specification is fully developed, the INFRAWEBS Semantic Web Service composer can be extended to create the orchestration on the basis of the workflow description.

12.2.4 Support for Semantic Web Service Application Providers

One of the main objectives of INFRAWEBS is to support organizations that want to create semantically enriched applications based on Semantic Web Services. In the previous sections the support for the creation of semantic descriptions via Semantic Web Service design or composition has been explained. These descriptions can also be used by Semantic Web Service application providers to create the basic functionality of their applications. However, in order to discover and execute these services, the application should be able to explore all possibilities provided by the INFRAWEBS runtime environment. At runtime, discovery of Semantic Web Services is done via matching a given user goal description against all service capability descriptions; hence, the first task of the application provider is to provide a mechanism for creating the goals.

A WSMO-based goal (Roman et al. 2006) has a structure similar to that of a WSMO Semantic Web Service and can be considered as a structured set of logical expressions written in a special language, WSML (Bruijn et al. 2005). We consider it to be absolutely unfeasible to assume that either the end user or a Semantic Web Service application provider will be able to write such expressions directly, or that it is possible to construct an algorithm able to automatically translate each possible natural language user query into the corresponding WSML logical expression. That is why the conceptual INFRAWEBS architecture assumes the presence of a (predefined) set of "general" WSMO-based goals that may be "reused" by the end users. Such general goals (called goal templates) should be prepared by the Semantic Web Service application provider at design time.

The assumption that the functionality of a service application can be fully described by a set of goal templates is still rather demanding to the application provider, since it requires goal templates to be prepared in advance for all possible user goals. Though we cannot further reduce this demand, we are, however, able to facilitate the application provider in satisfying it. In order to do this, we assume the following:

1. Each goal may be represented either by an atomic goal template (representing basic functionality of the application) or by a combination (composition) of some atomic goal templates and
2. The INFRAWEBS framework provides the application designer with necessary and easy-to-use tools both for goal template creation and for goal composition: the goal editor, part of the Semantic Web Service designer.

12.2.5 Running Semantic Web Service Applications

As discussed above, Semantic Web Service application functionality is provided by the Semantic Web Services included in its architecture. In the process of running such applications, the INFRAWEBS runtime environment is used to provide support for the following activities:

1. *Refinement of goal templates* During the design of the application, goal templates have been defined to represent the most common user requests to the application. These goal templates are included in the application user interface as specific forms where necessary data have to be entered by the user in order to use a certain functionality. When the user fills in these specific fields (slots), such as the desired destination for a flight, the application uses the INFRAWEBS framework to produce a concrete goal instance from the particular goal template.
2. *Service discovery* On the basis of the concrete goal, discovery compiles a ranked list of services that match this goal.
3. *Service selection* The application enables the user to select a suitable service from the list of matching services.
4. *Service execution* Finally, one of the selected Semantic Web Services can be executed to provide its functionality, and the results are appropriately presented to the user.

In INFRAWEBS these activities are performed through the service access middleware (SAM), which provides a single API for the semantically enabled applications to use. The actual execution of Semantic Web Services is carried out with the help of the Semantic Web Service executor (SWS-E) component (Scicluna et al. 2007).

Runtime Service Composition The INFRAWEBS user request modeling enables definition of "complex goals" which define independent user objectives that are interconnected by certain constraints. A typical example of a complex goal in the SFS scenario (see section 12.4.1) is the wish to book a flight for certain dates and reserve a room at a hotel in the destination city for the same dates. In this example the independent goals are booking a flight and making a hotel room reservation, but they are implicitly constrained by the same arrival and departure dates as well as the flight destination and hotel location.

In INFRAWEBS these constraints are modeled with WSML shared variables which specify that, for example, the hotel location slot has the same value as the flight destination.

Complex goals are also predefined by application providers at design time and capture any possible combination of "simple" goals that can be useful for the application functionality. In the case of the SFS test bed, composite goals are used to model different types of packages that can be created by the test bed user. Complex goals are also defined as goal templates that can be instantiated on the basis of the user input.

When complex goals are used, the discovery can find either atomic or composed services that match the goal instance, or, in some cases, no single service will match the goal. In such cases the INFRAWEBS runtime service composition mechanism (Agre and Marinova 2007) is used to provide the user with an appropriate solution.

12.3 Novel Design of WSMO-Based Semantic Web Services

A semantic WSMO-based description of a Web Service consists of three main parts (Roman et al. 2006):

1. *Top-level concepts* Describing service name spaces, used ontologies, and mediators, as well as service nonfunctional properties.
2. *Service capability* Describing what the service can do.
3. *Service choreography* Describing how the user can communicate with a semantic service.

The main parts of a Semantic Web Service description (service capability and transition rules) are represented via complex logical expressions written in WSML language, which combines a part of service choreography features of F-logic, description logic, and logic programming (Bruijn et al. 2005). Thus, "direct" creation of a WSML description of Semantic Web Services (e.g., by means of a text editor) is not an easy task, and requires strong knowledge of the formal logic, which significantly restricts the range of people able to accomplish such an activity. That is why we have decided to avoid this problem by constructing a special tool for designing Semantic Web Services: the INFRAWEBS Semantic Web Service designer. Its main design principles are the following:

1. *User-friendliness* The INFRAWEBS designer proposes an intuitive graphical way for constructing and editing service and goal descriptions, abstracting away as much as possible from the concrete syntax of the logical language used for implementing it. The WSML description of the semantic object under construction is automatically generated from the graphical models created by the user.
2. *Intensive use of ontologies* The process of constructing logical descriptions of semantic objects is ontology-driven. In each step of this process the user may select only those elements of the used ontologies that are consistent with the already constructed part of the object description.

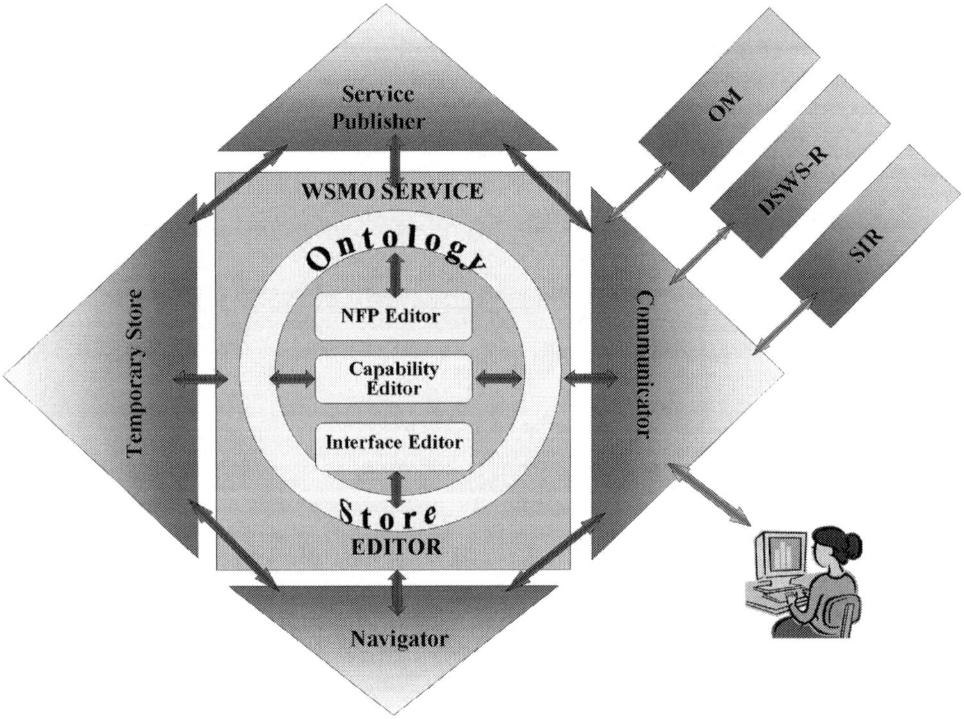

Figure 12.3
Conceptual Architecture of the INFRAWEBS Designer

3. *Reusability* Creation of semantic descriptions is facilitated by providing the designer with an opportunity to reuse existing, similar descriptions by applying a case-based reasoning approach.

The conceptual architecture of the INFRAWEBS designer, which implements the principles mentioned above, is shown in figure 12.3.

Temporary store is an abstract module representing a place where all local files produced or used by the INFRAWEBS designer are stored. Navigator is an abstract module centralizing the access to other INFRAWEBS designer modules. Communicator is responsible for communication with the user and external components such as organizational memory (OM), the distributed Semantic Web Service repository (DSWS-R) and semantic information router (SIR). Publisher is a module responsible for storing a semantic Web service description in an external (for the INFRAWEBS designer) storage—the DSWS-R. In order to guarantee the correctness and completeness of such a description, the publisher validates different parts of the description and augments them with some information needed to ensure the proper use of this service in the future. The WSMO service editor is an abstract module responsible for creating and editing the WSML description of the Semantic Web Service according to the WSMO framework. It combines three specialized graphical, ontology-driven editors and a specialized module for in-memory loading, visualization, and manipulation of WSML ontologies used by these editors.

12.3.1 The Use of Ontologies

A process for converting a nonsemantic Web Service into a WSMO-based Semantic Web Service may be seen as an interactive ontology-driven process of service annotation. Finding the appropriate set of ontologies is one of the initial steps the user has to do before creating a semantic description of a Web Service.

The INFRAWEBS framework assumes that all ontologies are stored in the distributed repository (DSWS-R). Thus, the process of finding ontologies is implemented in the INFRAWEBS designer as a complex procedure in which the user describes the expected content of the required ontology. The designer then translates this description into a query and sends it to the organizational memory, which matches the query against its internal (case-based) representations of ontologies and returns a set of ontologies most similar to the query.

All ontologies selected by the user are loaded into the ontology store, which is a global structure accessible for all semantic services loaded into the INFRAWEBS designer. Such an organization allows designing several new semantic services in parallel, using the same set of ontologies.

12.3.2 Graphical Creation of an SWS Description

Service Tree A description of a WSMO-based Semantic Web Service contains three types of information related to service identification (service nonfunctional properties, name spaces etc.), service advertisement (a logical description of service capability used for service discovery), and service choreography (a logical description of service behavior used for communication with and execution of the service). Although such information is very heterogeneous, it is displayed in the INFRAWEBS designer in a uniform way—as a tree in which internal (functional) nodes represent the roles of each specific portion of the information and are used for editing the tree structure; while the tree leaves serve as pointers to the content of each information portion (figure 12.4).

Graphical Models of WSML Logical Expressions In WSMO, logical expressions are used for representing service capability as well as conditional and conclusion parts of transition rules describing the service choreography. We have developed an approach in which the text (WSML) representation of such expressions is automatically generated from their graphical models (Agre and Dilov 2007). A WSML logical expression is graphically modeled by a labeled, directed acyclic graph (LDAG), which can contain five types of nodes:

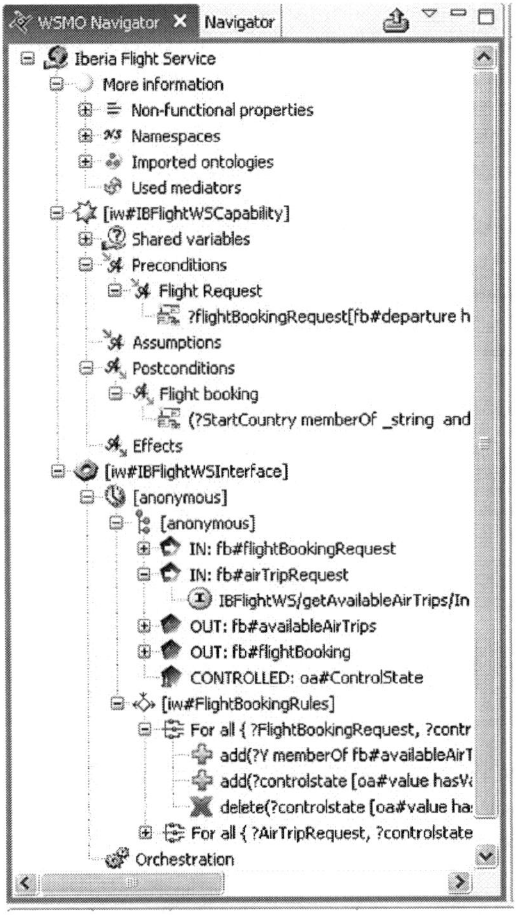

Figure 12.4
An example of service tree

1. A *root* node which may have only outgoing arcs The node is used for marking the beginning of the graphical model corresponding to the WSML logical expression.
2. Intermediate nodes called *variables* Such nodes can have several incoming and outgoing arcs. Each variable has a unique name and has a framelike structure consisting of slots represented by attribute–value pairs. Such a variable corresponds to a notion of a compound molecule in WSML (Bruijn et al. 2005).
3. Intermediate nodes called *relations* A relation node corresponds to a WSML statement $\mathrm{r}(\mathrm{Par}_1, \ldots, \mathrm{Par}_n)$, where *r* is a relation from a given ontology, and $Par_1, \ldots, Par_n$ are *WSML* variables–relation parameters. Graphically, each relation node is represented as a rectangle with a header containing the relation name and a row of relation parameters.

4. Intermediate nodes called *operators* that correspond to WSML logical *operators AND, OR, IF-THEN,*[5] *NOT, and Old-New*[6] Each node can have only one incoming arc and one (for NOT), two (for IF-THEN and Old-New), or more (for AND and OR) outgoing arcs.
5. Terminal nodes (leaves) called *instances* that cannot have any outgoing arcs An instance corresponds to the WSML statement *Var hasValue Instance*, where *Var* is a WSML variable and *Instance* is an instance of a concept from a given ontology.

The directed arcs of a graph are called *connections*. A connection outgoing from a variable or relation refines the variable (or relation parameter) value and corresponds to the WSML logical operator AND. A connection outgoing from an operator has the meaning of a pointer to the operator operand.

The proposed model allows considering the process of axiom creation as a formal process of LDAG expanding (and editing) and formulating some formal rules for checking (in relation to given ontologies) syntactic and semantic correctness of the constructed logical expressions.

Constructing a logical expression is considered as a repetitive process consisting of the combination of three main logical steps: definition, refinement, and logical development. The definition step is used for defining some general concepts needed for describing the meaning of axioms. During this step the nature of a main variable defining the axiom is specified. Such a step is equivalent to creating a WSML statement *?Concept memberOf Concept*, which means that the WSML variable *?Concept*, copying the structure of the *Concept* from a given WSML ontology, is created. Attributes of the concept, which are "inherited" by the axiom model variable, are called variable attributes. By default the values of such attributes are set to free WSML variables with the type defined by the definition of such attributes in the corresponding ontology.

The refinement step is used for more concrete specification of the desired properties of such concepts and may be seen as a specialization of too general concepts introduced earlier. This step is implemented as a recursive procedure of refining values of some attributes (or relation parameters) defined in previous step(s). In terms of our model, each cycle in such a step means an expansion of an existing nonterminal node–variable (or relation). More precisely, it means a selection of an attribute of an existing model variable, and binding its value to another (new or existing) node of the axiom model. The main problem is to ensure semantic correctness of the resulting (extended) logical expression. Such correctness is achieved by applying a set of context-sensitive rules determining permitted expansion of a given node.

The logical development step consists of elaborating the logical structure of the axioms, which is achieved through combination of general concepts by means of the logical operators AND, OR, IF-THEN, and NOT. Such operators may be added to connect two independently constructed logical expressions or be inserted directly into already constructed

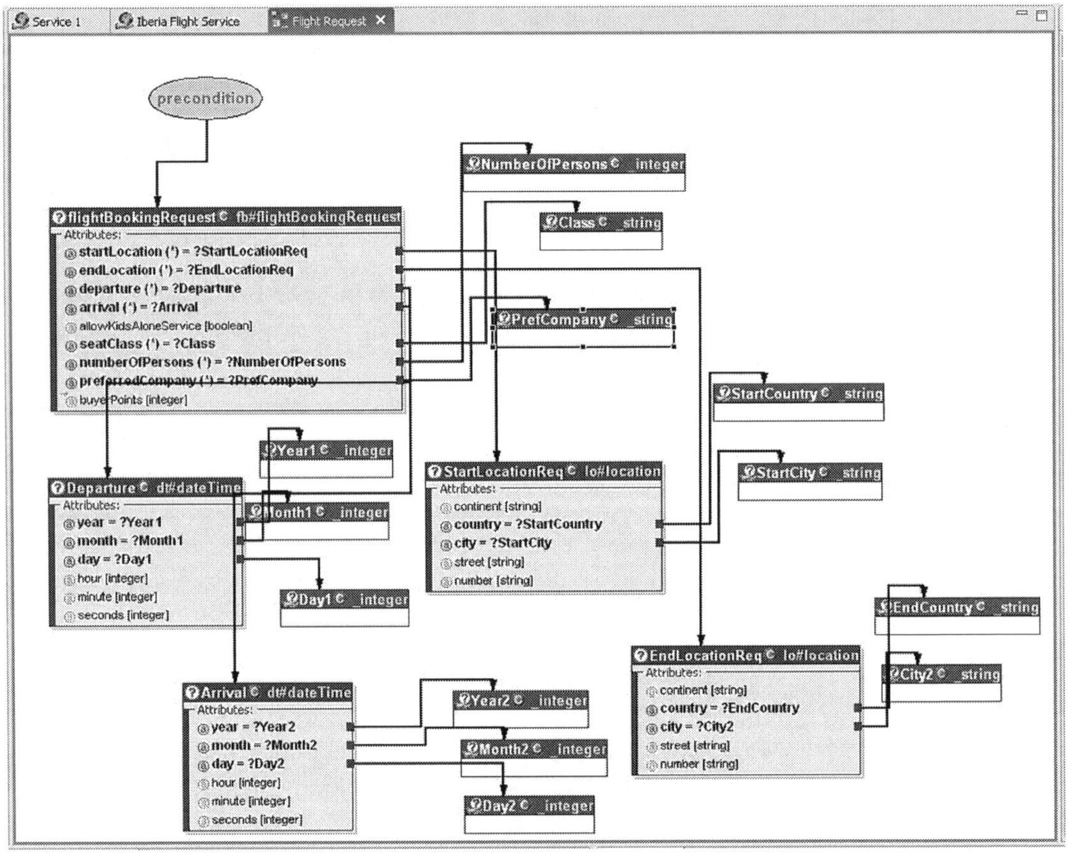

Figure 12.5
An example of a graphical model created by the INFRAWEBS Designer

expressions. The operation is controlled by context-dependent semantic and syntactic checks that analyze the whole context of the axiom. An example of a graphical model is shown on figure 12.5.

12.3.3 Reusing Descriptions of Existing Semantic Web Services

Although the usage of graphical models makes the process of designing WSML description of an SWS easier, it still remains a rather complex and time-consuming activity. The next step toward facilitating this process is to provide the service designer with an opportunity to reuse the descriptions of the existing semantic services.

Finding a Similar Service Description In order to be reused, WSMO descriptions of Semantic Web Services and other objects (goals, ontologies, mediators) are considered in the

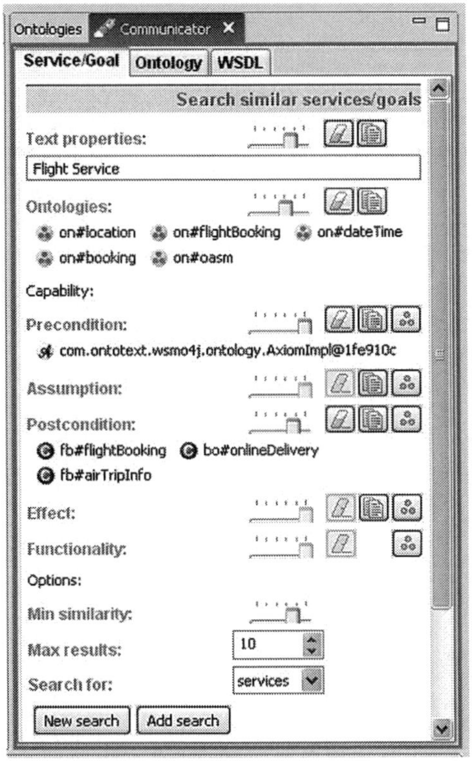

Figure 12.6
The service request form

INFRAWEBS framework not only as logical (WSML) representations of these objects but also as cases. A case is a triple {T, P, S}, where T is a type of the WSMO object stored (service, goal, or ontology) which determines the structure of the object representation P; P is a special representation of a WSMO object as a structured text; and S is the service IRI, which is used for locating the object in the remote distributed repository.

The user describes a semantic service to be found by filling out a standard form (figure 12.6), which is sent to the case-based memory (realized by the organizational memory). The form consists of three sections enabling construction of different queries based on the amount of information the user provides.

The "Text Properties" section allows the user to describe the desired functionality of a service by means of natural-language keywords. Nonfunctional properties of the semantic descriptions will be matched against these keywords, and services with the best match will be returned. The second section ("Ontologies") allows the user to find services using a set of ontologies similar to that specified in the request form. Ontology names are used by the organizational memory as keywords in the process of finding existing semantic services using the same (or a similar) set of ontologies.

The third section ("Capability") is devoted to ontological description of the capability of the desired service. Its first four subsections correspond to the sections of the service capability description according to the WSMO framework, and the last one ("Functionality") allows constructing a general description of the capability of a service to be found.

The first four subsections can be filled in the following two ways:

1. *Semiautomatic*, by selecting some ontological elements (concepts, instances, or relations) from the ontologies shown in the ontology store. In such a way the user can specify that she/he expects that the desired service should contain a similar set of ontology keywords in the WSML description of the corresponding section of its capability.
2. *Fully automatic*, by specifying the name of a service, whose corresponding capability description section will be used as an example of what the desired service should have in its capability section description.

When the user has no clear idea about the content of a concrete section of the desired service capability description or no "example" service descriptions exist, she/he can use the "Functionality" subsection to express her/his general idea of what ontology keywords the desired service capability description should have as a whole. That subsection can be filled by selecting ontological elements from all available ontologies.

The filled-in request form is translated into a complex XML query, in which each form subsection determines a separate (local) criterion for evaluating the similarity. The overall aggregated similarity is calculated based on a weighted sum of all local criteria (Agre 2006). The user can set the weight (from 0 to 1) for each criterion by means of a slider placed on the right of the line describing the corresponding form subsection (or section).

The query results returned by the organizational memory are represented as an annotated list of services ordered by the value of their ontological and lexical similarity coefficients.

Organizational Memory: INFRAWEBS's Case-based Memory Organizational memory (OM) is used in the INFRAWEBS framework for finding semantic (Semantic Web Services, ontologies, goals, etc.) and nonsemantic (WSDL files, BPEL files, etc.) objects stored in the INFRAWEBS information stores (distributed repository and semantic information router) based on the object content. In order to do this, the organizational memory considers all such objects as special text documents—"knowledge objects" having specific structure while each structured part of an object is written in a specific language (natural language and/or WSML) (Andonova et al. 2006). The structure of an object depends on its type and (for semantic objects) corresponds to main semantic parts representing the object accord-

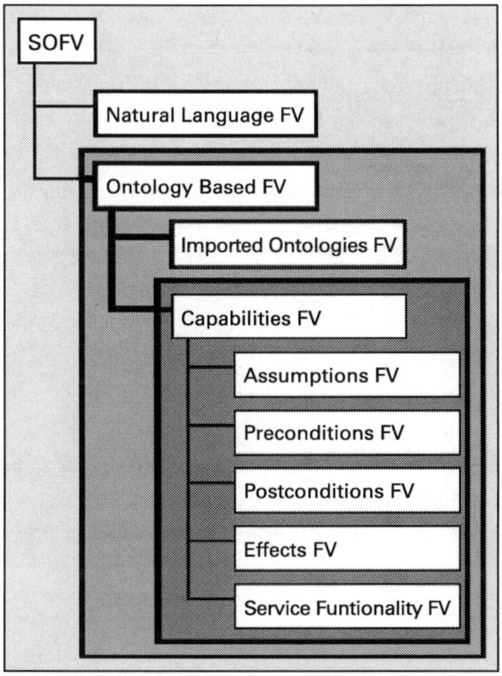

Figure 12.7
Structural Object Feature Vector (SOFV) for a SWS

ing to WSMO specification. By means of a special "filtering" procedure (specific for each object type) the organizational memory creates its internal "case" representation of each object {T, P, S}, where T is the object type (service, goal, etc.), P is the compressed representation of the object content as a structural object feature vector (SOFV), and S is the object identifier (IRI) and some natural language annotation briefly describing the object. An SOFV represents (see figure 12.7) a hierarchic collection of one-dimensional object feature vectors (OFV), sets of weighted keywords. Keywords may be natural-language words extracted from non-functional properties of an object, or ontology-based words extracted from a logical description of the object.

The organizational memory is equipped with different types of dictionaries—knowledge domain keywords, generic keywords, abbreviations, stop terms, and synonyms—and also maintains a list of keyword recommendations. The recommendations are automatically extracted from each new filtered object that is stored, and are added to the corresponding dictionaries. A fuzzy mapping between ontology-based dictionaries and natural-language dictionaries is maintained by the organizational memory, and is also used for retrieving semantic information by natural-language queries.

In order to provide efficient retrieval of knowledge objects, their case representations are organized in a hierarchical structure—a multilayer classification tree, in which internal nodes are centroids and leaves are concrete cases. Each centroid is a "typical" representative of a set of similar cases; splitting cases into different sets is done by means of a fuzzy concept matching clustering procedure (Nern et al. 2007). Each new case is placed into the classification tree based on its similarity to tree centroids. The resulting similarity coefficient is calculated based on a set of similarity functions that are different for each structural part of the case (see Agre 2006 for a detailed description of these functions).

12.3.4 Description Persistence and Publication

The main objective for creating a semantic service or other semantic objects (goal, ontology, etc.) is to allow it to be discovered and used by other users. In the INFRAWEBS framework this is achieved by publication of the object in a remote repository (the distributed repository component) which combines functionalities of a registry and a repository (Marinova et al. 2007). Whereas the repository component enables storage and management of WSMO descriptions within the scope of the organization (particularly the Semantic Web unit), the registry is responsible for their publication and propagation. The distributed repository provides functionality that can be used both to specify which Semantic Web Service descriptions should be publicly available for discovery (and for subsequent composition or execution) and to exchange them with the other registries in the p2p network.

This functionality can be used by Semantic Web Service providers that would like to advertise their services within the INFRAWEBS framework of partners. Published services can later be discovered and used by partners in accordance with the specified policies. Providers of composite services can discover and combine advertised services and then advertise the new composite service. Semantic Web Service application providers can publish new and composed services they provide to their clients.

In addition, advertisements of ontologies and goals can be published to enable their sharing and reuse. Ontology sharing is very important, since all kinds of WSMO descriptions are created on the basis of imported ontologies, and hence are usable only if these ontologies can be loaded.

Semantic description publication is a twofold process of first publishing WSMO object advertisements in the local registry, and then propagating them in the p2p network by exchanging messages between distributed repository components in different INFRAWEBS units (Semantic Web units). The major tasks associated with each of those two steps of description publication are the following:

1. *Uploading semantic objects to the repository* The INFRAWEBS designer and INFRAWEBS composer upload created WSMO descriptions to the distributed repository.

It is assumed that only valid WSML definitions are stored. As it has already been mentioned, the INFRAWEBS designer ensures that only syntactically correct descriptions of WSMO services and goals are created, and that all created descriptions are semantically consistent with the WSML ontologies used. That is why only the semantic completeness of created objects is verified with respect to the WSMO specification for the corresponding object. A WSMO service or a goal is considered as a complex object consisting of: the WSML description, all definitions of WSML ontologies mentioned in the object description, and the set of all graphical models corresponding to the logical expressions used for defining the object. All these elements are uploaded to the repository together with the WSML description of the object.

2. *Advertisement publication* An advertisement of a WSMO description is created and published in the registry with the help of a GUI component. When an advertised description has to be retrieved, service access middleware sends an asynchronous request to the distributed repository, and it is the registry's responsibility to locate the remote repository where the advertised description is stored and retrieve the description.

3. *Advertisement propagation* Description propagation is enabled by a subscription-notification mechanism that is supported by the registries. Each registry can subscribe to a partner registry and receive notifications for new, updated, or removed advertisements. When a new advertisement is published, the registry checks the propagation policy and determines which of the subscribed registries to notify. Having the policies on the advertisement level (instead of on the subscription level, as in UDDI) provides greater flexibility in business relations. In this way two businesses can partner in providing certain services while keeping their competitive advantages in others. After being notified, all registries in the INFRAWEBS framework will be updated and will present a consolidated set of advertisements of all their partner registries.

12.4 INFRAWEBS Implementation and Evaluation

The INFRAWEBS framework is implemented as an extensible enterprise service bus (ESB) middleware that exposes the public methods of the INFRAWEBS components and can be extended by any future components or services. Such an integrated INFRAWEBS framework (IIF) can be seen as the underlying infrastructure for communication and integration of all the components and, at the same time, as the unique selling point for exposing the functionality of such components to the external world in the form of services.

The integrated INFRAWEBS framework is delivered as a peer-to-peer network, with possible integration of components with different technologies within the peer. The IIF allows access to the methods of the components via a Java API or a Web Services wrapper, so any application able to use these technologies will be compatible with INFRAWEBS. It gives full native support for Java-based components and partial support for non-Java-based components using Web Service technology. In fact, there are components with different technologies within the stack of INFRAWEBS tools that have been integrated following this approach.

Most of the INFRAWEBS framework components are distributed as open-source code and can be downloaded from the INFRAWEBS Web site: HYPERLINK: http://www.infrawebs.eu.

The integrated INFRAWEBS framework has been evaluated in two test beds: the first is based on a travel agency scenario (López et al. 2005), and the second one is based on an e-government scenario (Riceputi 2006). The two test beds used both the design and runtime parts of the INFRAWEBS framework. In the design-time semantic information router, INFRAWEBS designer, INFRAWEBS composer, and organizational memory were initially used for annotating Web Services (represented as WSDL files) and defining goal templates and Semantic Web Service descriptions, which then were stored and published in the distributed repository component. In runtime the service access middleware component and organizational memory were used for creating concrete user goals, as well as for runtime composition and discovery of the corresponding Web Services able to satisfy these goals. Finally, the INFRAWEBS Semantic Web Service executor component was used for invocation of the discovered Web Services.

12.4.1 INFRAWEBS Test Beds

Two semantic Web Service applications have been developed using the INFRAWEBS framework: the STREAM Flows! system and an e-government application.

STREAM Flows! System The STREAM Flows! system (SFS) is the first prototype application of the INFRAWEBS framework which aims at overcoming such shortcomings of existing frequent flyer programs as impossibility of their users to contract services or a combination of services using a synchronous, real-time, anywhere, and anytime system. The customers of the STREAM Flows! system can obtain points by purchasing services. These services might be an airline ticket, a hotel booking, a car rental, or one of many others. Each service of the program has its counterpart in points, and these points can be consolidated and exchanged by one or more services.

The main functionality of the STREAM Flows! system allows the user to create new travel packages. First, the user chooses a package template to create a simple package, or combines templates to create a complex package. Alternatively, a predefined, complex package can be selected and automatically mapped to a composite goal template that will allow dynamic runtime composition of services (e.g., flight + hotel + car rental).

A typical scenario of using the STREAM Flows! system follows:

A package template is selected, for example, flight plus car rental plus hotel.

The user fills in the corresponding form, prompted by the application, to specify the parameters of travel. The STREAM Flows! system converts the form into a concrete composite WSMO goal and uses the service access middleware to discover the most suitable services able to satisfy this goal.

The service access middleware decomposes the goal into a set of composite or atomic subgoals (in the example, booking a flight, renting a car, and booking a hotel room) and finds a set of the best matching services for each subgoal. The resulting list of services is presented to the user, who can select the preferred service to be executed for each subgoal.

Selected services are sent for execution. Once the execution is done, the user is informed and can fulfill the contract form.

If some of the selected services cannot be executed because of some physical reasons (e.g., time-out errors, security errors, etc.), the STREAM Flows! system automatically presents to the user a list of services that are able to substitute for the service that has failed. The user can again select a service, and the execution of the new service composition continues.

The test bed has shown several benefits of using Web Service applications based on semantic descriptions of services:

1. *Runtime composition of services* The use of composite goal templates allows creation of dynamic composition of services in runtime.
2. *Selection of best offers based on Semantic Web Service discovery* The use of semantics allows finding the matches most appropriate to user requests.
3. *Comparatively easy addition of new services* In order to be potentially used by the application, a new service should be described only as a Semantic Web Service and published in a distributed repository.
4. *Ideally, no modifications to the code are required* The forms for specifying the travel parameters can be created dynamically, based on goal template slots (inputs), thus minimizing the impact on the maintenance of the application.
5. *Ease of use and integration* As a J2EE application, the STREAM Flows! system easily uses and integrates with all components of the integrated INFRAWEBS framework.

Opening a New Business The second test bed implements an e-government scenario related to the process of opening a new commercial activity (e.g., opening a new shop of an existing chain). Usually, the procedure for opening a new shop depends on local laws and regulations that can be changed as new government requirements are released. That is why the user should be familiar with the actualized list of documents and certificates required to open the new business activity. The user also has to ask for each document from the office or agency authorized to issue such a certificate. This process is time-consuming, as users need to travel to each agency to post the request, and sometimes to go back to get the certificate. The user must also know the proper sequence of actions if some relations or dependencies exist between services that issue certificates. This procedure may become even more complicated since each region inside a country has the freedom to require fewer or more documents and certificates for the same activity.

The implemented Semantic Web Service application allows the user to take advantage of semantic technology to accomplish all required activities from his/her personal computer, which allows a huge saving of time, error-free processes, and much faster responses.

The typical scenario of using the application is as follows:

1. The user has to define the shop profile and requirements.
2. The e-government application provides the user with a list of certificates that have to be obtained to satisfy the specified requirements, and the user uses his/her input to locate the services (agencies) able to issue such certificates.
3. The list of available agencies (services) that best match the user request is returned.
4. After the selection of the services, the execution starts. Typically this is a process that takes time and runs in the back end, so the service will send an e-mail to the user when the service is finished and has the expected result (the certificate).

This test bed offers interesting aspects that complement the results of the STREAM Flows! system test bed:

1. The e-government application is well ahead with current services offered to customers.
2. The e-government is a .NET (C#) application that uses the SOA implementation of the INFRAWEBS framework, which has proved the possibility of integration of different technologies using such an implementation.
3. The application can be used by government agencies to show the main advantages of semantic content being provided to their citizens, as well as how their internal costs will decrease owing to reduction of the required personnel.

12.4.2 Lessons Learned

The INFRAWEBS framework has been evaluated in two dimensions (Pariente et al. 2007):

1. *Environment dimension* Measuring the degree of satisfaction and fulfillment of the framework objectives regarding the two test bed results, based on the opinions of different framework users—designers, developers of test bed applications, and end users of the applications.
2. *System dimension* The system evaluation takes into account the overall service provision chain (annotation, design, composition, execution, quality of service of Semantic Web Services), focusing on the primary (innovation-related) questions that have been identified.

INFRAWEBS Advantages The evaluation has shown that INFRAWEBS offers a framework covering the whole life cycle of Semantic Web Services—from design and static composition to the discovery, runtime composition, execution, and monitoring of services. It gives the possibility for creating a new set of semantically enabled applications.

Moreover, INFRAWEBS is fully based on the current state of WSMO and provides advanced tools for the whole WSMO community. The INFRAWEBS design-time components offer graphical user interfaces for designing and publishing the semantic descriptions of WSMO-based Web Services and goals in a user-friendly way. They help the user to create semantic objects without any knowledge of the WSML language used for their descriptions.

All INFRAWEBS components make use of the integrated INFRAWEBS framework (IIF) to communicate with each other. Moreover, the IIF enables the integration of components of different technologies, and by using Web Service interfaces, it can be used as an open framework. The single API provided by the service access middleware component allows application providers to interact with the runtime environment without writing or reading any WSML expressions, which significantly facilitates the process of creating semantically enabled applications.

INFRAWEBS's Underlying Assumptions and Shortcomings Along with the benefits of INFRAWEBS, the evaluation process has identified the underlying assumptions and shortcomings that should be known for better understanding the applicability of the INFRAWEBS framework:

1. All INFRAWEBS components are developed in conformance with the current specification of WSMO. Since WSMO itself is in the process of active development, adjustments to the INFRAWEBS framework may be necessary in the future.
2. The current version of the INFRAWEBS framework does not support ontology mediation. All ontologies used are assumed to be known by all service and service application providers, and are shared using the distributed repository functionality.
3. User requests used for discovery are expressed as WSMO goals and are automatically transformed by the application, based on predefined goal templates and the mechanism for providing user input as values of slot variables. This assumption restricts the set of possible goals that can be formulated by the user, but allows users with no knowledge of WSML to use INFRAWEBS applications.
4. Runtime composition is possible only for goals created from templates using the INFRAWEBS goal editor.
5. Execution of WSMO services requires the presence of so-called adapters, which ground ontological concepts used in the semantic descriptions to the XML schema data types used in the WSDL descriptions of Web Services. Automatic creation of such adapters is an ongoing research topic, and that is why the current version of the INFRAWEBS framework does not provide tools for designing of such adapters.
6. Because of lack of clear specification of WSMO-based service orchestration, static composition in INFRAWEBS offers a limited support for orchestration—only on the functional level.
7. The INFRAWEBS choreography engine does not clearly guide the user during the execution process. A better engine would be a desirable future enhancement.

12.5 Related Work

The main results of the INFRAWEBS project can be evaluated from different points of view. Although the INFRAWEBS is fully based on the WSMO framework for modeling key elements of the Semantic Web technology, the definitions of main actors of this technology, as well as the SWS life cycle adopted by the INFRAWEBS, share many concepts with the SeCSE conceptual model of service-oriented systems (Colombo et al. 2005). Being restricted on semantic aspects of service-oriented computing technology, INFRAWEBS's conceptual framework has allowed clear identification of a set of necessary tools and components for analyzing, designing, and maintaining WSMO-based Semantic Web Services and SWS applications within the whole life cycle.

The necessity of intensive development of tools supporting Semantic Web Service technology, especially ones based on the WSMO framework, has been clearly recognized in the WSMO community. The ontology editing and browsing tool[7] is a plug-in for the Eclipse framework currently under development by the Ontology Management Working Group (OMWG).[8] The tool can be used to edit ontologies described within WSML documents.

A group of researchers from DERI is developing the Web Services modeling tool kit (WSMT),[9] a framework for the rapid creation and deployment of homogeneous tools for Semantic Web Services. In addition to several plug-ins for creating, visualizing, and mediating ontologies, the initial set of tools for the WSMT includes a WSML editor (Kerrigan 2007) aiming at providing a useful tool for describing and publishing WSMO-based Semantic Web Services. The main approach for realization of these goals is by using structural text editors, which of course simplify the process for creating WSML description of a service, but still require strong knowledge of WSML.

The analysis of existing tools for creating WSMO objects has shown that they are oriented mainly to researchers and developers working in the area of Semantic Web Services technology, rather than to the real users of such a technology: Semantic Web Service providers, brokers, and application providers. The end-user orientation of the INFRAWEBS designer is the basic feature making the product different from all similar research products developed in the area of Semantic Web Services.

A main shortcoming of the INFRAWEBS designer is the insufficient support that the designer provides to an "industrial" Web Service provider for filling the conceptual gap between the descriptions of "normal" and semantic (WSMO-based) Web Services. As future work in this direction we foresee more intensive use of WSDL description of the service (for example, for automatic generation of initial, rough WSML description of the semantic service state signature and choreography rules.

Another interesting result produced by the INFRAWEBS project is an innovative mechanism for Semantic Web Service discovery implemented in the service access middleware component of the INFRAWEBS framework. The work and approaches to service discovery are numerous and varied (see Kovács et al. 2007 for a comprehensive overview of such approaches).

The WSMO deliverable on discovery (Keller et al. 2004) suggests the keyword-based approach to be used in conjunction with the keywords given by capability editors and listed as nonfunctional properties (metadata about Web Services). However, the correctness and quality of such natural language descriptions are hard to ensure and control. The INFRAWEBS approach is different from the WSMO idea, because here the axioms are indexed instead of the nonfunctional properties. Since the proper formulation of the axioms is needed for the correct use of Semantic Web Services, the quality of the index data is implicitly ensured.

The INFRAWEBS matching algorithm combines a traditional information retrieval-based prefiltering step and a logic-based matching implemented in Prolog (Kovács et al. 2007). The logic-based step of discovery uses a novel technique based on Prolog-style unification of terms. This approach is able to find intersection and other types of service matches, and also provides possibilities to compare rank and explain service matches (or nonmatches). A solution is also provided to handle user preferences during discovery, which is becoming a more and more important aspect of Semantic Web Service usability.

12.6 Conclusion

In this chapter we have presented the main results of the IST FP6 INFRAWEBS project. The project has developed an easy and effective way of constructing and using semantic descriptions for existing and new Web Services.

The project adopts the WSMO (Web Service Modeling Ontology) and WSML (Web Service Modeling Language) standards and imposes no additional requirements on them. Therefore, the advanced software components developed during the project are of interest to the whole WSMO community.

One of the novel aspects in the approach of INFRAWEBS is the combination of the organizational memory and the Semantic Web Service designer. This tool allows a user to create a WSMO-based semantic description based on existing WSDL description of this service and a set of WSML ontologies. To ease this process, the organizational memory can be consulted to find similar descriptions that can serve as templates for the WSMO object under construction. In fact, the use of the organizational memory as a knowledge base holding knowledge about available Semantic Web Services makes the otherwise arduous process of constructing a WSMO-based Semantic Web Service application, requiring expert knowledge of the WSMO model and the Web Service Modeling Language, a task achievable by ordinary Web Service developers. Facilitating the task of WSMO object construction is an achievement of the project that has a potential impact on the adoption of Semantic Web Services on a larger scale.

In conclusion, we can say that INFRAWEBS is one of the first frameworks for semantic service engineering that covers the whole Semantic Web Service life cycle and allows creation of complex, semantically enabled applications.

Acknowledgment

The work published in this chapter is partly funded by the European Community under the Sixth Framework Programme, contract FP6–511723 INFRAWEBS. The work reflects only the authors' views. The Community is not liable for any use that may be made of the information contained therein.

Notes

1. http://www.infrawebs.eu.
2. http://www.wsmo.org.
3. http://www.nessieurope.com.
4. http://dublincore.org/.
5. This operator corresponds to Implies and ImpliedBy operators in WSML.
6. This operator can be used only for creating the update rules and corresponds to the WSML "=>" operator.
7. http://www.omwg.org/tools/dip/factsheets/OntologyEditorFactSheet.html.
8. http://www.omwg.org/.
9. http://sourceforge.net/projects/wsmt.

References

Agre, G. 2006. Using case-based reasoning for creating Semantic Web Services: An INFRAWEBS approach. In *Proceedings of EUROMEDIA 2006*, pp. 130–137.

Agre, G., and I. Dilov. 2007. How to create a WSMO-based semantic service without knowing WSML. In M. Weske, M.-S. Hacid, and C. Godart, eds., *WISE 2007 Workshops*. Berlin: Springer. LNCS 4832, pp. 217–235.

Agre, G., and Z. Marinova. 2007. An INFRAWEBS approach to dynamic composition of Semantic Web Services. *CIT: Cybernetics and Information Technologies* (Bulgarian Academy of Sciences) 7, no. 1: 45–61.

Agre, G., Z. Marinova, T. Pariente, and A. Micsik. 2007. Towards Semantic Web Service engineering. In *Proceedings of the First International Joint Workshop SMR2 2007 on Service Matchmaking and Resource Retrieval in the Semantic Web*, pp. 91–105.

Andonova, G., G. Agre, H.-J. Nern, and A. Boyanov. 2006. Fuzzy concept set based organizational memory as a quasi non-semantic component within the INFRAWEBS framework. In Bernadette Bouchon-Meunier, ed., *Proceedings of IPMU2006*, pp. 2268–2275.

Atanasova, T., H. Daskalova, V. Grigorova, and D. Gulev. 2006. Design & Realisation of Case-based Composition of SW Services in Design Time (Design-Time Composer). INFRAWEBS Deliverable D5.4.2.

Bruijn, J., H. Lausen, R. Krummenacher, A. Polleres, L. Predoiu, M. Kifer, and D. Fensel. 2005. D16.1—The Web Services Modeling Language (WSML). WSML final draft.

Colombo, M., E. Di Nitto, M. Di Penta, D. Distante, and M. Zuccal. 2005. Speaking a common language: A conceptual model for describing service-oriented systems. In *Service Oriented Computing ICSOC 2005: Third International Conference. Proceedings*, pp. 48–60.

Keller, U., R. Lara, and A. Polleres. 2004. D5.1v0.1. WSMO Web Service Discovery. WSML working draft.

Kerrigan, M. 2007. Developers Tool Working Group Status. Version 1, Revision 4. http://wiki.wsmx.org/index.php?title=Developer_Tools. (Accessed November 27, 2007.)

Kovács, L., A. Micsik, and P. Pallinger. 2007. Handling user preferences and added value in discovery of Semantic Web Services. In *Proceedings of the IEEE International Conference on Web Services* (ICWS 2007), pp. 225–232.

López, O., A. López Pérez, C. Pezuela, Y. Gorroñogoitia, and E. Riceputi. 2005. Requirement-Profiles & Technical Risk Management & Demonstration & Testbeds & Specification Checker. INFRAWEBS Deliverable D10.1–2–3–4.1.

Marinova, Z., G. Agre, and D. Ognyanov. 2007. Final Dynamic DSWS-R and Integration in the IIF. INFRAWEBS Deliverable D4.4.3.

Nern, H.-J., A. Boyanov, G. Andonova, T. Zaynelov, and G. Jesdinsky. 2007.

Organizational Memory and Recommender Tool. INFRAWEBS Deliverable D2.4.3.

Papazoglou, M., and D. Georgakopoulos. 2003. Service-oriented computing: Introduction. *Communications of the ACM* 46, no. 10: 24–28.

Pariente Lobo, T., A. López Pérez, and J. Arnaiz Paradinaz. 2007. Demonstrator. INFRAWEBS Deliverable D10.8.3.

Riceputi, E. 2006. Requirement Profile 2 & Knowledge Objects. INFRAWEBS Deliverable D10.5–6–7.2.

Roman, D., U. Keller, and H. Lausen, eds. 2006. Web Service Modeling Ontology. WSMO final draft.

Saarela, J. 2006. Specification & General SIR, Full Model & Coupling to SWS Design Activity. INFRAWEBS Deliverable D3.2–3–4.2.

Scicluna, J., J. Bruijn, D. Roman, J. Kopecky, T. Haselwanter, V. Momtchev, and Z. Marinova. 2006. Realization of SWS-E, Error Handling and QoS Monitor. INFRAWEBS Deliverable D7.3.2.

Scicluna, J., Z. Marinova, and G. Agre. 2007. D7.4.3 Final SWS-E and Running P2P-Agent. INFRAWEBS Deliverable D7.4.3.

Tzafestas, E. 2006. Security as immunity in virtual organizations. In *Proceedings of "Security in Autonomous Systems," Workshop at the International Conference ETRICS 2006.*

13 Enabling Data, Information, and Process Integration with Semantic Web Services: From a New Technology Infrastructure to a Compelling Demonstrator

Alessio Gugliotta, John Domingue, Vlad Tanasescu, Leticia Gutiérrez Villarías, Rob Davies, Mary Rowlatt, Marc Richardson, and Sandra Stinčić

13.1 Introduction

Web Services have attracted considerable attention from industry and academia in recent years, and current predictions indicate that the overall market for Web Service-based applications will be worth billions of dollars in the next few years (Zdnet 2005; MoreRFID 2005).

A key problem with Web Services, however, is that they are based on purely syntactic technologies. They thus rely on human developers to understand the intended meaning of the descriptions and to carry out the activities related to Web Service use—for example, finding, composing, and resolving mismatches between Web Service components.

The Semantic Web (Berners-Lee et al. 2001) is an extension of the current Web in which documents incorporate machine-processable meaning. The overall Semantic Web vision is that one day it will be possible to delegate nontrivial tasks, such as booking a holiday, to computer-based agents able to locate and reason with relevant heterogeneous online resources. One of the key building blocks for the Semantic Web is the notion of ontology. An ontology captures the main concepts and relations that a community shares over a particular domain. Within the context of the Semantic Web, ontologies facilitate interoperability as the underlying meaning of terms, for example within a Web document, can be made explicit for computer-based agents to support processing.

The objective of the project DIP—data, information, and process integration with Semantic Web Services (DIP 2004)—is to develop and extend Semantic Web and Web Service technologies in order to produce a new technology infrastructure for Semantic Web Services (SWS)—an environment in which applications can be automatically created from Web Services. The DIP case studies set out to demonstrate the enormous potential values and benefits of SWS in specific e-government, e-work, and e-commerce contexts.

In the present chapter, we consider some of the results of DIP and describe how they have been used to deploy a compelling real-world application in the e-government domain. According to the SeCSE conceptual model, our work lies at the level of identifying the various stakeholders that exploit, offer, and manage services. In fact, a close collaboration with the Essex County Council (ECC)—a large local authority in southeast England containing a population of 1.3 million—has been established to deploy a decision support system assisting the emergency officer in handling the dynamics of an emergency situation, and gathering information related to a certain type of event, faster and with increased precision. The resulting prototype provides a proof of concept of the benefits of using SWS technology in service-oriented architectures.

In terms of the NESSI framework described in chapter 1, the contribution of DIP is clearly focused in the semantic layer. The rest of the chapter is structured as follows. Section 13.2 introduces the SWS technology and highlights the expected added values by comparing other existing technologies; section 13.3 outlines the specific approach and associated framework for deploying SWS-based applications; section 13.4 details and demonstrates such an approach by showing how integration and interoperability emerge from such a model through a cooperative and multiple-viewpoint methodology; as a result of the experience of deploying a real-world application in the e-government domain, we report some lessons learned in section 13.5; and section 13.6 reports our conclusions.

13.2 Semantic Web Services

Semantic Web Services research aims to automate the development of Web Services based applications through the Semantic Web technology. By providing formal descriptions with well-defined semantics, it facilitates the machine interpretation of Web Services descriptions. The research agenda for SWS identifies a number of key areas of concern:

1. *Discovery* Finding Web Services which can fulfill a task. Discovery usually involves matching a formal task description against semantic descriptions of Web Services.
2. *Mediation* We can not assume that the software components which we find are compatible. Mediation aims to overcome all incompatibilities involved—for instance, at the level of data format, message protocol, and underlying business processes—by making use of semantic descriptions.
3. *Composition* Often no single service will be available to satisfy a request. In this case we need to be able to create a new service by composing existing components. AI planning engines are typically used to compose Web Service descriptions from high goals.

Several approaches have been introduced, although all of them are still undergoing research. A few examples include Web Service Modeling Ontology (WSMO 2005); OWL-S (OWL-S 2006), previously DAML-S; Semantic Web Services Framework (SWSF 2005); and WSDL-S (WSDL-S 2005), previously METEOR-S. The common underlying idea among these approaches is the use of ontologies to semantically represent the functional—and nonfunctional—properties of a Web Service. The differences mainly come from the described conceptual model of a Web Service (i.e., the kinds of features represented) and its level of abstraction.

13.2.1 WSMO

DIP adopted WSMO as the underlying epistemological framework. WSMO is a formal ontology for describing the various aspects of services in order to enable the automation of Web Service discovery, composition, mediation, and invocation. The metamodel of WSMO defines four top-level elements:

1. *Ontology* Provides the foundation for describing domains semantically. Ontologies are used by the three other WSMO components.
2. *Goal-related information* A goal description represents the user perspective of the required functional capabilities. It includes a description of the requested Web Service capability.
3. *Web Service-related information* A Web Service interface represents the functional behavior of an existing deployed Web Service. It includes a description of (a) functional capabilities, which represent the provider perspective of what the service does in terms of assumptions, effects, preconditions, and postconditions; (b) choreography, which specifies how to communicate with a Web Service; (c) grounding, which is associated with the Web Service choreography and describes how the semantic declarations are associated with a syntactic specification such as WSDL; (d) orchestration, which specifies the decomposition of Web Service capability in terms of the functionality of other Web Services.
4. *Mediators* In WSMO, a mediator specifies which WSMO top elements are connected and which types of mismatches between them can be resolved. WSMO defined four kinds of mediators: GG-mediator, which links different goals; WG-mediator, which connects Web Services with goals; OO-mediator, which enables components to import heterogeneous ontologies; and WW-mediator, which links Web Services to Web Services.

13.2.2 Added Values

The use of SWS introduces the following added values compared to other existing technologies for SOC:

1. *SWS vs. Web Services* Using Web Services, data and functionalities can be shared with anyone through the Internet. The syntactic definitions used in these specifications allow fast composition and good results in terms of application performance. However, they do not completely describe the capability of a service and cannot be understood by software programs. A human developer is required to interpret the meaning of inputs, outputs, and applicable constraints, as well as the context in which services can be used. Moreover, Web Services lack flexibility; for instance, if a new Web Service is deployed, the application developers need to remodel several syntax descriptions—introducing a cost—in order to integrate it in a specific context.

On the other hand, the SWS approach is able to model the background knowledge of a context together with the requested and provided capabilities, and hence to address automatic reasoning and reuse. In this way, service invocation, discovery, composition, and mediation are automated by adopting the best available solutions for a specific request, thus increasing the flexibility, scalability, and maintainability of an application. In particular, the clean ontological separation introduced by the four top elements of WSMO clearly introduces the idea of context. Goal and Web Service represent the user and resource provider viewpoints, respectively. Domain ontologies define the terminologies used for each view.

2. *SWS vs. other ontology-based approaches* Creating and managing ontologies is a bottleneck: understanding a domain, acquiring and representing knowledge, populating with instances, and evolving ontologies are big tasks for the application developers. In a complex domain such as e-government, centralized ontologies would require an unrealistic development effort with no guarantee of satisfactory results in terms of capturing domain knowledge. Moreover, government agencies deal with huge data sets (e.g., demographic, GIS, etc.) that cannot be easily transposed to ontology's instances. However, in the context of semantic-based applications, such a cost cannot be deleted, though it may be contained. SWS technology makes knowledge capture and maintenance simpler and more efficient. The only knowledge that needs to be modeled is related to the exposed functionalities of the Web Service. This means describing the concepts used by the Web Service only, such as inputs and output. Moreover, in WSMO-based approaches the knowledge-capturing process may be distributed among all of the stakeholders: each partner describes—and is responsible for—its particular domain. In this way, the several viewpoints—requesters described by WSMO goals and providers described by WSMO Web Services—can be independently and concurrently represented by the proper knowledge holders. Partners can also reuse their own existing ontologies.

Finally, a WSMO-based approach can support dealing with interoperability among very heterogeneous knowledge sources and mediation among the several viewpoints (users, multiple providers, etc.). WSMO mediators are mappings that solve existing mismatches and do not affect service descriptions.

13.3 Deploying SWS-based Applications: The IRS-III Approach

One of the results of DIP has been the definition of a domain-independent framework for deploying SWS-based applications, which integrate and interoperate multiple existing legacy systems—that is, data, information, and process sources. In the following, we introduce the three main elements of such a framework: IRS-III (Cabral et al. 2006), the core SWS environment; the generic application architecture; and the development methodology.

13.3.1 IRS-III

IRS-III—the Internet Reasoning Service—is a broker-based platform that provides a powerful execution environment for SWS. By definition, a broker is an entity which mediates between two parties, and IRS-III mediates between a service requester and one or more service providers. To achieve this, IRS-III adopts a Semantic Web-based approach and is thus founded on ontological descriptions. In particular, IRS-III incorporates and extends WSMO as the core epistemological framework.

Additionally, IRS-III supports the SWS developer at design time by providing a set of tools for defining, editing, and managing a library of semantic descriptions and also for grounding the descriptions to (1) standard Web Service with a WSDL description; (2) Web applications available through an HTTP GET request; (3) code written in a standard programming language (currently Java and Common Lisp).

One of the main aims for Web Services is to enable the interoperability of programs over the Internet. A reasonable extension of this is that as far as possible, SWS frameworks and platforms should also be interoperable. For this reason IRS-III has an OWL-S import mechanism and is interoperable with the WSMO reference implementations: for development WSMO Studio, http://www.wsmostudio.org, and for execution WSMX, http://www.wsmx.org.

The IRS-III Service Ontology The IRS-III service ontology forms the epistemological basis for IRS-III and provides semantic links between the knowledge-level components describing the capabilities of a service and the restrictions applied to its use. The WSMO conceptual model has been represented using OCML representation language (Motta 1998) and extended in the following ways:

1. *Explicit input and output role declarations* IRS-III requires that goals and Web Services have input and output roles, which include a name and a semantic type. The declared types are imported from domain ontologies. This makes the definition of goal and Web Services easier when complex choreographies are not required.
2. *Web Services are linked to goals via WG-mediators* If a WG-mediator associated with a Web Service has a goal as a source, then this Web Service is considered to solve that goal. An assumption expression can be introduced for further refining the applicability of the Web Service.
3. *GG-mediators provide data flow between subgoals* In IRS-III, GG-mediators are used to link subgoals within an orchestration, and thus they also provide data flow between the subgoals.
4. *Web Services can inherit from goals* Web Services which are linked to goals "inherit" the goals' input and output roles. This means that input role declarations within a Web Service are not mandatory, and can be used either to add extra input roles or to change an input role type.
5. *Client choreography* The provider of a Web Service must describe the choreography from the viewpoint of the client. This means IRS-III can interpret the choreography in order to communicate with the deployed Web Service.

6. *Mediation services are goals* A mediator declares a goal as the mediation service which can simply be invoked. The required transformation is performed by the associated Web Service.
7. *IRS-III component goals* The main components of IRS-III (e.g., the orchestration and choreography interpreters, and the handlers for the different WSMO mediators) are implemented using internal goal, Web Service, and mediator descriptions. Additionally, a number of utility goals, such as a number of arithmetic and list primitives, are incorporated.

Figure 13.1 depicts the main concepts and relations of the IRS-III service ontology. Note the link between goal (defining input and output roles) and Web Service (defining capability and interface) classes via the WG-mediator; dashed arrows represent relations inferred during Web Service discovery and selection phases. Further details about such semantic descriptions and their use are reported in the following section.

Finally, it is worthwhile to note that whenever we mention SWS descriptions, we refer to all the semantic descriptions introduced above, including not only Web Service descriptions but also their contexts of use, such as goals and mediators.

The IRS-III Core Functionalities A core design principle for IRS-III is to support capability-based selection and invocation of Web Services. When a client sends a request which captures a desired goal and, using the set of Semantic Web Service descriptions introduced in the previous section, IRS-III will take the following four actions.

First, it will discover potentially relevant Web Services. Given a goal, multiple WG-mediators can define such a goal as their source component. In turn, distinct capability descriptions can refer to a specific WG-mediator, and thus link to a goal. Finally, each capability description is part of a unique Web Service description. On the basis of the semantic descriptions above, a chain of backward reasoning can thus be defined to identify a pool of Web Services which can potentially satisfy a goal. In particular, a can-solve-goal relation (see figure 13.1) is inferred at runtime during the achieve-goal process. Table 13.1 shows the OCML definition of such a relation.

The sufficient conditions of the definition (:sufficient) specify the clauses to be proved when inferring such a relation. The IRS-III interpreter will fire the clauses in the order in which these are listed by finding any instance which makes the specific clause true. As a result, starting from a goal instance given in input (?goal), it is possible to identify (1) all of the WG-mediators (?mediator) which use such a goal as a source component; (2) the capabilities (?capabilities) which use the identified WG-mediators; and (3) the Web Services (?thing) which define the identified capabilities.

Second, it will select the set of Web services which best fit the incoming request. The selection process aims to identify the most appropriate Web Services to satisfy a goal, starting from the results of the previous phase (can-solve-goal relation). On the basis of the current goal inputs, the IRS-III interpreter will test the applicability conditions of

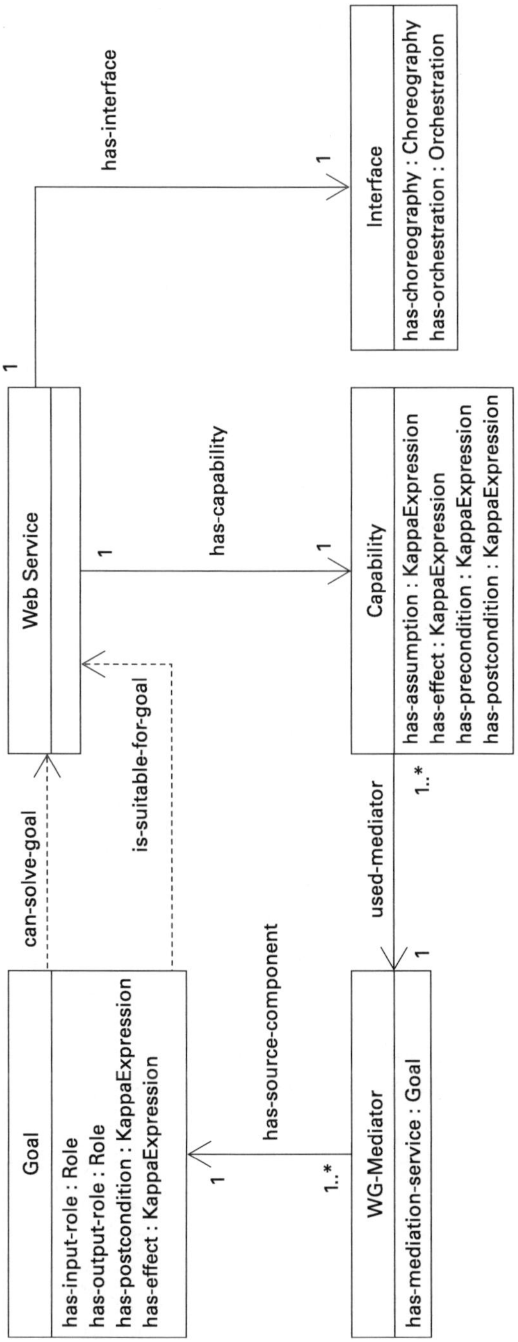

Figure 13.1
Main concepts and relations of the IRS-III service ontology

Table 13.1
OCML definition of can-solve-goal relation

```
(def-relation can-solve-goal (?goal ?thing)
  "Returns the web services which solve a goal.
   Uses the mediator to find the link"
  :sufficient (and (instance-of ?goal goal)
                   (= ?goal (the-slot-value ?mediator has-source-component))
                   (instance-of ?mediator WG-mediator)
                   (= ?mediator (the-slot-value ?capability used-mediator))
                   (instance-of ?capability capability)
                   (= ?capability (the-slot-value ?thing has-capability))
                   (instance-of ?thing web-service)))))
```

Table 13.2
Internal OCML function

```
(def-relation is-suitable-for-goal (?web-service ?goal)
  :iff-def (or (not (and (= ?capability
                             (the-slot-value ?web-service has-capability))
                          (instance-of ?capability capability)
                          (= ?exp (the-slot-value ?capability has-assumption))
                          (not (= ?exp :nothing))))
               (and (= ?capability
                             (the-slot-value ?web-service has-capability))
                    (instance-of ?capability capability)
                    (= ?exp (the-slot-value ?capability has-assumption))
                    (not (= ?exp :nothing))
                    (holds ?exp ?goal))))
```

each discovered Web Service. The aim is to infer the is-suitable-for-goal relation (see figure 13.1). An internal OCML function is thus invoked to (1) retrieve the applicability conditions—currently the assumptions defined in the capability description—of a given Web service and (2) test the applicability conditions according to the input roles defined in the given goal instance. Checking the OCML relation in table 13.2 is the core of such a function.

Sufficient and necessary conditions of the definition above (:iff-def) specify the clauses to be proved. Similar to the can-solve-goal relation introduced above, the IRS-III interpreter will fire the clauses. The "or" expression of the definition introduces two main cases. The first one manages the situation of Web Services which do not define any assumption. We assume that Web Services which do not define assumptions are applicable to the goal. In this way, for example, we can deal with general-purpose Web Services. The second one manages the situation of Web Services which define assumptions. The ?exp variable captures the stated assumption, which is expressed as a kappa expression. The latter is an OCML anonymous relation that takes as argument the invoked goal (?goal) itself and is satisfied if its clauses—OCML expressions referring to goal input values—hold for the given argument. The "holds" function invokes the IRS-III interpreter to test the retrieved kappa expression. If the kappa expression is satisfied, the Web Service is applicable to the goal.

Note that following this approach, several Web Services can be selected. The current policy selects the first suitable Web Service of the list, since a specific ranking mechanism is not defined. However, future work will concern improving current IRS-III selection with trust-based mechanisms (Galizia 2006), as well as considering capability precondition, postcondition, and effect definitions.

Third, it will invoke the selected Web Services while adhering to any data, control flow, and Web Service invocation constraints. Following the WSMO model, the interface class (see figure 13.1) provides information on how the functionality of the deployed Web Services is achieved, and the main interface components are orchestration and choreography. The semantic descriptions of the interface model are interpreted by IRS-III when the latter receives a request to achieve a goal. According to such descriptions, specific actions are performed. A choreography represents the interaction between IRS-III and the Web Service, and is described in IRS-III by a grounding declaration and a set of guarded transitions. The grounding specifies the conceptual representation of the operations involved in the invocation of a Web Service and their mapping to the implementation level. More specifically, the grounding definitions include operation-name, input-roles-soap-binding, and output-role-soap-binding. Guarded transitions can be seen as transition rules in the form of "If condition then fire event." The exposed conditions are mutually exclusive, so only one rule can fire at a time. Our overall view is that any message sent by IRS-III to a Web Service will depend on its current state, which will include a representation of the messages received during the current conversation. IRS-III uses a forward-chaining-rule engine to fire the transition rules belonging to a choreography, according to the current state. We have defined a set of choreography-specific primitives, implementing the events listed above, which can be used in transition rules. Our primitives provide an easy-to-use interface to control a conversation between the IRS and a Web Service: init-choreography initializes the state of the choreography; send-message calls a specific operation in the Web Service; send-suspend suspends the communication between IRS and the Web Service, without stopping the choreography execution; in received-suspend, the communication is suspended by the Web Service when for some reason it is not able to respond to an invocation; received-message contains the result of a successful send-message for a specific operation; and end-choreography stops the choreography.

During communication with a Web Service, the ontological-level descriptions need to be mapped to the XML-based representations used by the specific Web Service invoked. We provide two mechanisms which map (1) from the ontological level to XML (lower) and (2) from XML to the ontological level (lift). Both lift and lower mechanisms are implemented by OCML functions which can be customized according to the classes within the underlying ontology and the particular Web Services selected. In IRS-III, the orchestration is used to describe the model of a composed Web Service. At the semantic level the orchestration

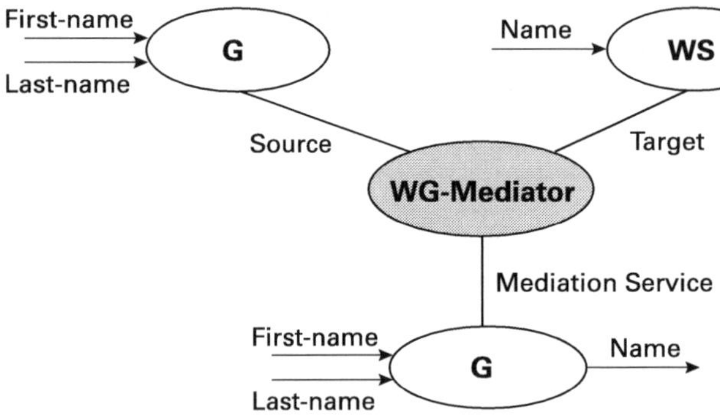

Figure 13.2
Use of mediation services for WG mediators

is represented by a workflow model expressed in OCML. The distinguishing characteristic of this model is that the basic unit within composition is a goal and not a Web Service. Thus, the model provides control and data flow constructs over a set of goals. Further, data flow and the resolution of mismatches between goals are supported by mediators. The set of control flow primitives which have been implemented so far in IRS-III are conditional, loop, fork, and join.

Fourth, it will mediate any mismatches at the data, goal, or process level. The brokering activity of IRS-III can be seen as a semantic mediation itself, which is further broken down into goal, process, and data mediation (Cabral and Domingue 2005). Goal mediation takes places during selection, and the types of mismatches that can occur are (1) the input types of a goal are different from the input types of the target Web Service; and (2) Web Services have more inputs than the goal. A WG-mediator is mainly involved in this mediation. Process mediation takes places during invocation—specifically, during orchestration—and the types of mismatches which can occur are (1) output types of a subgoal are different from the input types of the target subgoal; (2) output values of a subgoal are in a different order from the inputs of the target subgoal; and (3) the output of a subgoal has to be split or concatenated into the inputs of the target subgoals. A GG-mediator is mainly involved in this mediation. Data mediation is used by both goal and process mediation to map data across domain ontologies. An OO-mediator is mainly involved in this mediation. In IRS-III, a mediator declares a source component, a target component, and either a mediation service or mapping rules to solve mismatches between the two. The mediation service is just another goal that can be accomplished by published Web Services. For example in figure 13.2, a mediation service of a WG-mediator transforms input values coming from the source goal into an input value used by the target Web Services. The mediation goal is invoked and then accomplished when the respective mediator is considered by the IRS-III interpreter.

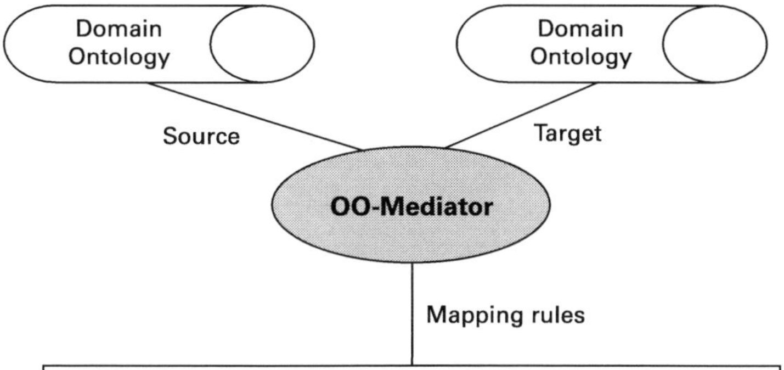


```
(def-concept-mapping citizen client)

(def-relation-mapping citizen-client-name-mapping
      ((has-client-name ?client ?value)
         if
         (maps-to ?client ?citizen)
         (has-citizen-name ?citizen ?value)))
```

Figure 13.3
Use of mapping rules for OO-mediators

Mapping rules are used between two ontologies, source and target components (see figure 13.3). They represent backward-chaining rules, based on three OCML main mapping primitives: maps-to, a relation created internally for every mapped instance; def-concept-mapping, which generates the mappings specified with the maps-to relation between two ontological concepts; and def-relation-mapping, which generates a mapping between two relations using a rule definition within an ontology. Since OCML represents concept attributes as relations, this primitive can be used to map between input and output descriptions.

13.3.2 Generic Application Architecture

Figure 13.4 depicts the generic application architecture of our approach.

From the bottom up, the four application layers are the following:

1. *Legacy system layer* Consists of the existing data sources and IT systems available from each of the parties involved in the integrated application.
2. *Service abstraction layer* Exposes (micro-) functionality of the legacy systems as Web Services, abstracting from the hardware and software platforms. In general, existing Enterprise Application Integration (EAI) software will facilitate the creation of required Web Services. For standard databases, for example, the necessary functionalities of Web Services can simply be implemented as SQL query functions. Note that this level may be populated with additional services which integrate the functionalities provided by the

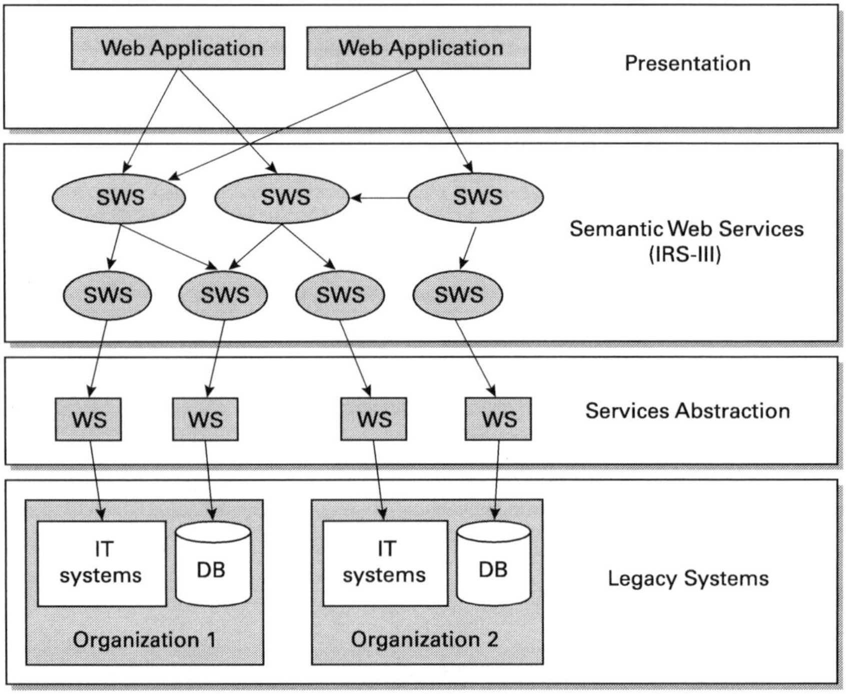

Figure 13.4
The generic application architecture

underlying legacy systems. Since IRS-III allows the description of different kinds of services (see section 13.3.1), the additional services are not necessarily standard Web Services.

3. *Semantic Web Service layer* Given a goal request, this layer, implemented in IRS-III, will (a) discover a candidate set of Web Services, (b) select the most appropriate, (c) mediate any mismatches at the data, ontological, or business process level, and (d) invoke the selected Web Services while adhering to any data, control flow, and Web Service invocation requirements. To achieve this, IRS-III utilizes the set of SWS descriptions supported by relevant domain ontologies. Note that we distinguish two main sets of SWS descriptions: basic SWS (bottom of the layer), which simply describe services available at the service abstraction layer and their context of use (e.g., the goal that can be fulfilled), and complex SWS (top of the layer), which require a composition and mediation of basic or complex SWS to fulfill complex goals.

4. *Presentation layer* A Web application accessible through a standard Web browser. The goals defined within the SWS layer are reflected in the structure of the interface and can be invoked either through the IRS-III API or as an HTTP GET request. The goal requests are filled with data provided by the user and sent to the Semantic Web Service

layer. We should emphasize that the presentation layer may be composed of a set of Web applications to support distinct user communities. In this case, each community would be represented by a set of goals supported by community-related ontologies.

As can be seen, the introduced architecture can be compared with well-known service-oriented architectures. The introduced added value resides at the Semantic Web Service layer, where integration and interoperability of existing heterogeneous services available on the Web are accomplished at runtime.

13.3.3 Development Methodology

In order to successfully create applications from SWS, as depicted in figure 13.4, four key activities need to be carried out:

1. *Requirements capture* The requirements for the overall application are captured using standard software engineering methodologies and tools. We do not advocate any particular requirements capture method but envisage that the resulting documents describe the stakeholders, the main users, roles, goals, any potential providers for Web Services, and any requirements on the deployed infrastructure and interfaces.
2. *Goal description* Using the requirements documents above, relevant goals are identified and semantically described in IRS-III. During this process any required supporting domain ontologies will be created from scratch or existing ontologies will be reused.
3. *Web Service description* Semantic descriptions of relevant Web Services are created within the IRS. Again, any domain ontologies required to support the Web Service semantic descriptions are either defined or reused as necessary.
4. *Mediator description* Mismatches between the ontologies used, and mismatches within and between the formal goal and Web Service descriptions, are identified, and appropriate mediators and mapping rules are created.

All of the above steps are carried out by SWS application developers. However, the first two steps are user/client-centric, and therefore involve discussions with the relevant client stakeholders and domain experts, whereas step 3 will require dialogue with the Web Service providers and domain experts. Steps 2 and 3 are mostly independent, and in the future we expect libraries of goals and Web Services to become generally available to support reuse. Finally, steps 2, 3, and 4 are supported by appropriate IRS-III clients for defining, editing, and managing a library of semantic descriptions.

Figure 13.5 shows the two IRS-III reference clients for the development process. A developer can adopt WSMO Studio for creating all SWS descriptions and then exporting them within IRS-III—an automatic translation from WSML (the WSMO reference language) to OCML is provided—as well as reuse the semantic descriptions available in IRS-III. The WSMO Studio snapshot (top of the figure) depicts the list of WSMO descriptions available in the selected IRS-III repository. The IRS-III browser is the reference tool for developing OCML descriptions of the IRS-III service ontology. Moreover, figure 13.5

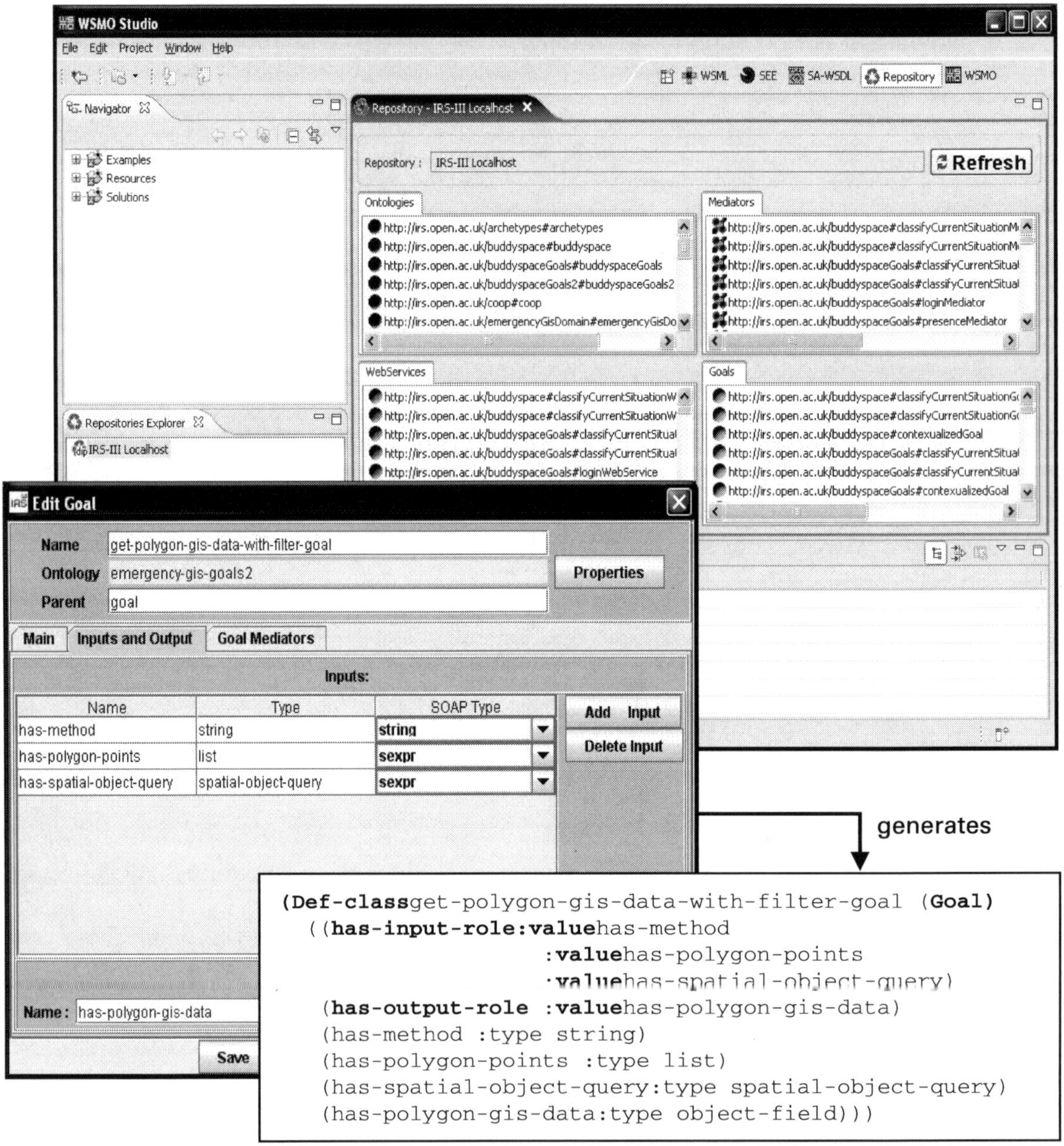

Figure 13.5
IRS-III clients supporting the development process: WSMO Studio and IRS-III browser

(bottom of the figure) shows the windows for creating goal descriptions and the generated OCML code.

As a result, we obtain a semiautomatic and interoperable knowledge acquisition process for the development of our applications.

13.4 A Compelling Demonstrator in the e-Government Domain

The full potential application of SWS technology requires large-scale testing domains. Since it is an enormous challenge to achieve interoperability and to address semantic differences related to the great variety of data sets and information technology solutions which should be networked, e-government is a very effective test bed for evaluating SWS frameworks. Moreover, it exhibits further significant characteristics which may indicate several research issues for SWS. For example, e-government is characterized by top-down prescribed constraints in key areas (e.g., laws, legal requirements, policies in the use of services and access to data); lack of centralized control; strong requirements to come to the same decisions in similar situations; a high requirement for nonfunctional properties such as security, privacy, and trust; and wide information imbalances between stakeholders, as well as multiple and heterogeneous stakeholders involved in the same process.

Therefore, the adoption of SWS in e-government appears to be a natural development. At present, Web Services are being introduced as infrastructure (often experimental) in some areas of government, and the broad awareness of need for semantic enrichment is increasing. However, since SWS are completely new—and are visible mainly to the academic/industrial research "e-government" sector—a measurable benefit to service and achievable cost savings, or "cashable benefits," will need to be established.

In the absence of golden standards, demonstrating real-world applications is an important first step to accomplish this goal.

13.4.1 Emergency Management System

In an emergency response situation there are predefined procedures which set out the duties of all agencies involved. A very wide range of agencies is often involved in the management of an emergency situation, potentially involving a huge data provision and communication requirement between them. Needs and concerns are escalated through a specified chain of command, but the organizations are independent of one another and decisions have to be made rapidly, based on knowledge of the situation—such as the type of problem, the site, and the population affected—and the data available.

However, many emergency-relevant resources are not available on the Web, and interactions among agencies or emergency corps usually occur on a personal/phone/fax basis. The resulting interaction is therefore limited in scope and slower in response time, contrary to the nature of the need for information access in an emergency situation.

Emergency-relevant data are often spatially related. Spatially related data (SRD) are traditionally managed with the help of geographical information systems (GIS), which allow access to different layers of SRD, such as highways, transportation, postal addresses index, and land use. GIS support decision making by facilitating the integration, storage, querying, analysis, modeling, reporting, and mapping of this data. The emergency management system (EMS) envisaged within the DIP use case will provide a decision support system which will assist the emergency planning officer to automatically gather and analyze relevant information in a particular emergency scenario, through the adoption of SWS technology. This should improve the quality of the information available to emergency managers in all the phases of emergency management: before (planning), during (response), and after (evaluation and analysis), thereby facilitating their work and improving the quality of their decisions in critical situations.

13.4.2 Prototype Definition

Several emergency-related scenarios were considered in order to pilot the prototype definition. With the collaboration of the ECC emergency planners, we decided to focus on a real past situation: "Heavy snowstorm around the Stansted area and M11 corridor (Essex, UK) on 31st January 2003," in which thousands of motorists were trapped overnight on some of Britain's busiest motorways (BBC News 2003). By focusing on a past event, we ensure the availability of real data. An additional advantage is the ability to compare the actions taken and the data available at that time, with the data and actions that would have been taken if an SWS-based emergency planning tool had been available.

As depicted in figure 13.6, there are three main actors which participate in this use case with different roles:

1. *Customer* (EPO) The end user that requests the services provided by EMS. The customer selects and invokes services through a user-friendly emergency planning interface. We envisage that this application will be used by the emergency planning officers in public organizations and other emergency partners (police, fire and rescue, ambulance service, National Health Service, Rover Rescue, etc.). As a result we obtain a cross-border application.
2. *Emergency planning and geographical information service providers* Governmental authorities, Ordnance Survey, Meteorological Office, emergency agencies, and commercial companies which provide specific emergency planning services and spatially related services through the Internet in the form of Web Services. They provide services to end users to improve collaboration in an emergency-based scenario.
3. *EMS* The broker between the customer and the providers. This management system holds all the functionalities for handling SWS—supporting automatic discovery, composition, mediation, and execution. It exposes services to end users, using existing emergency services and aggregating them into new, high-level services in order to improve collabora-

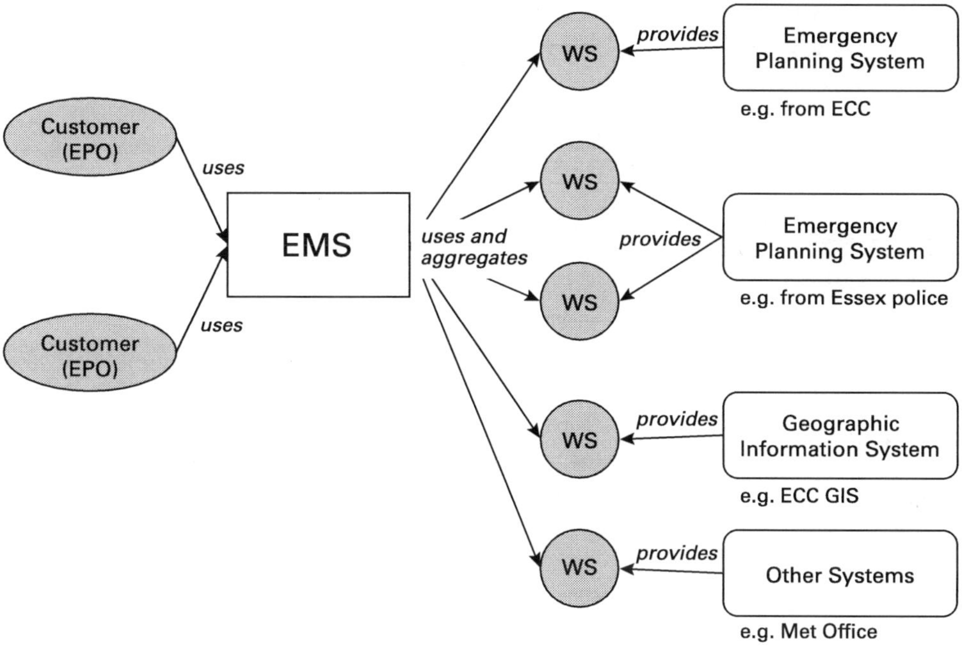

Figure 13.6
Prototype context diagram

tion in an emergency-based scenario. The EMS is considered to have a nonprofit governmental basis and to serve public interests in case of an emergency. It interacts with customers (emergency planners and heads of rescue corps) via a user-friendly interface allowing users to access and combine the different services provided by the service providers.

The current version of the prototype focuses on the planning phase only. Figure 13.7 depicts an example of an integrated process to be accomplished in a hazardous snowstorm situation, before planning an adequate emergency response.

The first goal of the scenario is to identify the affected area and the hazard level by analyzing snow data coming from the Meteorological Office. Then the EPO has—not necessarily in the following order—to locate suitable shelters for affected people by retrieving information from GIS of ECC and identify relevant people (rescue corps) available in the affected area by accessing appropriate communication systems. Each goal is not merely a retrieval operation, but also involves a goal decomposition that selects services and manipulates retrieved data according to situation-specific requirements.

Web Services will provide a first level of interoperability by encapsulating functionality regardless of the specific technologies/protocols of the providers' legacy systems. SWS

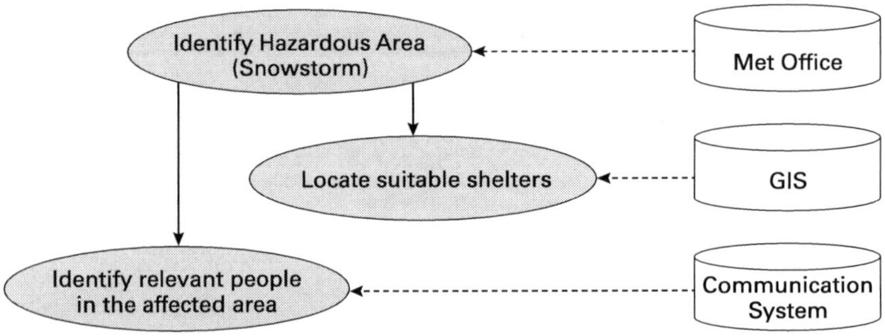

Figure 13.7
Example of emergency procedure in a hazardous snowstorm situation

descriptions will provide the second level of interoperability and integration by allowing automation of all the stages of the Web Service use as well as representing process and goal decompositions. In particular, all goals identified above will be represented by means of WSMO goals; the Web Services encapsulating existing functionalities will be represented by means of WSMO Web Services; further WSMO Web Services will be introduced to describe processes and goal decompositions, as well as additional services (section 13.3.2). Finally, WSMO mediators will map the link between the introduced WSMO descriptions and address mediation through appropriate mediation services (F4, "The IRS-III Core Functionalities").

In the rest of this section, we detail the prototype description by following the structure of the generic architecture and methodology introduced in sections 13.3.2 and 13.3.3.

Legacy System Layer The prototype aggregates data and functionalities from the following three sources:

1. *Meteorological Office* A national U.K. organization which provides environmental resources, particularly weather forecast data. Snowstorm data are stored in a dedicated database.
2. *ViewEssex* A collaboration between ECC and British Telecommunications (BT) which has created a single corporate spatial data warehouse. As can be expected, ViewEssex contains a wide range of data including those for roads, administrative boundaries, buildings, and ordnance survey maps, as well as environmental and social care data. Within the application we used building-related data to support searches for suitable rest centers.
3. *BuddySpace* is an instant messaging, client-facilitating lightweight communication, collaboration, and presence management (Eisenstadt et al. 2003) built on top of the instant messaging protocol Jabber (http://www.jabber.org/). The BuddySpace client can be accessed on standard PCs, as well as on PDAs and on mobile phones, which in an emergency situation may be the only hardware device available.

As many of the integrated real systems have security and access restriction policies, BT has created a single corporate spatial data warehouse where all Meteorological Office and ECC data sources have been replicated in order to work with them in a safe environment, thereby providing suitable Web Services to work with. However, the prototype represents how this system would work in a distributed environment with heterogeneous and scattered data sources over the Internet.

Service Abstraction Layer We distinguish between two classes of service: data and smart. The former refers to the three data sources introduced above, and are exposed by means of standard Web Services:

1. *Meteorological service* This service provides weather information—such as snowfall—over a specific polygonal spatial area.
2. *ECC emergency planning services* Using the ViewEssex data, each service in this set returns detailed information on a specific type of rest center within a given circular area. For example, "getHospitals" is a Web Service that returns a list of relevant hospitals.
3. *BuddySpace services* These services allow presence information on online users to be accessed.

Smart services represent additional services, as defined in section 13.3.2, and implement specific emergency planning, reasoning, and operations on the data provided by the data services. They are implemented in a mixture of Common Lisp and OCML and make use of the developed domain ontologies. In particular, we created a number of filter services that select the GIS data according to emergency-specific requirements—such as rest centers with a heating system, hotels with at least 40 beds, and easily accessible hospital. The criteria used were gained from our discussions with the EPOs. Note that although smart services make use of ontologies and introduce reasoning, they are not SWS. In principle, their functionalities can indeed be implemented in any programming language (e.g., Java). Therefore, smart services, as well as the standard Web Services introduced above, will be semantically described to create SWS.

Semantic Web Services Layer: Domain Ontologies In this and the next section, we focus on the semantic description defined within the Semantic Web Services layer. The following ontologies, reflecting the client and provider domains, were developed to support WSMO descriptions:

1. *Meteorology, emergency planning, and Jabber domain ontology* Representing the concepts used to describe the services attached to the data sources, such as snow and rain for the Meteorological Office, hospitals and supermarkets for ECC emergency planning, and session and presences for Jabber. If a new source and the Web Services exposing its data and functionalities are integrated, new domain ontology has to be introduced—also reusing existing ontologies. The services, composed of the data types involved as well as the

interface, have to be described in such an ontology, usually at a level low enough to remain close to the data.

To get the information provided by Web Services up to the semantic level, we introduce lifting operations that allows the passage of data types from a syntactic level (XML) to an ontological one (OCML) specified in the domain ontology definitions. These Lisp functions automatically extract data from SOAP messages and create the counterpart class instances. The mapping information between data types and ontological classes is defined at design time by developers.

2. *GUI ontology* This ontology is composed of GUI and user-oriented concepts. It maps the ontology elements which will be displayed to the elements of the particular user interface which is used; for example, stating that Google Maps API is used, or definirng "pretty names" for ontology elements. Note that although the choice of the resulting syntactic format depends on the chosen lowering operation (see below), concepts from the GUI ontology are used in order to achieve this transformation in a suitable way.

3. *Archetypes ontology* This is a minimal ontological commitment ontology aiming to provide a cognitively meaningful insight into the nature of a specialized object; for example, by conveying the cognitive ("naïve") feeling that a hospital, as a "container" of people and provider of "shelter," can be assimilated to the more universal concept of "house." The latter can be considered as an archetypal concept (i.e., based on image schemata, and therefore supposed to convey meaning immediately). It is, moreover, assumed that any client, though perhaps lacking the specific representation for a specific basic-level concept, knows its archetypal representation.

4. *Spatial ontology* This ontology describes geographical concepts of location, such as coordinates, points, polygonal areas, and fields. It also allows describing spatial objects as entities with a location and a set of attributes. The purpose of the GUI, archetypes, and spatial ontologies is the aggregation of different data sources on, respectively, a representation, a cognitive, and a spatial level. Therefore, we can group them under the term "aggregation ontologies." They allow the different data sources to be handled and presented in a similar way. Inversely to the lifting operations, lowering operations transform instances of aggregation ontologies into syntactic documents to be used by the server and client applications. This step is usually fully automated since aggregation ontologies are, by definition, quite stable and unique.

5. *Context ontology* The context ontology allows describing context n-tuples which represent a particular situation. In the emergency planning application, context n-tuples have up to four components: the use case, the user role, the location, and the type of object. Contexts are linked with WSMO goals (i.e., if this type of user accesses this type of object around this particular location, these particular goals will be presented). Contexts also help to specialize goal invocation (e.g., if we need information about gasoline stations in an area, the location part of the context is used to define this area, and input from the user is therefore not needed. For example, table 13.3 reports the definition of a localized emer-

Table 13.3
Definition of a localized emergency situation

```
(def-class snow-investigation-area (localized-emergency-type area-location-marker)
((has-requirements :default-value snow-hazard-level)
 (snow-hazard-level :type hazard-level :default-value zero)
 (has-observables :default-value snow-level)
 (snow-level :type float :default-value 0)
 (has-affordances
  :default-value GET-SNOW-DATA-AFFORDANCE
  :default-value GET-POLYGON-SNOW-DATA-AFFORDANCE
  :default-value LOGIN-AFFORDANCE)
 (has-following-situation
         :default-value snow-storm-hazard-situation
         :default-value snow-investigation-area)))

(def-instance GET-SNOW-DATA-AFFORDANCE spatial-affordance
  ((has-goal GET-SNOW-DATA-GOAL)
   (has-max-range-km 4)
   (has-input-roles-adapter GET-SNOW-DATA-ADAPTER)))
```

gency situation: the first step of a snow investigation. Each situation features specific requirements and affords the invocation of appropriate goals. The latter can provide observables which are then used to identify the following situation; among them, a possible one is testing the respective situation requirements. Note that the affordances actualize the link between contexts and goals, as well as define the adapters which can specialize a goal invocation.

Semantic Web Services Layer: WSMO Descriptions Figure 13.8 outlines how the ontologies and SWS descriptions stored within IRS-III link the user interface (application) to the Meteorological Office, ECC Emergency Planning, and BuddySpace Web Services (WSs). Starting from the application, counterclockwise, the italics words in the figure represent the main operations performed within IRS-III.

Note that the Web Service descriptions make use of domain ontologies—meteorology, ViewEssex, and Jabber—whereas the goal encodings rely on the GUI, archetypes, and spatial ontologies. Mismatches are resolved by mediation services linked to WG- and GG-mediators.

Figure 13.9 shows an example of the created SWS descriptions: Get-Polygon-GIS-data-with-Filter-Goal represents a request for available shelters within a given area. The user specifies a polygon area and the shelter type (e.g., hospitals, inns, hotels). The results obtained by querying ViewEssex need to be filtered in order to return shelters correlated to emergency-specific requirements only. The problems to be solved in this example include (1) discovering and selecting the appropriate ViewEssex Web Service; (2) meditating the difference in area representations (polygon vs. circular) between the user goal and available Web Services; (3) composing the retrieve and filter data operations. We outline below how the SWS representations in figure 13.9 address these problems.

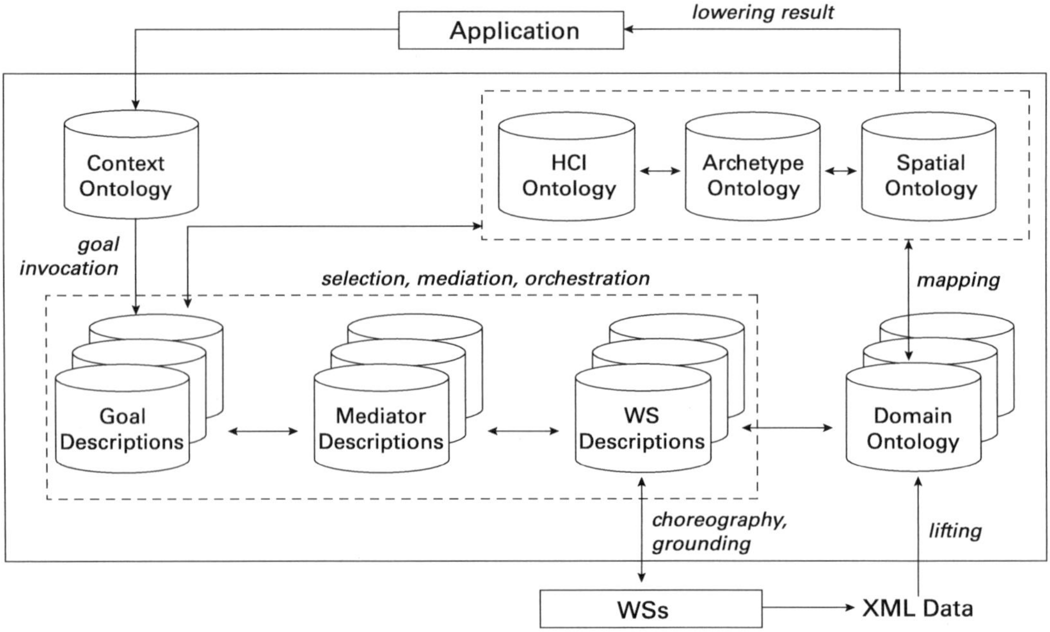

Figure 13.8
The use of semantics within the Semantic Web Service Layer

When the Get-Circle-GIS-Data-Goal is invoked, IRS-III discovers all Web Services that can solve it by means of the WG-mediator (first action under "The IRS-III Core Functionalities" above). Each semantic description of the ViewEssex Web Service defines the Web Service capability (i.e., the class of shelter provided by the Web Service). Table 13.4 reports an example of a kappa expression defining a capability assumption.

If the Web Service provides the class of shelters defined in one of the inputs of the goal, IRS-III selects it (second action under "The IRS-III Core Functionalities" above). In the example above, the Web Service is selected if the request class of shelters is hospital (hospitalquery).

In area mediation and orchestration, the Get-Polygon-GIS-data-with-Filter-Goal is associated with a unique Web Service that orchestrates three subgoals in sequence (third action under "The IRS-III Core Functionalities" above). The first one gets the list of polygon points from the input; the second one is the Get-Circle-GIS-Data-Goal described above; the third one invokes the smart service which filters the list of shelter data. Table 13.5 shows the IRS-III representation of such an orchestration.

The first and second subgoals are linked by three GG-mediators (fourth action under "The IRS-III Core Functionalities" above) which return the center, in the form of latitude and longitude, and the radius of the smallest circle that circumscribes the given polygon.

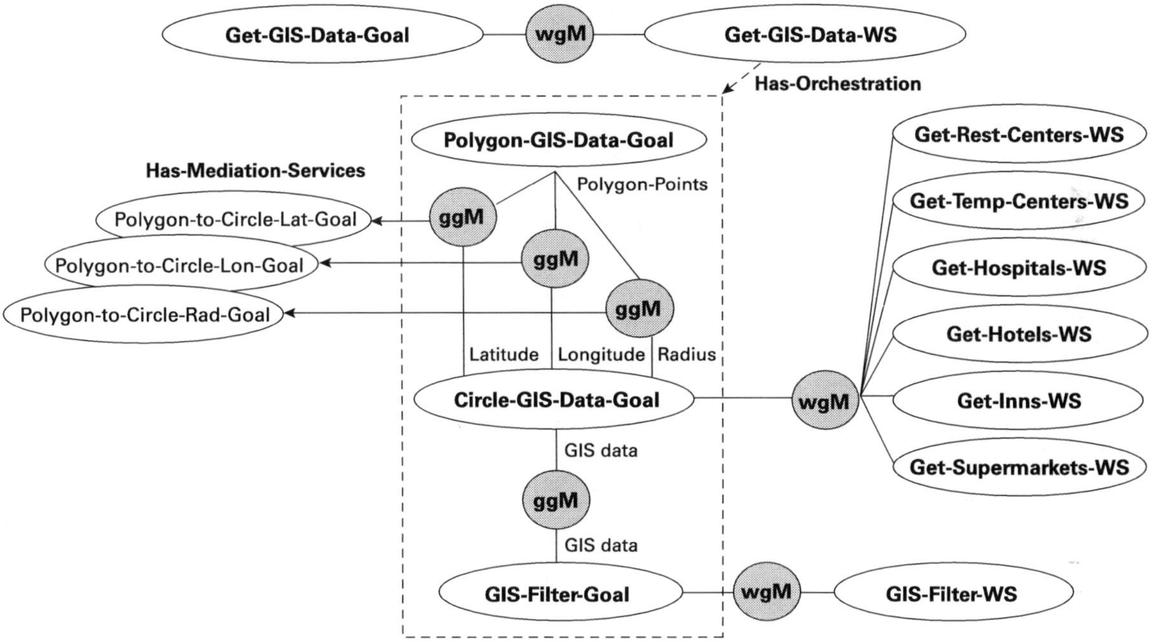

Figure 13.9
A portion of WSMO descriptions for the EMS prototype

Table 13.4
Example of a kappa expression defining a capability assumption

```
(DEF-CLASS GET-ECC-HOSPITALS-WEB-SERVICE-CAPABILITY (CAPABILITY) ?CAPABILITY
  ((USED-MEDIATOR :VALUE GET-GIS-DATA-MEDIATOR)
   (HAS-ASSUMPTION:VALUE
     (KAPPA(?WEB-SERVICE)
           (= (WSMO-ROLE-VALUE ?WEB-SERVICE'HAS-SPATIAL-OBJECT-QUERY)
              'HOSPITALSQUERY))))
```

Table 13.5
IRS-III representation of an orchestration

```
(DEF-CLASS GET-POLYGON-GIS-DATA-WITH-FILTER-WEB-SERVICE-INTERFACE-ORCHESTRATION
  ((HAS-BODY
    :VALUE ((ORCH-SEQUENCE
               CONVERT-POLYGON-POINTS-GOAL
               GET-CIRCLE-GIS-DATA-GOAL
               GIS-FILTER-GOAL)
            (ORCH-RETURN (ORCH-GET-GOAL-VALUE GIS-FILTER-GOAL))))))
```

To accomplish this, we created three mediation services represented by three distinct goals: Polygon-to-Circle-Lat-Goal, Polygon-to-Circle-Lon-Goal, and Polygon-to-Circle-Rad-Goal. Each mediation service is performed by a specific Web Service, exposing a Lisp function (the respective WG-mediator and Web Service ovals were omitted to avoid cluttering figure 13.9). The results of the mediation services and the class of shelter required are the inputs to the second subgoal. A unique GG-mediator connects the output of the second to the input of the third subgoal, without introducing any mediation service.

User Interface The prototype implementation is a Web interface using Google Maps for the spatial representation part of the application. The interface is built using the Google Web Toolkit (http://code.google.com/webtoolkit/), employing AJAX techniques on the client to communicate with a Java servlet, which itself connects to IRS-III through its Java API. A screencast of possible interactions and a live version of the prototype are available online at http://irs-test.open.ac.uk/sgis-dev/, to be used preferably with the Firefox Web browser.

13.4.3 Prototype Results

The application has been shown to the ECC emergency planners and other emergency stakeholders. On the basis of the obtained feedback, we decided to focus on developing a general-purpose platform that eases the integration of multiple data sources. This is an ongoing work on a new framework, named E-Merges, which focuses on geospatial data integration with Semantic Web Services (Tanasescu et al. 2007).

The resulting integration of new sources is relatively simple, although not entirely trivial. Indeed, IRS-III SWS integration allows the description of any XML data source available on the Web. From an expert point of view, our data source integration approach presents notable advantages compared to approaches based on standards such as the one demonstrated in the OWS-3 initiative, http://www.opengeospatial.org/initiatives/?iid=162.

These advantages are the following:

1. *Framework openness* Standards make integration easier but are not mandatory. Although the conformance to a specific standard ensures interoperability among systems following the same standard, the same specifications might not be used in systems adopting distinct specifications. For example, the three legacy systems of our prototype cannot conform to the same standard. Different data formats are lifted to the same concept in the spatial ontology.
2. *High-level service support* All the benefits of the underlying IRS-III platform, such as describing complex orchestrations through a full workflow model expressed in OCML; supporting data flow and solving mismatches through mediators; and defining how to interact with a single deployed Web Service (e.g., policies) on the basis of a set of forward-chaining rules (Cabral et al. 2006) are immediately available.

3. *Support to the emergency handling process* The conceptual distinction between goals and Web Services allows developers to easily design business processes known a priori (e.g., emergency procedure) in terms of composition of goals, and move the (automatic) identification of the most suitable service at runtime. One goal can be satisfied in different ways—according to a specific situation—by applicable Web Services developed within different agencies. As a result, organization processes behave in different ways according to their own set of operational procedures, requirements, and constraints.

Finally, in 2006 the prototype won a prize for the integration of Web scripting technologies with Semantic Web ones: http://www.semanticscripting.org/SFSW2006, and has been selected among the five finalists of the Semantic Web Challenge; see http://challenge.semanticweb.org/.

13.5 Lessons Learned

On the basis of challenges encountered—and the ways in which they were overcome—in the deployment of the application presented above, we now summarize the lessons learned, in terms of identifying the suitable scenario, following the adequate development process, verifying added values, and open challenges.

13.5.1 The Scenario

The first challenge regards the identification of proper scenarios where SWS technology can provide substantial benefits. On the basis of our experience, we can outline the following main features:

1. The scenario is a distributed and heterogeneous environment with a lack of centralized control, which provides a large number of alternatives (i.e., providing different functionalities in distinct situations) and competitive (i.e., providing the same functionalities in the same situation) services.
2. Provided services may also be connected to the external environment to access common data/resources already available on the Web; for instance, a user may request exchanging currencies using "today's best rate"; if our representation environment allows us to encode a current-rate relation which makes an external call to an appropriate Web Service or Web site, this not only will make life easier for the SWS developer but also make the resulting formal description more readable.
3. The scenario involves multiple stakeholders (clients and service providers) that need to collaborate. They represent the multiple viewpoints to describe.
4. The scenario is not static, but subject to changes and evolutions; the dynamism may involve the viewpoint descriptions (e.g., government policies, citizen needs, agencies' participation) or the service descriptions (e.g., changes in the service business process or new services provided by existing or new partners).

13.5.2 The Verified Added Values

The innovation in our research work is founded on the fact that our approach is the only feasible way to integrate across distributed heterogeneous systems where no central control is possible. Existing mature techniques would necessitate that different agencies harmonize their legacy systems or agree upon a unifying specification. However, the addition of a single new system would require a new consensus to be agreed upon. Conversely, in our approach:

1. Functionalities can be created by simply stating the workflow of WSMO goals to be accomplished. Orchestrating goals is simpler than orchestrating Web Services, since it abstracts from underlying technical details and is closer to the knowledge of domain experts. The orchestrated goals may belong to simple or complex SWS descriptions on top of several legacy systems. For example, in the proposed prototype, we developed SWS descriptions on top of three very different systems: Meteorological Office database, GIS, and instant messaging.
2. Each SWS description can link a goal to multiple Web Service descriptions. A given goal (e.g., Get-Circle-GIS-Data-Goal in our prototype) might be achieved by several Web Services. The most appropriate one is selected on the basis of the specific situation. As a result, the effective workflow (i.e., the actual sequence of service invocations) is known at runtime only. In a Web Service-based approach the functionalities are mapped at design time, when the actual context is not known. Moreover, if new Web Services will be available—for instance, providing data from further GIS—new Web Service descriptions can be simply introduced and linked to the existing goal (e.g., Get-Circle-GIS-Goal) by means of proper mediators—or reusing the existing one, if semantic mismatches do not exist—without affecting the current structure.
3. Heterogeneities are addressed by means of either mediation services or mapping rules associated with WG-, GG-, and OO-mediators. No central representations are thus necessary. In particular, the use of WG- and GG-mediators allows goal and process mediation, and thus a smooth crossing among services of distinct domains in the same workflow.
4. The instances of domain ontology concepts are not defined a priori; they are created at runtime (i.e., lifted), at the invocation of the Web Service. Therefore, we introduce multiple but small domain ontologies for supporting SWS descriptions. Each involved party is responsible for the respective domain ontology. This minimalist and distributed approach makes the management of ontologies (i.e., their evolution and maintenance) easy.

13.5.3 Open Challenges

The main remaining challenges identified are the following:

1. *SWS infrastructure* IRS-III and WSMO are the concerns of ongoing research, and some of its main features (e.g., orchestration, nonfunctional properties, and quality of services-based discovery) are still under development. Such aspects are likely to yield very useful results in e-government.

2. *Commercialization* The transition of the currently available systems into a stable and robust infrastructure is one of the major challenges that need to be solved before an SWS-based solution can be deployed into a productive environment. However, the prototyping development of carefully targeted applications with clear objectives can lead to real-world operational systems.
3. *Organizational and social aspects* The employees of governmental agencies usually perform tasks using well-established procedures; the inappropriately handled introduction of new processes or applications may lead to reluctance to use them. Active participation of stakeholders and end users in the design and development processes allows developers to deploy applications that respect current procedures and, at the same time, ease the work of staff, leading to improved acceptance.
4. *Privacy, security, and trust* These are fundamental requirements in e-government as well as other domains, such as e-commerce and e-work. At the syntax level, efficient solutions for addressing privacy and security issues already exist or there is relevant ongoing research. The semantic level should extend the syntactic solutions by ontologically describing security and privacy policies of accessing data and processes. Moreover, trust-based discovery of SWS is a crucial issue in order to avoid invocation of malicious or unreliable services, for which there are no defined standards by which SWS may expose their policies and trust features. The key to enabling a trust-based selection for SWS lies in a common ontological representation, where Web Service and client perform their trust guarantees and requirements (Galizia 2006).
5. *Standardization* It is still being debated which approach to follow between, as broadly described options, standardization versus integration (i.e., focusing on interoperation among several existing approaches). We believe that our approach is open to both solutions, and our results may contribute to the investigation of possible standards.

13.6 Conclusion

The technologies developed within DIP promise to do the following:

1. Provide added-value, joined-up services. Allowing the creation of interoperating services transparently to the users, and hence automate integration, reasoning, and mediation among heterogeneous data sources and processes available at distinct governmental levels.
2. Enable formalization of business processes in an unambiguous structure. Allowing the creation of a common understanding of processes, and visualization of the knowledge involved. This could eventually lead to a reengineering of the governmental systems and simplification of processes.
3. Reduce risk and cost by moving from "hard coding" services to reusable functionality, for example, through utility computing of shared services (e.g., payment platforms, legal resources, etc.); keeping organizations' autonomy in the description/management of their domain; increasing flexibility; enabling discovery of new or previously unknown services;

aggregating services on the basis of user preferences; providing better service to third parties and customers; and easily addressing the evolution and change of existing services and scenarios.
4. Provide better support to the front line by allowing one-stop, customer-focused, and multiple viewpoint access to services and shared information. However, demonstrating this requires the achievement of several prerequisites: creation of compelling demonstrators and prototypes, establishing visible standards, stable and mature technology and products, and convincing business cases. Perhaps more important, this may provide a way to address existing barriers and perceptions, such as trust in automated data sharing. Organizations are concerned about (1) ownership, control, and quality among service providers; and (2) security, data protection, confidentiality, and privacy issues.
5. Patchy awareness of Web Services. Stakeholders are often unclear about the distinction between Web Service and general services available via the Web.
6. Up-front infrastructure costs (e.g., investment in SWS). Organizations are reluctant to be the pioneers which take the initial financial "hit" in implementing SWS, as with almost any new technology.
7. Market development in terms of raising the awareness of potential SWS benefits, increasing pilot applications, and promoting the availability of working SWS platforms. Following our approach, we deployed a prototype of an emergency management system. In particular, we stressed all of the aspects associated with the development of SWS-based applications: knowledge acquisition, discovery, composition, and mediation.

Future developments of the prototype will be part of the framework E-Merges (Tanasescu et al. 2007). They will include an increase in the complexity of the integration ontologies (spatial, GUI, and archetypes) in order to allow multiple representation and an improved management of context to offer more cognitively sound features. Also, making the integration of new data sources even easier constitutes a long-term goal for the IRS SWS execution platform.

We believe that our work may contribute to raising awareness of the potential benefits of SWS, guide the efforts of new SWS-based applications and projects (e.g., LUISA: http://kmi.open.ac.uk/projects/luisa/ and http://www.ip-super.org/content/view/114/63/), and influence the standards and strategic environments so as to encourage the adoption of SWS technology.

Acknowledgment

The work published in this chapter is partly funded by the European Community under the Sixth Framework Programme, contract FP6–507483 DIP. The work reflects only the views of Alessio Gugliotta, John Domingue, Vlad Tanasescu, Leticia Gutiérrez Villarías, Rob Davies, Mary Rowlatt, Marc Richardson, and Sandra Stinčić. The Community is not liable for any use that may be made of the information contained therein.

References

BBC News. Thousands Trapped in Snow Storm. News.bbc.co.uk. January 31, 2003. http://news.bbc.co.uk/2/hi/uk_news/england/2712045.stm.

Berners-Lee, T., Hendler, J., and Lassila, O. 2001. The semantic Web. *Scientific American* 284(4): 34–43.

Cabinet Office, Emergency Planning College. 2006. Geographic Information Systems (GIS) & Integrated Emergency Management. http://www.epcollege.gov.uk/upload/assets/www.epcollege.gov.uk/0.pdf. (Accessed February 2007.)

Cabral, L., and Domingue, J. 2005. Mediation of Semantic Web Services in IRS-III. In *Proceedings of the First Workshop on Mediation in Semantic Web Services at ICSOC 2005*, pp. 1–16.

Cabral, L., Domingue, J., Galizia, S., Gugliotta, A., Tanasescu, V., Pedrinaci, C., and Norton, B. 2006. IRS-III: A broker for Semantic Web Services based applications. In *Proceedings of the 5th International Semantic Web Conference* (ISWC 2006), I. Cruz et al., eds. Berlin: Springer. LNCS 4273, pp. 201–214.

DIP. 2004. Data, Information, and Process Integration with Semantic Web Services—Objectives. http://dip.semanticWeb.org/objectives.html. (Accessed February 2007.)

Eisenstadt, M., Komzak, J., and Dzbor, M. 2003. Instant messaging + maps = powerful collaboration tools for distance learning. In *Proceedings of TelEduc03*, pp. 19–21.

Galizia, Stefania. 2006. WSTO: A classification-based ontology for managing trust in Semantic Web Services. In *Proceedings of 3rd European Semantic Web Conference*.

MoreRFID. 2005. Gartner Highlights Key Emerging Technologies in 2005 Hype Cycle. http://www.morerfid.com/details.php?subdetail=Report&action=details&report_id=508&display=RFID/. (Accessed February 2007.)

Motta, Enrico. 1998. An overview of the OCML modelling language. In *Proceedings of the 8th Workshop on Knowledge Engineering: Methods and Languages*.

OWL-S. 2006. OWL-S 1.2 Pre-Release. http://www.ai.sri.com/daml/services/owl-s/1.2/. (Accessed February 2007.)

SWSF. 2005. Semantic Web Services Framework. http://www.daml.org/services/swsf/. (Accessed February 2007.)

Tanasescu, V., Gugliotta, A., Domingue, J., Gutiérrez Villarías, L., Davies, R., Rowlatt, M., Richardson, M., and Stinčić, S. 2007. Geospatial data integration with Semantic Web Services: The eMerges approach. In *The Geospatial Web: How Geo-Browsers, Social Software and the Web 2.0 Are Shaping the Network Society*. Berlin: Springer.

WSDL-S. 2005. Web Services Semantic—WSDL-S 1.0. http://www.w3.org/Submission/WSDL-S/. (Accessed February 2007.)

WSMO. 2005. D2v1.2Web Service Modeling Ontology (WSMO). http://www.wsmo.org/TR/d2/v1.2/. (Accessed February 2007.)

Zdnet. 2005. SOA's Deep Impact on Software. http://blogs.zdnet.com/service-oriented/?p=399. (Accessed February 2007.)

14 AMIGO: Interoperable Semantic Services for the Smart Home Environment

Nikolaos Georgantas, Julia Kantorovitch, Ioanna Roussaki, Valérie Issarny, Jarmo Kalaoja, Ioannis Papaioannou, and Dimitrios Tsesmetzis

14.1 Introduction

The open networked smart home environment should allow the seamless integration of the various home devices that are now equipped with a network interface. This should further enable the functionalities provided by those devices to be dynamically integrated within the networked home system, in order to offer end users a rich variety of applications that will jointly exploit today's, mostly distinct, four application domains of the networked home:

- *Personal computing* (PC), based on home computers, printers, and Internet connection
- *Mobile computing*, manifested by the increasing use of home WiFi and Bluetooth networks connecting laptops, PDAs, and tiny personal devices
- *Consumer electronics* (CE), targeting multimedia in the home
- *Home automation or domotics*, adding intelligence to household appliances such as washing machines and lighting systems.

Usability of the networked home system calls for automatic discovery of devices and their functionalities, as well as application composability and upgradeability, and self-administration for easy installation and use. Service orientation (Papazoglou and Georgakopoulos 2003) appears as the appropriate architectural paradigm to cope with such requirements. By applying this paradigm, networked devices and their functionalities are abstracted as services which may be dynamically retrieved and composed, based on service discovery protocols as well as choreography and orchestration protocols associated with service-oriented architectures (Peltz 2003). Such features should be provided by the networked home system's middleware. The middleware should further support the following properties to address the extended usability and efficiency requirements:

- *Interoperability* Interoperability is necessary at all levels of the open networked home system, which integrates devices from the four application domains (PC, mobile, CE, and domotics), as well as from different manufacturers that use different communication standards and different hardware and software platforms. The supporting middleware should then provide software interoperability for services as well as for middleware components and protocols.

- *Context awareness* The networked home system should provide the user with services that take into account the user's situation, environment, requirements, and objectives. This property is known as context awareness, which should be established by the middleware, regarding both context data management and adaptation of the service behavior based on these data.
- *Quality of Service* (QoS) Usability of the networked home system will in particular be dependent upon the quality of service experienced by the users, which includes reliability, performance, and security. It is then required that the middleware integrate adequate support for QoS management, as well as QoS-based service selection and adaptation.

This chapter introduces the AMIGO service-oriented system approach for the open-networked home—which has been designed as part of the IST FP6 AMIGO project[1] on the development of a networked home system toward the ambient intelligence (AmI) vision—aiming to demonstrate all the aforementioned middleware properties. The key property targeted by AMIGO is interoperability. In contrast to most existing service architectures, the AMIGO approach does not impose any specific middleware technology. It allows heterogeneous technologies to be integrated, establishing interoperability at a higher, semantic, level. The AMIGO system architecture is built upon this fundamental principle.

Semantics of an entity encapsulate the meaning of this entity by reference to an established vocabulary of terms (ontology) representing a specific area of knowledge. In this way, semantics of entities become machine-interpretable, enabling machine reasoning on them. Such concepts come from the knowledge representation field and have been applied and further evolved in the Semantic Web[2] domain (Berners-Lee et al. 2001). The Web ontology language (OWL)[3] is a recommendation by W3C supporting formal description of ontologies and reasoning on them. A natural evolution from this has been the combination of the Semantic Web and Web Services,[4] the currently dominant service-oriented technology, into Semantic Web Services (McIlraith and Martin 2003). This effort aims at the semantic specification of Web Services toward automating Web Services discovery, invocation, composition, and execution monitoring. The Semantic Web and Semantic Web Services paradigms address Web Service interoperability (Tsounis et al. 2004; O'Sullivan and Lewis 2003).

Nevertheless, the AMIGO objectives are wider, that is, addressing service interoperability without being tied to any service technology. To this end, we establish semantic service modeling independently of underlying service technologies, elaborating appropriate ontologies for semantic service specification, accompanied by adequate tool support for the service developer. Based on the supported semantic service modeling, interoperability mechanisms can be developed and deployed to enable integration of heterogeneous services. Hence, we provide a runtime environment for the dynamic integration of our interoperable semantic services, supporting their dynamic discovery, composition, adaptation, and execution.

This book introduces a taxonomy of the various contributions coming from the surveyed IST FP6 projects with respect to the NESSI technology platform road map[5] and the service-oriented computing (SOC) road map (Papazoglou et al. 2006). This taxonomy spans from low-level infrastructure considerations to high-level semantic considerations in a service-oriented architecture and also addresses aspects that crosscut these different levels of abstraction. Even though AMIGO contributes to most of the layers identified in this taxonomy, its main objectives and concerns fall into the semantic layer. AMIGO contributes to the state of the art in semantic technologies by elaborating new ontologies, a semantic service description language, and a visual semantic modeling tool. Moreover, AMIGO identifies the need for service interoperability in the networked home or, more generally, in an open service environment and provides a solution based on semantics. Further, in this book the IST FP6 SeCSe project[6] conceptual model is introduced as a source of common terminology in the service-oriented computing field. We position the AMIGO approach with respect to this model in section 14.2.

The remainder of this chapter is structured as follows. Section 14.2 elaborates on semantic service modeling aspects of the AMIGO framework. It describes the AMIGO semantic vocabulary and language for service specification; it provides details on the QoS- and context-based specification of services; and it goes into tool-aided semantic service modeling, focusing on the VantagePoint tool developed for this purpose. Section 14.3 provides the basics of the dynamic integration of interoperable semantic services, and section 14.4 discusses related work. Finally, in section 14.5 conclusions are drawn and future plans are exposed.

14.2 Semantic Service Modeling

Interoperability between heterogeneous services in the AMIGO home is realized based on the semantic modeling of services. Semantic modeling allows a common description of services at a higher, technology-independent level, thus enabling integration of service architectures that differ in the ways that services are natively specified and interact, and in the employed communication protocols supporting their interaction. Semantic service modeling within AMIGO is based on two axes. First, we develop a set of ontologies modeling concepts/domains of interest, which can be used as a general-use vocabulary for describing services. Second, we develop a language (i.e., a set of ontologies, too) for semantically specifying services as a set of abstract attributes. The specification of a service using this language will refer to the aforementioned vocabulary for giving concrete values to the attributes of the service. Certainly, language and vocabulary should be in accordance with each other (e.g., addressing the same service attributes). Furthermore, as both vocabulary and language are ontologies aimed at describing services, we need to specify the boundary between them. Targeting diverse, heterogeneous services and service architectures, we have opted to make the language as generic as possible, not taking any design decisions that would restrict its range of application. Then, the vocabulary may be seen as a complement to the language, not only for giving concrete values to the attributes of the language but also for extending the language with new attributes that are appropriate for each specific case.

With regard to service modeling, the IST FP6 SeCSe project has proposed a conceptual model (Colombo et al. 2005) that describes actors, activities, and entities involved in a service-oriented scenario and the relationships between them. The SeCSe model can be used as a common base in service-oriented modeling. In our elaboration of the AMIGO semantic framework, we did not consider the SeCSe conceptual model, which was not available at the time. Nevertheless, several concepts present in the SeCSe model are included (even though using different terms) in the AMIGO ontologies and have driven the AMIGO middleware design and development. Thus, in the AMIGO networked home environment, services are software functionalities exposed by devices (service providers) and directly accessible by software clients (service consumers) and ultimately by human users; services can be stateful or stateless, and have concrete implementations and descriptions published on repositories; applications in the form of user tasks discover and integrate services based on abstract descriptions of their requirements, to be matched with published service descriptions; service discovery is supported by repositories, and the roles of service consumer and mediator—the latter being responsible for service composition—are assumed by a single entity on the user's device that also orchestrates component services into the resulting composite service. However, the AMIGO semantic framework introduces several core concepts (e.g., device, network, platform, protocol, connector) or domain-specific concepts (e.g., context, consumer electronics, domotics, mobile computing, personal computing, multimedia content)—actually, context is a core concept that depends on the domain—that are not covered by the SeCSe model. For core concepts, this is due to the fact that AMIGO focuses on interoperability between heterogeneous devices and service architectures. For domain concepts, this is because they derive from the specifics of the networked smart home environment.

In the following sections, the AMIGO vocabulary (14.2.1) and language (section 14.2.2) for semantic service specification are presented. The corresponding ontologies support both functional and nonfunctional service properties, in particular QoS and context with respect to the latter. As already mentioned, the language stays generic, allowing extension and enrichment. Further, we present a specialization for QoS and context semantics where both the language and the vocabulary are extended (section 14.2.3). Finally, to assist service developers in employing semantic technologies, we provide a tool for semantic service modeling which supports visual manipulation of ontologies associated with the home environment (section 14.2.4).

14.2.1 Semantic Vocabulary for Service Specification

The intensive user research (Röcker et al. 2005) performed in the AMIGO project provided us with ideas on how the home system could interact with people in a service-rich smart home environment. Based on this user research, we elaborated scenarios where the AMIGO home system does the following:

- Supports information and entertainment by proactively selecting music and personalized news for the users which may follow them everywhere in the house
- Assists in household tasks by setting home appliances or downloading recipes
- Controls ambient settings by adapting the light, audio, and video features in a room, for TV or personalized multiplayer game sessions.

We then analyzed these scenarios to identify the requirements for various domain ontologies and vocabularies toward coping with the heterogeneity of service descriptions. The resulting structure for the AMIGO service description vocabularies is depicted in figure 14.1.

The main rationale behind this structure is that vocabularies should support maintainability and future evolution of concepts related to a home. The domain vocabularies are extendable modules that provide detailed information about technologies and features of particular classes or specific models of home devices. New domain vocabularies can be added to cover more device manufacturers when needed. Any concepts from the higher-level (depicted in the lower part of figure 14.1) vocabularies can be specialized herein. For example, new device classes can be defined as subclasses of the higher-level AMIGO core domain device concept, and specific device models can be introduced as instances of device classes. The main part of vocabularies belongs to the AMIGO core domain vocabularies. These may also evolve: commonly used concepts from the lower-level domain vocabularies can be generalized and added herein. Furthermore, external generic ontologies, such as the foundation of intelligent physical agents (FIPA) device ontology,[7] may be imported or adapted herein. Also, the AMIGO-S service specification language ontology presented in 14.2.2, or any other semantic service description language, such as OWL-S,[8] can be imported here. The AMIGO core concepts provide a classification of concepts selected from the AMIGO core domain vocabularies that have important cross-domain relations. This reduces the need for the latter to import each other, thus improving the maintainability of vocabularies. In our elaboration of the above ontologies and classifications, numerous available sources of information have been considered: CCPP,[9] TvAnytime,[10] FIPA,[7] FIPAAV,[11] OMA,[12] DLNA,[13] MPEG7,[14] MPEG21,[15] and UPnP.[16] The complete AMIGO vocabulary ontologies, accompanied by guide documentation for the application and service developers, are publicly available.[17]

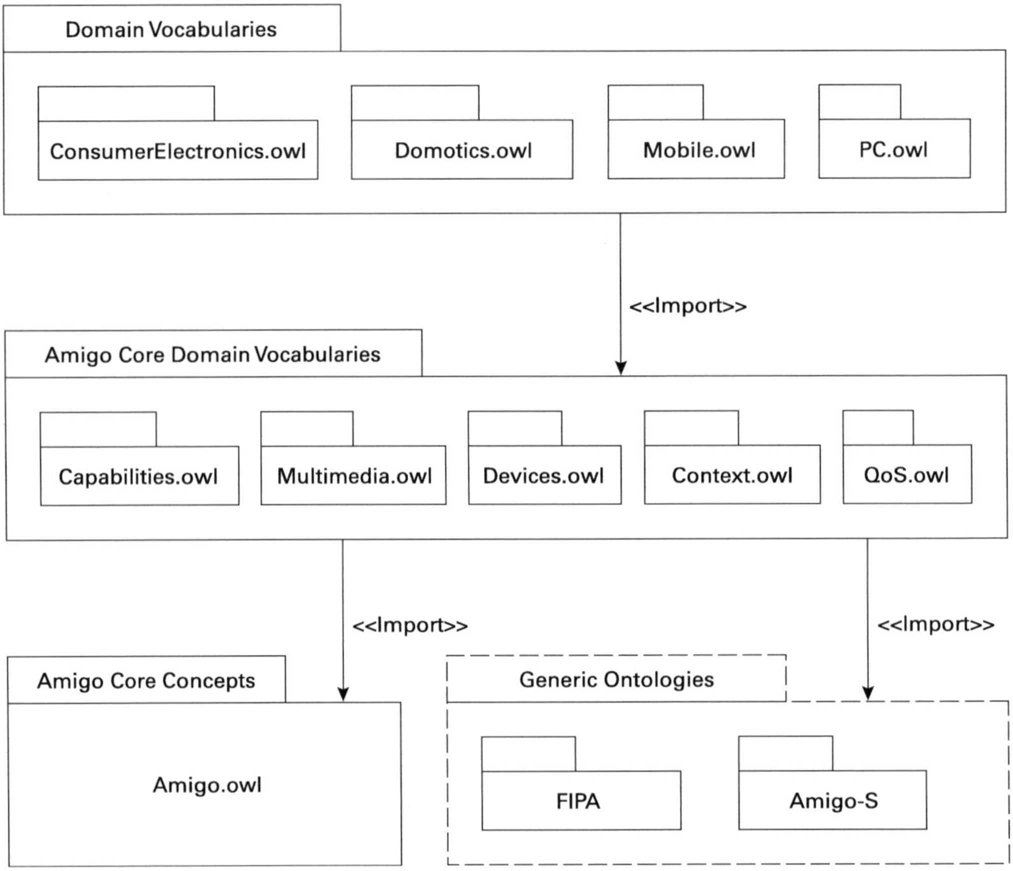

Figure 14.1
Structure for service description vocabularies

14.2.2 The AMIGO-S Semantic Language for Service Specification

To exploit the vocabulary ontologies in service description, we have elaborated AMIGO-S, a declarative language for semantic service specification. AMIGO-S builds upon OWL-S,[8] which is a widely used OWL-based ontology for semantically specifying Web Services. Our language considerably generalizes OWL-S toward supporting diverse service architectures, as well as nonfunctional service properties. Supporting the specification of any service architecture aims at realizing interoperability between these heterogeneous service architectures. Since each of these architectures employs native service specification and interaction schemes over a native middleware platform, both application-level and middleware-level interoperability should be enabled by AMIGO-S. More specifically, this requires that AMIGO-S provide at both levels the appropriate specification abstractions on which interoperability mechanisms may be built. In comparison, OWL-S supports only application-level interoperability while it imposes a single middleware infrastructure (i.e., Web Services). Herein, we define AMIGO-S in an informal manner, identifying its extensions with regard to OWL-S. A formal specification of the language can be found in AMIGO Consortium (2006a), and the source can be accessed online.[17] We illustrate our presentation of the language with a number of ontology diagrams elaborated using the Protégé[18] ontology editor. Our definition of AMIGO-S comprises the specification of service functional properties and nonfunctional properties, which are elaborated in the subsequent sections.

Specification of Service Functional Properties The AMIGO-S specification of service functional properties comprises the specification of service capabilities, service conversations, and underlying middleware.

Service Capabilities and Conversations Our specification of service capabilities and conversations relies on the OWL-S specification. The main new elements introduced by AMIGO-S are the following:

- We explicitly model a capability supported by a service—which may offer multiple capabilities—as a set of semantic IOPEs specifying the data inputs and outputs of the service, as well as the preconditions that need to be fulfilled for the execution of the service and the effects produced to the world (e.g., the environment of the service) by the execution of the service.
- We additionally model provided capabilities as capabilities supported by a service, and required capabilities as capabilities needed by a service, which will be sought on other networked services.
- We enable multiple conversation (process) scenarios of a service, one per capability.
- To be able to support any service-oriented architecture, we explicitly render the data types of the inputs and outputs of capabilities and of conversation operations (atomic processes) independent of a specific type system.
- We model application-level interaction with a service independently of the interaction model realized by the underlying middleware, such as RPC or event-based.
- To enable automated invocation of a service, we transcribe OWL-S conversations into executable BPEL[19] workflows, which is a widely accepted industrial standard, as further detailed in section 14.3.

Due to space limitations, we will not detail this specification further. (The interested reader may refer to AMIGO Consortium 2005, 2006a). Figure 14.2 depicts the specification of service capabilities and conversations in AMIGO-S.

Underlying Middleware Toward supporting multiple middleware platforms, AMIGO-S includes specification of the underlying middleware in the service specification.

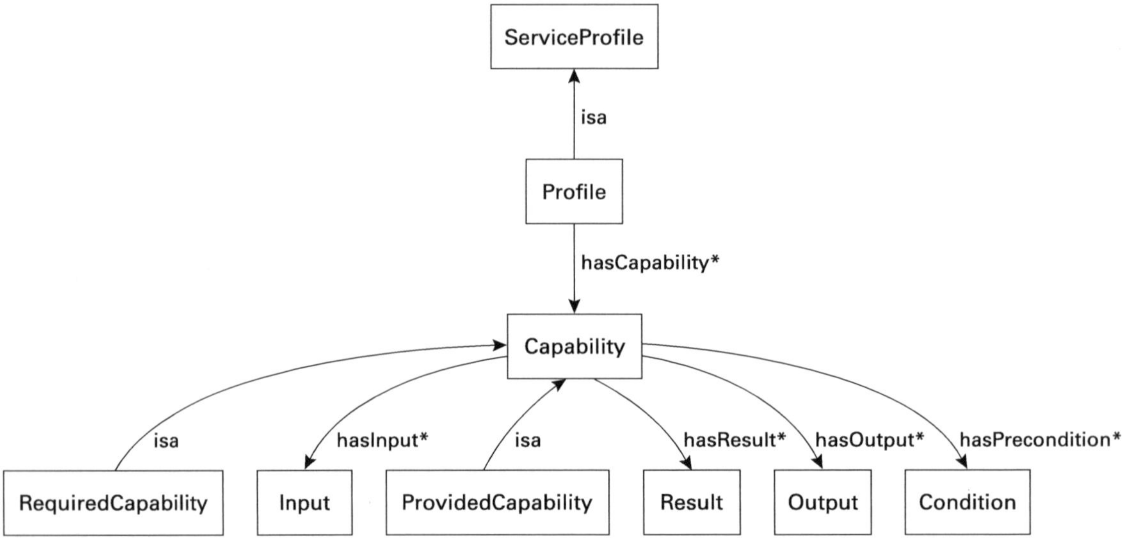

Figure 14.2
Specification of service capabilities and conversations

In a first step, we aim to support well-known middleware platforms integrating specific service interaction protocols coupled with well-known service discovery protocols. In AMIGO, we have elaborated middleware-layer interoperability mechanisms (both for discovery and for interaction) based on low-level semantic abstractions of relevant protocols. We specifically support interoperability between WS-Discovery, UPnP, and SLP, as well as between SOAP and RMI (AMIGO Consortium 2006b). Based on this work, the specification of underlying middleware supported by AMIGO-S may simply be a reference by name to a well-known middleware or to the employed discovery and interaction protocols. Then, interoperability between two services referencing each native middleware in its specification may be assessed directly on the basis of the availability of appropriate interoperability mechanisms between the referenced protocols.

A second step is to enable services to be deployed over any (discovery or interaction) connector, possibly associated to a specific capability/conversation of the service. Then, AMIGO-S should provide a complete specification of the connector, possibly incorporating external ontologies providing taxonomies of connector attributes. Based on such specification, interoperability between two connectors should be assessed and potentially dynamically realized. Initial results in this direction are presented in Georgantas et al. (2005). Figure 14.3 depicts the specification of underlying middleware in our language.

Furthermore, one of the features characterizing a middleware infrastructure or a connector is the supported interaction model, such as RPC or event-based. OWL-S adopts the interaction model of WSDL[20]/SOAP. We aim to support different interaction models,

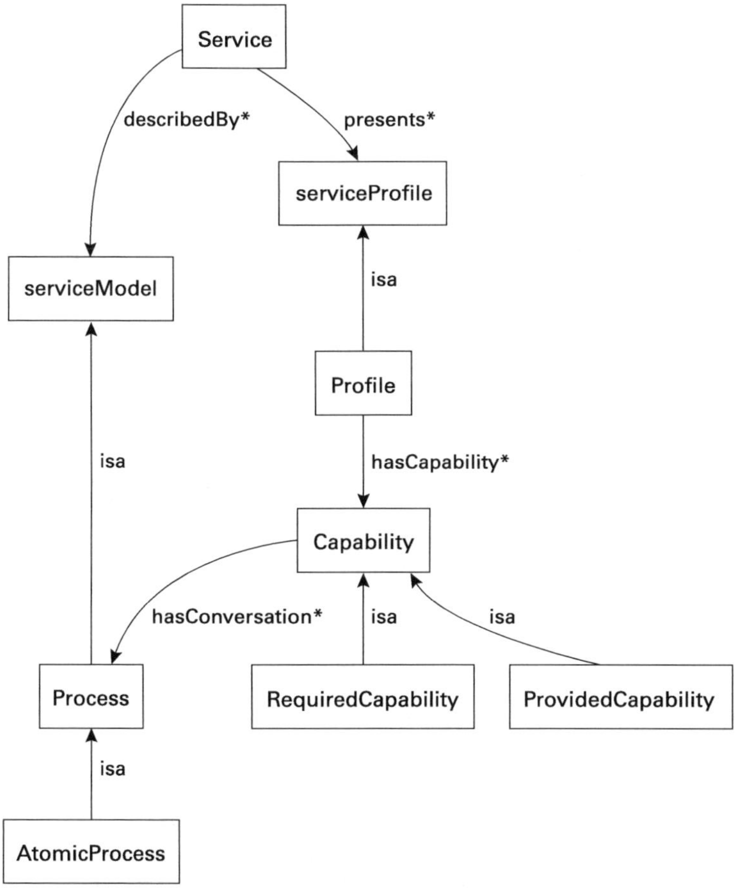

Figure 14.2
(continued)

and are particularly interested in event-based middleware or, more abstractly, in event-based connectors. The event-based interaction model is particularly suited for the dynamic, asynchronous AmI environment.

Finally, the data-type system independence discussed above should be complemented here by appropriate middleware-level support. Thus, our language should allow different type systems employed by the middleware. In OWL-S, when associating the service model to a concrete service grounding, OWL ontologies representing data types of inputs and outputs are mapped onto XML schema data types. AMIGO-S should enable mapping semantic data types to different syntactic data types (i.e., to different middleware type systems).

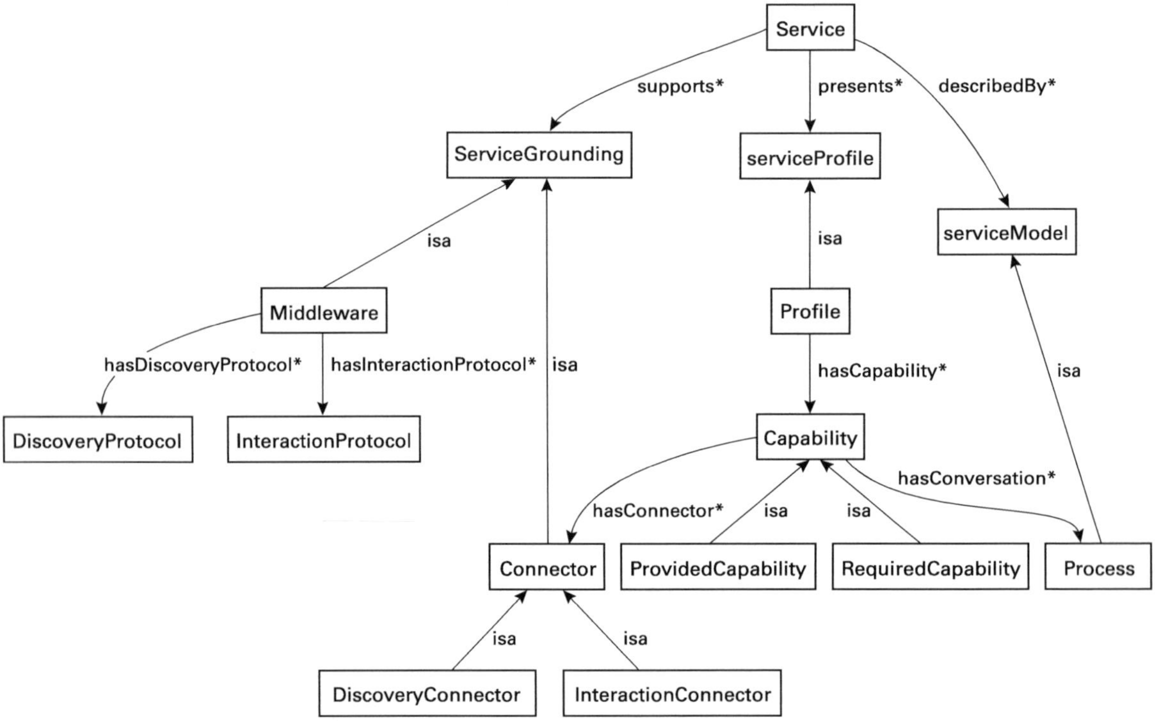

Figure 14.3
Specification of underlying middleware

Specification of Service Nonfunctional Properties The AMIGO-S specification of service nonfunctional properties comprises the specification of quality of service (QoS) and of service context.

Service QoS Aiming at a generic QoS specification not posing any restrictions on what QoS may be in the networked home environment, we do not define the specific QoS information that may be associated to a service. The fundamental class of our specification is the generic QoSParameter class, representing any QoS attribute. This generic specification can be further specialized into a more concrete QoS specification (as presented in section 14.2.3).

We initially introduce a general classification for service QoS, identifying the different system levels responsible for ensuring such QoS:

- *Application-level QoS* This is the QoS ensured by the service itself; for example, response time (performance) of a service is dependent on its computation efficiency, possibly based on programming optimizations.

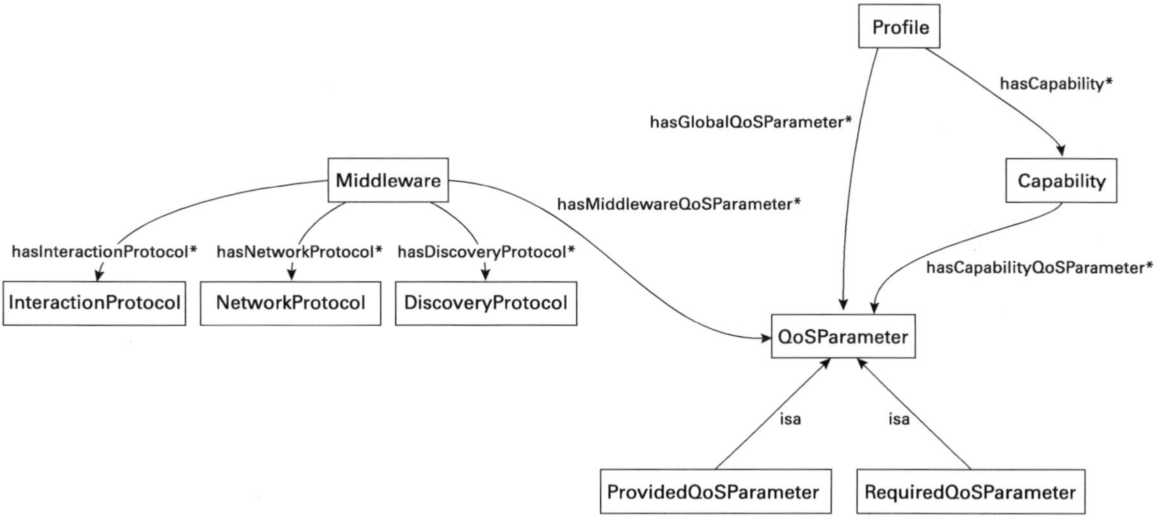

Figure 14.4
Specification of service QoS

- *Platform/system-level QoS* QoS also depends on the platform on which the service executes (e.g., service response time is also dependent on the system OS, CPU, memory, etc.).
- *Middleware-level QoS* Mechanisms deployed by middleware can affect QoS (e.g., middleware may support distributed replication of a server transparently for clients, in order to improve service response time in case of high load).
- *Network-level QoS* QoS certainly depends on the network connection between a service and its client (e.g., reservation of resources along the network path can guarantee sufficient bandwidth for timely delivery of a data stream).

Based on this classification, we identify the diffusion of QoS attributes in the service specification. Figure 14.4 depicts the specification of service QoS in AMIGO-S.

For specifying application-level and platform/system-level QoS, we extend the OWL-S service profile to include QoS attributes, which may be either global QoS attributes of the service or associated with a specific service capability. QoS attributes may be either provided or required in association with provided or required capabilities, respectively.

For specifying middleware-level and network-level QoS, related (provided or required) QoS attributes are added to the middleware (or connector) specification included in the service specification. In the case of network-level QoS, the middleware (or connector) specification may be extended to include underlying network protocols. These QoS attributes may imply—but not specify—employment of appropriate middleware-level or

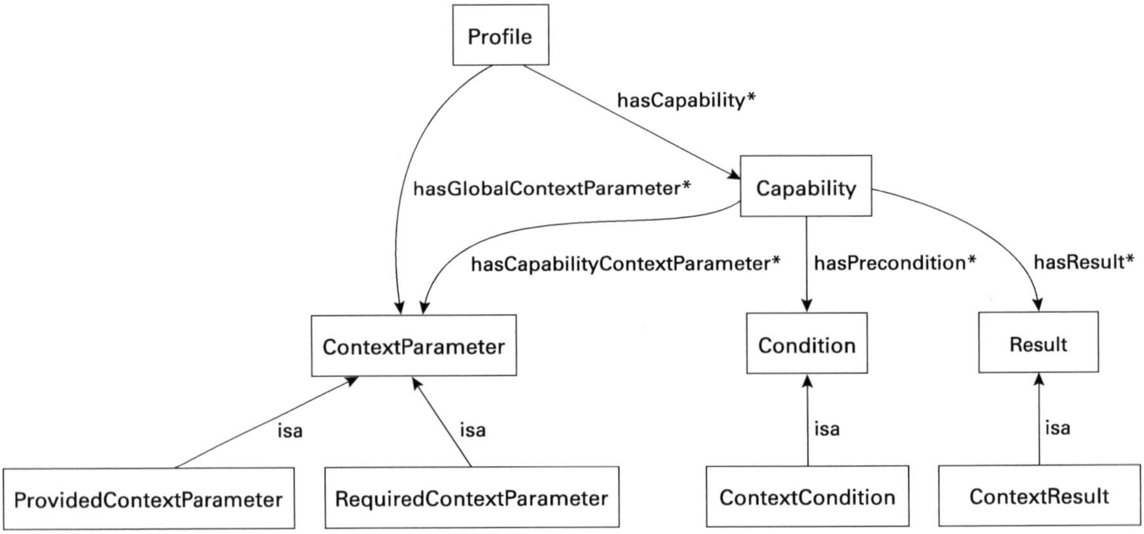

Figure 14.5
Specification of service context

network-level mechanisms (e.g., server replication or resource reservation, respectively). Network-level QoS mainly concerns multimedia streaming services of the CE domain in the AMIGO networked home.

Service Context Following the same approach as for QoS, we do not attempt to identify the concrete context information that may be associated with services. We have opted to include in AMIGO-S a generic service context specification, where the fundamental ContextParameter class representing any context attribute is introduced; no concrete context attributes are further identified (see figure 14.5). This generic context specification in AMIGO-S can be further specialized into a more concrete context specification (as presented in section 14.2.3).

Following this generic approach, we extend the OWL-S service profile to include context attributes. These attributes may be global context attributes of the service or may be associated with a specific service capability. Furthermore, both provided and required context attributes can be specified, thus enabling service and client context and context required by the client. Additionally, the adopted IOPE scheme describing a specific capability allows us to specify contextual preconditions and effects for each service capability. Finally, besides inputs (or outputs) provided by (to) its client, a service may have a number of context inputs (outputs). We consider this as part of the functional inputs/outputs of a service capability. Figure 14.5 depicts the specification of service context in our language.

14.2.3 Specializing the QoS and Context Specification

The AMIGO-S QoS and context specification presented in the previous section only identified the association of the generic QoSParameter and ContextParameter classes to specific elements of the service profile and service model. In this section, we go one step further, refining QoSParameter and ContextParameter. Specifically, we define four distinguished ontologies: the QoS language and vocabulary ontologies, as well as the context language and vocabulary ontologies. The presented ontologies have been implemented in OWL, using Protégé.

The AMIGO QoS language ontology (ALOqos) (Papaioannou et al. 2006) provides a standard generic model for the description of arbitrary QoS attributes while defining the nature of associations between QoS attributes and the way they are measured. In ALOqos, each QoS attribute is described by the classes subsequently presented. The core class of ALOqos is the QoSParameter that represents a generic QoS service property within a specific domain. It is related to various classes (i.e., Metric, QoSImpact, Aggregated, Relationship, and Type). The Metric class defines the manner in which each QoS parameter is assigned a value. In addition to the Value property, it carries the MetricType (e.g., int, long, string, boolean, etc.) and Unit (e.g., Kb, sec, bps) properties. As there are various ways to express quantities in terms of units, the Unit class has a relationship with the ConversionFormula class that is introduced to enable the transformation from one unit to another. ALOqos also supports statistical analysis elements over the monitored QoS parameters. This functionality is provided by the Statistics subclass of Metric that includes various statistical functions. The QoSImpact class represents the way the QoSParameter value contributes to the service quality perceived by the user. The Relationship class reflects the manner in which a QoSParameter is related to another QoSParameter and can be proportional or inversely proportional, and Strong, Medium, or Weak. In order to interrelate two QoSParameter objects, the InfluentialParameter mandatory object property has been introduced, which indicates the QoSParameter that has an impact on the "owner" QoSParameter of the relationship. The QoSParameter that is composed of two or more defined QoSParameters has the Aggregated property. Finally, the Type class represents the specific QoS category of the parameters and inherits from the AMIGO QoS vocabulary ontology described below.

An extended review of the literature on QoS taxonomies and classifications (e.g., Mani and Nagarajan 2002; Lee et al. 2003) formed the basis of the AMIGO work toward the design of a QoS vocabulary for interoperable semantic services. In the AMIGO QoS vocabulary ontology (AVOqos), all QoS parameters are instantiated as subclasses of the QoSParameter class of ALOqos. Subsequently, an overview of the main AVOqos classes is provided. The Performance class aggregates information that mainly depends on the properties of the network connection between the user and the service provider nodes. Its subclasses include Throughput, Latency, ResponseTime, Jitter, and ErrorRate. The Scalability class is used to describe the server's ability to increase its computing capacity

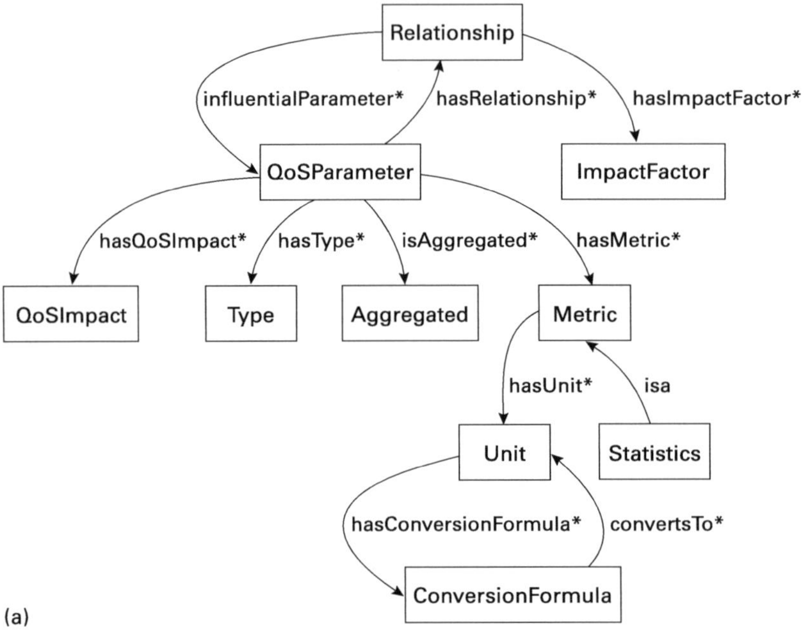

(a)

Figure 14.6
The Amigo QoS (a) Language and (b) Vocabulary Ontologies

and the system's ability to process more users' requests, operations, or transactions in a given time interval. The Availability class represents the probability that a server is up and running, and is measured by the MTTR (mean time to repair) and MTBF (mean time between failures) parameters. Accessibility refers to a node's ability to serve a service request. Accuracy refers to the accuracy of results in a numerical manner, and Capacity specifies the maximum number of requests a server is able to handle simultaneously. Cost represents the overall cost that results from service usage. The Configuration class of services is related to the interface update procedure and/or the adopted standards, and it provides information about the regulations the service complies with. It is measured by the following metrics: Stability, which represents how often the service interfaces are modified; SupportedStandard, which refers to the standards that the service complies with; and Regulatory, which refers to the probability of the fact that the service is compliant with a random regulation. The Integrity class represents the ability of a service to preserve data integrity during a transaction, and the Reliability class reflects the possibility that a service session will be completed successfully. The Security class indicates the security level a service provides and is expressed by the following subclasses: Confidentiality, Auditability, Authentication, Authorization, DataEncryption, and NonRepudiation.

The main classes of the ALOqos and AVOqos ontologies are illustrated in figure 14.6. (a and b respectively). The minimal height of the defined ontologies is a critical feature for

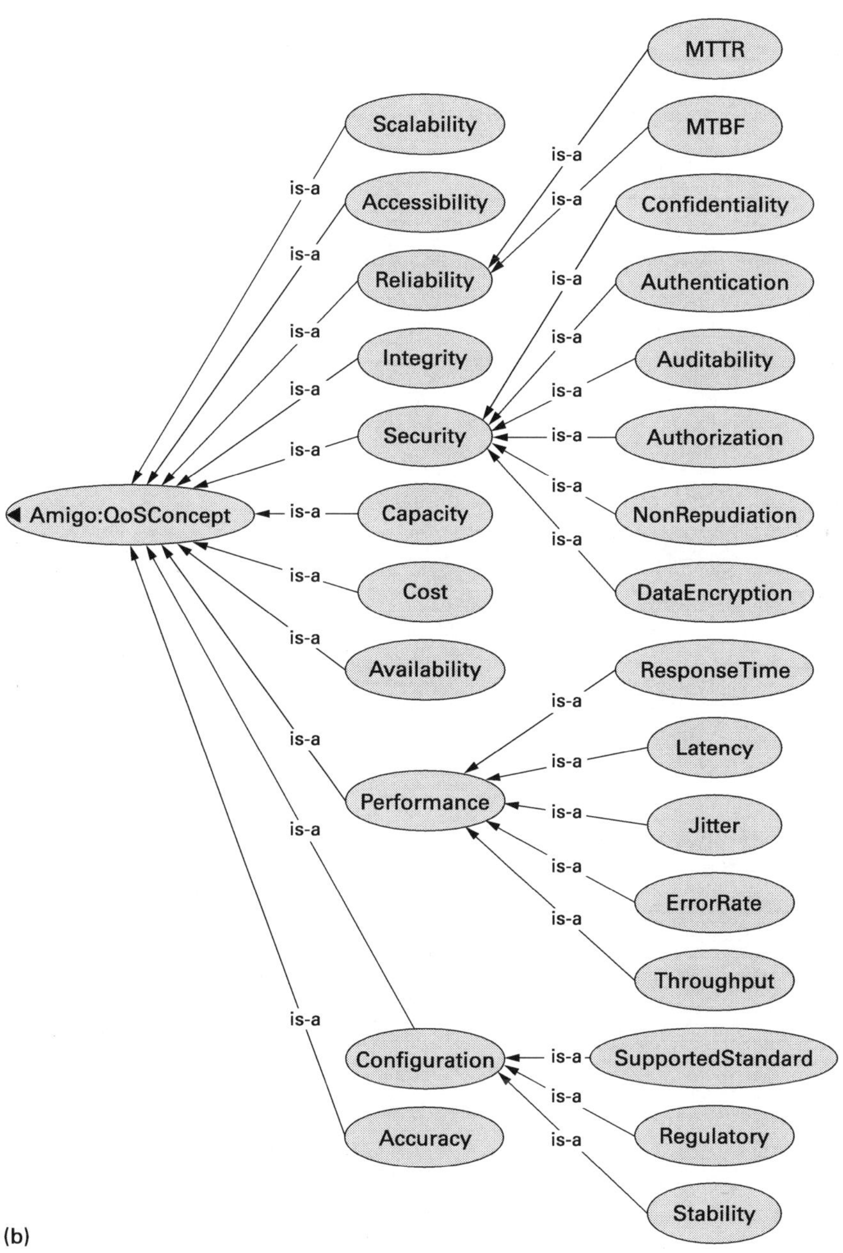

(b)

Figure 14.6
(continued)

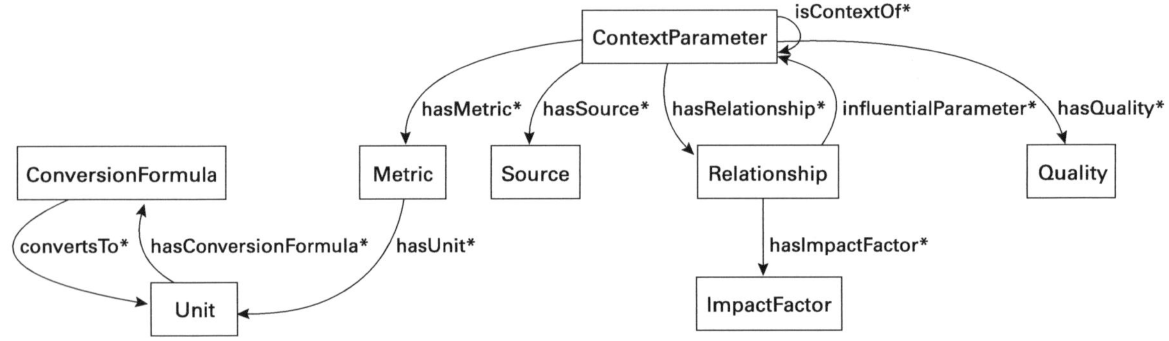

Figure 14.7
The Amigo Context (a) Language and (b) Vocabulary Ontologies

the QoS management system, as it demonstrates minimal complexity and thus has limited processing resource requirements.

The AMIGO context language ontology (ALOcontext) provides a standard generic mechanism for modeling arbitrary context information originating from various domains and is depicted in figure 14.7a. The main class of ALOcontext is the ContextParameter, which represents a piece of context information. We have structured ALOcontext similarly to ALOqos. ALOcontext is used to describe the information of each individual context type identified. These context types have been classified in the AMIGO context vocabulary ontology (AVOcontext) depicted in figure 14.7b, where all context parameters are instantiated as subclasses of the ContextParameter class of ALOcontext. Six core context domains have been identified in AMIGO that may potentially be used to build a complete information model of the conceptual and physical world: User, Social, Physical, Service, Device, and Network Context. Due to space limitations, we do not detail the ALOcontext and AVOcontext ontologies further.

14.2.4 Tool-Aided Semantic Service Modeling

As can be seen from the previous sections on the semantic vocabulary and language, the elaborated ontologies are pretty complex. Even simple ontologies can be difficult to access for nonpower users, not only end users but also domain experts such as application developers and service providers. In consequence, semantic service modeling can be a time- and effort-consuming process. Therefore, support tools are required to facilitate the adoption of semantic technologies.

Numerous freeware and commercial tools supporting development and use of ontologies are currently available: ontology editors, such as SWOOP,[21] Protégé,[18] and TopBraid Composer™[22]; application programming interfaces (APIs) for ontology languages, such as Jena[23] and OWL-S API[24]; reasoning tools, such as FaCT++,[25] Pellet,[26] and

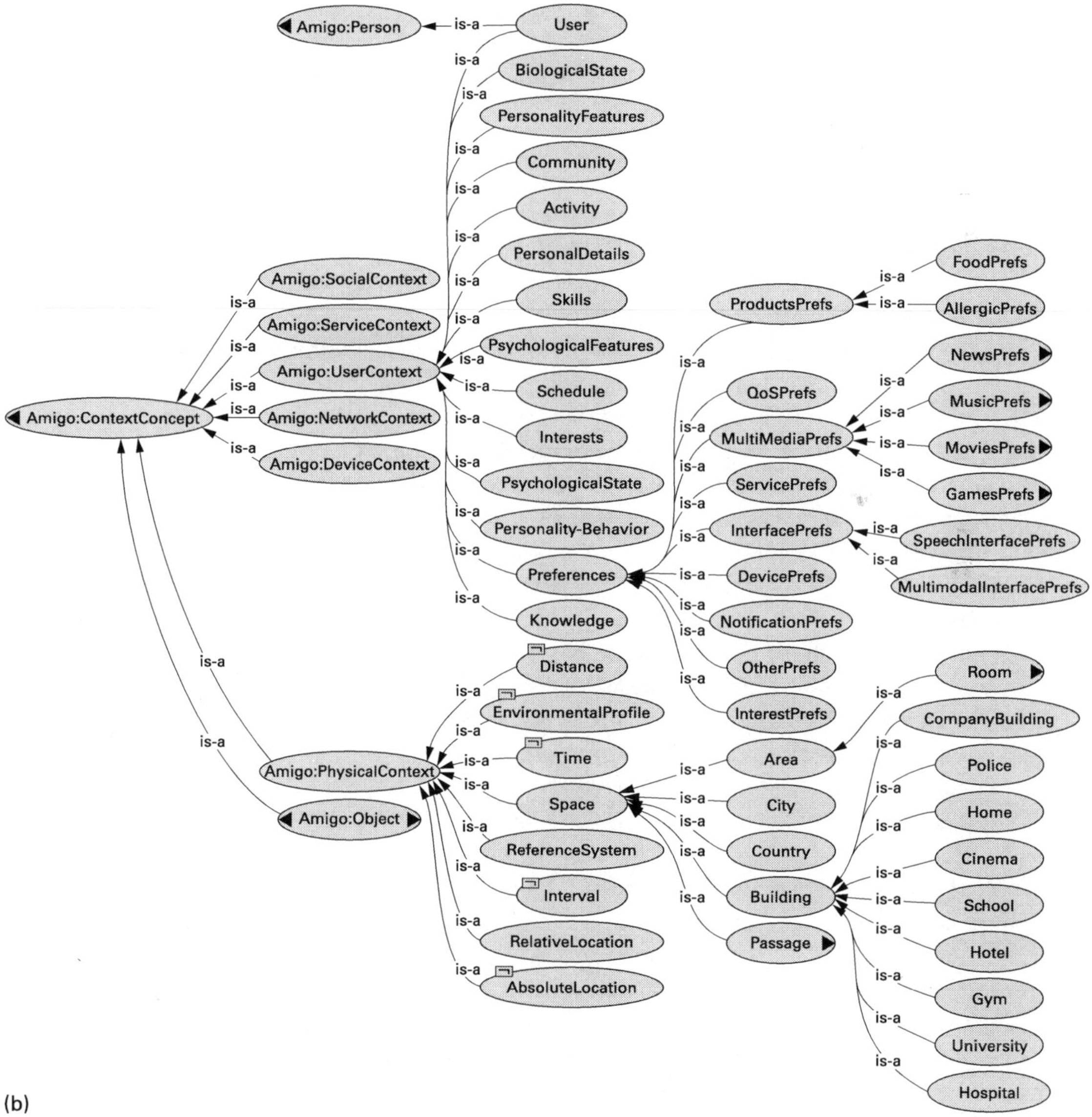

(b)

Figure 14.7
(continued)

RacerPro[27]; and service ontology-specific editors, such as OWL-S Editor[28] and WSMO Design Studio.[29]

However, what is missing in those tools, from the service modeling perspective, are features that would make the contextual semantic information related to service descriptions easier to understand, and foolproof to be used by an application developer. Moreover, the visualization support provided by generic ontology editors is limited to showing the abstract structural relations of the ontology classes and their instances. These tools are not well suited for the understanding of semantic relations in a complex, physical world or a dynamic application scenario, or for supporting creation of a model of such a scenario for application validation or testing purposes.

VantagePoint, the semantic support environment developed within AMIGO, is addressing the aforementioned shortcomings by visualizing the semantic information models related to contextual services in dynamic networked home application scenarios, and by providing visual editing as well as an interaction user interface for working with such models. It thus helps a developer to get familiar with the semantic information and rapidly start working with it.

More specifically, VantagePoint is an editor and viewer for contextual information described in OWL. Rather than providing a traditional class- and relation-oriented view for a designer, it displays a view of the application scene with rooms, objects, and persons (see figure 14.8) which form classes of the ontology. By clicking on these classes, the service developer can view and define relations in the ontology. By moving objects/persons, the constructed application can be simulated. A developer can use the visualizations to create contextual scenarios related to an AmI application in order to gain better understanding of the semantic models associated with the application.

VantagePoint provides two ways to visualize the spatial relations in the model: the bird's-eye view and the isometric view. The former is a ground plan view of the physical or abstract environment. It enables manipulating the model more accurately by making changes to its visual representation. The latter provides a 3D version of the representation, more intuitive and interesting to the user.

VantagePoint enables dynamic management of semantic contextual models. When a visualized model is manipulated by the service developer in the graphical view (i.e., devices and areas are added or removed), the changes are simultaneously added to the semantic model (i.e., OWL ontology files). The ontology classes can be related to external semantic information (e.g., semantic descriptions of services provided by a device). Such descriptions can be imported into the VantagePoint model to be further queried and used for service discovery and composition simulations. Various tools, such as the Protégé, OWL-S or WSMO editors, can be used to create and edit such information. Thus, VantagePoint is independent of the semantic language used to describe services.

VantagePoint uses the Jena interface to manage and query OWL ontologies. The tool offers a convenient user interface for specifying an SPARQL[30] query. Advanced users

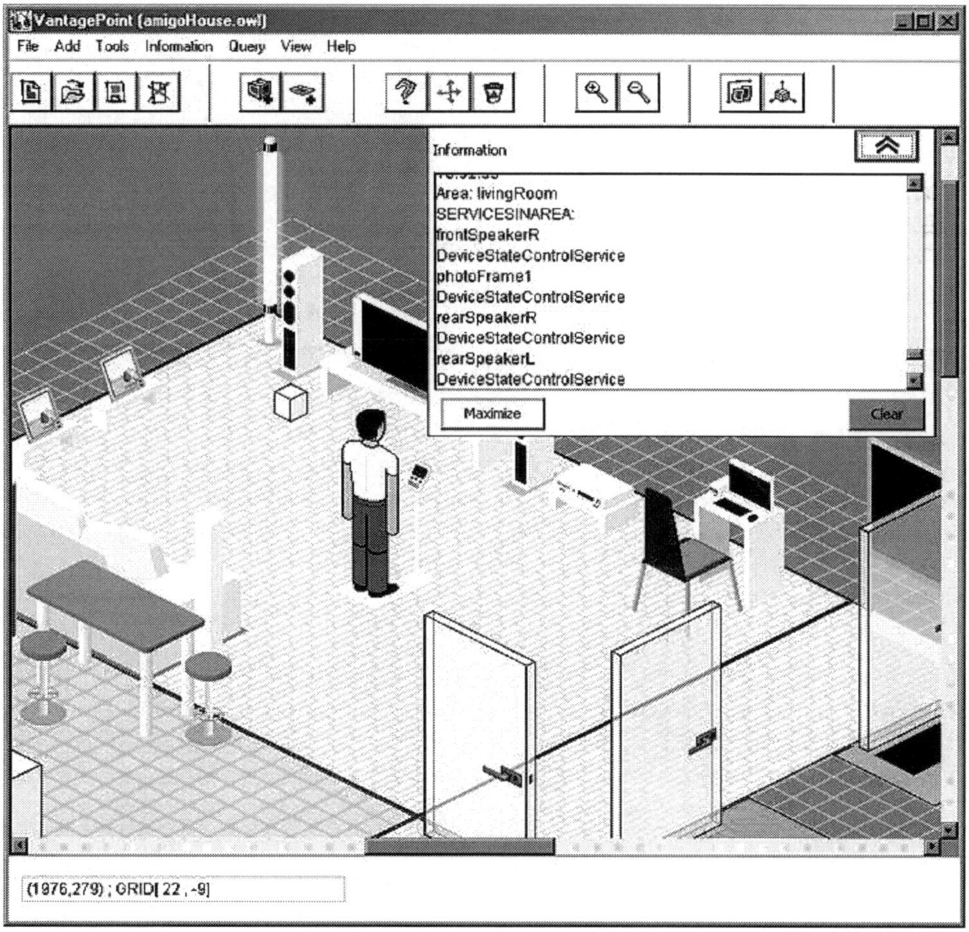

Figure 14.8
The VantagePoint tool

can specify their own sophisticated queries. For less advanced users, the tool provides some predefined query templates. Thus, information such as services presented in particular areas, services deployed by particular devices, status of devices, and information related to the persons located in the house can be easily obtained and provided to applications.

Simulation can be applied to see dynamic context changes in a much more illustrative manner than by observing changes in raw OWL files. Application developers can create visualizations of application scenarios and, by editing the visual model (e.g., moving items), simulate the contextual changes associated with the scenarios. Thus, they can see the results of semantic manipulations as in real life and notice practical errors without costly and time-consuming laboratory tests.

VantagePoint is still in the stage of development and improvement. Several real and imaginary home environments have been modeled using it. It has also been offered for testing to application designers within AMIGO. The obtained feedback is pretty positive. Furthermore, preliminary validation tests on efficiency and usability have been carried out. For example, time for loading the semantic model of an environment varies only a little, depending on the imported OWL ontology (3.3s for 999 versus 6.4s for 10230 RDF triplets). More information (tutorial, example source code, etc.) can be obtained online.[31]

14.3 Dynamic Integration of Interoperable Semantic Services

Based on the semantic service modeling detailed in the previous section, interoperability mechanisms can be elaborated at both application and middleware levels. We present herein an interoperability mechanism for dynamic composition of services focusing on the application level. To this end, we assume that middleware-level interoperability has been resolved by employing underlying middleware, the mechanisms evoked in the section on "Specification of Service Functional Properties."

Service composition aims at enabling distributed, dynamic, ad hoc, complex user applications to be deployed and executed in open AmI environments by exploiting the available services at the specific time and place. This system functionality may be decomposed into a number of functional steps. First, semantic service description, based on the elaborated language and vocabulary presented in the previous section, enables the composite service-based application and the component services to be described in a common, meaningful way. More specifically, services are accompanied by their concrete provided descriptions, and the application has an abstract required description and may thus be considered as an "expectation" not yet mapped on concrete service realizations. Furthermore, in open, dynamic environments, we do not know in advance either which services are available or their exact interfaces and behavior. Second, semantic service discovery enables locating in an ad hoc manner the available services that match semantically, and most probably approximately, the application's expectations. Third, a single service may prove sufficient for satisfying the application request; otherwise, service composition is carried out to combine a number of services toward reconstituting the application's required functionality. Fourth, as the composed services will most probably be close, but not exactly what the application expects, application adaptation is carried out to adjust the application's expectations to the available services. Finally, the adapted application is executed by invoking or orchestrating the single or multiple composed services.

Our objective has been to introduce a comprehensive approach to service description, discovery, composition, adaptation, and execution, collectively designated by the acronym SD-SDCAE. Regarding the SD part of SD-SDCAE, an application—coordinated by a user device and called a task—and services—located on several remote devices—are described by employing the AMIGO-S language introduced in section 14.2.2. Based on

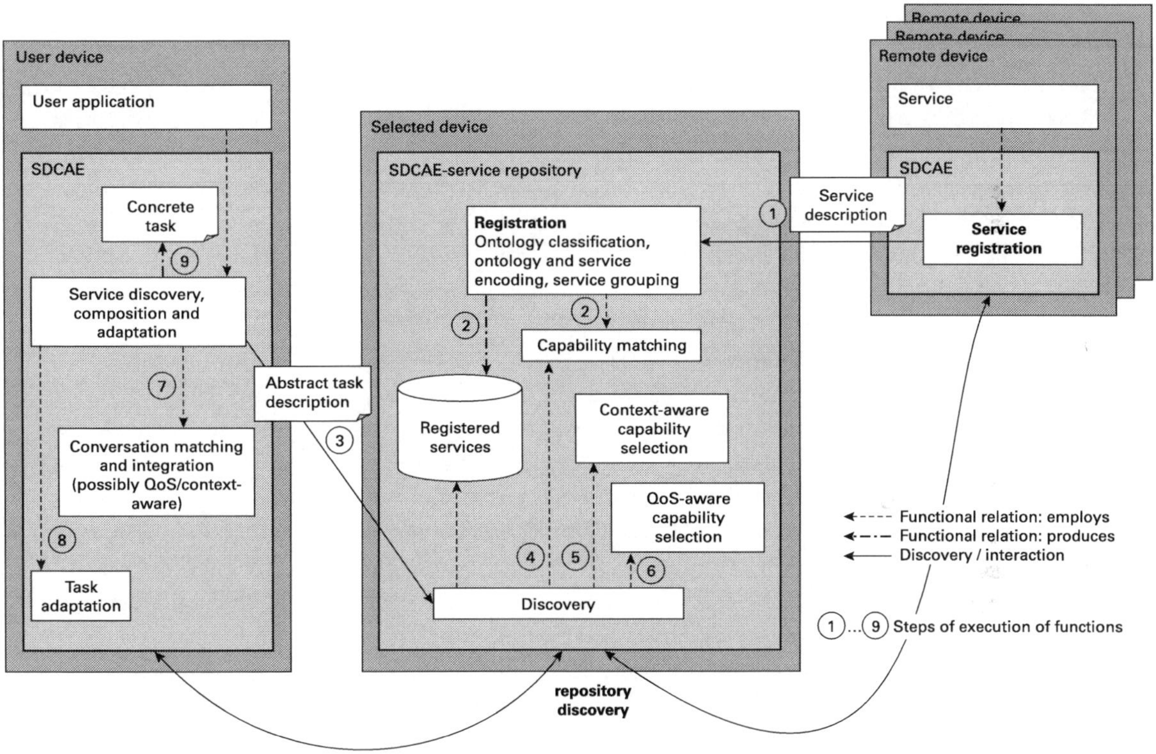

Figure 14.9
SDCAE reference system architecture (I)

the introduced SD, the objective of SDCAE is to enable the realization of applications by exploiting services available in the environment. We introduce a reference system architecture for SDCAE, which is depicted in figure 14.9. We identify SDCAE as a middleware-level functionality that is located on user devices, on other devices hosting services, and on a selected device hosting a service repository. The abstraction of a single service repository is only logical, whereas various realizations of the service repository may be physically employed serving different scalability requirements. SDCAE functionality is depicted in figure 14.9 as a sequence of steps discussed below.

In step 1, a service hosted by some device registers with the service repository by submitting its description. In step 2, registration of the service is treated internally by the service repository. In step 3, the user application located on the user device sends a discovery request for available services to the service repository submitting its abstract task description. Then, in step 4, the task description is matched with the descriptions of registered services in terms of capabilities, to identify services that may satisfy the application requirements.

Steps 2 and 4 have especially been the subject of our study and elaboration. First, semantic matching of service capabilities calls for adequate matching relations that not only can decide matching but also evaluate the degree of matching, as exact matching of the task's required capabilities with available service capabilities is rarely the case. Second, applying matching relations is based on the employment of existing ontologies and semantic reasoning tools; the latter are the object of intensive research within the knowledge representation community. However, such reasoning is particularly costly in terms of computing power and time; the most expensive part concerns classifying ontologies (i.e., producing expanded forms of them required for reasoning). Moreover, existing reasoning tools are not aimed at AmI environments, which involve resource-constrained devices and require acceptable response times for interactive applications. Thus, optimization is absolutely necessary for efficient semantic reasoning and matching within SDCAE. Optimization techniques in this direction include classifying ontologies offline and encoding ontologies—and, consequently, task and service semantic descriptions with numeric values, which reduces reasoning to numeric comparison. Furthermore, when matching within a service repository, a task description should be compared against all registered service descriptions. Grouping "similar" service descriptions in the service repository can provide another optimization to service matching and discovery. We have been working on efficient semantic service discovery and have achieved highly encouraging results so far, which are reported in Ben Mokhtar et al. (2006b).

After capability matching, context- and QoS-aware capability selection takes place in steps 5 and 6, respectively. This allows filtering out services identified in the previous step that do not satisfy the nonfunctional requirements of the application.

In the next step (step 7), conversations of services selected in the previous steps are integrated in an effort to reconstitute the task's target orchestration. We have been working on service conversation integration, where we translate conversations into finite state automata, thus transcribing the problem of conversation integration into an automata analysis problem. Again, results reported in Ben Mokhtar et al. (2006a) are highly encouraging in terms of performance.

Step 7 may be further enhanced by incorporating context- and QoS-awareness in conversation integration. This combines with the context- and QoS-aware capability selection of steps 5 and 6. A major challenge in this direction is to enable predictively aggregating context and QoS properties of the services being composed for assessing the context and QoS properties of the composition against the task's required properties. We have carried out initial work in this direction, which is reported in Ben Mokhtar et al. (2005a, 2005b).

After a successful composition of services, the task is adapted to the concrete services, in steps 8 and 9, to produce a concrete task (i.e., a task bound to concrete service realizations). Adaptation may include resolving syntactic incompatibilities between the task's required capabilities and the services' provided capabilities (e.g., in terms of names, data types, and order of input and output parameters); complementing or replacing parts of

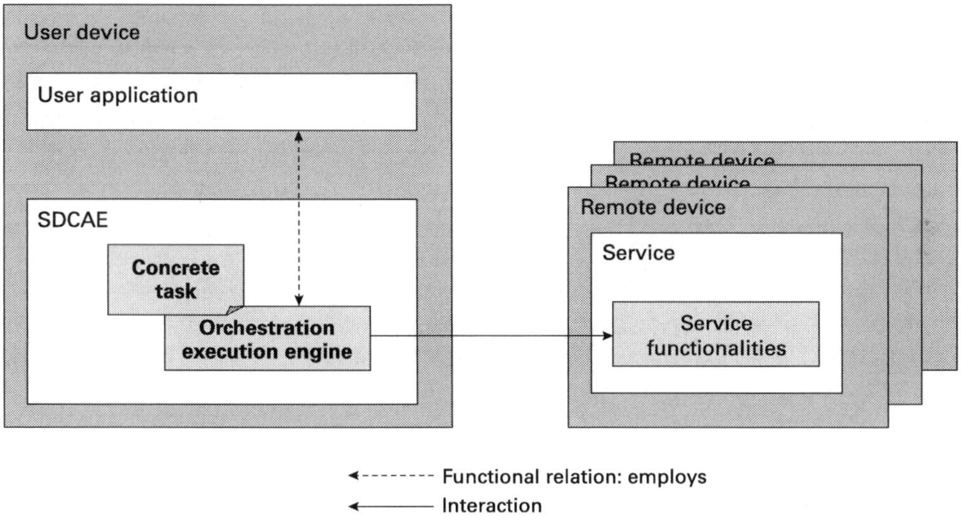

Figure 14.10
SDCAE reference system architecture (II)

the task orchestration with conversation fragments provided by the services; and possible adaptation in terms of context and QoS.

The final functional step of SDCAE is the execution of the resulting application, which is depicted in figure 14.10. To enable this execution, the concrete task description should be dynamically interpretable and executable by a specialized execution engine. So far, the descriptions of the task's orchestration and the services' conversations have been based on AMIGO-S, which actually adopts the process description language provided by OWL-S. However, OWL-S processes are not directly executable. Thus, we transcribe the concrete task into BPEL,[19] a widely used executable process language which, nevertheless, does not support semantics; thus, it could not be used at an earlier stage. Hence, finally, the concrete task runs on the execution engine, orchestrating the composed remote services to realize the target application.

14.4 Related Work

The AMIGO results presented in this chapter bring semantic services to the networked home environment. In this section, we discuss state-of-the-art research work in the related domains of AmI, with special focus on smart home environments, as well as semantic service modeling, engineering, and execution. By comparing with these approaches, we point out the contribution of AMIGO in these domains.

The Aware Home[32] project at Georgia Tech addresses challenges for the future home in a large experimental home laboratory. Research themes concern interactive experiences with people; sensing and perception technologies for awareness of human activity; social implications related to privacy; and context-aware software engineering (Dey et al. 2001). The latter work has influenced our approach to context discussed in section 14.2.3. At Xerox PARC, an approach called "recombinant computing" establishes preliminary interoperability between software components based on generic interfaces that any existing or future component may provide, irrespective of its specific functionality (Edwards et al. 2002). Full, specific interoperability between components is then enabled by leveraging mobile code. This effort supports ad hoc integration of components; however, it finally resorts to mobile code, which requires a specific support platform on every node. Whereas AMIGO interoperability is established at a semantic level, independently of the specific component technologies, interoperability mechanisms concretize the semantic interoperability into technology-specific mechanisms. In the PC and mobile domains, the EasyLiving project at Microsoft Research develops a prototype home architecture that allows typical personal computer-focused activities to move off a fixed desktop and into the environment (Brumitt et al. 2000). Device and service integration is based on an XML-based middleware. Hence, even if XML allows independence of operating system and programming language technologies, as in Web Services, EasyLiving enforces a specific service architecture on every home device. In the CE and domotics domains, a number of research efforts target device integration by imposing standard technologies. Thus, HAVi[33] (home audio/video interoperability) addresses integration of CE devices based on the IEEE 1394[34] bus standard, similarly to the InHoMNet[35] project. The Digital Living Network Alliance (DLNA)[13] elicits interoperability guidelines for media streaming systems. Finally, a number of technologies, each coming from a consortium of industrial players, such as OSGi,[36] UPnP,[37] Jini,[38] VESA,[39] Interactive TV,[40] DVB,[41] In-Home Digital Network (Bronnenberg 2002), and OpenCable,[42] are candidates for providing global or specific solutions to home networking middleware.

From the survey of related work, it is concluded that current research applicable to the networked home remains largely fragmented. Though employed paradigms come from fields where extensive research is being carried out, no attempt, to our knowledge, exists toward an open networked home system enabling integration of heterogeneous service architectures and the individual home application domains. The AMIGO approach is a big step toward this target.

Regarding semantic services, a widely employed approach concerning modeling, discovery, composition, and execution is OWL-S (Antoniou and van Harmelen 2004; Alesso and Smith 2004), which we discussed in section 14.2. Based on the Web Service Modelling Framework (WSMF; Fensel et al. 2002), another ontology called Web Service Modeling Ontology (WSMO; Roman et al. 2005) has been introduced. This effort develops both a formal generic ontology and a language for describing service functional and nonfunctional properties. WSMO includes mediators for resolving interoperability problems. A slightly different approach is proposed by the METEOR-S project.[43] METEOR-S aims to integrate base Web Services technologies, such as BPEL,[19] WSDL, and UDDI,[44] with Semantic Web technologies, thus enhancing existing standards, in order to automate service description and runtime. With respect to these Web Services-specific semantic approaches, the AMIGO approach is the only one that is not specific to a single service architecture: it integrates middleware-layer concerns, thus targeting interoperability between heterogeneous service technologies.

Some research efforts have focused on the semantics of the CE and domotics domains. Sommaruga et al. (2005) presents the DomoML-env ontology for household appliances, which uses parts of the European Home System, a home appliances classification. This approach enables element aggregation and integration of new devices into the home environment. However, each device is treated as a set of sensors and switches, without any specification-oriented characteristics, such as the protocols or software compliant with the device, which are essential in real-world applications. Another interesting taxonomy, not specific to home environments, is provided by Kim et al. (2005). In this work, technical specifications of CE appliances are attributes of an ontology that is used to map requirements and needs of different parties, enabling their communication via a common language. Whereas the presented CE and domotics ontology paradigms target only their specific application domain, the AMIGO semantic vocabulary approach attempts a global modeling approach of all application domains in the home, aiming to enable interoperability between them.

Regarding semantic QoS research, in Zhou et al. (2004) a QoS ontology language is defined that consists of three layers: the profile layer, used for matchmaking purposes; the property definition layer, defining property domain and range constraints; and the metrics layer, providing measurement details. A drawback of this approach is that the proposed ontology is quite limited, and the QoS ontology vocabulary is absent. The framework presented in Maximilien and Singh (2004) is based on agents. Service providers publish their services to registries, and service consumers use their agents to discover the desired service. The designed ontologies (language and vocabulary) enable agent-based dynamic Web Services selection. Although the proposed ontology language is quite complete, the metrics concept is absent. Tian et al. (2003) extend matchmaking mechanisms with the concept of the service broker. An advantage of this approach is that it enables users to monitor the status of the server. The proposed QoS ontology classifies QoS parameters in two main categories: network- and server/client-related. Nevertheless, it does not provide an advanced QoS ontology, but only a simple XML schema.

With regard to context-aware service modeling, SOCAM (service-oriented context-aware middleware; Gu et al. (2004) is based on a context model built around four main context concepts: person, location, activity, and computational entity (e.g., device, network, application, service, etc.). The context model is specified in OWL and addresses context sharing, reasoning, and knowledge reusing. It includes a generalized ontology and a domain-specific ontology which is coupled with the generalized ontology and is updated according to the changes in the contextual environment. COMANTO (COntext MAnagement oNTOlogy; Strimpakou et al. (2006) addresses the requirements of large-scale pervasive environments. It aims to support various stakeholders in sharing, collaborating, and synchronizing their context knowledge, thus providing a unified, well-structured scheme for semantic context representation. Nevertheless, it is not concerned with integrating the specified context semantics in service instances. SOUPA (Standard Ontology for Ubiquitous and Pervasive Applications; Chen et al. 2005) specifies OWL-based vocabularies concerning concepts such as agents, time, space, events, users, actions, and security. SOUPA borrows various terms from previous relevant work: the FOAF (friend-of-a-friend) ontology (Brickley and Miller 2003) to express personal information and relationships; the DAML-Time ontology (Pan and Hobbs 2004) to represent temporal constraints; RCC (regional connection calculus; Randell et al. 1992); and CoBrA (Chen et al. 2003) to incorporate spatial parameters.

For both QoS and context semantic modeling, the uniqueness of the AMIGO approach is that it introduces a generic specification not imposing any restrictions on what QoS or context may be in the networked home environment, thus allowing for interoperability and flexible specialization; we further provide one such specialization that particularly serves the networked home.

14.5 Conclusions

This chapter provided a selective description of the AMIGO middleware, focusing on the semantic service modeling and runtime functionalities it supports, and highlighting its advantages and innovative characteristics with respect to the related state of the art. The AMIGO semantic framework comprises the AMIGO-S service specification language and comprehensive vocabulary, a powerful combination suitable for the description of both functional and nonfunctional service properties in AmI home environments. The semantic modeling task is facilitated for the developer by the VantagePoint tool, offering a visual interface for contextual description and simulation of home environments. Finally, the efficient interoperable service composition mechanism deployed by the AMIGO middleware enables complex dynamic applications.

Throughout this chapter, it has been emphasized that the AMIGO project provides an open networked environment, which supports agile and seamless integration of heterogeneous devices, services, and service architectures. The AMIGO middleware architecture allows for various existent technologies, including middleware ones, establishing interoperability at the semantic level. It further supports semantically enriched services, integrating the four currently uncorrelated application domains within the networked home. The benefits for the AMIGO users are thus considerable, as they enjoy a rich variety of services that are transparently discovered, selected, composed, adapted, and integrated. Moreover, the provided interoperability, along with the context- and QoS-awareness of the services, offer a rich user experience. The AMIGO middleware with its semantic framework has the potential to promote the introduction of smart home services in the wide market and spread the advantages of ambient intelligence technologies over various user categories.

Acknowledgment

The work published in this chapter is partly funded by the European Community under the Sixth Framework Programme, contract FP6–IST-2004–004182 Amigo. The work reflects only the authors' views. The Community is not liable for any use that may be made of the information contained therein.

Notes

1. http://www.hitech-projects.com/euprojects/amigo/.
2. http://www.w3.org/2001/sw/.
3. http://www.w3.org/TR/owl-semantics/.
4. http://www.w3.org/TR/ws-arch/.
5. http://www.nessi-europe.eu.
6. http://secse.eng.it/.
7. http://www.fipa.org/specs/fipa00091/PC00091A.html.
8. http://www.daml.org/services/owl-s/1.2/.
9. http://www.w3.org/Mobile/CCPP/.
10. http://www.tv-anytime.org/.
11. http://www.fipa.org/specs/fipa00081/XC00081B.html#_Toc505481810.
12. http://www.openmobilealliance.org/.
13. http://www.dlna.org/home.
14. http://www.chiariglione.org/mpeg/standards/mpeg-7/mpeg-7.htm.
15. http://www.chiariglione.org/mpeg/standards/mpeg-21/mpeg-21.htm.
16. http://www.upnp.org/standardizeddcps/lighting.asp.
17. http://amigo.gforge.inria.fr/home/index.html.
18. http://protege.stanford.edu/.
19. http://www-128.ibm.com/developerworks/library/specification/ws-bpel/.
20. http://www.w3.org/TR/wsdl20.
21. http://code.google.com/p/swoop/.
22. http://www.topbraidcomposer.com/.
23. http://jena.sourceforge.net/.
24. http://www.mindswap.org/2004/owl-s/api/.
25. http://owl.man.ac.uk/factplusplus/.
26. http://pellet.owldl.com/.
27. http://www.racer-systems.com.
28. http://owlseditor.semwebcentral.org/.
29. http://www.wsmostudio.org/.

30. http://www.w3.org/TR/rdf-sparql-query/.
31. http://www.vtt.fi/proj/vantagepoint/.
32. http://awarehome.imtc.gatech.edu/.
33. http://www.havi.org/.
34. http://www.1394ta.org/.
35. http://cordis.europa.eu/data/PROJ_FP5/ACTIONeqDndSESSIONeq112422005919ndDOCeq1170ndTBLeqEN_PROJ.htm.
36. http://www.osgi.org/.
37. http://www.upnp.org/.
38. http://www.jini.org.
39. http://www.vesa.org/.
40. http://www.itvalliance.org/.
41. http://www.dvb.org.
42. http://www.opencable.com.
43. http://lsdis.cs.uga.edu/projects/meteor-s/.
44. http://uddi.xml.org/.

References

Alesso, H. Peter, and Craig F. Smith. 2004. *Developing Semantic Web Services*. Wellesley, Mass.: A. K. Peters.

AMIGO Consortium. 2005. Deliverable D3.1b: Detailed Design of the Amigo Middleware Core—Service Specification, Interoperable Middleware Core.

AMIGO Consortium. 2006a. Deliverable D3.2: Amigo Middleware Core.

AMIGO Consortium. 2006b. Deliverable D3.3: Amigo Middleware Core Enhanced: Prototype Implementation & Documentation.

Antoniou, Grigoris, and Frank van Harmelen. 2004. *A Semantic Web Primer*. Cambridge, Mass.: MIT Press.

Ben Mokhtar, Sonia, Damien Fournier, Nikolaos Georgantas, and Valérie Issarny. 2005a. Context-aware service composition in pervasive computing environments. In *Proceedings of the 2nd International Workshop on Rapid Integration of Software Engineering Techniques*.

Ben Mokhtar, Sonia, Jinshan Liu, Nikolaos Georgantas, and Valérie Issarny. 2005b. QoS-aware dynamic service composition in ambient intelligence environments. In *Proceedings of the 20th IEEE/ACM International Conference on Automated Software Engineering*.

Ben Mokhtar, Sonia, Nikolaos Georgantas, and Valérie Issarny. 2006a. COCOA: COnversation-based service COmposition in PervAsive computing environments. In *Proceedings of the IEEE International Conference on Pervasive Services*.

Ben Mokhtar, Sonia, Anupam Kaul, Nikolaos Georgantas, and Valérie Issarny. 2006b. Efficient semantic service discovery in pervasive computing environments. In *Proceedings of the ACM/IFIP/USENIX 7th International Middleware Conference*.

Berners-Lee, Tim, James Hendler, and Ora Lassila. 2001. The Semantic Web. *Scientific American* 284(4): 34–43.

Brickley, Dan, and Libby Miller. 2003. FOAF vocabulary specification. In RDF Web Namespace Document, RDFWeb. http://www.xmlns.com.

Bronnenberg, Wim. 2002. Interoperability in in-home digital networks. Paper presented at the IEEE 5th International Workshop on Networked Appliances.

Brumitt, Barry, Brian Meyers, John Krumm, Amanda Kern, and Steven Shafer. 2000. EasyLiving: Technologies for intelligent environments. In *Proceedings of the 2nd International Symposium on Handheld and Ubiquitous Computing*, pp. 12–29.

Chen, Harry, Tim Finin, and Anupam Joshi. 2003. An ontology for context-aware pervasive computing environments. *Knowledge and Engineering Review*, Special issue, "Special for Distributed Systems," 18(3): 197–207.

Chen, Harry, Tim Finin, and Anupam Joshi. 2005. The SOUPA ontology for pervasive computing. In Valentina Tamma, Stephen Cranefield, and Tim Finin, eds., *Ontologies for Agents: Theory and Experiences*, pp. 233–258. Berlin: Springer.

Colombo, Massimiliano, Elisabetta Di Nitto, Massimiliano Di Penta, Damiano Distante, and Maurilio Zuccalà. 2005. Speaking a common language: A conceptual model for describing service-oriented systems. In *Proceedings of the 3rd International Conference on Service Oriented Computing*. Berlin: Springer. LNCS 3826.

Dey, Anind, Daniel Salber, and Gregory Abowd. 2001. A conceptual framework and a toolkit for supporting the rapid prototyping of context-aware applications. *Human-Computer Interaction* 16(2–4): 97–166.

Edwards, Keith, Mark Newman, Jana Sedivy, and Shahram Izadi. 2002. Challenge: Recombinant computing and the speakeasy approach. In *Proceedings of the 8th ACM International Conference on Mobile Computing and Networking* (Mobicom).

Fensel, Dieter, Christoph Bussler, Ying Ding, and Borys Omelayenko. 2002. The Web Service modelling framework WSMF. *Electronic Commerce: Research and Applications* 1(2): 113–137.

Georgantas, Nikolaos, Sonia Ben Mokhtar, Ferda Tartanoglu, and Valérie Issarny. 2005. Semantic-aware services for the mobile computing environment. In *Architecting Dependable Systems III*. Berlin: Springer. LNCS 3549, pp. 1–35.

Gu, Tao, Xiao Hang Wang, Hung Keng Pung, and Da Qing Zhang. 2004. An ontology-based context model in intelligent environments. In *Proceedings of the Communication Networks and Distributed Systems Modelling and Simulation Conference*.

Kim, Wooju, DaeWoo Choi, and Sangun Park. 2005. Product information meta-search framework for electronic commerce through ontology mapping. In *Proceedings of the 2nd European Semantic Web Conference*. Berlin: Springer. LNCS 3532.

Lee, KangChan, JongHong Jeon, WonSeok Lee, Seong-Ho Jeong, and Sang-Won Park, eds. 2003. QoS for Web Services: Requirements and Possible Approaches. W3C Working Group Note. http://www.w3c.or.kr/kr-office/TR/2003/ws-qos/.

Mani, Anbazhagan, and Arun Nagarajan. 2002. Understanding Quality of Service for Web Services. IBM DeveloperWorks. http://www.ibm.com/developerworks/library/ws-quality.html.

Maximilien, Michael, and Munindar Singh. 2004. A framework and ontology for dynamic Web Services selection. *IEEE Internet Computing* 8(5): 84–93.

McIlraith, Sheila, and David Martin. 2003. Bringing semantics to Web Services. *IEEE Intelligent Systems* 18(1): 90–93.

O'Sullivan, Declan, and David Lewis. 2003. Semantically driven service interoperability for pervasive computing. In *Proceedings of the 3rd ACM International Workshop on Data Engineering for Wireless and Mobile Access*, pp. 17–24.

Pan, Feng, and Jerry Hobbs. 2004. Time in OWL-S. In *Proceedings of the 14th Annual Conference on Innovative Applications of Artificial Intelligence, Spring Symposium on Semantic Web Services*.

Papaioannou, Ioannis, Dimitrios Tsesmetzis, Ioanna Roussaki, and Miltiades Anagnostou. 2006. A QoS ontology language for Web-Services. In *Proceedings of the 20th IEEE International Conference on Advanced Information Networking and Applications*, vol. 1, pp. 101–206.

Papazoglou, Mike, and Dimitrios Georgakopoulos. 2003. Service-oriented computing. *Communications of the ACM* 46(10): 24–28.

Papazoglou, Michael, Paolo Traverso, Schahram Dustdar, and Frank Leymann. 2006. Service-oriented Computing Research Roadmap. ftp://ftp.cordis.europa.eu/pub/ist/docs/directorate_d/st-ds/services-research-roadmap_en.pdf.

Peltz, Chris. 2003. Web Services orchestration and choreography. *IEEE Computer* 36(10): 46–52.

Randell, David, Zhan Cui, and Anthony Cohn. 1992. A spatial logic based on regions and connection. In *Proceedings of the 3rd International Conference on Knowledge Representation and Reasoning*, pp. 165–176.

Röcker, Carsten, Maddy Janse, Nathalie Portolan, and Norbert Streitz. 2005. User requirements for intelligent home environments: A scenario-driven approach and empirical cross-cultural study. In *Proceedings of the Joint*

Conference on Smart Objects and Ambient Intelligence: Innovative Context-aware Services: Usages and Technologies. ACM Conference Proceedings, vol. 121, pp. 111–116.

Roman, Dumitru, Uwe Keller, Holger Lausen, Jos de Bruijn, Rubén Lara, Michael Stollberg, Axel Polleres, Cristina Feier, Christoph Bussler, and Dieter Fensel. 2005. Web Service modeling ontology. *Applied Ontology* 1(1): 77–106.

Sommaruga, Lorenzo, Antonio Perri, and Francesco Furfari. 2005. DomoML-env: An ontology for Human Home Interaction. In *Semantic Web Applications and Perspectives: 2nd Italian Semantic Web Workshop* (SWAP 2005).

Strimpakou, Maria, Ioanna Roussaki, Carsten Pils, and Miltiades Anagnostou. 2006. COMPACT: Middleware for context representation and management in pervasive computing environments. *International Journal of Pervasive Computing and Communications* 2(3).

Tian Min, A. Gramm, Tomasz Naumowicz, Hartmut Ritter, and Jochen Schiller. 2003. A concept for QoS integration in Web Services. Paper presented at the 1st Web Services Quality Workshop.

Tsounis, Athanasios, Christos Anagnostopoulos, and Stathes Hadjiefthymiades. 2004. The role of semantic Web and ontologies in pervasive computing environments. In *Proceedings of the Workshop on Mobile and Ubiquitous Information Access*.

Zhou, Chen, Liang-Tien Chia, and Bu-Sung Lee. 2004. DAML-QoS ontology for Web Services. In *Proceedings of the IEEE International Conference on Web Services*, p. 472.

15 Security and Dependability in the Evolving Service-centric Architectures

Aljosa Pasic, Daniel Serrano, Pedro Soria-Rodriguez, James Clarke, Pedro Carvalho, and Antonio Maña

15.1 Introduction

Traditionally, security and dependability have been regarded as secondary aspects in system design and development. They have always been treated as an afterthought and, in many cases, it was taken for granted that security and dependability (S&D) would be provided by external infrastructures. Therefore, ad hoc security and dependability solutions were developed to suit the specific needs of specific systems.

However, the "security-aware" belief that security must be a forethought and "built-in" component has gained popularity over the last few years. Although this belief acknowledges the need for integrating security into the design and development phases of information systems, in practice this integration has not yet been achieved. In current system development processes, security requirements are identified independently for each system component, such as servers storing and processing sensitive data or communication links using open networks, without explicitly considering the interdependences between them.

Today, rather standard security solutions or countermeasures (such as symmetric encryption, public key infrastructures, firewalls, and intrusion detection systems) are selectively employed for fulfilling typical security requirements such as authentication or confidentiality. Such security solutions provide "isolated" functionality, which is not always appropriate for the specific systems to be developed. These solutions may not even be effective for addressing the potential threats introduced by emerging environments such as service-based software systems.

Moreover, contextual information, such as legal requirements imposed by related laws and regulations, is usually overlooked or not given its requisite importance.

Assessment is an essential activity which should be performed in order to improve the existing system. During this activity, an analyst estimates current system state, identifies weak points, and proposes possible improvements. To perform the assessment, public standards such as the ISO/IEC 27002 (ISO 17799), the BSI ISO/IEC 20000 (best practices for service management processes), and, in some cases, the NIST Special 800 Series provide adequate detail for a general control framework. Moreover, the ISO/IEC 27002 (17799) and the BSI ISO/IEC 20000–2:2005 have specific practice recommendations regarding the infrastructure necessary to manage and apply security-related controls. Although cited as a fundamental requirement for proper and, therefore, certifiable application of the standards, neither the ISO 17799 nor the BSI ISO/IEC 20000–2:2005 defines a specific risk assessment method for determining the appropriate application of the controls. Furthermore, ISO/IEC 27005 (available 2007)—provides techniques for information security risk management that include information and communications technology security risk management and extend traditional approaches to risk management (Stoneburner et al. 2001; Freeman et al. 1997; Jenkins 1998; Bodeaum 1992; Alberts and Dorofee 2001; Bakry 2003; Mercuri 2003). The techniques are based on the general concepts, models, and management and planning guidelines laid out in part 1 of this international standard.

Other traditional approaches in security include the percentage of compliance with a security policy (Johansson and Johnson 2005b; Eloff and Eloff 2003; Eloff and von Solms 2000; Henning 2000). However, this does not account for specific needs of a particular system that ensures that the policy actually enforced corresponds to the formally described policy (the one whose assessment is actually checked by the above tools).

Threat modeling (Schneier 1999; van Lamsweerde 2004; van Lamsweerde et al. 2003; Sindre and Opdal 2000; McDermott and Fox 1999; Lin et al. 2003; Jürjens 2002) and approaches based on the economics of security (Bodin et al. 2005; Gordon and Loeb 2003; Schechter 2002, 2004a, 2004b; Schechter et al. 2003; Cavusoglu et al. 2004) evaluate designs of security systems (or system requirements) and analyze how the systems can be compromised. The approach is very subjective and, therefore, not very precise.

Experience shows that even for relatively small systems, it is difficult and often error-prone to fulfill security requirements simply by combining existing security mechanisms. Nevertheless, currently there are no development processes supporting the automatic and precise identification of security requirements and the correct choice of security mechanisms. On the contrary, expert knowledge in IT security is a prerequisite for applying existing security mechanisms. Unfortunately, such expertise is usually not available to the average system and software developer. Conversely, for large-scale systems, the complexity of the current and emerging computing environments and their security requirements has increased to the point where experience is not enough to guarantee adequate security.

The move toward services also increases the emphasis on relationships, negotiations, and agreements. This brings particular challenges for the area of security and dependability, which are traditionally very difficult to manage and measure. It also introduces the issue of accountability and liability, topics that have been heavily debated. The general assumption is that software and services will continue to be offered on a "best effort" basis, and so it becomes an interesting research question to understand how organizations can assure themselves and regulators that they have carried out due diligence in terms of setting up appropriate controls over their IT systems and processes, including security and dependability. In order to define which security actions and measures will be both required and beneficial for the evolving service architectures, a coherent framework for security actions and measures, as well as management of interactions and dependability on other architecture elements, has to be prepared.

There are a number of different factors and resultant consequences that should be taken into account when dealing with security in evolving service architectures:

1. Security is a nonfunctional requirement. Thus, it is difficult to capture with standard software design techniques.
2. Security is partly a human and social problem, and not just a technical one. Thus, it is difficult to capture in standard design languages.
3. There is no homogeneous way to represent security concerns and security mechanisms at different levels of software description. Thus, it is difficult to trace security issues along the phases of software development.

Although the current praxis of add-on security does not necessarily result in nonsecure systems, it has significant weaknesses:

1. The security requirements of the entire system may not all be satisfied by eliminating single, isolated weaknesses in the system. Furthermore, their fulfillment cannot be confirmed, since the requirements have not been clearly specified in the first place.
2. Different implementations of the system cannot be compared with respect to their security properties.
3. The security mechanisms introduced are not directly linked to the specific security requirements of the system. Linking between security mechanisms and requirements is particularly important in case of failures of security mechanisms, when the effects of attacks on the overall security of a system must be determined.

In order to achieve appropriate guarantees for the security of complex systems in open communication environments, the state of the art of development processes for secure systems has to be considerably improved. Such improvements should include methods for precise specification of security requirements and automated tools for classifying, selecting, adapting, and reorganizing existing security services, as well as for integrating them into software systems under development. Furthermore, special constructs for the expression of security requirements have to be integrated into existing modeling languages to support rigorous treatment of security issues throughout the entire development process.

In this chapter, we will present some of the results and conclusions from the ESFORS coordination action project (ESFORS Web site), which used focused workshops with the communities of ICT trust, security, and dependability, and software, services, and systems researchers, as well as an overview of relevant research initiatives, in which security and dependability issues are addressed at different layers of the NESSI framework (NESSI

Web site) and the research planes of the ICSOC road map (International Conference on Service-oriented Computing).

15.2 Security Engineering: From Foundation to Integration and Composition

The security engineering process lies at the very foundation of the ICSOC road map and NESSI framework. This discipline will draw together the areas of software and systems engineering, security engineering, and formal methods for the design and analysis of secure systems. In this manner, formal methods, a cornerstone for rigorous security engineering, can be made available for use within software engineering processes. Our vision of the process is that it must provide support to security engineers for the development of formally proven security solutions, but also to software engineers in the specification of their security requirements, the validation of their models against the security requirements, and the integration of proven security solutions into their models. We believe that this approach can be generalized to other fields as well, such as real-time systems, because it is based on defining a general collaborative framework that separates the work of experts in a specific field (security, in our case), allowing software developers to take advantage of the work of the experts and to integrate proven solutions into their models.

One of the main tasks of security engineers will be to analyze and define security properties. They will also use pattern design, formal modeling, and validation tools to create new specialized security solutions. They will formally prove that these solutions indeed provide the desired security services and, finally, they will integrate them into a library of security patterns. This library, in turn, will be used by system developers to fulfill security requirements in their models.

In order to include security requirements and solutions in the development process, we have to use some sort of common knowledge representation, for example, security patterns. A pattern describes a recurring problem that arises in a specific context and specifies a generic scheme with well-defined properties for its solution. Security patterns have appeared in the literature, where they have been used only as informal and often managerial measures of security, without any formal treatment and/or support for reasoning.

Security patterns, as well as other supporting mechanisms and measures (POSITIF Web site; S3MS Web site), should be semantically described. These semantic descriptions will include, among other characteristics, abstraction level, type of solution, applicability, context conditions, pre- and post-conditions, definition of parameters and, of course, the security properties provided or requested.

This semantic view of the security solutions enables us to move to more abstract levels and also to incorporate semantics about the context of application of those solutions. Additionally, it enables the implementation of the same security property through different S&D patterns, that is, different implementations of the same S&D class.

In summary, the semantic description of security properties and patterns enables the following:

1. The semantic categorization of patterns in a security solutions library, based on different parameters.
2. Considering the context of application of the pattern within the model, to locate the most appropriate pattern fulfilling the security requirements of the software model, based on semantic information.
3. Checking the interaction of different patterns providing different security properties in the model to be sure that such interaction does not cause cancellation or deterioration of some of them.
4. Validating the correctness of new security patterns incorporated by a security engineer.

At the next level of the NESSI framework (service integration layer) and the ICSOC road map (composition plane), we have to treat security aspects without separation from the treatment of other aspects (functional, performance, etc.) within the full software development cycle. Additionally, it should be possible to automatically process specifications in order to validate them and to find appropriate solutions in formally proven security knowledge bases.

In particular, we need methods that support the analysis of security requirements specified in the system models in order to find inconsistencies in the model (e.g., publishing confidential information on a public repository) with the aid of already defined semantic descriptions of the security properties.

We envisage that, for complex integration and composition of services, it will sometimes be necessary to compose different security aspects and properties before they can be integrated into the user model. Here, interdependencies between the newly integrated security mechanisms, previously introduced security, and the functional behavior of the system have to be considered.

15.3 Architecture for Secure Services

Web Services and software rely on the underlying architecture to guarantee a minimum service availability and protection of the information. Service availability is achieved with an architecture that is resilient to system failures (whether physical or logical). Likewise, the architecture needs to ensure that information leakage or manipulation at this level is not possible outside of the control of the upper layer (the services layer). This implies that network, storage, and computing infrastructures must be fitted with appropriate security measures to prevent service downtime and mishandling of the information transmitted and stored by these infrastructures.

A core problem for the infrastructure is how to ground service identity. Trusted Computing Group is working on provision of device identity, but once platforms have been virtualized, and components are routinely created, removed, cloned, and migrated, a sound and perhaps standard basis for reasoning about component identity will be needed.

Another problem is how to keep the management system separate from the "guest" services. This is a problem in current environments, as management agents normally have to run in the host operating systems of managed systems or applications. But the threat model is much greater in shared environments, where the managed services may be hostile both to each other and to the management system.

Many of the service infrastructure mechanisms may change the rules for how and where security should be applied and managed. As an illustration, today, IT departments concerned with application security have to worry whether the combination of application, OS, and network configuration produces the desired security. If trusted infrastructure can extend the richness and strength of enforced security policy, it will be possible to ensure that enterprise security policies are perhaps enforced independently of application configuration. For example, if an application is running on trusted infrastructure containing trusted services for identifying and isolating components, fewer account management and auditing controls will be needed within the application/service code. Similarly, if the infrastructure can dynamically deploy and enforce a security policy, there is less need for cumbersome processes to ensure that administrators are configuring and monitoring according to such policy.

15.3.1 Security Services in the Architecture

In addition to being secure in itself, the architecture needs to provide a set of security functions for use by the upper service layers. For instance, service providers will require identification and authentication facilities found in the architecture to establish authenticated communication with service consumers or other service providers. The architecture will also provide other basic security functions, such as tools to achieve confidentiality, integrity, or even nonrepudiation of information exchange at the service level. The service layer will make use of these functions in any number of possible combinations to obtain the desired protection of information, be it consumer-to-consumer security, service-to-consumer, service-to-service, or even within a subset of composed services.

We expect that a range of infrastructure security services will need to be available to higher-level services. For example, in the same way directory and single sign-on mechanisms simplify account management within enterprise IT architectures, there will clearly be a role for identity management services. The Liberty Alliance is already providing necessary standardization for interdomain identity management, but more may be needed to support identity services for fine-grained software components, services, devices, and perhaps other abstractions besides people. Moreover, grounding identity attestations will likely require new security services, such as integrity guarantees. Cryptographic techniques are likely to be used for these attestations, and this in turn makes cryptographic key management a necessary component or service.

The sharing of storage and network infrastructure implies research into mechanisms (encryption and/or policy enforcement, perhaps provided using virtualization as well as traditional storage and network components) to control this sharing. Moreover, new work is required to understand what service abstractions are needed to enable trusted deployment and operation in these shared contexts.

Finally, brought out by the assurance and audit requirements discussed in the scenario and business layers, there is the need for secure auditing services, applied both to the management system and for services within the infrastructure.

15.3.2 Securing the Architecture

In addition to the individual security technologies embedded in the architecture, other crucial elements are necessary for securing the architecture: security management practices and a system design in which appropriate and necessary separations are part of the structural properties.

Availability and information security properties in IT architectures must also scale, as architectures scale with the volume of operations or transactions they must support for the upper service layers. The nature of the architecture will also condition the security requirements of the architecture, for instance, in the case of an architecture that is deployed over different distant locations in contrast to an architecture that is confined to a single building. Securing the architecture will, therefore, be a process (as is the case with a proper security strategy) that needs to encompass requirements for various types of architecture properties.

Security policy tends to be stated in natural language and at a high/business level. The problem of how to translate these policies into the way security is managed at the application and infrastructure levels has been around for some time. Currently, organizations resolve this much more through people and process controls, rather than technology. Separating the problem into three layers has not removed this problem, although by introducing service notions, and focusing on automation, we provide a narrower context in which to study this problem.

15.4 Security Management and Monitoring

The service-centric view is also changing the way IT infrastructure and applications will be managed and delivered, and thus will be the context for end-to-end security management problems.

There are many aspects to security management. At the highest level, it is all about IT governance: What are the organization's IT-associated business risks, and are the controls/mitigations already put in place sufficient? Clearly, when the IT infrastructure is broken up into components being managed by different parties, and in many cases shared components, the whole methodology for creating controls and getting feedback will almost certainly change. Regulators and industries will still use traditional methods of assurance (i.e., IT auditors to ensure that the controls that have been endorsed are effective). Therefore, any change in approach to risks will have to be managed in conjunction with the audit community.

During the two years of the ESFORS project (2005–2007), there were several discussions in workshops between participants of FP6 RTD projects on the most appropriate methodology for the engineering of end-to-end security in service-oriented systems. Typically, European FP6 projects take either a top-down or a bottom-up approach to security requirement engineering. In GRID projects or projects focused on shared resource usage, the security of service-oriented communication infrastructures, for example, will depend largely on security implemented for communication between components through ESB (enterprise service bus). A set of trust, security, and dependability (TSD) message schemes and a set of common TSD command messages have to be agreed upon in order to use shared infrastructure. If the service bus is based upon a publish/subscribe pattern, we could also consider TSD properties an additional criterion for pattern refinements (besides service list or service functionality based). For example, a service composition layer could subscribe only on "trusted" services or only services with a specific minimum availability level.

On the other hand, in business process-driven projects, there are security requirements from end users that have been treated at the application level or business process level. Up to now, Business Process Management (BPM) tools have been used at design time and TSD has been often treated "as it should be," but the runtime environment and fine-grained security properties that are embedded in services now impose a new approach to BPM TSD design and control. One of the main challenges will be how to capture and treat high-level TSD requirements, how to use these during the service design and service-oriented integration, and how to link these to TSD of infrastructure elements.

Moving down a level, security management is also about managing security components and services. It will be very important to fold in expertise from current best practice for security management. Some of this is encoded in standards such as ITIL (ITIL Web site) and ISO 17799 (ISO 17799 Information Security Portal), but it is also important to gather input from different and actual operational environments. Financial decisions concerning spending on security will typically be made at a boardroom level by senior managers, and a security manager who is familiar with the issues and risks is not normally represented at this level. Measuring risk impact, usually done by estimations of service disruption cost or similar factors, may be straightforward, but quantifying savings that can be made through deployment of TSD mechanisms is a more complex issue. The change here will be how these current practices will apply and adapt when services are created out of aggregated component services of potentially different origin. Large numbers of factors need to be taken into account, including in-house vs outsourced security management, cost of the specialist skills and staff training cost, open source vs proprietary systems, existing ROI (return on investment) and ROSI (return on security investment) information, use of community knowledge (e.g., security patterns), trials and simulations, and use of CERT, Online Threat Model, and other decision support indicators.

Traditional computer security skills will be important to synthesize this data, but it will also be important to involve different skill sets. For instance, organizational and social scientists are likely to have a very different, yet relevant, view on how to assess the effectiveness of a people/process-based best practice in different contexts. Legal, risk, and auditing experts will be important to present different views on how agreements to share risk/security information between providers, as well as whether security agreements/contracts can be reached. However, it will be necessary to consider the inevitable challenges of integrating these diverse groups of experts, as gaps between requirements and capabilities may introduce additional challenges.

A key research question is how to deal with the complexity. Understanding the interdependence between technology components will be key, and even more important will be how to fold in operational and relationship-based factors. Research is required to understand any fundamental limits there may be to apply control over the IT. Similarly, what kinds of abstractions or models are appropriate to enable holistic or security governance and/or management of the aggregation of the IT an organization is using must be considered.

The resulting challenges are to find the right abstraction levels, techniques, models, and automated support of all aspects (people, processes, layers of technology, controls, practices, and so on) to drive configuration, evolution, and assessment of the security of services and/or the supply chain of federated services. Such an approach is needed to provide sufficient control and trust in the increasingly complex ICT systems upon which so much of the information society depends.

Appropriate models could provide a method to get to the heart of how to configure, change, and assess security of aggregated services; they should also drive the way we think about second-tier concerns such as SLAs, appropriate information sharing, trust, and assurance. Standards and protocols for access policy and audit should follow after these major concerns have been established.

15.5 Related Work

Although several approaches have been proposed for some integration of security, there is currently no comprehensive methodology to assist developers of security-sensitive systems. Lack of support for security engineering in those approaches for software systems development is usually seen as a consequence of (1) security requirements being generally difficult to analyze and model, and (2) developers lacking required expertise in secure software development. All this becomes a special concern when considering complex security requirements such as those associated with applications in e-commerce, e-government, e-finance, and e-health scenarios.

Existing approaches are not comprehensive enough in the sense that they focus either on some special stage of development (e.g., on design or implementation) or on a specific security aspect (e.g., access control). Moreover, they typically offer no guidance on how they can be integrated into current component- or model-based system development methods. Empirical studies confirm this view (Basin and Doser 2002; Jürjens 2001). In Jürjens (2001), the extension UMLSec of UML is used to express standards concepts from computer security, and it has been demonstrated on a process, with a combination of use case-driven and goal-directed approaches.

Concerning security for business processes, security aspects are introduced into business process and workflow models in Herrmann and Herrmann (1998) and Röhm et al. (1999). In this approach, security requirements are considered as inherent to business transactions and dependent on the circumstances of the applications. Although originally not based on UML, later work (Herrman and Herrmann 2002) includes an extension intended to support the development of an abstract UML-based business process specification. A model-driven architecture approach to security engineering, called Model Driven Security, is introduced in Basin et al. (2003). This approach, called SecureUML (Tryfonas et al. 2001), integrates role-based access control policies into a UML-based model-driven software development process. UMLsec (Vaughn et al. 2001) is proposed as an extension of UML for modeling security properties of computer systems, according to suggestions in Devanbu and Stubblebine (2000). UMLsec uses standard extension mechanisms to introduce new semantics into UML models but addresses only a few specific security requirements. Therefore, it does not support a security requirements engineering approach. Another recent approach proposes to integrate security and systems engineering, using elements of UML within the Tropos methodology (Castro et al. 2001; Mouratidis et al. 2003).

Use cases have been used to capture and analyze security requirements such as abuse cases (Sindre and Opdahl 2000), defined as an interaction between one or more actors and a system with a harmful result, and misuse cases (McDermott and Fox 1999), which describe functionality that the system should block. Use cases can describe requirements for special scenarios and are suitable to improve the intuitive understanding of security requirements.

UML lacks a formal semantics (France et al. 1997). However, a large community of researchers is currently exploring ways to close the gap between UML and formal specification languages. The work is supported by the UML Precise Group (PUML) (UML Precise Group), created for investigating the completeness of the UML semantics and for developing new approaches to using UML more precisely. We believe that new research results, maybe from FP7 projects, can complement this work by adding semantics for security and reliability requirements.

Several projects have been dedicated to issues that are relevant in the present context. The SEMPER project (Secure Electronic Marketplace for Europe; Lacoste et al. 2000) aimed at providing a comprehensive security framework for electronic commerce and business applications, concentrating on security architecture and services rather than secure systems development. The project COPS (Commercial Protocols and Services; Röhm and Pernul 2000) also concentrated on security services. COPS was intended to enable the design of an infrastructure for marketplaces supporting all phases of a market transaction. CORAS (Dimitrakos et al. 2002), on the other hand, aimed at developing a tool-supported framework for model-based risk assessment of security-sensitive systems. The methodology gives recommendations for the use of UML-oriented modeling in conjunction with risk assessment. Most recently, the CASENET project, whose main objective is the development of methods for the design and analysis of security protocols, started work on integrating security requirements specification into the process of application development. One of the most interesting approaches for introducing security into the development cycle is the one presented in Basin et al. (2003). Model Driven Security is a specialization of the MDA approach that proposes a modular approach to constructing modeling languages; it combines languages for modeling system design with languages for modeling security. This work introduces an application for constructing systems from process models, where they combine a UML-based process design language with a security modeling language for formalizing access control requirements. They are able to automatically generate security architectures for distributed applications from models in the combined language. There are more commercial tools, such as the ArcStyler® MDA-Security™ Cartridge (ArcStyler Cartridge Guide for ArcStyler Version 3.x for MDA-Security), which capture the skills of security experts and makes them available for other people who need to deliver secure systems. This tool uses an MDA approach also. Security engineering with patterns is currently a very active area of research (Schumacher and Roedig 2001). The Open Group is preparing a book on the subject (Open Group). Research into investigating a template for security patterns that is tailored to meet the needs of secure system development has been reported (Cheng et al. 2003); in it the UML notation is used to represent structural and behavioral aspects of design, and formal constraints to the patterns are used to enable verification.

The basic standard for security engineering is the SSECMM (Systems Security Engineering Capability Maturity Model). The model highlights the relationship between security engineering and systems engineering, regarding the former as an integral part of the latter and not an end unto itself.

15.6 Other Issues to Be Considered

15.6.1 Trust and Trustworthiness

It has been often said "Trust has no price, but it has enormous value," and in service-oriented software systems this becomes even more true.

In ESFORS and in NESSI Working Group on Trust, Security, and Dependability there are several notions of trust, ranging from the ones based on personal attitudes to the ones based on calculations that can be formally managed and evaluated.

Rapid adoption of ICT services depends on users and stakeholders trusting the technology, the service infrastructure, and the services (see iTrust 2005 for research contributions on trust). A crucial and complementary issue to achieving trust is the concept of trustworthiness of the components. This notion of trustworthiness is normally based on a set of assumptions about the adjudged behavior of the infrastructure entities on which to place trust. However, too many designs rely on assumptions that are not substantiated, potentially putting systems at risk. Meeting these assumptions without proper design and architecting principles is a hard task as computer systems become more modular, open, and geographically dispersed. The complexity of this task becomes overwhelmingly involved when simultaneous resilience against accidental and malicious threats is sought, as happens today.

At the ESFORS workshop held in September 2006 (report available at ESFORS Web site), a number of fundamental challenges were discussed and addressed:

1. Investigating the necessary but often forgotten link between trust (dependence on or belief in some system's properties) and trustworthiness (the merit of that system to be trusted, the degree to which it meets those properties or its dependability).
2. Investigating toward devising a global view of the relation between trust and trustworthiness, which encompasses not only the technological aspects (related to dependability, resilience, survivability, security, privacy, etc.) but also includes inter- and multidisciplinary fields that span ergonomics, usability, education, sociology, law, and governance.
3. Mechanisms to establish and maintain trust, both technical and nontechnical, with a special focus given to the use of service-oriented architectures, including difficulties in regard to security that can be related to the management of service contracts. Such difficulties include trust in process and service ownership (without a clear owner identification, the risk is extremely high for any organization), guidance, and authorization of dynamic reconfiguration of processes and services. These mechanisms should be mapped into the overall enterprise architecture vision, where a holistic view of dependencies can be depicted.
4. Mechanisms to develop solutions for trustworthiness, including, but not limited to, a discipline of secure services engineering; the provision of assurance of security and dependability properties for services and applications composed of them; the ability to validate these properties at design time and, in evolving architectures and applications, at runtime; and the ability to monitor, measure, test, and predict the security status of a system.

Among the several dimensions of trust are service provision trust (we trust a given service provider to offer a good service), delegation trust (we trust another party to act on our behalf), access trust (we trust an entity to access a service in the prescribed manner), and recommendation trust (we trust someone to recommend others for a given purpose).

If an ICT-based society is not be able to provide trustable services (services that are trusted because they rely on trustworthy components and trusted infrastructure), then such services, which nevertheless will be deployed owing to market pressure (1) will be perceived with suspicion by a large number of users; (2) information will be managed by a restricted group of "experts," increasing info-exclusion; (3) as it is managed, it may very well be mismanaged, becoming a big opportunity for cybercrime, e-fraud, cyberterrorism, and sabotage, which inevitably will result in a decrease in the number of users.

In regard to future software, services, and systems, trust will have to apply across the heterogeneous network infrastructure supporting the service-oriented architectures. The implementation, therefore, must follow both legislation and policy requirements that apply to a wide variety of networks and information servers.

The future trust research topics that were addressed in ESFORS workshops and NESSI WG meetings included some important subtopics:

1. *Security issues for trust management frameworks* We need to study the threat models that cope with malicious and cheating behavior of entities (collusion, defamation, free-riding attacks). Modeling, simulation, and validation techniques are necessary. In addition, trust often involves complex ID management issues, for example, those related to pseudonymity. We also need to consider privacy issues arising during trust negotiation, such as credential (attributes) disclosure.
2. *Introducing trust-related notions in service-level agreements* Service-level agreements must be able to deal with security requirements (e.g., authentication polices) as well as trust and dependability parameters. Contractual properties involving trust must be precisely defined. In addition, we need to define languages for expressing the desired service behaviors (normative behavior), as well as languages for representing evidence-gathering for supporting direct trust relationships.
3. *Autonomic trust management policies* Policy languages and mechanisms should be developed for continuously managing trust relationships, from their formation through evaluation, negotiation, and dissolution. Adaptive policy mechanisms should be developed, also based on advanced real-time monitoring frameworks. Both proactive and reactive monitoring techniques can be adopted (e.g., in case of negative events, the trust information could be spread to other users in a reliable way). Research in advanced policy languages, as well as on distributed enforcing mechanisms for specific trust policies, is also necessary.
4. *Semantics and ontology* Trust is often based on information context and tied to purposes. We need semantics models for exchanging and trading trust in different contexts and for different purposes.
5. *Integration with dependable building blocks* We need to study trust models associated with trusted computing. On one hand, trust models can use dependable building blocks to increase their attack resistance. For example, trusted computing has been proposed to mitigate a number of identity-based vulnerabilities quite common in trust models. On the other hand, trust models can be used to select the most trustworthy building blocks. This would force the manufacturers of dependable building blocks to improve the dependability of their building blocks, which are otherwise not used. In this latter case, although the

dependability of the building blocks cannot be managed, their dependability can still be improved. We need to study both sides of this integration between dependable building blocks, such as trusted computing or biometrics, and trust models.

6. *The value of trust* Trust is a derived demand: the need for trust arises from the booming growth of open networks. The value of a trustworthy entity/relation relies upon both minor costs incurred for trust failures and major revenues, when trust and confidence have a direct appreciation in the market (otherwise, we could think of some kind of pricing for trust and confidence through a utility function applied by the user of a trusted service).

15.6.2 Resilience of Service-Oriented Infrastructures

When it comes to resilience and dependability of services and service-oriented infrastructures (SOI), the separation within research projects is not always clear, as problems and solutions often overlap. The definitions from Servida (2006) describe dependability as a system property, survivability as a system capability, and resilience as a "system quality," which embraces both dependability and survivability because it captures the property and capacity of a system to (ideally) autonomously and gracefully tackle, adapt, respond, recover, self-heal, reconfigure, accommodate, and tolerate upsets/disruptions/failures/attacks.

In the Resist Network of Excellence (NOE; Resist NOE Web site), the first dependability issue that was identified for SOA applications was to improve the reliability of the runtime support of the Web Services (i.e., the platform on which the Web Service is executed). The second dependability issue is to tackle the problem at the level of actual SOA concepts (i.e., all protocols and software components used to interact with Web Services). Until recently, increased system performance or quality of service (QoS) has meant less security. Nevertheless, it is possible to build applications that gather the best of both worlds: high resilience at the level of arbitrary failure systems and high performance at the level of controlled failure systems. Distributed software paradigms, such as service orientation, have more places where faults can occur, but also have more potential for fault tolerance.

Through the innovative concept of architectural hybridization, several components with the capacity to tolerate vulnerabilities, attacks, and intrusions of different kinds and levels of severity are simultaneously supported (Hollnagel et al. 2006). For example, part of the system might be assumed to be subject to malicious attacks, whereas other parts are specifically designed in a different manner, to resist different sets of attacks. These hybrid failure assumptions are, in fact, enforced in specific parts of the architecture by system component construction, and are thus substantiated. In particular, trusting an architectural component doesn't mean making possibly naive assumptions about what a hacker can or can't do to that component. Instead, the component is specifically constructed to resist a well-defined set of attacks.

Resilience engineering in service architectures should rely on understanding safety and why accidents happen. In this, two significant insights become perceptible:

1. Adverse events are more often due to an unfortunate combination of a number of conditions than to the failure of a single function or component.
2. Failures are the reverse side of successes, meaning that if one doesn't hold, the other will, undesirably, take its place.

Both of these have their origin in performance variability and complement each other. The failure mechanisms behind adverse events are simply not known beforehand; otherwise, damage would have been avoided (hindsight approach). If we think of resilience as the ability to recover from or adjust easily to misfortune or change, as well as the capacity of systems to anticipate and adapt to the potential for surprise and failure, it becomes clear that this notion had gradually emerged as the logical way to overcome the limitations of existing approaches to risk assessment and system safety. Resilience engineering in service architectures is a paradigm that focuses on how to help people cope with the complexity of these architectures under pressure to achieve success, strongly contrasting with what is typical today (i.e., a paradigm of tabulating an error as if it were a thing, followed by interventions to reduce this count). One measure of resilience is, therefore, the ability to create foresight in order to anticipate the changing shape of risk before failure and harm occur.

Since the service-oriented infrastructure is going to be owned and managed by different stakeholders, each of its constituents can interact in many different, and sometimes unpredictable, ways, to a major extent owing to the concurrence existing between their functions and the intrinsic and surrounding events of the system. Modeling the accidents occurring in these systems in a way to understand their causes and gather knowledge to be further applied in a retrospective approach, in order to quickly react and avoid the same consequences, is not enough if we seek to provide the system with a much more powerful capacity which is to adapt itself in the face of major stress or misfortune. Therefore, we shall also be able to proactively perform some measurements of risk assessment for service-oriented infrastructures in a way to predict and avoid accidents, or at least to minimize their occurrence as much as possible.

In the European project DESEREC (DESEREC Web site), for example, a combination of three dimensions has been selected to deal with resilience in critical infrastructures: modeling and simulation approach, detection mechanisms, and response including reconfiguration. A similar combination could be applied to resilience in service infrastructures. Runtime reconfiguration is also considered in the FP6 project SERENITY (SERENITY Web site). In the IRRIIS project (IRRIIS Web site), on the other hand, the focus is on middleware components that would help to increase dependability, survivability, and resilience of infrastructures. Although resilience in service-oriented infrastructures has been investigated in the above-mentioned projects, which have ICT infrastructures as a part of critical infrastructures, resilience engineering for services has not yet been sufficiently addressed. The participants of the Resist NOE (Resist NOE Web site) collaborated with the ESFORS project on the common position paper that targets this issue. Resilient services should meet 4 criteria:

1. Availability (Is this service running right now?)
2. Reliability (How long can it run without failure?)
3. Safety (What will happen if the service fails?)
4. Maintainability (How easy is it to fix the service?).

One of the important issues will be classification of faults in services and service-oriented infrastructures (transient faults, intermittent faults, permanent faults) which lead to errors and failures in service-oriented software systems. An equally important issue is the business process resilience that relates to a group of services, and where design issues have to consider trade-offs between points of failure and efficiency. Service and process resilience is also considered in HIDENETS (HIDENETS Web site) in analyses of end-to-end resilience solutions for distributed applications and mobility-aware services in ubiquitous communication scenarios, such as ad hoc car-to-car communication with infrastructure service support. The use of off-the-shelf services and communication links will dramatically decrease the costs of market entry, and hence make such ubiquitous scenarios commercially feasible. However, as HIDENETS correctly mentions, if services and other software components are unreliable, even if we have reliable service-oriented infrastructures, the end-to-end system-level resilience solutions will not be satisfactory.

15.6.3 Privacy and Identity

Service providers will likely want to take advantage of the opportunity to provide offers that are highly personalized as the customer's needs become more numerous, specialized, and refined. However, user confidence is threatened by a lack of widely deployed and accepted privacy technologies that protect their personal data and let them feel comfortable with the security and privacy, and thus are reluctant to actively embrace the offered services. The release of personal data, therefore, must be under the customer's control. The service and its customers must have the means to build and sustain a trust relationship, like those proposed in European PRIME project (PRIME Web site). PRIME also proposed seven technical design principles for privacy-enhancing identity management:

1. Design must start from maximum privacy.
2. Explicit privacy rules govern system usage.
3. Privacy rules must be enforced, not just stated.
4. Privacy enforcement must be trustworthy.
5. Users need easy and intuitive abstractions of privacy.
6. Privacy needs an integrated approach.
7. Privacy must be integrated with applications.

Context-aware and personalized services that have to comply with current legislation such as the 2002/58/EC directive, which requires explicit consensus for the use of privacy-sensitive location, are the subject of the European FP6 project CONNECT (CONNECT Web site). The objective of this project is to satisfy users' need to control their context/

location privacy and, at the same time, the need to minimize the demands of user interaction for privacy authorization.

Project DISCREET (DISCREET Web site) has a very similar goal: to minimize and control the amount of personalized information made available in context-aware and personalized services. The project will develop a technical realization of a distributed unit of trust, which protects and keeps the data required for the subsystems of a complex networked service separate, using, for instance, anonymization and encryption techniques to make sure that only the absolutely necessary data will be provided to subsystems and subservices.

Similar user-centric connotations hold for service interaction with any identity system. A new identity ecosystem will need to provide systems that are flexibly accessible to people and services. This will require openness between system components and agreed-upon trust mechanisms. Identity data existing in multiple locations are commonplace, whether this is for political, physical, or legal reasons. However, the collection of fragmented identity data is becoming an increasing requirement of organizations for use by applications, as well as identity and access management solutions. A virtual view of identity data does not copy or synchronize data, as there should also be a requirement to provide a real-time view of data, which may exist in multiple deferring data repositories, such as directories or databases.

Another issue related to service ecosystems and identity management is that identities must be verified and approved before creation. This becomes a collaborative effort between people and services. Once created, the identity records and associated information must be maintained and updated as user access requirements change, and as policies change. Provisioning and identity management solutions simplify and automate such tasks as much as possible. Changes to the identity profile and access records are made from creation through user job role changes, policy changes, and up to and including employee termination or reassignment.

Finally, at the end of the identity control life cycle, it is often necessary to repudiate identity. This can involve invalidating or disabling a previously valid identity, its access profiles, and its authorization.

Research activities in the EU project FIDIS (fidis.net) include "identity of identity," profiling, interoperability of IDs and ID management systems, forensic implications, de-identification, high-tech ID, mobility, and identity.

15.7 Conclusion

Although the current praxis and solutions in TSD do not necessarily result in nonsecure service systems, they have significant weaknesses, such as that the security requirements usually focus on eliminating single, isolated weaknesses in the system. Often their fulfillment cannot be confirmed since the requirements have not been clearly specified in the first place and, in addition, different implementations and compositions of the service systems cannot be compared with respect to their security properties. This situation has begun to change, and both commercial software developers and the research community have started to pay due attention to TSD requirements right from the early phases of software and system engineering. Weaknesses are still found, but new efforts are emerging to address TSD requirements and problems in software and system engineering, to create architectures that include security services, and to provide security mechanisms embedded in these architectures.

However, in order to achieve the end-to-end vision of security, the individual security technologies embedded in the architecture layers need security management practices and a system design in which appropriate and necessary separations are part of the structural properties. Securing the architecture will therefore be a process (as is the case with a proper security strategy) that needs to encompass requirements from various types of architecture properties and different stakeholders.

Acknowledgments

The work published in this chapter is partly funded by the European Community under the Sixth Framework Programme, contract FP6–027599 ESFORS, within the Unit D4, ICT for Trust, Security and Dependability. The work reflects only the authors' views. The Community is not liable for any use that may be made of the information contained herein. Contributions to this chapter were also made by the European Technology Platform NESSI Working Group "Trust, Security and Dependability" members.

References

Alberts, C. J., and Dorofee, A. J. 2001. OCTAVE Criteria. Technical Report CMU/SEI-2001–TR-016, CERT.

ArcStyler Cartridge Guide for ArcStyler Version 3.x for MDA-Security. http://www.interactive-objects.com/products/mda-extensions/mda-security-with-arcstyler.

Bakry, S. H. 2003. Development of security policies for private networks. *International Journal of Network Management* 13, no. 3: 203–210.

Basin, D., and Doser, J. 2002. SecureUML: A UML-based modeling language for model-driven security. In *Proceedings of the 5th International Conference on the Unified Modeling Language*. Berlin: Springer. LNCS 2460.

Basin, D., Doser, J., and Lodderstedt, T. 2003. Model driven security for process-oriented systems. In *Proceedings of the Eighth ACM Symposium on Access Control Models and Technologies*, pp. 100–109. New York: ACM Press.

Bodeaum, D. 1992. A conceptual model for computer security risk analysis. In *Proceedings of the 8th Annual Computer Security Applications Conference*, pp. 56–63. New York: IEEE Computer Society Press.

Bodin, L. D., Gordon, L. A., and Loeb, M. P. 2005. Evaluating information security investments using the analytic hierarchy process. *Communications of the ACM* 48 , no. 2: 78–83.

Castro, J., Kolp, M., and Mylopoulos, J. 2001. A requirements-driven development methodology. In *Proceedings of the 13th International Conference on Advanced Information Systems Engineering*. Cavusoglu, H., Mishra, B., and Raghunathan, S. 2004. A model for evaluating IT security investments. *Communications of the ACM* 47, no. 7: 87–92.

Cheng, B. H. C., Konrad, S., Campbell, L. A., and Wassermann, R. 2003. Using Security Patterns to Model and Analyze Security Requirements. Technical Report MSU-CSE-03–18, Department of Computer Science, Michigan State University.

CONNECT Web site. http://www.ist-connect.eu.

DESEREC Web site. http://www.deserec.eu.

Devanbu, P. T., and Stubblebine, S. G. 2000. Software engineering for security. In *Proceedings of the 22nd International Conference on Software Engineering*. New York: ACM Press.

Dimitrakos, T., Raptis, D., Ritchie, B., and Stølen, K. 2002. Model based security risk analysis for web applications. In *Proceedings of Euroweb 2002*. DISCREET Web site. http://www.ist-discreet.org.

Eloff, J., and Eloff, M. 2003. Information security management—A new paradigm. In *Proceedings of the South African Institute of Computer Scientists and Information Technologists*, pp. 130–136.

Eloff, M. M., and von Solms, S. H. 2000. Information security management: An approach to combine process certification and product evaluation. *Computers & Security* 19, no. 8: 698–709.

ESFORS Web site. http://www.esfors.org.

Fidis Web site. http://www.fidis.net.

France, R., Evans, A., Lano, K., and Rumpe, B. 1997. The UML as a formal modeling notation. Presented at *OOPSLA'97 Workshop on Object-Oriented Behavioral Semantics*.

Freeman, J. W., Darr, T., and Neely, R. B. 1997. Risk assessment for large heterogeneous systems. In *Proceedings of the 13th Annual Computer Security Applications Conference*, pp. 44–50. New York: IEEE Computer Society Press.

Gordon, L., and Loeb, M. 2003. The economics of information security investment. *ACM Transactions on Information and System Security* 5, no. 4: 438–457.

Henning, R. 2000. Security service level agreements: Quantifiable security for the enterprise? In *Proceedings of the 1999 Workshop on New Security Paradigms*, pp. 54–60. New York: ACM Press.

Herrmann, G., and Pernul, G. 1998. Viewing business process security from different perspectives. In *Proceedings of the 11th International Bled Electronic Commerce Conference: Electronic Commerce in the Information Society*.

Herrmann, P., and Herrmann, G. 2002. Security-oriented refinement of business processes. In *Proceedings of the 5th International Conference on Electronic Commerce Research*.

Herrmann, P., Issarny, V., and Shiu, S. (Eds.). 2005. Trust management. In *Proceedings of the Third International Conference*, iTrust 2005, Lecture Notes in Computer Science, vol. 3477.

HIDENETS Web site. http://www.hidenets.aau.dk.

Hollnagel, Erik, Woods, David D., and Leveson, Nancy. 2006. *Resilience Engineering—Concepts and Precepts*. Aldershot, UK: Ashgate.

International Conference on Service-Oriented Computing. http://www.icsoc.org/.

IRRIIS Web site. http://www.irriis.org.

ISO 17799 Information Security Portal. http://www.computersecuritynow.com.

ITIL Web site. http://www.itil.co.uk/.

Jenkins, B. D. 1998. Security Risk Analysis and Management. Technical Report, Countermeasures, Inc.

Johansson, E., and Johnson, P. 2005a. Assessment of enterprise information security—An architecture theory diagram definition. In *Proceedings of the 3rd Annual Conference on System Engineering Research*.

Johansson, E., and Johnson, P. 2005b. Assessment of enterprise information security—Estimating the credibility of the results. In *Proceedings of the Symposium on Requirements Engineering for Information Security*.

Jürjens, J. 2001. *Towards Development of Secure Systems Using UMLsec*. Berlin: Springer. LNCS 2029.

Jürjens, J. 2002. Using UMLsec and goal trees for secure systems development. In *Proceedings of the 2002 ACM Symposium on Applied Computing*, pp. 1026–1030. New York: ACM Press.

Lacoste, G., Pfitzmann, B., Steiner, M., and Waidner, M. 2000. *SEMPER—Secure Electronic Marketplace for Europe*. Berlin: Springer.LNCS 1854.

Lin, L.-C., Nuseibeh, B., Ince, D., Jackson, M., and Moffett, J. 2003. Analysing Security Threats and Vulnerabilities Using Abuse Frames. Technical Report 2003/10, The Open University.

McDermott, J., and Fox, C. 1999. Using abuse case models for security requirements analysis. In *Proceedings of the 15th Annual Computer Security Applications Conference*, pp. 55–66.

Mercuri, R. T. 2003. Analyzing security costs. *Communications of the ACM* 46, no. 6: 15–18.

Mouratidis, H., Giorgini, P., and Manson, G. 2003. Integrating security and systems engineering: Towards the modelling of secure information systems. In *Proceedings of the 15th Conference on Advanced Information Systems Engineering*.

NESSI Web site. http://www.nessi-europe.com/Nessi/.

Open Group. Draft version of the Security Design Patterns technical guide available at http://www.opengroup .org/security/gsp.htm.

POSITIF Web site. http://www.positif.org.

PRIME Web site. http://www.prime-project.eu.org.

resist NoE Web site. http://www.resist-noe.org.

Röhm, A. W., Herrmann, G., and Pernul, G. 1999. A language for modelling secure business transactions. In *Proceedings of the IEEE Annual Computer Security Application Conference*.

Röhm, A. W., and Pernul, G. 2000. COPS: A model and infrastructure for secure and fair electronic markets. *International Journal on Decision Support Systems* 29, no. 4: 343–355.

S3MS Web site. http://www.s3ms.org.

Schechter, S. 2002. How to buy better testing. In *Proceedings of the International Conference on Infrastructure Security*. Berlin: Springer. LNCS 2437, pp. 73–87.

Schechter, S. E. 2004a. Computer Security Strength & Risk: A Quantitative Approach. Technical Report, Harvard University.

Schechter, S. E. 2004b. Toward econometric models of the security risk from remote attacks. In *Proceedings of the Third Annual Workshop on Economics and Information Security*.

Schechter, S. E., and Smith, M. D. 2003. How much security is enough to stop a thief? In *Proceedings of the 7th International Conference on Financial Cryptography*.

Schneier, B. 1999. Attack trees: Modelling security threats. *Dr. Dobb's Journal*, 24 no. 12: 21–29.

Schumacher, M., and Roedig, U. 2001. Security engineering with patterns. In *Pattern Languages of Programs 2001*.

SERENITY Web site. http://www.serenity-project.org.

Servida, A. 2006. Security and resilience in information society: The European approach. Paper presented at *International Conference on Emerging Trends in Information and Communication Security*.

Sindre, G., and Opdahl, A. L. 2000. Eliciting security requirements by misuse cases. In *Proceedings of TOOLS Pacific 2000*, pp. 120–131. New York: IEEE Computer Society Press.

Stoneburner, G., Goguen, A., and Feringa, A. 2001. Risk Management Guide for Information Technology Systems. Technical Report 800–30, National Institute of Standards and Technology. Available via http://csrc.nist.gov/publications/nistpubs/800–30/sp800–30.pdf.

Systems Security Engineering Capability Maturity Model (SSE-CMM). Model Description Document Version 3.0. Available at http://www.sse-cmm.org/model/ssecmmv2final.pdf.

Tryfonas, T., Kiountouzis, E., and Poulymenakou, A. 2001. Embedding security practices in contemporary information systems development approaches. *Information Management & Computer Security* 9, no. 4: 183–197.

UML Precise Group. http://www.puml.org.

van Lamsweerde, A. 2004. Elaborating security requirements by construction of intentional anti-models. In *Proceedings of the 26th International Conference on Software Engineering*, pp. 148–157.

van Lamsweerde, A., Brohez, S., De Landtsheer, R., and Janssens, D. 2003. From system goals to intruder anti-goals: Attack generation and resolution for security requirements engineering. In *Proceedings of the International Workshop on Requirements for High Assurance Systems*, pp. 49–56.

Vaughn, R., Henning, R., and Fox, K. 2001. An empirical study of industrial security engineering practices. *Journal of Systems and Software* (November) 61, no. 3: 225–232.

16 GridTrust—A Usage Control-Based Trust and Security Framework for Service-Based Grids

Philippe Massonet, Alvaro Arenas, Fabio Martinelli, Paolo Mori, and Bruno Crispo

16.1 Introduction

Grids have introduced a new model for distributed computing in which complex computing problems are solved using a dynamic pool of dispersed commodity-based resources. Grids have the potential to provide scalable and low-cost computing and storage. Next Generation Grids will push the model even further by incorporating the service-oriented paradigm, thus allowing Grids to provide scalable and low-cost service-based infrastructures for both business and scientific purposes. From the security point of view, Grids have introduced important challenges because the pool of resources and users is dynamic and managed by different administrative domains. Grid systems are open and dynamic. Current access-control technology in Grids provides only coarse-grained security: once a user has access to a resource, he can do anything he wants with it. The GridTrust consortium argues that coarse-grained access control leaves Grids inherently vulnerable, and that not only the access to a resource needs to be controlled, but also the usage that is made of the resource. This chapter describes the GridTrust framework that introduces fine-grained and continuous usage control in Grids, and provides the necessary services, tools, and methods to deploy it in OGSA-compliant Grids.

Next Generations Grids (NGG) are service-based Grids as defined by the NGG architecture (Next Generation Grids 2003). Grids allow the pooling of resources and users from different administrative domains in order to achieve common goals. Virtual organizations (VOs) define an extended domain to manage the resources and users from the different domains. Grid-based VOs can provide a sound technological infrastructure for a service-based economy. Grids can provide scalable and low-cost service-based infrastructures for both business and scientific purposes. As the underlying infrastructure, Grid-based VOs must be able to adapt to the changing needs of the business or scientific environment. They must be dynamic so that they can adapt to changes in the business or scientific environment: this means being able to add/remove users, services, or policies during the lifetime of the VOs.

From the security point of view, dynamic VOs have introduced important challenges because the pool of resources and users is dynamic and managed by different administrative domains. In the area of access control in Grids (Arenas 2005), many research issues in authentication have been explored. However, little research has been carried out on authorization. The objective of the IST GridTrust project (GridTrust 2006) is to develop the technology to manage trust and security for the Next Generation Grids, focusing on access control and, more specifically, authorization and trust management. The project adopts a vertical approach to tackling issues of trust and security from the requirement level down to the application, middleware, and foundation levels of the NGG architecture. Our emphasis is on models and tools to assist in reasoning about trust and security properties along the NGG architecture.

The resulting GridTrust framework is composed of policy-based trust and security services and policy derivation tools. The trust and security services use a new policy language based on the usage control model (Park and Sandhu 2004). The usage control model is a general model for trust and security in open and distributed systems. It generalizes existing access control models, and opens up new possibilities for trust and security in service-based Grids. The policy derivation tools and library provide support for producing the usage control policies for the policy-based trust and security services. The framework is integrated in the Open Grid Services Architecture (OGSA; Foster et al. 2002). It will allow Grid users to define and operate virtual organizations that are governed by trust and security policies. The definition and operation of the virtual organizations will be complemented at the local level by fine-grained, continuous usage control for Grids that will enforce the trust and security policies at the local level. The usage control model also covers privacy. Privacy is thus also covered in the GridTrust framework, in the sense that privacy policies can be represented as usage control policies. There is no dedicated privacy policy language similar to EPAL (Ashley et al. 2003) or P3P (Cranor 2003) in the GridTrust framework.

This chapter is organized as follows. Section 16.2 starts by describing dynamic virtual organizations and the types of dynamicity that are considered, and identifies trust and security challenges. Section 16.3 describes the state of the art on access control in Grids. Section 16.4 introduces the usage control model and policy language, as well as fine-grained and continuous usage control for Grids. Section 16.5 introduces the GridTrust framework that provides services and tools for usage control in Grids. Section 16.6 summarizes the main innovations in the GridTrust framework.

The NGG architecture is comparable to the NESSI framework presented in chapter 1 (NESSI 2006). It is composed of four layers: application, service middleware, foundation middleware, and network operating system. There is no explicit semantic layer, as in the NESSI framework; the semantic issues are distributed between the application and service middleware layers. The service middleware and foundation middleware are comparable to the service integration and infrastructure layers of NESSI. In the NGG architecture there is no explicit vertical security layer, as in the NESSI framework. The GridTrust framework addresses issues of security and trust in the service integration layer and the infrastructure layer. In this chapter the SeCSE conceptual model (see chapter 1) has been used as much as possible when compatible with the Next Generation Grid concepts.

16.2 Access Control and Trust Challenges in Dynamic Virtual Organizations

16.2.1 Dynamic Virtual Organizations

The ability to share resources using Grids enables organizations to collaborate, often in the form of workflows of services. The collaboration needs to be organized, and thus entails the creation of a new and virtual administrative domain called a virtual organization. A virtual organization (Arenas 2005; Wesner et al. 2005) is "a virtual temporary or permanent coalition of dispersed individuals, groups, organizational units or entire organizations that pool resources, capabilities and information to achieve common objectives." In a business context, when organizations collaborate with the aim of achieving a common objective, they are called virtual enterprises.

The dynamicity of the business environment means that organizations can join or leave the VO, that responsibilities within the virtual enterprise can change, or that the business opportunity changes. At the Grid infrastructure level, the VO thus needs to adapt rapidly and flexibly to changes in resources, services, service compositions, or policies.

Figure 16.1 shows an example of VO adaptation in a workflow. In this abstract workflow, organizations collaborate through the provision of services until an end result is provided to organization 5. The adaptation of the workflow that is illustrated is the replacement of service provider 3 with service provider 6. The workflow combines services

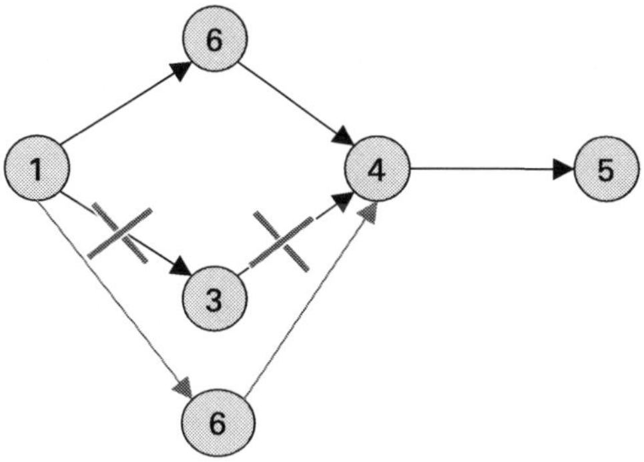

Figure 16.1
Dynamic changes in a VO-based service workflow

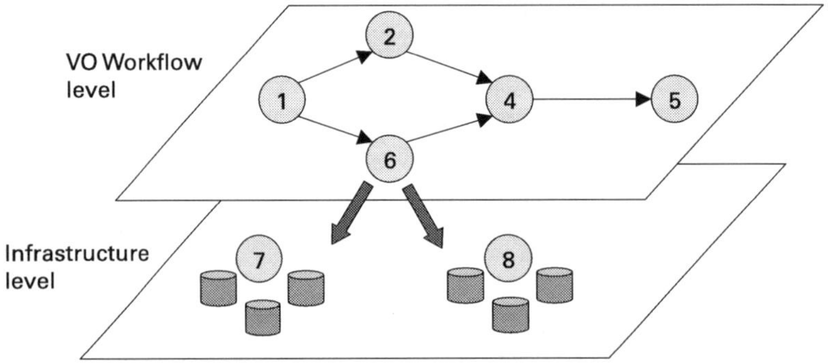

Figure 16.2
Selection of a hosting environment for service instance execution

from organizations 1 to 4 to provide organization 5 with a final result. In the above example, organization 3 stops providing the required service, and withdraws from the VO. An alternative service provider that provides a similar service is identified, and replaces organization 3 in the workflow. To support this type of adaptation, VOs thus need to be based on scalable, adaptive, secure, and dependable Grid architectures enabling the management of large networked distributed resources.

Changes in the business environment that lead to changes in the dynamicity of a VO can be handled manually by operators of the VO. However, if the changes become frequent and complex, the VO will quickly become unmanageable. VOs thus need to be self-organizing, fault-tolerant autonomous systems based on virtualization of resources.

16.2.2 Outsourcing in Grid-Based Virtual Organizations

Figure 16.2 shows that organization 6 provides a service to organization 4 and uses the Grid to complement its own resources to provide its services. In this case, organization 6 has to choose whether to execute a service instance for organization 4 on its resources or to outsource the execution to organization 7 or 8. During the VO and workflow lifetime, organization 6 will execute many instances of the service it has committed to providing. Each time it has to execute an instance, it can choose to execute on its own resources or outsource it to a service provider with the help of a service broker.

Figure 16.3 shows in more detail the relationship between the service requestor (organization 4), the service provider (organization 6), and the selected hosting environment (organization 7) for the service instance execution. The service instance is executed on the resources of the hosting environment. These resources are shared by different service instances from different service providers.

From the security and trust point of view, the trust and security policies of multiple stakeholders have to be taken into account:

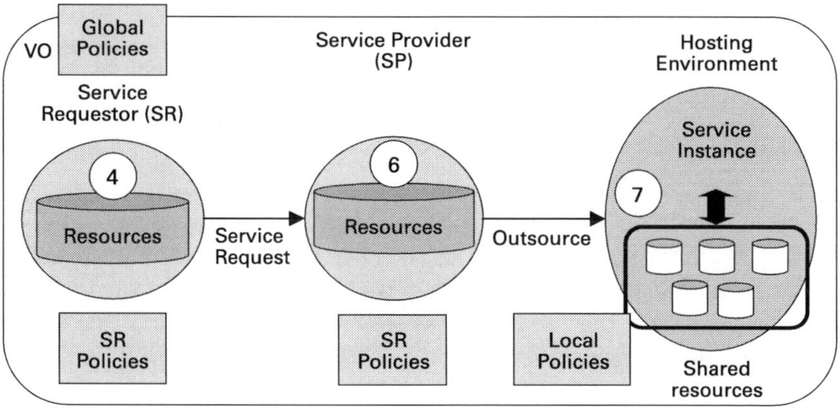

Figure 16.3
Outsourcing of service instances

1. *Global VO policies* The global VO trust and security policies define common policies that have to be respected by all VO members.
2. *Local policies* The hosting environment wants to protect its local resources from the service instances that are submitted by service providers from different administrative domains. The hosting environment does not necessarily know what these applications do, and thus needs to protect its resources and the other service instances running on the shared resources.
3. *Service provider policies* The service provider needs to protect the service instance and data that are outsourced to the hosting environment.
4. *Service requestor policies* The service requestor who provides data to the service provider might also want to control how its data are being handled from the security and trust point of view.

From the security point of view, prior work on access control has been based mainly on authentication and limited forms of authorizations—in the form of an access control list or other well-established means. However, these mechanisms do not scale up to large and dynamic virtual organizations (GridTrust 2007). Furthermore, the control is coarse-grained because Grid resource access is considered an atomic operation, and no further controls are executed after access to a resource is granted. Most of the authorization systems control access at the service level: control of access at the service level is coarse-grained, because there is no control on the use of resources by the service itself.

To overcome these problems, the GridTrust framework will provide an autonomic security management system that includes a set of mechanisms for policy management based on the continuous and fine-grained usage control of Grid resources, extended with trust-based approaches such as reputation systems.

16.2.3 Trust in Dynamic Virtual Organizations

Establishing and maintaining trust in dynamic VOs is fundamental, because sharing resources and confidential information requires a high degree of trust between the partners. Trust mechanisms have become complementary to security mechanisms. Security mechanisms typically protect resources from malicious users by restricting access to authorized users only. However, in many situations within distributed applications, one has to protect oneself from those who offer resources, so that the problem is in fact reversed. For instance, a resource providing information can act deceitfully by providing false or misleading information, and traditional security mechanisms are unable to protect against this type of threat. As noted in Josang et al. (2007), trust systems can provide protection against such threats. The difference between these two approaches to security was first described by Rasmusson and Janssen (1996), who used the term "hard security" for traditional mechanisms such as authentication and access control, and "soft security" for what they called social control mechanisms, of which trust is an example. Two approaches to trust are considered in the GridTrust framework: trust management based on credentials, and reputation-based trust.

16.3 Access Control in Grids

16.3.1 Standard Globus Security Support

The Globus Toolkit is a collection of software components that can be used to set up Grids. In particular, the Grid Security Infrastructure (GSI) is the set of these components concerning security issues. Figure 16.4 shows the main components of the Globus Toolkit version 4 (GT4); the components represented by green boxes are the ones related to security.

GT4 includes both non-WS components and WS ones. WS components were introduced in Globus version 3, and they exploit the Web Service (WS) technology. In the case of WS components, we refer to the security components as security services. In particular, these services are the following:

1. *Authentication* The standard authentication service of Globus exploits a public key infrastructure (PKI; Arsenault and Turner 2002), where X.509 end entity certificates (X.509 EECs) are used to identify entities in the Grid, such as users and services. These certificates provide a unique identifier, called the distinguished name (DN), and a public key to each entity. The user's private key is stored in the user machine. The X.509 EECs adopted by Globus are consistent with the relevant standards. The X.509 EECs can be issued by standard certification authorities and implemented with third-party software.
2. *Authorization* The standard authorization system of Globus is the gridmap. This mechanism is based on a file, the gridmap file, whose entries pair a local account to the distinguished name of each user that is allowed to access the resource. In this case, the security policy that is enforced is only the one defined by the privileges paired with the lo-

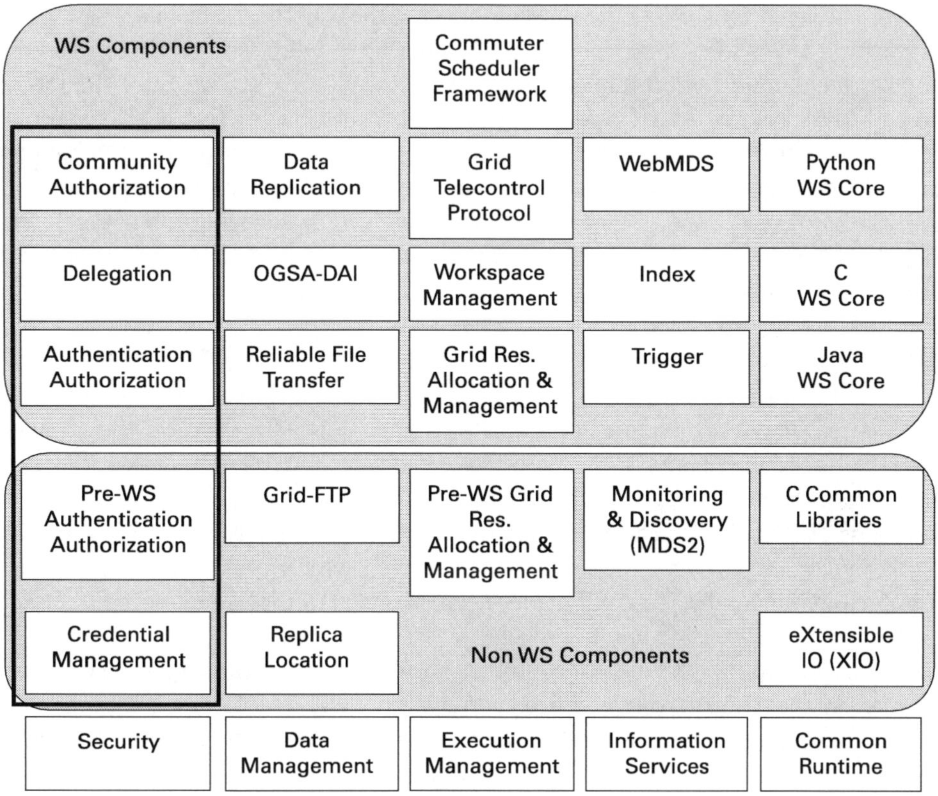

Figure 16.4
Globus Toolkit version 4 components

cal account by the operating system running on the underlying resource. The Globus Toolkit also provides some other simple authorization mechanisms that can be exploited by simply changing some configuration files, the security descriptors. These alternative mechanisms are self, identity, host, username, and SAMLCallout. As an example, the host authorization restricts the access only to users that submit their requests from a given host. Moreover, Globus allows the integration of third-party authorization services, exploiting the SAMLCallout authorization mechanism, that is based on the SAML AuthorizationDecision protocol (Welch et al. 2004). In this case, the external authorization system must run as a Globus service, and the security descriptors must be configured to refer to this service. The authorization service can run on the same machine as the Globus container, or even on a remote machine. This mechanism has been exploited to integrate well known authorization systems in Globus: Akenti, PERMIS, and Shibboleth, as described in the following sections.

3. *Delegation* Delegation reduces the number of times the user must enter his passphrase for the execution of his request. As a matter of fact, if a Grid computation involves several Grid resources (each requiring mutual authentication), requesting services on behalf of a user, the need to reenter the user's passphrase can be avoided by creating a proxy certificate. A proxy consists of a new certificate and a private key. The new certificate contains the owner's identity, modified slightly to indicate that it is a proxy, and is signed by the owner, rather than a CA. The certificate also includes a time notation after which the proxy should no longer be accepted. The interface to this service is based on WS-Trust (WS-Trust 2005) specifications.

16.3.2 External Authorization Services

As described in the previous section, the standard authorization systems provided by the Globus Toolkit are very coarse-grained and static. Hence, this authorization system does not address the real requirements of the Grid. As a matter of fact, the gridmap authorization system grants or denies access to a Grid service simply by taking into account the distinguished name (DN) of the Grid user that requested the access. It would be useful to consider other factors to define an access right. Moreover, once access to the resource has been granted, no more controls are executed. As an example, in the case of computational resources, once the right to execute an application has been granted to the Grid user, the application is started and no further controls are executed on the actions that the application performs on the Grid resource. Furthermore, especially in the case of long-lived accesses, it could be useful to periodically check whether the access right still holds. As a matter of fact, even if the access was granted when it was requested, during the access time some factors that influence the access right could have been changed. Then, the ongoing access could be interrupted.

Since the Globus Toolkit allows the adoption of an external authorization system, many solutions have been proposed by the Grid community to improve the authorization system. This section describes the main ones (GridTrust 2007):

1. *Community authorization service (CAS)* This is the virtual organization-wide authorization service (Pearlman et al. 2002). CAS manages a database of VO policies (i.e., the policies that determine what each Grid user is allowed to do as a VO member). CAS allows a VO to maintain its own set of policies and communicate those policies to Grid sites. Grid sites combine their local policies with the ones from CAS to obtain the policy to be enforced. This service issues proxy certificates to Grid users that embed CAS policy assertions. The Grid user contacts the CAS service to request a proper credential to request a service on a given resource. The credentials returned by the CAS server will be presented by the Grid user to the service it wants to exploit. Resource providers participating in a VO with CAS will deploy CAS-enabled services (i.e., services modified to enforce the policies in the CAS credentials).

2. *PERMIS* This is a policy-based authorization system proposed by Chadwick et al. (PERMIS 2007; Chadwick and Otenko 2002; Chadwick et al. 2004), which implements the role-based access control (RBAC) paradigm. RBAC is an alternative approach to access control lists (ACLs). Instead of assigning certain permissions to a specific user directly, roles are created for various responsibilities and access permissions are assigned to specific roles possessed by the user. The assignment of permissions is fine-grained in comparison with ACLs, and users get the permissions to perform particular operations through their assigned role.
3. *Akenti* The paramount idea of Akenti, proposed by Thompson et al. (Akenti 2004; Thompson et al. 2002) is to provide a usable authorization system for environments consisting of highly distributed resources and used by several stakeholders. By exploiting fine-grained authorization for job execution and management in Grid, Akenti provides a restricted access to resources by using access control policy which does not require a central administrative authority to be expressed and to be enforced (Chadwick et al. 2006).
4. *Shibboleth* Shibboleth (2007) is an Internet2/MACE project implementing cross-domain single sign-on and attribute-based authorization for systems that require interinstitutional sharing of Web resources with preservation of end user privacy (Chadwick et al. 2006). The main idea of Shibboleth is that instead of having to log in and be authorized at any restricted site, users authenticate only once at their local site, which then forwards the user's attributes to the restricted sites without revealing information about user identity. GridShib is a research project that investigates and provides mechanisms for integration of Shibboleth into Globus Toolkit (Welch et al. 2005; GridShib 2005; Chadwick et al. 2006). The focus of the GridShib project is to leverage the attribute management infrastructure of Shibboleth by transporting Shibboleth attributes as SAML attribute assertions to any Globus Toolkit PDP (Chadwick et al. 2006).

It should be noted that the use of context-based authorization has been studied in Grids. One application of context-based authorization extends RBAC with context constraints (Yao et al. 2005). In this approach, permissions are dynamically granted and adapted to users based on contextual information from the Grid environment.

It should also be noted that Grid X.509 certificates for authentication and authorization have built-in lifetimes. This opens up a number of vulnerabilities related to the use of lost, compromised, or otherwise invalid certificates. One approach to solve this is to allow certificates to be revoked, and maintain lists of revoked certificates to control the status of certificates before or during usage of resources. The use of online certificate status protocol (OCSP) for X.509 public key and attribute certificates has been considered (Mulmo et al. 2006).

OGSA components can be compared to the NESSI and SeCSE service infrastructure layer models. However, this comparison is outside the scope of this chapter.

16.4 The Usage Control Model and Policy Language

16.4.1 The UCON Model

The UCON model has been defined by Sandhu and Park (2003; Park and Sandhu 2004; Zhang et al. 2006). UCON is a new access control model that addresses the problems of modern distributed environments, where the subjects that access the resources could be unknown. One of the key features of UCON is that the existence of a right for a subject is not static, but depends on dynamic factors.

This is possible because, while the standard access control model is based on authorizations only, UCON extends this model with other two factors that are evaluated to decide whether to grant the requested right: obligations and conditions. Moreover, this model introduces mutable attributes paired with subjects and objects and, consequently, introduces the continuity of policy enforcement. In the following, we describe the UCON core components (i.e., subject, objects, attributes, authorizations, obligations, conditions, and rights).

Subjects and Objects The subject is the entity that exercises rights (i.e., that executes access operations) on objects. An object is an entity that is accessed by subjects through access operations. As an example, a subject could be a user of an operating system, an object could be a file of this operating system, and the subject could access this file by performing a write or read operation. Both subjects and objects are paired with attributes.

Attributes In the UCON model, attributes are paired with both subjects and objects, and define the subject and the object instances. Attributes can be mutable or immutable. Immutable attributes typically describe features of subjects or objects that are rarely updated, and their update requires an administrative action. Mutable attributes, in contrast, are updated often, as a consequence of the actions performed by the subject on the objects. The attributes are very important components of this model because their values are exploited in the authorization process. An important subject attribute is identity. Identity is an immutable attribute, because it does not change as a consequence of the accesses that this subject performs. A mutable attribute paired with a subject could be the number of accesses to a given resource the subject performed. The value of this attribute is obviously affected by the accesses performed by the subject on the resource. Another example of a mutable attribute could be the reputation of the subject. As a matter of fact, the reputation of a subject also could change as a consequence of the accesses performed by the subject on objects. Attributes are also paired with objects. Examples of immutable attributes of an object depend on the resource itself. For a computational resource, possible attributes are the identifier of the resource and its physical features, such as the available memory space, the CPU speed, the available disk space, and so on. The attributes of a file could be the price for reading it or its level of security (e.g., normal or critical file).

In the UCON model, mutable attributes can be updated before (preUpdate), during (onUpdate), or after (postUpdate) the action is performed. If the attribute is updated before the action, the new value could be exploited to evaluate the authorization predicate and to determine the right to execute this action, whereas if the attribute is updated after the execution of the action, the new value will be exploited for the next actions. The onUpdate of attributes is meaningful only for long-lived actions, when ongoing authorizations or obligations are adopted. When defining the security policy for a resource, the most proper attribute updating mode has to be chosen. As an example, if the reading of a file incurs a charge, then if the application tries to open a file, the security policy could state that at first, the subject balance attribute is checked, then the action is executed, and then the subject balance attribute is updated (postUpdate).

Rights Rights are the privileges that subjects can exercise on objects. Traditional access control systems view rights as static entities, for instance, represented by the access matrix. Instead, UCON determines the existence of a right dynamically, when the subject tries to access the object. Hence, if the same subject accesses the same object two times, the UCON model could grant him different access rights. Figure 16.5 represents rights as the result of the usage decision process that takes into account all the other UCON components.

Authorizations Authorizations are functional predicates that evaluate subject and object attributes and the requested right according to a set of authorization rules in order to

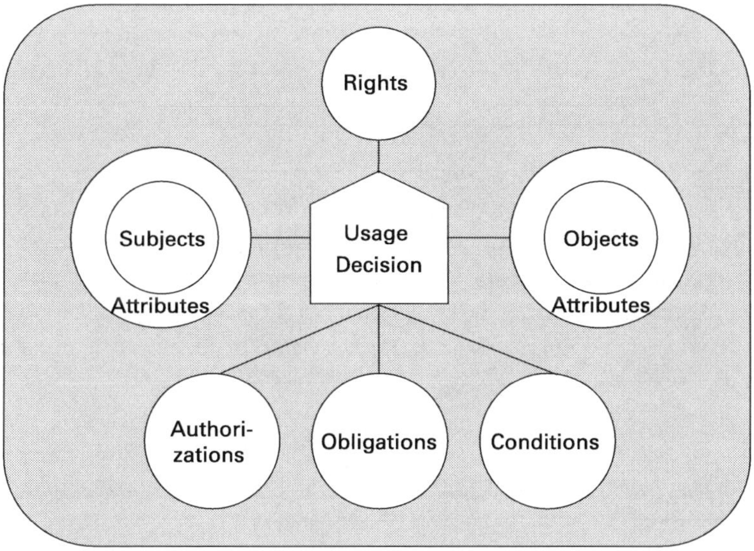

Figure 16.5
UCON components

take the usage decision. The authorization process exploits the attributes of both the subject and the object. As an example, an attribute of file F could be the price to open it, and an attribute of user U could be the prepaid credit. In this case, the authorization process checks whether the credit of U is enough to perform the open action on F. The evaluation of the authorization predicate can be performed before executing the action (preAuthorization), or while the application is performing the action (onAuthorization). With reference to the previous example, the preAuthorization is applied to check the credit of the subject before the file opening. OnAuthorization can be exploited in the case of long-lived actions.

As an example, the right to execute the application could be paired with the onAuthorization predicate that is satisfied only if the reputation attribute of the subject is above a given threshold. In this case, if during the execution of the application the value of the reputation attribute goes below the threshold, the right to continue the execution of the application is revoked for the subject.

Conditions Conditions are environmental or system-oriented decision factors (i.e., dynamic factors that do not depend upon subjects or objects). Conditions are evaluated at runtime, when the subject attempts to perform the access. The evaluation of a condition can be executed before (preCondition) or during (onCondition) the action. For instance, if access to an object can be executed during the daytime only, a preCondition that is satisfied only if the current time is between 8 a.m. and 8 p.m. can be defined.

OnConditions can be used in the case of long-lived actions. As an example, if the previous access is a long-lived one, an onCondition that is satisfied only if the current time is between 8 a.m. and 8 p.m. could be paired with this access, too. In this case, if the access has been started at 9 a.m. and is still active at 8 p.m., the onCondition revokes the access right to the subject.

Obligations Obligations are UCON decision factors that are used to verify whether the subject has satisfied some mandatory requirements before performing an action (preObligation), or whether the subject continuously satisfies these requirements while performing the access (onObligation). PreObligation can be viewed as a kind of history function to check whether or not certain activities have been fulfilled before granting a right. As an example, a policy could require that a user has to register or to accept a license agreement before accessing a service.

Continuous Usage Control The mutability of subject and object attributes introduces the necessity to execute the usage decision process continuously in time. This is particularly important in the case of long-lived accesses (i.e., accesses that last hours or even days). As a matter of fact, during the access, the conditions and the attribute values that granted the access right to the subject before the access could have been changed in a way such that

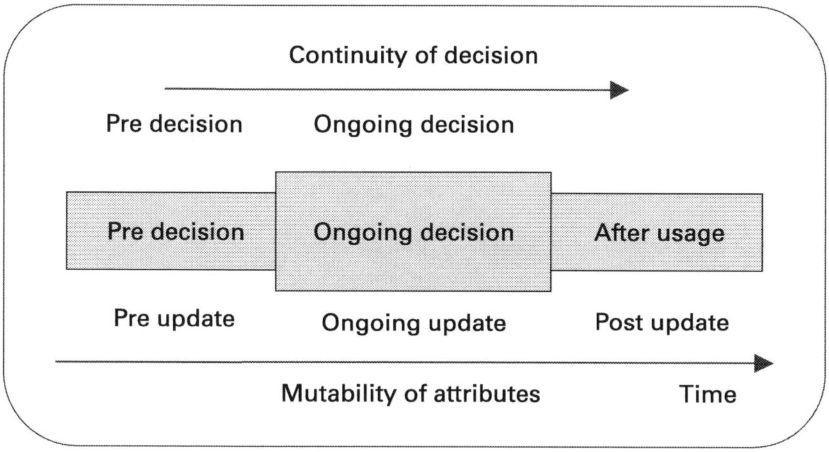

Figure 16.6
UCON continuity

the access right does not hold anymore. In this case, the access is revoked. Figure 16.6 represents the mutability of attributes and the continuity of access decisions.

16.4.2 Policy Specification

The policy language allows representing and combining the UCON components described in the previous section to implement the UCON model. Hence, the security policy describes the order in which the security-relevant actions can be performed; which authorizations, conditions, and obligations must be satisfied in order to allow a given action; which authorizations, conditions, and obligations must hold during the execution of actions; and which updates must be performed and when.

This section describes the components and composition operators of the policy language. We decided to adopt an operational policy language (Martinelli et al. 2006; Martinelli and Mori 2007) that we feel is closer to users' expertise than others that are more denotational. Since we deal with the sequence of actions, potentially involving different entities, we decided to use POlicy Language based on Process Algebra (POLPA).

Other variants are possible, and indeed concurrency theory presents many variants of process description languages. However, for the purposes of this chapter, the chosen policy language seems expressive enough to model the basic features of UCON models, as the next sections will show.

A policy results from the composition of security-relevant actions, predicates, and variable assignments through some composition operators, as described by the following grammar:

$$P ::= \bot \parallel \top \parallel \alpha(\vec{x}).P \parallel p(\vec{x}).P \parallel \vec{x} := \vec{e}.P \parallel P or P \parallel P par_{\alpha_1,\ldots,\alpha_n} P \parallel \{P\} \parallel Z$$

```
gvar[1]:=0. gvar[2]:=0.

([eq(gvar[2],0), eq(x1,"/directoryA/*"), eq(x2,READ)].open(x1,x2,x3).lvar[1]:=
x3.gvar[1]:= 1.
i([eq(x1,lvar[1])].read(x1,x2,x3)).
[eq(x1,lvar[1])].close(x1,x2)
)
par
([eq(gvar[1],0),eq(x1,"/directoryB/*"),eq(x1,READ)].open(x1,x2,x3).lvar[1]:=
x3.
gvar[2]:=1.
i([eq(x1,lvar[1])].read(x1,x2,x3)).
[eq(x1,lvar[1])].close(x1,x2)
)
```

Figure 16.7
Example of usage control policy: Chinese wall

where P is a policy, $\alpha(\vec{x})$ is a security-relevant action, $p(\vec{x})$ is a predicate, $\vec{x}$ are variables, and Z is a constant process definition $Z \doteq P$.

As an example, given that α and β represent actions and p and q are predicates, the following rule: $p(\vec{x}).\alpha(\vec{x}).q(\vec{y}).\beta(\vec{y})$ describes a behavior that includes the actions α, whose parameters $\vec{x}$ enjoy the conditions represented by the predicate p, followed by the action β, whose parameters $\vec{y}$ enjoy the conditions represented by the predicate q. In turn, β is followed by a policy P_1. Hence, this rule defines an ordering among the actions represented by α and β, because β can be executed only after α. The predicate p specifies the controls to be performed on the parameters and on the results of α, through conditions on $\vec{x}$. However, the predicate q could also include conditions on $\vec{x}$ to test the result of α.

Many different execution patterns may be described with this language. For instance, if we wish that the action δ is performed only after that α, β and γ have been performed (in any order) we may define the following policy: $(\alpha\ par\ \beta\ par\ \gamma);\ \delta$.

Figure 16.7 shows an example of a usage control policy. This usage control policy creates a Chinese wall between file directories "directoryA" and "directoryB." Initially the user can access files in any of the two directories. However, once he has opened a file in one of the two directories and started reading it, he can no longer access the files in the other directory.

16.4.3 Toward Usage Control in Grids

An initial attempt at providing continuous usage control for Grid computational services was developed in Martinelli et al. (2005). That work recognized the necessity of performing continuous and fine-grained authorization with behavioral policies expressed by means of process description operators. Some of the main concepts of usage control were introduced. Some new results appear in Koshutanski et al. (2006) and represent an attempt of some GridTrust researchers in this area. In this work credential management is exploited to enforce behavioral policies, and access control policies explicitly based on credentials are analyzed. This opened the interesting area of research for credential/trust negotiation that will be an active area of research for GridTrust.

After the starting of the GridTrust project, the same authors of the UCON model recognized the usefulness of their model for Grid and collaborative systems, and published (Zhang et al. 2006) an initial work in the area. The model is very basic since it does not yet allow obligations, and management of mutable subject attributes is fully centralized. As a matter of fact, mutable subject attributes are pulled by the system PDP from a centralized attribute repository of the VO. The updates of these attributes are performed by the PDP and reported to the centralized repository. Consistency among multiple copies of the same attribute is a problem when adopting a distributed version of the repository for subject-mutable attributes. This model clearly puts in evidence the necessity of specific authorization models for collaborative systems based on the usage control paradigm, and sustains the main claim of GridTrust research in this area. A peculiar claim is the need for continuous evaluations of policies and credentials (attributes), and the usage grant should be changed during runtime executions when attributes change.

An interesting evaluation of the potential models (either push or pull) for the credential retrieval by the policy decision point (PDP) is examined. The result is that for collaborative systems a hybrid mode must be considered: push for immutable and pull for mutable. This reflects the fact that the user may have interest in showing good value for mutable attributes, and the PDP should ensure it always has updated information. This is illustrated in figure 16.8.

Zhang et al. (2006) also recognize a role for reputation systems in collaborative environments, although they do not describe any reputation mechanism usable with the UCON model. The GridTrust framework also identifies the relationships between trust, reputation, and usage control policies.

16.5 The GridTrust Framework

The aim of the GridTrust framework is to introduce fine-grained and continuous usage control in Grids. The GridTrust framework provides the necessary services, methods, and tools to deploy it in OGSA-compliant Grids.

16.5.1 Overview of the GridTrust Framework

This section gives a high-level description of the GridTrust framework. The framework is composed of services and tools. The services all use usage control policies. The tools aim to assist designers in producing usage control policies.

Figure 16.9 shows the GridTrust framework services and tools. The framework addresses three layers of the NGG architecture: the Grid application layer, the Grid service middleware layer, and the Grid foundation layer. The framework is composed of trust

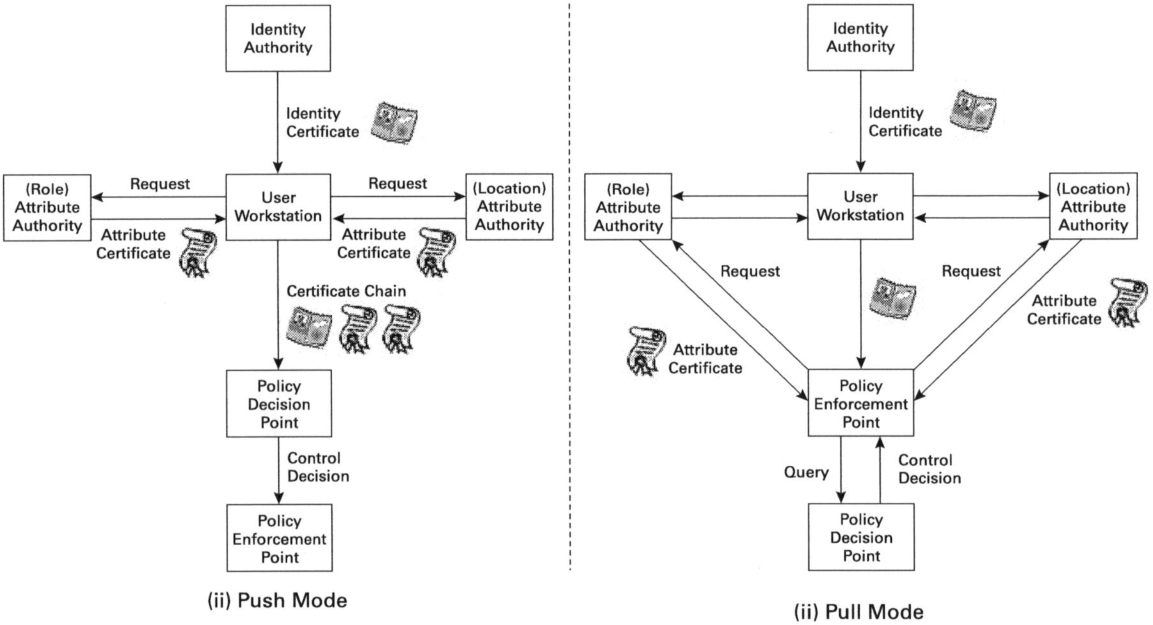

Figure 16.8
Push-Pull modes

and security services and tools, as indicated in the figure. The trust and security services are provided at the service middleware and Grid foundation middleware layers. The services all use usage control policies. The services at the service middleware layer are a secure resource broker (Bertino et al. 2004), a reputation service (Arenas et al. 2007; Resnick et al. 2000), and a service-level usage control service. At the Grid foundation middleware layer, fine-grained continuous computational usage control (Baiardi et al. 2004; Martinelli et al. 2005; Martinelli and Mori 2007) is provided.

The GridTrust framework policy tools aim to produce the security and trust policies needed by the different services. At the application level a requirements tool helps analysts define security and trust goals and requirements, and produces high-level security and trust policies. A policy refinement tool takes the abstract security and trust policies as input and refines them into service- and computational-level usage control policies. These usage control policies are used by the different trust and security services.

16.5.2 Framework Services and Tools

Services The services at the service middleware layer are the following: a secure service/resource broker (Bertino et al. 2004), a reputation service (Arenas et al. 2007; Resnick et al. 2000), service-level usage control service, and GridTrust-aware VO management.

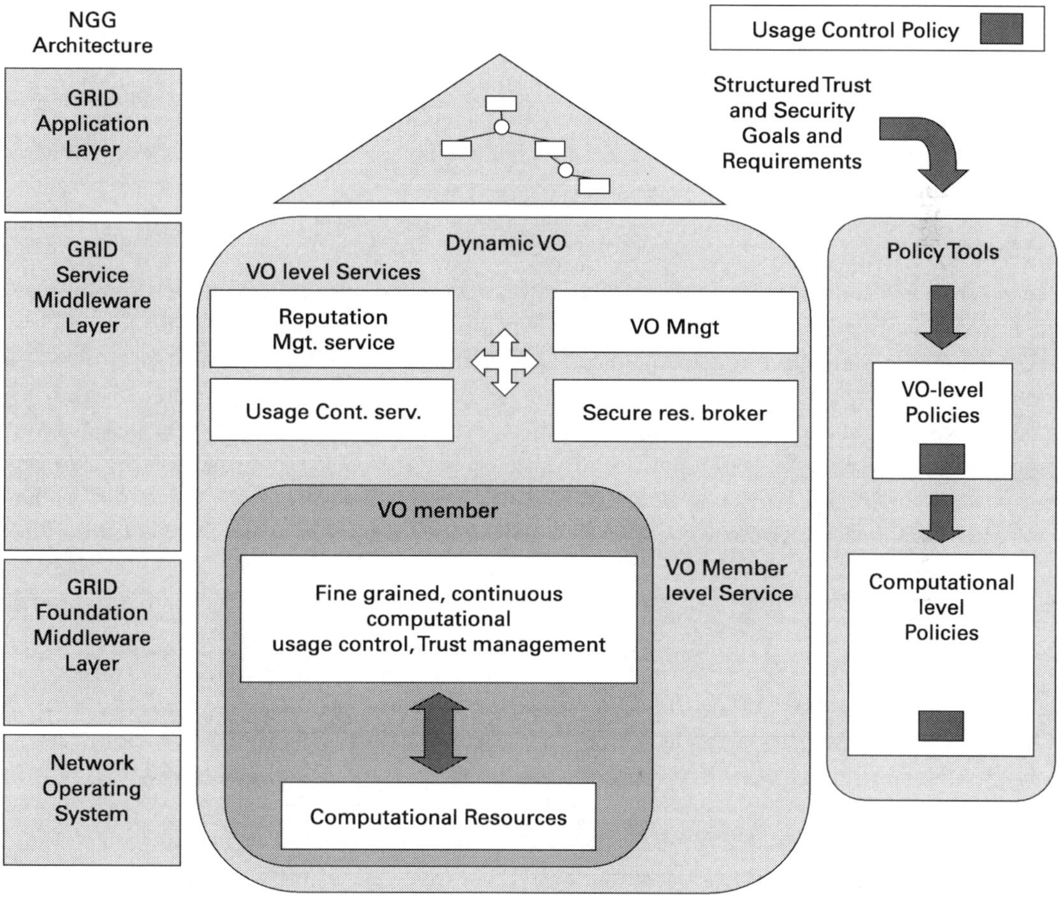

Figure 16.9
GridTrust framework services and tools

The secure service/resource broker takes into account security policies when searching for service providers, so that only service providers with security policies that are compatible with the service requestor security policies are selected (Bertino et al. 2004). The security component, which could be part of a metascheduler service, finds the list of nodes where a user is authorized to run his/her jobs. Performance and scalability are taken into account in the design of the security component: the aim is to reduce as much as possible the number of rules that need to be evaluated for each user request. The security is embedded in a security component that can be integrated into other service/resource brokers. We assume one secure resource broker per VO, but several VOs can coexist and overlap.

The reputation service measures the reputation (Arenas et al. 2007; Resnick et al. 2000), and is based on a utility-based model for reputation that has been tailored for service-oriented computing. The model builds the reputation from information provided by monitoring systems, making it suitable for service-oriented settings such as Grids. The monitoring information is provided by the computational usage control service.

The service-level usage control service controls the usage that is made of resources, using the same usage control techniques described below. This is achieved by replacing the default implementation of the OGSA authorization service with the usage control service. The VO management service provides VO management with the integrated GridTrust trust and security services.

At the Grid foundation middleware layer, fine-grained continuous computational usage control is provided (Martinelli et al. 2005). This usage control is integrated into the OGSA Grid resource allocation management (GRAM), and allows low-level usage control policies to be enforced. Details of the integration can be found in (Martinelli et al. 2005). It is continuous because program execution is monitored and policies are history-based. It is fine-grained because all system calls are monitored, and usage control policies can be expressed in terms of these systems calls, such as "open socket" or "open file." The computational usage control is integrated with Role-based Trust-management Markup Language (RTML) credential-based trust management (Colombo et al. 2007). The implementation provides an RTML-based inference engine, managing trust and reputation credentials.

Policy Tools The above policy-based trust and security services use usage control policies. An important open issue is the design of these usage control policies for the different stakeholders identified in section 16.2.1 and at different levels (service and computational) in the NGG architecture, as discussed in section 16.5.2. The GridTrust framework provides tools and a library of patterns for defining abstract usage control policies and refining them into more concrete policies to be used by the GridTrust trust and security services.

Initial trust and security requirements are defined in the KAOS requirements language (van Lamsweerde 2004), and are built by reusing abstract trust and security patterns (Dallons et al. 2007). The policies expressed in the abstract policy language can be refined into concrete policy language, using the GridTrust refinement tool that is based on the B refinement method (Abrial 1996).

16.6 Conclusions and Innovation in the GridTrust Framework

This chapter has argued that existing approaches to authorization in Grid-based VOs are inherently vulnerable. It argued that not only the initial access to a resource needs to be controlled, but also the usage that is made of the resource. One promising approach to address the vulnerabilities is proposed by the usage control model.

The generality of the usage control model allows a wide range of trust and security policies to be defined. With respect to existing access control models, it introduces the concepts of mutable attributes for subjects and objects, obligations, and continuous enforcement of usage control policies.

The GridTrust framework proposes a set of trust and security services to provide high levels of trust and security in open and dynamic Grid-based VOs. The framework brings several innovations to the state of the art in Grid trust and security.

It introduces usage control, and more specifically the UCON model, into Grids (Martinelli et al. 2005, 2006; Martinelli and Mori 2007). With respect to existing access control models that have been developed for Grids, it improves the state of the art by introducing mutable attributes for subjects and objects, obligations, and continuous enforcement of usage control policies. Furthermore, usage control is enforced in GridTrust at two levels: the computational level and the service level. The computational level allows local trust and security policies to be enforced continuously and in a fine-grained manner. The service-level usage control allows the global VO-level policies to be enforced in a continuous but coarse-grained manner.

A second innovation is the combination of brokering and security (Bertino et al. 2004) in a scalable manner. Current resource brokers do not take security policies into account when identifying resources. Resource brokers return candidate resources that match the user resource request but might not be compatible with the user's trust and security policies. However, this is discovered only after or during negotiation with the resource provider. The main advantage of the secure resource broker is that it returns only available resources from service providers whose security policies are compatible with the requesting user's security policies.

A third innovation is the combination of security with reputation (Arenas et al. 2007; Resnick et al. 2000). Globus already provides some reputation services. Reputation is used for service discovery and selection. In the GridTrust framework, reputation is used for a different, new purpose. It aims to use reputation for authorization decisions: the policy decision point takes reputation into account when taking usage decisions. Reputation can also be updated based on respect for or violation of usage control policies.

A fourth innovation is the derivation of usage control policies from business-level security goals and requirements. The trust goals and security goals can represent the wishes of the different stakeholders involved: service requestors, service providers, resource providers (including hosting environments), and the virtual organization as a whole.

Acknowledgment

The work published in this chapter is partly funded by the European Community under the Sixth Framework Programme, contract FP6–033817–GridTrust. The work reflects only the authors' views. The Community is not liable for any use that may be made of the information contained therein.

References

Abrial, J.-R. 1996. *The B-Book*. New York: Cambridge University Press.

Akenti Web site. 2004. http://dsd.lbl.gov/security/Akenti/papers.html.

Arenas, A., Cosmin Silaghi, G., and Silva, L. 2007. A utility-based reputation model for service-oriented computing. In *Proceedings of the CoreGRID Symposium*.

Arenas, A. E., ed. 2005. Survey Material on Trust and Security. CoreGRID Internal Deliverable.

Arsenault, A., and Turner, S. 2002. Internet X.509 Public Key Infrastructure. Roadmap. Internet Draft, draft-ietf-pkix-roadmap-09.txt. http://tools.ietf.org/html/draft-ietf-pkix-roadmap-09.

Ashley, P., Hada, S., Karjoth, G., Powers, C., and Schunter, M. 2003. Enterprise Privacy Authorization Language (EPAL 1.1) Specification. IBM Research Report. http://www.zurich.ibm.com/security/enterprise-privacy/epal.

Baiardi, F., Martinelli, F., Mori, P., and Vaccarelli, A. 2004. Improving grid service security with fine grain policies. In *Proceedings of On the Move to Meaningful Internet System 2004: OTM Workshops*. Berlin: Springer. LNCS 3292, pp. 123–134.

Bertino, E., Mazzoleni, P., Crispo, B., Sivasubramanian, S., and Ferrari, E. 2004. Towards supporting fine-grained access control for Grid resources. In *Proceedings of the 10th IEEE International Workshop on Future Trends of Distributed Computing Systems*.

Chadwick, D., and Otenko, A. 2002. The PERMIS X.509 role based privilege management infrastructure. In *Proceedings of the 7th ACM Symposium on Access Control Models and Technologies*, pp. 135–140. New York: ACM Press.

Chadwick, D., Otenko, A., and Welch, V. 2004. Using SAML to link the GLOBUS Toolkit to the PERMIS authorization infrastructure. In *Proceedings of the Eighth Annual IFIP TC-6 TC-11 Conference on Communications and Multimedia Security*.

Chadwick, D. W., Novikov, A., and Otenko, A. 2006. GridShib and PERMIS integration. In *Proceedings of the TERENA Networking Conference*. http://www.terena.org/events/tnc2006/programme/presentations/show.php?pres_id=200.

Colombo, M., Martinelli, F., Mori, P., Petrocchi, M., and Vaccarelli, A. 2007. Fine grained access control with trust and reputation management for Globus. In *GADA'07*. Berlin: Springer. LNCS 4804.

Cranor, L. 2003. P3P: Making privacy policies more useful. *IEEE Security & Privacy* 1(6) (November–December): 50–55.

Dallons, G., Massonet, P., Molderez, J. F., Ponsard, C., and Arenas, A. 2007. An analysis of the Chinese wall pattern for guaranteeing confidentiality in Grid-based virtual organisations. In *Proceedings of the First International Workshop on Security, Trust and Privacy in Grid Systems*.

Foster, I., Kesselman, C., Nick, J., and Tuecke, S. 2002. The Physiology of the Grid: An Open Grid Services Architecture for Distributed Systems Integration. Globus Project. www.globus.org/research/papers/ogsa.pdf.

GridShib Project Web site. 2005. http://grid.ncsa.uiuc.edu/GridShib.

GridTrust Project. 2007. Deliverable D3.1—Survey on Access and Usage Control for Grids. http://www.gridtrust.eu.

GridTrust Project Web site. 2006. http://www.gridtrust.eu.

Josang, A., Ismail, R., and Boyd, C. 2007. A survey of trust and reputation systems for online service provision. *Decision Support Systems* 43, no. 2: 618–644.

Koshutanski, H., Martinelli, F., Mori, P., and Vaccarelli, A. 2006. Fine-grained and history-based access control with trust management for autonomic Grid services. In *Proceedings of the International Conference on Autonomic and Autonomous Systems*.

Martinelli, F., and Mori, P. 2007. A model for usage control in Grid systems. In *Proceedings of the First International Workshop on Security, Trust and Privacy in Grid Systems*.

Martinelli, F., Mori, P., and Vaccarelli, A. 2005. Towards continuous usage control on Grid computational services. In *Proceedings of the Joint International Conference on Autonomic and Autonomous Systems and International Conference on Networking and Services*.

Martinelli, F., Mori, P., and Vaccarelli, A. 2006. Fine Grained Access Control for Computational Services. Technical Report TR-06/2006. Istituto di Informatica e Telematica, Consiglio Nazionale delle Ricerche, Pisa.

Mulmo, O., Helm, M., Luna, J., Manso, O., and Sova, M. 2006. OCSP Requirements for Grids. https://forge.gridforum.org/sf/go/doc4852.

Next Generation Grid(s). 2003. European Grid Research 2005–2010. Expert Group Report. Available at http://www.cordis.lu/ist/grids.

NESSI Web site. 2006. http://www.nessi-europe.com/Nessi/.

Park, J., and Sandhu, R. 2005. The UCON ABC usage control model. *ACM Transactions on Information and System Security* 7(1).

Pearlman, L., Welch, V., Foster, I., Kesselman, C., and Tuecke, S. A. 2002. Community authorization service for group collaboration. In *Proceedings of the IEEE 3rd International Workshop on Policies for Distributed Systems and Networks.*

PERMIS Web site. 2007. http://sec.cs.kent.ac.uk/permis/index.shtml.

Rasmusson, L., and Janssen, S. 1996. Simulated social control for secure Internet commerce. In C. Meadows, ed., *Proceedings of the 1996 New Security Paradigms Workshop.* New York: ACM Press.

Resnick, P., Zeckhauser, P., Friedman, R., and Kuwabara, K. 2000. Reputation systems. *Communications of the ACM* 43(12) (December): 45–48.

Sandhu, R., and Park, J. 2003. Usage control: A vision for next generation access control. In *Workshop on Mathematical Methods, Models and Architectures for Computer Networks Security.* Berlin: Springer. LNCS 2776, pp. 17–31.

Shibboleth Project Web site. 2007. http://shibboleth.internet2.edu/.

Thompson, M., Mudumbai, S., Essiari, A., and Chin, W. 2002. Authorization policy in a PKI environment. In *Proceedings of the 1st Annual PKI Research Workshop.*

van Lamsweerde, A. 2004. Elaborating security requirements by construction of intentional anti-models. In *Proceedings of ICSE '04, 26th International Conference on Software Engineering*, pp. 148–157. New York: ACM Press and IEEE Press. Available via ftp anonymous: //ftp.info.ucl.ac.be/pub/publi/2004/avl-Icse04–AntiGoals.pdf.

Welch, V., Barton, T., and Keahey, K. 2005. Attributes, anonymity, and access: Shibboleth and Globus integration to facilitate Grid collaboration. In *Proceedings of the 4th Annual PKI R&D Workshop.*

Welch, V., Siebenlist, F., Chadwick, D., Meder, S., and Pearlman, L. 2004. Use of SAML for OGSA Authorization. https://forge.gridforum.org/projects/ogsa-authzV.

Wesner, S., Schubert, L., and Dimitrakos, T. 2005. Dynamic virtual organizations in engineering. In *Proceedings of the German–Russian Workshop.*

WS-Trust. IBM. Web Service Trust Language (WS-Trust). 2005. http://specs.xmlsoap.org/ws/2005/02/trust/WS-Trust.pdf.

Yao, H., Hu, H., Huang, B., and Li, R. 2005. Dynamic role and context-based access control for Grid applications. In *Parallel and Distributed Computing, Applications and Technologies.*

Zhang, X., Nakae, M., Covington, M., and Sandhu, R. A usage-based authorization framework for collaborative computing systems. In *Proceedings of the 11th ACM Symposium on Access Control Models and Technologies.* New York: ACM Press.

Zhang, X., Parisi-Presicce, F., Sandhu, R. S., and Park, J. 2006. Formal model and policy specification of usage control. *ACM Transactions on Information and System Security* 8(4): 351–387.

17 Security-by-Contract (S×C) for Software and Services of Mobile Systems

Nicola Dragoni, Fabio Martinelli, Fabio Massacci, Paolo Mori, Christian Schaefer, Thomas Walter, and Eric Vetillard

17.1 Introduction

The paradigm of pervasive services (Bacon 2002) envisions a nomadic user traversing a variety of environments and seamlessly and constantly receiving services from other portables, handhelds, embedded, or wearable computers. Bootstrapping and managing security of services in this scenario is a major challenge.

We argue that the challenge is bigger than the "simple" pervasive service vision because it does not consider the possibilities that open up when we realize that the smart phone in our pocket *already* has more computing power than the PC on our desk 15 years ago.

Current pervasive services, including context-aware services, do not exploit the computational power of the mobile device. Information is provided to the mobile user anywhere, but the computing infrastructure is centralized (Harter et al. 2002). Even when it is decentralized to increase scalability and performance (Chakraborty et al. 2007; Diot and Gautier 1999), it does not exploit the devices' computing power.

We believe that the future of pervasive services will be shaped by *pervasive client downloads*. When traversing environments the nomadic user not only invokes services according to a Web Service-like fashion (in either push or pull mode) but also downloads new applications that are able to exploit computational power in order to make a better use of the unexpected services available in the environment.

A tourist, upon landing at the airport in a historical city might download a *tourist guide* application that can route her rented car to those touristic hot spots that are among her particular interests. The application is configured with touristic hot spots and, in order to determine the route to those hot spots, the application needs to interact with the car's navigation system to determine the current location and to update the route planning (but only if confirmed by the driver), and may send travel tips to selected driver's companions.

This is a pervasive service download because it offers local services; we want it exactly where we need it (e.g., via a Bluetooth link at the airport), without the bother of a long and frustrating Web search before departing; we want to use it on our mobile phone or PDA without connecting to a remote route planner each and every time.

Table 17.1
Security enforcement points

Development	Deployment		Execution
(I) at design and development time	(II) after design but before shipping the application	(III) when downloading the application	(IV) during the execution of the application

Such scenarios create new threats and security risks on top of the "simple" pervasive service invocation because they violate the heart of the security model of mobile software in Java (Gong and Ellison 2003) and .NET (LaMacchia and Lange 2002; Paul and Evans 2004):

1. A pervasive download is essentially untrusted code whose security properties we cannot check and whose code signature (if any) has no degree of *trust*.[1]
2. According to the classical security model, it should be sandboxed; its interaction with the environment and the device's own data should be limited.
3. Yet this is against the whole business logic, as we made this pervasive download precisely to have lots of interaction with the pervasive environment!
4. In almost all cases, however, this code will be trustworthy, having been developed to exploit the business opportunities of pervasive services.

Another example is services for mobile workers in a ubiquitous environment who not only have to share data with each other but also, if they are from different enterprises, may share their applications as well (Montagut and Molva 2005). Web browser plug-ins, Web clients, and collaborative tools are other examples.

The current security model is highly unsatisfactory: if we download a client in order to use a service, we trust it either fully or not at all. In contrast, we need a flexible mechanism that allows the owner of the mobile platform to control which actions of a given application are allowed on the platform. The enforcement of the platform security policies can be taken at different stages of the mobile application's life cycle. Each stage will have different functionality constraints, as shown in table 17.1.

(I) can be achieved by appropriate design rules and requires developer support; (II) and (III) can be carried out through (automatic) verification techniques. Such verifications can take place before downloading (*static verification*; Skalka and Smith 2000; Nordio et al. 2004) by developers and operators, followed by a *trusted signature* or as a combination of pre- and postloading operations, such as through *in-line monitors* (Erlingsson and Schneider 2000) and *proof-carrying code* (Appel and Felten 1999; Necula 1997); (IV) can be implemented by *runtime* checking (Martinelli et al. 2005). Each method has different technical and business properties. For example, from an operator's viewpoint:

1. Working on existing devices would rule out runtime enforcement, and favor static analysis. Monitors might be used (for properties that could not be proved), but on-device proof would then not be possible.

Table 17.2
Enforcement technology strengths and weaknesses

Criteria	Static Analysis	In-lining	Runtime
Works with existing devices	√	?	×
Works with existing applications	?	×	√
Does not modify applications	√	×	√
Offline proof of correctness	√	√	×
Load-time proof of correctness	×	√	×
May depend on runtime data	×	√	√
Does not affect runtime performance	√	?	×

2. Operators distrusting the certification process could rely on runtime checks, at the price of upgrading devices' software.
3. An operator who wants to be able to run existing applications would prefer runtime enforcement.

Table 17.2 shows some of the possible strengths and limitations of each different technology. The basic idea behind the S^3MS project (www.s3ms.org) is to put together these enforcement technologies in order to build the security-by-contract framework.

17.2 Our Vision

We advocate the notion of *security-by-contract* (S×C) as a mechanism to make possible the trustless dissemination of trustworthy code in the pervasive service scenario that we have just described. The key idea behind S×C is that a digital signature should not just certify the origin of the code, but rather to bind the code with a contract.

Loosely speaking, a *contract* is just a set of rules describing the security behavior of the *mobile application* with its host platform. Some examples of security-relevant rules are silently initiating a phone call or sending an SMS, memory usage, secure and insecure Web connections, access to the user's address book, confidentiality of application data, and constraints on access from other applications already on the platform. We discuss informally the syntax in section 17.3 and refer to Aktug and Naliuka (2007) for details. A mobile application can take a number of forms, such as a Java plug-in for a browser or a .NET assembly to be installed on the mobile phone's virtual machine. Essentially it is a piece of code that we download on our mobile platform in order to use some services in the surrounding environment.

To understand how this apparently minor addition can dramatically change the reality of pervasive services, let's consider the life cycle of a mobile client. Figure 17.1 summarizes the phases of the application/service life cycle in which the contract-based security paradigm is present. Still, mobile systems will be more customizable and trustworthy, and third-party services can be used securely.

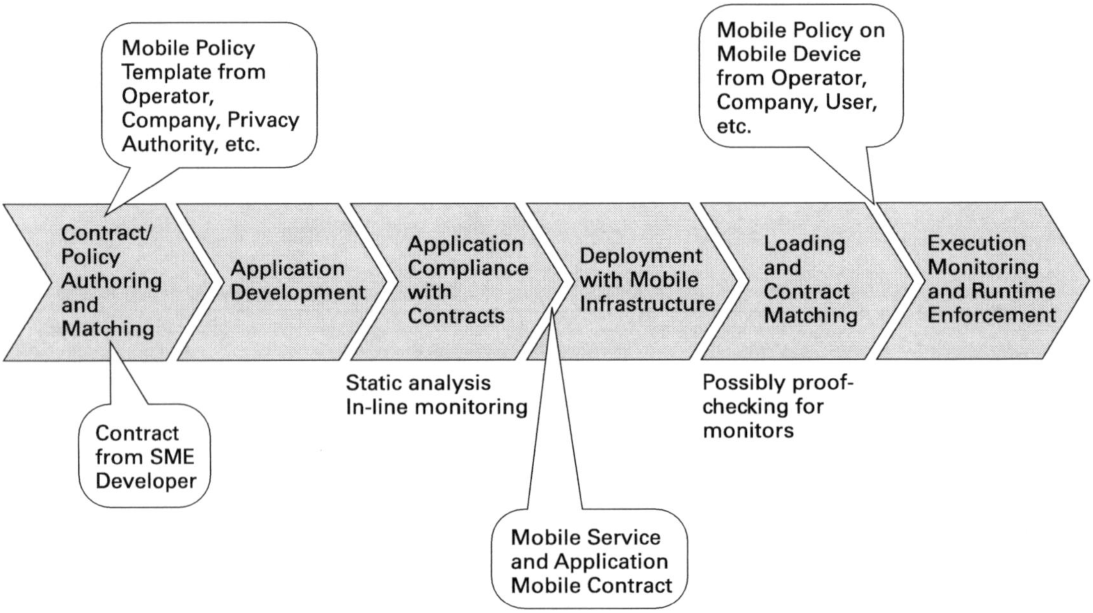

Figure 17.1
Application/service life cycle

At development time a service provider could check its downloadable client (the mobile application) against a contract template that is provided by operators or other service brokers. *Static analysis* could be efficiently used to check that a mobile application satisfies the template contract. We discuss this possibility in section 17.4.

At the other end of the life cycle, end users, operators, or companies managing the platform may deploy a *platform policy*, describing the security behavior expected (or at least desired) from all applications to be downloaded on the platform. At this stage we don't need a separate language, and contracts can also be reused for policies. At deployment time (i.e., when clicking the "download" button) the contract should be accepted by the platform, depending on the actual security policy that the platform has. This *matching* step must be supported to avoid the situation in which users wishing to download a service client simply click through their way by accepting all possible bad actions. We discuss the key issues behind matching in section 17.5.

During the execution of the mobile application the platform might opt for *runtime monitoring* the application anyhow (for example, in cases where contract matching failed or there is no trusted signature binding together code and contract). We discuss how this can be done in section 17.6.

The whole architecture of S×C can itself be represented as a service-oriented infrastructure where each of the above-mentioned services (matching, static analysis, etc.) can be represented as a service. We analyze the security functionalities and the threat models of S×C as an SOA in section 17.7.

Finally, we conclude our chapter with some remarks on the role of security in the broader outlook of S×C.

17.3 What Is a Security Contract?

A security contract is just a claim on the security-relevant actions of the mobile applet (i.e., the client downloaded on the platform in the pervasive services scenario). In the S×C framework we defined a contract specification language (ConSpec) where a single contract/policy consists of a *list of disjoint rules* (for instance, rules for connections, rules for a personal identification module [PIM], and so on), and each rule is defined according to the following grammar:

⟨RULE⟩:=
SCOPE [OBJECT ⟨class⟩|
SESSION|
MULTISESSION]
RULEID ⟨identifier⟩
⟨formal specification⟩

Rules can differ in both SCOPE and RULEID. Scope definition reflects at which scope (OBJECT, SESSION, MULTISESSION) the specified contract will be applied. The tag RULEID identifies the area of the contract (which security-relevant actions the policy concerns, such as "files" or "connections").

Intuitively, the session scope defines behavior that can belong to a single execution of the mobile code. The multisession scope defines rules with "memory" that describe properties that ought to be true across subsequent executions of the code.

We assume that SCOPE and RULEID divide the set of security-relevant actions into *noninterleaving sets*, so that two rules with different SCOPEs and RULEIDs (in the same contract specification) cannot specify the same security-relevant actions. This assumption allows us to perform matching as a number of simpler matching operations on separate rules, as we will show in section 17.5.

The ⟨formal specification⟩ part of a rule gives a rigorous and not ambiguous definition of the behavior (semantics) of the rule. Since several semantics might be used for this purpose (such as standard process algebras, security automata, and Petri nets), in the framework of the S^3MS project the industry partners of the consortium have done a careful requirements analysis in order to capture the key business needs (see www.s3ms.org). Some of the examples of desired security "contracts" for mobile applications are detailed below:

1. Send no more than a given number of messages in each session.
2. Load each image from the network only once.

3. Do not initiate calls to international numbers.
4. Make calls only to fixed premium SMS numbers.
5. Do not send MMS messages.
6. Connect only to the origin domain.
7. The length of each SMS message sent must not exceed the payload of a single SMS message.

Such requirements have been further distilled in the minimal characteristics of contractual features that should be captured and demonstrated:

1. *Permitting or prohibiting the activation or deactivation of a security-relevant service* (e.g., opening a communication, sending an SMS message, starting an application, modifying the address book).
2. The *presence of past events as a prerequisite for allowing a present event* (e.g., user confirmation before an SMS message is sent or an image is downloaded).
3. *Cumulative accounting of events* (e.g., downloading at most 5MB of images and sending at most 3 SMS messages).

The next step is of course the *specification of the security-by-contract language* that is able to capture the above features. We refer to Aktug and Naliuka (2007) for details, and here informally show some examples in order to give a taste.

Example 3.1 Requirements G-37 (MOBIUS 2006) *ConSpec: "The MIDlet only establishes HTTP connection."*

```
SCOPE Session
SECURITY STATE
BEFORE javax.microedition.io.Connector.open(java.lang.String url)
PERFORM
  url.startsWith("http:") -> {skip;}
BEFORE javax.microedition.io.Connector.open(java.lang.String url, int mode)
PERFORM
  url.startsWith("http:") -> {skip;}
BEFORE javax.microedition.io.Connector.open(java.lang.String url, int mode, boolean
time-outs)
PERFORM
  url.startsWith("http:") -> {skip;}
```

Example 3.2 Let us consider an application's contract which includes two rules: one for using HTTPS network connections and the other for restricting the sending of messages.

The application uses only HTTPS network connections.
No messages are sent by the application.
The corresponding ConSpec specification follows:

```
MAXINT 10000 MAXLEN 10

RULEID HIGH_LEVEL_CONNECTIONS
SCOPE Session
SECURITY STATE
boolean opened = false;
BEFORE javax.microedition.io.Connector.open(string url)
PERFORM
  url.startsWith("https://") && !opened -> {opened = true;}
  url.startsWith("https://") && opened -> {skip;}

RULEID SMS_MESSAGES
SCOPE Session
SECURITY STATE
BEFORE javax.wireless.messaging.MessageConnection.send
  (javax.wireless.messaging.TextMessage msg)
PERFORM
  false -> {skip;}
AFTER javax.wireless.messaging.MessageConnection.send
  (javax.wireless.messaging.TextMessage msg)
PERFORM
  false -> {skip;}
```

An example of automata-based specification of the above rules is given in figure 17.2. In particular, the automaton on the left corresponds to the formal specification of the HIGH_LEVEL_CONNECTIONS rule, while the automaton on the right corresponds to the SMS_MESSAGES rule. Discussing the details of such specifications is outside the scope of this paper because it would require the introduction of the underlying automata theory. Interested readers are invited to consult Bielova et al. (2008).

17.4 Static Analysis

Static analysis provides a way to verify that an application's code complies with the application's declared contract. It needs to be performed before actually deploying the application, as the technology is too complex to be run on the target device. Static analysis therefore needs to be used in conjunction with other technologies, which will help relay the proof provided by a static analysis tool to the actual device, such as the following:

1. *Digital signatures* The most classical way to use static analysis is to make the use of a static analysis tool one of the conditions for the generation of a digital signature for an application, for instance, as part of a systematic certification program.
2. *Proof-carrying code* The static analysis tool is used to build a correctness proof, which is sent over with code and verified on the device. This technology relies on the fact that it is

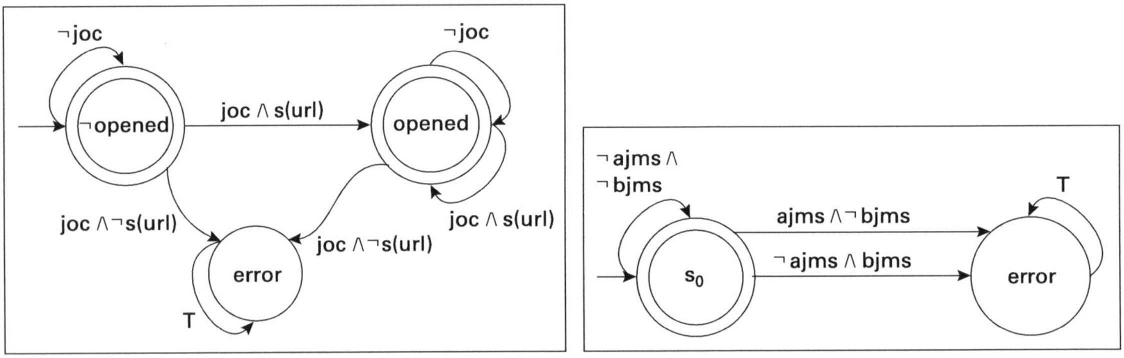

(a) Automaton 1 **(a) Automaton 2**

Abbreviations for JAVA APIs:

joc ≐ io.Connector.open(url)
s(url) ≐ url.startsWith("https://")
ajms ≐ after MessageConnection.send(message)
bjms ≐ before MessageConnection.send(message)
s_0 ≐ initial state, the system is staying in this state until it sends the message

Figure 17.2
Automata for the contract of example 3.2

much easier to verify a proof than to infer the information required to build it. It is, for instance, used by the Java bytecode verifier used in all Java ME devices.
3. *On-the-fly analysis* The static analysis tool runs during the deployment process. This of course supposes that the tool can run fast enough, and that the deployment process occurs over a secure connection, in order to guarantee that the application actually originates from a server that uses the appropriate static analysis tools.

Such technologies are not the main focus of the S^3MS project, which looks at the core technologies required for the use and enforcement of contracts, while minimizing the impact on the infrastructure itself. The fact that several technologies can be used for enforcement is actually an advantage for S×C, as it reduces the constraints on the deployment of the technology. In particular, the fact that S×C can rely on digital signatures is a very strong point, because all mobile application frameworks already support digital signatures as a way to guarantee that an application has been properly certified, so the adaptation of the device for supporting S×C static analysis can be minimal. In some cases, it simply consists of the use of a specific public key.

There is a strong incentive for application developers to use static analysis tools during the development process: static analysis tools are in essence imperfect, because they need to reason on an approximation of the application's behavior. Therefore, they are often unable to prove that an application verifies a property, although it actually does so. Static analysis tools usually make assumptions about the developer's behavior, and each tool favors some programming habits that happen to suit the way in which the tool is built. Here are two examples of such habits:

1. *Programming patterns* Most static analysis tools are able to get better results if the developers provide code that matches specific programming patterns. Such patterns are usually well known, and often correspond to the typical uses of APIs.
2. *Program annotations* Some static analysis programs are able to use additional information entered by the developer as annotations. This information is used to make the analysis more precise, usually at points where the algorithms have difficulties inferring the information by themselves. Annotations can also be a way to make the analysis of a program faster.

Both programming patterns and program annotations can be useful with the algorithms used in S×C. To show the feasibility of the approach, the S^3MS project has extended an industrial tool used to enforce security policies defined by operators. It is based on a rather simple analysis that in turn is based on abstract interpretation. The analysis is interprocedural, but it relies heavily on a method-local analysis. In particular, the tool infers very limited information about sequences of operations across methods. The Java ME static analysis tool is therefore not intended to be the only code–contract compliance verification method. Its objective here is to verify as many contract properties as possible, in order to reduce the runtime overhead. Initially, the Java static analysis tool has been designed for the verification of a fixed set of rules, most of them hard-coded.

The purpose of this section, then, is to expose the development of generic verifiers in the tool. *Generic verifiers*, which are well suited for contract verification, satisfy the high-level business requirements specified in S×C. They can be used either offline, before the deployment, or online, during the deployment (if the performance level is sufficient).

In the context of the S^3MS project, the static analysis implemented by Trusted Logic is able to determine a Java virtual machine state (stack, frame, heap) as well as any action on this state (API method invocation or heap accesses). On the contrary, it is not able to enforce temporal security requirements (e.g., delay between operations). Thus, *API usage*, *API usage restrictions*, and *mandatory sequences* can be only partly verified by the static analysis.

17.4.1 API Usage (Restrictions)

This is the simple category of generic verifiers to implement in the Java static analysis tool. The characteristics of such a verifier should be as follows:

1. It requires registration (for instance, through the Java listener mechanism) to a fixed list of API method events identified by the method signature.

2. It should be able to compare expected (contract) and observed (static approximation) registered method arguments, possibly ignoring some of the arguments: in the Connector .open ("http://"*, READ, *) expected expression, the time-out parameter could take any value.
3. The argument comparison is delegated to the abstract domain of each type of value, and the precision of the contract may differ from one value to another.

In the context of the S^3MS project, the tool should at least support the following expressions:

Boolean domain A requirement on boolean values could be expressed by a concrete value in the tuple {*true*, *false*} or by any value (*).
Integer domain A requirement on integer values could be expressed by a concrete value in each associated range (such as [–128, 127] for byte) or by any value (*).
Floating point domain Floating point values are not supported by ConSpec similar to integer values (a concrete value or any value).
String domain String requirements are the most important elements in the context of Java mobile application certification, since strings are used for any sensitive operations in the application, such as connection URLs. Thus, any standard string comparisons in Java should be supported by both ConSpec and the static analysis tool. A minimal list of string requirements must contain string prefix(es) and string suffix(es) requirements, string equality, and string length.
Reference domain Reference requirements should be limited to the tuple {*null*, ⟨*not_null*⟩, *}. In addition, the ⟨*not_null*⟩ requirement may specify a specific instance type for simple references, whereas for arrays it may specify an array element type, a dimension, and an array length.
Mandatory sequences Some of the sequencing requirements could be expressed in a generic manner, too. In the context of the S^3MS project, the Java static analysis tool supports only sequencing requirements that are limited to sequences of events local to a method body. Thus, it could explore the application control flow graph regardless of the concurrency issues on mobile applications.

A generic verifier handling sequencing requirements has the following characteristics:

1. It should be able to extract the association state variable updates and related events from the ConSpec policy.
2. Then, it should construct in a generic manner a control flow graph branch that should be matched to the analyzed one.

Example 4.1 Below is an example of the definition of the Möbius security requirement G-27 (MOBIUS 2006) in ConSpec: "The application does not send messages in a loop."

```
SCOPE Session
SECURITY STATE
boolean loop = false;
BEFORE enterloop // Unexisting event modifier
PERFORM
TRUE -> {loop = true;}
BEFORE exitloop // Unexisting event modifier
PERFORM
TRUE -> {loop = false;}
BEFORE javax.wireless.MessageConnection.send(javax.wireless.Message msg)
PERFORM
!loop -> {skip;}
```

17.5 Contract–Policy Matching

In order to define the matching between a contract and a policy, we abstract from a particular formal specification,[2] identifying the necessary abstract constructs for combining and comparing rules. Moreover, we assume that rules can be combined and compared for matching only if they have the same scope. This assumption allows us to reduce the problem of combining rules to the one of combining their formal specifications, without considering scopes.

We have identified the following abstract operators. (*Spec* indicates a generic specification, and *C* and *P* indicate a generic contract and policy, respectively.):

[Combine Operator $\bigoplus$] $Spec = \bigoplus_{i=1,\ldots,n} Spec_i$

It combines all the rule formal specifications $Spec_1, \ldots, Spec_n$ in a new specification *Spec.*
[Simulate Operator $\approx$] $Spec^C \approx Spec^P$

It returns 1 if rule formal specification $Spec^C$ simulates rule formal specification $Spec^P$, 0 otherwise.

[Contained-By Operator $\sqsubseteq$] $Spec^C \sqsubseteq Spec^P$

It returns 1 if the behavior specified by $Spec^C$ is among the behaviors that are allowed by $Spec^P$, 0 otherwise.

[Traces Operator] $S = \text{Traces}(Spec)$

It returns the set *S* of all the possible sequences of actions that can be performed according to the formal specification *Spec.*

We assume that the above abstract constructs are characterized by the following properties:

Property 5.1 $\text{Traces}(Spec_1 \oplus Spec_2) = \text{Traces}(Spec_1) \cup \text{Traces}(Spec_2)$

Property 5.2 $Spec_1 \sqsubseteq Spec_2 \Leftrightarrow \text{Traces}(Spec_1) \subseteq \text{Traces}(Spec_2)$

Property 5.3 $Spec_1 \approx Spec_2 \Rightarrow \text{Traces}(Spec_1) \subseteq \text{Traces}(Spec_2)$

Definition 5.1 (Exact Matching) Matching should succeed if and only if by executing the application on the platform, every trace that satisfies the application's contract also satisfies the platform's policy.

$\text{Traces}(\bigoplus_{i=1,\ldots,n} Spec_i^C) \subseteq \text{Traces}(\bigoplus_{i=1,\ldots,m} Spec_i^P)$

Definition 5.2 (Sound Sufficient Matching) Matching should fail if by executing the application on the platform, there might be an application trace that satisfies the contract and does not satisfy the policy.

Definition 5.3 (Complete Matching) Matching should succeed if by executing the application on the platform, each trace satisfying the contract also satisfies the policy.

By applying definition 5.2 we might reject "good" applications that are too difficult or too complex to perform. On the other hand, definition 5.3 may allow "bad" applications to run, but it will certainly accept all "good" ones (and "bad" applications can later be detected, for instance, by runtime monitoring).

The algorithm is *generic* since it does not depend on the formal model adopted for specifying the semantics of rules. Namely, it is defined by means of the abstract constructs just discussed. Therefore, to actually exploit the algorithm, it will be sufficient to have an implementation of such constructs in the formal language adopted for specifying rules.

As shown in figure 17.3, the matching algorithm takes as inputs two rule sets, R^C and R^P. They represent, respectively, the contract and the policy to be matched. The algorithm checks whether or not R^C "matches" R^P.

Algorithm 1 lists the pseudo code of the MatchContracts function, which represents the root function of the whole algorithm. Basically, the algorithm works as follows. First of all, both rule sets R^C and R^P are partitioned according to the scope of the rules. As already mentioned, this partition is necessary because in the S×C framework, comparison of rules starts only within a certain scope.

The algorithm creates two sequences of scope specific rule sets (one for the contract and one for the policy), and checks if each rule set in the sequence of the contract matches the corresponding rule set in the sequence of the policy (lines 3–11). In other words, we match rules within the same scope. The match is checked by calling the MatchRules function (lines 4–6) that we discuss in the next paragraph. If all succeeds (line 11), then the contract matches the policy. Otherwise, matching fails.

Algorithm 1 MatchContracts Function

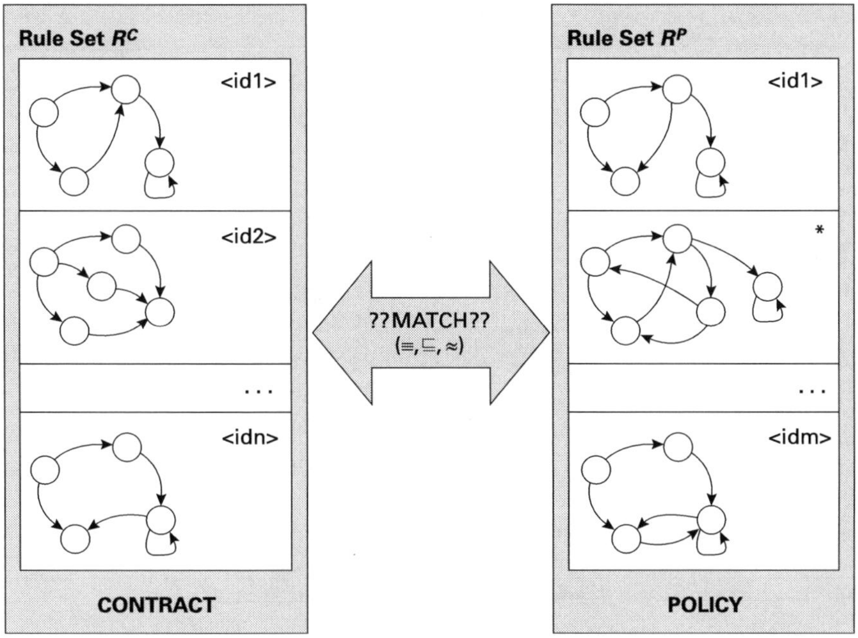

Figure 17.3
Contract-policy matching problem

Input: rule set R^C, rule set R^P
Output: 1 if R^C matches R^P, 0 otherwise

```
Partition R^C according to the SCOPE of the rules
Partition R^P according to the SCOPE of the rules
if rules with SCOPE SESSION do match (call to the MatchRules function) then
    if rules with SCOPE MULTISESSION do match (call to the MatchRules
    function) then
        for all classes in policy do
            if rules with SCOPE OBJECT do match (call to the MatchRules
            function) then
                skip
            else
                return(0)
            end if
        end for
        return(1)
    end if
end if
return(0)
```

Matching rules with the same scope is performed by the MatchRules function (algorithm 2). Since the rules of the two input sets R^C and R^P have the same scope, before starting the match the algorithm cleans R^C and R^P, removing the tag SCOPE from each rule. As a consequence, two sets L^C and L^P of pairs ($ID^{C/P}$, $Spec^{C/P}$) are built, where ID identifies a specific rule. Now the algorithm is ready to perform the contract–policy match. Each pair in L^P is compared with the set L^C by means of the MatchSpec function (line 4). When a match is not found for a pair (line 6), the MatchSpec function returns 0 and that pair is stored in a rule set L^P_{failed} (line 7).

If for all rules in L^P there exists a match with L^C (i.e., the MatchSpec function returns 1 for each pair in L^P so that $L^P_{failed} = \varnothing$, then the match between rules succeeds and the algorithm returns 1. Otherwise, if $L^P_{failed} = \varnothing$ (i.e., there are no rules in L^C that match the rules of L^P_{failed}), then the algorithm performs a last "global" check. More precisely, the combination of the rules in L^C is matched with the combination of the rules in L^P_{failed} (line 13). If also this match does not succeed, then the algorithm returns 0; otherwise it returns 1.

Algorithm 2 MatchRules Function

Input: rule set R^C, rule set R^P (both containing rules with the same SCOPE)
Output: 1 if R^C matches R^P, 0 otherwise
1: Remove tag SCOPE from all the elements of R^C and save the new list L^C
2: Remove tag SCOPE from all the elements of R^P and save the new list L^P
3: **for all** (ID^P, $Spec^P$) in L^P **do**
4:     **if** there exists a rule in L^C that matches (ID^P, $Spec^P$) (call to the MatchSpec function) **then**
5:         skip
6:     **else** [may return $\varnothing$ for efficiency]
7:         add the element (ID^P, $Spec^P$) to the list L^P_{failed}
8:     **end if**
9: **end for**
10: **if** L^P_{failed} is empty **then**
11:     return(1)
12: **else**
13:     call MatchSpec with the combination of the contracts in L^C and the combination of the policies in L^P_{failed} and return the result
14: **end if**

The MatchSpec function (algorithm 3) checks the match between a set of pairs $L^C = \langle (ID^C_1, Spec^C_1), \ldots, (ID^C_n, Spec^C_n) \rangle$ and a pair (ID^P, $Spec^P$), representing, respectively, the rules of the contract and a rule of the policy to be matched. The function returns 1 in two situations:

1. There exists a pair (ID^C, $Spec^C$) in L^C that matches (ID^P, $Spec^P$).
2. The combination of all the specifications in L^C matches (ID^P, $Spec^P$).

Otherwise, the function returns 0.

Matching is performed as follows. If there exists a pair (ID^C, $Spec^C$) in L^C such that ID^C is equal to ID^P (line 1), then the algorithm checks the hash values of the specifications $Spec^C$ and $Spec^P$. Matching succeeds if they have the same value (line 2). Otherwise, the algorithm checks if $Spec^C$ simulates $Spec^P$ (line 4). If this is the case, then the matching succeeds; otherwise, the more computationally expensive containment check is performed (line 6). If this check also fails, the algorithm ends and matching fails (because the rules with the same *ID* must have the same specification).

If there exists no pair in L^C such that ID^C is equal to ID^P (line 11), then the algorithm checks the match between the combination of all the specifications in L^C and (ID^P, $Spec^P$) (line 12).

Algorithm 3 MatchSpec Function

Input:
Output: 1 if L^C matches (ID^P, $Spec^P$), 0 otherwise
1: **if** $\exists$ $(ID^P, Spec^P) \in L^C$ and $ID^C = ID^P$ **then**
2: **if** $\text{HASH}(Spec^C) = \text{HASH}(Spec^P)$ **then**
3: return(1)
4: **else if** $Spec^C \approx Spec^P$ **then**
5: return(1)
6: **else if** $Spec^C \approx Spec^P$ **then**
7: return(1)
8: **else** [Restriction: if same ID, then same specification must match]
9: return(0)
10: **end if**
11: **else**
12: MatchSpec($(*, \bigoplus_{(ID^C, Spec^C) \in L^C}), (*, Spec^P)$)
13: **end if**

17.6 Runtime Enforcement on Java ME

Java 2 Micro Edition (J2ME) consists of three distinct layers, the mobile information device profile (MIDP), the connection limited device configuration (CLDC), and the kilo virtual machine (KVM), as shown in figure 17.4. Each of these layers provides a specific security support.

The security support provided by the CLDC (JSR139 2003) concerns the low level and the application-level security. To execute the MIDlet, the CLDC adopts a sandbox model, which requires that the MIDlet has been preverified; the MIDlet cannot bypass or alter

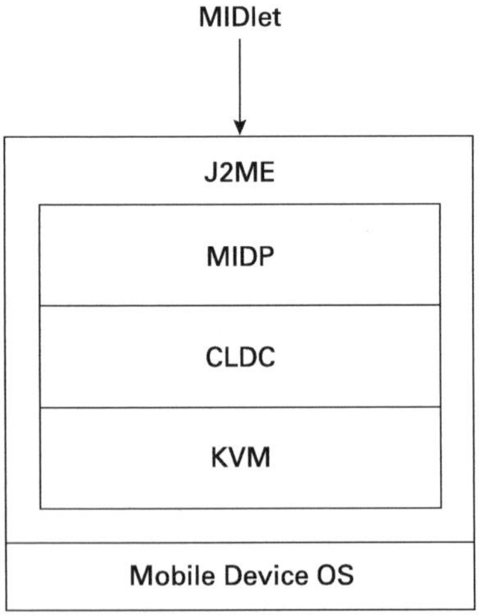

Figure 17.4
Java 2 Micro edition run-time environment

standard class loading mechanisms of the KVM; only a predefined set of APIs is available to the MIDlet; the MIDlet can load only classes from the archive it comes from (i.e., from the Jar file including it); and, finally, that the classes of the system packages cannot be overridden or modified.

The security support provided by the MIDP (JSR118 2002; JSR118 Addeddum 2002) defines a set of protection domains, and pairs a set of permissions with each of these domains. Each MIDlet that runs on the device is bound to one of these protection domains, and this determines the value of its permissions. A protection domain is assigned to a MIDlet depending on who signed the MIDlet itself, and can be untrusted, trusted, minimum, and maximum. If the MIDlet is not signed, then it is paired with the untrusted protection domain. The permissions refer to the operations that the MIDlet can perform during its execution, and the value that can be paired with them can be either allowed or user. As an example, the javax.microedition.io.Connector.http permission refers to HTTP connections. If the value is allowed, the permission is granted; otherwise, a user interaction is required to enter the value of this permission.

17.6.1 S×C Security

The S×C framework enhances the J2ME standard security support by enforcing security policies at runtime, the last stage of the application life cycle described in figure 17.1. The security policy is defined through the ConSpec language, as previously seen for contracts, and defines which security-relevant actions the MIDlet can perform during its execution. In particular, the actions we are interested in are the methods of the J2ME core classes that perform interactions with the underlying device.

As an example, opening a connection with a remote partner is considered a security-relevant action because the connection could be exploited by the MIDlet to send personal data to an unknown entity; on the other hand, the conversion of an integer value into a string is a negligible action from the security point of view. The policy pairs each method with a set of conditions that must be satisfied before and/or after the execution of the method itself. For example, these conditions may concern the value of the method parameters or the value of some policy variables.

With respect to the static analysis, the runtime enforcement can evaluate conditions that depend on input data. As an example, if we want the security policy to allow connections with remote servers only if the target URL begins with a given prefix, such as http://www.google.it/, this control can be implemented by pairing a condition that checks the URL parameter value before the execution of the open connection method. This value could be obtained by the MIDlet as an input parameter or as a result of a previous operation. The security policy can also take into account the state of the execution, or define dependencies among the execution of actions (i.e., it can define the order in which actions are performed). As an example, the security policy can state that only three HTTP connections can be opened at the same time, or that further HTTP connections cannot be opened after an HTTPS connection has been opened.

With respect to the standard J2ME security support, the security policies supported by the S×C framework define finer granularity controls and a history-based monitoring of the MIDlet. The policy defines the sequences of operations that the MIDlet can execute. In this way, the right of the MIDlet to execute an action does not depend only on the actions, but also on all the other actions that have previously been executed by the MIDlet.

From the architectural point of view, the enforcement of a security policy during the execution of a MIDlet is performed through the integration in the J2ME architecture of two components: a policy decision point (PDP), which evaluates the current security- relevant action against the security policy, and a MIDlet monitoring component, which intercepts the security-relevant actions performed by the MIDlet during its execution, invokes the PDP for the evaluation of the policy, and enforces the decision taken by the PDP. This implies that the S×C runtime support works with existing MIDlets, but requires the upgrade of the software of mobile devices.

Several solutions can be possible to integrate the MIDlet monitor component into the J2ME architecture. As an example, the system's calling for the KVM to perform on the operating system of the underlying mobile device could be intercepted by the monitor and considered as security-relevant actions. However, this solution has not been adopted because we are interested in monitoring the MIDlet behavior at the methods level. Moreover, since the set of system calls could be different on distinct mobile devices, defining the security policy in terms of system calls prevents the portability of the security policy.

Another solution is the one that exploits the permissions defined by MIDP. In this case, the monitor could be embedded in the MIDP component that evaluates the permission that is invoked by the J2ME every time an action that involves a permission is executed. As an example, let us suppose that the MIDlet asks to open an HTTP connection with a remote URL by exploiting the javax.microedition.io.Connector class of the MIDP. In this case, the value of the javax.microedition.io.Connector.http permission decides whether the HTTP connection can be established. However, this solution defines as security-relevant actions only the ones that are also paired with a permission. Moreover, this solution does not allow performing the test of the security policy after the execution of the security-relevant action, because the MIDP permissions are evaluated only before the execution of the action.

The adopted solution is based on the modification of the J2ME platform. We chose a subset of the methods of the API provided by MIDP and CLDC as set of security-relevant actions, and the MIDlet monitoring component has been embedded in the J2ME architecture by modifying the source code of these methods. The modification simply consists in inserting the invocation of the PDP at the beginning and at the end of the source code that implements these methods. In this way, every method of the J2ME could, in principle, be defined as a security-relevant action. If the result of the invocation of the PDP is negative (i.e., the execution of the action is denied according to the security policy), a SecurityException error is thrown by the method. The MIDlet could be instrumented to manage this exception, and in this case it continues running; otherwise, it fails. The resulting architecture is described in figure 17.5.

The policy decision point (PDP) is the component of the architecture that decides whether a given security-relevant method can be performed in a given state according to

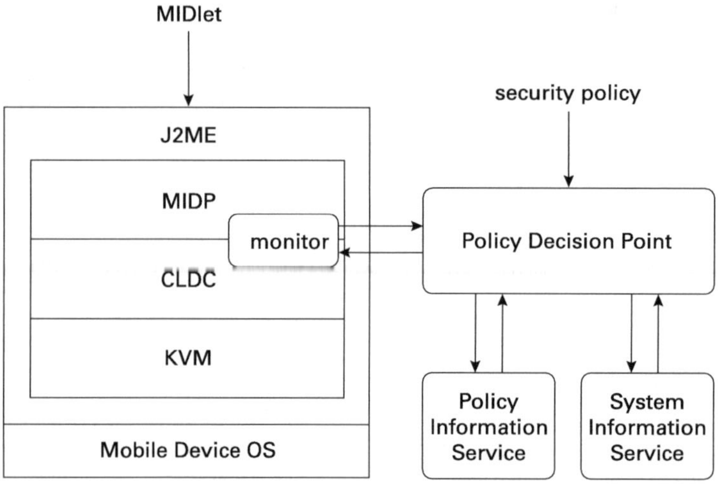

Figure 17.5
Java 2 Micro edition run-time monitoring

the policy. The PDP is invoked by the MIDlet monitor twice for each security-relevant method that the MIDlet tries to execute, and this invocation reports to the PDP the method's full name, its parameters, the name of the MIDlet, an ID of the MIDlet, and a flag that specifies whether the invocation has been made before or after executing the method.

To evaluate the security policy, the PDP could need the value of some policy variables. As an example, a policy could allow opening a further network connection only if this MIDlet has opened less than X connections. In this case, the number of connections is represented by a policy variable, and the PDP has to retrieve the value of this variable to decide whether a new connection can be opened, and to increase the variable value to represent the fact that a new network connection has been opened. In these cases the PDP interacts with the policy information service (PIS). The PIS is a further component of the S^3MS framework architecture that is in charge of managing the state of the policy. The PDP could also need some information about the current state of the device to evaluate the policy. As an example, a policy could state that an SMS message can be sent only if the battery level is above a given threshold. In this case, the PDP interacts with a further component of the architecture, the system information service (SIS). In particular, the following information can be requested from the SIS: get date and time, get CPU load, get free memory size, get network type, get battery level.

17.7 S×C as a Service-Oriented Architecture

This section presents the service-oriented architecture of the S×C framework in the spirit of the SeCSE conceptual model. The architecture consists of several layers, defines the S×C services provided by the S×C framework, and has been designed with the following goals in mind:

1. The application/service life cycle (as shown in figure 17.1) is quite complex and at least two stakeholders are involved: developer and user. The developer is the subject that wrote the application code, and the user is the mobile device owner who wants to execute the application. Another stakeholder is the application provider, who distributes the applications to the users. However, the stakeholders' number is often bigger when some framework tasks are outsourced to third parties. Obviously, the various phases of the development, deployment, and execution cycle require that data elements are to be exchanged between stakeholders. Consequently, one set of functions of the S×C architecture is concerned with protection of the communication and the data elements exchanged between stakeholders.
2. In a real business model some support for accounting, charging, and billing needs to be provided, which requires that service usages (e.g., downloading the client) can be attributed to a specific entity.
3. For a certification process, trust relationships between stakeholders need to be established. We do not require that this be done explicitly, but we rely on a certification infrastructure that manages public key certificates for digital signatures. The word "trust" here

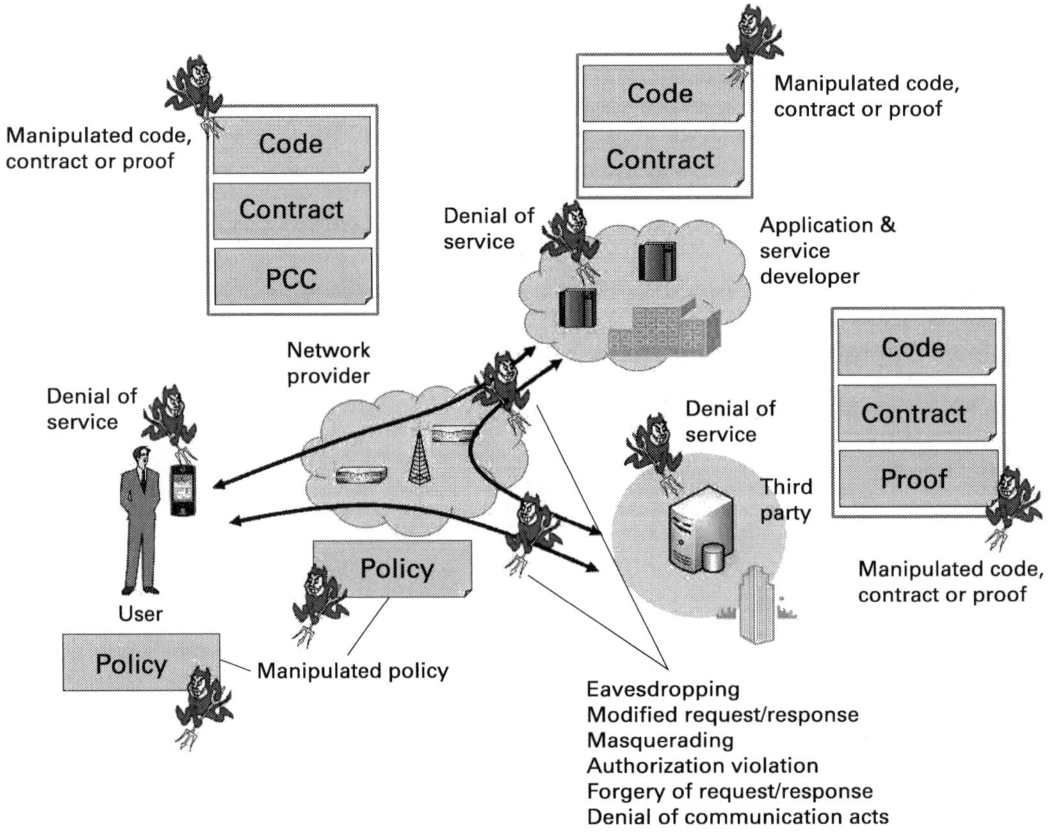

Figure 17.6
Threat analysis

refers to the authenticity and integrity of exchanged data elements such as code, contract, proof, and policy. Specifically, authenticity and integrity of data elements become important when the in-lining of code (i.e., code is added to the byte code of an application) for contract and policy compliance is done by a third party.

In order to define the architecture, we have carried out a careful threat analysis which is reported in the S^3MS deliverables and is synthesized in figure 17.6. It combines parties and data elements, and identifies possible threats.

Code, contracts, and policy are maintained in the domain of the application, service developer, and operator, and therefore the protection that they need is guaranteed by the S×C framework itself. Let's consider the case of static analysis:

1. *By the developer* In that case, the developer uses the static analysis tool during the development process in order to verify that the application matches its contract. A successful

result, in which the static analysis tool is able to prove that the application actually complies with its contract, can then be used by the developer to support claims about the innocuousness of the application.
2. *By the application provider* The application provider acts as a producer and distributor of the application, pushing it for deployment by network and portal operators. After reviewing the application's contract and ensuring that it is compatible with typical policies, the application provider will verify, as part of the quality assurance process, that the application actually satisfies its contract, before offering it for deployment.
3. *By the application portal/network operator* The operator in charge of the application's deployment (whether it is an application portal operator or a network operator) usually has contractual obligations regarding the content that it proposes for downloading. It will therefore verify that an application's contract matches its policies, and that the corresponding application matches its application contract.

Another example, the proof of compliance, may be given as PCC (proof-carrying code; see Necula 1997), in which case it is maintained in the domain of the developer. Policies are a concern of the user and the mobile network operator. In the S^3MS project, KTH has developed a PCC for Java that is currently visible on the Web site of the project, among the deliverables.

The analysis of the threats in the communication between the stakeholders during the application life cycle showed a number of low-level security issues that do not rely on the S×C feature, and therefore must be secured independently: eavesdropping, modifying request or response, masquerading, forgery of request or response, authorization violation. The first four threats obviously impact the overall security of S×C, as no guarantees on the authenticity and integrity of S×C components and policy can be given without providing some security mechanisms for S×C. DoS attacks can be run against any of the parties and may block them from providing services. As an example, running a DoS attack against a party that performs the contract–policy matching prevents the users that need this service from executing their applications. Taking the threat analysis and goals from above into account, and following the definition of a security architecture given in Shirey (2000), a layered S×C architecture with a strict separation between and allocation of services to the layers is motivated. Our proposed S×C architecture differentiates four layers, as depicted in figure 17.7.

The service/application layer defines the top layer of the architecture and rests on the S×C layer. The services being provided depend on the usage scenario of the service layer:

1. The user experiences the application layer as the layer where the downloaded mobile applications are being executed.
2. For the developer the layer integrates the development tools that are being used for the implementation of the mobile application.
3. The third party runs its certification process in this layer.

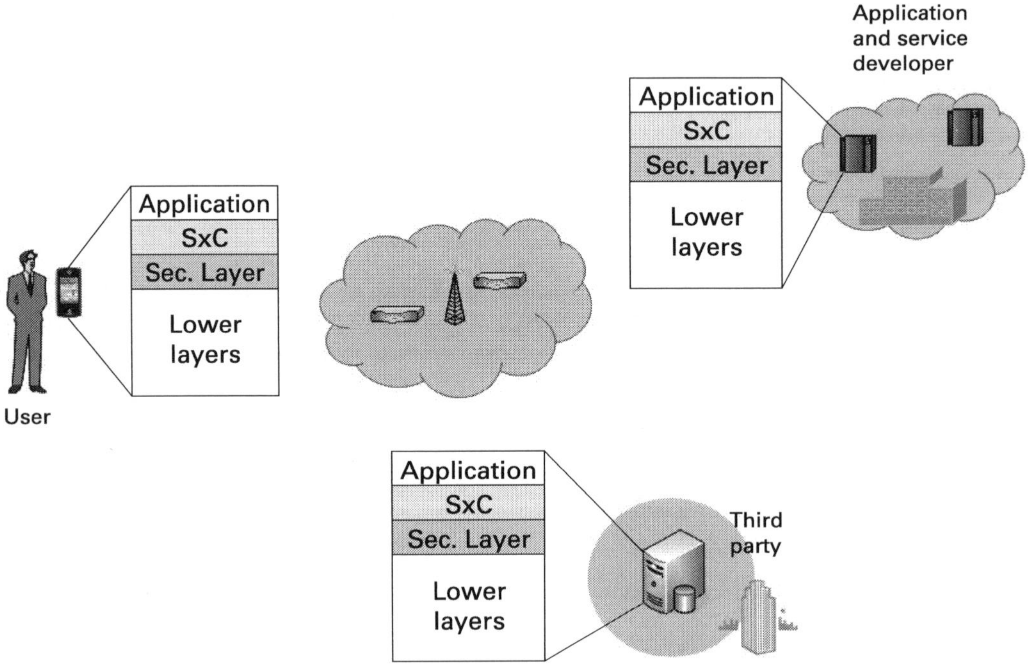

Figure 17.7
S × C architecture

The S×C services, being part of the S×C layer, are detailed on the left column of table 17.3. These services are invoked by the user to download code (from the developer or a third party) and to initiate specific S×C services. The services map to the enforcement methods that are applicable along the software life cycle. To run an application on a mobile device, a user may first get the application code and the contract, analyze code and contract to check their compliance, perform the matching of contract against the platform policy, and then, if all previous steps have been successful, execute the downloaded application. Eventually, the execution may be monitored. Similar interaction patterns can be derived for the other S×C services:

1. **get(Code, Contract).** This service returns the requested code and contract from either the developer or a third party.
2. **analyze(Code, Contract).** Code and contract are analyzed for compliance and, if successful, a positive result is returned to the caller; and a negative result otherwise.
3. **in-line(Code, Contract).** The code is submitted to the in-lining service for code and contract compliance assurance. This service returns the in-lined code (i.e., code that has been rewritten in order to embed a monitor directly in the code itself).

4. **in-line(Code, Policy).** The code is submitted to the in-lining service for code and policy compliance assurance. This service returns the in-lined code.
5. **match(Contract, Policy).** Contract and policy are analyzed and the compliance of contract to policy is checked. If compliance can be established, a positive, otherwise a negative, result is returned.
6. **monitor(Code, Policy).** The monitoring of the code with respect to the policy is initiated. The monitoring terminates if a policy violation is detected.
7. **check(Code, Contract, Proof).** The proof is checked against the given code and contract. If the check is successful, a positive result is returned; otherwise, a negative result is returned.
8. **proofGen(Code, Contract).** The compliance of code and contract is established and a respective proof is returned.
9. **manage(Policy).** The service enables a party to create, update, or delete its own policies. An updated policy is returned (in case of the deletion of a policy, nothing is returned).

Depending on the complexity of the code, its contract, and the policies to be obeyed, execution of some of the S×C services is demanding with respect to computational power and memory capacity of the executing devices. Considering mobile applications being executed on current constrained mobile devices, it is obvious that some services cannot be executed on these platforms. This requires outsourcing respective services. In table 17.2 we consider two interesting cases from the business model perspective of S×C for pervasive services, which also take into account the relative computational complexity of each of the tasks. In the local services model the device is powerful enough to perform most tasks by itself or rely on the developer to check a number of them. In the *remote services* model (value-added service model, in the terminology of mobile operators) the S×C services are offered by a third party, such as the mobile operator of the nomadic device.

The developer can use proof-carrying code (Necula and Lee 1998) for the proof of compliance of code and contract. Later on, the user checks the correctness of the proof-carrying code on his device by calling the respective *check* S×C service. This proof checking is restricted in complexity and can be done on the user's mobile device.

Code and contract compliance by in-lining is a service that should be carried out by a third party only. If it is done by the developer, the user does not get any evidence that the in-lining has been performed correctly. The third party, on the other hand, as part of the certification process, asserts that the in-lining is correct and covers all of the properties of the contract.

Last, monitoring execution of the mobile application code for policy compliance is reasonably to be done on the mobile device only.

The second and third columns of table 17.3 extend this discussion to all S×C services. Further, with *online* we refer to a service that might be executed on demand (i.e., a communication with the pervasive environment is established in order to set up a channel between the developer's, third party's or user's devices. A service is offered *offline* if a service

Table 17.3
S × C services

Service	Local	Remote
get(Code, Contract)	online	online
analyze(Code, Contract)	N/A	offline
inline(Code, Contract)	N/A	offline
inline(Code, Policy)	on-device	online/offline
Match(Contract, Policy)	on-device	online
monitor(Code, Policy)	on-device	N/A
check(Code, Contract, Proof)	on-device	online
proofGen(Code, Contract)	N/A	offline
manage(Policy)	on-device	online/on-device

is requested and executed in advance. This is an option for the *in-lining* of code for contract compliance, which can be done far in advance of the actual mobile application code download.

17.7.1 Security Layer

Whenever S×C services require the cooperation of an external party, this holds for all the S×C services marked *online* or *offline* in table 17.3, the S×C layer calls the services of the security layer to protect the communication between the parties.

The interactions between the described layers are as follows. Assuming that the user of the mobile device is performing a download of an application from the application and service developer, then the user calls the respective method of the S×C layer (i.e., get(Code) from (Developer)). Further, this call is mapped into a call to the security layer. The security layer subsequently maps this call into a sequence of method calls to set up a connection with the developer; performs authentication of the developer; gets the package containing code, contract, and signature; checks the signature for correctness; extracts code and contract from the received package; and hands code and contract back to the calling S×C layer, which in turn gives the code and contract back to the application layer.

17.7.2 Lower Layers

These layers simply support the security layer in its communication with other mobile devices and servers. We assume the lower layers comprise a TCP/IP protocol stack.

17.8 Conclusions

The S^3MS project belongs to the area of service-oriented computing and addresses issues—security and trust—that cut across all three research planes of the SOC road map (foundation, composition, and management and monitoring; see the Introduction to this volume). The S^3MS project designed and developed a contract-based approach to develop secure service in the mobile device scenario. The project concerns at least the three characteristics that the SOC road map defines for transversal services (semantics, nonfunctional characteristics, and quality of services). The S^3MS project addresses nonfunctional characteristics of services, such as security and trust in the mobile device scenario, where contracts define the semantics of the applications from the security point of view. From the point of view of the quality of service (QoS), in the case of the S^3MS project we can talk of quality of protection (QoP), since the quality attribute that is guaranteed by the S×C framework is security. Hence, all the stakeholders of the S^3MS scenario exploit this approach (i.e., the services provided by the S×C framework) to develop, deploy, and execute new secure services for mobile devices. As an example, in the S×C model, application developers are responsible for delivering a security contract together with each application. Contracts are written using the language defined by the S×C framework, and will be managed by the other stakeholders of the scenario with the services provided by the the S×C framework, too.

We have proposed a framework and a technological solution for trusted deployment and execution of communicating mobile applications in heterogeneous environments where a *contract-based security mechanism* lies at the core of the framework. In S×C a contract is a claim by a mobile application on the interaction with relevant security and privacy features of a mobile platform. We have shown how the compliance of the contract with the application can be verified, how contracts can be matched by policies during deployment and how they can be enforced during development, at time of delivery and loading, and during execution of the application by the mobile platform.

We argue that in the long term a new paradigm will not replace, but enhance, today's security mechanisms, and will provide a flexible, simple, and scalable security and privacy protection mechanism for future mobile systems. It will allow a network operator and a user to decide what an application is allowed to do, prevent bad code from running, and allow good code to be easily designed and deployed.

In this way we hope to build the basis for a concrete opening of the software market of nomadic devices to trusted third-party applications, without sandboxing and without the burden of roaming trust infrastructure.

Acknowledgment

The work published in this chapter is partly supported by the European Community under the Sixth Framework Programme, contract FP6–27004–S^3MS. The work reflects only the authors' views. The Community is not liable for any use that may be made of the information contained therein.

Notes

1. Most software is from small companies which cannot afford the expenses necessary to obtain an operator's certification, and thus will not run as trusted code.

2. Interested readers can find in Dragoni et al. (2007) an example of exploitation of our matching algorithm for automata-based rule specification.

References

Aktug, I., and Naliuka, K. 2007. Conspec—A formal language for policy specification. In *Proceedings of the First International Workshop on Run Time Enforcement for Mobile and Distributed Systems* (REM2007).

Appel, A. W., and Felten, E. W. 1999. Proof-carrying authentication. In *Proceedings of the 6th ACM Conference on Computer and Communications Security*, pp. 52–62. New York: ACM Press.

Bacon, J. 2002. Toward pervasive computing. *IEEE Pervasive Computing* 1(2): 84–86.

Bielova, N., Dalla Torre, M., Dragoni, N., and I. Siahaan. 2008. Matching Policies with Security Claims of Mobile Applications. In *Proceedings of the Third International Conference on Availability, Reliability and Security (ARES'08)*, Barcelona, Spain, 2008, IEEE Computer Society Press.

Building Bug-free O-O Software: An Introduction to Design by Contract. Eiffel Manual. http://archive.eiffel.com/doc/manuals/technology/contract.

Chakraborty, D., Dasgupta, K., Mittal, S., Misra, A., Gupta, A., Newmark, E., and Oberle, C. 2007. Businessfinder: Harnessing presence to enable live yellow pp. for small, medium and micro mobile businesses. *IEEE Communications* 45(1): 144–151.

Diot, C., and Gautier, L. 1999. A distributed architecture for multiplayer interactive applications on the Internet. *IEEE Network* 13(4): 6–15.

Dragoni, N., Massacci, F., Naliuka, K., and Siahaan, I. 2007. Security-by-contract: Toward a semantics for digital signatures on mobile code. In *EuroPKI 2007. Proceedings of the Fourth European PKI Workshop: Theory and Practice*, pp. 297–312. Berlin: Springer.

Erlingsson, U., and Schneider, F. B. 2000. IRM enforcement of Java stack inspection. In *IEEE Symposium on Security and Privacy*, p. 246. New York: IEEEComputer Society Press.

Gong, L., and Ellison, G. 2003. *Inside JavaY™ 2 Platform Security: Architecture, API Design, and Implementation*. Pearson Education.

Harter, A., Hopper, A., Steggles, P., Ward, A., and Webster, P. 2002. The anatomy of a context-aware application. *WiNet* 8(2–3): 187–197.

JSR 118. 2002a. Mobile Information Device Profile for Java 2 Micro Edition. http://jcp.org/aboutJava/communityprocess/final/jsr118/index.html.

JSR 118 Addendum. 2002b. Security for GSM/UMTS Compliant Devices Recommended Practice. Addendum to the Mobile Information Device Profile. http://www.jcp.org/aboutJava/communityprocess/maintenance/jsr118/.

JSR139. 2003. The Connected Limited Device Configuration Specification. http://jcp.org/aboutJava/communityprocess/final/jsr139/index.html.

LaMacchia, B., and Lange, S. 2002. *.NET Framework Security*. Addison Wesley.

Martinelli, F., Mori, P., and Vaccarelli, A. 2005. Towards continuous usage control on Grid computational services. In *Proceedings of the International Conference on Autonomic and Autonomous Systems and International Conference on Networking and Services*, p. 82. New York: IEEE Computer Society Press.

MOBIUS (Mobility, Ubiquity and Security). 2006. Deliverable D1.2, Framework- and Application-specific Security Requirements. http://mobius.inria.fr/twiki/pub/DeliverablesList/WebHome/Deliv1–2corrected.pdf.

Montagut, F., and Molva, R. 2005. Enabling pervasive execution of workflows. In *Proceedings of the 1st IEEE International Conference on Collaborative Computing: Networking, Applications and Worksharing*.

Necula, G. C. 1997. Proof-carrying code. In *Proceedings of the 24th ACM SIGPLAN–SIGACT Symposium on Principles of Programming Languages* (POPL '97), pp. 106–119.

Necula, G. C., and Lee, P. 1998. Safe, untrusted agents using proof-carrying code. In *Mobile Agents and Security*, pp. 61–91. London: Springer.

Nordio, M., Medel, R., Bavera, F., Aguirre, J., and Baum, G. 2004. A framework for execution of secure mobile code based on static analysis. In *Proceedings of the Quantitative Evaluation of Systems, First International Conference* (QEST '04), pp. 59–66. Washington, DC: IEEE Computer Society.

Paul, N., and Evans, D. 2004. .NET security: Lessons learned and missed from Java. In *Proceedings of the 20th Annual Computer Security Applications Conference*, pp. 272–281.

RFC 2828. 2000. *Internet Security Glossary*.

Skalka, C., and Smith, S. 2000. Static enforcement of security with types. *ACM SIG-PLAN Notices* 35(9): 34–45.

18 The ATHENA Framework for Cross-Organizational Business Processes

Matthias Born, Ulrike Greiner, Sonia Lippe, Rainer Ruggaber, Timo Kahl, Jörg Ziemann, and Frank-Walter Jäkel

18.1 Introduction

One of the trends in the global market is an increasingly complex collaboration among enterprises. Over 90 percent of CIOs consider collaboration a "strategic necessity" or "very important" (AMR 2005). Organizations that are transforming themselves into "networked organizations" need to interact with a wide community of buyers, sellers, and partners. Numerous new business opportunities and business solutions are created for enterprises that work effectively and efficiently together in business networks. Interoperability, as the organizational, operational, and technological ability of an enterprise to cooperate with its business partners, is a prerequisite to support these types of collaborations.

Insufficient interoperability is a major impediment to the adoption of new business models that could enhance productivity and competitiveness. It produces inflexibility and slow adoption to changing markets. Organizations are willing to invest 30–40 percent of their IT budgets on integration (Phifer et al. 2003; AMR 2005). However, integration projects today are time-consuming and face a set of numerous, interrelated interoperability issues concerning ICT (information and communication technology) systems, semantic agreement, strategy, management, and culture. Examples are incomplete models for value assessment of interoperability projects, proprietary data formats and proprietary semantics, many incompatible standards, and hard-coded transformations and processes. From a technical viewpoint, interoperability issues develop when provided characteristics of a system do not match what is required for a certain collaboration. Interoperability thus is not a product or component that is developed and that can be added to an existing IT Infrastructure. Interoperability is a characteristic of a system that allows for automated exchange of information and meaningful use of this information.

At its most fundamental level, the concept of interoperability is simply about making things work together. Interoperability issues can arise on all levels throughout the enterprise. Generally we can distinguish business-level interoperability challenges and technical concerns. To address interoperability issues of all kinds appropriately, ATHENA has developed an interoperability framework and a reference architecture that relate the different

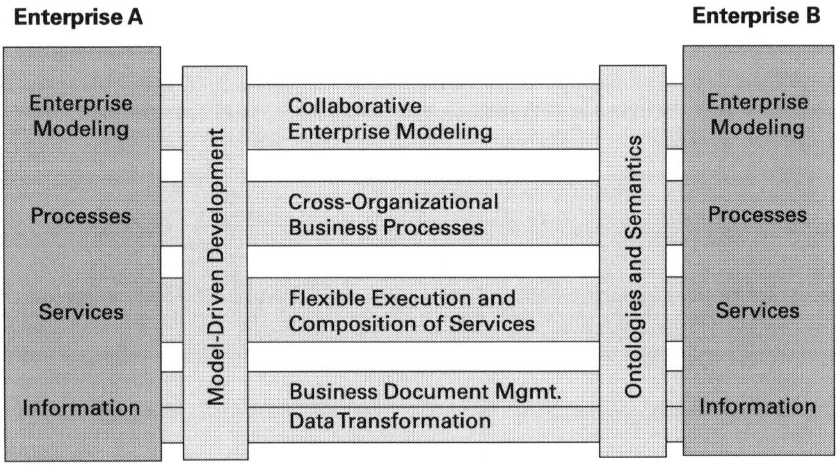

Figure 18.1
ATHENA reference architecture (simplified view)

areas in which interoperability issues can occur, and thus outline the solution space of the technical results developed in ATHENA. Figure 18.1 provides a simplified view of the ATHENA reference architecture.

The reference architecture relates the interoperability artifacts of two collaborating enterprises on the following levels: enterprise modeling (including business aspects), processes, services, and information. For each of these levels ATHENA has developed a model-driven interoperability approach in which models are used to formalize and exchange the interoperability artifacts that must be negotiated and agreed upon.

Collaborative enterprise modeling concerns the exchange and alignment of models for describing business aspects, processes, organizations, products, and systems in the collaboration context. Cross-organizational business processes (CBPs) focus on linking the processes of two or more business entities to model and implement their interaction. (A discussion of related work in these two areas can be found in the respective sections below.) Flexible execution and composition of services are concerned with identifying, composing, and executing various applications. The information aspect is related to management, exchange, and processing (including transformation) of different documents, messages, and other information structures exchanged between business partners. Many stakeholders with different ways to communicate are involved in design and implementation of CBPs, as well as many different modeling languages. To overcome the semantic barriers resulting from this heterogeneous environment and to avoid wrong interpretations of syntactic descriptions, precise, computer processable meaning must be associated with the models expressed on the different levels. This problem theoretically could be solved if all involved stakeholders would use the same modeling language, and this modeling language would also comprise machine-interpretable, unambiguous elements. But in practice the different stakeholders use different languages with different concepts. For example, the exact meaning of "event" varies in different business process modeling languages. Therefore we propose the use of additional semantic annotations to clearly specify business process elements in cross-organizational scenarios.

In this chapter we focus on the process level of the ATHENA reference architecture. With respect to the taxonomy of contributions used in this book (see chapter 1), the content of this chapter falls in the vertical area of "interoperability." We present a framework developed in ATHENA to model and implement CBPs. A successful implementation of CBPs requires a clear understanding of the common processes across all involved stakeholders. It also needs a structured approach to interlink internal (private) processes of an enterprise into a CBP. Ideally the implementation of CBPs starts on the business level, using enterprise models to identify business structures between and within companies as well as their interrelations. The main target is to achieve a common agreement between all stakeholders involved (process owners). Based on this agreement, an interim level between design and execution (technical level) is used to perform a detailed execution-oriented modeling and evaluation in a platform-independent way. The technical-level models allow the generation of data and formats that are required for automated process execution.

Besides requiring different kinds of information for different stakeholders, companies also need means to selectively expose information to their business partners. Therefore, the ATHENA CBP framework also comprises a concept for process abstraction to hide information if necessary. Following the ATHENA reference architecture, the ATHENA CBP framework focuses on service-oriented architectures as the execution infrastructure for CBPs.

The remainder of this chapter is structured as follows. We start with the analysis of a collaboration scenario and present requirements for a CBP modeling and execution framework. After discussing related work, we present the design framework and the execution environment. We close with a presentation of piloting activities from the ATHENA project and some conclusions.

18.2 E-Procurement Case Study

In this section we will motivate and illustrate the concepts that are introduced in this chapter on the basis of a generic e-procurement process. We present requirements for modeling and enacting CBPs that have been derived from several case studies in various industries (e.g., furniture, aerospace, automotive), from users in the ATHENA project.

The process describes the interaction between a manufacturer, a retailer, and a supplier (see figure 18.2). We focus on the quotation and order part. The scenario consists of two processes: the retailer–manufacturer collaboration and the manufacturer–supplier

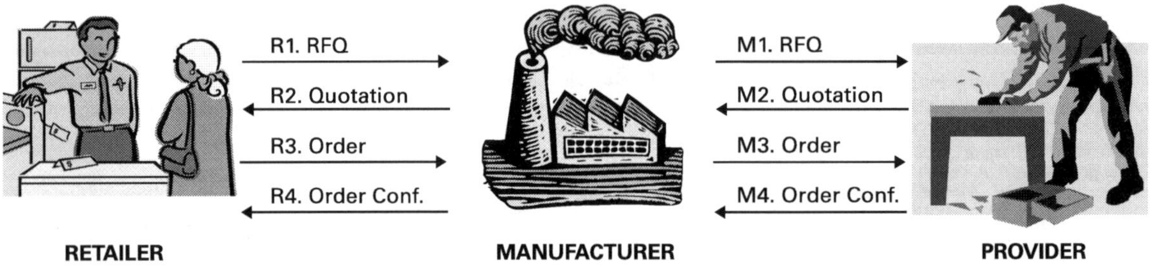

Figure 18.2
E-Procurement scenario

collaboration. The former starts when the retailer prepares a request for quotation (RFQ) for a new project. The RFQ is sent through the Internet to the manufacturer's sales department. The sales department takes care of RFQ processing and contacts other departments (e.g., product design) to complete the quotation. The retailer accepts the quotation and responds with an order. During order processing, the procurement department of the manufacturer has to order material in case the warehouse is understocked. This triggers the manufacturer–supplier collaboration, which consists of the same message exchanges. After delivery is confirmed for all materials, the final order confirmation is sent to the retailer.

18.2.1 Requirements for Modeling Framework

A detailed analysis of modeling several scenarios revealed the following challenges that have to be addressed by an industry-spanning modeling framework for CBPs (see also Lippe et al. 2005):

1. A modeling language should allow for efficient assembly of CBPs, including CBP internal information flow and interface descriptions.
2. It is necessary to provide a level of abstraction on which the partners first agree on the business goals of their collaboration. To implement the collaboration with ICT systems, the involvement of technical staff is necessary. Thus a modeling framework should support different graphical modeling languages meeting the needs of all involved stakeholders, from the business level down to technical experts.
3. The internal business processes of each partner have to be linked into a CBP without revealing confidential private information (e.g., calculation of discount rates) through so-called process abstraction.
4. Simplified process adoption has to be achieved. For example, a supplier interacting with different manufacturers should not require different private processes for each collaboration he is involved in.
5. Depending on the level of trust between the collaborating partners, a scalable exposition of internal processes should be possible.

18.2.2 Requirements for Execution in a Service-oriented Environment

From the ATHENA user scenarios we also derived a set of requirements with respect to the enactment of CBPs in a service-oriented environment. We focus on the CBP aspects of the enactment architecture, meaning that we leave out the more general requirements for technical architectures and systems, such as reliability, scalability, and performance. In particular, we have derived the following requirements:

1. *CBP collaboration environment for operating CBPs* The architecture must support the CBP collaboration to (co)operate (i.e., observe and execute [send, receive, and broker] the running CBPs).
2. *Different interoperability strategies and means* In order to interoperate with the architecture, the CBP partners must be able to choose among different interoperability strategies and interaction means. Three alternatives are identified: (1) the CBP partner wants to use its own business process engine, (2) the CBP partner wants to make a technical bridge to its own legacy systems (e.g., ERP system), or (3) the CBP partner wants to make a full adoption (i.e., apply an interoperable internal business process execution platform).
3. *Multicast interactions* Multicast interactions are important because the CBP must cater for more complex interactions between collaborators than just binary interactions.
4. *Automatic transformation of business documents* The transformation of business documents in the data interchange between CBP partners must be done automatically. The architecture should support data interchange standards.

18.3 Related Work

In this section we discuss related work, in particular that on process-modeling and enterprise-modeling frameworks. In the last part of this section we also consider related projects.

We have analyzed different modeling languages with respect to how well they address the requirements specified above (see table 18.1 and Lippe et al. 2005). CBP assembly considering CBP internal data flow and CBP interface descriptions is well supported by nearly all approaches. An exception to this is RosettaNet, a consortium of major information technology, electronic components, semiconductor manufacturing, telecommunications, and logistics companies that aims at creating and implementing industry-wide, open e-business process standards. It focuses on the definition of common business procedures and reflects data flow only partially.

Regarding the support of a process abstraction, we identified insufficient support for modeling of process abstraction and linking internal processes to CBPs. Even though CBPs can be modeled and interfaces between the partners can be specified, we observe a shortcoming in explicitly linking internal processes to CBPs. None of the analyzed approaches offers a suitable mechanism to link private processes to CBPs, enabling information hiding and simplified process adoption at the same time. Only WS-BPEL (Andrews

Table 18.1
Comparison of process modeling languages

Requirement	Fully supported	Partly supported	Not supported
CBP assembly	EPC IEM Business Scenario Maps BPDM UML ebXML BPML XPDL WS-BPEL/WS-CDL	RosettaNet	
Process abstraction concept		WS-BPEL/WS-CDL	EPC IEM Business Scenario Maps UML BPML XPDL BPDM ebXML RosettaNet
CBP modeling framework		EPC IEM Business Scenario Maps BPDM UML RosettaNet BPML WS-BPEL/WS-CDL XPDL	ebXML
Support for business-level users	EPC IEM Business Scenario Maps BPDM UML	BPML	ebXML RosettaNet XPDL WS-BPEL/WS-CDL
Support for technical users	ebXML BPML XPDL WS-BPEL/WS-CDL	BPDM RosettaNet	EPC IEM Business Scenario Maps UML

et al. 2003), a merger of IBM WSFL and Microsoft XLANG) partially meets this requirement, as it has the notion of "abstract processes" that can be used to model abstract views of business processes. To define CBPs, WS-CDL (W3C 2004) may be used in combination with WS-BPEL, as it provides a global, message-oriented view of a process involving multiple Web Services. However, WS-BPEL is an execution-oriented language to be used by IT experts, not business experts. Therefore, WS-BPEL is relevant mainly at the execution level of the overall ATHENA process framework. Furthermore, the abilities of WS-BPEL to model multiple view processes per role and private process are limited, thus requiring that the user maintains one private process per abstract process. Some other approaches offer constructs which might be used to model abstractions of processes, but they do not support flexible hiding of private information. For instance, with UML the data and organizational and functional views of a CBP can be modeled with class diagrams. For modeling the process view, activity diagrams are most suitable, especially with all their new features introduced by UML 2.0 (OMG 2007b), such as interaction and composition structure diagrams. A general weakness of UML is the fact that UML as a general-purpose modeling approach lacks primitives for intuitively describing business processes (partly addressed by BPDM; OMG 2007c). UML 2.0 also does not support automatic generation of view processes from private processes, particularly of multiple view processes on the same private process to address multiple interactions, which is an important aspect of the ATHENA process framework.

With respect to the requirement of a CBP modeling framework, tool support is offered for most modeling languages, mainly with graphical user interfaces. However, they often support only either the business experts (e.g., EPC, Horrmann et al. 1992; IEM, Mertins and Jochem 1999; Spur et al. 1996; or business scenario maps, SAP 2004) or the technical experts (e.g., BPML, BPMI 2007; XPDL, WfMC 2002; WS-BPEL), or modeling of platform-independent control flow, as in model-driven architectures (MDA; OMG 2007a). The last is supported by BPDM (OMG 2007b), which defines an abstract metamodel for business process definition. Thus this metamodel provides a common abstraction for multiple business process or workflow definition languages. We did not find an approach that gives comprehensive modeling support on all levels.

Second, we consider modeling frameworks in our discussion of related work. Different modeling frameworks have previously been defined for business process or enterprise modeling. These include the "framework for information systems architecture" (Zachman framework; Zachman 1987) and the "architecture of integrated information systems" (ARIS; Scheer 1999). Both frameworks offer modeling support from different user perspectives. The ARIS architecture distinguishes between organization, function, output, information, and control views. The purpose of the Zachman framework is to provide a basic structure which supports organization, access, integration, interpretation, development, and management of a set of architectural representations of the organizations' information systems. Although both frameworks combine different user perspectives and allow modeling on different levels of abstraction, the focus of these frameworks is on internal process modeling. They lack methods which allow modeling of cross-organizational collaborations, as a creation of an external view of the organization (as required for CBPs) is not supported.

The UN/CEFACT modeling methodology (UMM) is specifically designed to provide a modeling procedure for specifying CBPs in a technology-neutral, implementation-independent manner (UN/CEFACT 2003). However, there is no notion of process abstraction and no support for linking internal processes to CBPs without revealing confidential internal information.

Third, we relate the ATHENA framework to results from other research projects. In particular we cover TrustCoM, SUPER, ECOLEAD, DBE, INTEROP, R4eGov, and ArKoS.

TrustCoM (TrustCoM 2007) aims to develop a framework for trust, security, and contract management in dynamic virtual organizations. In contrast to ATHENA, which focuses more on BPM-related issues, the TrustCoM project deals with security and trust issues of collaborative business processes. The infrastructure developed within the project enables a secure and global management of business processes and is based on open standards for Web Services.

The SUPER project (SUPER 2007) is working to improve the modeling and management of business processes inside an enterprise. It attempts to decrease the gap between the business level and the IT level. In order to shift the control to the business expert during the BPM life cycle, SUPER is analyzing how semantic technologies can be used to lower the complexity of existing process models and improve the quality and creation of new process models. Unlike ATHENA, SUPER is more concerned with how semantic technologies, such as Semantic Business Process Discovery, Semantic Business Process Composition, and Semantic Business Process Mediation, can help in the overall BPM life cycle of one enterprise. There are only minor tasks defined within the project that deal with collaborative business processes.

ECOLEAD (ECOLEAD 2007) aims at developing technologies for networks of collaborative enterprises. Three focus areas are addressed: breeding environments, dynamic virtual organizations, and professional virtual communities. Within the project, foundations, mechanisms, and tools for establishing, operating, and managing collaborative networked organizations are developed. The challenge is to use modeling methodologies, languages, and tools that are suited for the particular characteristics of the virtual organizations. The ECOLEAD project does not aim at developing new modeling frameworks and methodologies, and does not focus on all the interoperability problems and their solutions, which are investigated in ATHENA. The challenge for ECOLEAD is to find and build on approaches that support virtual organization management from different aspects.

DBE (DBE 2007) is focusing on a platform approach to realize service-oriented architecture for small and medium enterprises (SMEs), but also to support services related to cultural and trust aspects. In contrast, ATHENA has developed a federated approach for midsize and large companies which could be adapted to smaller companies. The ATHENA approach supports an independent realization of the external connection for each company. On that basis the companies can be connected in an interoperable manner configured by a model-based concept. In ATHENA, mostly the concepts, procedures, and architecture have been developed. A connection between both approaches could be a good solution for the future. The ATHENA architecture might be a connection point between SME platforms based on the DBE approach and systems of larger companies.

INTEROP-NoE (INTEROP 2007) was a network of excellence regarding interoperability research for networked enterprises' applications and software. A major result of the project is the INTEROP-VLab, promoting interoperability across Europe, which was established in the spring of 2007. INTEROP-VLab is funded by national or regional organizations, mostly associations of research organizations and industry. INTEROP-NoE was a partner project of ATHENA. Consequently, topics such as the synchronization of enterprise models, the approach around model-driven interoperability (MDI), the annotation requirements for models, and semantic aspects of interoperability had a lot of synergies between the two projects. However, the results are different because INTEROP was more research-driven, whereas ATHENA started with the viewpoints of industrial and IT companies. Related to the CBP approach, the INTEROP MDI and model synchronization can provide means to handle models developed independently and combined afterward.

R4eGOV (R4eGOV 2007) investigates solutions for "interoperability in the large" by supporting CBPs between public administrations in Europe (e.g., Europol and Eurojust). R4eGov builds on the ATHENA solutions, and also models and correlates view processes of public administrations on various levels of technical detail. It will further refine these concepts following the needs of the R4eGov e-government use cases which have specific requirements regarding secure information handling and also will show a high degree of human involvement.

The research project ArKoS (ArKoS 2007) deals with the development of an architecture for the management of collaborative scenarios consisting of methods, a tool support, and an integration platform. The architecture is used for the integrated support of cooperation- and coordination-intense cross-enterprise business processes. To achieve this aim, existing concepts, modeling methods, and tools are tested for their practicability. These are to be expanded in accordance with the requirements and to be redesigned if required. The industry-indifferent framework provides a generic solution concept which is subsequently transferred into an industry-specific reference model for the building industry. Thus, in contrast to ATHENA, this framework especially fits the requirements of the construction industry.

18.4 Design of Cross-Organizational Business Processes

18.4.1 Dimensions of the Framework

In order to model an entire enterprise and its interfaces, different modeling dimensions are necessary. Modeling frameworks which previously have been applied to enterprise modeling (e.g., the Zachman framework or ARIS) offer modeling support for various dimensions of an enterprise. Although both frameworks combine different user perspectives and allow modeling on different levels of abstraction (see also section 18.3), they lack methods which allow modeling cross-organizational collaborations, as a creation of an external view on the organization is not supported. The modeling methodology described in this chapter aims at developing easy-to-understand collaborative business process models that are transformable to Web Service protocols. Thus, the framework consists of two dimensions:

1. Modeling levels from design to execution of the CBP
2. Aggregation and filtering of information through an additional abstraction layer.

The first dimension of the modeling framework deals with the requirements of different modeling users and stakeholders involved in the business process. These levels are similar to the different types of models used in model-driven architectures (OMG 2007a). However, as the focus is specifically on modeling cross-organizational business processes, different names are chosen for the three levels to distinguish the more MDI-related approach as described in Elvesater et al. (2005) from the general approach of model-driven architectures. The framework incorporates the following levels (see figure 18.3):

1. *Business level* This level represents the business view on the cooperation and describes the interaction of the partners. The CBPs modeled on this level allow for analyzing business aspects, such as costs or involved resources.
2. *Technical level* This level provides a more detailed view on the CBP, representing the complete control flow of the process in a platform-independent manner. Nonexecutable

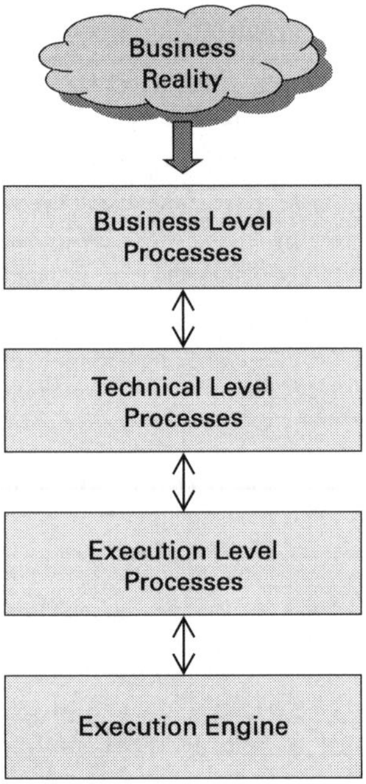

Figure 18.3
Modeling levels of CBP framework

tasks are not considered. Also, the message exchange between single tasks is modeled and can be analyzed. This supports reuse of the process models, as they can be ported to various execution platforms.

3. *Execution level* On this level the CBP is modeled in a platform-specific manner (i.e., in the modeling language of a concrete business process engine). This also includes the specification of services that execute activities and service interfaces provided by partners for exchanging messages.

In order to realize all requirements defined earlier, it was necessary to define another framework dimension. We introduced another abstraction layer which provides a systematic way that allows partners to selectively expose internal information and interweave process steps to CBPs. In the following, internal processes are defined as private processes which are known only to the owning organization and are not exposed to the outside world. The abstraction of information is achieved by the introduction of view processes as an additional abstraction layer between the private processes and the CBP model, as proposed by Schulz (2002; Schulz and Orlowska 2004).

The concept of creating views to provide abstract information about internal processes was introduced by Liu and Shen (2001). It is derived from views as they are used in database systems, and the authors present a formal model of processes and extend it to virtual process views providing transformation rules. While the views in the initial work are used only to provide necessary information about processes to other company internal departments, they extend their work for the purpose of CBPs. Parallel to this work Chiu et al. (2002) introduced workflow views to control visibility of internal processes and to enable interoperability of e-services. The main focus in this work is on combining views of different partners with composite e-services (CBPs) and the implementation of the views with contemporary Web Services. A mapping mechanism to ensure the coupling between private processes and views in all circumstances is not provided. Schulz takes up the concept of views, discusses it in the context of mediated and unmediated communication, and formalizes the dependencies between private processes, process views, and CBPs (Schulz 2002; Schulz and Orlowska 2004).

View processes provide a process-oriented interface toward business partners. View processes are an abstraction of the private processes, containing information that needs to be published for the purpose of an interaction. Several tasks of a private process can be combined in one view task. This leads to the following definition: A view process abstracts information from one or more private processes, and thus enables companies to hide critical information from unauthorized partners. It is an interface to the outside world which extracts only that kind of information which is necessary for the interaction with one or more potential partners. Thus, a view process can be seen as general interaction description of one or more private processes from the perspective of one partner.

Whereas a view process describes allowed interactions from the perspective of one partner, a CBP describes these interactions from a neutral perspective, capturing all allowed

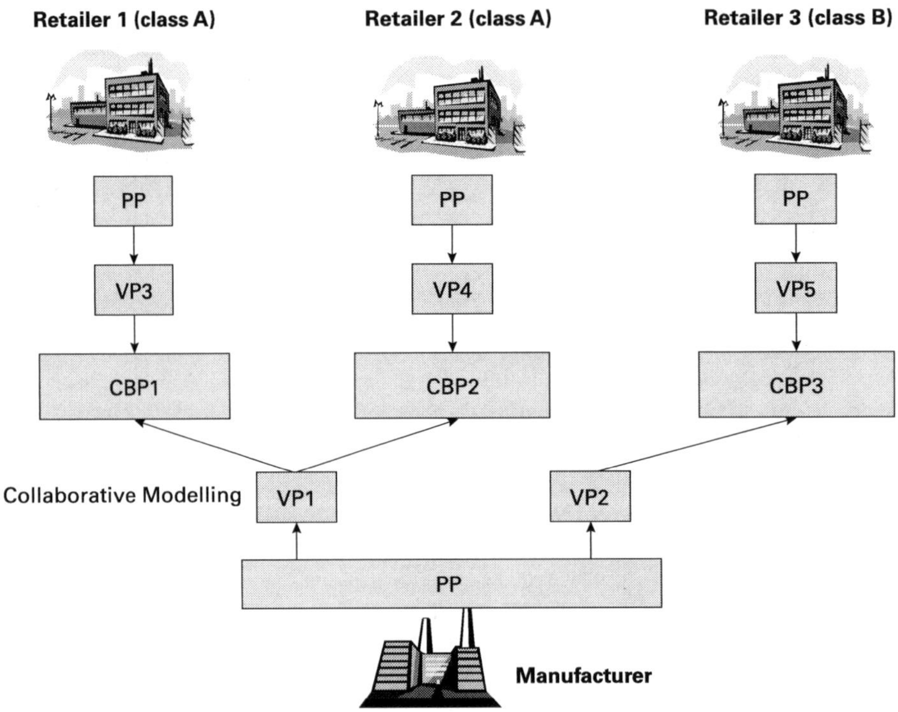

Figure 18.4
Private Processes (PP), View Processes (VP), and Cross-Organizational Business Processes (CBP)

interactions between all partners. One view process can contain interactions with different partners. Sometimes a view process suffices to describe all allowed interactions of various collaborating enterprises: if all interactions of the CBP happen only between the partners and the enterprise that provides the view process. Although more technical definitions of view processes reduce them to descriptions of digital message exchanges (see Bussler 2002), on the conceptual level partner interactions regarding money ("payment received") or material (e.g., "deliver container") can also be described in a view process. Figure 18.4 describes the view approach, using the e-procurement scenario as an example.

As described in the scenario analysis, the manufacturer works with several retailers. The manufacturer has to share his view process with the retailers in order to interact with them. The view process may vary depending on the class to which a retailer belongs. The manufacturer wants to hide his discount system from certain retailers; the solvency check should always be hidden. Thus he creates two different view processes, VP1 and VP2. Within both view processes the solvency check is hidden, but in VP1 the discount system is visible. Both view processes can be used for the interaction with different retailers, and thus one view

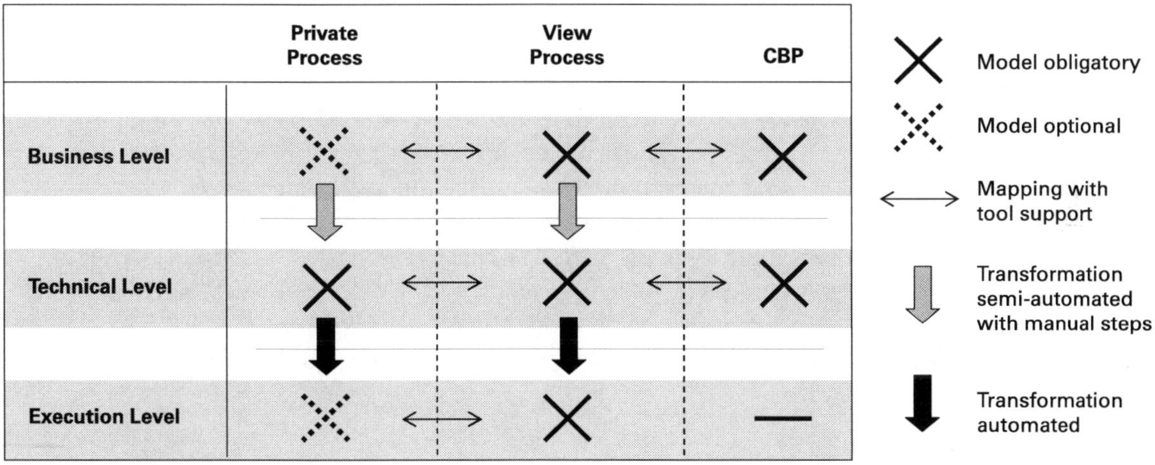

Figure 18.5
Modeling framework

process can be part of various CBPs. The CBP is created collaboratively by the manufacturer and the respective retailers.

18.4.2 Structure of the Framework

The framework structure incorporates the following (see figure 18.5):

1. Different stakeholders involved in modeling cross-organizational business processes, their different perspectives and needs
2. The selective hiding of internal process steps while offering a mechanism to expose CBP-relevant information to partners.

At each intersection between the two framework dimensions, a possible process model can be identified to capture tasks and relationships of cross-organizational interactions. Thus, it is ensured that all relevant perspectives on CBP models, as well as the processes required for the view concept, are properly captured and modeled.

Models can be distinguished as either mandatory or optional models for the CBP implementation (figure 18.5). On the business level it is compulsory for all involved parties to create a view model, specifying the externally visible business context for a specific CBP scenario. This can be used for partner communication on the management or the business analyst level. Also required is a CBP model which specifies from a high-level business perspective how the partner processes are interwoven.

The interenterprise coordination builds on a distributed business process model in which partners manage their own part of the overall business process. A CBP specifies tasks that each of the parties is required to perform as agreed in their contract (specified in terms of business-level models). Although the CBP model will not be executed, and therefore does not exist on the execution level (Schulz and Orlowska 2004), it is required for the specification of the message exchange on the technical level. It can be used for monitoring in the actual enactment phase. A process view can be considered a proxy for its corresponding private process. In other words, a process view is outsourcing its implementation to its corresponding private process (Schulz and Orlowska 2004). Therefore, it is mandatory that both models are specified on the technical level. The framework allows for creating various views on the same internal processes when interacting in different contexts. It is the intent that a process modeler can leave a private process unchanged and create a special view process which can be adapted to satisfy specific business requirements. This is possible on all levels of abstraction.

18.4.3 Annotation for Model Mapping and Transformation

We propose to use mappings and transformations between process models to support the user in not having to fully regenerate process models manually when moving through the framework (see figure 18.5 for an overview of the necessary transformations and mappings). In this section we discuss how annotation can support the horizontal mappings and the vertical transformations in the modeling framework. By "annotation" we mean giving additional information that is necessary to generate correct technical process models later on. Two different elements of business process models have been identified for which annotations are beneficial:

1. Elements describing the structure of the process model. These comprise the nature of activities in the process (e.g., to wait, to receive a message, etc.) as well as control flow elements such as logical connectors.
2. Elements describing information, material, or other artifacts that are used by the process activities (e.g., business documents, material that is sent, money that is received).

In collaborative scenarios, the process structure captures the sequence in which information, money, or products are exchanged. Annotations with a precise description of the intended meaning of activities make it easier for a partner to correctly adapt his own processes to view processes of his partners. However, the annotation of the process structure should not be limited to characteristics of process activities, but also should describe characteristics of control flow elements. For example, (Van der Aalst 2002) shows that logical operators, representing an important part of the control flow, are defined ambiguously in many workflow languages and can be interpreted in different ways. An annotation of these elements would allow describing the precise semantics of control flows and facilitate their correct automatic interpretation and transformation.

The second kind of model elements to be annotated is the content of the information exchanged in a CBP. This helps to avoid misunderstandings and enables automated transformations (e.g., two companies exchanging a business document describing a product can use different descriptions).

Annotation of View Processes for Horizontal Mapping The annotation of business process models to precisely describe the intended behavior is of particular use for mapping of private processes to view processes to CBPs. We will explain that with an example. Figure 18.6 shows the CBP in which the retailer requests and receives a quote for goods from the manufacturer.

On the left, the view process of the manufacturer is illustrated; on the right, the view process of the retailer. The view process of the retailer shows that he waits only three days for an answer; if he does not receive one in this period, the RFQ process will be terminated. Though this is a very simple CBP, several of its elements should be refined by annotation (for example, business documents, process activities, and events).

The meaning of activities can be made more precise by annotating them. For example, with respect to activities to send and receive the RFQ, it is unclear if the message is going to be sent by post, by e-mail, by EDIFACT, or some other means. This could be clarified with an annotation specifying the actual channel.

Events can also be made more precise. Take as an example the "3 days passed" event. The manufacturer cannot tell exactly how much time he has to answer the RFQ: "3 days" could mean 3×24 hours, it could mean noon of the third day after receipt, or it could mean midnight of the third day. Annotation would specify this period more precisely, and ambiguities could be avoided during modeling the CBP.

Annotation for Vertical Model Transformation Annotation of models at the business level (e.g., EPCs or IEM) can also support vertical transformation. In the vertical direction, technical realizations of business models are created. Therefore, it is necessary that the elements of a business-level model can be matched to elements of the technical models. This is difficult, because activities described in the model are usually aimed at business analysts and not intended for interpretation by IT systems. For example, a function may be described by the label "Wait for arrival of message from supplier." This function could be automated on the execution level (e.g., using an event mechanism). But in practice, the function names are described differently by different persons and are not necessarily as precise as in the example. Therefore, current approaches to such model transformations require the description of processes in a certain syntax: they demand that all processes that should be automated are described in a certain manner (see, for example, Ziemann and Mendling 2005). This limits descriptions of activities to a certain vocabulary and prevents business analysts from using a language natural for them. In contrast, if these functions, apart from a text label created by the business analysts, were further described by structured annotations related to the technical level, their exact meaning could be captured and used to automate the transformation to the technical level.

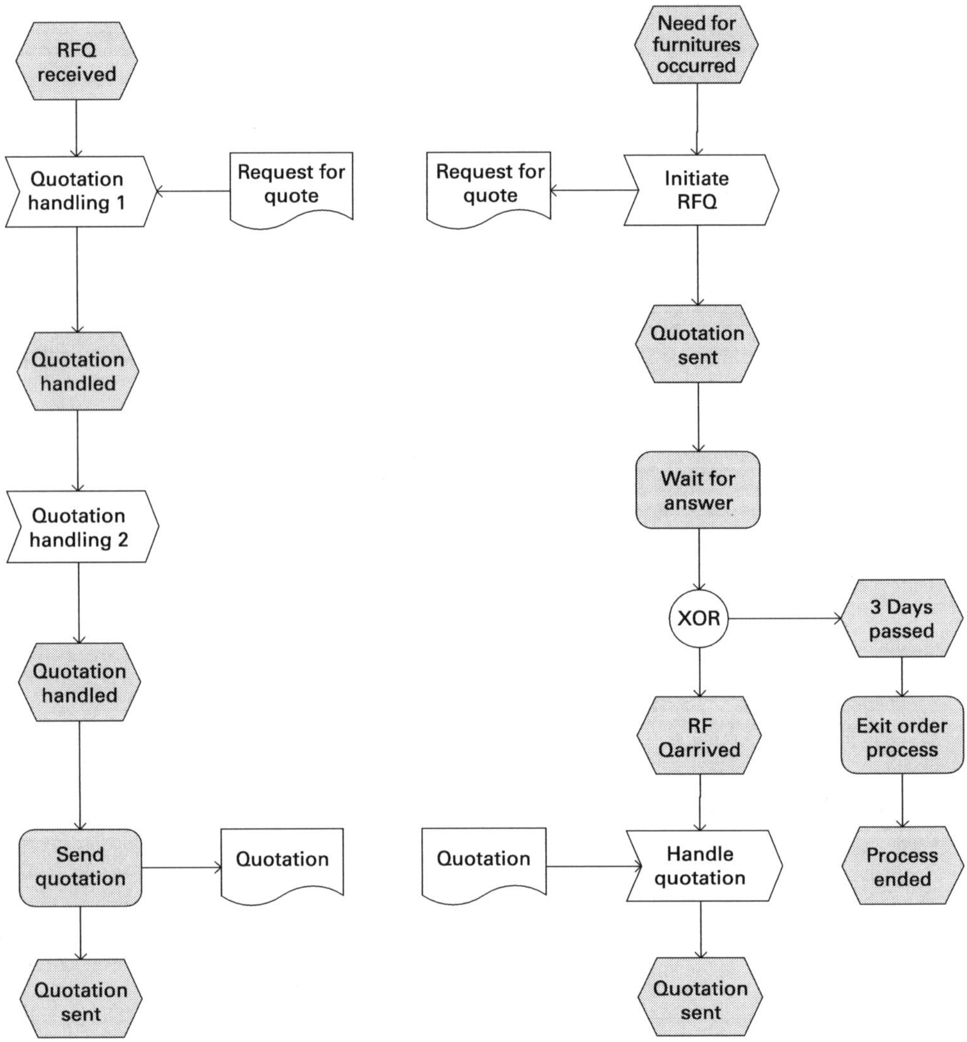

Figure 18.6
An RFQ process from the manufacturer (left) and the retailer point of view (right)

Figure 18.7 shows processes annotated with information related to their transformation to a technical-, and finally an execution-level representation. Each process describes the information used in elementary Web Service functions. For example, if a process step is realized by the synchronous invocation of a Web Service, the corresponding EPC model should contain information on the outgoing and ingoing variables as well the Web Service specification. The other functions describe the information necessary for the asynchronous invocation of a Web Service, the receiving of a message from a Web Service, and the reply to a message received before.

18.4.4 Modeling Procedure

To complete the modeling framework, a modeling procedure is required that describes in which order models have to be created to make best use of the framework and to ensure the best possible integration of existing models. Concerning the creation of views and CBPs, three possible procedures can be identified.

1. In an inside-out approach, each company starts with the identification of its private processes and the creation of interaction-specific views (see the dashed arrows 1 in figure 18.8). The views are then combined into CBPs (dashed arrows 2). Depending on how well the process views of the process partner fit, variations on their own view might be necessary to finalize the modeling activities (dashed arrows 3).
2. In an outside-in approach, the partners start by identifying a common picture of the interaction in terms of a CBP model. Each partner then has to create its views according to the process steps that he will be executing. This also might need iterations for redefining the CBP (solid arrows 1 and 2 in figure 18.8). As a last step the partners have to define their private processes (solid arrows 3).
3. In the third scenario, one partner starts with its private processes and offers a process view to its partners. The partners can use this process-based interface to link that process view to their internal processes via their process views. This would conform to a bottom-up approach for one partner and a top-down for the others. Which procedure is suitable depends on existing partner processes and the relationship between the different organizations.

In terms of the different levels of abstraction, the current practice in process modeling is the outside-in approach. CBPs are first defined on the business level, refined on the technical level, and then implemented into an executable model for each partner (TrustCoM 2007; INTEROP 2007). Further research should address an approach in which models of existing organization-internal processes can be made available on the business level, providing information about existing executable processes. Managers could use this information while negotiating with business partners and an improved adoption of existing processes could be achieved.

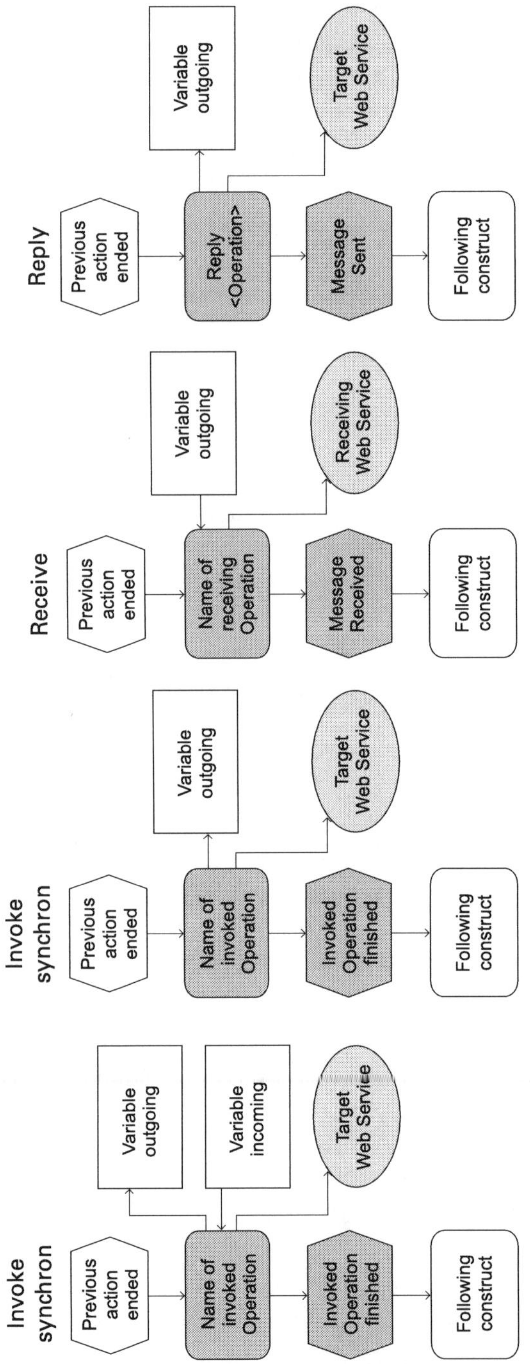

Figure 18.7
EPC Functions annotated for transformation to technical level artifacts

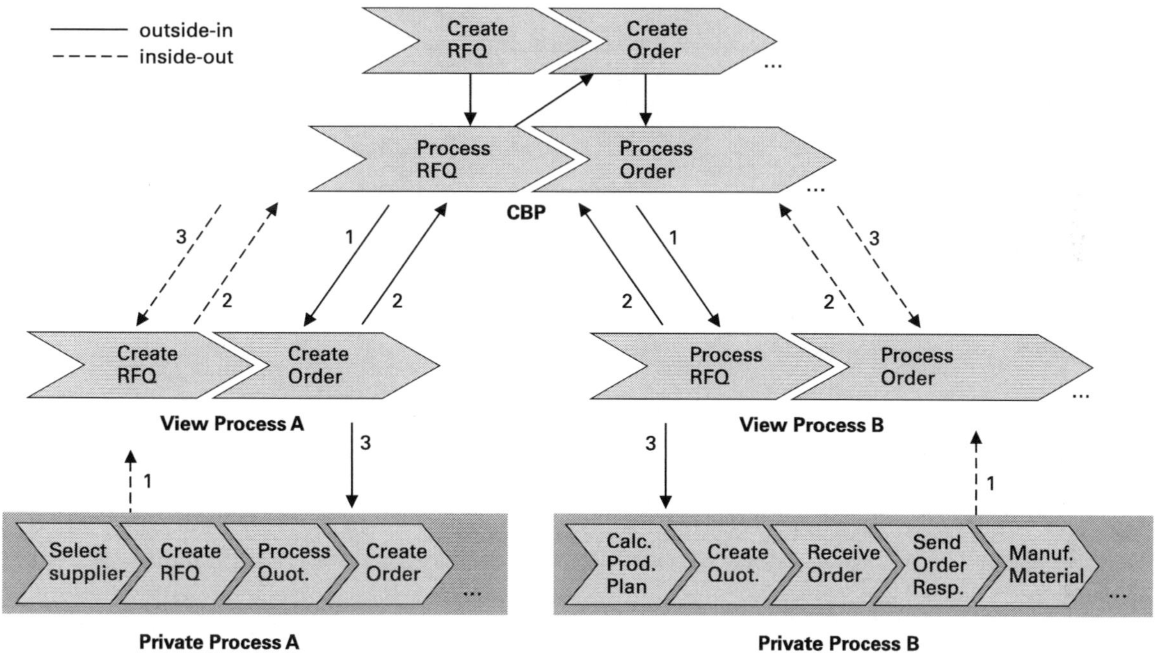

Figure 18.8
Modeling procedures (outside-in vs. inside-out) illustrated with processes from the eProcurement scenario

18.5 Execution of Cross-Organizational Business Processes

18.5.1 Enactment Architecture for CBPs

In the following, we outline the building blocks of an architecture for the enactment of CBPs. One characteristic of the architecture is that it does not make any assumptions about the distribution of the building blocks among the involved partners. For instance, there can be several process engines linked in a decentralized way as well as a central CBP engine that is responsible for correlating the different processes.

We start with the definition of high-level building blocks and then refine those building blocks in further steps. Our goal is to define a process enactment architecture that allows for the execution of CBPs defining the necessary components (such as tools, information, repositories) for participating organizations. The need for privacy, on the one hand, and information and activity sharing, on the other hand (as outlined in section 18.2.1), have to be the guiding principles in the architecture. Therefore, we can identify three main blocks on the highest level of abstraction (see figure 18.9):

1. Company internal components
2. Interface components
3. CBP components.

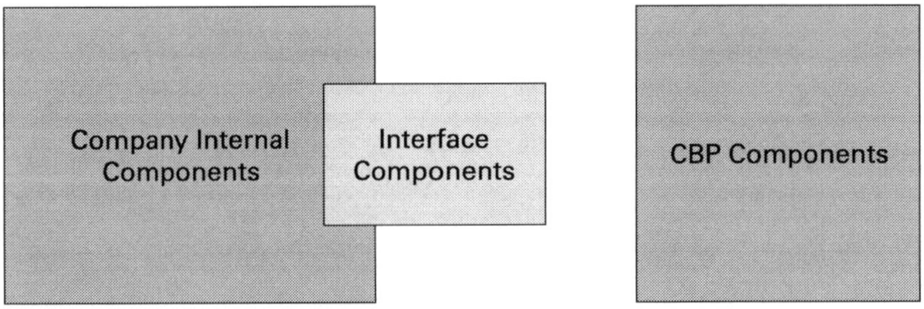

Figure 18.9
Top level architectural building blocks

The company internal components contain all building blocks which are encapsulated inside the company and are not accessible by partners. For instance, these are all components that are linked to the modeling and execution of private processes or to the invocation of internal applications.

The CBP components are accessible by all partners. They represent the information that has to be shared between partners in order to define and execute CBPs. They can also contain information that is necessary to monitor and analyze the CBP execution if this is required in a particular business scenario.

The interface components link company internal components with CBP components. They represent the information that is published by the companies in order to take part in CBPs (for instance, view processes of the partners' private processes).

From here we take a more detailed look into the building blocks, considering the company internal components as a black box, as we define the architecture on a generic level independent of the partners' internal system landscape. Figure 18.10 depicts the interface and CBP components for the architecture. The interface components are the following:

1. *Enactment engine for view processes* An engine is required which is responsible for executing the views that make up a CBP.
2. *Internal application gateway* This serves as an interface to the internal applications or business services encapsulating applications.
3. *External partner gateway* A component is required that acts as a gateway to the external world and the partners.
4. *View processes repository* A repository is needed to store the view processes. This can be separated from the private process repository, which might already exist.
5. *Event and document correlation* The event and document correlation is responsible for identifying the CBP instance to which an incoming message belongs. It consists of two parts: "message to process instance mapping," which identifies the relevant process instance, and semantic document mapping, which maps incoming messages into a format that the partner can understand. It also maps outgoing messages into a format the

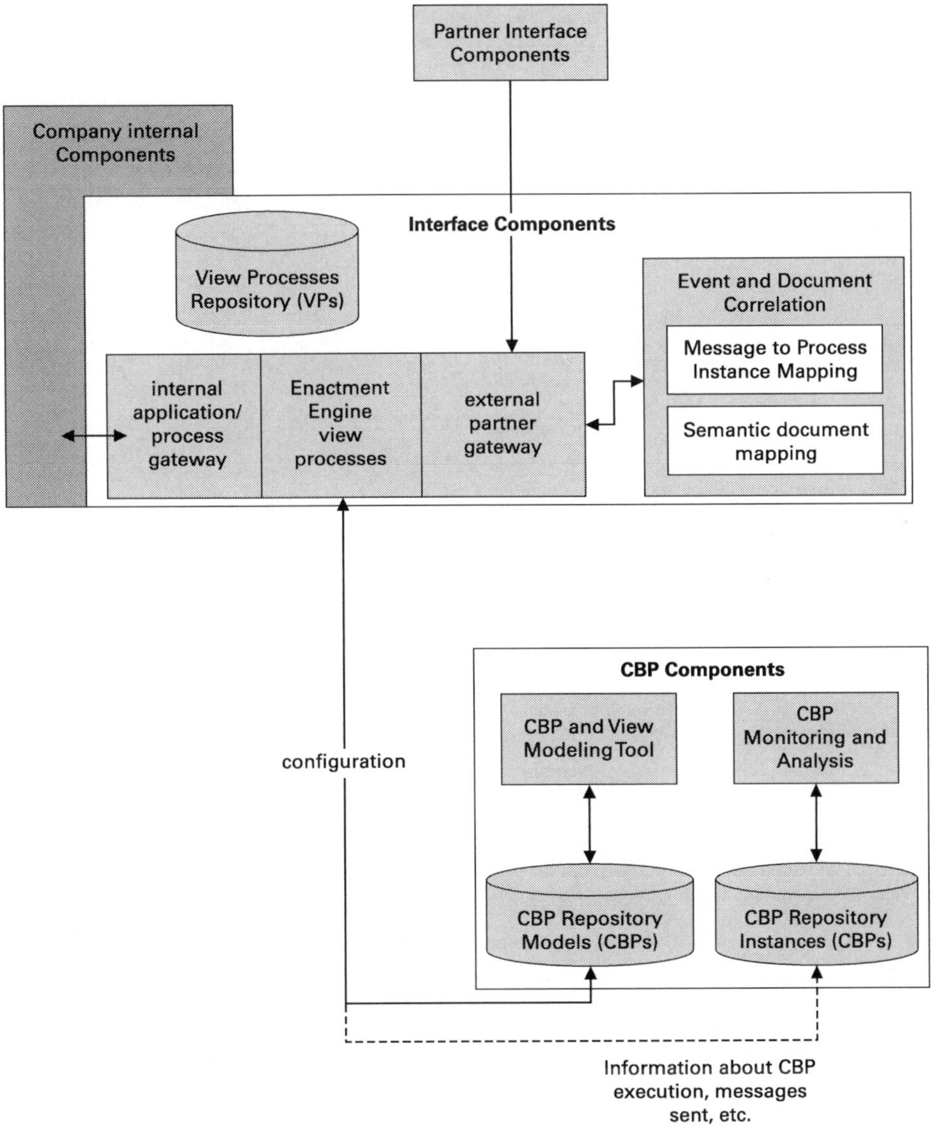

Figure 18.10
Common building blocks for CBP enactment architecture

receiving partner can interpret appropriately. This can be supported by annotation of the exchanged documents as described above.

The enactment engine for view processes executes the view processes of the partners that are part of a CBP instance. By executing the views, the CBP is executed. The enactment engine for view processes communicates over the internal application gateway with internal business services representing the private processes. The enactment engine exchanges (i.e., sends and receives) messages with partners using the external partner gateway. This gateway calls the event and document correlation to map messages or extract correlation information from them. The information is used internally in the enactment engine for view processes.

The CBP components are the following:

1. *CBP and view modeling tool* This component is used by the participating companies to define their view processes based on their private processes, and to define the overall CBP which uses the views.
2. *CBP monitoring and analysis tool* This component may be used to monitor actual executions of CBP instances and to analyze data offline that has been stored during execution of CBP instances.
3. *A repository for storing both the CBP definition and the execution data (i.e., process instances)* The process definition is used for a CBP-driven configuration of the engine. The information for the instance repository is derived from the execution data generated by the view engine.

18.5.2 Service-Based Enactment Architecture

Following the ATHENA reference architecture outlined in the introduction, we refine the enactment architecture for CBPs to a service-based enactment architecture. The architecture has to combine two requirements. First, we have to address the execution of Web Services inside a private process. Such Web Services are those that are called inside a company. Second, we have to address the execution of interface services. Those services have to connect several partner views, so that a CBP can be executed in a decentralized way. Each partner knows only the interface services of the other partners, and will publish its own inbound interfaces to the outside world.

Web Services and interface services can be modeled as task profiles. In general, a task profile describes the functionality that a task performs at runtime. This business functionality is modeled in a task management tool (extending the CBP enactment architecture) and assigned to a task model during the design phase of a business process. The process task in the process modeling tool simply references task profiles (see figure 18.11). This concept allows us to reuse task profiles for several process tasks in the same or different process models. The following example will clarify this idea. Consider two simple business processes. The first one is a time recording process, in which a manager needs to approve

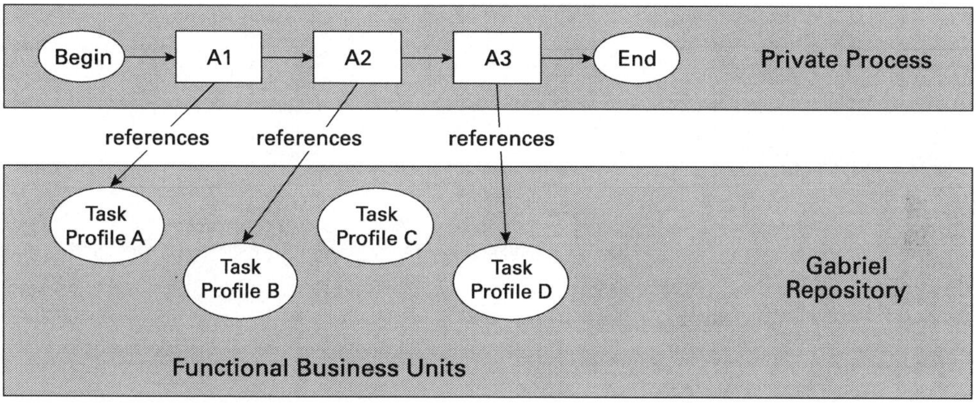

Figure 18.11
Assignment of a task profile

the expenses and time recorded. The second process is a leave request. Both processes need an approval task to perform the business functionality. We can assign the same task profile to both processes in the process modeling tool.

Task profiles can be of different types. We distinguish between service task profiles, interface profiles, and user task profiles. During process enactment, each task profile will result in an actual task instance that is responsible for executing the business logic (see figure 18.12).

User tasks require human interaction in order to be completed. It is the responsibility of the task management tool to make sure that the different instances are activated and delegated to the right user. We will not further discuss user tasks here, as we want to focus on an automated CBP enactment based on a service-oriented architecture.

Service task profiles represent tasks that will automatically trigger a Web Service at runtime. A service does not need any human interaction. Instead, the task management tool is responsible for updating the status, sending the relevant data to the service, and, in the case of a synchronous service call, importing the response back to the process data.

The goal of interface profiles is to enable different process engines to interact with each other. The communication is based on Web Services because other process engines, such as a WS-BPEL engine, are also supporting this standard. The partners who are participating in a CBP should provide well-defined interfaces in the form of Web Service definitions that do not include any proprietary process information. Nevertheless, when two processes are communicating with each other, they need to agree on some kind of correlation information. This ensures that each process can identify to which process step from which process instance an incoming message has to be assigned.

As we see, both the service task profiles and the interface profile are dealing with Web Service calls. Therefore, the task management tool needs to enable the execution of

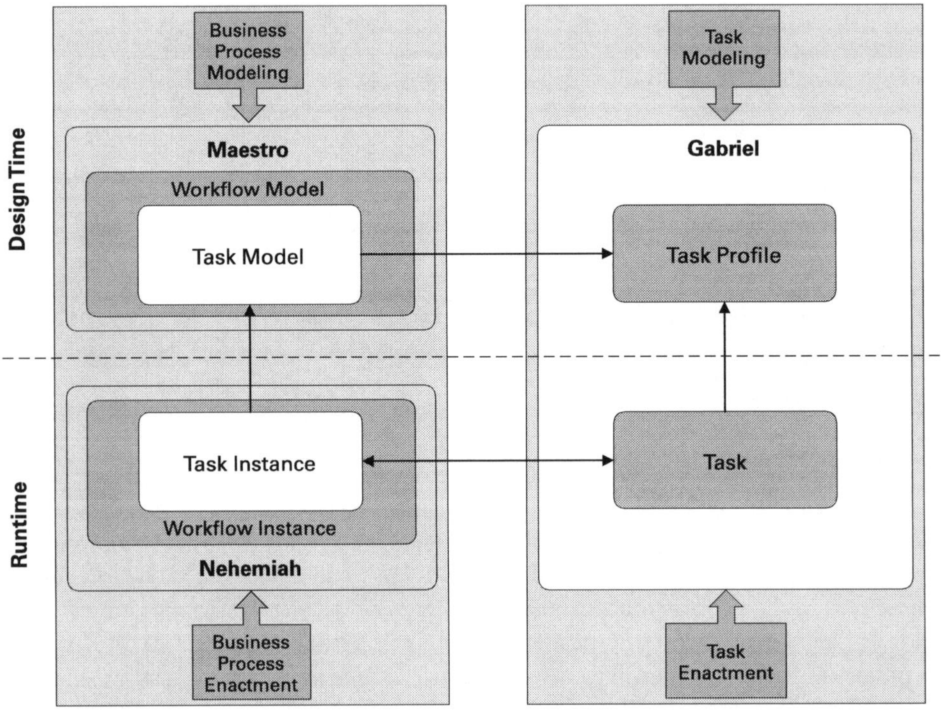

Figure 18.12
Association between process management and task management tools

Web Services. Furthermore, regarding the interface profiles, the task management tool needs to provide a general inbound interface that other process engines can call. The general relationship between the process modeling and enactment tools and the task management tools is outlined in figure 18.12.

18.6 Piloting in ATHENA

18.6.1 Implementation of the Modeling Framework

The implemented prototype of the modeling framework (figure 18.5) includes an integrated chain of modeling languages and tools (figure 18.13) that demonstrate the feasibility of the ATHENA process framework. The solution focuses on providing a direct path between business-level process description and the design and execution of business processes. The following modeling languages and tools are used on the different levels:

1. On the business level, ARIS Toolset (Scheer 1999) and MO^2GO (Mertins and Jaekel 2006): These two modeling tools are chosen to illustrate the capability to follow the CBP

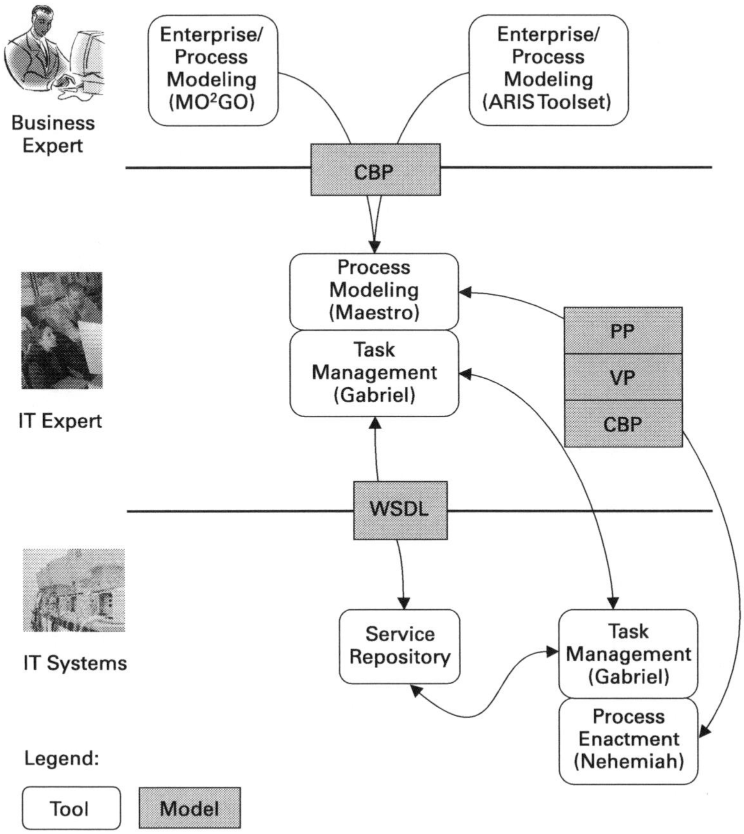

Figure 18.13
Integrated tool chain of the ATHENA process framework pilot

concept in different tools and methodologies. ARIS Toolset supports EPCs (event-driven process chain) (Horrmann et al. 1992) and MO^2GO supports integrated enterprise modeling (IEM; Mertins and Jaekel 2006; Spur et al. 1996). Both languages offer graphical notations which are easy to understand for business analysts and allow them to analyze business aspects, such as costs and involved resources. Thus both languages fulfill the requirements for business-level modeling in general but both languages need concepts which allow for a collaborative modeling.

2. On the technical level, the process modeling tool Maestro (SAP Research 2005b), together with the design time part of the task management tool Gabriel (SAP Research 2005a): This tool provides a more detailed view on the CBP, representing the complete control flow and message exchange of the process. The graphical notation allows replacement or deletion of non-IT-executable tasks which should not be considered on this level. Additionally the task profiles for the interface services are assigned.

3. On the execution level, the process engine Nehemiah (SAP Research 2005c), together with the runtime part of the task management tool and a service repository: The process engine supports the CBP enactment architecture outlined above and is able to execute the CBP in a service-based environment.

The integrated tool chain ensures that the business processes agreed upon by process owners and business managers on a business level, independent of a specific technical implementation or service description, can be coherently transformed to technical and, further, execution-level description following the ATHENA process framework. In the tool chain CBP models are exchanged between the business level and the technical level. On the technical level these models are extended by IT experts with information about private processes, view processes, and Web Services for enactment. These models can then be transformed into models executable by the process engine. In the following we discuss the different modeling levels in more detail.

Business-Level Modeling with ARIS Toolset and MO²GO In order to enrich the EPC with functionalities required to model CBPs, new constructs have been implemented. To abstract from sensitive process information, the EPC is extended by the object type *process module*. This construct depicts a closed logical unit that reflects a reasonable and clearly limited part of a business process. A process module can substitute for a single function as well as a subprocess. To supplement correlation between view and private process models, each view process has a unique ID. A similar mechanism is defined as a process type for IEM.

An example for using process modules is shown in figure 18.14. In this figure the private process of the manufacturer's order processing is shown on the left side. This process contains two sensitive subprocesses: the checking of the solvency of the retailer and the calculation of a price discount. If the retailer orders more than ten products a month, a 10 percent discount is given; in all other cases the retailer gets no discount. This process has to be distributed to several retailers in order to show them the sequence of the order processing, so that they can inform their staff and configure their workflow engines. The manufacturer wants to hide his discount system from certain retailers; the solvency check should always be hidden. Thus, he creates two different views of the same internal process for two classes of retailers by subsuming the area labeled "abstraction area 1" and "abstraction area 2" into process modules.

Apart from creating views of private processes in a collaborative scenario, it is also necessary to define the business scenario on a high level of abstraction. Therefore, a new model is proposed that enables business experts to specify the scenario in an abstract manner while hiding sensitive process information (see figure 18.15). The model aims at adapting and optimizing the complete collaboration; therefore all organizations involved are displayed. It gives an overview of all view processes that are part of the CBP, including the organizational units that are in charge of the respective process steps. On this level of

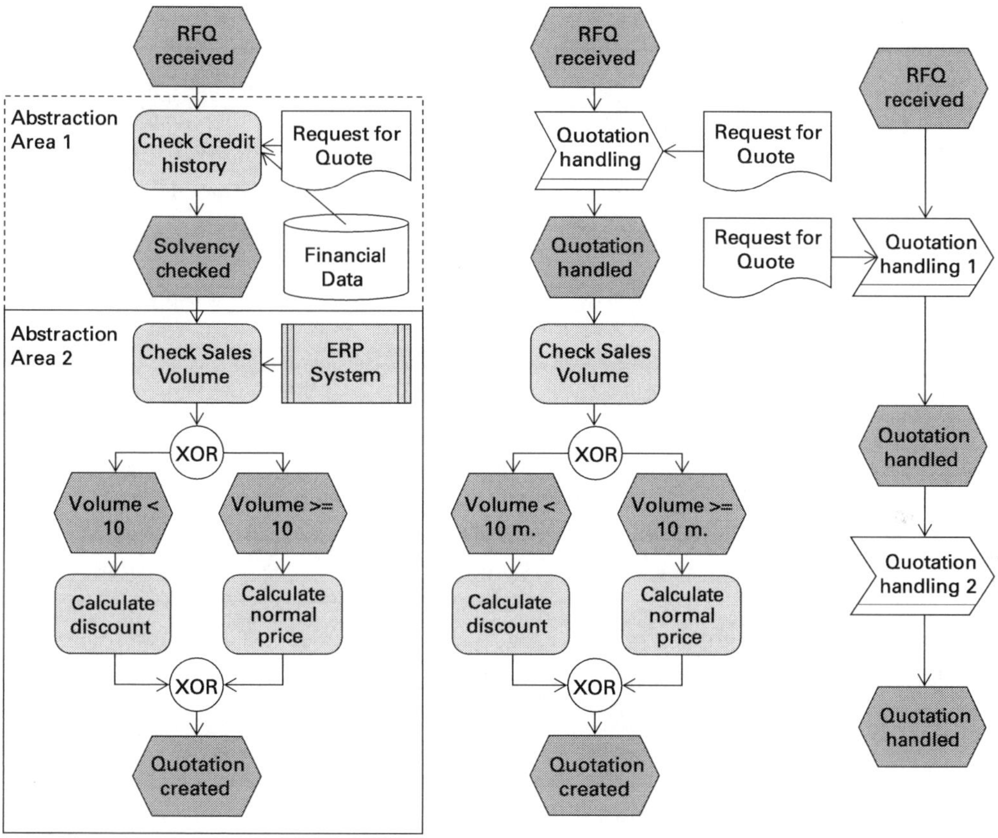

Figure 18.14
Private process of manufacturer and derived view processes for retailers

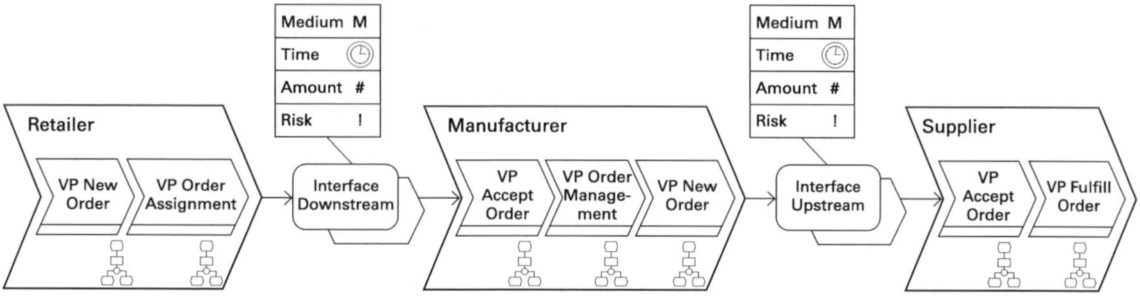

Figure 18.15
CBP: overall view

abstraction it is not easy to organize the interaction between the participants because of the lack of information concerning the internal procedure within the linked process modules. One way of dealing with this problem is describing the needed input as well as the produced output of the view processes. The direction of the connection shows whether the object for the view process is input or output. The specification regarding time, amount, and quality gives an example about possible attributes that should/could be taken into account.

Vertical Transformation to the Technical Level In the following we briefly present an annotation-based vertical transformation from MO^2GO to the technical-level modeling tool. This mechanism is used as an interface to the modeling tool in order to avoid the transfer of nonexecutable process steps to the technical level.

The objective of this export is to generate a model which consists only of executable actions. For this purpose the process steps in the model must be categorized according to their type of execution. This is realized with the help of an enumeration attribute "ExecutionType," defined for the action class in MO^2GO with three possible values: EX, NEX, and UEX. Only actions annotated as EX (executable) or UEX (executable with user interface) are exported; those actions that are annotated as NEX (nonexecutable) are not exported. The resulting model of a business process consists only of executable tasks and therefore must be executable itself. Figure 18.16 shows an example for a transformation of processes from the e-procurement case study.

Technical-Level Modeling After transforming process models to technical-level models and importing them into the process modeling tool, the view processes are linked to existing private processes to realize the information-hiding principle and are also connected to the final CBP. In this step the message exchange between the view processes also is specified. The modeling tool supports the creation of the CBP with a graphical modeling interface and a wizard that leads the user through the necessary design steps. It also generates all technical information describing the linkage between private processes and view processes that is then relevant for the process execution.

The user also specifies the services that are called during runtime to execute the different steps in the private processes of the partners during technical-level modeling. Additionally, he specifies the interface services over which information is exchanged with partners. This information is necessary to actually execute the CBP.

CBP Enactment The CBP modeled on the technical level is enacted using the process engine. It can directly import process models from the technical-level modeling tool. The transformation from technical-level to execution-level process models happens directly when storing the process models in the repository of the process engine. In the case study, all partners use the process engine developed in ATHENA that exchanges messages via

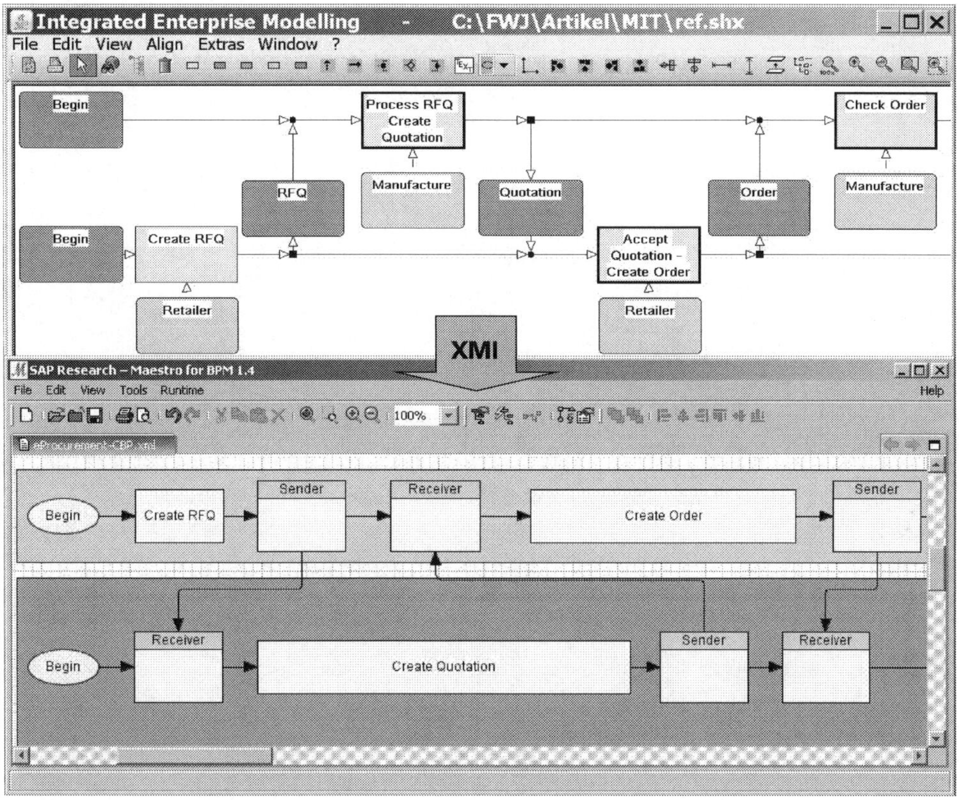

Figure 18.16
Transformation of a MO^{2}GO model to a technical level model

interface services. Thus, no central engine is needed to control the process, but we achieve a fully distributed enactment of the CBP. As an alternative to using the engine at each partner, the scenario could also be that only one of the partners uses the ATHENA engine and the other partners use different process engines (e.g., WS-BPEL engines) to enact their private and view processes. This would work in the same way as the partners communicate completely via interface services.

The process engine provides a browser-based user interface that allows the users to monitor the progress of the execution. Figure 18.17 shows a snapshot of the CBP for the e-procurement case study comprising the view processes from four different partners: the retailer (first row from the top), the manufacturer (sales department, second row from the top), the procurement department (third row from the top), and the supplier (fourth row from the top). All partners communicate via interface services that are assigned to the nodes labeled Sender and Receiver. The edges between the nodes represent the links.

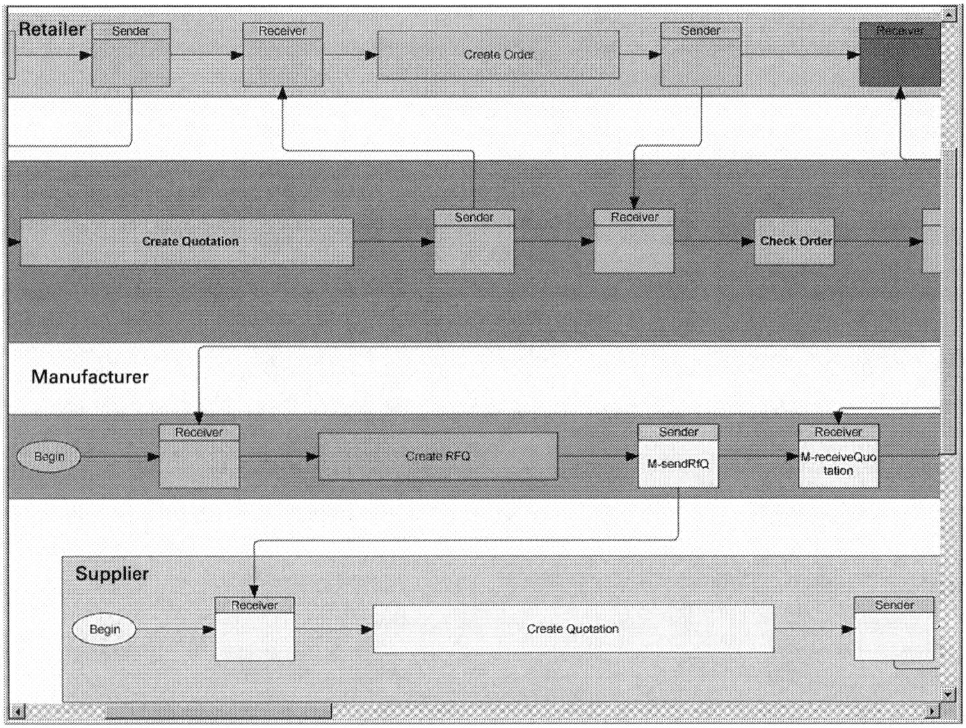

Figure 18.17
CBP monitoring in ATHENA process engine

In the user interface we also use color coding of the activities to visualize the current execution state of the CBP. We distinguish the following execution states:

1. An activity is still to be executed and has not yet been activated (e.g., the Create Quotation activity in the supplier view process).
2. An activity is activated and can be executed next (e.g., the Create RFQ activity in the manufacturer procurement view process).
3. An activity is currently running (meaning that it has been started and is executed or waiting for input, e.g., a receiver node).
4. An activity has been completed (e.g., the Create Order activity in the Retailer process).

18.7 Conclusion

Interoperability requires a consolidated and consistent understanding across all stakeholders. To ensure a correct cooperation between two or more entities, it is mandatory to build an appropriate process model. This can lead to an amplification of all cross-interface activities and constraints between the entities. In this chapter we presented the ATHENA project. Business-level models (e.g., enterprise models) illustrate the organizational business aspects as a prerequisite for the successful technical integration of IT systems and their configuration. The technical model derived from the business-level model secures the technical realization of the process interaction and represents the bridge to the process execution.

The greatest demand for further research can be seen in closing the gap between conceptual and technical models. This requires a formalization of transformation methods, especially in a methodologically sound transfer of process models into ICT configurations. Another aspect that requires further research is the use of supporting tools that ease the task of exchanging process models between different enterprises and to distinguish between private processes, view processes, and CBPs. User-specific views on the business process models will enable new user groups to work with business process models, as the example of intuitive metaphor-based process modeling shows. Moreover, ICT can actively support business process management by checking, verifying, or even automatically negotiating consistency and interoperability of models.

Acknowledgment

The work published in this chapter is partly funded by the European Community under the Sixth Framework Programme, contract FP6–507849 ATHENA. The work reflects only the authors' views. The Community is not liable for any use that may be made of the information contained therein.

References

Locke, B., Shepherd, J., Davis, W. 2005. The Enterprise Resource Planning Spending Report, 2005–2006. http://www.amrresearch.com/Content/View.asp?pmillid=18905 2005.

Andrews, T., et al. 2003. Business Process Execution Language for Web Services, Version 1.1. http://www.oasis.org.

ArKoS Consortium. 2007. Project Web site. http://www.arkos.info/.

BPMI. 2007. BPML Specification. http://www.bpmi.org/bpml.esp.

Bussler, C. 2002. Public process inheritance for business-to-business integration. In *3rd VLDB Workshop on Technologies for E-Services* (TES 2002).

Chiu, D. K. W., Karlapalem, K., Li, Q., and Kafeza, E. 2002. Workflow view based e-contracts in a cross-organizational e-services environment. *Distributed and Parallel Databases* 12(2–3): 193–216.

DBE Consortium. 2007. Project Web site. http://www.digital-ecosystem.org/DBE_Main/about.

ECOLEAD Consortium. 2007. Project Web site. http://ecolead.vtt.fi/.

Elvesater, B., Hahn, A., Berre, A., and Neple, T. 2005. Towards an interoperability framework for the model-driven development of software systems. In *1st International Conference on Interoperability of Enterprise Software and Applications*.

Horrmann, W., Kirsch, J., and Scheer, A.-W. 1992. Modellierung mit ereignisgesteuerten Prozeßketten: Methodenhandbuch. In A.-W. Scheer, ed., *Veröffentlichungen des Instituts für Wirtschaftsinformatik*, no. 101.

INTEROP Consortium. 2007. Project Web site. http://www.interop-noe.org/.

Lippe, S., Greiner, U., and Barros, A. 2005. A survey on state of the art to facilitate modeling of cross-organisational business processes. In *1st GI Workshop XML4BPM–XML Interchange Formats for Business Process Management*.

Liu, D.-R., and Shen, M. 2001. Modeling workflows with a process-view approach. In *Seventh International Conference on Database Systems for Advanced Applications*.

Mertins, K., and Jaekel, F. W. 2006. MO^2GO: User oriented enterprise models for organizational and IT solutions. In P. Bernus, K. Mertins, and G. Schmidt, eds., *Handbook on Architectures of Information Systems*, 2nd ed., pp. 649–663. Berlin: Springer.

Mertins, K., and Jochem, R. 1999. *Quality-Oriented Design of Business Processes*. Boston: Kluwer Academic Publishers.

OMG. 2007a. Model Driven Architecture. http://www.omg.org/mda/.

OMG. 2007b. Unified Modeling Language. http://www.uml.org.

OMG. 2007c. Business Process Definition Metamodel—Request for Proposal. OMG Document. http://www.omg.org/cgi-bin/doc?bei/03-01-06.

Phifer, G., Hayward, S., and Flint, D. 2003. Technologies That Enable Business Process Fusion. Report by Gartner. http://www.gartner.com/.

R4eGov Consortium. 2007. Project Web site. http://www.r4egov.eu/index.php.

SAP. 2004. SAP Business Maps. Technical report. http://www.sap.com/solutions/businessmaps/c-businessmaps.

SAP Research. 2005a. Gabriel. ATHENA Deliverable. http://www.athena-ip.org.

SAP Research. 2005b. Maestro for BPM. ATHENA Deliverable. http://www.athena-ip.org.

SAP Research. 2005c. Nehemiah Process Engine. ATHENA Deliverable. http://www.athena-ip.org.

Scheer, A. W. 1999. *ARIS—Business Process Modeling*, 2nd. ed. Berlin: Springer.

Schulz, K. 2002. Modelling and Architecting of Cross-Organisational Workflows (Ph.D. thesis, School of Information Technology and Electrical Engineering, University of Queensland, Australia).

Schulz, K. A., and Orlowska, M. E. 2004. Facilitating cross-organisational workflows with a workflow view approach. *Data & Knowledge Engineering* 51(1): 109–147.

Shen, M. X., and Liu, D. R. 2001. Coordinating interorganizational workflows based on process-views. In *Database and Expert Systems Application*. Berlin: Springer. LNCS, pp. 274–283.

Spur, G., Mertins, K., and Jochem, R. 1996. *Integrated Enterprise Modelling*. Beerlin: Beuth.

SUPER Consortium. 2007. Project Web site. http://www.ip-super.org/.

TrustCoM Consortium. 2007. Project Web site. http://www.eu-trustcom.com/.

UN/CEFACT. 2003. UN/CEFACT Modeling Methodology User Guide. http://www.ifs.univie.ac.at/untmg/artifacts/UMM_User_Guide_2003–09–22.pdf.

van der Aalst, W. M. P., ter Hofstede, A. H. M., Kiepuszewski, B., and Barros, A. P. 2002. Workflow Patterns. QUT technical report, FIT-TR-2002-02. Brisbane, Australia: Queensland University of Technology.

W3C. 2004. Web Services Choreography Description Language Version 1.0. http://www.w3.org/2002/ws/chor/.

WfMC. 2002. Workflow Process Definition Interface—XML Process Definition Language, v.1.0. WfMC document WFMC-TC-1025. http://www.wfmc.org/standards/xpdl.htm.

Zachman, J. A. 1987. A framework for information systems architecture. *IBM Systems Journal* 26(3): 276–292.

Ziemann, J., and Mendling, J. 2005. Transformation of EPCs to BPEL—A pragmatic approach. In *7th International Conference on the Modern Information Technology in the Innovation Processes of the Industrial Enterprises*.

19 Dependability in Service-Oriented Systems

Johannes Osrael, Lorenz Froihofer, Piotr Karwaczyński, Jaka Močnik, and Karl M. Goeschka

19.1 Introduction

Dependability is becoming more and more important for service-oriented architectures, especially if the service-oriented paradigm is to be applied in critical, vital systems—such as air traffic control systems, health care systems, nuclear power plants, chemical refineries, or public transportation.

Dependability is the "ability of a system to avoid service failures that are more frequent or more severe than is acceptable" (Avizienis et al. 2004). It is an integrating concept and comprises the following attributes:

- *Availability* is the "readiness for correct service."
- *Reliability* is the "continuity of correct service."
- *Safety* is the "absence of catastrophic consequences for the user(s) and the environment."
- *Integrity* is the "absence of improper system alterations."
- *Maintainability* is the "ability to undergo modifications and repairs."

Dependability in traditional, tightly coupled systems is well understood today, and a plethora of architectures, protocols, and tool kits exists for these systems (e.g., group membership systems, replication protocols, and failure detectors). Unfortunately, the inertness of many of today's software systems turns them into obstacles rather than enablers for dependability: large-scale, complex, highly dynamic, and heterogeneous software systems that run continuously often tend to become brittle and vulnerable after a while. According to Mary Shaw (2002), this is partly caused by some of the following: (1) most users are inarticulate about their precise criteria for dependability and other system qualities; (2) it is impossible to reasonably predict all combinations of environment evolvement and failure scenarios during design, implementation, and deployment; (3) the system may be too complex to predict its internal behaviors precisely. Consequently, we argue that software needs to become more "elastic" during runtime in order to be able to provide the expected trust and dependability. The loose coupling inherent in the service paradigm promises to support this kind of coupling between a system's components.

On the other hand, according to recent Gartner studies (http://www.gartner.com), service-oriented computing is not yet well understood, and in particular the loose coupling (e.g., through asynchronous behavior) is not deployed effectively in today's service-oriented systems. Rather, we can see a trend in which service-oriented computing is used as "yet another technology"—basically just wrapping existing systems and components behind Web service interfaces. Though this approach allows for immediate reuse of some dependability research results (as we will show in section 19.2), for replication in data-centric service-oriented systems, it will clearly not be possible to address the challenges of service-oriented systems of the future characterized by massive-scale, cross-organizational heterogeneity and dynamics.

Consequently, the additional research challenges arise from the following questions: (1) How can true loose coupling help to make traditional tightly coupled systems more dependable? How can the dependability of tightly coupled systems be improved by relaxing the coupling between the systems' constituents to achieve more loosely coupled systems? (2) How can dependability be achieved and guaranteed in truly loosely coupled and highly dynamic, flexible, and heterogeneous environments, in order to foster the true potential of the service oriented paradigm?

In terms of the taxonomy of this book (see chapter 1), dependability is a crosscutting concern in service-oriented systems, and thus is placed in a vertical layer (primarily in the management services layer) of the NESSI framework. Moreover, dependability cuts through all research planes of the SOC road map and is thus placed on the perpendicular axis.

19.1.1 Chapter Overview

In the DeDiSys (Dependable Distributed Systems) project, we have addressed dependability techniques for both data-centric and resource-centric services. *Data-centric service-oriented systems* have the main focus on data and its processing. Relational database management systems are most often used for persistent storage of the data. Examples of data-centric distributed systems are booking engines and online marketplaces. *Resource-centric service-oriented systems* are mainly concerned with usage or management of resources (e.g., processing power). Aspects such as time, capacity, protocols, or resource allocation come into consideration here. Resource-centric systems are often deployed on a Grid and follow the peer-to-peer paradigm.

Section 19.2 discusses how traditional replication techniques can be applied in data-centric service-oriented systems and presents a middleware architecture for replication of services.

Section 19.3 focuses on the trade-off between availability and quality of service (QoS), and introduces a system for balancing these attributes in resource-centric distributed systems such as Grids (Foster et al. 2004) or peer-to-peer networks. The framework can be used, for instance, by hardware utility providers to match provided and requested capabilities.

Section 19.4 discusses related work, and the chapter closes in section 19.5 with conclusions and remarks on future work.

19.2 Replication in Data-centric Service-Oriented Systems

Replication is a well-known technique to enable fault tolerance—one of the means to achieve dependability—in traditional distributed systems such as distributed object systems, distributed process systems, or distributed databases. Before presenting a middleware architecture for replication of services, the most important replication techniques will be discussed. For a detailed discussion on replication options and replication middleware for service-oriented systems see Osrael et al. (2007a).

19.2.1 Replication Techniques

Though replication of stateless services is comparatively easy to achieve, replication of stateful services requires synchronization of the replicas' state. A stateful service either encapsulates state or persists it in an external data store, such as a file or a database. The latter type of stateful service can be modeled as a stateless "access" service plus a stateful resource. Thus, for this type of service, state synchronization of replicas can be performed either via the underlying data store (i.e., a database or file replication system) or on the service level. The following replication techniques can—in principle—be applied on both the service and the data levels of a service-oriented system.

Active Replication In active replication (Schneider 1993), all replicas receive and process the clients' requests. Thus, replicas need to behave in a deterministic way (state machine). That is, given the same initial state, replicas need to reach the same final state if the same operations are processed in the same order at all replicas. In contrast to primary backup replication, active replication is a symmetric solution—the same code runs on all replicas. Failures are transparent to the client as long as one replica receives the client invocations. The difficulty in active replication is to ensure that all replicas process the operations in the same order. Ordering guarantees might be weakened if semantics of operations such as commutativity of operations are taken into account.

Primary Backup Replication In the original primary backup approach (Budhiraja et al. 1993), which is also known as *passive replication*, only one of the replicas (the primary) processes clients' requests and forwards the updates to the other replicas (backups).

Ordering of operations is easier to achieve than in active replication since all operations are directed to the primary. However, the primary replica may become a bottleneck. If the primary crashes, a new one needs to be selected.

Coordinator–Cohort Replication The coordinator–cohort replication model (Birman et al. 1985) is similar to the primary backup model in the sense that only one replica—the coordinator—processes a client's requests and propagates the updates to the other replicas—the cohort. However, the coordinator can change for every invocation. Coordinator–cohort replication requires distributed concurrency control (distributed locking), deadlock detection, and deadlock removal mechanisms.

19.2.2 Replication Middleware Architecture[1]

According to ObjectWeb (2007), "in a distributed system, middleware is defined as the software layer that lies between the operating system and the applications on each site of the system." The purpose of middleware is to reuse infrastructure code and avoid reinvention of the wheel for each application. Replication is one of the crosscutting concerns that will be provided by middleware for highly reliable systems.

Only a few Web Service replication middleware solutions exist so far (see, e.g., Salas et al. 2006; Ye and Shen 2005; Liang et al. 2003; Osrael et al. 2007d), some of them obviously not fault-tolerant (e.g., FAWS; Jayasinghe 2005). Although different technologies are used for the existing solutions, they share many architectural commonalities and only few differences. We have analyzed (for more details, see Osrael et al. 2006) and compared these existing solutions with distributed object replication middleware such as FT-CORBA (CORBA) and derived an architectural pattern for replication middleware, as shown in figure 19.1.

The identified architectural pattern contains six major components:

- An *invocation service*, providing the invocation logic (interception of client invocations, conveyance of the transaction context, etc.)
- A *multicast service* for reliable, ordered dissemination of operations
- A *monitoring service* for detection of faults in the system (e.g., crash of a service)
- A *replication manager*, mainly for maintenance of object/service groups and overall configuration of the replication logic

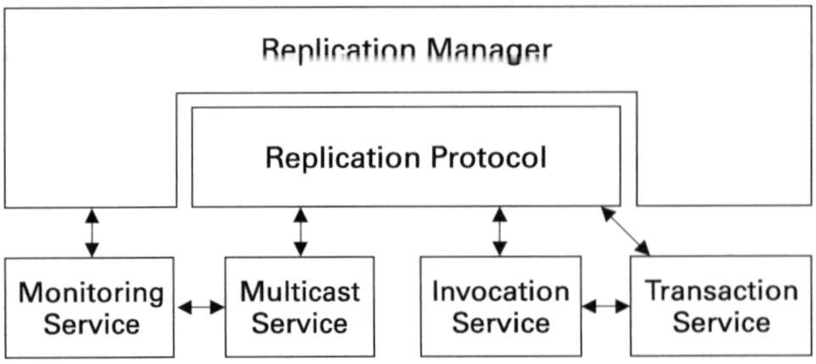

Figure 19.1
Replication middleware architecture

- A *replication protocol* unit for providing the actual replication logic (e.g., primary backup protocol)
- An optional *transaction service* for supporting transactions on replicated entities.

In order to provide fault tolerance for the middleware infrastructure itself, the components reside on every node of the system. That is, if they are not naturally distributed such as the algorithms implemented by the components (multicast, group membership, etc.), the middleware components are replicated as well. Thus, single points of failure are avoided.

Besides these six major components, replication middleware typically comprises further supportive components (e.g., some kind of persistence service for object-relational mapping).

19.2.3 Similarities of Object and Service Replication Middleware

As argued in (Osrael et al. 2006), not only different service but also service and object replication middleware systems (e.g., FT-CORBA [CORBA]) share many commonalities and only subtle differences—primarily caused by different technologies (see Osrael et al. 2007b). That is, the middleware architecture shown in figure 19.1 is feasible in both distributed object and service-oriented systems, as we have also proved in our prototype implementations (e.g., see Osrael et al. 2007b).

Interactions Figure 19.2 shows the interactions of the main components of this architecture for primary backup replication. Client invocations are intercepted by the invocation service in order to trigger the replication logic. First, the replication protocol requests the location of the primary copy from the replication manager. If it does not reside on the current node, the invocation is redirected to the node hosting the primary. The invocation is processed by the primary, and afterward the update is propagated (via either state transfer or operation transfer) to the backup replicas.

Invocation Service Ideally, replication should not change the way a client invokes a service. Thus, invocations of clients need to be intercepted by a so-called invocation service in order to trigger the replication logic. State-of-the art middleware such as the Java-based Axis2 SOAP engine (Perera et al. 2006) or Microsoft's new SOAP-based communication platform Windows communication foundation (WCF), which is part of the .NET framework (Microsoft) 3.0, provides many options to intercept invocations and thus ease the implementation of replication middleware.

Monitoring Service Replication middleware needs to take appropriate action in case of a fault—thus monitoring of services is required. For instance, in a primary backup replication, the middleware has to react if the primary crashes, and promote a backup to a new primary.

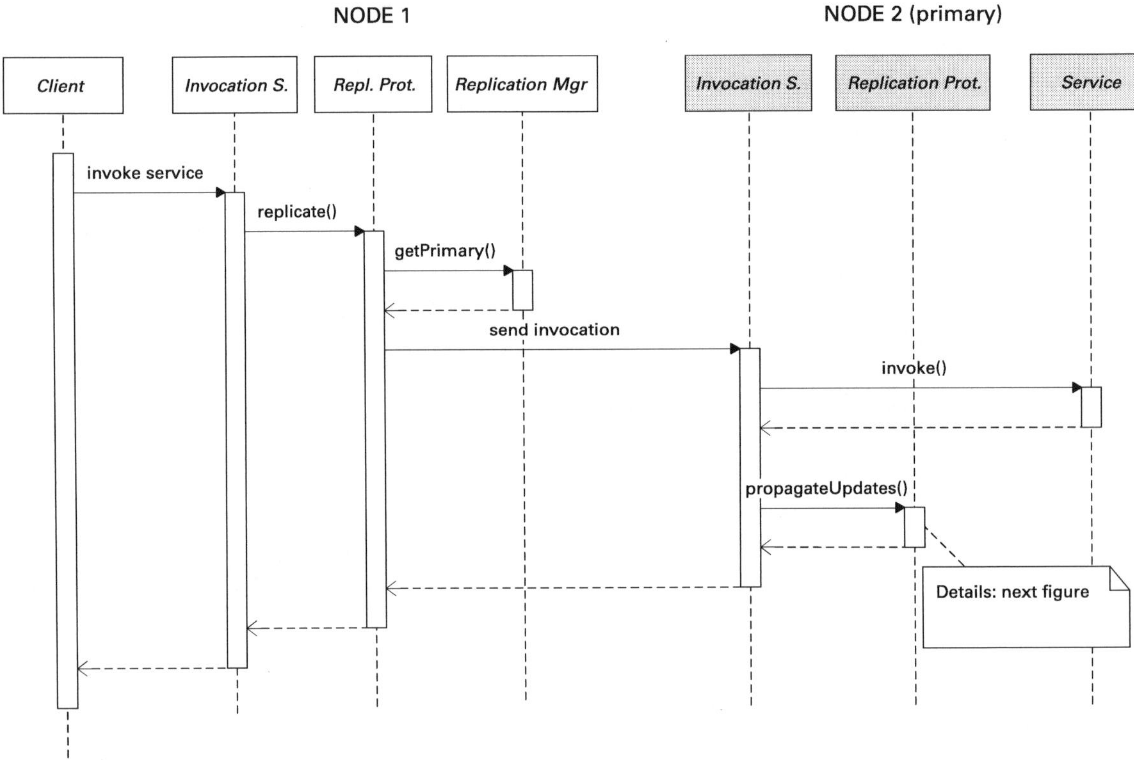

Figure 19.2
Interactions between key components

Group membership services typically provide monitoring on a node-level basis. Replicas of a certain service constitute a logical group. Thus, instead of addressing each replica separately, the group as a whole can be addressed; for instance, a message can be sent to a group. Group membership services monitor the members of a group and notify interested parties (typically the group members) about membership changes.

Vogels and Re (2003) proposed WS-Membership, a monitoring and membership service for Web Services.

Multicast Service Replication requires reliable multicast primitives as well. For instance, in a primary backup replication, updates need to be propagated from the primary to the backups. In active replication, atomic multicast is required. Reliable multicast services are typically combined with a group membership service since group membership changes have to be taken into account when a multicast is sent to a group. The combination of group membership service and group communication primitives is referred to as a view-oriented group communication system (Chockler et al. 2001). Group communication systems provide multicast primitives to (object, process, service) groups with configurable delivery and ordering guarantees.

The following ordering guarantees can be distinguished:

1. *FIFO multicast* primitives guarantee that messages are received in FIFO order. If message m is sent before message m′, then every group member that receives both messages will receive m before m′.
2. *Causal multicast* primitives guarantee that messages are received in causal order. If message m causally precedes m′, then every group member that receives both messages will receive m before m′.
3. *Total order multicast* primitives guarantee that messages are received in the same order at all correct group members. Defago et al. (2004) provide a comprehensive taxonomy and survey of total order protocols.

Reliability is defined in the context of view delivery (i.e., "reliability guarantees restrict message loss within a view" (Chockler et al. 2001). *Sending view delivery* guarantees that a message is sent and delivered in the same view. *Same view delivery* is weaker and guarantees that a message is "delivered at the same view at every process that delivers it" (Chockler et al. 2001).

The use of a group communication tool kit is not mandatory for any replication middleware, but its use is highly recommended since it significantly reduces implementation complexity for the middleware programmer (Osrael et al. 2007b).

Replication Manager A certain component is necessary to manage replicated services, including tasks such as storing thc location and rolc (c.g., primary, backup) of replicas, and maintaining service groups' general configuration of the replication middleware, such as the replication style. Typically, this component is called the replication manager (e.g., in FT-SOAP; Liang et al. 2003).

The replication manager is targeted to a specific family of replication protocols (e.g., primary backup replication protocols). Ideally, a replication manager can serve different replication protocols and thus allows changing the replication protocol. Most often, this is possible only if the replication protocols belong to the same family or adhere to a similar model. For instance, a primary backup replication manager cannot be immediately used for quorum consensus replication protocols (e.g., Gifford 1979).

The interface of a simple primary backup replication manager might—among others—contain methods for getting the location of the primary and backup replicas. In contrast, a replication manager for quorum consensus protocols does not distinguish between primary and backup replicas, but requires methods for retrieving read-and-write quorums of replicas.

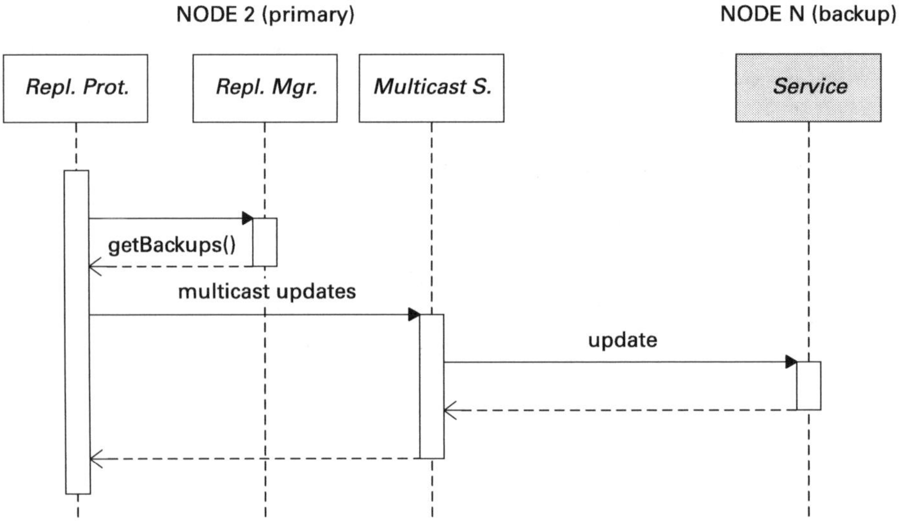

Figure 19.3
Update propagation

Replication Protocol Two options for implementing the actual replication logic (e.g., update propagation, recovery) are the most common. Either the protocol is implemented as a separate component or it is embedded in the replication management unit. The first variant eases the change of the protocol, which might be necessary, for instance, owing to system evolvement.

Figure 19.3 depicts one aspect of the replication protocol for the primary backup variant: update propagation. The replication protocol queries the replication manager to get the location (or group ID) of the backup replicas and then uses the multicast service to propagate the updates to the backup, which applies the update.

Transaction Service Finally, replication middleware should also provide transactional support. However, transactions in replicated service environments are rather difficult to implement since they need to be performed on replicated services. Therefore, only a few service replication frameworks have addressed this issue so far. For instance, WS-Replication has been successfully tested in combination with long-running transactions as defined in the Web Services composite application framework (Arjuna et al. 2003).

Obviously, there is a need for further research to examine replication in combination with different Web Service transaction models. For instance, Web Service replication middleware could build upon the WS-AtomicTransaction (IBM et al. 2005) and WS-BusinessActivity (IBM et al. 2005) specifications. The former is targeted to short-running

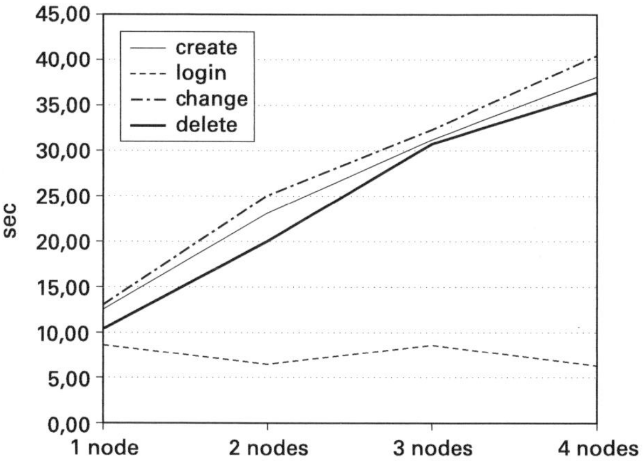

Figure 19.4
Update propagation performance in WLAN setting (Weghofer 2007)

ACID (atomicity, consistency, isolation, durability) transactions, and the latter to long-running transactions.

19.2.4 Axis2-Based Web Service Replication Middleware

We have implemented a Web Service replication middleware (Weghofer 2007; Osrael et al. 2007d) built-upon the Java-based Axis2 SOAP engine (Perera et al. 2006). The middleware closely follows the architectural pattern presented in the previous section and provides a variant of primary backup replication using operation transfer. The entry point to the replication system is the invocation system, which is based on the Axis2 handler concept. Axis2 handlers are customizable message interceptors. Incoming SOAP messages are cut out of the Axis IN-flow, propagated to the other replicas, and injected into their IN-flow. Monitoring and multicast primitives are provided by the Spread group communication tool kit (Amir et al. 2000).

Figure 19.4 shows the performance of our framework for up to three backup nodes: For the experiment (Weghofer 2007), a simple user account management Web Service has been used which provides methods for creating a user account, changing a user account, deleting a user account, and for log-in. The latter method has "read" semantics, and the former have "written" semantics. Invocations are submitted directly to the primary node, which is connected with the backups via an 11Mbit wireless network. The results depicted in figure 19.5 are the median of several iterations of 400 consecutive calls of each of the Web Service methods. While the overhead in this setting with a relatively slow network (which resembles a wide area network) is not negligible, other experiments in a 100Mbit network (see Weghofer 2007; Osrael et al. 2007d) indicate that the performance overhead by replication remains acceptable in a local setting.

```
<Policy>
  <ExactlyOne>
    <All>
      <Bandwidth>300</Bandwidth>
    </All>
  </ExactlyOne>
</Policy>
```

Figure 19.5
Provided policy document

19.3 Dependability in Resource-centric Systems

So far, this chapter addressed dependability concepts (in particular replication) for data-centric service-oriented systems. Another dependability concept—which is independent of the work presented in the previous section—has been developed in the context of the DeDiSys project for resource-centric service-oriented systems and is presented in this section.

It is of crucial importance for business scenarios that the service is delivered to the consumer according to consumer's requirements; guaranteed quality of service is a must if parts of a business process are to be entrusted to third-party service providers. In order to ensure this, on one hand the consumers must be able to identify the providers that can deliver the service according to their requirements. On the other hand, the providers must be aware of these requirements and deliver the service accordingly, by means of per-consumer allocation of (limited) resources implied by the consumer's requirements. Clearly, best-effort service, the most common service delivery method used nowadays, can not ensure this.

Similarly to data-centric service-oriented systems as discussed in the previous section, resource-centric service-oriented systems may be able to tolerate faults if they utilize redundancy. To this end, their components should be replicated on system nodes; in the extreme case, on all nodes (completely decentralized approach). In large, even global-scale service-oriented systems, possible failures do not stem only from faults of hardware and software. Another class of failures may be observed in provisioning of resources. Each consumer served requires the provider to allocate a part of the computing resources available to it for that consumer. The unpredictable behavior of large numbers of independent consumers, often competing for the same service, results in constantly changing availability of resources, and thus in changing capabilities of the service providers to deliver service to consumers. Redundancy may be helpful here as well: if more resources are provided than the consumers need, availability of the entire system does not suffer. This is hard to achieve, though, owing to the unpredictability, dynamics, and open nature of such systems, as service providers and consumers constantly join and leave the system, voluntarily or involuntarily; belong to different administrative domains, thus lacking centralized control; and are completely independent. As the example of the World Wide Web shows, overload of individual service providers, being overwhelmed by a sudden increase in consumer requests, is a common problem in such systems. Instead of the providers servicing at least a subset of the consumers in a satisfactory manner, all competing consumers are de facto denied service, as it is delivered too poorly, too late, or—most often—both.

The dynamic nature of the described systems does not allow the application developer to make reliable a priori assumptions about the service providers present in the system, their locations, and their capability to satisfy consumer requirements for the delivered service. No decisions with regard to the providers being used by any consumer can be made at the time of building or deploying a system. Instead, such decisions have to be postponed until runtime, until the very moment a consumer needs to invoke a provider's operation, as the latest up-to-date information about the system needs to be leveraged to make that decision. Service providers need to determine the nonfunctional properties (quality of service, time assertions, security parameters, etc.) of the service that can be provided based on the computing resources available to them, and to advertise them to potential consumers. We call these properties of the service *provided capabilities*. Consumers should use this information to discover and use the provider that can fulfill their requirements, which we call *requested capabilities*, best.

Furthermore, not only should the consumers consider how a provider may deliver the service. The providers also need to be aware of the consumers' requested capabilities. In this manner, providers are able to allocate their resources in order to deliver the service in accordance with the requested capabilities. This results in controlled service delivery, thus preventing overloads, denial of service attacks, and unsatisfactory service. In the worst case, the providers must deny requests from consumers whose requirements cannot be fulfilled, or fulfillment of which would violate fulfillment of other consumers being serviced concurrently.

Unfortunately, such an approach can render the providers unavailable to many consumers. It is worth considering the fact that a large class of applications can be served at different levels of requirements' satisfaction, ranging from optimal to minimal but still acceptable satisfaction (Močnik et al. 2006). When optimal satisfaction cannot be provided to all concurrent consumers, the providers should attempt to satisfy them at a lower—but still acceptable—level, thus increasing the availability of the providers at the expense of consumers' satisfaction.

In order to provide for such behavior, we need to extend the existing service-oriented specifications and middleware with means to do the following:

- Describe provided and requested capabilities
- Evaluate the providers with regard to how their provided capabilities satisfy the requested capabilities of the service consumer

- Discover the best (with regard to the above evaluation) provider for a consumer
- Enable dynamic trading of consumer satisfaction for provider availability.

This approach was investigated in the DeDiSys project and is explained in the following sections.

19.3.1 Capabilities

According to WS-Glossary, a capability is *a named piece of functionality (or feature) that is declared as supported or requested by an agent*. In the scope of our work, we explicitly distinguish between provided capabilities and requested capabilities.

- Provided capabilities are the properties of the service that may be provided by a service provider.
- Requested capabilities are specified by service consumers searching for a service provider to use.

In order to represent the capabilities in a machine-readable format, we chose to use the Web Services Policy framework (WS-Policy), an established method for specifying capabilities and constraints of Web Services. In the terms of WS-Policy specification, a service provider advertises its provided policy document that contains one or more policy alternatives, each containing a set of policy assertions that describe *how* the provider can deliver its service. The service consumer, on the other hand, uses the requested policy document to query for an appropriate provider. Once again, a requested policy document may contain multiple policy alternatives, each with a set of policy assertions stating requirements that must be met by the provider. Different alternatives may satisfy the requester at different levels and should be evaluated accordingly. Different policy assertions are not prescribed by the WS-Policy specification. As they are specific to an application domain, it is up to an application, a cooperating service provider, and a consumer to define them.

As an example, consider a service provider offering relaying of arbitrary streams between clients and a consumer wishing to use such a provider for relaying audio and video streams of a video conference among four participants. The provider advertises that up to 300kbps may be relayed with the document in figure 19.5, whereas the consumer uses the document in figure 19.6 to query for an appropriate provider. The consumer is most satisfied with providers that offer over 400kbps bandwidth, which allows it to use high-quality video and audio streams between all participants, but can make do with providers offering 200kbps bandwidth (the consumer will compensate for lower bandwidth by using lower-quality video streams), or even with servers capable of relaying only 32kbps (the consumer will drop video streams and only attempt to relay audio streams).

Matching is also supported by the specification with the process of document intersection. Intersection of provided and requested policy documents will yield another document, containing only the policy alternatives that are acceptable to both parties: on one hand, they are satisfactory for the consumer, and on the other hand, the provider can pro-

```
<Policy>
  <ExactlyOne>
    <All>
      <Bandwidth>400</Bandwidth>
    </All>
    <All>
      <Bandwidth>200</Bandwidth>
    </All>
    <All>
      <Bandwidth>32</Bandwidth>
    </All>
  </ExactlyOne>
</Policy>
```

Figure 19.6
Requested policy document

vide the properties asserted by these alternatives. An intersection of documents in figures 19.5 and 19.6 is shown in figure 19.7. Clearly, only the less demanding two alternatives can be provided—it is up to the consumer to choose one of them. An intersection of policy documents from an incompatible provider and requester would yield an empty policy document.

The system architecture is built around a discovery service, named the Dependable Discovery Service, or DDS (Močnik et al. 2006; Kwiatkowski et al. 2006), and the processes of service advertising and service discovery. Service discovery encompasses the search for services implementing the desired interface, and matching of advertised provided capabilities of these services against the requested capabilities of the service requester that initiated the discovery process.

Requested and provided capabilities of services are inherently related to resources. Since using and managing low-level, distributed resources (CPU, bandwidth, storage space, data) is tedious, the capabilities are exposed by services as higher-level named pieces of functionality and are characterized by specific features. Consequently, services can be perceived as *abstract resources* (WS Glossary).

In contrast to classic discovery services (Coulouris et al. 2001), the DDS improves the selection process by taking into account the consumers' minimal requirements, optimal requirements, and information on how to evaluate providers that meet these requirements differently. With this information, the DDS is able to accurately match the requested capabilities with the provided capabilities of the available service providers.

According to the terminology discussed in Vinoski (2003), the DDS could be denoted as a trading service that is partly static (it does not evaluate capabilities dynamically during discovery) and partly dynamic (it does not rely on capabilities advertised when a service provider joined a system—they are readvertised periodically, or after significant change

```
<Policy>
  <ExactlyOne>
    <All>
      <Bandwidth>200</Bandwidth>
    </All>
    <All>
      <Bandwidth>32</Bandwidth>
    </All>
  </ExactlyOne>
</Policy>
```

Figure 19.7
Intersection

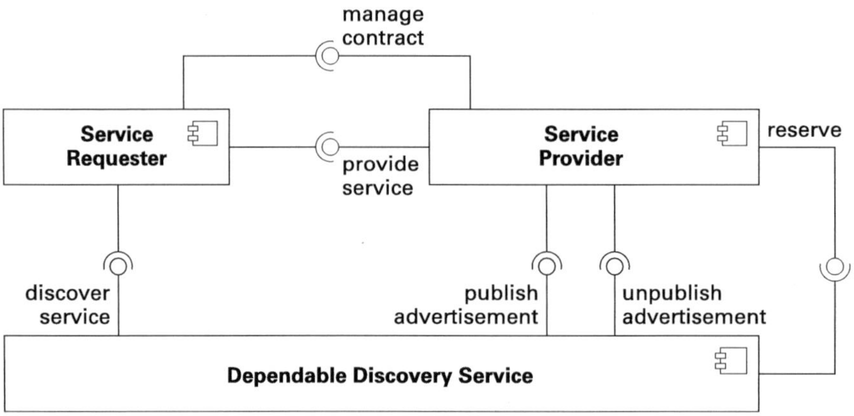

Figure 19.8
Key components and interfaces of a DDS-based service-oriented system

occurs). Its key distinctive features (e.g., as compared to the CORBA trading service (Object Management Group) are suitability for large-scale, frequently and unpredictably changing environments; flexibility in expressing provided/requested capabilities; and complete decentralization.

The architecture of a service-oriented system that makes use of the DDS is shown in figure 19.8. The three major architectural components are detailed below.

Service Requester A service requester uses the DDS to discover service providers that have implemented the requested interface and provide capabilities sufficient for the requester's needs. Discovery yields a contract with the discovered service provider, which is used by the latter to determine how the service will be delivered.

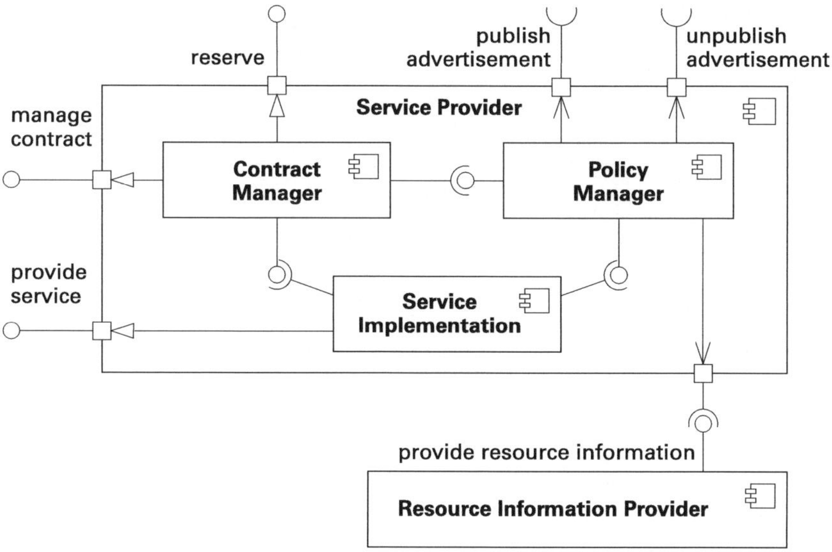

Figure 19.9
Subcomponents of a Service Provider

Service Provider The subcomponents that jointly implement a service provider are shown in figure 19.9.

The service implementation is the fundamental component of a service provider. It exposes its specific functions to the outside world in close cooperation with the policy manager and the contract manager.

The policy manager handles the currently provided capabilities of the provider. It is responsible for construction and advertising of the policy documents containing these capabilities. The process of identification and/or calculation of capabilities uses the knowledge of the local resources provided by the resource information provider and the current contracts (confirmed or reserved) consuming some of the capabilities. All that is required of a DDS-compliant service provider is to define a few callbacks for calculation of the service policy based on available resources and its augmentation based on allocation of existing resources to currently served consumers. Having collected all necessary information, the policy manager publishes the advertisement of a service provider that comprises the following:

- The implemented service interface (used by service requesters as the key for discovery)
- The service address, which can be any (usually a technology-specific) address that allows the requester to contact the service provider (in our work we use WS-Addressing end point references of Web Services)

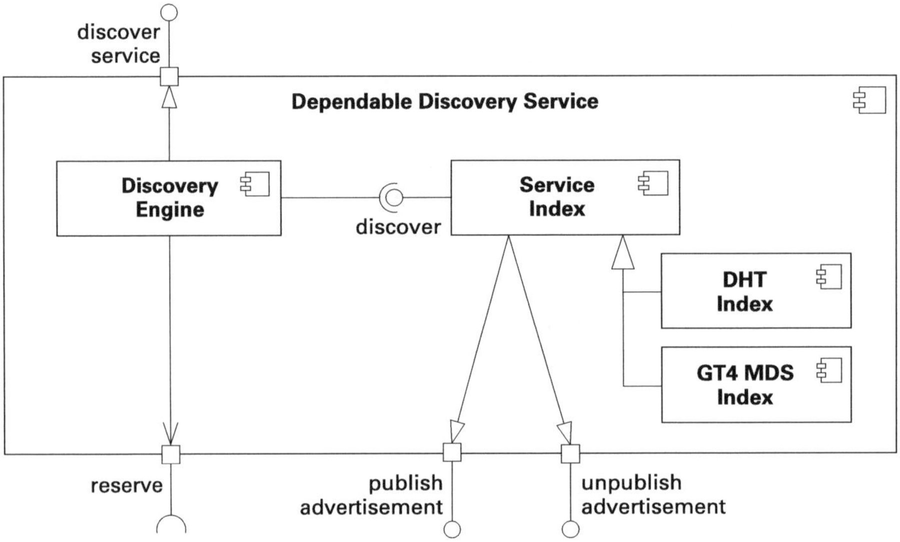

Figure 19.10
Internal structure of the Dependable Discovery Service

- The provided policy for interaction with a service requester, including the provided capabilities.

The contract manager handles reservations of contracts performed by the DDS and manages established contracts of service requesters, including allocation of contracted capabilities for requesters invoking operations of the service provider.

Dependable Discovery Service The internal structure and interfaces of the dependable discovery service are shown in figure 19.10.

The two basic components that constitute the dependable discovery service are the discovery engine and the service index.

Discovery Engine All discovery requests are invoked via the discovery engine, which utilizes the service index to discover all service instances providing the requested interface.

Then, the discovery engine parses the specification of requested capabilities and provides capabilities of all discovered providers: application-specific assertions are mapped to Java objects, using plug-ins provided by the consumer, one for each application-specific assertion type. Provided capabilities are matched against provided capabilities of the discovered providers, and successful matches are then evaluated according to consumers' criteria.

Service providers that match the requested capabilities are ranked according to the evaluation, and the policy documents resulting from the match (for an example, see figure

19.7) are used to form a candidate contract with a provider. The discovery engine attempts to reserve such a contract first with the best evaluated provider, and if this fails (owing to capabilities having changed in the meantime) continues with the other providers in decreasing order of evaluation. As soon as one of the providers is successfully reserved for the client, the reserved service contract is returned to the consumer. The consumer must confirm the reserved contract and may then use the provider according to the contract: a special SOAP header is passed in all subsequent provider invocations in order to let the provider identify the consumer and serve it according to the established contract.

The Service Index The service index is used to map interface descriptions to sets of advertisements of service providers implementing that interface. It provides a simple API that enables service providers to publish their advertisements and remove a previously published advertisement. Furthermore, the service index is used by the discovery engine to search for advertisements of service providers implementing the requested interface.

The service index by itself may, but is not required to, use the information on requested capabilities during the discovery process to refine the search, and only provide results matching the requested capabilities. The final matching of all discovered service providers is performed by the discovery engine component in any case.

The index state is maintained using soft-state mechanisms; published advertisements expire after some time, and should be republished prior to expiration. Such an approach prevents stale advertisements of services that have crashed or have ungracefully quit cluttering the index. It also forces the services to advertise (relatively) fresh information, making the index contents better reflect the real state.

The service index is an abstraction that allowed us to use the same code base to implement systems with different storage backend implementations. On one hand, we have implemented a hierarchical index provided by the MDS Index hierarchy in a Globus tool kit 4 (Foster 2005) environment (the GT4 MDS index component in figure 19.9), suitable for smaller environments. On the other hand, larger environments are better served by our implementation of a distributed index built on top of a distributed hash table (DHT; Balakrishnan et al. 2003) on an overlay network (the DHT Index component in figure 19.10).

The DHT index, constructed according to the peer-to-peer paradigm, plays a vital role in improving the dependability of a system. In contrast to the GT4 MDS index, it does not introduce any single points of failure; it is redundantly distributed over all system nodes and all these parts are functionally equal. Consequently, failures of any system node (and thus a part of the DHT index) do not hinder the index as a whole. However, it may require some time for self-reconfiguration.

The service index provides functionality similar to UDDI registries (Oasis 2004), but these were considered inappropriate to be used in its place owing to the following:

- The UDDI specification prescribes a Web Service interface to the registry, which we want to avoid because of performance issues.
- Registries are commonly implemented as heavyweight Web Services with a relational database as the storage backend: such an implementation consumes too much resources.
- Our work needs only a very small subset of functionality that the registries should support according to the full UDDI specification.

Also, prescribing the use of UDDI registries would remove the aforementioned abstraction that allows us to plug in different index implementations according to the system's needs. However, a service index using one or more UDDI registries as the storage backend could be implemented, thus preserving this abstraction while making use of existing UDDI registry deployments.

19.3.2 Trading Consumer Satisfaction for Availability

Trading must first be allowed by the service consumer. This is done by specifying multiple requested policy alternatives and an evaluation plug-in that evaluates providers by matching different requested alternatives differently: providers capable of delivering service according to more satisfactory alternatives should be evaluated better. Thus, the discovery engine will select the optimal (most satisfactory) providers if any are available; otherwise it will fall back to less satisfactory ones, effectively trading consumer satisfaction for availability of the service provider.

In order to verify whether our trading paradigm improves availability of real-life applications, we have tested a prototype implementation of our extensions to the Apache Axis Web Services stack on a sample time-constrained, computation-intensive application performing a Monte Carlo simulation in order to evaluate a bond portfolio with regard to different market conditions. Since many sets of input parameters describing the market must be considered in order to deliver a trustworthy result, the consumer is more satisfied if the provider is able to analyze more sets of input parameters. Also, the time for result delivery is limited.

In reality, tens of thousands of such analyses should be performed, but in order to shorten our testing time, we have chosen 60 analyses as the optimal value, but the consumers would settle for as few as 10 analyses if availability of the providers was limited. The time limit for result delivery was chosen to be one minute. Our approach leveraging the trading paradigm (marked Trading) was compared with best-effort service delivery (marked No AC), common on the World Wide Web today, and with service delivery with admission control (marked No trading), where the providers served the consumers either if optimal service was possible or not at all. Three test cases were inspected:

1. A healthy system overloaded with service consumers; i.e., the cumulative resources of all providers are not sufficient to optimally serve all the consumers. (See figure 19.11)

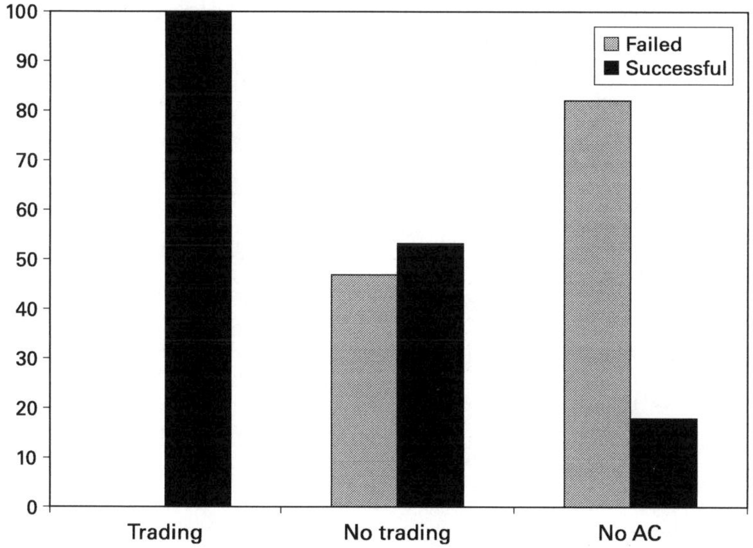

Figure 19.11
Test case 1: Successful consumers in a healthy system

2. A healthy system with third-party load imposed on the service provider's resources, further reducing resources, i.e., independent programs consuming CPU time. (See figure 19.12)
3. A system in which provider failures both reduce resources and force consumers to resubmit their requests to other providers with even less time available. (See figure 19.13)

In all test cases, the test system consisted of four Monte Carlo service providers, and a single node was used to run all consumers, using a thread-per-client model. Provider nodes were capable of serving exactly one consumer optimally within the time limit of one minute. One hundred consumers were spawned during the test, their arrivals being modeled as a Poisson process with an average rate of 0.2/s (i.e., on average, one new requester was spawned every five seconds). Also, arrival of third-party load and provider node failures in test cases—(2) and (3), respectively—was modeled as Poisson processes with an average rate of 0.01 (i.e., on average, one new CPU-intensive program is started or one node fails every 100 seconds).

The consumers were classified in two classes: *successful*, which were delivered at least 10 analyses, and *failed*, which were denied service or were delivered fewer than 10 analyses.

As the results show, in all tested scenarios, use of the trading paradigm clearly outperforms the other two approaches with regard to availability of the service providers, and thus the ability of consumers to function in conditions of underprovisioned resources.

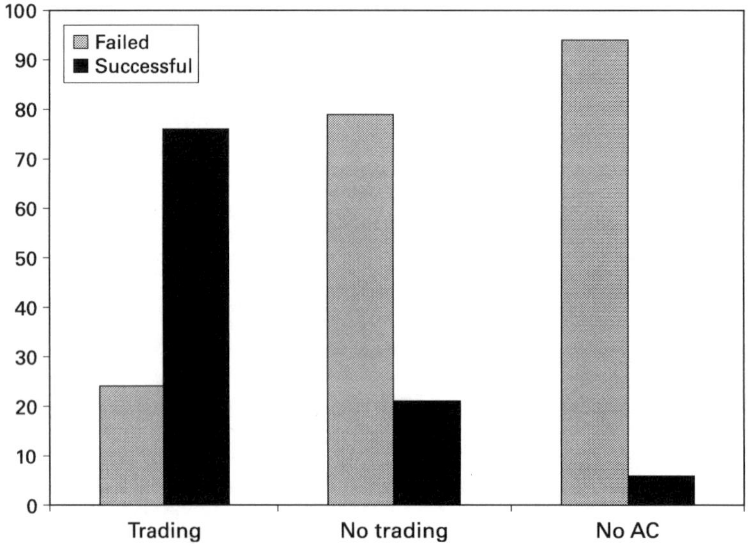

Figure 19.12
Test case 2: Successful consumers in presence of third-party load

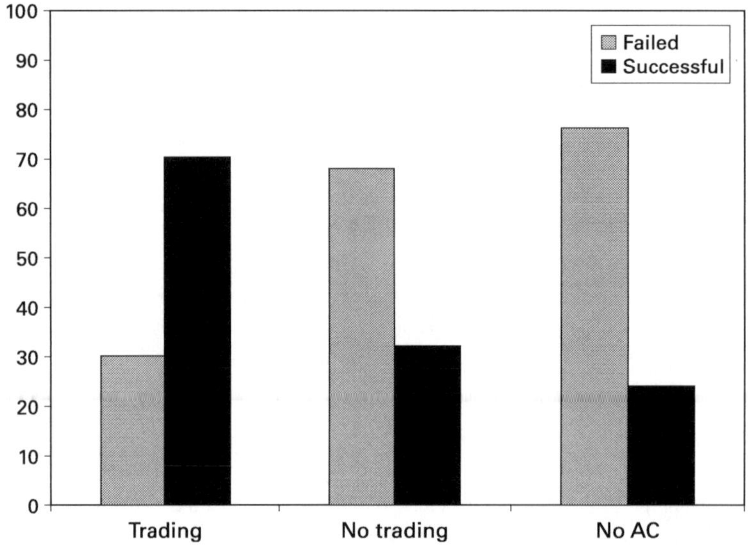

Figure 19.13
Test case 3: Successful consumers in presence of node failures

19.4 Related Work

Related work is threefold.

19.4.1 Service Replication Middleware

Our architectural pattern for replication middleware has been derived from both object and service replication middleware solutions. Among the Web Service middleware systems we have considered the following.

The WS-Replication (Salas et al. 2006) middleware offers transparent active replication, based on the Axis1 SOAP engine. The major components in WS-Replication are a *Web Service replication component* and a *reliable multicast component*. The former enables active replication of Web Services, and the latter—called WS-Multicast—provides SOAP-based group communication. Moreover, WS-Multicast performs failure detection (which is required for group communication) by a SOAP-based ping mechanism. WS-Multicast can also be used independently from the overall WS-Replication framework for reliable multicast in a Web Service environment. The SOAP group communication support has been built on the JGroups tool kit. Currently, WS-Multicast is not available on an open-source basis, so we used the Spread group communication tool kit in our own Axis2-based replication framework (Weghofer 2007; Osrael et al. 2007).

The middleware presented in Ye and Shen (2005) offers transparent active replication based on group communication. The system implements the TOPBCAST (Hayden and Birman 1996) probabilistic multicast protocol on top of the JGroups tool kit. Both synchronous and asynchronous interaction between the client and the Web Service are supported.

FT-SOAP (Liang et al. 2003) provides primary backup replication and is built upon the Java-based Axis1 SOAP engine. As in the FT-CORBA architecture (CORBA), FT-SOAP comprises a replication manager, a fault management unit, and a logging and recovery unit.

To our knowledge, except for our own comparison (Osrael et al. 2006), no previous architectural comparison of replication middleware for distributed objects and services exist. Our own Axis2-based replication middleware (Weghofer 2007; Osrael et al. 2007d), which closely follows the pattern we have presented, is different from the existing solutions since it (1) is based on the latest Web Service specifications (e.g., in contrast to FT-SOAP) and (2) it provides a different replication protocol: a variant of primary backup replication using operation transfer instead of state transfer.

19.4.2 Discovery in Large-Scale Distributed Systems

Runtime discovery is a necessity in all distributed systems, where the properties of the participating nodes are not known a priori. This problem was first tackled in heterogeneous and dynamic clusters, where not all worker nodes can serve all jobs all the time; thus, matching of jobs against worker nodes that will execute them is required. The Condor workload management system (Thain et al. 2002) was one of the first systems to provide such functionality in a comprehensive and sophisticated manner. Aimed primarily at cluster installations, Condor supports large Grid deployments by using the Globus tool kit remote job execution infrastructure as the backend. Condor uses the ClassAd language (Raman 2000) for both node advertisements and queries.

The first problem one encounters when attempting to deploy such a service in a large-scale, widely distributed environment is the sheer volume of advertised objects (resources, services, etc.) and the traffic required to maintain consistent and up-to-date information about all the advertised objects. Furthermore, it is imperative that the discovery service itself should provide a high level of dependability, as it is a central element of our design; the discovery service should be highly available and reliable, and provide up-to-date information about the whole system. Hence, centralized approaches do not prove adequate; they are overwhelmed by the amount of data that needs to be stored and the query and update traffic directed at them.

The discovery service must itself be distributed in order to cope with such conditions. The hierarchical approach used by Globus tool kit's MDS (Foster 2005), connecting multiple instances of the MDS Index service in a treelike hierarchy, is better suited to such environments, distributing the information over a hierarchy of MDS Index instances and thus lowering the amount of information stored on and traffic directed at any single MDS Index instance in the hierarchy. However, failure of any MDS instance in the hierarchy results in a partition of the hierarchy; clients using the Index instance in one partition cannot access the information stored in instances of the other partition. UDDI registries (Oasis 2004), on the other hand, provide fault tolerance by means of replication of data, but the requirement for strong consistency among replicas negatively impacts performance in a highly dynamic system, where advertisements are constantly updated; UDDI registries are better suited to predominantly static environments.

Thus, a fully distributed approach should be investigated. Algorithms from the domain of peer-to-peer systems seem promising, as they provide natural fault tolerance, load balancing of the stored information, and update and query traffic over all the nodes in the system. Peer-to-peer resource discovery has been investigated in Iamnitchi and Foster (2002), and an overview of models and systems for resource discovery based on peer-to-peer paradigm is presented in Trunfio et al. (2007). Today, many such systems exist (Gupta et al. 2005; Hauswirth and Schmidt 2006; Caron et al. 2006) and manage to cope well with the issues caused by quantity of data and network traffic, providing reasonably dependable function. Most of these systems provide only means for discovery of low-level system resources, such as hardware and software platforms, and processing and storage capabilities of the computer nodes, often with a fixed vocabulary of resource types. Due to the heterogeneity of the nodes, the constantly changing state of their resources, and possible differences in the implementation of functionally same services owned by different providers, such information is of little use to the service consumers. As an example, consider that in order to utilize data on CPU power and load for estimating the time the service would take to complete a job, the consumer would have to know the details of service implementation. Obviously, services should describe their capabilities on a higher level, which is more meaningful to the service consumer (Močnik et al. 2006). As an example, consider a service providing a Monte Carlo simulation to its consumers; it should advertise the number of solutions it can analyze in an hour, not the current CPU load.

19.4.3 Matching and Negotiation of Service Properties

According to discussion in section 19.3, in order to create dependable service-oriented systems, it is of utmost importance for the service consumer, be it an end user or another *composite* service, that the service provider delivers the service in accordance with the consumer's requirements regarding the nonfunctional service properties. Dynamic composition that allows such behavior requires the process of discovery to take into account not only the functional properties of the service but also a set of nonfunctional properties. This part of the discovery process is often referred to as *matching* or *selection*, and has been investigated primarily in relation to quality-of-service-aware SOAs (Toma et al. 2006; Maximilien and Singh 2004; Yu et al. 2007; Tian et al. 2004; Anselmi et al. 2007).

Finally, following the selection, the desired service properties need to be negotiated between the consumer and the selected provider, resulting in a form of a contract, often referred to as a service-level agreement (SLA), which states the nonfunctional properties that the service delivered should provide.

Languages for specification of nonfunctional properties of Web Services and frameworks for SLA creation and monitoring have been devised (the WSLA framework, Ludwig et al. 2002; SLAng, Skene et al. 2004; the WS QoS framework, Tian et al. 2004; QoS Policies, Maximilien and Singh 2004).

Instead of inventing a new language, our work leverages a widely used standard (WS-Policy) for expressing the required or provided capabilities as well as SLAs, leaving individual providers to extend them as necessary with their specific policy assertions. Also, the matching and selection process is performed solely by the consumer and the discovered (functionally adequate) providers, which proves essential for building open, widely distributed, and highly dynamic service-oriented systems. First, no global consensus on the specification of nonfunctional properties is required, as only the requesters and providers that cooperate need to recognize and interpret specific policy assertions that specify nonfunctional properties. Other parts of the system, including all constituent nodes of the distributed service index, need not know anything about specific assertion semantics. Another advantage is that the matching and selection algorithms are solely in the domain of the consumer, allowing it to optimize these processes according to its own needs by means of pluggable matching and match evaluation modules.

19.5 Conclusion and Future Work

Dependability is a key factor if service-oriented computing is to become a success story even in critical areas such as public safety or air traffic control. In the DeDiSys project, we have focused in particular on dependability in data-centric and resource-centric service-oriented systems.

With respect to the first kind of systems, we have contributed a replication middleware architecture pattern which has proved its usefulness in both service-oriented systems and distributed object systems. The main conclusion stemming from this work is that many traditional dependability concepts, such as replication, failure detection, and group communication, can be adopted (or adapted) for service-oriented systems. Nevertheless, service-oriented systems of the future, such as ultralarge-scale systems, will require additional research to address the challenges of massive scale, cross-organizational heterogeneity and dynamics (Osrael et al. 2007c).

Future work for our replication middleware is (1) the combination with service-oriented transaction techniques and (2) the introduction of a security concept for the framework.

With respect to resource-centric systems, we have contributed an abstract architecture that supports the concept of increasing provider availability at the expense of consumer satisfaction. This approach was proved to increase availability when there is underprovisioning of resources by experimental evaluation of our prototype. The prototype implementation specifically caters to very large, highly dynamic, and open-service-oriented systems. On the one hand, the peer-to-peer-based service index provides a service registration and discovery infrastructure that performs well in the case of large numbers of unreliable and unpredictable member nodes. On the other hand, the proposed approach to describing provider capabilities and consumer requirements, and decentralized discovery, matching, and evaluation of providers, allow seamless runtime integration of new providers with new capabilities that have no centralized control over the system.

Future work for our dependable discovery service includes extensions to enable automatic composition of multiple services into more complex services. The matching framework should be extended to allow for reasoning on the capabilities of composite services based on the capabilities of the composed services. Thus, arbitrary complex workflows could be automatically managed. Also, integration with and extension of existing related standards/specifications and technologies, such as WS-Agreement (Gridforum 2006) and WS-BPEL (Web Services Business Process Execution Language, OASIS 2007), should be considered.

Acknowledgment

The work published in this chapter is partly funded by the European Community under the Sixth Framework Programme, contract FP6–4152 DeDiSys. The work reflects only the authors' views. The Community is not liable for any use that may be made of the information contained therein.

Note

1. This subsection is based on an earlier work: J. Osrael, L. Froihofer, and K. M. Goeschka, "What service replication middleware can learn from object replication middleware," in *Proceedings of the 1st Workshop on Middleware for Service Oriented Computing in Conjunction with the 7th International ACM/IFIP/USENIX Middleware Conference*, pp. 18–23. http://doi.acm.org/10.1145/1169091.1169094. © 2006, Association for Computing Machinery, Inc. Included by permission.

References

Amir, Y., C. Danilov, and J. Stanton. 2000. A low latency, loss tolerant architecture and protocol for wide area group communication. In *Proceedings of the International Conference on Dependable Systems and Networks*, pp. 327–336. Washington, DC: IEEE CS.

Anderson, D. P., and G. Fedak. 2006. The computational and storage potential of volunteer computing. In *Proceedings of the Sixth IEEE International Symposium on Cluster Computing and the Grid (CCGRID'06)*, pp. 73–80. Washington, DC: IEEE CS.

Anselmi, J., D. Ardagna, and P. Cremonesi. 2007. A QoS-based selection approach of autonomic Grid Services. In *Proceedings of the 2007 Workshop on Service Oriented Computing*, pp. 1–8. New York: ACM Press.

Arjuna, Fujitsu, IONA, Oracle, and Sun Microsystems. 2003. Web Services Composite Application Framework WS-CAF Ver. 1.0. http://developers.sun.com/techtopics/webservices/wscaf/primer.pdf.

Avizienis, A., J.-C. Laprie, B. Randell, and C. Landwehr. 2004. Basic concepts and taxonomy of dependable and secure computing. *IEEE Transactions on Dependable and Secure Computing* 1(1): 11–33.

Balakrishnan, H., M. F. Kaashoek, D. Karger, R. Morris, and I. Stoica. 2003. Looking up data in P2P systems. *Communications of the ACM* 46(2): 43–48.

Birman, K. 2006. The untrustworthy Web Services revolution. *IEEE Computer* 39(2): 98–100.

Birman, K., T. Joseph, T. Raeuchle, and A. El Abbadi. 1985. Implementing fault-tolerant distributed objects. *IEEE Transactions on Software Engineering* 11(6): 502–508.

Budhijara, N., K. Marzullo, F. Schneider, and S. Toueg. 1993. "The primary-backup approach." In S. Mullender, ed., *Distributed Systems*, 2nd ed., pp. 199–216. Wokingham, UK: ACM Press, Addison-Wesley.

Caron, E., F. Desprez, and C. Tedeschi. 2006. Dynamic prefix tree for service discovery within large scale Grids. In *Proceedings of the 6th IEEE International Conference on Peer-to-Peer Computing* (P2P '06), pp. 106–116.

Chockler, G., I. Keidar, and R. Vitenberg. 2001. Group communication specifications: A comprehensive study. *ACM Computing Surveys* 33(4): 427–469.

Coulouris, G. F., J. Dollimore, and T. Kindberg. 2001. *Distributed Systems: Cconcepts and Design.* Addison-Wesley.

Defago, X., A. Schiper, and P. Urban. 2004. Total order broadcast and multicast algorithms: Taxonomy and survey. *ACM Computing Surveys* 36(4): 372–421.

Feiler, P., R. Gabriel, J. Goodenough, R. Linger, T. Longstaff, R. Kazman, M. Klein, L. Northrop, D. Schmidt, K. Sullivan, and K. Wallnau. 2006. *Ultra-Large-Scale Systems.* Pittsburgh, PA: Software Engineering Institute, Carnegie Mellon University.

Foster, I. 2005. Globus toolkit version 4: Software for service oriented systems. In *Proceedings of the IFIP International Conference on Network and Parallel Computing*, pp. 2–13. Boston: Springer.

Foster, I., C. Kesselman, and S. Tuecke. 2001. The anatomy of the Grid: Enabling scalable virtual organizations. *International Journal of High Performance Computing Applications* 15(3): 200–222.

Gifford, D. K. 1979. Weighted voting for replicated data. In *Proceedings of the 7th Symposium on Operating Systems Principles*, pp. 150–162. New York: ACM Press.

Gridforum. 2006. Web Services Agreement Specification WS-Agreement. http://www.ogf.org.

Gupta, A., Divyakant Agrawal, and Amr El Abbadi. 2005. Distributed resource discovery in large scale computing systems. In *Proceedings of the 2005 Symposium on Applications and the Internet* (SAINT '05), pp. 320–326. Washington, DC: IEEE CS.

Hauswirth, M., and R. Schmidt. 2005. An overlay network for resource discovery in Grids. In *Proceedings of the 16th International Workshop on Database and Expert Systems Applications*, pp. 343–348.

Hayden, M., and K. Birman. 1996. Probabilistic Broadcast. Technical report. Ithaca, N.Y.: Cornell University.

Iamnitchi, A., and I. Foster. 2004. A peer-to-peer approach to resource location in Grid environments. In *Grid Resource Management: State of the Art and Future Trends*, pp. 413–429. Norwell, MA: Kluwer Academic Publishers.

IBM, BEA Systems, Microsoft, Arjuna, Hitachi, and IONA. 2005. Web Services Transactions Specifications. http://www-128.ibm.com/developerworks/library/specification/ws-tx/.

Jayasinghe, D. 2005. FAWS for SOAP-based Web Services. http://www-128.ibm.com/developerworks/webservices/library/ws-faws/.

Jgroups. The Jgroups Project. http://www.jgroups.org/.

Kwiatkowski, J., P. Karwaczyński, and M. Pawlik. 2006. *Dependable Information Service for Distributed Systems.* Berlin: Springer. Lecture Notes in Computer Science 3911.

Laprie, J.-C. 2005. Resilience for the scalability of dependability. In *Proceedings of the 4th International Symposium on Network Computing and Applications*, pp. 5–6. Washington, DC: IEEE CS.

Liang, D., C.-L. Fang, C. Chen, and F. Lin. 2003. Fault tolerant Web Service. In *Proceedings of the 10th Asia–Pacific Software Engineering Conference*, pp. 310–319. Washington, DC: IEEE CS.

Ludwig, H., A. Keller, A. Dan, R. Franck, and R. King. 2002. Web Service Level Agreement (WSLA) Language Specification. IBM Corporation. http://www.research.ibm.com/wsla/.

Maximilien, M. E., and Singh, M. P. 2004. Toward autonomic Web Services trust and selection. In *Proceedings of the 2nd International Conference on Service Oriented Computing*, pp. 212–221. New York: ACM Press.

Microsoft. NET Framework 3.0. http://msdn2.microsoft.com/en-us/netframework/.

Močnik, J., and P. Karwaczyński. 2006. An architecture for service discovery based on capability matching. In *Proceedings of the 1st International Conference on Availability, Reliability, and Security* (ARES '06), pp. 824–831. Washington, DC: IEEE CS.

Močnik J., M. Novak, and P. Karwaczyński. 2006. A discovery service for very large, dynamic Grids. In *Proceedings of the 2nd International Conference on e-Science and Grid Computing*. Washington, DC: IEEE Press.

Oasis. 2004. UDDI Version 3.0.2. http://uddi.org/pubs/uddi_v3.htm.

Oasis. 2007. Web Services Business Process Execution Language Version 2.0. http://www.oasis-open.org/committees/tc_home.php?wg_abbrev=wsbpel.

Object Management Group (OMG). 2004. Common Object Request Broker Architecture: Core Specification v3.0.3. http://www.omg.org/technology/documents/formal/corba_iiop.htm.

Object Management Group. Trading Object Service Specification. 2000. http://www.omg.org/docs/formal/00-06-27.pdf.

ObjectWeb. 2007. What's Middleware. http://middleware.objectweb.org.

Osrael, J., L. Froihofer, and K. M. Goeschka. 2006. What service replication middleware can learn from object replication middleware. In *Proceedings of the 1st Workshop on Middleware for Service Oriented Computing in Conjunction with the 7th International ACM/IFIP/USENIX Middleware Conference*, pp. 18–23. New York: ACM Press. http://doi.acm.org/10.1145/1169091.1169094.

Osrael, J., L. Froihofer, and K. M. Goeschka. 2007a. Replication in service oriented systems. In P. Pelliccione, H. Muccini, N. Guelfi, and A. Romanovsky, eds., *Software Engineering and Fault Tolerance.* Singapore: World Scientific Publishing.

Osrael, J., L. Froihofer, and K. M. Goeschka. 2007b. Experiences from building service and object replication middleware. In *Proceedings of the 6th IEEE Symposium on Network Computing and Applications.* Washington, DC: IEEE CS.

Osrael, J., L. Froihofer, and K. M. Goeschka. 2007c. On the need for dependability research on service oriented systems. In *Fast Abstract Proceedings of the 37th Annual IEEE/IFIP International Conference on Dependable Systems and Networks*. Washington, DC: IEEE CS.

Osrael, J., L. Froihofer, M. Weghofer, and K. M. Goeschka. 2007d. Axis2-based replication middleware for Web Services. In *Proceedings of the International Conference on Web Services 2007*. Washington, DC: IEEE CS.

Perera, S., C. Herath, J. Ekanayake, E. Chinthaka, A. Ranabahu, D. Jayasinghe, S. Weerawarana, and G. Daniels. 2006. Axis2, middleware for next generation Web Services. In *Proceedings of the International Conference on Web Services*, pp. 833–840. Washington, DC: IEEE CS.

Raman, R. 2000. Matchmaking Frameworks for Distributed Resource Management. PhD. dissertation, University of Wisconsin at Madison.

Rappa, M. A. 2004. The utility business model and the future of computing services. *IBM Systems Journal* 43(1): 32–42.

Salas, J., F. Perez-Sorrosal, M. Patino-Martínez, and R. Jiménez-Peris. 2006. WS-Replication: A framework for highly available Web Services. In *Proceedings of the 15th International Conference on the World Wide Web*, pp. 357–366. New York: ACM Press.

Schiper, A. 2006. Group communication: From practice to theory. In *Proceedings of the SOFSEM 2006 Conference: Theory and Practice of Computer Science*, pp. 117–136. Berlin: Springer.

Schneider, F. 1993. Replication management using the state-machine approach. In S. Mullender, ed., *Distributed Systems*, pp. 17–26. Wokingham, UK: ACM Press/Addison-Wesley.

Shaw, M. 2002. Self-healing: Softening precision to avoid brittleness. In *Proceedings of the 1st Workshop on Self-healing Systems*, pp. 111–114. New York: ACM Press.

Skene, J., D. Lamanna, and W. Emmerich. 2004. Precise service level agreements. In *Proceedings of the 26th International Conference on Software Engineering*, pp. 179–188.

Thain, D., T. Tannenbaum, and Miron Livny. 2002. Condor and the Grid. In F. Berman, G. Fox, and T. Hey, eds., *Grid Computing: Making the Global Infrastructure a Reality*. John Wiley & Sons.

Tian, M., A. Gramm, H. Ritter, and J. Schiller. 2004. Efficient selection and monitoring of QoS aware Web Services with the WS QoS framework. In *IEEE/WIC/ACM International Conference on Web Intelligence*, pp. 152–158. Washington, DC: IEEE CS.

Toma, I., D. Foxvog, and M. C. Jaeger. 2006. Modelling QoS characteristics in WSMO. In *Proceedings of the 1st Workshop on Middleware for Service Oriented Computing*, pp. 42–47. New York: ACM Press.

Trunfio, P., et al. 2007. Peer-to-peer resource discovery in Grids: Models and systems. In *Future Generation Computer Systems*. Amsterdam: Elsevier Science.

Vinoski, S. 2003. Service discovery 101. *IEEE Internet Computing* 7(1): 69–71.

Vogels, W., and C. Re. 2003. WS-Membership—Failure Management in a Web-Services World. http://www2003.org/cdrom/papers/alternate/P712/p712–vogels.html.

W3C. Web Services Description Language WSDL 1.1. http://www.w3.org/TR/wsdl.html.

Weghofer, M. 2007. Implementierung und Evaluierung von WebService Replikationsmechanismen. Master's thesis, University of Applied Sciences Technikum Wien.

WS-Glossary. Web Services Glossary. http://www.w3.org/TR/ws-gloss/.

WS-Policy. Web Services Policy (WS-Policy) Framework. ftp://www6.software.ibm.com/software/developer/library/ws-policy.pdf.

Ye, X., and Y. Shen. 2005. A middleware for replicated Web Services. In *Proceedings of the 3rd International Conference on Web Services*, pp. 631–638. Washington, DC: IEEE CS.

Yu, T., Y. Zhang, and K.-J. Lin. 2007. Efficient algorithms for Web Services selection with end-to-end QoS constraints. *ACM Transactions on the Web 1(1)*.

20 Consolidating Research Results: The Industrial Perspective of NESSI

Stefano de Panfilis

20.1 Introduction

All the preceding chapters describe a tremendous effort by European organizations to move in the direction of building sound technological foundations to support the service economy.

The challenges of these efforts originated from the Lisbon Agenda[1] and have been discussed and substantiated in many documents, among them the NESSI Vision document.[2] The elaboration of this vision is discussed in the NESSI Strategic Agenda, volume 1, Framing the Future of the Service Oriented Economy,[3] in which the NESSI Framework (discussed in chapter 1) is part of an overall perspective: the NESSI holistic model (see figure 20.1). This model not only depicts the technological foundations (reflected in the research area "NESSI Framework"), but also delineates research directions which are needed in order for these technologies to become effective. These directions are the understanding of business domain peculiarities (reflected in the research area "NESSI Landscape") and of all the implications a full transition to a service economy has for societal aspects (reflected in the research area "NESSI Adoption"), such as new skills, organizational models, and laws and regulations.

In this perspective there is still a lot of work to be done. Even if building blocks for the NESSI Framework are being developed, in order to integrate all these results into a coherent framework it is necessary to create a common understanding. In the next sections we elaborate possible scenarios and introduce the notion of NEXOF (the NESSI Open Service Framework), which is meant to define a referential approach and environment into which European research efforts can fit. NEXOF, together with the building blocks coming out of the different research projects, aims to become a service environment which can be used to the advantage of all service economy stakeholders and European citizens. The following section describes possible scenarios that can be realized through NEXOF.

20.2 Imagine a World...

20.2.1 NEXOF—Promoting Collaborative Services to Ease Business Expansion across Europe

Imagine a young inventor who has just come up with a startling new idea. He is alone, without any means to move from idea to implementation. Even with the current level of connectivity and information at hand, finding the right partnership is at best difficult. But imagine what could be possible when the virtual communities that are emerging today are taken to the next level. New services will provide the inventor with a personalized access to potential collaborations across the world—collaborations with predefined qualities, partnerships that can take his invention from idea to product.

20.2.2 NEXOF—Supporting Secure Services to Implement a Full Chain of Events

Imagine yourself in a foreign European city. Suddenly an accident happens. You are taken away by ambulance, in an unknown city, where a foreign language is spoken.... The ambulance takes you safely to the best hospital. The traffic lights turn to green whenever the ambulance approaches, in a permanent and personalized connection mode between the vehicle and the road infrastructure. While you are being transported, your medical information is being downloaded, analyzed, translated into a foreign language, and sent to the hospital. It is being shared between the ambulance attendants and the hospital physicians.

Today, technologies could implement this exchange of information—but this is much more than information—it is the exchange of critical, protected, and sensitive data between countries, public and private organizations, and human beings. And, in addition, they need to be exchanged without delay.

It is about sharing this information at a level that has yet to be achieved. It is about building service infrastructures and raising the awareness of public health authorities to make this unprecedented sharing safe, secure, realistic, and immediate.

20.2.3 NEXOF—Service Infrastructures to Create Virtual Learning Environments

Imagine a world which transforms each visit to the museum into a personalized cultural experience. One in which selecting the picture you want to know more about does not deliver standardized information but adapts to your expectations. It provides you with an in-depth analysis or, on the contrary, limits itself to a high-level view. It adapts to the amount of time you want to spend in the museum, and you can preselect your learning approach, share it with your friends, capture the essence of art—just the way you want it.

20.3 The NESSI Holistic Model

The above scenarios are just a few of many possible examples which describe how we envisage European industry will make use of service technologies for the benefit of citizens,

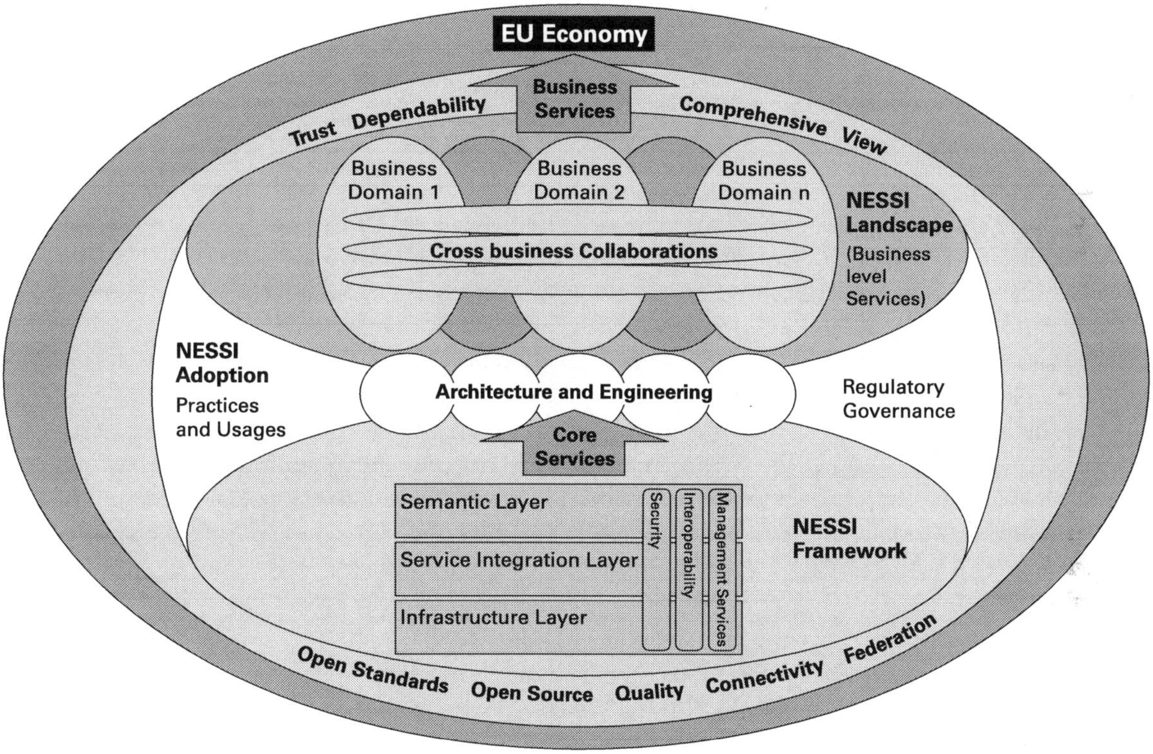

Figure 20.1
The NESSI holistic model

as a driver for the evolution toward a fully employed service economy which will effectively benefit from the Future Internet.

Contributing to the Future Internet is a wonderful challenge in which many people and organizations are involved, and because of this, there is the need for a comprehensive, consistent, and coherent common understanding. This the aim of the NESSI holistic model, which embraces the whole service area and, as depicted in figure 20.1, gives services research a complete and integrated perspective in the transformation process of the European economy. The model defines the three main constituent parts of the context:

- ICT technologies, represented by the *NESSI Framework*, where the services are engineered. Future scenarios will be characterized by large distributed systems with many data collection points, operations, and computers that transform data into knowledge and help humans coordinate the execution of complex tasks. Large amounts of data will be generated by sensors, transmitted via wireless channels to ground stations, and then moved through fast optical technology to powerful computational infrastructure. The results will be visualized on different devices according to the context of use. A crucial missing piece is a software infrastructure facilitating a seamless and cost-effective composition of services in this new era of the Web. This software infrastructure should support pervasive and ubiquitous application scenarios in which machines dissolve across the Net into a set of special-purpose and domain-specific appliances.

- The *NESSI Landscape*, where the services as implemented by the NESSI Framework are applied to specific businesses, organizational goals, and domains, and where cross-domain cooperation is analyzed, as it is expected that the current segmentation into separate business domains (such as automotive and health care) will be relaxed. The NESSI Landscape also aims at enabling tight interactions between systems of agile service-oriented businesses in an always changing market.
- The set of instantiation mechanisms based on regulations, rules and policies, and new skills which, constituting the *NESSI Adoption*, make services real, and thus usable by the consumers. Indeed, the fact that service-based systems will be implemented and deployed is not sufficient to have these systems efficiently adopted by citizens. Several barriers have to be addressed, and to do so, NESSI will develop its adoption strategies along three main axes:

1. Entering the service economy will possibly require organizations not only to master service infrastructures, but also to reinvent their business models.
2. The long-term adoption of service technologies will be sustained by the development of expertise in knowledge domains that are relevant to a service-oriented economy. This could be achieved by setting up education programs and promoting the development of open cross-disciplinary communities of experts in Europe.
3. Compliance with and evolution of regulations and governance procedures. The dynamicity of new service-based business models might require a different understanding, since current regulations might appear in some cases to be too restrictive with respect to the full adoption of the envisaged new models. In addition, the new service era might raise new issues (e.g., social, economic), unforeseen by regulators and requiring new regulations. A typical example of the relationship between technological and social issues is the capability of service-based systems to establish or maintain valid contracts on behalf of the organizations or human beings running them.

20.4 The NESSI Open Service Framework

Recent and continuous advances in mobile communications and embedded solutions are transforming the environment, at home, at work, and on the go, into an intelligent interface to information—shielding users from the complexity of software, networks, and computers; this is the Future Internet, which is apparent in new Networks, the "Internet of

Things," the "3D Internet," "Internet of Content," and the "Internet of Services." It is the aim of NEXOF to be a key technological environment that will make all of this happen.

With respect to the NESSI holistic model, NEXOF is intended to support the whole model so that NEXOF, the NESSI Open Service Framework, is an *integrated*, *consistent*, and *coherent* set of technologies, methods, and tools intended, as stated by the NESSI vision document, to do the following:

- Provide the European industry and the public sector with efficient services and software infrastructures to improve flexibility, interoperability and quality
- Master complex software systems and their provision as service-oriented utilities
- Establish the technological basis, the strategies, and the deployment policies needed to speed up the dynamics of the services ecosystem
- Develop novel technologies, strategies, and deployment policies that foster openness, through the increased adoption of open standards and open source software, as well as the provision of open services
- Foster safety, security, and the well-being of citizens by means of new societal applications, enhanced efficiency of industry and administrations, and competitive jobs.

The overall architectural goal of NEXOF is to be an open service framework, implementing the whole NESSI Framework, ranging from the infrastructure up to the interfaces with the end users; leveraging research in the area of service-based systems, of which this book provides an optimal compendium; and to consolidate and trigger innovation in service-oriented economies for the benefit of the whole European economy.

The referential nature of NEXOF requires it to be complete. To this end NEXOF will deploy the following:

1. *A Reference Architecture*, to define and specify the main concepts needed to allow the building of NEXOF instances. In turn the reference architecture is made of (a) a model, which defines the main concepts from the technology, business, and citizens' viewpoints; and (b) specifications, to formalize the model into open specifications facilitating precise implementations of the service environment according to different domains, technologies, and business scale. The model captures an abstract vision of the architecture providing a set of components and describing at a high level the interaction between these components. The specifications provide detailed interfaces among the components. Rules, principles, and policies govern the decisions taken to create the architecture.
2. *A Reference Implementation* to make NEXOF real and concrete, serving as the guide for further NEXOF instantiations by different organizations, for different domains and adopting different technological approaches. The reference implementation is not just an application, but a complex of methods, tools, and technologies, released as open source, allowing derivative works which are needed to design, build, manage, and operate NEXOF instances.

3. *A compliance test suite*, to validate NEXOF instances and related provided services, not only to be fully operational but also to be compliant with the reference architecture, so as to assure maximum interoperability among different instances and provided services.

20.5 Concluding Remarks

The effort needed and the ambition to implement a framework such as NEXOF are substantial. Nevertheless, we are conscious that projects and initiatives which are within the scope of NEXOF are running, as illustrated in this book, and will be in place in the near future. Therefore, when implementing NEXOF we should concentrate on the "added value" of building such a comprehensive integrated, consistent, and coherent reference framework incorporating as many existing or emerging relevant results and solutions as possible. To this end, possibly inheriting from the wide and active world of the communities, new and specific approaches in terms of project management should be adopted and put in place to guarantee an adequate level of surveying and measuring of the state of the art, and methodologies and policy for their integration into NEXOF.

This should be an open approach through which all the NEXOF achievements are made available to other research, experimental, or commercial initiatives as a reference from which to experiment with new ideas and identify new research gaps, keeping in mind that the independent character of NEXOF will foster its adoption and usage by large businesses as well as the dynamic world of SMEs.

Acknowledgment

The work presented in this chapter will be partly funded by the European Community under the Seventh Framework Programme, contract FP7–ICT-216446 NEXOF-RA.[4] The work reflects only the author's views. The Community is not liable for any use that may be made of the information contained therein.

Notes

1. Lisbon European Council: Presidency Conclusions (24/03/2000 No. 100/1/00).
2. http://www.nessi-europe.com/Nessi/Portals/0/Nessi-repository/Publications/Flyers/2005_09_Vision_V2.pdf.
3. http://www.nessi-europe.com/Nessi/Portals/0/Nessi-repository/Publications/Flyers/2006_02_NESSI_SRA_VOL_1.pdf.
4. http://www.nexof-ra.eu/.

21 S-Cube: The Network of Excellence on Software Services and Systems

Mike P. Papazoglou and Klaus Pohl

21.1 Introduction

This book shows that the research community in the area of service-oriented computing in Europe is growing. The aim of the Software Services and Systems (Research) Network (S-Cube) is to develop this community further and to establish a unified, multidisciplinary, vibrant research community, which will achieve worldwide scientific excellence by defining a broader research vision and perspective, and shape the software-service-based Internet. S-Cube intends to accomplish its mission by meeting the following objectives:

1. Realigning, reshaping, and integrating research agendas of key European players from diverse research areas, and synthesizing and integrating diversified knowledge, thereby establishing a long-lasting foundation for steering research and for achieving innovation at the highest level.
2. Inaugurating a Europe-wide common program of education and training for researchers and industry, thereby creating a common culture that will have a profound impact on the future of the field.
3. Establishing trust relationships with industry (and NESSI; see chapter 20 in particular) to achieve a catalytic effect in shaping European research, strengthening industrial competitiveness and addressing main societal challenges.

21.2 Research Agenda

Today's approach to service-oriented architectures is a technology evolution, which will enable future technologies, architectures, and approaches to emerge. Once SOAs are achieved, the next step is to go beyond technology alone and continue the evolution by aligning technology with business value. However, the conventional SOA approach neither addresses the separation of overarching concerns, such as the orchestration and coordination of services, the engineering and evolution of services, the development and deployment of industrial-strength, service-based applications, nor does it distinguish between the functionality required for developing application-related services and that of technical services (at the systems level) required for composing, monitoring, and managing services. Such a logical separation of functional SOA concerns can provide facilities for ensuring consistency across the organization at all levels (both technical and business), high availability of services, and orchestration of multiple services as part of mission-critical composite applications—all essential requirements for industrial-quality services.

21.2.1 Current Approaches and Open Problems

Currently, common practice for the development of service-based systems distinguishes three functional layers to realize service-based systems. (See the NESSI framework and the SOC road map, explained in chapter 1.):

1. The service infrastructure layer supports the description, publishing, discovery, and binding of services, and provides the runtime environment for the execution of service-based systems and applications. It provides service communication primitives that utilize the basic service middleware, constructs that connect heterogeneous services and service description and location primitives that support the discovery of services.
2. The service composition and coordination layer supports the aggregation of multiple services into a single composite service offered to service clients or used as discrete services in further service compositions. By relying on the services infrastructure, service composition controls and coordinates the execution of the constituent services in the composition, and manages dataflow as well as control flow among them.
3. The business process management layer provides end-to-end visibility and control over all parts of a long-lived, multistep business process that spans multiple applications and human actors in one or more organizations. It provides the mechanisms for expressing, understanding, representing, and managing an organization in terms of a collection of business processes (composed services that are furnished from service composition) and may involve human actors.

Currently, there are several serious architectural limitations and assumptions that permeate the services functionality stack described above. Although several communities address fundamental issues inherent in the three functional layers, many crucial service issues are neglected, while in some cases solutions are too specialized and do not deliver on their promises or are rendered moot by new technological advances. There is an abundance of important open research problems that require immediate research scrutiny. Some typical open research problems include the following:

1. *Sophisticated service functionality, including adaptation and proactiveness* The next generation of end-to-end service networks will require service-based systems that can adapt themselves to unexpected changes of, for instance, technology, regulations, and market opportunities, and can operate within a mixed environment of people, content, and systems. Service-based systems will thus possess the ability to continuously adapt and morph themselves in reaction to unexpected environment challenges and changing user require-

ments, and the differentiated services will reflect the unique requirements and user context where they apply. In addition, the next generation of services will have to be able to predict problems, such as potential degradation scenarios, future erroneous behavior, and exceptions/deviations from conventional behavior, and move toward resolving them, if required, under the guidance and supervision of human actors, before they occur.

2. *Holistic methodologies for engineering and adapting service-based systems* Novel engineering methodologies are needed to unify business context and IT resource-centric engineering approaches, in order to facilitate future, sophisticated hybrid service-based systems that cannot be addressed with today's limited engineering approaches. These methodologies should allow the service provider, as well as the lay end user, to compose and adjust service-based systems according to their actual needs.

3. *End-to-end quality provision and SLA compliance* Future, truly proactive service-based systems should guarantee end-to-end quality and compliance with SLAs and/or regulations. They should monitor, detect, and resolve problems in applications before services are impacted. End-to-end quality provision implies that the different quality characteristics (such as reliability or performance) must be understood across all three functional layers—service infrastructure, service composition, and business process management—and must be handled in a uniform way.

Any research group or even research community in isolation cannot deliver the innovation that is required to address the major research challenges, such as the ones mentioned above. Addressing those research challenges requires the synergy and integration of a variety of research communities, including business process modeling, Grid computing, service-oriented computing, software engineering, automated planning, human–computer interaction, information retrieval, and semantics.

21.2.2 Research Approach

To address the future research challenges outlined above, S-Cube aims for the following joint research objectives:

1. *Service-based systems engineering and adaptation methodologies* The objective is to jointly develop the next generation of service engineering and adaptation methodologies which, by combining different competences, take a holistic view and empower service composers, service providers, as well as lay end users to compose and adjust service-based systems. These methodologies should support the realization of business goals and processes in service-based systems, as well as the exploration of services and discovery of services on the basis of service design principles.

2. *Service technologies* The objective is to jointly design and develop the next generation of well-designed and interrelated realization mechanisms for service-based systems to support the engineering and functional adaptation of service-based systems at the infrastructure level, the service composition, and the business process management level.

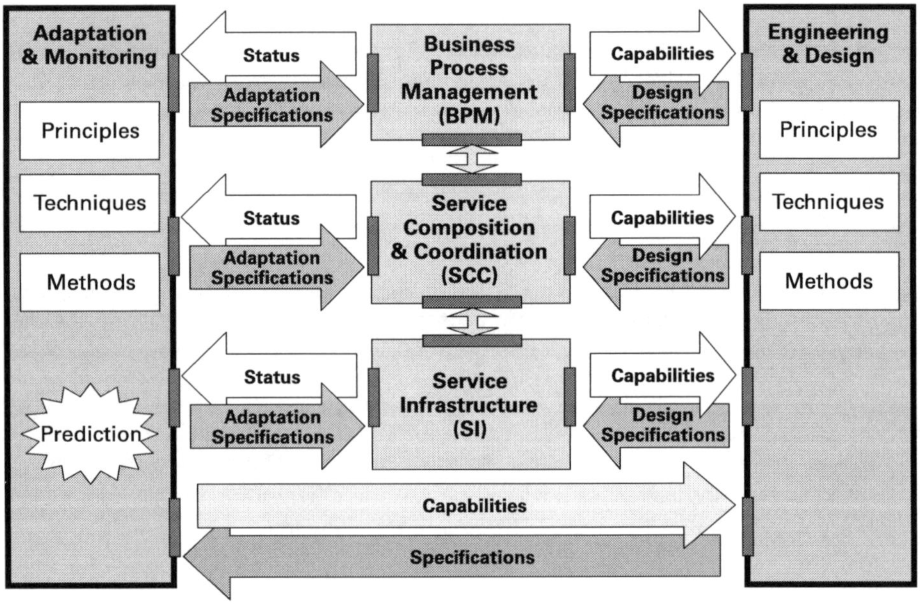

Figure 21.1
Conceptual S-Cube architecture

S-Cube research is organized around the five functional layers depicted in figure 21.1. The functional layers of the S-Cube model largely overlap with the NESSI framework and the SOC road map which were introduced in chapter 1. The conceptual S-Cube architecture combines the three functional layers of service infrastructure (SI), service composition and coordination (SCC), and business process management (BPM) with service engineering and design (SED) and service adaptation and monitoring (SAM). The services technologies (SI, SCC, BPM) and engineering principles and methodologies (SED, SAM) equip the organization of the future with the functionality and flexibility that enable it to develop new service value systems and applications. In addition to services and business processes, it intends to support human processes, including issue identification, escalation, and resolution. Most of all it will keep human actors, such as designers, business analysts, and developers, involved in the decision-making process and ensure that they remain amenable to changes in work patterns related to their role. In the S-Cube architecture, cooperating organizations form the nodes in an adaptive virtual organization network that can sense, react, and respond to demand, and leverage its technology and business assets (including knowledge about the environment, SLAs, policies, regulations, and users) to adapt itself to challenges, such as complying with future technology requirements, regulations, or industry guidelines, and emerging market opportunities.

With a foundation of these five functional layers, advanced service features (such as simulation and historical analysis) can be applied not only to the human components of complex business processes but also to the performance of service elements that participate in a service composition and the ensuing business process. For example, both the per-use cost and latency introduced by accessed service functions can be modeled and simulated as first-order participants in large and complex business processes that span a variety of organizations. This allows for true process improvement at all process levels, such as constituent services (services that make up a service composition), hosting infrastructure, and runtime environment.

We briefly sketch the research objective of S-Cube in terms of these five interrelated key areas in the following:

1. *Service infrastructure* (SI) The most basic building block in the next-generation services architecture is the SI segment. This segment supports services communication primitives and utilizes the basic service middleware and architectural constructs that connect heterogeneous systems, provide multiple-channel access to services, and introduce the runtime environment for the execution of services. This runtime infrastructure allows defining basic interactions involving the description, publishing, finding, and binding of services.
2. *Service composition and coordination* (SCC) The SCC segment encompasses functionality necessary for the aggregation of multiple (possibly singular) services into a single composite service offering. Coordination controls the execution of the constituent services in a composition by relying on the SI and manages data flow as well as control flow among them (e.g., by specifying workflow processes and using a workflow engine for runtime control of service execution).
3. *Business process management* (BPM) The BPM segment provides the mechanisms for expressing, understanding, representing, and managing an enterprise in terms of a collection of business processes (composed services that are furnished from the composition segment in figure 21.1) that are responsive to a business environment of internal or external events. Organizations use BPM to coordinate work between people and systems, with the ultimate goal of improving organizational efficiency, responsiveness, and reliability; strategic measures (business performance management); and their correlation as the basis for process improvement and innovation.
4. *Service engineering and design* (SED) The SED segment provides the knowledge, mechanisms, and methodology (collectively referred to as capabilities in figure 21.1) to appropriately interweave the constructs found in the segments of service infrastructure, service composition and coordination, and business process management with the aim to develop healthy and well-functioning service-based applications. It provides design guidelines which, in conjunction with environment and QoS knowledge, help create the most meaningful execution environment for the service application at hand. To assist in composing services in a manner that guarantees that composite services do not lead to spurious results

and that the overall process behaves in a correct and unambiguous manner, the SED provides guidelines and corresponding mechanisms (heuristics) to the service composition and coordination section. Moreover, the SED provides guidelines to manage the entire services life cycle—including identifying, designing, developing, deploying, finding, applying, provisioning, evolving, and maintaining services. It also assists in establishing a services-based platform and programming model, which includes connecting, deploying, and managing services within specific runtime infrastructure facilities.
5. *Service adaptation and monitoring* Finally, SAM is directed toward monitoring the activities of a distributed services ecosystem, making management decisions, and performing control actions to modify and fine-tune the behavior of the entire services network, especially in cases where individual services adapt their functionality and characteristics.

The service-based engineering framework provides the services infrastructure with environment knowledge, such as information about the environment where services run, servers, legacy applications, backend systems, physical connectivity characteristics, and so on. It also includes properties that can identify and describe a particular service or resource (underlying a service), metrics, and resource state. Metrics provide information (mainly QoS) and operations for measurements of a service, such as throughput, utilization, service availability, response time, transaction rate, service throughput, service idle time, security aspects, and so on. Metrics are, for instance, used to simulate the impacts of changes to a process to measure its effect on numerous variables, including cost, profitability, resource utilization, throughput speed, and other critical business objectives.

Figure 21.1 also illustrates that the SED and SAM segments work closely together to jointly handle evolving (adaptable) services and processes by exchanging specialized information. To achieve this synergy, the SAM contains knowledge required to predict, sense, and respond as required for service and process adaptability. Functionality and knowledge of this segment guarantee the effective monitoring of service activities, nonintrusive introduction, and/or nondisruptive departure of evolvable services in overlay networks and distributed infrastructures. The efficient management of services entails new methodologies in monitoring large networks as well as the creation of innovative frameworks for dynamic management of scalable services and the underlying service infrastructure. To this end the SAM provides design knowledge and mechanisms (capabilities) to ensure that service compositions are able to function in spite of changes in behavior of constituent services in the composition. The intention is to catch and repair faults and predict behavior (to the extent possible) so as to reduce as much as possible the need of human intervention for adapting services to subsequent evolutions. The SAM uses knowledge of business events that cause changes to processes to recognize and respond to these events and manage process changes on a timely basis. It detects the complex event patterns that lead to process changes and correlates the relationships between possibly independent or isolated events and event-driven processes, such as causality, membership, and timing.

21.3 Concluding Remarks

What makes the S-Cube architecture a unique point of departure from the traditional way of developing SOA-based applications is its disjunctive, composite nature, in which each segment of the architecture is the result of its own deeply specific problem-solving techniques and expressive potentialities. Each segment in the architecture describes a logical separation of functionality and defines its own set of constructs, capabilities, and responsibilities. However, it leans on constructs of associated segments to accomplish its mission and the overall objective of the architecture, which is to provide facilities for ensuring application consistency across the organization, high availability of services, and orchestration of multiple services as part of mission-critical composite applications—all essential requirements for developing next-generation, industrial-strength service-based applications. Wherever possible, the research will build on the results described in this book.

Awareness of industrial needs is a prerequisite for the industrial relevance of S-Cube's results. To this end the S-Cube architecture overlaps significantly with the NESSI holistic model described in chapter 20. Besides the cutting-edge, long-term research challenges, S-Cube will initiate targeted shorter-term research projects triggered by industry needs. Therefore, common scenarios and business cases will be identified and industry best practices, reference models, and application guidelines will be obtained from industrial partners. Knowledge will be transferred from research outcomes, prototypes, and test beds to industry.

Acknowledgment

The work presented in this chapter will be partly funded by the European Community under the Seventh Framework Programme, contract FP7–ICT-215483 S-CUBE. The work reflects only the authors' views. The Community is not liable for any use that may be made of the information contained therein.

About the Authors

Gennady Agre is an assistant professor in the AI Department of the Institute of Information Technologies, Bulgarian Academy of Sciences. He is an author of more than 80 scientific papers on aspects of case-based reasoning, machine learning, data mining, and Semantic Web Services. In the INFRAWEBS project Dr. Agre was a creator of the INFRAWEBS Semantic Web Service Designer and the method for runtime composition of Semantic Web Services.

Javier Aguiar holds a telecommunications engineering degree from the University of Valladolid, Spain. Currently he is professor in the Telecommunications School in the University of Valladolid, and his research is focused on multimedia overpacket networking. He participates in several IST and EUREKA projects managing technical activities, participated in ETSI STF 294, and cooperated with companies in the telecommunication sector.

Danilo Ardagna received the Ph.D. degree in computer engineering in 2004 from the Politecnico di Milano, from which he graduated in December 2000. He worked for six months at the IBM T. J. Watson Research Center, in the Performance Analysis and System Optimization Group. He is now an assistant professor of information systems in the Dipartimento di Elettronica e Informazione of Politecnico di Milano. His research interests include Web Services composition, autonomic computing, and computer system costs minimization.

Liliana Ardissono (Ph.D., 1996) is associate professor in the Department of Computer Science of the University of Turin. She has worked in the area of intelligent user interfaces and adaptive hypermedia, focusing on user modeling and personalization for Web-based systems and digital TV. She has also dealt with the design and development of multiagent architectures supporting personalized, ubiquitous services. She is now working in the area of Web Service composition and Web Service choreography management.

Alvaro Arenas is a member of the research staff at the STFC Rutherford Appleton Laboratory in the United Kingdom. He holds a D.Phil. in computation from Oxford University. His research interests include software engineering for distributed and concurrent systems, dependability, and trust and security of information systems. His work focuses on the application of formally based methods and tools to the design and development of secure architectures and software within areas such as safety-critical systems, Grids, and knowledge-based systems.

Tatiana Atanasova is a computer scientist at the Institute of Information Technologies, Bulgarian Academy of Sciences. She is a member of the Modeling and Optimization Lab, where she conducts research in conceptual data modeling, data integration, and workflows. She has contributed to the design and development of the INFRAWEBS ontology-based approach for organizing semantic services workflow components.

George Athanasopoulos is a Ph.D. candidate in the Department of Informatics and Telecommunications of the National and Kapodistrian University of Athens. He holds a diploma from Department of Computer Engineering and Informatics of the University of Patras. Since 2002 he has participated in several research projects. His research interests include service-oriented computing with a focus on the context-adaptable composition of heterogeneous services, distributed systems, software architecture modeling, and modern programming methodologies.

Marco Autili received a first-class honors degree in Computer Science in April 2004, and a Ph.D. in Computer Science in April 2008 from the University of L'Aquila. Currently, he is a Research Assistant at the Computer Science Department of the University of L'Aquila. His main research areas are component-based software engineering, service-oriented architectures, and temporal property specification. His main works include the formalization of an architectural approach to the automatic synthesis of distributed adapters for correctly assembling black-box components. He is currently investigating how to exploit the synthesis technique to compose software services. He also formalized a scenario-based visual language for specifying temporal properties called Property Sequence Chart.

Carlos Baladrón received an M.Eng. degree in telecommunications engineering and is a Ph.D. candidate at the University of Valladolid, Spain, where he has worked on several European and national projects as a researcher. Currently, he is Technical Coordinator of the OPUCE project. He is interested in, and has performed research on, service engineering and SOA systems, next-generation networks (NGNs), and quality of service over NGNs.

Luciano Baresi is an associate professor in the Dipartimento di Elettronica e Informazione at the Politecnico di Milano. He also has held positions at the University of Oregon and the University of Paderborn (Germany). He has published or delivered more than 60 papers in the most important national and international journals and at conferences. His research interests are modern and flexible software systems, with special emphasis on service-oriented applications, autonomic systems, and fully flexible infrastructures. Further information is available at http://home.dei.polimi.it/baresi.

Alejandro Bascuñana Muñoz obtained the Ph.D. degree in 2006. He is a senior systems engineer in the Innovation Unit of Ericsson Spain. He has participated in several research projects included in the European Framework Programs, on topics such as beyond 3G technologies, smartcards, and smart payment systems. His current main interests include user-centric service creation environments, mashup platforms, and intelligent agents.

Leire Bastida is an R&D engineer at the European Software Institute in Spain. She has a broad working experience in industrial and research projects related to the service-centric systems engineering, model-driven development, and enterprise interoperability technologies. Her main research interests are focused on software engineering covering business process modeling, service-oriented architectures, and open source development. In this line, she has collaborated in projects that include SeCSE, ATHENA, and SODA, generating results that have been published in the proceedings of international conferences.

Sonia Ben Mokhtar is a research associate at University College London. In 2007 she received her Ph.D. in computer science from University Pierre et Marie Curie (Paris VI) while studying at INRIA-Rocquencourt in the ARLES Research Group, working mainly on distributed software composition in mobile environments.

Arne-Jørgen Berre is chief scientist at SINTEF and associate professor at the University of Oslo. He has served as technical manager for many IST projects, including Eureka Software Factory, DISGIS, ACE-GIS, ATHENA, SWING, and SHAPE. He is involved in service modeling, standardization with the UML Profile and Metamodel for services (UPMS) in OMG, and interoperability standardization in ISO/TC211 and the Open Geodata Interoperability Consortium. He heads the Norwegian SOA in Practice network.

Piergiorgio Bertoli (http://soa.fbk.eu/people/bertoli) is senior consultant at FBK, where he collaborates with the Service-Oriented Applications Research Group. He has ten years of experience in the research areas of planning and formal methods. He is contributing to the adoption of advanced techniques developed in those areas for the purposes of supporting the development of service-oriented applications.

Antonio Biscaglia works for DeltaDator S.p.A., where he is a product manager in the Local Government Business Unit. He has extensive experience and competence in the management of Italian local taxes. He was responsible for significant developments in the interoperability of complex systems, such as banks and central/local governments.

Laura Bocchi received a Ph.D. in computer science at the University of Bologna, Italy. Her doctoral work concerned the formal investigation of transactional aspects in the Web/Grid service architectures. She is currently a research associate at the University of Leicester, in the United Kingdom, funded by the IST-FET Integrated Project SENSORIA (Software Engineering for Service-Oriented Computers). She is interested in formal models for composition and coordination in service-oriented systems, and she is contributing to the development of the Sensoria Reference Modeling Language (SRML).

Stefano Bocconi received a Ph.D. in the Netherlands in 2006. His thesis work, developed at CWI in Amsterdam, is in the field of automatic generation of multimedia presentations. He is currently a research contractor in the Department of Informatics at the University of Turin and is involved in research on Web Service diagnosis and dynamic TV.

Matthias Born works as a research associate at SAP Research in Karlsruhe, Germany. Currently he is doing active research in the area of semantic business process modeling and is involved in the Integrated Project SUPER. Before that he mainly participated in the ATHENA project on Enterprise Interoperability, where his main focus was on modeling cross-organizational business processes in heterogeneous networks. He holds a diploma in business computing from Albstadt-Sigmaringen University.

Andrei Boyanov is a chief executive officer of active solutions and member of the Linux Professional Institute technical advisory board. Having completed postgraduate work at the University of Sofia, he has been a computer engineer and an instructor of higher learning for staff members in the domain of system networks under Linux since 1998. His main works include training materials for LPI certification courses and studies in the domain of fuzzy classification.

Rolv Bræk is a professor of system and service engineering at the Norwegian University of Science and Technology. He has more than 30 years of experience in the model-based design of distributed systems in both industry and academia. Currently his main research interest lies in methods, tools, and platform support for rapid and incremental service engineering based on UML 2.0 collaborations.

Pietro Braghieri received his degree in electronic engineer in 1987 at the University of Bologna. He has 20 years of experience in design and software development on several platforms and technologies. Since 2002 he has been working on complex systems based on Web/J2EE and SOA architectures. Currently he is the Technical Director of the Local Government Business Unit for DeltaDator S.p.A..

Cinzia Cappiello received a Laurea degree in computer engineering and a Ph.D. degree in 2001 and 2005, respectively at the Politecnico di Milano, where she currently holds a post-doctoral position. Her interests are methodologies to support the ERP projects and data quality methods and tools.

Belén Carro is associate professor in the Signal Theory and Communications and Telematics Engineering Department of the University of Valladolid, where she received her Ph.D. in 2001. She is in charge of the CIT laboratory, where she acts as Research Manager and is involved in several European projects—mainly in the areas of service engineering, personal communications, IP broadband communications, NGN, and voice-over IP and quality of service. Currently she is the principal investigator of the OPUCE project.

Pedro Carvalho received a degree in informatics (computer science and engineering) from the Faculty of Sciences of the University of Lisbon, with specialization in computer systems and networks. He is currently working in his dissertation for the M.Sc. degree, on the topic of virtualization and trusted computing. Other research interests focus on the application of dynamical systems and chaos theory in airplane modeling for the creation of "catastrophic oracles" suitable for safety preservation.

Imrich Chlamtac is the president of CREATE-NET and the Honorary Bruno Kessler Professor at the University of Trento. He is a fellow of the IEEE, a fellow of the ACM, a Fulbright Scholar, and the recipient of the ACM Award on Mobility and the IEEE Award on Wireless Personal Communications. He has published over 400 refereed journal and conference articles, and is listed among ISI's Highly Cited Researchers in Computer Science. He is the co-author of several books, including the first book on local area networks (1980) and the Amazon.com best seller, *Wireless and Mobile Network Architectures* (John Wiley and Sons).

Allan Clark is a research associate at the Laboratory for the Foundations of Computer Science at the University of Edinburgh. He has completed his Ph.D. dissertation, which describes a functional programming language of his own design for use in low-level programming, and since then has been working on performance modeling and in particular with the process algebra PEPA.

James Clarke is a program manager at Waterford Institute of Technology and has been involved since 1995 in the technical and managerial work involved in advanced pan-European research, development, and coordination projects. In 2008, he became manager of a newly accepted Call 1 FP7 project titled INCO-TRUST, which stands for International Co-operation in Trustworthy, Secure and Dependable ICT Infrastructures. In Framework Programme 6, he was the coordinator of the IST SecurIST project (http://www.securitytaskforce.eu) and worked on the IST ESFORS project (http://www.esfors.org). Previously, he worked for eight years at LAKE Communications (http://www.lakecommunications.com/) in Ireland as a manager involved in a number of FP4–FP6 projects.

Luca Console (Ph.D. 1991) is full professor of computer science and chair of the Communication Sciences School at the University of Turin. His research interests are in areas of artificial intelligence ranging from knowledge representation to automated reasoning (with specific attention to model-based reasoning and intelligent agents for adaptive systems). He has published about 100 papers in international journals, books, and conference proceedings, and is co-editor of the Readings in MBD collection. He has been a local coordinator for four EU-funded projects (VMBD, IDD, CAWICOMS, and AUTAS) and member of the executive board of the Monet I and II EU-funded Network of Excellence (chairing the Automotive Task Group of Monet II). He is a member of the editorial boards of international journals, twice chaired and twice organized the International Workshop on Principles of Diagnosis (DX), and has been a member of the Program Committees of several international conferences. He was an invited speaker at IJCAI 99, and received the Artificial Intelligence Prize 95, for young researches in AI working in Italy.

Marie-Odile Cordier is full professor at the University of Rennes, in France, and carries out her research activities at Irisa-Inria; she is currently the scientific leader of the DREAM team (Diagnostics, REasoning and Modeling). Her main research interests are in artificial intelligence, focusing on model-based diagnosis, online monitoring, model acquisition using model-checking techniques, and inductive logic programming and temporal abductive reasoning. She has been responsible for several industrial projects and has published numerous papers in international conference proceedings and scientific journals. She has been an ECCAI fellow since 2001 and has served as a Program Committee member and as an area chair for several international conferences (Ijcai, Ecai, DX, KR, etc.), and is a member of editorial committees of a few specialized journals.

Bruno Crispo received an M.Sc. in computer science from the University of Turin and a Ph.D. in computer science from the University of Cambridge. He is currently an associate professor of computer science at the University of Trento in Italy. His research interests are security protocols, authentication, authorization, and accountability in distributed systems and Grids, and sensor security. He has published several papers on these topics in refereed journals and in the proceedings of international conferences.

Jesús Gorroñogoitia Cruz is a software architect and technical consultant in the services area of Atos Research and Innovation (ARI), a department of Atos Origin SAE (Spain). He is working on both national and international (mainly European Community FP funded) IT research and innovation projects in areas such as Semantic Web Services, model-driven development, and open source software.

Philippe Dague received the engineering degree from the École Centrale de Paris in 1972, and the Ph.D. degree in theoretical physics from the University Paris 6 in 1976. He was a mathematics assistant at the University of Poitiers, then at the University Paris 6, from 1976 to 1983. From 1983 to 1992, he was a research engineer in computer science at the IBM Paris Scientific Center. He received the *habilitation à diriger des recherches* degree in computer science in 1992 from the University of Paris 6. From 1992 to 2005, he was professor of computer science at the University of Paris-Nord 13, where in 1999 he founded and led the Artificial Learning, Diagnosis, and Agents Group of the Laboratoire d'Informatique de Paris-Nord (LIPN). Since 2005 he has been professor of computer science at the University Paris-Sud 11, Adjunct Director of the Laboratoire de Recherche en Informatique (LRI), a member of the Artificial Intelligence and Inference Systems Group, and Director of the Computer Science Department of the Engineering School. His research activity deals with artificial intelligence techniques for Engineering, in particular, bridging the control engineering and the AI MBD approaches, building qualitative models from numeric design models or from specifications, distributed diagnosis for discrete-event systems, and diagnosability analysis. He has applied these techniques to various fields in partnership with private industries, national industries (National Research Center for Telecommunication, CNET; National Network of Research in Telecommunication, RNRT; National Center for Space Studies, CNES; National Network of Research and Innovation on Software Technologies, RNTL; National Research and Innovation Program in Earth Transports, PREDIT), and European projects (Brite-EuRam III, FP5 Streps, NoE, ESA, FP6 Streps). He has been a member of the Program Committees of more than 35 conferences, and is the author of about 60 papers in international or national conference proceedings and journals, and of several books.

Rob Davies is partner in MDR Partners, a company specializing in European research projects in fields such as e-government, e-learning, and cultural heritage.

Stefano de Panfilis is the Director of the research and development laboratories of Gruppo Engineering, leading a team of about 100 researchers in Italy and elsewhere in Europe in the field of software engineering. He graduated cum laude in mathematics from the University of Rome "La Sapienza." Since April 1994, he has participated in various European-funded R&D projects. Since its beginning, he has been deeply involved in the NESSI initiative. He is the coordinator of the Strategic Research Agenda Committee of NESSI. He has authored several scientific papers. He is member of the board of directors of OW2 and has been a member of several international conferences' Program Committees.

Elisabetta Di Nitto is an associate professor in the Dipartimento di Elettronica e Informazione at the Politecnico di Milano. Her current research interests are mainly in software engineering, in particular on process support systems, service-centric applications, dynamic software architectures, and autonomic computing. She has served on the Program Committees of international conferences. She is also member of the editorial board of the SOCA journal and has co-edited a Springer monograph, *Test and Analysis of Web Services*.

Massimiliano Di Penta is assistant professor at the University of Sannio, Italy. His main research interests include software maintenance and evolution, reverse engineering, program comprehension, and service-centric software engineering. He is author of more than 90 papers that have appeared in journals and in proceedings of conferences and workshops, and has been involved as general chair; program chair; or Steering, Organizing, or Program Committee member in several software engineering conferences and workshops. He is a member of IEEE and ACM. Further information is available at http://www.rcost.unisannio.it/mdipenta.

John Domingue (http://kmi.open.ac.uk/people/domingue) is the Deputy Director of the Knowledge Media Institute at The Open University, United Kingdom. He has published more than 100 refereed articles in the areas of Semantic Web Services, the Semantic Web, ontologies, and human–computer interaction. Currently he is the Scientific Director of SUPER, a large EU project which integrates Semantic Web Services and business process modeling. Dr Domingue also currently sits on the Steering Committee for the European Semantic Conference Series.

Nicola Dragoni received an M.S. degree in computer science in 2002 and a Ph.D. in computer science in 2006 from the University of Bologna. In 2006 he worked as postdoctoral researcher at the same university and visited the MIT Center for Collective Intelligence. In 2007 he joined University of Trento as research fellow. His current research interests include service-oriented computing, trust, negotiation, and security for mobile systems.

Khalil Drira, Ph.D., has been a senior researcher at LAAS-CNRS since 1992. His research interests include software architecture, QoS management, self-healing, component-oriented software, model-driven coordination, cooperative networked software, formal design, and collaborative and communicating systems. He is or has been involved in various research projects, has published regular and invited papers in proceedings of international conferences and in journals, and has co-edited a number of proceedings, two books, and one special journal issue on these subjects.

Daniele Theseider Dupré (Ph.D., University of Turin, 1994) is associate professor of computer science at the Università del Piemonte Orientale. His research interests are in artificial intelligence and model-based reasoning, with emphasis on diagnostic reasoning for physical and software systems.

Johann Eder (Ph.D. University of Linz, 1985) is full professor of informatics (workflow) at the University of Vienna. He serves as Vice President for Natural Science and Technology of the Austrian Science Funds. He holds a diploma in engineering and a doctorate in technology from the University of Linz. His research interests include databases, information systems, and knowledge engineering. Current research projects include workflow management systems, in particular time management and exception handling, temporal data warehouses, and interorganizational business processes. Professor Eder has co-authored one book, co-edited 11 books and proceedings, and published more than 90 papers in fully reviewed international journals and conference proceedings. He has served on numerous Program Committees for international conferences and as editor and referee for international journals and conferences.

Frank Eliassen is a professor and leader of the Research Group on Networks and Distributed Systems at the University of Oslo. He is also a senior researcher and project manager at Simula Research Laboratory. He has been doing research in the area of distributed systems since the early 1980s. In later years he has mainly been working on adaptation middleware, focusing on support for self-adaptation of QoS-aware applications and services. He received his degrees from the University of Tromsø.

Antonio Sánchez Esguevillas coordinates innovation activities in the Services line at Telefonica I+D, Spain. He holds a Ph.D. degree (with honors) and is an adjunct professor at the University of Valladolid. His current research interests are in the areas of services and applications: personal services (mobility, communications, ambient intelligence), digital home, enterprise, and e-health. He is an IEEE senior member and a member of the editorial board of *IEEE Communications* magazine, and currently serves on the TPC of ICC '08 and ICC '09, VTC-Spring '08, Healthcom '08, and PIMRC '08.

José Luiz Fiadeiro is professor in the Department of Computer Science, University of Leicester, which he joined in November 2002 after having held academic positions at the Technical University of Lisbon and the University of Lisbon, and visiting research positions at Imperial College, King's College London, PUC–Rio de Janeiro, and SRI International. His most recent work has focused on the engineering of complex software-intensive systems, including the methodological and scientific challenges raised by service-oriented computing.

Jacqueline Floch is a senior scientist at SINTEF ICT, Norway's largest independent research institution. She is currently Technical Manager for the SIMS project. Her research interests include software architecture, model-driven service engineering and service validation. She received her doctorate in engineering in telematics from the Norwegian University of Science and Technology.

Lorenz Froihofer is a research assistant at the Vienna University of Technology, where he received his Ph.D. in computer science with distinction in 2007 for his dissertation "Middleware Support for Adaptive Dependability through Explicit Runtime Integrity Constraints." Since 2004 he has been working on the EU IST FP6 project DeDiSys (Dependable Distributed Systems). His primary research interests are in the areas of distributed systems, software engineering, and dependability and security.

Gerhard Friedrich has been full professor since 1997 at the Alpen-Adria University, Klagenfurt, Austria, where he directs the Research Group on Intelligent Systems and Business Informatics and heads the Institute for Applied Informatics. He received his Ph.D. at the Technical University of Vienna and was a guest researcher at the Stanford Research Institute and at the Corporate Research Division of Siemens AG. Before coming to the University of Klagenfurt, he was head of the Technology Center for Configurators and Diagnosis Systems of Siemens Austria, where under his supervision numerous knowledge-based systems were successfully implemented. He has published more than 100 articles in highly renowned journals and proceedings of conferences. He serves as an editor of *AI Communications* and is associate editor of the *International Journal of Mass Customisation*. He and his team conduct research in the areas of knowledge-based systems for configuring products and services, knowledge-based advisory systems, distributed knowledge-based systems, knowledge acquisition, integration of knowledge-based systems, diagnosis and repair of processes, and self-healing Web Services.

Mariagrazia Fugini is associate professor of computer engineering at the Politecnico di Milano. She received the Ph.D. in computer engineering in 1987, and has been a visiting professor at the University of Maryland, the Technical University of Vienna, the University of Stuttgart, and the Polytechnic University of Catalunya. Her research interests are in information system security, software reuse, information retrieval, information systems development and re-engineering, and e-government. She participated in the TODOS, ITHACA, F3, WIDE and DEAFIN UE projects, working on information system development and reengineering, software reuse, data security, information retrieval tools, and workflow and Web application design. She is involved in the EU projects WS-DIAMOND (Diagnosis in Web Services and Self-healing Systems) and SEEMP (Single European Employment Marketplace), working on security, interoperability, Web-based information systems for public administration, and Web Services for citizens and enterprises. She is coauthor of the book *Database Security* (Addison-Wesley, 1995). She cooperates with the Italian public administrations in the design of portals for services to employment, and in ASI projects on security of satellite data archiving and management.

Roberto Furnari received a Laurea degree in computer science in 1999 at the University of Turin. He spent six years as a software engineer at Sinedita, an ICT company in Turin, and is currently a Ph.D. student in computer science within the Doctoral School of Science and High Technology of the University of Turin. His main research interests are in Web Service orchestration and choreography.

Nikolaos Georgantas is senior researcher at INRIA Paris-Rocquencourt. In 2001 he received his Ph.D. in electrical and computer engineering from the National Technical University of Athens. His research interests include distributed systems, middleware, ubiquitous computing, and service-oriented architectures. He is currently working on ad hoc system interoperability in pervasive computing environments based on semantic technologies, specifically leading the work package related to ambient intelligence middleware for the networked home in the EU IST AMIGO project.

Stephen Gilmore is a reader in computer science at the University of Edinburgh. He is the Edinburgh site leader for the SENSORIA project and is in charge of the work package on model-driven development. His research interests include performance evaluation of computer systems using stochastic models derived from process algebra models. His recent work has been on extending the applicability of these process algebras to large-scale and scalable systems.

Karl M. Goeschka is a senior researcher at the Vienna University of Technology and is coordinator of the EU project DeDiSys (Dependable Distributed Systems). Before that, he was Chief Scientist and Director of Corporate Research at Frequentis Austria, world market leader in safe communications for air traffic control. He has co authored over 100 scientific articles, conference presentations, and books. Recently, he organized a track at ACM SAC 2006–2008, and workshops at IEEE ARES, EDOC, and ACM Middleware.

Laurent-Walter Goix graduated with distinction in telecommunication engineering from INSA Lyon and received a master's degree in telecommunications from TILS. He is a senior research engineer at Telecom Italia labs, Turin, Italy. He has more than eight years of experience on VoIP and NGN service platforms, focusing on service creation, management, and delivery. His current interests are context awareness, Web2.0, and converging

NGN/IT mobile service platforms. He is a regular OMA delegate and scientific manager of IST OPUCE.

Anna Goy is a researcher in the Department of Informatics of the University degli Studi in Turin. She obtained a Ph.D. in cognitive science at the same university, where she participates in the research and development activity of the Intelligent User Interface Group. Her research interests include adaptive hypermedia and Web technologies.

Ulrike Greiner is senior researcher and project manager at SAP Research Switzerland. Previously she was a researcher at the SAP Research Center in Karlsruhe, Germany, where she was mainly involved in the ATHENA project on enterprise interoperability. Her current responsibilities include research on interoperability, modeling and enactment of business processes (especially cross-organizational), user-centric process modeling, and ICT value engineering. She holds a Ph.D. in computer science from the University of Leipzig.

Roy Grønmo is a researcher at SINTEF and a Ph.D. candidate at the Department of Informatics, University of Oslo. He has been a member of more than ten Program Committees of international workshops and conferences. He has experience from a number of EU projects in FP5 and FP6, including DISGIS, ACE-GIS, SODIUM, and MODELWARE. His research interests include model-driven development, service-oriented computing, and aspect orientation.

Karim Guennoun received the M.S. degree in computer science from Paul Sabatier University in 2002 and the Ph.D. from the same university in 2006. He currently holds a postdoctoral position at LAAS-CNRS. His research interests include software architecture description, verification, and management applied to service-oriented dynamic architectures. He is author of more than 20 papers on these subjects in international conference proceedings and journals.

Alessio Gugliotta (http://kmi.open.ac.uk/people/alessio) received his Ph.D. in computer science at the University of Udine in March 2006. Since January 2006, he has been a research fellow at the Knowledge Media Institute of The Open University (United Kingdom). His current research focuses on knowledge modeling, service-oriented computing, and Semantic Web Services and their application within multiple domains, such as e-government and e-learning. His main works include the publication of a book about Web technologies (http://www.catalogo.mcgraw-hill.it/catLibro.asp?item_id=1849).

Svein Hallsteinsen is a senior research scientist at SINTEF, in Trondheim, Norway. He is currently the Technical Manager of MUSIC IST and had the same position in MADAM IST. He has an M.S. in physics and applied mathematics from the Norwegian University of Science and Technology in Trondheim.

Andreas Hess obtained his Ph.D at the University of Dublin, where he used combined techniques from machine learning and semantic web to automatically learn meaningful, machine-understandable descriptions of web services. He then moved to the Vrije Universiteit Amsterdam to further develop and apply these techniques in the context of the EU-sponsored WS-DIAMOND project. Being very much interested in commercial applications of these advanced technologies, Andreas is currently working at the Lycos search engine, again combining machine learning with semantic web techniques to improve the behavior of the Lycos search engine.

Hjørdis Hoff is an information architect at Det Norske Veritas and previously was a reasearcher at SINTEF. She holds an M.Sc. degree in computer science from the University of Oslo. Her role in SODIUM was dual: Project Manager for SINTEF and researcher in the project. She has experience from a number of EU projects in FP5 and FP6, including SODIUM, SWING, DISGIS, ATHENA, and ACE-GIS. Her main professional interests are semantic interoperability, model-driven development, service-oriented computing, and systems engineering.

Matthias Hölzl received his diploma in mathematics in 1999 and his Ph.D. degree in computer science in 2002. He was a member of the DFG project "Constraint-Funktionale Programmierung" and is currently a senior researcher at the Ludwig-Maximilians-Universität in Munich and Executive Manager of the project SENSORIA. He has published on theoretical foundations and practical applications of constraint programming, service-oriented architecture, and model-based architectures for intelligent reasoning and adaptation in open-ended environments.

John Hutchinson is a research associate in the Computing Department at Lancaster University, United Kingdom. His primary research interest is process support for software development using reusable components and services, especially where these are "off-the-shelf." He has published widely on various aspects of service-oriented and component-based software engineering.

Jyrki Huusko received his degree in theoretical physics with minor concentrations in mathematics and information technology from the University of Oulu. He is currently with the VTT Technical Research Center of Finland as a research team leader in seamless networking. His research topics have included lowly parallel clusters networking, medium access control mechanisms, and cross-layer mechanisms for TCP/IP protocols and multimedia delivery. His current research interests include future autonomic networks and services, future Internet, and post-IP mobility solutions.

Valérie Issarny is Directress of Research at the Paris-Rocquencourt Research Center, where she heads the INRIA ARLES project team (http://www-rocq.inria.fr/arles/). Her research interests are in the areas of software engineering and middleware, in particular, investigating solutions to ease the development of software systems enabling ambient intelligence/pervasive computing based on the exploitation of advanced networking technologies. She was coordinator of the IST FP6 PLASTIC STREP project (http://ist-plastic.org/).

Volodymyr Ivanchenko is a Ph.D. student at the Alpen-Adria University in Klagenfurt, Austria. He is a member of the Intelligent Systems and Business Informatics Research Group, led by Prof. Gerhard Friedrich. In 2005 he received his master's degree at the National Technical University, Kharkov Polytechnic Institute, Kharkov, Ukraine. During his study he worked in the Ukrainian IT companies, government institutes, and production. In 2004–2005 he participated in the student-exchange program KUK2 and worked for one of the Austrian IT companies. His research interests are in the areas of artificial intelligence, dataflow systems, workflow technologies, Web Services, diagnosis and repair of processes, and the theory of complexity.

Frank-Walter Jaekel, the holder of diplomas in engineering and informatics, is a senior researcher in the Corporate Management Division at IPK-Berlin. He is responsible for the development of the business process modeling tool MO^{2}GO, and leader for reengineering and software development projects in research and industry (consultancy). He was a work package leader in the EU projects IMSE, PLANTFABER, MISSION, and INTEROP-NoE, and was involved in the CBP development in ATHENA. He has published papers on enterprise modeling, distributed simulation, and enterprise interoperability in national and international journals.

Timo Kahl holds a diploma in industrial engineering and management from the Technical University of Kaiserslautern. Since 2004 he has been a researcher at the German Research Center for Artificial Intelligence (DFKI) in Saarbrücken. He was involved in national and international research and consulting projects at DFKI (e.g., INTEROP, research consulting on business rules, and ATHENA). His research concentrates on collaborative business and business process management.

Jarmo Kalaoja received the M.Sc. degree in electrical engineering from the University of Oulu, Finland, in 1988. He is a research scientist at the VTT Technical Research Center of Finland in Oulu. His main research topics have been domain analysis, generative and model-based software development, software product line architectures for embedded systems, and middleware for service-oriented and P2P-based software systems.

Julia Kantorovitch is a research team leader in the Software Architectures and Platforms Group at VTT. She received her M.Sc. degree in physics in 1999, and a licenciate in technology in 2003, from the University of Oulu, Finland. Her research interests are in wireless networks management, Internet protocols and technologies, and semantic Web technologies applied to the domain of networked services management.

Piotr Karwaczyński received his M.Sc. degree in computer science with distinction from the Wroc aw University of Technology in 2003. Currently he is completing his Ph.D. thesis. His research interests focus on large-scale decentralized systems. Since 2003 he has been a research assistant at the Institute of Applied Informatics, Wroc aw University of Technology. At the university he was responsible for the cooperation with the EU FP6 project Dependable Distributed Systems and the international PlanetLab initiative.

Nora Koch is a researcher at the Institute of Informatics of the Ludwig-Maximilians-Universität, Munich (LMU) and is a project manager at F.A.S.T. GmbH. She has been involved in European and national projects since 1995. She leads the Web Engineering Group of the LMU responsible for the development of the UWE methodology. Her main research interests focus on metamodeling and model-driven development of Web applications and Web Services. She is the author of more than 70 publications.

Janne Lahti received his master's degree in telecommunications from the University of Oulu, Finland, in 2005. He is currently employed as a research scientist by the VTT Technical Research Center of Finland. His research topics have included mobile multimedia systems and mobile digital rights management. His current research interests include future autonomic services, service mobility, mobile service creation technologies and near field communication.

Xavier Le Guillou received the M.S. degree in computer science from the University of Rennes 1 in 2005. Since then, he has been a Ph.D. student at the same university, working with the DREAM research team at IRISA, focusing his work on the diagnosis of distributed discrete event systems using chronicle models.

Marek Lehmann (Ph.D. 2005) is an assistant professor of computer science in the Department of Knowledge and Business Engineering of the University of Vienna. He received his B.Sc. (1999) and M.Sc. (2001) in computer science from Poznan University of Technology in Poland, and his doctorate in technology (2005) in computer science from the University of Klagenfurt in Austria. His research interests include databases and information systems, system integration, data transformations, workflow management systems, and Web Services.

Yingmin Li obtained her bachelor's degree in computer science from Peking University, and her MBA in management from CNAM, Paris. Since 2006, she has been a Ph.D. student at LRI, University Paris-Sud 11. The subject of her thesis is monitoring and diagnosis of complex Web services.

David Linner began as software engineer for large-scale business applications in 2001. During his computer science studies at the Technical University of Berlin (TUB), he joined the Fraunhofer Institute FOKUS. In 2006 he received his degree in computer science. Since then he has been a research assistant with the Open Communication Systems (OKS) Group of the TUB and the Fraunhofer Institute FOKUS. He oversees research and development of distributed service platforms in industrial and publicly funded research projects. Currently he is working on the BIONETS project supported by the European Union.

Sonia Lippe is a project manager at the SAP Research Project Management Office, where she is mainly responsible for EU projects. She develops and implements project management standards within SAP Research. Previously, she was a researcher with SAP Research in Brisbane, Australia, where she was mainly involved in the ATHENA project, focusing her research on business processes and interoperability. She holds a master's degree in information systems from the University of Münster, Germany.

José-Manuel López-Cobo was born in 1972 in Granada, Spain. He holds a degree in computer engineering from the University of Málaga and is currently working on his Ph.D. in the field of SWS. He has been working on research projects since 1999. He has been employed at Atos Origin and iSOCO as Technical Research Manager of the R&D Department, being responsible for the management of projects including SWWS, DIP, INFRAWEBS, TAO, LUISA, and SUPER. Currently he works at iSOCO as Research Manager, dividing his time among research and commercial projects.

Neil Maiden is professor of systems engineering and head of the Centre for Human–Computer Interface Design, an independent research department in City University's School of Informatics in London. He has been directing interdisciplinary research in requirements engineering since 1992. He has published over 120 papers in journals and conference and workshop publications. He was program chair for the 12th IEEE International Conference on Requirements Engineering in Kyoto in 2004. He is editor of *IEEE Software*'s "Requirements" column.

Antonio Maña received his M.Sc. and Ph.D. degrees in computer engineering from the University of Málaga in 1994 and 2003, respectively. In 1995 he joined the Department of

Computer Science of the University of Málaga, where he is currently an associate professor in the Computer Science Department. His present research activities include security and software engineering, information and network security, application of smart cards to digital contents commerce, software protection, and DRM. He has more than 60 peer-reviewed publications. He has participated in several EU-funded projects and is currently the Scientific Director of the FP6 SERENITY project and the UMA's principal investigator of FP6 GST and GREDIA projects. He is a member of the editorial board of the *International Journal of Electronic Security and Digital Forensics (IJESDF)* and a reviewer for several other international journals. He is a member of various professional and scientific societies and work groups, and is actively involved in the organization of research and educational activities.

Jürgen Mangler is a research and teaching assistant at the Department of Knowledge and Business Engineering of the Faculty of Computer Sciences, University of Vienna. He is currently working on his Ph.D. thesis under supervision of Prof. Eder and Prof. Schikuta. He received his Master of Business Informatics (Mag.rer.soc.oec.) from the University of Vienna. He has been working on various projects since 1995, and has been a member of the Department of Knowledge and Business Engineering since 2002.

Annapaola Marconi (http://soa.fbk.eu/people/marconi/) is a researcher in the Service-oriented Applications Research Group at FBK. Her main research interests include service-oriented computing, Web Service composition, and automated synthesis of code. In particular, most recently she has worked on the problem of automatically synthesizing process-level compositions of Web Services starting from the description of the component services and from control-flow and data-flow composition requirements.

Zlatina Marinova studied computer science at Sofia University, Bulgaria, where she obtained her M.Sc. degree in 2002, writing a thesis on planning in multi-agent systems. She joined Ontotext Lab of the Sirma Group Corporation in 2003. She has participated in a number of EC IST research projects, including SWWS, DIP, INFRAWEBS and TAO. In INFRAWEBS she led the development of repository and registry infrastructure for Semantic Web Services.

Fabio Martinelli (M.S. in computer science, University of Pisa 1994, Ph.D. in computer science, University of Siena 1999) is a senior researcher of the Institute of Informatics and Telematics (IIT) of the Italian National Research Council (CNR). His main research interests involve security and privacy in distributed and mobile systems, and foundations of security and trust. He was the initiator of the International Workshop series on Formal Aspects in Security and Trust (FAST).

Fabio Massacci received an M.Eng. in 1993 and Ph.D. in Computer Science and Engineering at University of Rome "La Sapienza" in 1998. He joined University of Siena as an assistant professor in 1999, was visiting researcher at IRIT Toulouse in 2000, and joined Trento in 2001, where he is now full professor. His research interests are in security requirements engineering, formal methods, and computer security. His h-index on Google Scholar is 20, and his h-index normalized for individual impact (hI_norm) is 13 (in June/2008). He is currently scientific coordinator of multimillion euros industry R&D European projects on security and compliance.

Philippe Massonet is manager of the Requirements Engineering Team and Scientific Coordinator at CETIC, the Belgian Center of Excellence in ICT. He holds degrees in computer science and business administration. His research interests focus on software and knowledge engineering methodologies in general, with a special interest in requirements engineering methodologies, formal methods, agent-oriented software engineering methodologies, and Grid computing. He is currently coordinator of the IST project GridTrust.

Philip Mayer is a research associate and doctoral candidate in the Research Group on Programming and Software Technology at LMU in Munich. He received his master's degree in computer science at the University of Hannover in 2006. His main research interests lie in the area of automated program transformations, in particular refactoring, program analysis, and tooling. He is currently working on the EU research project SENSORIA, on development of service-oriented software systems.

Matteo Melideo is a project manager and the head of the Unit on Service Engineering in the R&D Lab of Engineering Ingegneria Informatica S.p.A. Currently he is the coordinator of the SeCSE project. He has more than ten years of experience as a software engineer, in particular on workflow management systems, component-based software development, and service-oriented computing.

Tarek Melliti has been an assistant professor at the IBISC (Informatique Biologie Intégrative et Systèmes Complexes) laboratory, located at the University of Evry Val-Essonne (France), since 2006. He obtained his Ph.D. in computer science in 2004. His research has dealt with formal methods applied to orchestrated and choreographed Web Services composition and adaptation. Recently, his research has focused on model-based Web Services diagnosis and diagnosability.

András Micsik is a senior research associate at the Computer and Automation Research Institute of the Hungarian Academy of Sciences (SZTAKI) in Budapest. He received the Ph.D. in 2001 at the Eötvös Loránd University in Budapest (ELTE). He has been active in the research on digital libraries and computer-supported cooperative work. Currently, his main interest is the application of Semantic Web technologies in group work. He is author of more than 40 publications in English.

Daniele Miorandi is the head of the Pervasive Area at CREATE-NET, Italy, where he is leading a group working on pervasive computing and communication environments. He is the coordinator of the European project BIONETS (www.bionets.eu). He has published more than 50 papers in international refereed journals and conference proceedings. He has served on the Steering Committees of international events (WiOpt, Autonomics, ValueTools), for some of which he was a co-founder (Autonomics and ValueTools). He also serves on the Technical Program Committee of several conferences in the networking field, including IEEE INFOCOM, IEEE ICC, and IEEE Globecom.

Jaka Močnik has been involved in research in the area of distributed systems since his undergraduate study, working on massively parallel simulations of physical phenomena and visualization of the results at the Jozef Stefan Institute in Ljubljana, Slovenia. He has developed systems for load balancing of IP traffic and cluster management, and telecommunications software. His current research interests lie in the domain of large-scale, globally distributed systems, focusing on SOA and peer-to-peer systems.

Stefano Modafferi received his Ph.D. in information engineering at the Politecnico di Milano, where he is now a postdoctoral fellow in the Dipartimento di Elettronica e Informazione. He is involved in several national and international projects. His interests are mainly the design of information systems and the design of advanced orchestration for Web Services including topics of "mobile" and "self-healing."

Paolo Mori is a researcher at the Institute of Informatics and Telematics (IIT) of the Italian National Research Council (CNR). His main research interests involve security and privacy in Grids. He is currently participating in the IST project GridTrust.

Enrico Mussi received a university Laurea degree in computer engineering and a Ph.D. degree, in 2002 and 2006, respectively, from the Politecnico di Milano, where he currently holds a postdoctoral position. His research interests are in self-healing Web systems, in adaptive information systems, and in mobile applications. He cooperated on the VISPO (adaptive systems in virtual enterprises and environments) and MAIS (Adaptive Multichannel Information Systems) projects.

H.-Joachim Nern is the Chef Executive Officer of the German company Global IT&TV GmbH and leader of the consulting platform Aspasia Knowledge Systems. He is the author or co-author of more than 100 scientific papers related to automation, information retrieval, knowledge management, and system theory. For the INFRAWEBS project his main work included contributions to the overall system architecture and the design of the clustering and classification module of the organizational memory.

Isabel Ordás holds a telecommunication engineering degree from Centro Politécnico Superior at the University of Zaragoza (Spain). She joined Telefonica I+D as a scholarship holder in 2003. Since then, she has been involved in several research projects related to instant messaging, VoIP, and NGN technologies. Currently, she is working on the OPUCE project, mainly on work-package dealing with use case description, requirements, and high-level architecture and interface definition.

Johannes Osrael received his doctoral degree in computer science with distinction from the Vienna University of Technology in 2007. Since 2004 he has been working on the framework Programme 6 project DeDiSys (Dependable Distributed Systems) and has conducted research on replication in distributed object and service-oriented systems. His primary research interests are in the areas of distributed systems, dependability, and service-oriented systems.

Michael Pantazoglou is a Ph.D. student and research scientist at the Department of Informatics and Telecommunications of the National and Kapodistrian University of Athens. He holds a diploma in informatics and telecommunications from the same institution. He has participated in several research projects. His research interests include service-oriented technologies with a focus on service discovery, P2P computing, and the application of information retrieval and natural language processing techniques in data management.

George A. Papadopoulos is a professor in the Department of Computer Science at the University of Cyprus. His research interests include software engineering, mobile computing, open and distance learning, distributed computing, cooperative information systems, and service oriented computing. He has published over 100 papers, and he serves on the editorial boards of five international journals. He has been involved in over 30 internationally and nationally funded projects (total budget for his participation is around 4 million euros).

Ioannis Papaioannou received his diploma (with honors) from the Computer Engineering and Informatics Department of the University of Patras, Greece, in July 2004. He is currently a Ph.D. candidate in the Electrical and Computer Engineering Department of the National Technical University of Athens. His research interests include computer networks, wireless and mobile communications, Web Services, mobile intelligent agents, automated negotiations, and machine learning.

Michael P. Papazoglou holds the chair of computer science and is Director of the INFOLAB at the University of Tilburg in the Netherlands. He serves on several international committees and on the editorial boards of nine international scientific journals. He has chaired numerous well-known international scientific conferences in computer science and has authored/edited 15 books and over 150 scientific journal articles and refereed conference papers. His two most recent books are *E-Business: Organizational and Technical Foundations* (John Wiley, 2006) and *Web Services: Principles and Technology* (Addison-Wesley, 2007). He is the Scientific Director of S-Cube.

Tomás Pariente has a bachelor's degree in telecommunications engineering from the UPM (Spain). His technical expertise is mainly in semantic technologies. He has worked for Indra Sistemas, and since June 2006 he has been project manager and technical consultant for EU-based projects in semantic technologies in ATOS Origin. He is involved in several working groups in this technology. He has worked on EU projects such as Ontologging, SmartGov, OntoGov, and INFRAWEBS, and is currently involved in the NeOn and LUISA projects.

Aljosa Pasic has studied and worked at the universities of Zagreb, Croatia, Sarajevo, Bosnia and Herzegovina, and Eindhoven, The Netherlands. He was employed by Cap Gemini (Utrecht, The Netherlands), and in January 1999, he joined the Sema Group Spain (now part of Atos Origin) as the manager for the Spanish Council of Justice project. He also has worked for the Dutch Ministry of Defense, the government of the Canary Islands, the Cyprus government, and the European Commission. His current position is head of the Advanced Information Management Unit, where he manages a number of EU projects, such as IMPULSE (Improving Public Services), E-COURT, and CB-BUSINESS (all of them in the area of e-government), and SPARTA, SECURE-PHONE, and SECURE-JUSTICE (the area of security). He is also the Chairman of the NESSI Working Group on Trust, Security, and Dependability. Since 2003 he has been certified as a Project Manager Professional (PMP); he is also a member of the Project Management Institute.

Nearchos Paspallis is a research associate in the Department of Computer Science, University of Cyprus. He is currently leading the context work package of MUSIC IST; in the past he has also worked for MADAM IST (both FP6 projects). He has a B.S. in computer engineering and informatics from the University of Patras, and an M.S. in computer science from the University of California, Santa Barbara.

Cesare Pautasso is an assistant professor in computer science at the University of Lugano, Switzerland. In 2007, he was a researcher at the IBM Zurich Research Lab and an *Oberassistent* at ETH Zurich. His computer engineering degree is from the Politecnico di

Milano (2000), and his Ph.D. in computer science is from the ETH Zurich (2004). His research focuses on Grid computing, software composition, Web 2.0, mashups, and scientific workflow management. Visit www.pautasso.info for more information on his current activities.

Yannick Pencolé, Ph.D., has been a CNRS research fellow at LAAS-CNRS since 2006. He received his Ph.D. at the University of Rennes 1 in 2002 and worked as a postdoctoral fellow at the Australian National University from 2003 to 2006. His research interests include diagnosis and diagnosability of discrete-event systems, and his published papers are mainly about diagnosis and diagnosablility of distributed DES.

Barbara Pernici is full professor of computer engineering at the Politecnico di Milano. She has a doctorate in engineering (Laurea) from the Politecnico di Milano and an M.S. in computer science from Stanford University. Her research interests include workflow information systems design, cooperative information systems, Web-based information systems, virtual enterprises, adaptive information systems and Web Services, data quality, office and information systems conceptual modeling, computer-based design support tools, reuse of conceptual components, temporal databases, and applications of database technology. She has published more than 40 papers in international journals, co-edited 12 books, and published about 150 papers at the international level. She has participated in several ESPRIT and IST European projects (TODOS, ITHACAEQUATOR, F3, and WIDE). She coordinates several National Research Council and Italian research projects. She has been on the Program Committee of international conferences (VLDB, SIGMOD, ER, ECOOP, CAISE, Mobis, BPM, ICSOC, ECOWS, ICWS, WWW, ICDE, IFIP TC8 and IFIP WG 8.1 and 8.4 working conferences), and referee for several international journals. She is member of the editorial board of *Requirements Engineering Journal, Journal on Cooperative Information Systems*, and *Journal on Database Management*. She serves as elected chair of IFIP TC8 Information Systems and of IFIP WG 8.1 (Information Systems Design and Evaluation).

Giovanna Petrone is a researcher in the Computer Science Department, University of Turin, working with the Intelligent User Interfaces Group. Her research projects include the definition of a conversational model for Web Services, aimed at supporting complex interactions. She gained extensive international experience as a software engineer and architect at several companies, including Sun Microsystems.

Claudia Picardi is a researcher at the Department of Informatics of the Università degli Studi di Torino. She obtained a Ph.D. in computer science at the same university. Her research is mainly in the field of artificial intelligence; her interests are focused on model-based diagnosis.

Stefano Pintarelli, a software engineer, received his degree in 2001. His first notable accomplishment was the project Net Quality, in cooperation with LII (Laboratorio di Ingegneria Informatica). The project focused on multimedia broadcast streaming. Currently he is working for DeltaDator as a senior development engineer on Centura, Java, Oracle, and SqlServer environments.

Marco Pistore (http://soa.fbk.eu/people/pistore) is a senior researcher at FBK, where he leads the Group on Service-oriented Applications and directs the Laboratory of Interoperability and E-Government. His main research interests include theory of concurrent systems, formal methods, automated synthesis of code, and their application to the design of service-oriented applications. He has been responsible for research and industrial projects on SOC and Web Services technologies, and for their adoption in application domains such as telco, logistics, and e-government.

Klaus Pohl holds the chair of software systems engineering at the University of Duisburg-Essen, Germany, and is adjunct professor at the University of Limerick, Ireland. He is the funding Scientific Director and Chief Scientific Adviser of Lero, the Irish Software Engineering Research Centre. He serves on several international committees and has chaired numerous well-known international scientific conferences. He has authored/edited over 20 books/proceedings and over 130 refereed papers. He is a Vice Chair of the Steering Committee and member of the Executive Board of NESSI, the European Technology Platform on Software and Services, and is the Coordinator of S-Cube.

Xavier Pucel received an engineering degree, specializing in computer science, from the Institut National des Sciences Appliquées (INSA) and a master's degree from Paul Sabatier University, both in Toulouse, France, in 2005. He currently holds a Ph.D. position at LAAS-CNRS, Toulouse. His research interests are in model-based diagnosis, diagnosability, distributed approaches, and application to service-oriented applications.

Rosario Pugliese is associate professor of computer science in the Department of Syistems and Informatics of the University of Florence. He is the author of some 60 publications in international journals, books, or edited conference proceedings. His research results include a prototype language for agents' interaction and mobility (KLAIM), a process calculus for specifying and analyzing service-based applications (COWS), and analysis techniques for concurrent systems and cryptographic protocols.

Ilja Radusch received his M.Sc. in computer science from the University of Technology, Berlin (TUB). Since 2003 he has been a researcher with Open Communication Systems (OKS), and with Fraunhofer FOKUS since 2005. Since 2006 he has been a group leader at OKS. He is working in the field of car-2–car communication, sensor and ad hoc networks, and context-aware services. His responsibilities include several projects for industry partners such as Deutsche Telekom (pervasive gaming, online community life) and DaimlerChrysler (SIM-TD), as well as research projects for the German Ministry of Education and Research (AVM) and the European Union (e-Sense, BIONETS). He is also a lecturer in various courses at the TU Berlin.

Pierre-Guillaume Raverdy is a research engineer at INRIA-Rocquencourt, on the ARLES research team (http://www-rocq.inria.fr/arles/). He has an extensive background in conceiving and implementing innovative middleware services and applications in both academic and industrial research laboratories. His research interests are in the areas of service life cycle management, and mobile and pervasive computing.

Marc Richardson is a senior researcher in the Next Generation Web Research Group, part of Research and Venturing at British Telecommunications PLC. He joined BT in 2001 as a developer of knowledge management applications, and was involved in the formation of a successful knowledge management spin-off company, Exago, which is now part of Corpora PLC. His work is currently focused on research of the Semantic Web and its application in the telecommunications domain.

Gianluca Ripa received his Laurea degree from the Politecnico di Milano. He is currently working at CEFRIEL, a research center located in the Milan area, as a software engineering specialist. His research interests are in the area of software engineering, in particular, in service-oriented systems and in automatic negotiation of SLAs.

Sophie Robin is associate professor at the University of Rennes and performs her research activities at IRISA (DREAM research team since a few years). She has been involved in different research projects and worked on the role of frame-based models in reasoning and abstraction before becoming interested in modeling for diagnosis. She is now focusing her work on monitoring distributed discrete event systems using chronicles models.

Ioanna Roussaki received her Ph.D. in telecommunications and computer networks from the National Technical University of Athens (NTUA) in 2003. Since 1999, she has been a research associate at NTUA and has participated in several research projects on ubiquitous and pervasive computing, context awareness, mobile and personal communications, virtual home environment, mobile agent systems, e-negotiations, algorithms, and service engineering. Since April 2008, she has been a lecturer at NTUA specializing on pervasive systems.

Mary Rowlatt is Customer Relations Manager at the Essex County Council. She was the main contact in the e-government work package within the European-funded project DIP (Data, Information, and Process Integration with Semantic Web Services). Her main tasks encompassed the management of the relationships between the work package members and the involved stakeholders within the Essex County Council.

Laurence Rozé, Ph.D., is associate professor at INSA (Rennes, France) and performs her research activities at IRISA (DREAM team). She received a master of research in computer science in 1993, and a Ph.D. in artificial Intelligence in 1997, in Rennes. Her research interests lie in diagnostic and monitoring. She has been involved in different application projects, including supervision of telecommunication networks, monitoring of web service.

Rainer Ruggaber is a senior researcher at SAP Research Center, Karlsruhe, Germany. His responsibilities include the project management of SAP's contribution to THESEUS, including the project management of the TEXO Use Case. He also has been the Scientific Coordinator of the ATHENA research project. He holds a Ph.D. from the University of Karlsruhe. His current interest is in the development of Internet services from vision to reality.

Richard T. Sanders is a research scientist at SINTEF ICT. He is currently leading the SIMS project. He has worked with methods and languages for software engineering for many years. He received his doctorate of engineering in telematics from the Norwegian University of Science and Technology.

Anne-Marie Sassen studied informatics at the University of Leiden in The Netherlands and received her Ph.D. from the Technical University of Delft in 1993. After working for several years as a researcher for the Netherlands Organization for Applied Scientific Research TNO, in the field of knowledge-based systems and control systems, she joined the system integration company Atos Origin as a project manager. Since 2005 she has worked for the European Commission as a project officer, responsible for projects in the field of service engineering.

Christian Schaefer received his diploma in computer science from the University of Karlsruhe, Germany. Since September 2003 he has been a researcher for DoCoMo Euro-Labs in Munich, Germany. His main research interests are the enforcement of security policies in distributed systems, with a focus on usage control and security of mobile handsets.

Andreas Schroeder is a research assistant at the Institute for Informatics of the Ludwig-Maximilians-Universität in Munich. He completed his diploma thesis with honors in 2005, specifying a query algebra and describing efficient algorithms for the implementation of Xcerpt, a rule-based query language for semistructured data with advanced language constructs. His current work focuses on modeling and analysis aspects of service orchestrations in UML, and design concepts for self-adaptive software systems.

James Scicluna is a researcher at the University of Innsbruck, in the STI-Innsbruck Research Institute. He is an active member of the WSMO, WSML and WSMX working groups whose main focus is the development and implementation of Semantic Web Service technologies, and is also a member of the SEE OASIS Program Committee. His main research interests are Semantic Web Service Composition and Workflow languages. He has worked on European Union projects including INFRAWEBS and SUPER.

Marino Segnan is a researcher in the Computer Science Department, University of Turin, working with the Advanced Service Architectures Group. His recent research activities deal with interaction models for Web Services, choreographies, and monitoring. His earlier work focused on the realization of a qualitative simulation tool for model-based diagnosis. He has worked with several companies, mainly on projects involving integrated development environments, user interfaces, compilers, and transaction management.

Daniel Serrano is a Ph.D. student in the Computer Science Department at the University of Málaga, as well as at ATOS Origin Innovation and Research. He holds an M.Sc. degree in computer science and a postgraduate master's degree in software engineering and artificial intelligence, both of them from the University of Málaga. His principal research interests are in the area of automated software engineering and security engineering. He is a research assistant in the SERENITY project, and he previously participated in the ASD project funded by the regional government of Andalusia.

Jürgen Sienel completed his studies incomputer science at the University of Stuttgart in 1992 with a *Diplom-Informatiker* degree, and since then has worked for Alcatel Research and Innovation (now part of Bell Labs), where his current interest is focused on service-oriented network infrastructures, IMS evolution. and alternatives. He is also Work Package Manager for Service Life Cycle Management in OPUCE. He has been named Distinguished Member of the Alcatel-Lucent Technical Academy.

Alberto Sillitti is assistant professor at the Free University of Bolzano, Italy. He is a professional engineer collaborating with public institutions and companies. He is involved in several European Union-founded projects in the software engineering area. His research areas include software engineering, component-based software engineering, Web and mobile services, agile methods, and open source. He has been program chair, Organizing Committee member, or Program Committee member for several software engineering conferences and workshops.

Pedro Soria-Rodriguez, CISSP, is currently head of the Security Unit of Atos Research & Innovation (R&D arm of Atos Origin Spain), leading an information security research team involved in several security-related European projects (MASTER, ESFORS, SecurePhone, SERENITY, Serket). His professional experience in the United States and Europe in information security spans both military and commercial applications, encompassing the design and development of technology for IT security systems, as well as consulting and auditing of information security management systems. He holds the CISSP certification, has passed the CISM exam, and received B.S. and M.Sc. degrees from Worcester Polytechnic Institute, Worcester, Massachusetts.

George Spanoudakis is a professor of software engineering in the Department of Computing of City University in London. He has more than ten years of experience in managing research projects, and more than 75 peer-reviewed publications. He has been on the Program Committees of more than 40 international conferences and workshops, associate editor of the *Journal of Software Engineering and Knowledge Engineering*, and Program Committee co-chair of SEKE '06 and SEKE '07.

Stephan Steglich received his M.Sc. in computer science (1998) and his Ph.D. in computer science (2003) from the TU Berlin in 2003. His fields of interest include context awareness, user interaction, and adaptive systems. In 1998 and 1999 he worked intensively in the research area of intelligent mobile agents. Since 1999 he has conducted research in the area of user-centric communication. He has been involved in a number of projects which were related to human–machine interaction, UMTS/VHE, personalization, and user profiling. He manages international- and national-level research activities, and has been an organizer and a member of the Program Committees of several international conferences. He has actively participated in standardization activities in his research areas. He lectures on mobile telecommunication systems and advanced communication systems at the TU Berlin.

Sandra Stinčić is a researcher in the Next Generation Web Research Group, part of Research & Venturing at British Telecommunications PLC. She joined BT in 2005 as a developer of Semantic Web applications after graduating from the University of Zagreb (Croatia) Faculty of Electrical Engineering and Computing. She has been involved in projects related to the Semantic Web and Web Services, including the EU 6th Framework Data Information and Process Integration with Semantic Web Services and Semantic Knowledge Technologies. Her current work is focused on research on the Semantic Web and its application in the telecommunications domain.

Audine Subias received her Ph.D. in 1995, and her *habilitation à diriger des recherches* in 2006, both from Paul Sabatier University in Toulouse, France. Since 1997 she has been an associate professor at the Institut National des Sciences Appliquées (INSA), working at LAAS-CNRS as a member of the Diagnosis, Supervision, and Control Group for several years. Her research interests include detection and diagnosis of discrete-event systems, and mainly model-based diagnosis.

Amirreza Tahamtan is a research and teaching assistant in the Department of Knowledge and Business Engineering of the University of Vienna. He is also working on his Ph.D. thesis in the fields of distributed information systems and Web Service composition. He received his M.S. degree in computer sciences with distinction from Vienna University of Technology. He was a research assistant from 2001 to 2005 at the Department of Neurology, Medical University of Vienna.

Vlad Tanasescu is a postgraduate student at KMi—Open University, with a background in computer science and philosophy. He is applying Semantic Web Services to geographical information systems in eMerges, the application he designed as part of his Ph.D. work. Other work includes research on differences, an attempt at finding a common ground for various KR paradigms used in GIScience, and extreme tagging, a study of emerging semantics by the tagging of tags.

Annette Ten Teije is lecturer at the Vrije Universiteit Amsterdam (Ph.D. in 1997 from the University of Amsterdam on the automatic configuration of diagnostic knowledge-based systems). She has been a visiting research scientist at the Imperial Cancer Research Fund in London, and was a lecturer at the University of Utrecht before joining the Vrije Universiteit. She has published 25 research papers, many of them in proceedings of leading conferences. Relevant work for WS-DIAMOND is (among others) the study of model-based diagnostic methods, verifying safety properties for knowledge-based systems, and the automated configuration of Web Services (in the EU-funded IBROW project under the FET-O program).

Marcel Tilly received a master's degree in physics at the Technical University of Dortmund. Since then he has worked for more than ten years on developing and consulting on software engineering. Most recently his work has been primarily focused on model-driven development and service-oriented architecture. He is co-author of a book about Web development and has been a speaker at several conferences. In 2006 he joined the European Microsoft Innovation Center in Aachen as a Program Manager.

Michele Trainotti is a system architect at the Laboratory of Interoperability and E-Government in Trento, Italy. His main interests include service-oriented architectures, e-government solutions, and distributed systems in general. He has worked at the ITC-IRST Research Institute on the ASTRO research project (http://astroproject.org/) as a system architect for the ASTRO suite.

Rubén Trapero received his master of engineering degree in telecommunications engineering from Universidad Politécnica de Madrid (UPM). He had joined the Electrical Engineering and Computer Science Department at UPM in 2003 working in the area of identity based services and peer-to-peer mobile services. Since then, he has been involved in several European and national projects as a technical researcher while conducting his Ph.D. work. His research interests include identity management and services engineering over convergent networks.

Paolo Traverso is Head of Division at ITC/IRST. Service-oriented applications is one of his main recent research interests, especially in the field of automated composition of distributed business processes. He is on the editorial board of the *Journal of Artificial Intelligence Research (JAIR)*, of the *Journal of Applied Logic (JAL)*, of the *International Journal of Cooperative Information Systems (IJCIS)*, and of the *European Transactions in Artificial Intelligence (ETAI)*. Since 2005, he has been a fellow of the European Coordinating Committee in Artificial Intelligence.

Louise Travé-Massuyès received a Ph.D. degree in control in 1984 and an engineering degree specializing in control, electronics, and computer science in 1982, both from the Institut National des Sciences Appliquées (INSA) in Toulouse, France, and an award from the

Union des Groupements d'Ingénieurs de la Région Midi-Pyrénées. She was awarded a *habilitation à diriger des recherches* by Paul Sabatier University in 1998. She is currently Research Director of the Centre National de Recherche Scientifique (CNRS), working at LAAS, Toulouse, France, where she has been the scientific leader of the Diagnosis, Supervision, and Control Group for several years. She is responsible for the scientific area "modeling, control, and system Optimization, which oversees four research groups in the field of continuous and discrete automatic control. Her main research interests are in qualitative and model-based reasoning and applications to dynamic systems supervision and diagnosis. She has been responsible for several industrial and European projects and has published more than 100 papers in international conference proceedings and scientific journals. Her recent and current responsibilities include membership of the IFAC Safeprocess Technical Committee; membership of Conseil National des Universités for Section 61; co-leader of the French Imalaia Group; and Scientific Director of the Joint Academic–Industrial Laboratory AUTODIAG with IRIT and the company ACTIA. She is a senior member of the *IEEE* Computer Society.

Aphrodite Tsalgatidou is a permanent member of the Faculty of the Department of Informatics and Telecommunications of the National and Kapodistrian University of Athens, since 1995. She holds an M.Sc. and a Ph.D. in computer science from the University of Manchester, England. Her current research focuses on service interoperability, discovery and composition, peer-to-peer systems, and business process management and interoperability. She is the Director of the S3 Laboratory (www.s3lab.com), which pursues research in service engineering and software engineering. Aphrodite was the Technical Manager of SODIUM.

Dimitrios Tsesmetzis received the electrical and computer engineer's diploma from the National Technical University of Athens (NTUA) in July 2002. He received the third Ericsson's Award for his thesis, "Research and Analysis of Coon Open Policy Service (COPS)." He is currently a Ph.D. candidate in the Electrical and Computer Engineering Department of NTUA. His research interests include computer networks, Semantic Web and Web Services, algorithms, and distributed systems.

Elpida Tzafestas is an electrical and computer engineer, and has studied artificial intelligence in France. She is a research scientist in intelligent systems at the Institute of Communication and Computer Systems in Athens, Greece. She has authored over 70 papers in journals, conference proceedings, and books, and she has taught several courses on human–computer interaction and intelligent and complex systems. Her interests include artificial life, behavior-based AI, autonomous agents, complex systems, cognitive science, and enactive user interfaces design.

Frank Van Harmelen (Ph.D. in 1989 from Edinburgh on metalevel reasoning) is professor of knowledge representation and reasoning in the Department of Artificial Intelligence of the Vrije Universiteit Amsterdam. He is author of a book on metalevel inference, editor of a book on knowledge-based systems, editor of a book on knowledge management on the Semantic Web, and the author of the first available textbook on Semantic Web languages. He has published over 100 papers, many of them in leading journals and conference proceedings. He has made key contributions to the CommonKADS project by providing a formal basis for the conceptual models. More recently, he was one of the designers of OIL, which was the basis for a W3C standardized Web ontology language. He was a key member of the W3C Working Group on Web Ontology Languages, responsible for the OWL Web Ontology Language. He was the 2002 Program Chair of the European Conference on Artificial Intelligence, and General Chair of the 2004 International Semantic Web Conference.

Eric Vetillard is the CTO of Trusted Labs, a spin-off from Trusted Logic that provides security-related services. He is in particular responsible for the security evaluation of embedded Java platforms and applications (Java Card, J2ME), and for the development of static analysis tools. Previously, he had been chief architect at Trusted Logic, and Java architect at Gemplus. He is the Technical Chairman of the Java Card Forum, in which he has participated since its inception in 1997, contributing to all Java Card specifications. He is a regular speaker at industrial and academic conferences. He holds an M.S. from Florida State University, and a Ph.D. from the University of Marseille-Méditerranée.

Thierry Vidal, Ph.D., is a *maître de conférences* at ENI, Tarbes; a member of the research group INRIA; and associate professor at ENIT; he was also seconded to INRIA as a research scientist. In June 1990 he received the engineering degree in computer science from the ENSEEIHT Engineering School, Toulouse. In September 1995 he was awarded a Ph.D. in artificial intelligence by Paul Sabatier University (UPS), Toulouse. His research interests are in the development of fault diagnosis expert systems with a specific knowledge acquisition tool (MACAO), and in-time planning and scheduling (efficient and complete management of heterogeneous and uncertain constraints). He is also involved in constraint-based temporal reasoning, numerical constraints (dates and durations), uncertain durations, consistency and controllability in temporal constraint networks, scheduling and resource allocation, application-dependent graph decomposition techniques, complexity, efficiency versus expressivity and, in the application domain, production management and machining design.

Leticia Gutiérrez Villarías, M.Sc. in computing and mathematics, was the ontology engineer for the e-government work package within the European-funded project DIP (Data, Information, and Process Integration with Semantic Web Services). Her main tasks encompassed increasing e-government service-providing efficiency via Semantic Web Services, leading research into ontologies, and disseminating the benefits of Semantic Web technologies in the e-government sector.

Thomas Walter is Project Manager in the Security Technology Lab of DoCoMo Euro-Labs. He received the degree of *Diplom-Informatiker* from the University of Hamburg and the degree of *Doktor der Technischen Wissenschaften* from the ETH Zurich. Since 2002, he has been engaged in research and development of application security support for next-generation mobile communications. Before joining DoCoMo Euro-Labs, he was a researcher and lecturer at ETH Zurich.

Martin Wirsing has been the head of the research group Programmierung und Software-Technik at the Ludwig-Maximilians-Universität, Munich, since 1992. His recent research has focused on software engineering for distributed mobile systems, and Web applications and their mathematical foundations. He is author or editor of more than 20 books and has published more than 170 scientific papers. In addition, he is President of the Scientific Committee of INRIA and member of several other international scientific committees.

Jörg Ziemann studied information systems at the University of Göttingen, the University of California, and the University of Hamburg. Since 2004 he has been a researcher at the German Research Center for Artificial Intelligence (DFKI). His research concentrates on model-driven development of service-oriented architectures. He has worked on European research projects including ATHENA IP, Interop NOE, and R4eGov. He has published more than 20 articles in conference proceedings, journals, and books, and is currently working on his Ph.D. thesis.

Arian Zwegers is a Project Officer at the European Commission's Directorate General Information Society and Media, in the Software & Service Architectures and Infrastructures Unit. He received a Ph.D. from the Eindhoven University of Technology in The Netherlands for his contribution to the system architecting field, which focused on reference architectures, shop floor control architectures, and modular software design. After receiving his Ph.D., he worked for the Center for Manufacturing Technology of Philips Electronics, Baan Development in The Netherlands, and PlatteConsult in Brussels.

Index

Made in United States
Orlando, FL
04 November 2026

90209472R00317